ENCYCLOPEDIA OF
EUROPEAN SOCIAL HISTORY

ENCYCLOPEDIA OF
EUROPEAN SOCIAL HISTORY

FROM 1350 TO 2000

VOLUME 5

Peter N. Stearns

Editor in Chief

Charles Scribner's Sons

an imprint of the Gale Group

Detroit • New York • San Francisco • London • Boston • Woodbridge, CT

Copyright © 2001

Charles Scribner's Sons
An imprint of the Gale Group
1633 Broadway
New York, New York 10019

1 3 5 7 9 11 13 15 17 19   20 18 16 14 12 10 8 6 4 2

Printed in United States of America

Library of Congress Cataloging-in-Publication Data
Encyclopedia of European social history from 1350 to 2000 / Peter N. Stearns, editor-in-chief.
     p.   cm.
     Includes bibliographical references and index.
     ISBN 0-684-80582-0 (set : alk. paper) — ISBN 0-684-80577-4 (vol. 1)—ISBN
0-684-80578-2 (vol. 2) — ISBN 0-684-80579-0 (vol. 3) — ISBN 0-684-80580-4 (vol. 4)
— ISBN 0-684-80581-2 (vol. 5) — ISBN 0-684-80645-2 (vol. 6)
     1. Europe—Social conditions—Encyclopedias.   2. Europe—Social life and
customs—Encyclopedias.   3. Social history—Encyclopedias.   I. Stearns, Peter N.
HN373 .E63 2000
306′.094′03—dc21
                                                                            00-046376

The paper used in this publication meets the requirements of ANSI/NISO Z39.48–1992 (Permanence of Paper).

CONTENTS OF THIS VOLUME

Section 19   Culture and Popular Culture

Popular Culture   3
 Peter Burke

High Culture   15
 Arthur Mitzman

Magic   29
 Stuart Clark

Festivals   41
 Mack P. Holt

The Reformation of Popular Culture   53
 Ann W. Ramsey

Language   67
 Peter Burke

Consumerism   77
 Gary S. Cross

Drinking and Drugs   89
 Thomas E. Brennan

Honor and Shame   103
 Robert A. Nye

Memory and the Invention of Traditions   115
 Tamara L. Hunt and Scott Hughes Myerly

Humor   131
 Benjamin Roberts

Music and Dance   141
 William Weber

Section 20   Modern Recreation and Leisure

Policing Leisure   155
 John K. Walton

Sports   167
 Allen Guttmann

Holidays and Public Rituals   185
 Scott Hughes Myerly and Tamara L. Hunt

Consumer Leisure   201
 Charles Rearick

Vacations   219
 John K. Walton

Travel and Tourism   229
 Stephen L. Harp

Section 21   Religion

Belief and Popular Religion   249
 Keith P. Luria

Church and Society   263
 Andrew Barnes

Judaism   275
 Jay R. Berkovitz

Catholicism   287
 Keith P. Luria

Protestantism   301
 Andrew Pettegree

Eastern Orthodoxy   313
 Gregory L. Freeze

Section 22   Education and Literacy

Schools and Schooling   329
 Paul F. Grendler

Higher Education   353
 Charles R. Day

Teachers   365
 Scott J. Seregny

Printing and Publishing   377
 Thomas Cragin

Literacy   391
 R. A. Houston

Reading   407
 Daniel P. Resnick and Jason Martinek

CONTENTS OF THIS VOLUME

Journalism   419
    Thomas Cragin

Section 23   Everyday Life

Material Culture   435
    Whitney A. Walton
Standards of Living   451
    Norman Pounds
Housing   461
    Craig Keating

Domestic Interiors   471
    Rineke van Daalen
Clothing and Fashion   483
    Beverly Lemire
Food and Diet   497
    Kolleen M. Guy
Animals and Pets   507
    Kathleen J. Kete
Toys and Games   521
    Gary S. Cross

CONTENTS OF OTHER VOLUMES

VOLUME 1

Alphabetical Table of Contents   xiii

List of Maps   xvii

Introduction   xix

Chronology   xxiii

List of Abbreviations   xliii

Section 1   Methods and Theoretical Approaches

Generations of Social History   3
    Geoff Eley

The Sources of Social History   31
    Mary Lindemann

The Annales Paradigm   41
    Peter Burke

Marxism and Radical History   49
    Bryan D. Palmer

Interdisciplinary Contacts and Influences   61
    Louise A. Tilly

Cliometrics and Quantification   71
    Michael P. Hanagan

Cultural History and New Cultural History   83
    C. E. Forth

Gender Theory   95
    Bonnie G. Smith

Microhistory   105
    Karl Appuhn

Comparative European Social History   113
    Hartmut Kaelble

Section 2   The Periods of Social History

Periodization in Social History   125
    Peter N. Stearns

The Medieval Heritage   131
    Constance B. Bouchard

The Renaissance   143
    John Martin

The Protestant Reformation and the Catholic Reformation   153
    Ronnie Po-Chia Hsia

The Early Modern Period   165
    Jonathan Dewald

The Enlightenment   179
    Brian Dolan

The French Revolution and the Empire   193
    Isser Woloch

The Nineteenth Century   205
    Timothy B. Smith

The World Wars and the Depression   219
    Jay Winter

Since World War II   229
    Donna Harsch

Section 3   Regions, Nations, and Peoples

Principles of Regionalism   243
    John Agnew

Britain   257
    Brian Lewis

Ireland   271
    David W. Miller

France   283
    Jeremy D. Popkin

The Low Countries   297
    Wim Blockmans

The Iberian Peninsula   307
    Montserrat Miller

Italy   321
    Lucy Riall

Central Europe   337
    Mary Jo Maynes and Eric D. Weitz

The Nordic Countries   357
    Panu Pulma

The Baltic Nations   371
    Alfred Erich Senn

East Central Europe   379
    Steven Béla Várdy and Emil Neiderhauser

Russia and the East Slavs   405
    Rex Wade

The Balkans   421
    Maria Bucur

The Jews and Anti-Semitism   433
    Michael C. Hickey

Roma: The Gypsies   449
    David M. Crowe

Section 4   Europe and the World

The World Economy and Colonial
    Expansion   461
    Gayle Brunelle

Explorers, Missionaries, Traders   475
    Stephen Maughan

Emigration and Colonies   489
    Kenneth Orosz

Imperialism and Domestic Society   503
    Laura Tabili

Imperialism and Gender   515
    Nupur Chaudhuri

America, Americanization, and
    Anti-Americanism   523
    Rob Kroes

Immigrants   533
    Panikos Panayi

Racism   545
    Gisela Kaplan

VOLUME 2

Section 5   Processes of Social Change

Modernization   3
    Peter N. Stearns

Technology   13
    Kristine Bruland

Capitalism and Commercialization   23
    Robert S. Duplessis

Protoindustrialization   39
    Gay L. Gullickson

The Industrial Revolutions   51
    Patrick K. O'Brien

War and Conquest   67
    Jeremy Black

Science and the Scientific Revolution   77
    John Henry

Secularization   95
    Hartmut Lehmann

Communications, the Media, and
    Propaganda   101
    Tom Wolfe

Section 6   Population and Geography

The Environment   115
    Richard H. Grove

Migration   133
    Leslie Page Moch

The Population of Europe: Early Modern
    Demographic Patterns   145
    David Levine

The Population of Europe: The Demographic
    Transition and After   159
    Michael R. Haines

The European Marriage Pattern   171
    David Levine

Birth, Contraception, and Abortion   181
    John M. Riddle

The Life Cycle   193
    Sherri Klassen

Health and Disease   205
    Kenneth Kiple

Death   219
    David G. Troyansky

Section 7   Cities and Urbanization

Urbanization   237
    Alexander Cowan

The City: The Early Modern Period   249
  Christopher R. Friedrichs
The City: The Modern Period   263
  Josef Konvitz
The Urban Infrastructure   277
  Nicholas Papayanis and Rosemary Wakeman
Shops and Stores   291
  Montserrat Miller
Urban Institutions and Politics: The Early
  Modern Period   301
  Christopher R. Friedrichs
Urban Institutions and Politics: The
  Modern Period   307
  Theresa M. McBride
Street Life and City Space   313
  W. Scott Haine
Suburbs and New Towns   329
  Alexander Cowan

Section 8   Rural Life

Agriculture   343
  James R. Lehning
Land Tenure   357
  Liana Vardi
Serfdom: Western Europe   369
  Liana Vardi
Serfdom: Eastern Europe   379
  Boris Gorshkov
Peasant and Farming Villages   389
  Palle Ove Christiansen
Collectivization   403
  Lynne Viola
Estates and Country Houses   413
  Priscilla R. Roosevelt
Fairs and Markets   425
  Montserrat Miller

Section 9   State and Society

Absolutism   439
  David Parker
The Liberal State   449
  Adrian Shubert
Democracy   463
  Charles Tilly

The Welfare State   477
  Steven Beaudoin
Civil Society   489
  Guido Hausmann
Nationalism   499
  Caroline Ford
Fascism and Nazism   509
  Alexander J. De Grand
Communism   519
  Eric D. Weitz
Bureaucracy   533
  Don K. Rowney
Military Service   545
  Michael Neiberg

VOLUME 3

Section 10   Social Structure

Social Class   3
  Charles Tilly
Social Mobility   19
  Hartmut Kaelble
The Aristocracy and Gentry   27
  Jonathan Dewald
The Middle Classes   39
  Margaret Hunt
Professionals and Professionalization   57
  James C. Albisetti
Students   67
  Keith Vernon
Artists   79
  Alexander Varias
The Military   97
  Michael Neiberg
Artisans   107
  Peter N. Stearns
The Petty Bourgeoisie   111
  Daniel T. Orlovsky
Working Classes   121
  Dick Geary
Servants   139
  Bridget Hill

Peasants and Rural Laborers   149
　　Cathy A. Frierson
Slaves   165
　　Richard Hellie
Marginal People   175
　　Timothy B. Smith

Section 11　Social Protest

Collective Action   189
　　Charles Tilly
Moral Economy and Luddism   205
　　John G. Rule
Urban Crowds   217
　　Michael P. Hanagan
Revolutions   227
　　Michael D. Richards
Labor History: Strikes and Unions   253
　　Michael P. Hanagan
Socialism   267
　　Eric D. Weitz
Gender and Popular Protest   279
　　Anna K. Clark
New Social Movements   289
　　Gisela Kaplan
Student Movements   301
　　Brendan Dooley
Modern Protest Politics   311
　　Marco Giugni

Section 12　Deviance, Crime, and Social Control

Crime   335
　　Pieter Spierenburg
Prostitution   351
　　Kathryn Norberg
Witchcraft   361
　　J. A. Sharpe
Banditry   373
　　Paul Sant Cassia
Juvenile Delinquency and Hooliganism   383
　　Kathleen Alaimo
Police   399
　　Haia Shpayer-Makov
Punishment   413
　　Abby M. Schrader

Madness and Asylums   429
　　Peter Bartlett

Section 13　Social Problems and Social Reform

Charity and Poor Relief: The Early Modern
　　Period   447
　　Brian Pullan
Charity and Poor Relief: The Modern
　　Period   453
　　Timothy B. Smith
Social Welfare and Insurance   467
　　Young-Sun Hong
Alcohol and Temperance   483
　　George Snow
Orphans and Foundlings   497
　　David L. Ransel
Developmental and Physical Disabilities:
　　The "Blind," "Deaf and Dumb," and
　　"Idiot"   507
　　David Wright
Public Health   517
　　Dorothy Porter

VOLUME 4

Section 14　Gender

The Development of Gender History   3
　　Bonnie G. Smith
Patriarchy   15
　　Merry E. Wiesner-Hanks
Women and Femininity   25
　　Bonnie G. Smith
Men and Masculinity   37
　　Peter N. Stearns
Feminisms   45
　　Laura E. Nym Mayhall
Gender and Work   55
　　Merry E. Wiesner-Hanks
Gender and Education   69
　　Linda L. Clark

Section 15　The Family and Age Groups

History of the Family   85
　　David Levine

Kinship   101
    Andrejs Plakans
The Household   109
    Richard Wall
Inheritance   125
    Julie Hardwick
The Family and the State   135
    Roderick G. Phillips
Courtship, Marriage, and Divorce   145
    Joanne M. Ferraro
Motherhood   161
    Ellen Ross
Child Rearing and Childhood   175
    Colin Heywood
Youth and Adolescence   193
    Andrew Donson
Widows and Widowers   207
    Sherri Klassen
The Elderly   219
    David G. Troyansky
Generations and Generational Conflict   231
    Elizabeth Townsend

Section 16   Sexuality

Sexual Behavior and Sexual Morality   243
    Lisa Z. Sigel
Illegitimacy and Concubinage   259
    Anne-Marie Sohn
Puberty   269
    Alexandra M. Lord
Masturbation   279
    Lesley A. Hall
Pornography   291
    Lisa Z. Sigel
Sex, Law, and the State   301
    Roderick G. Phillips
Homosexuality and Lesbianism   311
    Randolph Trumbach

Section 17   Body and Mind

The Body and Its Representations   327
    Lisa Z. Sigel

Cleanliness   343
    Virginia Smith
The Senses   355
    Constance Classen
Gestures   365
    Herman Roodenburg
Manners   371
    Cas Wouters
The Emotions   383
    Rineke van Daalen
Anthropometry   397
    John Komlos and Robert Whaples
Medical Practitioners and Medicine   409
    Matthew Ramsey
Childbirth, Midwives, Wetnursing   427
    Amanda Carson Banks
Psychiatry and Psychology   439
    Roger Smith

Section 18   Work

Work and the Work Ethic   451
    Peter Shapely
Preindustrial Manufacturing   467
    Steven A. Epstein
Factory Work   479
    Barbara Bari
Middle-Class Work   495
    Peter N. Stearns
Work Time   501
    Gary S. Cross
Child Labor   513
    Colin Heywood

VOLUME 6

Biographies   1
Directory of Contributors   375
Index   389

ALPHABETICAL TABLE OF CONTENTS

A

Absolutism   2:439

Agriculture   2:343

Alcohol and Temperance   3:483

America, Americanization, and
    Anti-Americanism   1:523

Animals and Pets   5:507

The *Annales* Paradigm   1:41

Anthropometry   4:397

The Aristocracy and Gentry   3:27

Artisans   3:107

Artists   3:79

B

The Balkans   1:421

The Baltic Nations   1:371

Banditry   3:373

Belief and Popular Religion   5:249

Birth, Contraception, and Abortion   2:181

The Body and Its Representations   4:327

Britain   1:257

Bureaucracy   2:533

C

Capitalism and Commercialization   2:23

Catholicism   5:287

Central Europe   1:337

Charity and Poor Relief: The Early Modern
    Period   3:447

Charity and Poor Relief: The Modern
    Period   3:453

Childbirth, Midwives, Wetnursing   4:427

Child Labor   4:513

Child Rearing and Childhood   4:175

Church and Society   5:263

The City: The Early Modern Period   2:249

The City: The Modern Period   2:263

Civil Society   2:489

Cleanliness   4:343

Cliometrics and Quantification   1:71

Clothing and Fashion   5:483

Collective Action   3:189

Collectivization   2:403

Communications, the Media, and
    Propaganda   2:101

Communism   2:519

Comparative European Social History   1:113

Consumerism   5:77

Consumer Leisure   5:201

Courtship, Marriage, and Divorce   4:145

Crime   3:335

Cultural History and New Cultural History   1:83

D

Death   2:219

Democracy   2:463

Developmental and Physical Disabilities:
    The "Blind," "Deaf and Dumb," and
    "Idiot"   3:507

The Development of Gender History   4:3

Domestic Interiors   5:471

Drinking and Drugs   5:89

E

The Early Modern Period   1:165

East Central Europe   1:379

Eastern Orthodoxy   5:313

The Elderly   4:219

Emigration and Colonies   1:489
The Emotions   4:383
The Enlightenment   1:179
The Environment   2:115
Estates and Country Houses   2:413
The European Marriage Pattern   2:171
Explorers, Missionaries, Traders   1:475

F

Factory Work   4:479
Fairs and Markets   2:425
The Family and the State   4:135
Fascism and Nazism   2:509
Feminisms   4:45
Festivals   5:41
Food and Diet   5:497
France   1:283
The French Revolution and the Empire   1:193

G

Gender and Education   4:69
Gender and Popular Protest   3:279
Gender and Work   4:55
Gender History   4:3
Gender Theory   1:95
Generations and Generational Conflict   4:231
Generations of Social History   1:3
Gestures   4:365

H

Health and Disease   2:205
High Culture   5:15
Higher Education   5:353
History of the Family   4:85
Holidays and Public Rituals   5:185
Homosexuality and Lesbianism   4:311
Honor and Shame   5:103
The Household   4:109
Housing   5:461
Humor   5:131

I

The Iberian Peninsula   1:307
Illegitimacy and Concubinage   4:259

Immigrants   1:533
Imperialism and Domestic Society   1:503
Imperialism and Gender   1:515
The Industrial Revolutions   2:51
Inheritance   4:125
Interdisciplinary Contacts and Influences   1:61
Ireland   1:271
Italy   1:321

J

The Jews and Anti-Semitism   1:433
Journalism   5:419
Judaism   5:275
Juvenile Delinquency and Hooliganism   3:383

K

Kinship   4:101

L

Labor History: Strikes and Unions   3:253
Land Tenure   3:357
Language   5:67
The Liberal State   2:449
The Life Cycle   2:193
Literacy   5:391
The Low Countries   1:297

M

Madness and Asylums   3:429
Magic   5:29
Manners   4:371
Marginal People   3:175
Marxism and Radical History   1:49
Masturbation   4:279
Material Culture   5:435
Medical Practitioners and Medicine   4:409
The Medieval Heritage   1:131
Memory and the Invention of Traditions   5:115
Men and Masculinity   4:37
Microhistory   1:105
The Middle Classes   3:39

Middle-Class Work   4:495

Migration   2:133

The Military   3:97

Military Service   2:545

Modernization   2:3

Modern Protest Politics   3:311

Moral Economy and Luddism   3:205

Motherhood   4:161

Music and Dance   5:141

N

Nationalism   2:499

New Social Movements   3:289

The Nineteenth Century   1:205

The Nordic Countries   1:357

O

Orphans and Foundlings   3:497

P

Patriarchy   4:15

Peasant and Farming Villages   2:389

Peasants and Rural Laborers   3:149

Periodization in Social History   1:125

The Petty Bourgeoisie   3:111

Police   3:399

Policing Leisure   5:155

Popular Culture   5:3

The Population of Europe: The Demographic Transition and After   2:159

The Population of Europe: Early Modern Demographic Patterns   2:145

Pornography   4:291

Preindustrial Manufacturing   4:467

Principles of Regionalism   1:243

Printing and Publishing   5:377

Professionals and Professionalization   3:57

Prostitution   3:351

Protestantism   5:301

The Protestant Reformation and the Catholic Reformation   1:153

Protoindustrialization   2:39

Psychiatry and Psychology   4:439

Puberty   4:269

Public Health   3:517

Punishment   3:413

R

Racism   1:545

Reading   5:407

The Reformation of Popular Culture   5:53

The Renaissance   1:143

Revolutions   3:227

Roma: The Gypsies   1:449

Russia and the Eastern Slavs   1:405

S

Schools and Schooling   5:329

Science and the Scientific Revolution   2:77

Secularization   2:95

The Senses   4:355

Serfdom: Eastern Europe   2:379

Serfdom: Western Europe   2:369

Servants   3:139

Sex, Law, and the State   4:301

Sexual Behavior and Sexual Morality   4:243

Shops and Stores   2:291

Since World War II   1:229

Slaves   3:165

Social Class   3:3

Socialism   3:267

Social Mobility   3:19

Social Welfare and Insurance   3:467

The Sources of Social History   1:31

Sports   5:167

Standards of Living   5:451

Street Life and City Space   2:313

Student Movements   3:301

Students   3:67

Suburbs and New Towns   2:329

T

Teachers   5:265

Technology   2:13

Toys and Games   5:521

Travel and Tourism   5:229

U

Urban Crowds   3:217

The Urban Infrastructure   2:277

Urban Institutions and Politics: The Early Modern
        Period   2:301

Urban Institutions and Politics: The Modern
        Period   2:307

Urbanization   2:237

V

Vacations   5:219

W

War and Conquest   2:67

The Welfare State   2:477

Widows and Widowers   4:207

Witchcraft   3:361

Women and Femininity   4:25

Work and the Work Ethic   4:451

Working Classes   3:121

Work Time   4:501

The World Economy and Colonial
        Expansion   1:461

The World Wars and the Depression   1:219

Y

Youth and Adolescence   4:193

COMMON ABBREVIATIONS USED IN THIS WORK

A.D.	*Anno Domini,* in the year of the Lord		i.e.	*id est,* that is
AESC	*Annales: Économies, Sociétés, Civilisations*		IMF	International Monetary Fund
ASSR	Autonomous Soviet Socialist Republic		MS.	manuscript (pl. MSS.)
b.	born		n.	note
B.C.	before Christ		n.d.	no date
B.C.E.	before the common era (= B.C.)		no.	number (pl., nos.)
c.	*circa,* about, approximately		n.p.	no place
C.E.	common era (= A.D.)		n.s.	new series
cf.	*confer,* compare		N.S.	new style, according to the Gregorian calendar
chap.	chapter		OECD	Organization for Economic Cooperation and Development
CP	Communist Party		O.S.	old style, according to the Julian calendar
d.	died			
diss.	dissertation		p.	page (pl., pp.)
ed.	editor (pl., eds.), edition		pt.	part
e.g.	*exempli gratia,* for example		rev.	revised
et al.	*et alii,* and others		S.	*san, sanctus, santo,* male saint
etc.	*et cetera,* and so forth		ser.	series
EU	European Union		SP	Socialist Party
f.	and following (pl., ff.)		SS.	saints
fl.	*floruit,* flourished		SSR	Soviet Socialist Republic
GDP	gross domestic product		Sta.	*sancta, santa,* female saint
GDR	German Democratic Republic (East Germany)		supp.	supplement
GNP	gross national product		USSR	Union of Soviet Socialist Republics
HRE	Holy Roman Empire, Holy Roman Emperor		vol.	volume
ibid.	*ibididem,* in the same place (as the one immediately preceding)		WTO	World Trade Organization
			?	uncertain, possibly, perhaps

ENCYCLOPEDIA OF
EUROPEAN SOCIAL HISTORY

Section 19

❧

CULTURE AND POPULAR CULTURE

Popular Culture   3
Peter Burke

High Culture   15
Arthur Mitzman

Magic   29
Stuart Clark

Festivals   41
Mack P. Holt

The Reformation of Popular Culture   53
Ann W. Ramsey

Language   67
Peter Burke

Consumerism   77
Gary S. Cross

Drinking and Drugs   89
Thomas E. Brennan

Honor and Shame   103
Robert A. Nye

Memory and the Invention of Traditions   115
Tamara L. Hunt and Scott Hughes Myerly

Humor   131
Benjamin Roberts

Music and Dance   141
William A. Weber

POPULAR CULTURE

Peter Burke

Definitions of popular culture abound, whether it is viewed primarily as peasant culture, oral culture, unofficial culture, the culture of custom, the community, culture created by the people or for the people. Despite or sometimes because of this abundance, some historians have questioned whether popular culture is a useful category of analysis at all. To discuss this question is the fundamental aim of this article. After a short discussion of the historiography of the subject, the remaining pages will be devoted to problems, notably the problem of the sources; the problem of defining the key terms "popular" and "culture"; the twin problems of hegemony and resistance; and the problem of mass culture.

HISTORIOGRAPHY

Popular culture was long neglected by historians because ordinary people were considered beneath the "dignity of history." Although earlier European antiquaries had sometimes written with more or less condescension about popular customs, a serious interest in the culture of ordinary people on the part of the learned began not among historians but among men of letters, such as Sir Walter Scott and Johann Gottfried Herder. A movement developed, from the late eighteenth century onward, to collect traditional popular poetry before the new urban and commercial society destroyed it. This interest in the "folk" spread from poetry to music, painting, and building and to the beliefs and customs described from the middle of the nineteenth century onward as folklore (*Volkskunde, folclore,* and so on). Open-air museums of peasant housing and material culture were founded in Denmark, Norway, Sweden, and elsewhere in the later nineteenth century.

One of the main reasons for this new interest was that the people, especially the peasantry, were believed to have preserved the cultural heritage better than other social groups had done. Around 1800 in many parts of Europe, a return to this heritage was regarded as an antidote to the corruption of different national cultures by the imitation of foreign models on the part of the upper and middle classes, especially in the cities. It was no accident that this "discovery of the people" took place in the age of nationalism or that more interest was shown in popular culture in central and eastern Europe and in Scandinavia than in western Europe, more in Scotland than in England, and more in Britanny or Languedoc than in the Île-de-France.

Until the 1960s most historians were content to leave the study of popular culture to the folklorists. However, two shifts of interest combined to place the study of popular culture on the agenda of historians at this time. First was the rise of history from below. Following the example of E. P. Thompson in Britain and like-minded scholars in other countries, historians of culture and society increasingly found a place for ordinary people in their narratives. Second, the turn toward the new cultural (or sociocultural) history meant that historians of the "popular classes" found a place for culture alongside their discussions of the standard of living or political action.

However, to give culture a greater importance than before was to do more than simply widen the historian's agenda, as the debate over Thompson's *Making of the English Working Class* (1963) shows clearly enough. Thompson's book was criticized by his fellow Marxists for what they called its "culturalism," a deviation from the economic interpretation of history. They had not expected to hear so much about broadside ballads or to learn about the symbolism of food and initiation ceremonies and the iconography of riots or to be told that John Bunyan's *Pilgrim's Progress* was a foundation text of the working-class movement or to read about the culture of the English radicals or that of the weaving communities of Yorkshire and Lancashire.

As this example suggests, although new approaches to history are normally designed to solve problems, they often raise problems of their own. In the field of popular culture, the two most fundamental problems revolve around, although they cannot be reduced to, the difficulty of defining the two key terms, "popular" and "culture."

THE PROBLEM OF THE SOURCES

All historians have to grapple with the problem that their access to the past is indirect, but historians of popular culture face the problem of mediation in an unusually acute form, as the following observations may suggest.

1. Historians of the culture of ordinary people are often condemned to see it through the eyes of elites, including the antiquarians and folklorists who collected much evidence that would otherwise have been lost but also added their own interpretations of it. We know a good deal about elite views of popular culture and all too little about the reverse.

2. The alien eyes through which we see so much of popular culture are sometimes literally foreign, the eyes of travelers, because in early modern Europe in particular, festival culture and everyday culture alike were taken for granted in the region itself, so that only outsiders found it sufficiently surprising to bother to record it. It would be difficult indeed to write the history of the Carnival of Venice without the testimony of a succession of foreign visitors who described what they saw or asked the locals what it meant, visitors such as the fifteenth-century German nobleman Arnold von Harff or the seventeenth-century English gentleman John Evelyn. However, foreign visitors notoriously misunderstand what they see and even what they hear in a strange environment.

3. The eyes through which a historian observes popular culture may also be hostile eyes, for example, the eyes of reformers, whether clerical or lay, intent on purifying the culture from paganism, superstition, immorality, or disorder.

4. Much of popular culture is oral; some would define it as essentially oral. Yet in the age before the use of the tape recorder, the oral survives only through written evidence, which necessarily distorts it. The performative element in popular culture is even more elusive, the verbal descriptions and occasional images providing no more than an approximation to the lost reality.

5. Historians of culture, like historians of society, want to discover what the norms were in particular places and times. Since these norms were taken for granted at the time, historians are condemned to discovering them from the breaches, reconstructing what should have happened from stories about what went wrong—from a tavern brawl that led to manslaughter to Carnival in the city of Romans in Dauphine in 1580—analyzed by the French historian Emmanuel Le Roy Ladurie, in which local social and religious conflicts, exacerbated rather than appeased by the festivities, led to a massacre.

6. When, in the most favorable conditions, the sources allow the historian to view popular culture from inside, the participants who have left first-hand accounts do not form a random sample of the whole but are the more self-conscious individuals, generally the more prosperous, literate, and urban.

7. In any case, different kinds of ordinary people participated to different degrees. The visibility and audibility of young adult males in festivals from carnival to charivari will be obvious enough. The majority of the community, including women, remained relatively invisible and inaudible. Following the sources closely, historians run the risk of assuming the consensus of the community and overlooking possible differences, distinctions, and conflicts.

8. Surviving sources privilege major celebrations in major cities at the expense of the more common rural festivities, which were smaller in scale and often escaped the notice of visitors and reformers alike.

All these problems are serious, but none of them rules out the possibility of writing history at all. Better-documented examples illuminate others for which the evidence is more fragmentary, while different sources for the same event or activity may confirm or supplement one another.

THE PROBLEM OF THE POPULAR

For some nineteenth-century scholars, "the people" included everyone. It was synonymous with the nation, and in some European languages the same word (*narod* in Russian, for example) is used in both contexts. For others, the term rightly referred only to the peasantry, thus excluding the urban working classes, who were thought to have no traditions of their own. Today, historians still have problems with the concept of the popular. From an economic point of view, the people might be described as the relatively poor. In political terms, they are what the Italian social theorist Antonio Gramsci called the "dominated classes" (*classi*

Carnival in Venice. Painting by Canaletto (Giovanni Antonio Canal) (1697–1768). Bowes Museum, County Durham, U.K./The Bridgeman Art Library

subalterni), in other words, the powerless. A strictly cultural definition is more difficult. The people might be described as the formally uneducated, more exactly, as those who have not had access to higher education and may not even have attended school. It will be noted that these three definitions are essentially negative, describing the people as those who lack what other groups possess. In similar fashion, popular culture has often been described if not defined in terms of residues, what is left over after "high" culture (Michelangelo, Shakespeare, Descartes, Beethoven, and so on) has been subtracted—leaving us with folk songs, folktales, and folklore. The disadvantages of defining any object of historical study in terms of what it lacks rather than what it possesses should be obvious enough.

The binary model. Another general problem is that of the cultural distance between the elites and the people in a given place and time. Where earlier historians either argued or, more frequently, assumed that the upper classes lived in a different cultural world from ordinary people, much work in cultural history has dealt, following the Russian cultural theorist Mikhail Bakhtin, with interactions, exchanges, or negotiations between the two. For Bakhtin, the cultural distinction between high and low was not a distinction between social groups but rather one between the official and the unofficial. He emphasized the importance of unofficial occasions, such as Carnival, and unofficial locales, such as the marketplace.

Late-twentieth-century studies confirmed Bakhtin's suggestion by showing that sixteenth-century European nobles, for example, participated in what we call "popular culture" at least on some occasions in the year, such as Christmas and Carnival—the rituals associated with the annual cycle of the seasons offer the clearest example of common participation by different social groups. The wives and daughters of the nobility participated still more fully in everyday popular culture at this time partly because their level of literacy was generally lower. The elites were bicultural just as they were bilingual in the sense of being able to speak a standard or literary form of the vernacular as well as to communicate with ordinary people in the local dialect.

This biculturalism of individuals and groups facilitated exchanges between cultures or subcultures. It has long been known that certain cultural items, romances of chivalry, for example, have descended in the social hierarchy over the centuries, forming part of what the German folklorists called "sunken cultural property" (gesunkenes Kulturgut). Movement also took place in the opposite direction, as in the case of dance. The European upper classes regularly appropriated styles of dancing from the peasants, attracted by the vigor and spontaneity of these dances but gradually refining them until the need to borrow reasserted itself. In some cases it is possible to trace a complete circle of appropriation and adaptation between the culture of shepherds, let us say, and aristocratic pastoral.

It is virtually impossible to discuss interactions of this kind without using terms such as "learned" and "popular," or "high" and "low." In other words, we need the dichotomy in theory even when we are engaged in undermining it in practice. At the very least it provides historians with a useful kind of shorthand or a model in the sense of a deliberate simplification that enables the user to understand a more complex reality somewhat better. Some scholars, particularly those interested in cities, have advocated a three-tier rather than a two-tier model, finding a place for an apparently distinctive third or middle-class culture. One example is found in the American historian Louis Wright's *Middle-Class Culture in Elizabethan England* (1935) with its descriptions of printed books or booklets that encourage self-improvement, give instructions in domestic relations or guidance to godliness, or offer accounts of the wonders of nature and of travel. Another comes from a perceptive study of nineteenth-century Sweden, by Jonas Frykman and Orvar Löfgren, in which the bourgeoisie are presented as defining themselves first against the culture of the aristocracy and then against the culture of the working class.

The problem is that on close inspection, this middle-class culture often turns out to have many elements in common with the other two. In those cases it therefore seems preferable, on the grounds of intel-

lectual parsimony, to work with a binary model on one condition: that the frontier between the two cultures is not regarded as too sharp or too stable. Historians need a model that enables them to discuss not only degrees of cultural distance but also change over time. The binary model allows them to do this and also to distinguish the directions of cultural movement, upward or downward.

The logic of appropriation. Unfortunately, the conceptual problems of historians of the popular do not end at this point. As the French scholar Roger Chartier has argued, it is extremely unwise to try to define the popular in terms of particular texts, images, festivals, or other items given the different uses and meanings of the same artifact or practice when it is appropriated by different individuals or groups. In France at the end of the seventeenth century, for example, certain folktales (fairy tales, as we sometimes call them) that had long circulated among the peasantry were appropriated by the lords and ladies who surrounded Louis XIV. However, the stories changed their meaning when they were transported from the cottage to the court, just as Marie Antoinette in pastoral garb was no ordinary shepherdess. In his own work on French chapbooks, the so-called *Bibliothèque Bleue* (so called because the booklets were bound in cheap blue paper), Chartier has tended to focus on the texts, studying their careers or trajectories as they were adapted to the needs of different communities of readers and listeners.

This approach is both valid and valuable. However, it surely needs to be complemented by another approach, which might be described as a "social history of culture." The traditional, more or less Marxist sociology or social history of culture, which aligned ideas, artifacts, and performances with different social groups (usually social classes) has often been criticized as too simple and reductionist. For instance, according to the French theorist Michel de Certeau (a major influence on Chartier), the old sociology of culture failed to take account of the phenomenon of appropriation, of what he called the creative or productive aspect of consumption, the different uses and meanings of the same item in different settings. Certeau viewed culture as a kind of bricolage in which the users were continually producing something new out of old materials.

However, the social history of culture is capable of being revised to take account of these suggestions. A new social history of culture might usefully center on what might be called the logic of appropriation, in other words, the principles underlying the selection and combination of texts, images, and so on by a particular social group in a particular setting at a particular time. The British sociologist Dick Hebdige's well-known study of some British popular subcultures of the 1960s and 1970s, notably the Rastas, mods, and punks, argued that it was precisely by bricolage that these groups created their own styles, but that each style also had a social meaning. How can we discover this logic of appropriation? Such an investigation might well start from a social rather than a cultural definition of the popular, such as the attitudes and values of ordinary people as they are expressed or embodied in practices and in artifacts. Of course social groups are to some extent culturally constructed—defined by their style of life—but only to some extent, since there are real and sometimes extreme contrasts in wealth and power underlying the lifestyles of different classes or "estates."

The advantage of this social definition is that it leaves open for empirical investigation two fundamental problems. The first is whether or not there are cultural divisions within the subordinate groups taking the form either of cultural stratification (the richer and the poorer peasantry, for example) or of what has been called segmentation into subcultures—male and female, old and young, urban and rural, not to mention occupational subcultures such as soldiers, sailors, beggars, thieves, shepherds, cobblers, and so on. In order not to forget this variety, it might be advisable to employ the term "culture" in the plural and speak of learned cultures, popular cultures, religious cultures, and so on.

The second problem is whether or not particular cultural items are shared (in a given place at a given time) between ordinary people and elites, either ruling classes or specialists in what is variously called "high" or "learned" culture (priests, intellectuals, and so on). What is often called popular religion, for instance, might be better described as the religion of the laity or as unofficial religion—although we should not forget that ordinary people sometimes developed their own forms of religious organization, such as Catholic confraternities and Protestant lay preaching.

An alternative description might be "local religion," a point made by the American anthropologist William Christian in a study of religion in the region around Toledo in Spain in the later sixteenth century. Focusing on chapels, shrines, relics, indulgences, and the collective vows that villages made to saints to invoke their aid against natural disasters, Christian argues that "the vast majority of sacred places and moments held meaning only for local citizens," including in this group the local elites as well as ordinary people.

How much or how little different social groups have in common culturally has varied a great deal in

British Rastafarians. Malcolm Willidon and John Mills stand outside a community center in London, 15 August 1979. ©HULTON GETTY/LIAISON AGENCY

the last five hundred years of European history. From the sixteenth century onward starting in Italy, historians have discerned a movement of withdrawal from popular culture on the part of the nobles, the clergy, and finally the middle classes, male and (somewhat later) female, beginning in Italy and spreading to France, England, the Netherlands, Spain, central Europe, and finally, Scandinavia and Russia. A vivid example comes from a 1986 study of early modern Barcelona. The author, James Amelang, speaks of a "retreat to the balcony" by urban elites; "direct participation in communal ceremonies gave way to observation, as the ruling class abandoned the street in favor of the balconies and inner salons of its mansions" (p. 196). The speed of this process of withdrawal must not be exaggerated. It was perhaps never complete, and in the twentieth century, if not before, the movement went into reverse. All the same, the concept of withdrawal has the advantage of suggesting links between a number of more specific changes, from the rise of private Carnival parties among elites to the abandonment of dances and taverns by the Catholic clergy after the reforms enacted at the Council of Trent.

THE PROBLEM OF CULTURE

"Culture" is if anything an even more difficult concept than "popular," and students of this topic have experimented with different definitions and research strategies. The first solution to the problem, adopted by the folklorists of the nineteenth century (if indeed it was a conscious solution and not an unconscious assumption), was to treat popular culture as a set of popular equivalents of the main forms and genres of high culture, in other words folk music, folktales, folk art, folk drama, and so on. This was for the most part what they chose to collect. A second solution, more open ended, was to focus on performances and especially on festivals, above all on Carnival—not only the central rituals (processions, dances, mock trials, and executions) but also the informal practices that surrounded them, the songs, the masks, the violence, and so on. Carnival has been studied with most care in the major cities along the urban spine of Europe—Naples, Rome, Florence, Venice, Basel, Nürnberg, and Cologne. These were the locales in which the most spectacular performances took place from the later Middle Ages onward for the sake not only of the citizens but of villagers from the surrounding countryside, not to mention the foreign visitors who arrived in increasing numbers from the late seventeenth century onward. From the nineteenth century onward, however, there is also increasing evidence of Carnival at the village level in Italy, France, Germany, and elsewhere.

Whether or not ordinary people used to spend most of their year looking forward to Carnival and other festivals or remembering past ones, it is clear that their culture cannot be reduced to such events. The late-twentieth-century solution to the problem, "What is popular culture?" was to approach it through the study of everyday life. Following the lead of anthropologists and the philosophy of the "cultural construction of reality," historians used the term "culture" more and more widely to speak of "political culture," "print culture," "culinary culture," "housing culture," the "culture of poverty," "the culture of the factory," the "culture of consumption," and so on. Among the advantages of this approach is the fact that the gendering of popular culture appears more clearly in the study of the everyday than in that of festivals, whether one thinks of distinctive female attitudes to sexuality or violence, or of women's access to certain cultural spaces, from the public square to the tavern.

However, if all human activities are to be described as culture, there seems no point in using the term at all. Cultural historians have stuffed so many different items into their sack that it is on the verge of bursting. A possible solution to this problem might be to define cultural history, like cultural studies, in terms of an approach (or a discourse) rather than a field in the conventional sense. The approach might be described as one emphasizing values, attitudes (including what the British critic Raymond Williams called "structures of feeling"), and symbols, wherever they are to be found, as they are expressed or embodied in artifacts (images, tools, buildings) and in actions, whether everyday practices or special performances. It is also concerned with what the Russian semiotician Juri Lotman called the poetics of culture, the unwritten rules and unspoken assumptions underlying everyday life.

Unfortunately, these concepts too present obstacles. The notion of a cultural rule has been criticized by the French social theorist Pierre Bourdieu as too rigid. On the other hand, his alternative to it, "habitus," might be said to have the opposite disadvantage—it is too flexible and elusive. The idea of the "everyday" is also more ambiguous than it may look, since in different contexts it has different meanings—private as opposed to public, popular as opposed to elite, routine as opposed to creative, and normal life as opposed to special occasions.

Perhaps the safest way to operate with the concept of culture is to treat it as historians have learned to treat the popular. In other words, not to focus on the everyday in itself but rather on the relation between the everyday and its opposite, the extraordinary, including in this category major events like the Renaissance, the Reformation and the French Revolution. The German sociologist Max Weber had a word for this process of interaction. One of the recurrent themes in his work was what Weber called *Veralltäglichung*. Usually but not quite accurately translated as "routinization," the term refers to the incorporation of novelties into everyday practices. It might be rendered as "quotidianization," "domestication," or even "familiarization"—a choice that has the advantage of reminding us that the "defamiliarization" advocated by some European writers early in the twentieth century was precisely an attempt to combat this process and to force people to look at their everyday reality with fresh eyes.

THE PROBLEMS OF HEGEMONY AND RESISTANCE

The study of popular culture, like the study of the everyday, has sometimes been criticized by politically committed historians as a kind of escapism, a retreat from the political. In the case of some scholars, this criticism may have been on target, but the links between politics, the everyday, and popular culture have been pointed out by a number of scholars.

Some of these scholars view popular culture as a means of political control or of "social" control as sociologists used to say. This theory goes back a long way. Roman elites thought that the people could be controlled by "bread and circuses." In the late Middle Ages, Carnival was already viewed as a period of license that would enable society to function normally the rest of the time. Marx called religion the opium of the people, and this idea has been extended to include elements of secular culture such as escapist literature.

A more subtle explanation of the fact that governments and ruling classes have often more or less had their way, taken over from Antonio Gramsci by some historians of popular culture, is the idea of "cultural hegemony." The essential idea is that the ruling class rules not, or not only, by naked force but rather by infecting other social groups with its values or worldview, so much so that ordinary people may come to accept the dominance of the church, the monarch, the aristocracy, and so on as unquestionable, as natural, as no more than common sense. Thus the popular image of the "three estates," which circulated in Europe in the form of cheap woodcuts as well as in literary texts, portrayed society as a division of labor blessed by God between those who pray, those who fight, and those who work in the strict sense of the term. Subaltern or dominated groups often structure their world through models provided by the dominant group. In that sense the dominated groups may be described as "muted," the term coined by the British anthropologist Shirley Ardener to describe the culture of one of the most important of these groups—women.

The principal alternative to the opium theory, however, is its exact opposite, the idea of popular culture as encouraging or underpinning resistance to changes initiated by governments or ruling classes. Open resistance sometimes took the form of rebellion, its forms or language colored by the local culture as many historians have argued with reference to the Peasants' War in Germany; the "barefoot" rebellion of Normandy in 1639 *(Va-nu-pieds)*; the revolt of the serfs, led by Pugachov, in eighteenth-century Russia; or the Luddite riots in early-nineteenth-century England.

Another form of resistance is more subtle. Muted groups often have a way of subtly changing the interpretation of the ideas or symbols handed down to them by the ruling classes. The creative appropriation discussed earlier, in the section on the idea of the pop-ular, may be linked to what are sometimes described as "counterhegemonic strategies," a phrase that may exaggerate the degree of self-consciousness and planning involved. Popular revolt, for instance, has not infrequently been justified in terms of official religious values. One famous example is that of the German peasants who rose against their masters in 1525 claiming that serfdom was unjust because Christ died for all men. Another is that of the Neapolitans who claimed that the Blessed Virgin (more exactly, a particular manifestation, the Virgin of the Carmine) was on their side in their revolt against Spanish rule in 1647. Alternatively, appeal may be made to a dead ruler for support against a living one, as the Norman rebels in 1639 appealed to Louis XII, who was said to have wept whenever he asked his people for money, against his successor Louis XIII, who had recently increased the burden of taxation. The songs, stories, and plays that treat outlaws or bandits as heroes, from Robin Hood to the mid-twentieth-century Sicilian Salvatore Giuliano, should not be forgotten because they justify resistance. No wonder then that Henry VIII was advised to forbid plays about Robin Hood on the grounds that they encouraged disobedience to royal officials.

To study popular resistance through rebellion alone, however, is like studying popular culture through its festivals, forgetting everyday life. Open revolt, however spectacular, was relatively rare. As the American political scientist James Scott was one of the first to emphasize, resistance to officials, landlords, or factory owners has often taken more everyday forms such as going slow, poaching, or sabotage, and the repertoire of these forms is part of popular culture—it is, after all, a form of knowledge and it may also have a symbolic meaning.

In any case, popular political culture was not just a matter of resistance. There were traditions of self-government at the village level in many parts of Europe, the German *Gemeinde* being a particularly well-known example. In Sweden the peasantry were represented in the Diet *(Riksdag)* as a separate estate of the realm. In many early modern cities, the craft guilds played a significant part in municipal politics. From the sixteenth century on, the role of ordinary people, especially urban males, in politics gradually became more important at the level of the state as well as the locality. The impetus to this increased political participation and political consciousness was one of the consequences of the Reformation. The religious wars in France, for example, and the revolt of the Netherlands against Philip II were civil wars in which local elites divided by religion appealed to the people for support, forming unstable coalitions with them.

Something similar happened in the course of the so-called revolutions of the 1640s, notably, the English Civil War. In all these cases, a crucial element in the mixture was print. Printed pamphlets produced by both sides to justify their cause had the long-term effect of involving ordinary people in supralocal (if not national) issues more deeply than before.

The French Revolution both fitted the pattern of the earlier revolts and went beyond it. Once again, divided elites appealed to the people, and once again, print played an important part in the movement. However, there was a larger role for ordinary people on this occasion. The new political culture was more egalitarian than its predecessors, witness the attempt at the elimination of distinctions of dress, for example. Festivals were organized on a grander scale than before, allowing more people to participate.

Retrospectively at least, 1789 appears as a watershed in the history of popular culture, especially since it more or less coincided with the first stages of the longer industrial revolution. Traditional revolts continued in rural areas, such as the Rebecca Riots in Wales or the War of the Demoiselles in the Ariege in 1829, in both of which cases male rebels dressed as women. In cities, on the other hand, we see increasing participation by ordinary people in large-scale political movements such as the revolutions of 1848 and 1917. There was also more popular participation in everyday politics, thanks to the gradual extension of the vote.

The extension of the vote was linked to the spread of schools, the spread of schools to the rise of newspaper reading, and this in turn to increased political awareness. In England universal education was made compulsory after the extension of the vote to artisans in 1867. As a Victorian cabinet minister joked, "We must educate our masters." Universal primary education was also necessary to inculcate loyalty to the nation-state, to turn "peasants into Frenchmen" as the American historian Eugen Weber put it. In Russia a literacy campaign followed the revolution, while posters and films also promoted "mass mobilization." We have reached the problem of "mass culture."

THE PROBLEM OF MASS CULTURE

It has often been argued or at least asserted that a major change in European culture took place around 1800. It was about that time that traditional popular culture was replaced or, more exactly, began to be replaced by mass culture. The culture that the folklorists were collecting and recording was in terminal decline.

Where popular culture "grew from below," to employ the incisive formulation of Dwight Macdonald, "Mass Culture is imposed from above."

Discussions of "mass culture," at their height between the 1930s and the 1960s, present two problems in particular. In the first place, description, narrative, and analysis were closely linked to critique, to rejection. The critique was often formulated in terms of inauthenticity or spuriousness. Mass culture was viewed not as a culture but as an absence of culture or an anticulture. The intellectuals who criticized mass culture viewed the masses as the "other," in a way not so very different from earlier condemnations of "superstition," "license" or disorder.

In the second place, there was the problem of nostalgia, of idealizing or romanticizing earlier forms of popular culture from different periods. For example in *The Uses of Literacy,* a study of publications and entertainments such as magazines, popular music, and television, the English critic Richard Hoggart contrasted the "candy-floss world" of the 1950s, with its "sex in shiny packets," with what he described as an "older order," the more authentic working-class culture of his youth in Leeds in the 1930s. Needless to say, other critics located the golden age of popular culture considerably earlier than Hoggart, in 1900, for example, or in 1800. Take the music hall or its French or German equivalents at the end of the nineteenth century. Does this new institution exemplify the creativity of popular culture or, on the contrary, the rise of a mass culture turning ordinary people into passive spectators (as television would later be said to do)? The history of spectator sports such as boxing (institutionalized in England by the eighteenth century) and horse racing (institutionalized by the seventeenth century) leads to similar conclusions.

If only homemade culture qualifies as "popular," while commercialized culture is mass culture, then the latter has a much longer history than is usually admitted. In England, France, and elsewhere, the eighteenth century has been described as the age of the first "consumer society" in the sense that certain manufactured goods, such as clothes and furniture, were now cheap enough for ordinary people to buy. As for commercialized entertainment, one need look no farther for it than the theater of the fairground in Paris and elsewhere or the races at Newmarket. But why stop in the eighteenth century? The rise of the permanent theater in the late sixteenth century in London and Madrid gave opportunities to Shakespeare and Lope de Vega, but all the same it was commercialized and passive entertainment for a broad section of the urban population. The prevalence of print was already allowing "stars" of the entertainment

Rebecca Riots. Welsh protesters attack a toll gate on a private toll road. The "Rebecca riots" began in 1839. Engraving, ninteenth century. PRIVATE COLLECTION/BRIDGEMAN ART LIBRARY

world to emerge, among them the Londoners Richard Tarlton, the clown, and John Taylor, the waterman-poet. Both men knew how to add to their reputation with publicity stunts, such as dancing all the way from London to Norwich or sailing from London to York. Does this mean that mass culture had already arrived by 1600?

A more precise and so a more useful concept than mass culture is that of a "culture industry," central to the Frankfurt school of critical sociology. The industrial revolution, so it is argued, led to the mass production of culture. To be more precise, it led to a proliferation of standardized objects such as cheap prints, still cheaper in the age of the steam press than they had been in the early modern period. According to Marx, mass production led to the transformation of the people into the masses.

In contrast to Marx and the Marxists of the Frankfurt school, some late-twentieth-century analysts of popular culture, notably Michel de Certeau, emphasized the freedom of individual consumers to resist mass culture, for example, by making their own selection from the mass-produced objects available to them and by endowing these objects with personal meanings. Some of the British youth cultures or subcultures of the 1970s, such as the Rastas, mods, and punks mentioned in an earlier section, exemplify this process with particular clarity. However, the style of

these rebellious subcultures has in turn been incorporated by the producers of mass culture, notably in the garment industry.

In any case the training of children was also standardized in the, nineteenth and twentieth centuries with the rise of compulsory school attendance in one European country after another, replacing informal methods of instruction in the family, the field, or the workshop by a more official, formal, or institutional culture. The British anthropologist Ernest Gellner described this process as the rise of "universal high culture." It might be more exact to speak of an attempt to introduce pupils to a high culture that was national or Western rather than local. The standardizing or leveling tendencies of the schools were reinforced by those of youth organizations such as the Hitler-Jugend and the Russian Komsomol, founded in a fascist and a communist country, respectively, in the twentieth century and an integral part of what has been called the "propaganda state." In the USSR in the 1920s, for example, the regime favored revolutionary songs and the patriotic music of Glinka and Tchaikovsky over traditional folk music.

All the same, in practice culture was also shaped by class. E. P. Thompson was a sharp critic of the traditional view of culture as the expression of communal values, thus privileging shared meanings over conflicts of meaning. Ironically, he has himself been criticized for the communitarian model of worker's culture that underlies his famous *Making of the English Working Class.* To go beyond this communitarian model, it may be useful to turn to Pierre Bourdieu, whose ethnography of contemporary France stressed the extent to which the bourgeoisie and the working classes have each defined themselves in contrast to the other. Was this also the case in nineteenth-century England? To the argument that schools introduce high culture to everyone, Bourdieu replies by stressing the hierarchy of schools and other institutions of higher education and the inequality of access to institutions at the top of the ladder. In other words, universal education did no more than replace one form of cultural stratification with another, while the cultural hegemony of the elite persists.

The culture of the school can also be resisted, a process described by Paul Willis in a study of working-class male adolescents in Birmingham in the 1970s. However, resistance had its price. The rebels who did not take school seriously ended up in unskilled working-class jobs.

POSTINDUSTRIAL OR POSTMODERN CULTURE

Studies of the postindustrial or postmodern age have important implications for historians of contemporary popular culture. The increase in leisure, whether voluntary (owing to a reduction of working hours) or enforced (owing to unemployment) obviously has important cultural consequences. So does the late-twentieth-century globalization of culture. It undermines the nineteenth-century nationalization of cultures, reducing cultural variety in the world as a whole while at the same time increasing choices at the level of the individual and leading to cultural hybridization on a scale and at a speed previously unknown. The decline in the importance of literacy in an age of television and home computers is also of great significance for the future history of popular culture. Of the changes in progress in the 1990s, however, the one most central to the theme of this essay is the breakdown of the old barriers between elite and popular cultures. It is the inverse of the movement of withdrawal in the early modern period, discussed above. Almost everyone watched the same television programs, for instance, and thus participated in a common culture, even if many minorities—not only elites—had a second culture of their own.

In the last few years of the twentieth century, a certain reaction among historians against the idea of popular culture arose. To some extent this reaction was justified by the crude dichotomies sometimes employed in the past. However, this response may also be a projection onto the past of the situation in which, to quote Susan Sontag, "the distinction between 'high' and 'low' culture seems less and less meaningful." Late-twentieth-century analysts perceived a danger that historians of the early twenty-first century would forget the existence of the barriers of birth, wealth, and education that were so important in the cultural history of Europe in the previous five centuries or more.

See also other articles in this section.

BIBLIOGRAPHY

Amelang, James. *Honored Citizens of Barcelona: Patrician Culture and Class Relations, 1490–1714.* Princeton, N.J., 1986.

Anderson, Patricia. *The Printed Image and the Transformation of Popular Culture, 1790–1860.* Oxford, 1991.

Bailey, Peter. *Leisure and Class in Victorian England: Rational Recreation and the Contest for Control, 1830–1885.* 2d ed. London and New York, 1987.

Bakhtin, Mikhail. *Rabelais and His World.* Translated by Helene Iswolsky. Cambridge, Mass, 1968.

Bourdieu, Pierre. *Distinction: A Social Critique of the Judgement of Taste.* Translated by Richard Nice. Cambridge, Mass, 1984. Translation of *La distinction.*

Burke, Peter. *Popular Culture in Early Modern Europe.* 2d ed. Aldershot, U.K., 1994.

Capp, Bernard. *The World of John Taylor the Water-Poet 1578–1653.* Oxford, 1994.

Certeau, Michel de. *The Practice of Everyday Life.* Translated by Stephen Rendall. Berkeley and Los Angeles, 1984. Translation of *L'invention du quotidien.*

Chartier, Roger. "Culture as Appropriation: Popular Cultural Uses in Early Modern France." In *Understanding Popular Culture.* Edited by Steven L. Kaplan. Berlin, New York, and Amsterdam, 1984.

Christian, William A., Jr. *Local Religion in Sixteenth-Century Spain.* Princeton, N.J., 1981.

Davis, Natalie Z. *Society and-Culture in Early Modern France.* Stanford, Calif., 1975.

Davis, Robert C. *The War of the Fists: Popular Culture and Public Violence in Late Renaissance Venice.* New York, 1994.

Frykman, Jonas, and Orvar Löfgren. *Culture Builders: A Historical Anthropology of Middle-Class Life.* New Brunswick, N.J., 1987.

Ginzburg, Carlo. *The Cheese and the Worms.* Translated by John and Anne Tedeschi. Baltimore, 1980. Translation of *Il formaggio e i vermi.*

Gramsci, Antonio. *Selections from Cultural Writings.* Edited by David Forgacs and Geoffrey Nowell-Smith. Translated by William Boelhower. Cambridge, Mass., 1985.

Harris, Tim, ed. *Popular Culture in England, c. 1500–1850.* London, 1995.

Hebdige, Dick. *Subculture: The Meaning of Style.* London, 1979.

Hoggart, Richard. *The Uses of Literacy.* London, 1957.

Hutton, Ronald. *The Rise and Fall of Merry England: The Ritual Year, 1400–1700.* Oxford, 1994.

Kenez, Peter. *The Birth of the Propaganda State: Soviet Methods of Mass Mobilisation, 1917–29.* Cambridge, U.K., 1985.

Le Roy Ladurie, Emmanuel. *Carnival in Romans.* Translated by Mary Feeney. London, 1980. Translation of *Le Carnaval de Romans.*

Lotman, Juri, and Boris Uspenskii. *The Semiotics of Russian Culture.* Edited by Ann Shukman. Ann Arbor, Mich., 1984.

Macdonald, Dwight. "A Theory of Mass Culture." In *Mass Culture: The Popular Arts in America.* Edited by Bernard Rosenberg and David M. White. Glencoe, Ill., 1957. Pages 59–73.

Sahlins, Peter. *Forest Rites: The War of the Demoiselles in Nineteenth-Century France.* Cambridge, Mass., 1994.

Scott, James C. *Domination and the Arts of Resistance: Hidden Transcripts.* New Haven, Conn., and London, 1990.

Scribner, Robert W. *For the Sake of Simple Folk: Popular Propaganda for the German Reformation.* Rev. ed., Oxford, 1994.

Sider, Gerald. *Culture and Class in Anthropology and History.* Cambridge, U.K., 1986.

Stites, Richard. *Russian Popular Culture: Entertainment and Society since 1900.* Cambridge, U.K., 1992.

Te Brake, Wayne. *Shaping History: Ordinary People in European Politics, 1500–1700.* Berkeley and Los Angeles, 1998.

Thompson, Edward P. *Customs in Common.* London, 1991.

Thompson, Edward P. *The Making of the English Working Class.* London, 1963.

Weber, Eugen. *Peasants into Frenchmen: The Modernization of Rural France 1870–1914.* Stanford, Calif., 1976.

HIGH CULTURE

Arthur Mitzman

Although there is no consensus among historians as to the definition of high culture, for many the term evokes the ivory tower of art for art's sake, mandarin aversion to raucous public entertainments, and highbrow disdain for politics. Because of this assumption of a willed distance from mundane, everyday life, elective affinities between high culture and the normal concerns of social history seem lacking. Where social historians have dealt with it, they have been more preoccupied with its relevance to the broader agendas of social history—that is, popular culture, demographic trends, or institutional intermediaries for cultural formation like schools and publishing houses—than with its contents, which they have left to specialists in literary and intellectual history. Under the influence of postmodern theory, in the late 1980s and 1990s social historians turned away from questions of social stratification and power toward broadly cultural matters of gender, textuality, print culture, and identity. This shift, however, has not increased their professional interest in the conventional terrain of high culture.

Nonetheless, the standard references to "culture" in modern European history link it to high rather than popular culture and consistently show high culture besmirched with political and social involvement. In general many of the turning points in the evolution from ancien régime to modern society have been associated, rightly or wrongly, with high culture. In Germany the term is used in the romantic nationalist defense of German *Kultur*—whether against Latin civilization, as in Jakob Burckhardt's title *Die Kultur der Renaissance in Italien* (1860; *The Civilization of the Renaissance in Italy*), or, after 1872, against Rome-centered Catholicism in Bismarck's *Kulturkampf* (cultural war). In Belgium the revolutionary birth of the nation in 1830 was triggered by an opera performance, a high culture ritual. In France conservative enemies of the French Revolution attributed that upheaval to the anti-Christian rationalism of the High Enlightenment. A century later the concept of the "intellectuals" was inseparable from the intervention of creators of high culture, like Anatole France, Marcel Proust, and Émile Zola, who defended Alfred Dreyfus in the "affair" that led to the definitive separation of church and state in the Third Republic. To the extent that most of these political events involved social conflict and that the various movements of high culture implicated in those events were shaped by the rapidly changing social institutions, ideologies, and mentalities of the modern era, "high" culture merits scrutiny by social historians.

The significance of high culture for historians is here limited to its meaning in modern Europe from the Renaissance to the twenty-first century. Assuming the relevance of certain literary, anthropological, sociological, and depth-psychological perspectives, this discussion proceeds from four theoretical points of departure: Friedrich Nietzsche's distinction in *The Use and Abuse of History* between celebratory, "monumental" high culture and negative, satiric, parodistic, deprecatory, "critical" high culture; the Weberian concept of an ongoing rationalization and centralization of all aspects of society; the Freudian concept—not altogether unrelated to the Weberian one—of culture as sublimation of instinctual impulse; and Pierre Bourdieu's notion of "cultural capital." Frameworks for the discussion are the dialectical relation between "high" and "low" in Western culture, as discussed in anthropologically informed literary theory; Robert Muchembled's notion of a *mission civilisatrice* (civilizing mission) directed at the lower orders of society by the social strata embodying the high culture; and the complex question, provocative to intellectual historians, sociologists, and social historians alike, of the relation between high culture, cultural capital, educational institutions, ideologies, and intellectual paradigms, which might be called the question of the sociology of knowledge.

The first section of this article distinguishes the anthropological notion of culture from high culture. It differentiates between high culture's monumental and critical sides and between modern secular and premodern religious high cultures, tracing the historically shifting boundaries between "high" and "low." The second section discusses the various underpinnings of modern secular high culture. On the one hand are the religious and psychological bases for the evolving opposition of high and low; on the other are the institutional and ideological bases of that distinction in the culture of the modern world. This section also posits the paradoxical blurring of high and low in art, literature, and music. The third section presents the increasing predominance of critical elements in the secular high culture of the modern era in terms of the emergence of formal criteria—the autonomization of thought and aesthetics, bohemia, and abstraction—and concludes with a summary of the critical theory of the Frankfurt school. The final section focuses on the paradoxical relationships between autonomization and universities as cultural monuments, between postmodernism and political economy, and between high culture and cultural capital.

SOME DISTINCTIONS

Anthropologists view culture as the totality of that part of the human environment that has been more or less consciously created by humankind. Since 1970 this notion of culture largely has been taken over by both cultural and social historians. Agricultural systems and implements, ideologies, cities, architectural styles, automobiles, information technology, poems, weapons of mass destruction are all, as conscious creations, expressions of human culture.

A narrower meaning of culture excludes from such creations those that are indispensable, or at least materially useful, for human survival and focuses on those that are viewed by the society that produced or inherited them as agreeable. Such creations are useful in the nonmaterial sense of being edifying or pleasing to eye, ear, or mind. On what basis within this latter category is the historian to distinguish between high and low? On the one hand, any distinction between high and low culture remains an artificial construction based on the values of those who make the distinction rather than on an evidential reality. On the other hand, historical analysis of the contents of such constructions in particular societies has yielded many answers to the question of the sociology of knowledge.

With this paradox in mind, a workable definition of high culture is that which signifies the spiritual, intellectual, and aesthetic achievements viewed by the hegemonic strata of a particular society as worthy of emulation and continuance. This definition appears to stress the monumental, self-celebratory side of culture; but to understand the concept it is crucial

to realize that a critical, satiric aspect has frequently accompanied it, even been integrated into it.

Although high cultures are normal in the history of civilization, arguably Western society since the Renaissance is a unique case. In most of the world's major civilizations, the monumental aspects have predominated and have been inseparable from religious traditions, rituals, and beliefs cultivated by either a priestly caste or a religiously colored, bureaucratic mandarinate. Such civilizations, including ancient Egypt, Confucian China, and the Christian Middle Ages, were stratified so sharply by sacralized social privilege and distinction, frequently taking the form of caste systems, that specifically cultural differences between high and low were usually less important than the social ones embedded in sacred hierarchies of power and privilege. For example, medieval Europe had two parallel high cultures, that of the feudal aristocracy, based on a religiously sanctioned code of chivalry, and that of the church, which monopolized literacy and intellectual debate. Nonetheless, even in the Christian Middle Ages parodies and inversions of both the clerical and the aristocratic cultures originated in and supplemented the high cultural heritage. The musical play-inversion of rites and hierarchies, *la fête de l'âne* (the feast of the ass), which introduced an ass into the church as bishop, was performed by apprentice clergy in cathedrals during the ten-day holiday after Christmas. The vernacular masterpieces of Boccaccio, Chaucer, and Dante ridiculed the vice and folly of the powerful as well as of the common people of the medieval world.

In the Western version of high culture that developed between the sixteenth and the twentieth centuries, the hegemonic strata came to distinguish themselves by their identification with and support for literary, artistic, musical, and intellectual achievements of an increasingly nonreligious character. The gradual disappearance of a religiously sanctioned hierarchical social order, together with the accelerating degree of social mobility, blurred social contrasts that formerly were taken for granted. A shopkeeper who became a wealthy banker was avid for the insignia of distinction, and an aristocrat who fell on bad times no longer was guaranteed privileged status by birth and title alone. In this context the contrast between those associated with the achievements of the secular high culture and those associated by idiom, taste, and mentality with the culture of the common people became more important. The common people were assumed to have a merely customary, contingent, or mercenary character, viewed as base or barbaric, expressive of a low popular or mass culture. But the high culture that was the fruit of family values and education and that permitted identification with the hegemonic strata—Bourdieu's "cultural capital"—became an important supplement to economic capital.

Paradoxically, however, in the contemporary world the concepts of high and low culture appear more and more difficult to distinguish, particularly since the development of modern media. A clear-cut distinction between the elite and the popular in cinema and television is hard to find, and the impact on culture of the diffusion of texts and images through the Internet has further complicated matters. The inexpensive reproduction of art and music has led some critics to repudiate the mass diffusion of such works as inauthentic, reserving the notion of high culture for works and performances that are created and appreciated directly, without electronic or other means of reproduction or amplification. Walter Benjamin, for example, distinguished original works of art from their reproductions by the "aura" attached to the original.

This problem of shifting boundaries between high and low is, of course, anything but new. There are many historical examples of cultural artifacts, once considered "elite," that became "popular" and vice versa. "Classics" easily have become popularized under certain circumstances, for example, through the films or musicals that have brought works of Victor Hugo, George Bernard Shaw, or William Shakespeare to the masses. Paradoxically, many of the plays and novels that have become part of the "high" culture heritage, including those of the three men just mentioned, were originally presented to the public in theaters and imprints intended for a popular audience. Indeed the source of modern dramaturgy lies in the vernacular mystery plays of the Middle Ages that, though originating in the clergy, became a phenomenon of the urban lay culture by the early fourteenth century. Most of the survivals from past cultures, such as Gothic cathedrals, the works of the Greek philosophers, the writings of Dante, Boccaccio, and Chaucer, revered since the eighteenth century by those who viewed them as testimonies to the sublimity of the human spirit, blurred the distinction between elite and popular.

As the automatic sacralization of power and privilege that characterized the Middle Ages was called into question, it became desirable and necessary for the ruling strata to add cultural distinction to the other attributes of power. The bases of such questioning multiplied in the modern era. The Reformation, which at least at a spiritual level denied hierarchy; the mercantile individualism of the urban cultures; the rationalism spurred by feudal absolutism; and after the French Revolution, the democratic ideologies of nationalism and socialism—all undermined the religiously endorsed hierarchies that shaped most of Western culture.

Thus the modern concept of a high culture, which links the cultivation of aesthetic, intellectual, and ethical sensibilities to a secular worldview, has been coterminous with the postmedieval evolution of literate elites, whose social hegemony depended, in their eyes, on their capacity to distinguish themselves culturally from inferiors. Cultural (as distinct from social) contempt for what was "low" or popular became increasingly evident in Renaissance and baroque Europe among an increasingly literate and luxury-loving aristocracy, who disdained the rituals, beliefs, and idioms of common people, physical labor, and apart from the city-states of northern Italy and Flanders, commercial activity. Cultural contempt also appeared in the value the subsequent bourgeois society placed on brainpower and the refinement of feeling as opposed to muscle power and violent emotion.

THE EVOLUTION OF
SECULAR HIGH CULTURE

Religion and psyche. Although the concept of a secular high culture became common coin only in the modern world, its origins are implicit in the historical development of morality and religious ideas. To the extent that religions evolved from local beliefs (shamanism, totemism, animism) linking the supernatural to natural phenomena into a belief in some kind of transcendent, rationally comprehensible, omniscient, and omnipotent being, the newer faith viewed the older one as of a lower order. Where distinctions were made between heavenly (divine or moral) and earthbound (diabolic or immoral) supernatural forces, the earlier religions were associated with the earthbound. Emmanuel Le Roy Ladurie's *Montaillou: The Promised Land of Error* (1979) demonstrates this association in the operations of the fourteenth-century inquisition in a southern French town.

This high-low opposition, the basis of subsequent distinctions between high and low culture, occurs frequently in cultural history. The ancient Greek contrast between the gods of Olympus and their chthonic predecessors is one example, as are the various myths and legends of the classical and Christian traditions depicting a winged hero (Perseus, Saint George, or Saint Michael) rescuing a maiden from the clutches of a multiheaded hydra or dragon associated with the underworld. Shakespeare's opposition (in *The Tempest*) of Prospero and Caliban is a secularized variant on this: the cultivated seer versus the barbarian

The Magic Flute. Costumes for Mozart's *Die Zauberflöte (The Magic Flute),* nineteenth-century engraving. MUSEUM DER STADT WIEN, VIENNA/THEARTARCHIVE

"wild man." Christianity's denigration and suppression of medieval nature religions, whose traces in the countryside persisted well into the nineteenth century, is an example. Another instance is the scorn among austere and "elevated" Christian reformers for clerical corruption and for the compromises, such as cults of the saints and carnival festivals, the Catholic Church made with the older religious beliefs. Tied up with religious notions of a higher culture was a slow transformation of morality and notions about human sexuality. The development of conscience (the evolution from "shame" to "guilt" cultures) accompanied both the change in the psychological locus of religious conviction from matriarchal (natural) to patriarchal (heavenly) belief systems and, independent of the matriarchy-patriarchy split, the change in social ethic from aristocratic honor to bourgeois virtue. As Norbert Elias, following Freud, showed, this latter evolution also involved mounting repression of affects that might lead to gross behavior, violence, or uncontrolled sexuality (associated with the lower body) and an increased emphasis on civility, tolerance, and ratiocination (associated with the head).

This valorization of intellectual capacities in the medieval and early modern world was long associated with the concept of a "higher" Christian sublimity, both religious and aesthetic; but for the French mon-

archs of the seventeenth century, that valorization was a means to curb the grossness and impulsive violence of the court aristocracy. Later, it was a means for Deist bourgeois successors to the Christian-feudal tradition to establish their own cultural identity against that imposed by the old regime. One of the icons of European high culture, Mozart's *The Magic Flute* (1791), provides an outstanding example of such a post-Christian religious identity. This opera reveals an artful integration of many of the themes of high versus low. It also shows the ambivalent relationship between the monumental and the critical sides of high culture characteristic of the era of the French Revolution and the dependence of the critical aspect on elements of the popular culture.

The Magic Flute demonstrates that the "superior" morality of high-culture Freemasonry was not simply directed against the "low" culture of the populace. To the contrary, the bird catcher Papageno, although given to buffoonery, is an emblem of virtue. Indeed the opera's initial performance in 1791 took place in a popular theater, evidence that the enlightened bourgeois and the popular were not sharply separated at that time. Like Mozart's other major operas, *The Marriage of Figaro* (1786) and *Don Giovanni* (1787), *The Magic Flute* sets the ethical standards of the enlightened bourgeois against the waning feudal-clerical social order of the old regime as high versus low. In *The Marriage of Figaro,* Count Almaviva is trapped by his petit bourgeois majordomo and his long-suffering wife into giving up his licentious ways. In *Don Giovanni* the libidinous aristocrat is literally swallowed up by the underworld for his conscienceless sexual violence. *The Magic Flute* represents an early version of the moral consciousness of Europe's new middle-class culture, which in its Masonic form was more inclined to seek models in the religious rituals and consciousness of ancient Egypt than in those of classical antiquity.

Institutional and ideological bases of the evolution to a secular high culture. In general the notion of high culture in the eighteenth and nineteenth centuries prioritized a classical literature that began in Greek and Roman antiquity. This development was largely dependent on two interrelated cultural phenomena that some observers consider the basis of both nationalism and modern society as a whole: mass literacy and printing. For these achievements to become widespread—ultimately catalyzing the modern distinction between high and low culture—four changes were necessary: the triumph of political centralization over feudal anarchy, the imposition of uniform vernacular languages on the innumerable patois of Europe's regions, the valuing of literature written in a uniform language, and an organized educational system accompanied by some kind of merchant capitalism. Culturally speaking, these various aspects of the ongoing rationalization and centralization of social power constitute the unity of the era of European history from the Renaissance to the twenty-first century.

During this period the consciousness of a distinction between high and low culture flourished, but its origins can be traced back to the various vertical culture clashes of the late medieval period. Elias, in his theory of the "civilizing process," focused on the efforts of French royal courts to curtail the violence and incivility of aristocratic vassals by importing standards and "manner books" from the more advanced courts of Renaissance Italy. But Robert Muchembled and others applied Elias's idea more broadly to the

---

THE MAGIC FLUTE

As *The Magic Flute* begins, the hero, Tamino, who will subsequently be initiated into an Egyptianate religion of sun-worshiping Deists, is chased by a huge serpent, a monster of the underworld. Tamino is rescued by three female servants of the Queen of the Night, who gives him the task of rescuing her daughter from the clutches of Sarastro, a villainous usurper and successor to her husband as high priest of the solar circle. The opera makes clear that the Queen of the Night, not Sarastro, is the true villain. Analysis of the text and music of the opera and the backgrounds of its collaborators—particularly Mozart and Emanuel Schikaneder, who commissioned the opera, signed his name to the libretto, and played the role of Papageno in the initial production—suggests that the solar cult is a thinly disguised version of Masonic beliefs and rituals. Late-eighteenth-century Austrian Freemasonry, to which all the important collaborators belonged, embraced High Enlightenment Deist ideas of a superethical monotheism deemed compatible with the moral teachings of most major world religions.

The conflict between Sarastro and the Queen of the Night is thus a conflict between high and low, that is, between heavenly and terrestrial, light and dark, sun and moon, true religion (Deism or Freemasonry) and false (by implication Catholicism). Overlapping these is the symbolic opposition between male (patriarchal) and female (matriarchal) principles. Women are not condemned altogether as evil and irrational—the daughter of the Queen of the Night is initiated into the mysteries of the cult alongside the hero—but the opera follows Enlightenment stereotypes in viewing them as intellectually dependent on men and given to evil passions when outside the male controlling influence. When, after the evil female does everything in her power to murder Sarastro, saying, "My heart is seething with hellish vengeance," Sarastro, foils all plots against him, revealing the generous wisdom of a philosopher-king in dealing with her: "Within these sacred portals, revenge is unknown . . . enemies are forgiven." Thus does the opera show the superiority of reason over violent emotion.

history of the early modern epoch. Muchembled, in *Popular Culture and Elite Culture in France, 1400–1750* (1985), demonstrated that similar attitudes characterized the efforts of the church to Christianize the common people in the late medieval and early modern periods. In this case, however, the repression of the pre-Christian belief system on the grounds of superstition, immorality, and ungodly violence actually involved a diffusely conceived and executed "civilizing offensive" of a Christian culture, which saw itself as higher, against a partly pagan popular culture, which Christians viewed as lower. This offensive mission was part and parcel of the valorization of intellectual and ethical capacities and of a higher Christian sublimity, both religious and aesthetic, visible in the philosophy of Nicolas de Malebranche and François de Fénelon and in the music of Johann Sebastian Bach and Marc-Antoine Charpentier. In baroque art, for example, in the work of Nicolas Poussin, huge canvases commissioned by the church expressed Christian sublimity through biblical subjects. Other paintings evoked for royal and feudal patrons heroic themes from classical antiquity, themes with which the aristocratic elites of the period identified.

As in Mozart's operas, comparable religious values with non-Christian or post-Christian presuppositions permeated the new bourgeois culture. Nonetheless, a certain ambiguity, also evident in *The Magic Flute,* characterized the relation of high to low in the modern era both before and after the French revolutionary watershed.

FROM THE "MONUMENTAL" PREMODERN TO THE "CRITICAL" MODERN

Even under the Old Regime, a number of important writers later associated with high culture, such as François Rabelais, the poet François Villon, and the playwrights Shakespeare and Molière, produced a major part of their oeuvre with little regard for the monumentalist norms that guided the work of most of their fellow creators. Genial creators made as much use of popular language and legend as of high-culture form. This tendency continued in the romantic era, for example, in the "grotesque," carnivalesque aspects of Hugo's oeuvre, and in the twentieth century, in works by James Joyce. In the work of the seventeenth-century English poet John Donne, religious sublimity coexists with an erotic passion that certainly escapes the confines of Christian sublimity. Donne's poems suggest the complexity of the high culture of the time and anticipate the coexistence of the sacred and the

erotic in the work of the nineteenth-century French poet Charles Baudelaire. Other examples include the complex relationship between the sixteenth-century love stories and religious poetry of Marguerite de Navarre and the mingling of the sacred and the erotic in the poetry of Elizabeth Barrett Browning.

During and after the demise of the Old Regime, this complex relation of the producers of high culture to the values and dogmas of the social elites that supported them intensified. Coinciding with the political and economic modernization of Europe, the aesthetic triumphs of high culture in the two centuries after the French Revolution reveal that the creative figures of modernism were elaborately connected both to the official morality of the bourgeois society that was their frequent social origin and source of support and to the "underworld" morality and perspectives of the popular culture normally denigrated by the dominant bourgeoisie. On the one hand, the developing high culture of Western art, literature, music, and social and philosophical speculation has been caught up in an ongoing professionalization and autonomization such that artists, thinkers, and musicians have created increasingly for their peers rather than for the economically and politically powerful. On the other hand, their social ties to the powerful have been frequently attenuated by a profound criticism of official morality and by a felt need, both ideological and creative, to infuse the common people with culture. This latter impulse was shaped by two mass ideologies, sometimes compatible and sometimes at loggerheads, that accompanied the processes of modernization: nationalism and socialism.

Following the French Revolution, a new social framework allowed an uneasy cohabitation of the trend toward professionalization with the impulse toward cultural populism. Via the impersonal marketplace and the individualization of social relations, the cultural creators gained increasing independence from the hegemonic classes. The patronage of wealthy nobles, royal courts, and high churchmen had been embedded in the hierarchical society of the old regime along with the aristocratic salons in which writers, artists, and musicians often found their wealthy patrons. The telltale sign of a sea change in the relation of the artists and intellectuals to society, and thereby in the significance of high culture, was the replacement, during the period of postrevolutionary romanticism, of the salon with the coterie of independent, like-minded artists and writers. Various circles of romantic novelists, poets, artists, and critics collected around the Schlegels in Germany, around William Wordsworth and Samuel Taylor Coleridge and later around Lord Byron and Percy Bysshe Shelley in England, and around Hugo and his friends in France. These circles were all premised on the material possibility of earning a living as a writer or artist directly through the marketplace. In *Illusions perdues* (1837–1843), Honoré de Balzac portrayed brilliantly the functioning of coteries and salons in the era of the French Restoration (1815–1830). Salons and elite patronage never completely lost their influence over the production of high culture, and aristocratic libertinism and love of luxury were important elements in the aesthetic critique of bourgeois society by high culture poets and intellectuals of the nineteenth and twentieth centuries, particularly in the art for art's sake movement. But after romanticism the institutional frameworks inherited from the Old Regime waned steadily in influence; the popular press, cost reductions in print technology, and university positions enabled artists and writers to determine the form and content of their creativity. Although social paradigms continued to be important in shaping individual creativity, they were attenuated when transmitted through the marketplace.

An important side effect of this relative independence from the taste and desires of elite patrons was the creation of bohemian subcultures, as in Schwabing, Montmartre and the Latin Quarter in Paris, and Greenwich Village and SoHo in New York, that nurtured communities of relatively free artists, writers, and composers. It is to a considerable degree within such subcultures that the two principal and often contradictory tendencies of modern thought and aesthetics—professionalization and autonomization, and cultural populism, making art and ideas the advocate of the suffering masses—have manifested themselves.

Historically, painters and sculptors frequently were of humble origins. In the Middle Ages, because of a tight association between traditional artisan crafts and the paintings and sculptures, largely of wood, later revered as high art in museums, the creators almost never signed their names to their work. This changed only in the Renaissance culture of the northern Italian cities, such as early thirteenth-century Siena, where individual painters were becoming recognized. More than two centuries later the transformation of anonymous artisan into artist was repeated in the metamorphosis of the goldsmith Benvenuto Cellini into a renowned sculptor.

Despite their individuality, Renaissance artists had little room to determine their own subjects, and the content of post-Renaissance visual art continued to reflect the monumentalist, self-celebratory tastes of the ruling elites. The baroque and classical painters of the ancien régime, uniformly subsidized by elite patrons, portrayed scenes from antiquity and religious history intended to augment the grandeur of church, state, and feudality. In the Netherlands, where a burgher elite ruled over the newly liberated eleven provinces, artists portrayed bourgeois interiors, the peasantry, and everyday life but in conformity with a new paradigm. The important exception in the history of French painting is the seventeenth-century work of the brothers Antoine, Louis, and Mathieu Le Nain, who also painted the peasantry. This aspect of their work was long forgotten and was finally brought to public attention in the 1850s by the writer Champfleury, a friend of the realist painter Gustave Courbet. In general artists remained dependent on elite patronage. Even in the French revolutionary epoch, older painters such as Jacques-Louis David continued the classical style and its antique subject matter, merely bending its significance toward the celebration of the new value of civic liberty. Younger artists like Antoine-Jean Gros and Jean-Auguste-Dominique Ingres adapted the existing style to the contemporary situation, particularly in the celebration of Napoleonic military valor.

With the exceptions of the preimpressionist experiments with light and color by the romantic landscape artist J. M. W. Turner and the Pre-Raphaelite circle in England, the important nineteenth-century movements and innovations in the plastic arts were French. After Waterloo, French romantic artists, such as Eugène Delacroix and Théodore Géricault, began to emphasize their own styles and tastes. But apart from his well-known allegorical painting *Liberty Leading the People* (1831), the closest Delacroix came to depicting ordinary people was his romanticized gypsies and his colorful scenes of North African life. Although the new bourgeois elites paid considerable sums for portraits of themselves and their families, paintings of ordinary Europeans, most of whom were peasants in the nineteenth century, were rare before 1848. Only artists with an engraving background, like Honoré Daumier, Grandville, and Charles Johannot, regularly expressed cultural populism through lithographs in popular reviews and books, thus reflecting the social and political radicalism of artisan revolutionaries and democratic revolutions.

Modern art began around 1848 in the new school of realism represented by Courbet and Jean-François Millet. For the first time in France ordinary peasants became a common subject of paintings, as did circles of artists and writers, a clear sign of the developing autonomy and self-awareness of groups of creative figures. The cultural populism implicit in Courbet's work was representative of the brief revolutionary period in which it first appeared, but interestingly the genre of peasant paintings long outlived

Bacchanal before a Herm. Painting (c. 1634) by Nicolas Poussin (1594–1665). NATIONAL GALLERY, LONDON/THE BRIDGEMAN ART LIBRARY

the radicalism of the French Second Republic. The Bonapartist empire that followed derived its legitimacy from popular referenda, in which the support of the peasantry was crucial. As long as the peasants were depicted as long-suffering but not revolutionary, Courbet and his friends could continue to paint them. In other words, the shift from a radical to a conservative cultural populism, matching the transition from the Second Republic to the Second Empire, occurred largely unnoticed in the visual arts. A friend of Pierre-Joseph Proudhon and Baudelaire, Courbet made public his feelings about the Second Empire in 1871, when, as president of the Paris Commune's fine arts committee, he ordered the destruction of a major Bonapartist symbol, the Vendôme column, a gesture for which he was punished after the commune was crushed.

The public greeted realism in painting with the same kind of incomprehension that has greeted most artistic innovations since the French Revolution. Courbet was dubbed the "leader of the school of ugliness," partly because of the somber tints of his palette and partly because of the unlovely character of the rural population he so "realistically" presented. Although impressionism, the artistic movement that followed realism, had a brighter palette, it was not given a better reception. Although the countryside depicted by impressionists was frequently the lush, summery landscape of southern France, and the women represented usually bourgeois beauties on holiday, the painters' brush strokes and other techniques made a picture coherent at a certain distance but incomprehensible when looked at up close. Impressionism took the first steps toward abstraction of color and form, and this emphasis on the formal aspects of art pleased philistine tastes no more than had realism.

Impressionism's new formal concerns had double origins, one social, the other technical. Socially, with the increasing autonomization of art, artists produced for one another, which, as with classical music throughout the nineteenth and twentieth centuries, made contemporary art increasingly inaccessible to the contemporary lay public. Technically, the artists in the last third of the nineteenth century, the era of impressionism, confronted the fact that, for the first time in history, a machine—the camera—could more accurately reproduce visual reality than the most talented painter. This mimetic aspect of the new technology encouraged artists to focus on what the camera could not do, organize color and form not imitatively but imaginatively. Moreover at the end of the nineteenth century the emphasis on time as a constituent element of reality, for example, by Henri-Louis Bergson and subsequently by Proust, was picked up by impressionist artists in a way that prefigured cubism and futurism's efforts to represent change and motion in two-dimensional canvases. During roughly the same time span (1880–1930), symbolist, surrealist, and expressionist art attempted to depict emotional states that were only loosely related to visual reality. The terminus of this increasing distance from traditional representation was abstract expressionism. All these movements were partly the result of the autonomization of the plastic arts, partly the creative artist's

response to the camera, and partly reactions to the accelerating pace and complexity of social existence and the theories that reflected it.

Despite their trend to abstraction, many modern artists have been vitally concerned with the "social question." Vincent van Gogh and Camille Pissarro, both related to impressionism, showed such engagement in the nineteenth century, as did Pablo Picasso, one of the first cubists, and many French artists in the twentieth century. Other artists, particularly those associated with the fin de siècle symbolist movement, like Gustave Moreau and Puvis de Chavannes, continued to treat the classic themes of antique myths dear to the high culture notions of the bourgeoisie but with an effort to penetrate the myths' emotional significance. European surrealism would later make similar efforts. The admiration expressed by André Breton, a leading surrealist, a communist, and a Trots-

Masked Ball at the Opera. Painting (1873) by Édouard Manet (1832–1883). National Gallery of Art, Washington, D.C., Gift of Mrs. Horace Havemeyer in memory of her mother-in-law, Louisine W. Havemeyer

kyist, for Moreau's symbolist painting warns against any facile association of the more traditional high culture of the symbolist movement with bourgeois conservatism.

The social history of modern literature is in many ways similar to that of modern art. Literature experienced an increasing sense of independence from the dominant class whose values it was expected to represent. It too went through phases of romanticism, realism, and simultaneously with impressionism, naturalism. The tight connection between impressionism and naturalism is illustrated by the friendship between the founder of the naturalist school, Zola, and one of the principal impressionists, Paul Cézanne. Zola crafted one of his major novels, *L'oeuvre* (1886), around this relationship. With the exceptions of cubism and abstract expressionism, the other artistic movements mentioned—symbolism, futurism, surrealism, and expressionism—all had literary equivalents.

Literary romanticism was initially more important in Germany and England than in France; only in France did it parallel the development of romanticism in the visual arts. The common denominator of all romanticisms was their correspondence to the principal social and political trends between the French Revolution and the revolution of 1848. The literary high culture of the postrevolutionary epoch revealed the increasing weight of the critical as opposed to the monumental side of high culture. On the one hand, writers expressed the individualism of the liberal era both in their appreciation and emulation of individual genius, military or literary, and in their striving to earn their bread independent of official patronage. On the other hand, they also voiced the new sense of collectivism that emerged in that era. The circles of poets, critics, playwrights, and novelists, even when their social origins were aristocratic or upper bourgeois, echoed the revolutionary consciousness of the masses. They often cast this consciousness in the mold of nationalist sentiment, which was more common in Germany, or of the utopian strivings of artisan socialists, as in the social romanticism of some French writers, such as Eugène Sue, George Sand, Jules Michelet, and Pierre Leroux, in the 1840s. Both the individualist and collectivist values of the romantics fed their criticism of bourgeois conformity.

Technology and education helped popularize literature and reinforced authors' leanings toward cultural populism. Improvements in printing techniques made books and newspapers cheaper throughout the century. Economically, from the 1830s on writers like Balzac, Sand, Sue, Zola, and Charles Dickens published their novels in feuilleton installments, which provided a regular source of income. Ideologically, the reactions of a more literate popular public sometimes had a radicalizing effect on authors.

Subsequent literary movements of the nineteenth and twentieth centuries—realism and naturalism in particular—shed much of the diffuse social idealism and stylistic excesses of romanticism but retained and accentuated the romantic devotion to the craft of the artist, an aspect of the developing professionalization of cultural creation. They also accentuated the critical, parodistic, even subversive element in literature. Examples include the mid-century French novelist Gustave Flaubert, the poet Arthur Rimbaud, the playwright Alfred Jarry, and the French and German circles of expressionism, dadaism, and surrealism.

This critical element went deeper than merely siding with the popular victims of the new liberal order. Entangled within all of these movements from romanticism to naturalism and symbolism, writers liberated from upper-class patronage set themselves critically against the dominant liberal values of the nineteenth century. For some this meant a recourse to the remnants of Old Regime aristocratic values that were libertine and luxury-loving but also distinctly anti-utilitarian. Among those were the French school of *l'art pour l'art* (art for art's sake) as represented by Théophile Gautier and Baudelaire and in Germany the poetic circle of Stefan George. Writers such as Wordsworth and some of the German romantics immersed themselves in alternative religious conceptions that emphasized the "eternal recurrence" of the world of nature. In the juxtaposition of "natural harmony" to the jarring and depressing world of commerce and industry, a number of romantics, such as the historian Michelet, came close to expressing later ecological concerns.

Many creative figures of nineteenth- and twentieth-century high culture emerged from circles of rebellious bourgeois youth. Such circles peppered the social landscape from roughly the end of the eighteenth century to the middle of the twentieth century and fed the ongoing critique of the dominant values of the elites. The adolescent groups of friends, beginning with German, English, and French romanticism, imprinted oppositional values on a wide variety of important creative figures, from Wordsworth and Coleridge to the German expressionists and French surrealists. Flaubert was powerfully influenced by a group of adolescent intimates, which is reflected in his *L'éducation sentimentale* (1869). Oppositional values were at the heart of the German youth movement, which started in an elite Gymnasium in Berlin, and the student-based youth rebellion of the period 1965 to 1975.

A number of these themes—nature as an alternative to industrial society, the distance from liberal utilitarian values, and an increasing appreciation of the sexual passions and an opposition to their repression in high Victorian culture—appear in the work of two Austrian writers of the late nineteenth century, Arthur Schnitzler and Hugo von Hofmannsthal, and in the work of two English novelists of the early twentieth century, E. M. Forster and D. H. Lawrence. In general the critical element in modern high culture wavered between this more profound, often philosophical dissent from its monumental, self-celebratory aspect and the cultural populist denunciation of social injustice.

This wavering shows up in the evolution, between 1930 and 1970, of the Frankfurt school, the group of German philosophers, sociologists, and psychoanalysts specifically associated with critical theory. Continuing the Hegelian-marxist tradition in German thought, most of the principal figures in this group focused, until the middle of World War II, on the critique of fascism as a fusion of traditional authoritarianism and monopoly capitalism in its anticommunist phase. During this period critical theory represented a sophisticated marxism that was nonetheless a version of cultural populism. The course of the war seems to have convinced many of them that the responsibility for modern barbarism lay deeper than any traditional leftist interpretation could account for. Indeed it was inherent in the Western notion of rationality, particularly in its empiricist, liberal, instrumental, and nondialectical forms. That rationality posited the domination of reason over nature and emotion and impeded empathy with human suffering. This turn took shape in a series of books and articles that began with Max Horkheimer's wartime *Eclipse of Reason* (1947) and a book he coauthored with Theodor Adorno, *Dialektik der Aufklärung* (1947), which posed fundamental questions about the character of the rationalism propagated by the High Enlightenment. It continued to Herbert Marcuse's seminal works *Eros and Civilization: A Philosophical Inquiry into Freud* (1955) and *One-Dimensional Man* (1964). Following its transformation during World War II, the Frankfurt school provided an essential commentary on modern high culture, analyzing critically its philosophical presuppositions, condemning its ties to inhuman systems of exploitation and mass destruction, and defending and resuscitating its aesthetic protagonists who resisted its norms. It particularly defended poets and artists who refused the limitation on feeling and imagination mandated by the monumental, self-celebratory side of the "official" culture's instrumental rationalism.

The work of Jürgen Habermas carried the critical theory begun by Horkheimer and Adorno into the late twentieth century. Habermas's work exhibits little of the specifically Hegelian, marxist, and Freudian presuppositions of his predecessors. Poststructuralist and postmodern theorists attacked those assumptions as "essentialist," that is, as presupposing—by positing the reality of abstract ideas like the dialectic, capitalism, and the id—some kind of real essence, a subject capable of historical action. Habermas attempted to recast critical theory on bases less susceptible to such attacks. He replaced the Frankfurt school's opposition between instrumental and dialectical reason with a differentiation between official and private discourse. This differentiation parallels the distinction, posed by the sociologist Ferdinand Tönnies, between the psychological analogues of society and community, *Kürwille* and *Wesenwille*. In the face of postmodern critiques of "essentialism," Habermas thus retained the utopian element in critical theory. In his view the expansion of those private spheres of discourse and their social underpinnings create a new normative basis for philosophy and "a community of needs and solidarity" as well as "a community of rights and entitlements" (Benhabib, 1986, pp. 339).

CONCLUDING PARADOXES

The extensive discussion of the historical interaction between the monumental-celebratory and the critical aspects of modern high culture leads to a related problem: the extremely complex tension between

(1) processes of autonomization in the arts and the intellectual disciplines,
(2) the institutionalizing of intellectual and cultural production in universities,
(3) changing paradigms or discourses about literature, art, science, and society in the nineteenth and twentieth centuries,
(4) changes in modes of production and in the norms of political economy, and
(5) high culture as the "legitimate culture" or the "cultural capital" (in Bourdieu's terms) of hegemonic elites.

Bourdieu attempted to order the paradoxical connection between the autonomization of the aesthetic sphere—the emphasis by the creators and appreciators of visual art, literature, and music on purely formal questions divorced from narrative, social, or ethical content—and the elites' use of the new formal criteria as a badge of their distinctive cultural prowess. The paradox is that this autonomization—initially in the social and economic frameworks of coteries, bohemian communities, and literary reviews—developed after the disintegration of the ancien régime as a symbol of the emancipation of writers and artists from aristocratic patronage. The emergence of autonomization coincided with a historically unprecedented outburst of criticism, by poets and other writers, of the new society that had afforded them this freedom. Among the devotees of art for art's sake were, in France, Gautier, Flaubert, Baudelaire, and Stéphane Mallarmé; in Germany, the George Kreis and Thomas Mann; and in England, Oscar Wilde. These artists frequently had only contempt for the high bourgeoisie, who a generation or two later embraced as sublime their separation of aesthetics from ethics and transmitted their works to posterity in deluxe bindings.

The institutional independence of poets, artists, and intellectuals was, however, historically circumscribed. It continued to exist for poets like Ezra Pound, William Butler Yeats, and T. S. Eliot and for novelists like Proust, Joyce, and Joseph Conrad until well after World War II. The social space of intellectual and artistic freedom remained open for philosophers and critics like Jean-Paul Sartre and Edmund Wilson until the mid-twentieth century. It is undeniable that most aesthetic production and virtually all critical work in philosophy and social thought in the late twentieth century was written, painted, sculpted, or composed by members of university or college faculties. A fundamental path for social historians of culture, then, is to trace and comprehend the development of new ties and new dependencies between, on the one hand, the intellectual and poet and, on the other, the economic and social power elites that control universities.

Flowing out of this dependency is a further question concerning the relationship, within the academic dispensation, between the autonomization of high culture production, the paradigms and ideological parameters that shape it from within, and the changes in the dominant mode of production that mold the perspectives of the powerful entrepreneurs and other public figures who govern the universities. For example, does a certain correspondence exist between the deconstructionist side of postmodern thought and the decentralizing production methods that since Henry Ford have swept global industrial centers? Do both reflect the triumph of a liberal or neoliberal worldview that emphasizes the individual and denies the collective? That worldview posits the need for "flexibility" of labor, condemns public spending, especially on the poor, and denies the "social question" even as it rejects structural thinking, "essences" and fixed "subjects," and demands the universal acceptance of "risk" and "chaos." This linking of postmodern and neoliberal perspectives has been resisted by academic radicals, who argue that postmodernist aesthetics imply the transgression of conventional discourse. Moreover such radicals have purported to defy the individualism of neoliberal thought by pointing to the support of postmodernism for "identity studies," a field that deals with the values and interests of collectivities, particularly of ethnic and gender groups. Those hostile to the postmodernist position, however, have argued that this radical postmodernism touches on collectivities only as individual entities without intrinsic connection to humankind as a whole or to collective notions like class or nation that used to be considered an integral part of it. Thus they undermine any concept of a social justice applicable to all people and make it impossible to theorize a "just society." In the 1950s and 1960s American cold war propaganda agencies easily exploited and manipulated avant-garde aesthetic creations by covertly subsidizing individuals and organizations, anticipating the rupture between aesthetics and ethics in postmodernism. Thus the "transgression" of conventional ethics by the late-modernist autonomization of aesthetics may be quite compatible with the dominant liberal ideologies of the second half of the twentieth century.

An additional link between contemporary ideologies and postmodern high culture surfaces in information technology, which has inspired industrial and financial practices since Ford and has shaped the postmodern view of the world. Instantly downloading information onto the computer screen has conditioned automated production methods and the international financial market, and it also has encouraged the ahistorical and "playful" way of thinking of postmodern philosophers and literary critics. Technology has had another parallel impact on economy and high culture, the elimination of as many costly "permanent" positions as possible in factories and offices. The ease of subcontracting in computerized production has been mirrored in universities in a proliferation of poorly paid, nontenured positions and in the shifting of much professional production to underfunded and academically substandard junior colleges or branches of state universities. Finally, the postmodern dismissal (as "essentialist") of notions like "the nation" and "the working class" has coincided with the factual undermining of both phenomena by neoliberal globalization and computerization.

Merely granting the possibility of correspondences between the preconditions and precepts of postmodernism and those of neoliberal ideology raises two final questions for the social historian confronting contemporary high culture. What does the autonomization of aesthetics and intellectual disciplines, so bravely launched in the nineteenth century, signify in an epoch in which the producers of art and thought may reflect, both in their organizational dependence and in their intellectual and aesthetic paradigms, the worldview underlying the current mode of industrial production and exchange? The second question flows from the observation that both the monumental and the critical aspects of high culture have always been dependent on a notion of the present as imbedded in a continuum that moves between past and future. Given the symbiosis between the neoliberal celebration of the end of history and the virtual denial of history mandated by postmodern criticism and philosophy, are either of these aspects, particularly the critical, valid?

See also **The Medieval Heritage** *(volume 1);* **Secularization; Communications, the Media, and Propaganda** *(volume 2);* **Artists** *(volume 3);* **Belief and Popular Religion** *(volume 5); and other articles in this section.*

BIBLIOGRAPHY

Abrams, M. H. *Natural Supernaturalism.* New York, 1973.

Allen, James Smith. *In the Public Eye: A History of Reading in Modern France, 1800–1940.* Princeton, N.J., 1991.

Anderson, Benedict. *Imagined Communities.* New York, 1983.

Arato, Andrew, and Eike Gerhardt, ed. *The Essential Frankfurt School Reader.* New York, 1993. Includes essays by T. W. Adorno, Walter Benjamin, Erich Fromm, Max Horkheimer, and Herbert Marcuse.

Bakhtin, Mikhail. *Rabelais and His World.* Cambridge, Mass., 1968.

Benhabib, Seyla. *Critique, Norm, and Utopia: A Study of the Foundations of Critical Theory.* New York, 1986.

Bourdieu, Pierre. *Distinction: A Social Critique of the Judgement of Taste.* Translated by Richard Nice. London, 1984.

Brombert, Victor. *Victor Hugo and the Visionary Novel.* Cambridge, Mass., 1984.

Cassagne, Albert. *La théorie de l'art pour l'art: En France chez les derniers romantiques et les premiers réalistes.* 2d. ed. Paris, 1959.

Chailley, Jacques. *The Magic Flute: Masonic Opera.* Translated by Herbert Weinstock. London, 1972.

Chambers, E. K. *The Mediaeval Stage.* 2 vols. Oxford, 1903.

Chevalier, Louis. *Labouring Classes and Dangerous Classes in Paris in the First Half of the Nineteenth Century.* Translated by Frank Jellinek. London, 1973.

Clark, T. J. *The Absolute Bourgeois: Artists and Politics in France, 1848–1851.* London, 1973.

Clark, T. J. *Image of the People: Gustave Courbet and the 1848 Revolution.* London, 1973.

Craig, Hardin. *English Religious Drama of the Middle Ages.* Oxford, 1955.

Duby, Georges. *Le temps des cathédrales: L'art et la société, 980–1420.* Paris, 1976.

Eagleton, Terry. *The Illusions of Postmodernism.* Oxford, 1997.

Elias, Norbert. *Über den Prozess der Zivilisation: Soziogenetische und psychogenetische Untersuchungen.* 2 vols. Basel, Switzerland, 1939.

Febvre, Lucien. *Amour sacré, amour profane.* Paris, 1971.

Febvre, Lucien. "Civilisation." In *A New Kind of History: From the Writings of Febvre.* Edited by Peter Burke. Translated by K. Folca. London, 1973. Pages 219–257.

Gay, Peter. *The Bourgeois Experience: Victoria to Freud.* 5 vols. New York, 1984–1998.

Gellner, Ernest. *Nations and Nationalism.* Oxford, 1983.

Ginzburg, Carlo. *The Cheese and the Worms. The Cosmos of a Sixteenth-Century Miller.* Translated by John Tedeschi and Anne Tedeschi. Harmondsworth, U.K., 1983.

Gombrich, E. H. *The Story of Art.* Oxford, 1984.

Gossman, Lionel. *Between History and Literature.* Cambridge, Mass., 1990.

Graña, César. *Bohemian versus Bourgeois: French Society and the French Man of Letters in the Nineteenth Century.* New York, 1964.

Howarth, W. D. *Sublime and Grotesque: A Study of French Romantic Drama.* London, 1975.

Huyghe, René. *La relève du réel: la peinture française au XIXe siècle: Impressionnisme, symbolisme.* Paris, 1974.

Jacoby, Russell. *The End of Utopia: Politics and Culture in an Age of Apathy.* New York, 1999.

Jacoby, Russell. *The Last Intellectuals: American Culture in the Age of Academe.* New York, 1987.

Jay, Martin. *The Dialectical Imagination: A History of the Frankfurt School and the Institute of Social Research, 1923–1950.* Boston, 1973.

Kreuzer, Helmut. *Die Boheme: Analyse und Dokumentation der intellektuellen Subkultur vom 19. Jahrhundert bis zur Gegenwart.* Stuttgart, Germany, 1971.

Le Goff, Jacques. *Time, Work, and Culture in the Middle Ages.* Translated by Arthur Goldhammer. Chicago, 1980.

Le Roy Ladurie, Emmanuel. *Montaillou: The Promised Land of Error.* Translated by Barbara Bray. New York, 1979.

Lindsay, Jack. *Gustave Courbet: His Life and Art.* London, 1973.

Löwy, Michael, and Robert Sayre. *Révolte et mélancolie: Le romantisme à contre-courant de la modernité.* Paris, 1992.

Marienstras, Richard. *New Perspectives on the Shakespearean World.* Translated by Janet Lloyd. Cambridge, U.K., 1985.

McCole, John. *Walter Benjamin and the Antinomies of Tradition.* Ithaca, N.Y., 1983.

Mitzman, Arthur. *Michelet, ou, La subversion du passé.* Paris, 1999.

Mozart, Wolfgang Amadeus. *Die Zauberflöte.* (The magic flute.) Libretto to Colin Davis recording. Translated by Robert Jordan. Philips, 1984.

Nietzsche, Friedrich. *The Use and Abuse of History.* Indianapolis, Ind., 1957.

Palmer, Bryan D. *Descent into Discourse: The Reification of Language and the Writing of Social History.* Philadelphia, 1990.

Ringer, Fritz K. *The Decline of the German Mandarins: The German Academic Community, 1890–1933.* Cambridge, Mass., 1969.

Saunders, Frances Stonor. *Who Paid the Piper?: The CIA and the Cultural Cold War.* London, 1999.

Schorske, Carl E. *Fin-de-Siècle Vienna: Politics and Culture.* New York, 1980.

Thiesse, Anne-Marie. "L'éducation sociale d'un romancier: Le cas d'Eugène Sue." *Actes de la Recherche en Science Sociale* 32–33 (April–June 1980): 51–63.

Wiggershaus, Rolf. *The Frankfurt School: Its History, Theories, and Political Significance.* Translated by Michael Robertson. Cambridge, Mass., 1994.

MAGIC

Stuart Clark

The word "magic" has been in widespread use throughout modern European history as a label to designate social phenomena. Precisely what it designates, however, remains elusive, for neither social scientists nor social historians have succeeded in defining it. This is partly because what magic has signified has varied from age to age and context to context; it is a classic example of a concept whose meaning and application are always a function of local circumstances. For late-twentieth-century historians, though not for many in the past, this makes any attempt to define it in a transhistorical manner not merely difficult but undesirable. Partly, too, magic has most often been something disapproved of, and "magical" a term of refusal. This is especially true in the sphere of religion, where magic has invariably been a concept employed either to stigmatize competitor faiths or to proscribe beliefs or behavior deemed to be irreligious. It is in this sense that magic has been the "other" of Judeo-Christian religious tradition from biblical times through to the present day. Western science has also had a major part in investing magic with oppositional meanings, in this case between the cogency and rationality of orthodox scientific or medical practice on the one hand and the error and irrationality of the magician on the other. Here magic has mostly been bad or pseudo science, as defined by the scientific establishment of the day.

One striking consequence of this for the social historian is that it can be difficult to find anyone in the past who accepted "magic" as a correct description of what they thought or did, let alone any who called themselves "magicians." A glaring example comes from the Protestant Reformation of the sixteenth century. The two major leaders of Protestantism, Martin Luther and John Calvin, along with all their colleagues and successors, argued that Catholicism itself was merely a form of magic, with its many miracles, its exorcisms and votive prayers for the dead, and the transubstantiations of the Mass as the most prominent examples. One could hardly expect their Catholic contemporaries—or, indeed, Catholic historians of

the Reformation since—to agree with this. But such has been the power behind this particular piece of labeling that only in the late twentieth century do we realize that to talk about pre-Reformation religion as "magical" is to use an essentially Protestant vocabulary.

There are some important exceptions to this principle, as we shall see; the Renaissance magus, the ceremonial magicians of the eighteenth, nineteenth, and twentieth centuries, and even the magical healers and diviners of the European countryside have not lacked self-recognition or been solely defined by those hostile to them. Nevertheless, magic has mostly been a term of attribution and its social history must, in consequence, be a history of how that attribution came to be made and how it has been contested. Some people have indeed been magicians and have practiced a magic they themselves have defined and developed. Usually, however, it is a question of which individuals or groups have used the concept of magic to label other individuals or groups and for what reasons.

Naturally, scholars too have indulged in the same labeling. The early academic history of anthropology in Europe, for example, was marked by the adoption, under the influence of the two traditions already mentioned, of distinctions between magic and religion and between magic and science that were almost entirely stipulative and dismissive of the magical practices of other cultures. Pioneer anthropologists like James Frazer and Edward Tylor tended to conceive of magic in terms of ignorance of natural causes and fear of inexplicable phenomena and to call any practice "magical" if it appeared, in their eyes, to control by supernatural means what could not be controlled by technological ones. Some historians of preindustrial European society and its culture have taken the same view, interpreting popular festivals, for instance, as attempts to cope magically with technological inadequacy and its consequent emotional tensions. Historians of science, too, have not always been careful to avoid the Whiggish sentiment that many aspects of medieval and early modern science were magical in nature. By the 1990s, however, to describe an aspect of any culture, past or present, as magical was thought to beg serious questions. Indeed, magic has come to be seen as a cultural construction, there being nothing in our attitudes to ourselves or to the world that is inherently magical. Once again, then, the task of social history becomes that of understanding how this construction came about and how it has been utilized and discussed in various sociocultural settings.

THE RENAISSANCE MAGUS

The intellectuals of the Renaissance are the most significant of those who very definitely enunciated their own theory of magic. Indeed, they had a very highly developed notion of the seriousness and importance of magic, which they called *magia*. With an illustrious pedigree stretching back to ancient Persia and to the mythical Egyptian philosopher Hermes Trismegistus, it signified the pursuit by adepts of a highly elevated and esoteric form of wisdom based on the perceived presence in the world of mystical patterns and intelligences possessing real efficacy in nature and in human affairs. In the cases of the Italian Neoplatonist Marsilio Ficino and the German occultist Heinrich Cornelius Agrippa, causation was seen in terms of an organically related hierarchy of powers. Influences descended from the angelic or intellectual world of spirits to the stellar and planetary world of the heavens, which in turn governed the behavior of earthly things and their physical changes. The magician was, in consequence, someone who sought to ascend to a knowledge of these superior powers and then accentuate their normal workings by drawing them down artificially to produce wonderful effects. This conception of magic was reinforced by the further idea that man was a microcosm and that the proportions and harmony of his body therefore resembled those of the universe. Hence the well-known depictions of the human frame with the arms and legs outstretched to meet the circumference of a perfect circle.

There is no doubt that men like Ficino and Agrippa, and other magicians of this kind, like the Italian Giovanni Pico della Mirandola and the Welshman John Dee, thought of their studies as the highest form of natural philosophy. For them magic had only positive connotations. But it is also easy to see why they aroused the hostility of churchmen, who often saw their work as demonic. *Magia* was as much an act of mystical illumination as a piece of science; here the magician aimed at a priestlike role and his wonders competed with the miracles of religion. In the early

AGRIPPA ON MAGIC

Magick is a faculty of wonderfull vertue, full of most high mysteries, containing the most profound contemplation of most secret things, together with the nature, power, quality, substance, and vertues thereof, as also the knowledge of whole nature, and it doth instruct us concerning the differing, and agreement of things amongst themselves, whence it produceth its wonderfull effects, by uniting the vertues of things through the application of them one to the other, and to their inferior sutable subjects, joyning and knitting them together thoroughly by the powers, and vertues of the superior Bodies. This is the most perfect, and chief science, that sacred and sublimer kind of phylosophy, and lastly the most absolute perfection of all most excellent philosophy.

— *From Heinrich Cornelius Agrippa,* Three Books of Occult Philosophy, *first published in 1533.* —

sixteenth century the Paduan philosopher Pietro Pomponazzi even argued that the secret forces studied by the magicians could explain away such miracles in naturalistic terms. Theologians and clergymen suspected that magical wonders were beyond nature altogether and, knowing that they could not be God's work, attributed them to the collaborative power of demons. Here is a good example, therefore, of the turning of a word with positive associations into a pejorative; magia became mere magic. Nevertheless, the three occult sciences that made up the practical applications of *magia*—astrology, alchemy, and natural magic, together with their derivatives in the field of medicine—enjoyed a great vogue in the sixteenth and seventeenth centuries. Indeed, these were often considered the most demanding, most innovative, and most rewarding kinds of science to practice. Their concentration on hidden causes made them intellectually challenging, and their promise of marvelous effects made them exciting as observational and empirical practice and offered material and political rewards, as well as renown.

It was once normal to assume that Renaissance *magia* was inimical to proper science and that astrology, alchemy, and the like were pseudosciences that had to be swept away before modern science could develop. But this was to accept at face value the retrospective judgments made by modern scientists themselves, once *magia* had become outmoded and depreciated. Late-twentieth-century historians were much more likely to avoid this anachronism by recognizing the vital contribution the occult sciences made to natural philosophy throughout the early modern period and even to the kind that developed in later-seventeenth-century Europe. John Dee was the first major English exponent of Euclidean mathematics; Francis Bacon, the great propagandist for scientific reform on empirical lines, wished to make *magia* a central part of his program, once he had purged it of what he regarded as its more fanciful and esoteric practices; and Isaac Newton, it is now well known, pursued alchemy no less fervently than physics or optics. More fundamentally, historians are also far more aware of the difficulty in making any conceptual distinction between science and magic in this context. Throughout the early modern period, the concept of magic encouraged researchers in many disciplines to see their activity in the empirical and interventionist terms that defined science from the eighteenth century onward.

A good individual example of how *magia* had a crucial role in what we now think of as a classic scientific "revolution" comes from the field of astronomy. The heliocentricism of Copernicus, announced in his *De revolutionibus orbium coelestium* of 1543, was heavily influenced by a traditional magical reverence for the sun as a symbol of the divinity and of knowledge. During the Renaissance, this tradition found expression, above all, in the writings of Ficino, whose enthusiastic follower Domenico Maria da Novara was professor of astronomy at Bologna and an associate of Copernicus. Copernicus himself described the sun as "enthroned" in the heavens and as "the lamp, the mind, the ruler of the universe," citing Hermes Trismegistus on the same theme, and Neoplatonists like Giordano Bruno were among the keenest early supporters of the Copernican system.

Of particular significance for social history, historians in the late twentieth century were also becoming increasingly aware of the great significance of the occult sciences in the political circles in which many magicians then moved and received patronage, notably those of monarchical courts and aristocratic households. Magic offered a vocabulary for rulership and the exercise of authority, just as it provided a pattern for science. The powers of rulers were often seen in divine and mystical terms in Renaissance Europe and their ability to provide solutions to political problems was regarded as thaumaturgical and charismatic. Magic provided a way of conceptualizing these ideals.

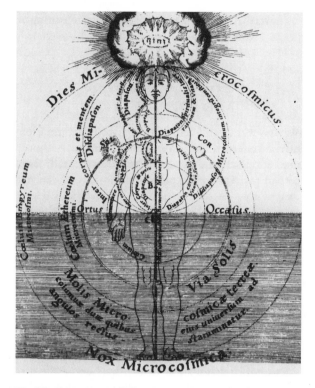

Fludd's Diagram. In "The Harmonic Intervals of Man" Robert Fludd (1574–1637) proposed to relate the human body to the wider universe. ©HULTON GETTY/LIAISON AGENCY

It also worked in secret ways, as did princes in the realm of *arcana imperii* (secrets of state). The processes of alchemy, in particular, were often applied allegorically to the problems of maintaining order and harmony in societies divided by religious and other conflicts. Natural magic likewise helped to promote the keen interest in marvels and the setting up of *Wunderkammern* (cabinets of curiosities) that typified courtly and aristocratic notions of power and knowledge in this period. An example of the application of magic to government can be seen in Bacon's utopian work *New Atlantis,* which appeared in eight editions between 1626 and 1658. It contains the vision of a society ruled by men who combine the functions of politicians, priests, and natural philosophers. Another illustration is the sustained interest shown in the magical or "occult" sciences at the court of the emperor Rudolf II in Prague between 1583 and 1612. Above all, perhaps, it is the figure of Prospero in Shakespeare's last play, *The Tempest,* that best captures the relationship, ambivalent at times, between the art of ruling and the practice of magic. In some respects, Prospero is a Baconian figure, a natural magician seeking knowledge and control of nature's secret powers;

he nevertheless renounces magic before returning to power as the duke of Milan.

THE REFORMATIONS AND POPULAR MAGIC

Whatever their differences, the religious Reformations of the sixteenth and seventeenth centuries—Protestant and Catholic alike—were fundamentally concerned to improve lay piety and morality. What historians now see as the social impact of religious change in this period consisted chiefly in this—getting ordinary men and women to take religious values and solutions more seriously in every aspect of their individual and communal lives. This applied in particular to the trials and tribulations of everyday life in the preindustrial countryside and to the more concrete steps often taken to prevent misfortune and alleviate distress. Study after study has shown how, all over Europe, ordinary people regularly appealed not to their own consciences or to the collective conscience of the church, as their priests urged them to do. Instead they turned to local practitioners skilled in healing, divination, exorcism, and astrology to help solve their everyday problems. They did this frequently in cases of suspected witchcraft but any kind of misfortune, anticipated or experienced, could justify a visit to the "cunning" man or woman. Alternatively, they might use their own traditional folk remedies, since the techniques employed by the specialists were, in principle, accessible to all.

Those who practiced these techniques presumably thought that they worked in a straightforward causal way; they were simply techniques for dealing with an illness, a bad crop, a theft, or an unrequited love. Although they themselves sometimes called them "magic"—and, indeed, "good" or "white" magic—they did so without any implication of inefficacy. Churchmen, by contrast, were convinced not only that they diverted attention from concepts like providence, sin, and repentance, but that they were also empty of all effect, appearing to work only because the devil intervened to make them do so. They were suspicious, too, of the scraps of real religion often mixed up in these folk techniques, especially religious objects and words (like holy water or candle wax, saints' names, and prayerlike incantations). Universally, they were known as "superstitions" by the orthodox, but "magic"—now "evil" or "black" magic—was also the label used to denounce them. By the end of the sixteenth century, vast areas of lay culture were, in principle, susceptible to the charge. It was made in countless sermons, catechisms, confes-

A LUTHERAN PREACHER'S DEFINITION OF MAGIC

This definition of magic was offered by the Lutheran preacher and writer Bernhard Albrecht in a book denouncing popular magic, published in 1628: Magic occurs "when anyone uses something in God's creation, such as herbs, wood, stones, words, times, hours, gestures and the like, or seeks to bring about some effect, other than God has decreed, with the assistance and support of devils, either to reveal hidden or future things, or to obtain unnatural things, supposedly to help a neighbor."

sors' manuals, works of casuistry, and specialist books about witchcraft and demonism, and it could be applied to many popular forms of agriculture and domestic production; behavior to do with marriages and parenting; attempts to find lost goods or hidden treasure, or to be lucky in gambling; the widespread belief in omens and propitiousness; foretelling the future; the interpretation of dreams; and the casting of lots. Particularly prominent was the accusation that popular medicine was full of magic. For two centuries and more, disapproving clerics, and other intellectuals and professionals, condemned a vast array of traditional folk practices to do with protecting and preserving the body because they were irreligious and deemed not to work.

Intellectually, then, the two Reformations were an attempt to reinforce the boundary between what was deemed to be religion and what was deemed to be magic (although as we saw earlier, religious enemies accused each other of performing magic, too). The social consequences associated with this campaign have been the subject of many studies of early modern communities going through what can only be described as a process of acculturation. Some experts, like the French historian Robert Muchembled, have attributed the upsurge in witchcraft trials to the social strains that resulted. The European countryside became divided by commitment to the new religious ideals, projecting onto witches the fears, anxieties, and guilty feelings aroused by the cultural revolution being imposed from above; thus, witches were creations of the attack on magic. Other historians have concentrated on the issue of whether this revolution actually succeeded in changing lay behavior and eradicating magic from people's lives. The most pessimistic verdict in this debate was that of Jean Delumeau, who argued controversially that even in France the population had not become fully Christianized on the eve of the Revolution in 1789. Whatever its successes or failures, however, the attack on popular magic between the sixteenth and eighteenth centuries was a crucial part of probably the most sustained attempt ever made in European history to change fundamentally the beliefs and behavior of the general population.

Easily the most authoritative and influential attempt to absorb the whole subject of magic into the mainstream social history of early modern England was Keith Thomas's *Religion and the Decline of Magic* (1971). By borrowing the method of thick ethnographical description from social anthropology Thomas was able to show the embeddedness of magical practices, especially those to do with personal fortune and misfortune, in the daily lives of ordinary men and women in the period. The book provided an immensely rich panorama on the subjects of magical healing, the work of the "cunning men" and other magic professionals, the popularity of astrology, and the fears about witchcraft. More than this, Thomas juxtaposed the history of popular culture in these areas with the Protestant Reformation in England, showing how deeply interrelated the two were and how concerned the religious reformers were to take every suggestion of magic out of religious belief and practice. Most controversially Thomas offered an account of the decline of magic not solely in terms of intellectual criticism, or in relation to technological improvements that made contemporaries gradually less vulnerable to an environment they had hitherto had difficulty in managing, but as an aspect of the development of the notion of self-reliance and of faith in unaided human capacities.

TRADITIONAL FOLK PRACTICES

Typical instances of traditional folk practices are diagnosis by measuring a person's belt or girdle; healing by charms or other forms of words or by symbols (especially the misuse of religious words or symbols); healing by wearing amulets; the belief in the evil eye and in illness by bewitchment or by being touched; the attribution of various powers to body parts or substances (notably blood and semen); many practices to do with determining the sex of a child during gestation; the opening of chests or doors to relieve labor pains; and the curing of a wound by treating the weapon that inflicted it.

Witches. Witches at a cauldron. English engraving, 1489.
PRIVATE COLLECTION/THE BRIDGEMAN ART LIBRARY

MAGIC AND MISFORTUNE IN MODERN EUROPE

Partly as a result of Keith Thomas's thesis, evidence that popular faith in magic has continued down to the present is often presented as a case of the "survival" of superstition after it was supposed to have disappeared under the influence of better religion, better education, and better insurance policies. This is a further instance of the labeling that invariably accompanies the concept of magic. Even in Judith Devlin's pioneering study, *The Superstitious Mind,* where the peasants of nineteenth-century rural France were reported to have beliefs in magical healing, apparitions, witchcraft, possession, and prophecy that were scarcely different from those of their medieval predecessors, magic was still associated with intellectual irrationality and confusion and with emotional trauma. During the twentieth century it was sensationalized and exoticized in newspaper reports, collected and treated as an archaeological relic by folklorists, and explained away by rationalist and functionalist anthropologists. Once again, however, what the social historian has to recognize is that magic has gone on being appealing not as an archaism or a substitute for better solutions but as applicable to specific situations deemed to be directly relevant to it. This is especially true of the misfortunes associated with witchcraft and of the management of health, love, and money.

Witchcraft has been a continuous presence in modern European societies even though the last legally sanctioned executions of witches took place in the eighteenth century. Communities have gone on fearing the witch's malice, have gone on identifying witches in their midst, and, in consequence, have gone on resorting to counterwitchcraft. Magic, always a powerful apotropaic in this area, has thus retained its relevance, and "unwitchers," cunning men and women, "witch doctors," and other magical specialists have kept their clients. In the Netherlands, in the province of Drenthe, both the church and civil authorities took action against magicians of this sort long after they had ceased to punish witches. In France, the studies of historians like Matthew Ramsey and Bernard Traimond have shown how crucial to the moral and social economy of rural communities were the *devins* and other healers who diagnosed illness by witchcraft and treated its symptoms. Traimond looks, in particular, at the stories of a Basque barber-surgeon in Bayonne around 1750 and of three unwitching specialists, two of whom were unfrocked priests, in Bordeaux in the 1800s. The folk magic and rural superstitions of Germany in the eighteenth and nineteenth centuries have likewise been the subject of the studies of the social historian Eva Labouvie.

Counterwitchcraft by no means exhausted the repertoire of magic in these and other countries. Treasure seeking (a male preserve), divination, and techniques for enhancing love also figured prominently. But a diminution in the role and scope of witchcraft cases and their narrowing social complexion—they became restricted to the countryside, to the lower socioeconomic classes, to nonprofessionals, and to women—did mean a corresponding reduction in the importance of magical remedies. Even so, and whatever its precise form, or the sex or social position of those involved, popular magic has proved to be a rich resource for the historian interested in the social and cultural dynamics of modern communities.

Twentieth-century versions of magic of this sort were certainly not lacking. Unwitchers were still practicing their skills virtually everywhere in Europe, well-

---

A DANISH WITCH DOCTOR

In Drenthe in 1862 newspaper accounts of a witch doctor named Sjoerd Brouwers reported that he recommended that an eighteen-year-old girl suffering from nausea, headaches, backache, and stomachache should rub her toes between twelve and one o'clock at night with pig's blood in which a cock's head had been boiled. After this her father had to ride her around the house three times in a wheelbarrow. The medicines were to be buried and every other day before sunrise they were to be smelled. Two weeks after this report, the newspaper announced that the girl had been delivered of a chubby boy. (Gijswijt-Hofstra, 1999, p. 111)

---

integrated in witchcraft "systems" and, indeed, occupying a key position in them. This was nowhere more dramatically shown than in the Bocage in the 1970s, when the French anthropologist Jeanne Favret-Saada found herself "caught" so personally in the witchcraft episodes she was studying that she came herself to be seen as both bewitched and an unwitcher. A witchcraft case in the Dutch town of Sliedrecht in 1926 involved a prominent and widely consulted witch doctor, Lambertus Lelie, and in 1954 in Sarzbüttel, northwest of Hamburg, a witch doctor named Waldemar Eberling who had been seeing clients for decades was put on trial accused of illegal medical practice.

LEARNED AND CEREMONIAL MAGIC FROM THE EIGHTEENTH TO THE TWENTIETH CENTURIES

Eventually the occult sciences of the Renaissance were overtaken in the scientific mainstream by different assumptions about nature and different styles of natural inquiry. Astrology, alchemy, and natural magic decisively lost ground, the first not least through its seventeenth-century links with radicalism. Most of the natural effects previously ascribed to magical or occult causation were explained away by eighteenth-century physics and chemistry. It became customary in "enlightened" circles to ridicule the magic of previous eras as the product of superstition, irrationality, and ignorance. The French philosopher and historian Voltaire declared magic to be "an impossible thing" and thought that magicians were mostly imposters. It is important to see this disparagement as a social and ideological phenomenon, as well as an intellectual one, with magic becoming a point of reference for a whole set of assumptions about modernity and progress. It was said to be the product of "enthusiasm" and deception—precisely the sorts of things most troublesome to increasingly commercialized societies. Denouncing magic was a way of establishing the values of order and politeness and other cultural boundaries appropriate to such societies. In effect, it was an aspect of ideological changes driven by conflict. Above all, it was a way of making a social distinction between the classes thought to be most and least committed to the new enlightened values.

On the other hand, we should not be misled by the language used by the "enlightened" crusaders against magic into thinking that the European elites could not continue to mix what were proclaimed to be incompatible beliefs. The occult and the supernatural had a posthumous life in the art and literature of this period. Suppressed, they returned, migrating into the world of the Gothic and into romanticism, where the supernatural could be made sublime and its terrors enjoyed without risk. The "decline of magic" is also seriously compromised by the presence in European high culture of the eighteenth and nineteenth centuries of new forms of occult science—labeled "pseudo" sciences by the dominant Newtonianism. Alchemy and astrology survived enough to continue to appeal, alongside new studies like animal magnetism, physiognomy, and phrenology. Franz Anton Mesmer, whose "mesmerism" resembled the magnetic theories of the Renaissance natural magicians, for whom magnetism was always the classic occult quality, behaved like a magus and even a shaman, though always protesting scientific respectability. The physiognomical teachings of the Swiss pastor Johann Kaspar Lavater were likewise reminiscent of the magical traditions of the past.

At the same time, ceremonial or ritual magic, another former ingredient of Renaissance neo-Platonism, enjoyed a fresh popularity, especially among the members of the secret societies and benefit clubs that flourished to an extraordinary extent from the eighteenth century onward. Freemasonry, in particular, was committed to magical rites derived from the wisdom of ancient civilizations and the transmission of secret skills and crafts down the ages, and designed to initiate members. Its key symbols included the pentagram, the five-pointed star central to magical tradition. Ronald Hutton writes that "it is difficult to overvalue the importance of Freemasonry in nineteenth-century British culture. It was patronized by royalty, existed in every part of the nation and in town and countryside alike, and was an accepted part of local life" (p. 5). Magic also appealed strongly to the antirationalist trends in nineteenth-century society, and a revival of learned interest in it occurred in the final decades, notably around the French enthusiast Alphonse Constant ("Eliphas Levi"), the Societas Rosicruciana in Anglia (founded in 1866), and, from 1888 until about 1900, the Hermetic Order of the the Golden Dawn, which actually practiced a ritual magic based on Greek, Hebrew (cabalistic), and Christian traditions. Among the best known members of this last order was the Irish poet W. B. Yeats.

One other aspect of the nineteenth century's interest in magic should be noted, though it has nothing to do with the *practice* of magic. This is the emergence of many attempts to explain the place of magic in human thought and society, and not simply to condemn it as wrongheaded as the eighteenth-century thinkers had done. Magic became more and more the subject of academic investigation—by theorists of cultural change and secularization, by folklorists, antiquarians, and anthropologists, even by psychopathologists. Chief among the sociological theories that emerged was that of the "positivists" Auguste Comte and Herbert Spencer, both of whom argued that human consciousness had progressed through successive stages in which first theology, then metaphysics, and finally science had a dominating influence. This kind of metanarrative historicized magic by giving it a historical role at an appropriate moment of human development, much as Émile Durkheim later suggested a social-functional role for it. Such scholarly explanations have in fact had a profound effect on the historiography of magic ever since; they testify to magic's power to resonate in the minds of Europeans even when they neither believe in it nor seek to perform it.

MAGIC AND PAGAN WITCHCRAFT

Twentieth-century Britain saw a remarkable development of pagan witchcraft, known as Wicca, in which magical elements are prominent. As Ronald Hutton has shown, these elements stem partly from the traditions of ceremonial magic already discussed and partly from the continued practice of magic into the modern age in its popular form by cunning folk, conjurers, charmers, and users of "natural medicine." This last tradition bequeathed to modern pagan religion not only a store of operative magical techniques but a number of those who practiced them as well.

Masonic Ritual. "Meeting of Freemasons for Reception of Masters," anonymous French engraving, eighteenth century. At right, a future member of the lodge waits under a cloth for his initiation. BIBLIOTHÈQUE NATIONALE DE FRANCE, PARIS/©COLLECTION VIOLLET

From the first, Wicca was portrayed by its followers as a vehicle for magical powers and with rituals designed to release and manipulate them. It was inspired in part by Aleister Crowley's *Magick in Theory and Practice* (1929), the most important exposition of the techniques of ritual magic from the early part of the century, but it also included elements from traditional *grimoires,* descriptions of witchcraft practices by the anthropologist Margaret Murray, and initiation ceremonies borrowed from Freemasonry and from the Golden Dawn. During the 1950s the leading Wiccan, Gerald Gardner, was continuously revising its rituals by drawing on these and other sources. The second main branch of the movement, the Alexandrian, after Alex Sanders, was likewise based on cabalistic and other forms of ritual magical working. More recently still, pagans have looked more critically at the sense in which Wicca continues the practices of an "Old Religion," but still its magical core remains. As Hutton has said, "at the heart of its mysteries lies a particular notion, and experience, of the transformative power of something which is called magic" (p. 71).

The central aim of this magic is not just personal development and self-knowledge but concrete powers—powers to see and know, to create and move, and to heal. These are acquired both by releasing and expanding abilities thought to lie hidden in each individual and by tapping into the workings of the cosmos, much as magic has always been conceived to operate by synchronisms between the microcosmic and macrocosmic levels of things. In Hutton's view,

Wicca is thus a religion that negotiates with supernatural beings in a way normally reserved for magicians; that is, by seeking to direct forces that would in conventional religious contexts be seen as beyond human control. For this purpose deities are drawn by ritual means to join with the individual, who is seen both as a priestess or priest, passively serving and praising the divine, *and* as a witch, constraining the divine to cooperate. In social terms the practice of magic by modern Wiccans reveals the capacity for independence and organization characteristic of the small group of religious enthusiasts, while also exemplifying what Hutton calls the "privatization" of religion in the mid- to late twentieth century. However, unlike other manifestations of the phenomenon known to sociologists of religion as New Religious Movements, pagan witchcraft does not, according to Hutton, "depend heavily upon one or a few charismatic leaders. It does not appeal overwhelmingly to a particular age group or cultural group. It does not offer a radical break with existing family and social relationships; and it does not challenge the wider culture as a whole" (pp. 77–78).

MAGIC AND SATANISM

The second part of the twentieth century also saw the creation of groups who call themselves "satanists." A huge mythology concerning their supposed devil worship also arose, but it bore no resemblance to the actual beliefs and behavior of satanists. Among these

36

groups magic has had a role as both practice and ideology, though the numbers involved make this a marginal social phenomenon. Ironically, it is the mythology that has been of greater interest and significance to social historians and anthropologists of religion. A leading analyst of both the American and British manifestations of satanism is Jean La Fontaine, who said that modern satanists are yet further practitioners—

if self-taught—of the learned and ceremonial (or ritual) magic that we have seen to be so crucial to the European Renaissance, the development of Freemasonry, the nineteenth-century occult revival, and twentieth-century enthusiasts like Aleister Crowley (for whom magic was "magick" and a way of rescuing the self, in both its spiritual and bodily manifestations, from the burdens of social convention). The Church of Satan founded in California in 1966 by Anton Szandor LaVey, for instance, proclaimed a threefold magical power in its rituals—the power to attract love and desire, the power to give help, and the power to destroy—while the rituals themselves depended heavily on the magical symbol of the pentagram and the magical god Baphomet. Its offshoot, the Temple of Set, as its name makes clear, has proclaimed strong links with ancient Egyptian magic and its beliefs include the magical idea of the transformative power of the subjective will aided by rituals.

The mythology surrounding satanism crystallized in the modern world in accusations of devil worship accompanied by child abuse and led to well-publicized cases of intervention by social work professionals and would-be prosecutors. What is of interest to social historians here, once again, cannot be an actual magical practice since no independent evidence to corroborate the accusations has been found. Instead, it is the social phenomenon of such accusations that is itself under scrutiny, preeminently so in La Fontaine's authoritative study of the subject, *Speak of the Devil* (1998). Mainly, the analysis has fallen on the emergence in recent decades of revivalist and fun-

Rosicrucianism. Poster advertising the Rosicrucian Salon, Paris, 1892. MIRROR SYNDICATION, LONDON

THEOSOPHY

Theosophy, a movement founded in 1875 and inspired by the Russian noblewoman Helena Petrovna Blavatsky, was popular in North America, Europe, and India. Its main belief, like that of the pansophical claims of the Renaissance magi, was that a single wisdom lay behind the differences in world religions and philosophies. Blavatsky herself also practiced magic, in the sense of attempting to make voices and objects appear from nothing (psychokinesis), and also popularized the notion of reincarnation in the West. (Hutton, 1999, p. 10)

damentalist "New Christian" movements, anxious, like their Reformation predecessors, to brand all other religions as unbiblical and satanic. For these movements devil worship has always been a historical reality rather than what it is for historians—a social and cultural construction extending back through the ages to embrace medieval heresy, early modern witchcraft, and modern Freemasonry, and now active again in the form of all sorts of supposed modern depravities. First in the United States and then in Europe, these have come to include the ritual sexual abuse of children, accusations being fueled by the testimony of new converts remembering their own satanic pasts, by other adults "satanically" abused in childhood, and by children suggestively interviewed by "experts." The uncanny resemblance between these sources of "evidence" and those that led to the witch-hunts of the sixteenth and seventeenth centuries has now become apparent. We return, then, to the distinction that has been constitutive of the social history of magic in the modern world, the distinction we started with—between actual practice and the allegation of practice.

See also **The Protestant Reformation and the Catholic Reformation** *(volume 1); and other articles in this section.*

BIBLIOGRAPHY

Clark, Stuart. "French Historians and Early Modern Popular Culture." *Past and Present* 100 (1983): 62–99.

Delumeau, Jean. *Catholicism between Luther and Voltaire: A New View of the Counter Reformation.* Translated by Jeremy Moiser, with an introduction by John Bossy. London, 1977. Translation of *Le catholicisme entre Luther et Voltaire.*

Devlin, Judith. *The Superstitious Mind: French Peasants and the Supernatural in the Nineteenth Century.* New Haven, Conn., 1987. Argues that the escapism and anxiety evident in the magic of rural France are not incompatible with cultural modernity.

Favret-Saada, Jeanne. *Deadly Words: Witchcraft in the Bocage.* Translated by Catherine Cullen. Cambridge, U.K., and New York, 1980. Translation of *Mots, la mort, les sorts.*

Gijswijt-Hofstra, Marijke. "Witchcraft after the Witch-trials." In Marijke Gijswijt-Hofstra, Brian P. Levack, and Roy Porter. *Witchcraft and Magic in Europe: The Eighteenth and Nineteenth Centuries.* The Athlone History of Witchcraft and Magic in Europe, 5. London, 1999. Pages 95–189.

Hutton, Ronald. "Modern Pagan Witchcraft." In Willem De Blécourt, Ronald Hutton, and Jean La Fontaine. *Witchcraft and Magic in Europe: The Twentieth Century.* The Athlone History of Witchcraft and Magic in Europe, 6. London, 1999.

Labouvie, Eva. *Verbotene Kunste: Volksmagie und landlicher Aberglaube in den Dorfgemeinden des Saarraumes (16.–19. Jahrhundert).* St. Ingbert, Germany, 1992.

La Fontaine, Jean. "Satanism and Satanic Abuse Mythology." In Willem De Blécourt, Ronald Hutton, and Jean La Fontaine. *Witchcraft and Magic in Europe: The Twentieth Century.* The Athlone History of Witchcraft and Magic in Europe, 6. London, 1999.

La Fontaine, Jean. *Speak of the Devil: Tales of Satanic Abuse in Contemporary England.* Cambridge, U.K., and New York, 1998.

Luhrmann, Tanya M. *Persuasions of the Witch's Craft: Ritual Magic and Witchcraft in Present-Day England.* Oxford, 1989.

Ramsey, Matthew. *Professional and Popular Medicine in France, 1770–1830: The Social World of Medical Practice.* Cambridge, U.K., and New York, 1988. Pages 229–276. Considers folk healers, *magia,* and witches.

Tambiah, Stanley Jeyaraja. *Magic, Science, Religion, and the Scope of Rationality.* Cambridge, U.K., and New York, 1990. Examines magic as a concept in the intellectual history of Western thought.

Thomas, Keith. *Religion and the Decline of Magic: Studies in Popular Beliefs in Sixteenth and Seventeenth Century England.* London and New York, 1971. A magisterial study of the changing relationship between religion and magic that transformed the social history of popular beliefs.

Traimond, Bernard. *Le pouvoir de la maladie: Magie et politique dans les Landes de Gascogne, 1750–1826.* Bordeaux, France, 1988.

FESTIVALS

Mack P. Holt

Festival, feast, fête—these are all words that derive from the Latin *festum,* meaning a celebration or an occasion for celebration, such as a holiday (or holy day). Thus, the history of festivals in the modern West is necessarily linked to eating and drinking, Christianity, work and leisure, and the history of rituals generally. Moreover, the history of festivals in the West from the Renaissance to the present is distinctly diverse. A cornucopia of local, regional, national, and some nearly universal festivals have existed all over Europe since the high Middle Ages. They range in scope from festivals marking rites of passage—births and marriages, for example—to feasts denoting a specific time of the calendar year—the harvest in early autumn and new millennium celebrations being obvious examples—to religious feasts such as Carnival and Easter (with Lent in between), to nationalist festivals—Bastille Day in France being the best known. The experience of European festivals is so diverse that no short summary can possibly be complete. What follows is less a comprehensive survey of European festivals from the Renaissance to the present than an essay that attempts to sketch out some of the major types of festivals and assess how they have changed over time. The principal claim made is that the functions of these festivals evolved and changed between 1500 and 2000. In the late Middle Ages most festivals served many purposes, but one thing they all shared was the ability to build and cement an idea of community. Many, in fact, delineated the boundaries of the community itself: between the sacred and the profane, between insider and outsider, or just between the orthodox and the unorthodox. Even though definitions of community, the sacred, insiderness, and orthodoxy have changed over the centuries, some of these functions have remained. What changed in the nineteenth and twentieth centuries, however, was that participation in these festivals evolved from a largely collective and social experience to one much more individual and commercial. That is not to argue that a utopian "world we have lost" has been replaced by less satisfying modern commercialism. Nor is it suggested that community and capitalism are mutually exclusive. Changes over time do help us better understand ourselves, however, as a closer look at several specific examples of these changes will make clear.

CARNIVAL

The word carnival comes from *carne,* meaning flesh. And as the etymology of this word in most Latin-based languages indicates, this means animal flesh, or meat, as well as human flesh. Thus Carnival has always been associated with the consumption of flesh as well as the carnal sins of the flesh—gluttony and lechery—two of the seven deadly sins for Christians in the late Middle Ages. It may seem a genuine irony, then, that Carnival's entire raison d'être was its link to Lent and the feast day of Easter itself, that link being the purification and satisfaction of sin through the sacrament of penance. Usually in the form of a three- to six-day period of feasting culminating in Shrove Tuesday (Mardi Gras, Fastnacht, and so on), Carnival preceded the beginning of Lent in the liturgical calendar, which always falls on Ash Wednesday. Thus Carnival was a festival of the flesh that marked the transition from a carnal period of behavior to a penitential regime of abstinence from flesh altogether during Lent—both from meat and from sex, even between husbands and wives. The Lenten season lasted from Ash Wednesday until Easter Sunday, the single most important feast day on the liturgical calendar, where the consumption of flesh was resumed once again, traditionally in the form of the paschal lamb. Carnival was the first half of an inseparable duality, of which the other half was Lent. Carnival was a period of feasting, meaning shops were supposed to be closed, with leisure replacing work, while Lent was a period of fasting and purification. The whole was designed as a means of preparing the sinner, via confession and penance on the one hand and abstinence of flesh on the other, for the holiest feast of all, the consumption of Christ's own flesh in the sacrament of the Eucharist on Easter Sunday.

But why did clerical and political authorities condone such explicit gluttony and lechery during Carnival? How could such deadly sins be a precursor to, much less a vital part of, preparation for the sacred experience of the mass? The answer does not lie in the "safety-valve theory" proposed by some social anthropologists, whereby ecclesiastical and secular authorities allowed the masses to let off a little steam for a few days once a year to keep the lid on the boiling cauldron of social tensions that were inevitable in a hierarchical society. By letting the laity turn their world upside down during Carnival, so the theory goes—allowing gender roles, social roles, and even political roles to be reversed, with men dressing as women and peasants dressing as kings—the world would remain more or less right side up the rest of the liturgical year. While this argument may doubtless contain an element of truth, it does not explain why premodern authorities seemed to condone, or at least turn a blind eye to, behavior and comportment that would have profaned the sacred any other time of the year. A much better explanation is depicted in Pieter Brueghel's painting *The Fight between Carnival and Lent.* On the left side a fat and corpulent peasant is mounted astride a beer barrel, with a roasting spit for a lance on which a pig's head is skewered. On the ground beside him are playing cards, dice, and other things associated with gambling, while his assistants offer him jugs of wine, beer steins, and a grill for roasting meat. This "carnal knight" is engaged in battle with his opposite, an emaciated cleric sitting in a chair pulled by two women. His lance is a long oven paddle on which are two fish, the only allowable flesh during Lent. Beside him are the loaves, pancakes, and pretzels that made up the rest of the Lenten diet. The point of this image is not just that Carnival and Lent were polar opposites and in competition with each other, but that they were engaged in as part of a common process of penitential satisfaction of sin. The object of the feasting of Carnival was to emphasize and bring to light the entire corpus of sin from the previous year, so that it could then be eviscerated and ultimately confessed and satisfied during Lent itself. This dialectical relationship between carnival and Lent was perhaps best depicted in Rabelais's fictitious king of the Carnival, Quaresmeprenant, whose very name indicates the symbiotic relationship between the two (*carême-prenant* is the French name for this pre-Lenten period). Rabelais's writings are full of references to Carnival, and many writers, above all Mikhail Bakhtin, have been misled into believing that Carnival's origins lay rooted in folklore and popular culture instead of in the penitential season of Lent.

This was a festival of carnality. It was usually symbolized by some kind of stock carnival figure or effigy, traditionally the figure of a fat man, which was paraded around during a feast and ceremoniously burned at the end of it. Gluttony was the order of the day, and lots of meat, especially from fat animals such as pigs or boars, was consumed with relish, washed down by large quantities of beer in northern Europe and wine in the south. There was also a considerable amount of sexual display and insult involved. Brothels, protected and even run by local officials in many municipalities throughout Europe before the Reformation, were obviously in much demand during Carnival. And overtly sexual symbols and metaphors were explicitly displayed in many of the festivities, from the huge, fat sausage that was carried through the streets in Königsberg and the even more graphic phallus that was paraded through the streets of Naples, to the more common sexual icons of cocks and bears. For this short period sexual propriety seemed to be suspended, as passions that were supposed to be tightly reined during the rest of the year became unbridled.

Carnival was also a period when other passions were unleashed: insult, envy, and anger among them. Fistfights were common everywhere and even ritualized in some places, such as Venice, where young men carried out their territorial and familial struggles under the guise of ritual. That violence might be the natural by-product of a world turned upside down should not be too surprising, and its ubiquity is yet another strike against the safety-valve theory. If women were temporarily allowed to fulfill the roles of men—to be "on top," to use Natalie Davis's wonderful phrase—or if peasants were allowed to play the role of kings, this might help eliminate enough steam in the social boiler to keep the entire structure from exploding. On the other hand, turning the world upside down might, by allowing violence and displaying alternatives, threaten the very social order the process was supposed to protect. The riot and massacre that broke out in the French town of Romans in Dauphiné during Carnival in 1580 may be the best known, thanks to Emmanuel Le Roy Ladurie, but there were plenty of other such violent incidents that grew out of Carnival in Naples, Switzerland, Corsica, and elsewhere to suggest that this was far from an isolated episode. It is thus largely irrelevant to argue whether the function of Carnival was to reinforce the social order (the safety-valve theory) or to undermine it: it could do both.

The chronology and geography of Carnival are also instructive. Despite the claims of many scholars, Carnival does not appear to be an ancient pagan rite that was appropriated by Christianity for its own purposes (as was the case with so many Christian rituals). In fact, there is little evidence of Carnival anywhere in Europe before the twelfth century. So it appears to be entirely a medieval and Christian phenomenon. Nor was Carnival practiced uniformly throughout Europe. Most of the features described above were largely restricted to southern Europe: almost the entire Mediterranean region including Spain, Italy, and the islands, as well as most of France, Austria, Switzerland, and much of Germany. In northwestern Europe— Brittany and other parts of northern France, the British Isles, most of the Low Countries, parts of northern Germany, and all of Scandinavia—the festivities of Carnival were limited to little more than the ritual eating of pancakes on Shrove Tuesday. There might have been regular Shrove Tuesday football match accompanied by some Morris dancers and other festivities here and there, but in essence, the carnality was largely missing. So how is the geography of Carnival to be explained?

John Bossy is surely right to stress that the answer lies in Carnival's foundation in and links to the sacrament of penance. The Roman liturgy of the sacrament was a largely collective and entirely public affair. Christians were required to confess their sins, as well as satisfy them before God through an act of penance, before they could participate in the Eucharist on Easter Sunday. The confession was a public one, as the sinner openly confessed his sins to the priest and to God; although he or she was not specifically addressing the other parishioners present, they obviously were able to hear what was going on. Then the priest would place his hands on the head of the penitent as a public sign of reconciliation to God and his neighbor. The act of penance to be performed afterward varied widely, but it was also intended as a public sign of contrition and reconciliation. This often took the form of public penitential processions, as large numbers of penitents collectively sought to expiate their sins through the ritual of parading through the streets of their town or village. In short, in the Roman liturgy penance was a social sacrament whose function was not only preparation for the Eucharist, but also the reconciliation of everyone in the community to each other as well as to God. It is evident, however, that the Roman liturgy's hold on the laity was not so secure the farther one ventured from Rome. Indeed, by the high Middle Ages it had already disappeared in many parts of northern Europe, and in others it had never been established at all, as local liturgies were introduced from the beginning. In most of northern Europe confession and penance had never been so public and collective as in the south. Given the communal and collective nature of Carnival itself,

Carnival in Venice. Festival of the last Thursday of Carnival in Venice. Painting by Gabriel Bella (fl. 1700–1750). GALLERIA QUERINI STAMPALIA, VENICE/SCALA/ART RESOURCE, NY

it is not a surprise that it tended not to catch on in most of northern Europe. Carnival was hardly resistant to exportation to foreign cultures, however, as its adoption by many Jews and Orthodox Christians makes clear. Nevertheless, it does appear that the geography of Carnival is tied to the history of penance.

Reform attacks on Carnival. That geography was seriously threatened, however, by the reformations of the sixteenth and seventeenth centuries, Protestant as well as Catholic. Luther, Calvin, and most other Protestant reformers, by accepting Erasmus's revised translation of Matthew 4:17, rejected penance as a sacrament altogether, and it is thus no surprise that the carnality of Carnival became a prime target of their anti-Catholic attacks. Perhaps more surprising is how quickly many Catholic reformers also came to attack Carnival. Again, the link with the sacrament of penance is instructive, as both Protestant and Catholic reformers alike sought to transform a collective and social ritual into an individual and private practice. The innovator on the Catholic side was Carlo Borromeo, archbishop of Milan. Borromeo's bright idea was the invention of the confessional box in 1565, which quickly put to rest the social aspects of the sacrament. With confessions no longer made in public, and with a barrier between priest and penitent to prevent the laying on of hands, the function of reconciliation to the community soon took a backseat to reconciliation with God. And with the sacrament of penance shorn of its communal and public face, there was not much point left in celebrating Carnival, especially as it invoked so many sins of the flesh.

The Catholic Church's rejection of Carnival was just one thread in a much broader tapestry of social and moral reform that arose out of the Catholic Reformation in general and the Council of Trent in particular. Like the much vaunted "reformation of manners" so associated with the Puritans and other Protestants, Catholic post-Tridentine piety had as its ultimate goal the reestablishment of the kingdom of Christ on earth through a stricter policing of moral discipline. Although Calvin's Geneva may be more closely associated with moral discipline in the public eye than Counter-Reformation Catholicism, it is nevertheless true that Borromeo's program in Milan was just as great a source of Reformation discipline as anything conjured up by the Protestants. Indeed, this was one of the principal goals shared by all reformers, Protestants and Catholics alike, which, despite their theological differences, made them allies in a war against the common enemy of carnality. And when both churches as well as the state nearly everywhere in Europe began to mount serious anti-Carnival campaigns, it is no surprise that in the long run they were successful. By the late seventeenth and early eighteenth centuries, in fact, Carnival was just a shadow of its former medieval self in the cities and urban areas, even in southern Europe. Although resistance was far stronger in the rural countryside, where the reach of church and state was less secure, it is nevertheless clear that the Protestant and Catholic Reformations had a significant impact on the practice of Carnival by 1700. Although the festival continued to exist, it was largely shorn of much of its carnal and virtually all its penitential functions.

By the late eighteenth century in Paris, for example, the rituals were already becoming more commercialized. For the elite, more conscious than ever of distinguishing themselves from the masses, there were a number of privately organized masked balls and banquets, above all the famous ball held every year at the Paris Opera. For the popular classes, there were also more restrained public masked balls, and food and drink tended to be available in great quantities outside the city walls, where taxes were lower. There were also processions of artisans' guilds, the most prominent of which was that of the butchers, who paraded a fat ox—*le boeuf gras*—through the streets of Paris nearly every year until 1870, the only interruption being the years of the Revolution (1790–1800). Although this is clearly evidence that flesh had not disappeared entirely from Carnival, brothels and other overt signs of sexuality were largely absent. Moreover, during the years of the Second Empire (1851–1869) Napoleon III clamped down on the celebrations even further by attempting to curtail street masking. The masked balls declined as a result, including the Opera ball, and as the suburbs were

brought into the city limits, even the excesses of food and drink were no longer available. In the years after 1870 Carnival became less a social and even more a commercial enterprise. In Paris, as in many other European cities, large department stores and other commercial institutions tried to revive the festival. About all that they could sustain, however, were a few parades, as popular participation declined precipitously. By 1900 little remained of Mardi Gras in Paris except for a parade and a few neighborhood balls. The day of Mardi Gras itself was no longer either a feast day recognized by the church or a holiday recognized by the state. What had once been perhaps the single most anticipated festival in the entire calendar, with members of all social classes looking forward to its excesses, had become by the twentieth century just another workday.

To suggest that Carnival had disappeared from Europe completely is not entirely true, however, as it was revived in the New World in the late nineteenth century at the very moment it was waning in the Old. This epilogue demonstrates that Carnival could survive in the twentieth century only as a commercial venture. Both the American and Brazilian reincarnations of the festival—in New Orleans and Rio de Janeiro respectively—depend on tourism to survive, and both show how far individualism and commercialism have replaced community as the focus. In New Orleans it was local social clubs, known as krewes, that in the 1870s created Mardi Gras by holding their own balls and parading through the French Quarter on Shrove Tuesday. While many of these clubs remain exclusive and parochial even at the beginning of the twenty-first century (the anti-Black and anti-Semitic elements of some of these clubs is well known), some such as the Rex krewe started selling tickets to tourists and other outsiders as early as 1872. Already by 1900 more than 100,000 tourists were flocking to New Orleans every February. The Hermes and Bacchus krewes, founded in 1937 and 1969 respectively, were devoted to tourism from the beginning and now work with the New Orleans Chamber of Commerce, bringing in nearly half a million visitors at Carnival time. The city's own tourist bureau estimates that by the 1970s the two weeks leading up to Mardi Gras generated more than fifty million dollars annually in tourist revenues, roughly 10 percent of all revenues brought into the city by visitors each year. And if added to that are another twenty-five million dollars each year in locally generated revenue in preparation for the event, it is clear that the city of New Orleans, as well as the state of Louisiana, has come to rely on the celebration of Carnival in its own form of Mardi Gras as a major source of revenue. To be sure, this modern form of American Carnival may contain many more carnal elements—prostitutes and *le boeuf gras* are still very visible in New Orleans—and rites of inversion than its European counterparts of the eighteenth and nineteenth centuries, but it is now entirely a commercial spectacle. And the carnality is for sale year-round in New Orleans, not just during Mardi Gras.

The Brazilian Carnival in Rio de Janeiro has its own narrative, but one that moves in a similar direction. It too was transformed into a commercial enterprise via tourism, and as with Mardi Gras in New Orleans, Carnival in Rio began and is still structured around social clubs that hold balls and parades. Unlike the krewes in New Orleans, however, the samba schools in Brazil are less exclusive and less exclusively upper and middle class. Whereas in New Orleans the black population was traditionally excluded from Mardi Gras and forced to hold its own parades in the black quarters of the city, in Rio there has always been a more inclusive and communal atmosphere at Carnival. Nevertheless, the parades of the samba schools, like the parades of the krewes in New Orleans, have now become dominated by commercialism, each vying to outspend and outdo the others. As in New Orleans, the tourist industry is what drives as well as funds most of this activity in Rio. The major difference in Rio is its geography. Being in the southern hemisphere means that Carnival in Rio contains none of the elements associated with the end of winter and beginning of spring as in Europe; it is the end of the summer in Brazil, and the beach in Rio has proven to be just as commercially viable a site for Carnival as Bourbon Street in New Orleans. And for its participants in both hemispheres today, any association with penitence and preparation for Lent has long since disappeared; Carnival is now in the business of entertainment.

NEW YEAR

Celebrating the end of one year and the beginning of another, unlike Carnival, goes back to the pre-Christian era of the earliest societies. What constituted a year, however, varied widely from one society to the next, though most did eventually coalesce around a model that fit into the changing seasons of the harvest year. It was the Romans who first moved the West onto an exclusively solar calendar. The early Roman calendars were lunar calendars, basing the length of the year (354 days) on the cycles of the moon. In 46 B.C.E. Julius Caesar mandated that the Romans switch to a solar calendar of 365¼ days, with an extra day added every fourth year. The Romans marked the end of one year at the end of December and the beginning of another starting in January with a special festival and celebration.

When Christianity finally became the official Roman religion after the conversion of Constantine in the early fourth century, the Church did not entirely replace the Julian calendar with a new one of its own. Instead, it appropriated the old calendar and many of its festivals, replacing Roman festivals with Christian festivals. The Church did alter the numbering of the years—making the year one that of the year of the birth of Christ, as opposed to the year of the founding of the Roman Republic—and also altered the beginning of the year, changing it from January 1 to Easter Sunday. The celebration of the new year was transformed in the early fourth century at the Council of Nicaea in 325, when Easter itself was fixed to the cycle of the moon: the first Sunday after the first full moon after the spring equinox (that is, no earlier than March 22 and no later than April 25). Thus, from 325 the festival celebrating the New Year was the same day as the festival celebrating the birth of Christ. And because the preceding evening was still during Lent—a fast day instead of a feast day—New Year's Eve clearly did not mean much to premodern sensibilities.

The impetus for a more secular celebration of the New Year came in the sixteenth century, and as with Carnival, the Protestant and Catholic Reformations played a role. First, several states—France, for example, in 1564—decided unilaterally to switch the beginning of the year back to the Roman date of January 1. This had less to do with any desire to secularize New Year celebrations than the fact that with New Year's Day not being fixed, virtually every year had a different number of days, which was already causing problems in contracts, leases, and rents that normally lasted for the duration of a calendar year. It was the shift away from the Lenten season that ultimately provided New Year celebrations with a more secular focus. Although the modern idea of champagne and New Year's Eve parties is a much more recent invention—champagne did not even exist until the late seventeenth century, when it was allegedly invented accidentally by a French monk, Dom Pérignon—it was not too much of a leap for Europeans in the eighteenth century to revive the older Roman pagan rituals of feasting to celebrate the New Year, usually on New Year's Day itself. There were few public rituals or celebrations of note until much later, but Europeans everywhere generally celebrated the New Year with family and friends, exchanging greetings and wishes of good fortune and prosperity for the coming

New Year's Eve. Revelers in front of the Arc de Triomphe, Paris. CORBIS

year. Good luck rituals varied from one part of Europe to the next. In Austria and Hungary, for example, pigs were believed to bring good fortune and live pigs were often let loose in the streets of Vienna and Budapest. In other places the eating of certain foods at the New Year was believed to bring good luck throughout the rest of the year—from special New Year's cakes, ales, or other delicacies, to more traditional meats, fish, and vegetables. The emphasis everywhere was on sharing food, drink, and greetings and good wishes with family and friends.

The New Year's Eve gatherings we know today are much more modern. New Year's Day was St. Sylvester's Day in the Roman church (and St. Basil's Day in the Orthodox church in much of eastern Europe) and a special mass or celebration marking the eve of St. Sylvester still survives in many places. For most, however, the idea of gathering in public crowds for a collective and entirely secular celebration of the New Year—whether in Trafalgar Square in London, the Champs Élysées in Paris, the Ringstrasse in Vienna, the Puerta del Sol in Madrid, or St. Mark's Square in Venice—did not really begin until the end of the nineteenth century. This escalated in special years marking the end of centuries, and New Year's Eve in 1899 saw a significant increase in the festivities. With the end of the millennium in 1999, commercialism

came to dominate the celebrations, as every hotel, restaurant, resort, and tourist attraction competed with one another for the vast sums that were shelled out by a population with more money to spend on entertainment. While pedants pointed out that the *real* millennium would not begin until 1 January 2001, it was nevertheless clear that Europeans could accept the cultural construction of their calendar. What mattered most was that the festivities still had meaning for many that were bound up in building communities of friends and family. The survival of such traditional practices as Hogmanay in Scotland—gifts for small children—or the same country's celebration of the first guest to cross the hearth after the stroke of midnight on New Year's Eve with a convivial drink, for example, demonstrate how many rituals have survived the advent of commercialism.

Indeed, some of the commercial practices associated with contemporary celebrations of the New Year are not only based on much older and more traditional practices, but have sustained them and guaranteed their survival. The sending of special New Year's greeting cards, ubiquitous nearly everywhere in Europe apart from the British Isles (and the United States), where greeting cards are sent to friends and family at Christmas, is one such example. Obviously, it was not until the greeting card industry arose in the late nineteenth century that specially printed greeting cards emerged as a means of wishing someone a prosperous New Year. These cards became immediately popular. The custom was based, however, on the much older custom of exchanging greetings and wishes of prosperity in person or via a handwritten note or letter. And while many Europeans today might question whether a printed greeting card at New Year is as personal or as meaningful an expression as a handwritten note, it is nevertheless true that these cards continue to maintain ties of community and sociability in their own way. The same can be said of many of the other ways contemporary Europeans celebrate the New Year. Even though wine merchants might make up to a quarter of their annual profits from champagne sales at New Year, and while hoteliers and restaurateurs may do likewise, it seems clear that these annual celebration—even the overly hyped millennium celebrations of 31 December 1999—are almost never just individualist expressions of conspicuous consumption. They are almost always observed collectively with friends and family, and even the most commercially explicit of them usually take note of the actual passing of the old year and the beginning of the new year at midnight. And it is this passing of the year, the continual and perpetual clicking over of the calendar, however the calendar year is measured, that ties us to all our ancestors and renders us human. In this sense, the celebrations of the New Year have always been festivals of life and the continuity of humanity: ringing out the old and ringing in the new.

BASTILLE DAY: JULY 14

Festivals marking nationalist holidays are a relatively recent phenomenon. Until there were nation-states, as opposed to dynastic states, fully supported by the nationalist movements of the nineteenth century, there were no holidays invoking the beginning or creation of a particular nation. One of the first of these new nation-states was France, which was transformed by the French Revolution of 1789–1799 from a dynastic monarchy to a republic. But which particular event of this transformation should be celebrated as the national holiday? The storming of the Bastille (14 July 1789)? The Tennis Court Oath (20 June 1789)? The renunciation of privileges by the nobility and clergy (4 August 1789)? The opening of the first representative assembly (1 October 1791)? The overthrow of the monarchy (10 August 1792)? The beheading of Louis XVI (21 January 1793)? In fact, it was not until nearly a century later, in 1880, that 14 July, was decreed to be the national holiday of France: the date of the capture by a Paris crowd of the Bastille, an old fortress used as a municipal jail that held only a handful of insignificant prisoners. The choice of date itself was a highly politicized one in 1880, as politicians of the Third Republic from both the left and the right sought to use the national holiday as a symbol to confirm their own narratives of the Revolution itself. July 14 was a compromise that privileged neither the Orleanists and Bonapartists on the right nor the militant radicals and heirs of the Jacobins on the left. In 1880 and for a good time thereafter, the national holiday of France and the ways it was celebrated were fraught with political baggage that truly imbued it with a sense of the tensions inherent in the construction of a nation.

The first such celebration of Bastille Day, as it is now commonly known, occurred during the Revolution itself, and indeed, as Mona Ozouf has amply demonstrated, it was part of the Revolution. Kings had used rituals and festivals for political purposes for centuries, usually in an attempt to reinforce their power and authority, so it was only natural that the revolutionaries should do the same. The Festival of Federation in Paris on 14 July 1790 looked back not so much to the humble events of the year before, but ahead to the revolution still to come. It embodied an exhilarating sense of newness and beginning, at the same time functioning as a means of forging a new community of citizens. The long military parade of troops, including retired veterans as well as young children, formed a major part of the festivities and is still part of Bastille Day rituals. The revolutionaries also took an oath of allegiance and then celebrated with a special meal together to cement their ties of community. What is particularly striking about this commemoration of the events of one year earlier is that it was duplicated in thousands of small towns and villages all over France, with explicit efforts to time the parades, oaths, and celebratory dinners in the provinces to occur simultaneously with their counterparts in the capital. Again, the emphasis was on the togetherness, unity, and cohesion of the body social. The seizure of the Bastille the year before was seen as a sharp break with the past, a watershed that marked a new future of French men and women as citizens rather than royal subjects. And even if the Revolution as it unfolded could not ultimately deliver all that was promised and implied in the Festival of Federation in July 1790, it marked the beginning of a long series of festivals that ultimately came to shape the revolutionary regime: the Festival of Reason (10 November 1793), the Festival of the Supreme Being (8 June 1794), the Festival of Victories (29 May 1796), and the Festival of Liberty (29 July 1798) being only the best known. Like the revolutionary calendar invented by the revolutionaries to replace the Gregorian calendar—renaming the months after the seasons and renumbering the years with the revolutionary Year I marking the abolition of the monarchy and declaration of France as a republic by the Convention in September 1792—the festivals of the French Revolution played a vital political and social role in cementing the break with the Old Regime's values of hierarchy and distinction and helping to forge a new sense of nation around the ideals of liberty, equality, and fraternity. That it took nearly a century to create a national holiday out of Bastille Day only indicates the ambiguities and tensions that remained within the new republic in France as well as the political struggles over how the history of the revolution would be told.

The political battles before 1880, however, were only a foretaste of what was to come. For about a decade thereafter the supporters of the new national holiday continued to use it to forge a sense of nation for the many rural provinces that had remained largely untouched by either industrialization or the republican state. Those on the left also used the national holiday as a means of fighting some of their own political battles, especially the creation of secular public schools, which had political and religious as well as educational implications, since the Catholic Church had been a staunch opponent of the Revolution since 1789, as well as an outspoken critic of the Third Republic in France. For those on the right the celebration of the new national holiday after 1880 was something entirely different. For them 14 July 1789 was just the prelude to the Terror, and the Revolution as a whole was seen as something destructive that broke down the proper and divinely ordained political and social order of the Old Regime. They mounted a frenzied but ultimately unsuccessful effort to establish 28 June 1689 (the date when a seventeenth-century nun had a vision of the Sacred Heart) as a replacement for 14 July 1789. For many Catholics 1889 marked not the centennial of the detested Revolution, but the bicentennial of the miracle of 1689.

The centennial celebrations of 14 July 1889, however, proved to be a total defeat for the right. The government of the French Third Republic mounted the Universal Exposition in Paris to mark the hundredth anniversary of Bastille Day. And they commissioned a new Paris landmark to replace that symbol of the Old Regime, the Bastille, which had long since been torn down. Although it was immediately denounced by many on the right as modernism gone amok, the Eiffel Tower stood in the minds of its creators as a stark contrast with the former Bastille: one a symbol of the medieval world of superstition and despotism, the other a modern symbol of reason and progress. The events of 14 July 1889 mirrored those of 14 July 1790 all across France: military parades, special meals, followed by public dances and balls in village and town squares throughout the republic. It was clear that the national holiday quickly had become not only public, but also a popular holiday. As long as a republican government remained in power—and the Third Republic lasted until it was replaced in 1940 by the Vichy regime—this would remain the case. While extremists on both sides of the political spectrum would continue to propagate criticisms of the government through attacks on Bastille Day and even some demonstrations against the festivities on 14 July, these never amounted to much.

Celebrations were interrupted during World War II, and the first celebration of Bastille Day in six years on 14 July 1945 was very poignant. On the one hand, it was a celebration of freedom and liberty from occupation, with all parties more or less able to celebrate French liberty. On the other hand, it marked a political struggle between the supporters of General Charles de Gaulle, who had led the Free French government in exile during the war, and the communists and socialists. De Gaulle wanted 14 July to commemorate more a national than a republican holiday, reflecting a mythical and almost eternal France fighting against oppression, symbolized by Joan of Arc, Henry IV, Napoleon, Clemenceau, and de Gaulle himself. And while he managed to dominate electoral politics in France for more than two decades after the war, de Gaulle ultimately lost out in his effort to transform the national holiday into something else. The festivities of 1945 repeated all the rituals as they had been before the war, and there were no monuments to Joan of Arc or Napoleon, a sign that France had returned to normalcy despite nearly six years of foreign occupation.

The old political struggles between left and right were not totally eliminated, however, as the bicentennial of the French Revolution in July 1989 made clear. The political tensions were exacerbated by the fact that the new president of the republic, the socialist François Mitterand, had just soundly defeated one of the leaders of the right, Jacques Chirac, the mayor of Paris. As the celebrations of the bicentennial were destined to focus on Paris, despite the traditional provincial celebrations, the battleground loomed large as both Mitterand and Chirac sought to outdo—and outspend—each other on a commercial celebration of the bicentennial. What worked against and ultimately overshadowed this political rivalry between left and right was the crushing of the Chinese student demonstrations in Tiananmen Square by the Chinese government in May 1989. The events in China had a dramatic effect on the celebrations in Paris two months later. First, Chirac's effort to bring some attention to the city of Paris (that is, to his own municipal government in the capital) and to take away some of the attention inevitably showered on the federal government and President Mitterand fell completely flat. Although he was a solid republican, unlike some on the far right, Chirac's idea was to mark the hundredth anniversary of the Eiffel Tower in June rather than to commemorate the Revolution itself. The resulting spectacle and light show, in which no expense was spared, was both a critical and popular failure. The aging rock stars hired to evoke a sense of Parisian destiny—Johnny Halliday and Stevie Wonder among them—did not help matters. For his part, President Mitterand felt obliged to invite some of the Chinese students to participate in the grand parade scheduled to march down the Champs Élysées in Paris on the evening of July 14, and they completely stole the show. In the end, it did not matter, as the Chinese student presence only reinforced the notion that the French Revolution was a universal revolution, fought for all humanity rather than just for France. The millions of francs spent on the events were of course another sign that commercialism had played a big role, as was the case in most modern festivals. But despite

Bastille Day under the Third Republic. Dancing in the street on Bastille Day, 14 July 1930. ©HULTON GETTY/LIAISON AGENCY

all that, a sense of French nation was spelled out in stark relief by the festivities of July 1989, a nation to which both Chirac and Mitterand, as well as their respective supporters, could claim to belong. If anything, the nation had grown to be too inclusive for a few. The National Front Party used the celebrations to demonstrate against the foreigners living in France, and on the morning of 14 July the citizens of Dijon in Burgundy, a region dominated by the right, woke up to find storefronts and shop windows littered with the graffiti "Bi*sang*tennaire," an allusion to the bloody violence of the Revolution that was being celebrated throughout France. For most French men and women, however, their national holiday has remained much more a holiday than a paean to the nation.

CONCLUSION

There is no question that the festival tradition declined in Europe; the forces of industrialization, in particular, added to earlier reform attacks. In early modern Europe (depending on the religion prevalent in an area) festival days could total eighty or more per year, although specific calendars varied from locality to locality. Reform attacks dented the tradition, although even Protestant Britain saw efforts at revival as late as the eighteenth century. With nineteenth-century industrialization, employers and public authorities attempted to institute further discipline. Fes-

tivals cost working time, they assembled potentially menacing crowds, and they inspired a spontaneity that was itself suspect. Urbanization reduced community familiarity, another pillar in the festival tradition. Many festivals shrank in importance, and in the long run the rise of private leisure, including vacations, replaced some of their functions. Important festivals remained, however, including new ones associated with political identity. In Eastern Europe, these included great twentieth-century communist innovations such as May Day. In western Europe, changes in the character of festivals particularly highlighted the growth of commercialization.

Some festivals naturally illustrate the transition from a ritual of sacred community to secularism and commercialism better than others. Perhaps the best example of all is Christmas, the Christian festival celebrating the birth of Christ. Protestants and Catholics alike in the sixteenth century had railed against the pagan practices that had become part of the Christmas celebrations since the Middle Ages: Yule logs, evergreen trees decorated with candles, and decking the halls with holly and ivy had always been part of the ancient festival of light at the celebration marking the winter solstice. Even the date of Christmas was chosen to coincide with these pagan rituals, as no one knew the actual date of Christ's birth. Puritans in seventeenth-century England had attempted to outlaw all such pagan practices during their brief moment in power in the

Bicentennial Bastille Day. A large crowd gathers on the Place de la Bastille in Paris on 14 July 1989. ©PETER TURNLEY/CORBIS

gland, the practice of exchanging gifts and greeting cards was not generally associated with Christmas at all. And by 1900 a cohort of commercial institutions proudly displaying their own Santa Clauses helped to fuel the market for gift giving that only exacerbated this transition further. By the end of the twentieth century Christmas had become a season rather than a single day of festivities. And with up to a third of all retail sales for the year coming in the Christmas season, it was primarily a season of shopping. Despite the best efforts of Christian churches everywhere across Europe to stem the tide, it was already a battle lost.

Other festivals, such as the Feast of St. John (24 June), have achieved more mixed results. Just as Christmas was assigned a day on the Christian calendar to coincide with the pagan celebration of the winter solstice, the Feast of St. John the Baptist was assigned to coincide with the summer solstice, or midsummer's eve, celebrations. Bonfires have been lit on the eve of St. John's Day since the Middle Ages in towns and villages across Europe. And while modern fireworks have replaced the bonfires in many places, the rituals of these festivities follow a traditional and well-worn path. To be sure, the bonfires are no longer believed to be purifying agents that function to ward off evil spirits as they did in their ancient beginnings, but neither do they have much explicit connection with the Feast of St. John the Baptist. Although no one could claim that this festival has become commercialized, it is now just entertainment and has been shorn of its religious roots.

There are a host of other festivals that could be cited to demonstrate how the ways that Europeans have celebrated important events with feasts and other celebrations have changed over time since the Renaissance. What seems clear, however, is that rituals of feasting and the celebration of holidays of some kind are as much a part of human society as any other aspect of life. That the events that Europeans celebrate and how they have chosen to celebrate them have changed over the last five centuries is hardly a revelation. What is significant is that festivals continue to matter in a variety of ways. That the control of Carnival or of Bastille Day, for example, has been so hotly contested only underscores the continued significance of these rituals. And that many of them have become commercialized almost to excess does not alter the fact that they still function in a variety of ways to delineate boundaries of the community and to promote a sense of connection to the human past. In an information age of the instant and immediate, this matters. Moreover, while contemporary festivals may seem more oriented toward commercial entertainment and leisure

1650s—to no avail. The fact is that Christmas was never a major Christian holiday before the nineteenth century and had always been far overshadowed by Easter. In the nineteenth century in Great Britain a fortuitous series of events not only resurrected the celebration of Christmas, but proceeded to turn it into the commercial excess it has now become. A combination of attempts by several large London department stores to stir up sales in the bleakness of midwinter, combined with the commercial and popular success of Charles Dickens's novel *A Christmas Carol,* resulted in a series of new rituals that were cloaked in the guise of Christian celebration, but that were above all else a bastion of conspicuous consumption. The invention of Santa Claus, or Father Christmas as he is called in some countries, shows how a relatively obscure medieval Christian saint could be transformed into a jolly old man in a red suit who brought presents to all young children on Christmas Eve (Santa Claus being the Germanic form of Saint Nicolas). Prior to this Victorian invention in nineteenth-century En-than those in the premodern world, they nevertheless maintain the capacity to tell us much about who we are and how the world we live in got to be the way it is.

See also other articles in this section.

BIBLIOGRAPHY

Amalvi, Christian. "Bastille Day: From *Dies Irae* to Holiday." In *Realms of Memory: Rethinking the French Past*. Volume 3: *Symbols*. Edited by Pierre Nora. Translated by Arthur Goldhammer. New York, 1997. Pages 117–169.

Bossy, John. *Christianity in the West, 1400–1700*. Oxford, 1985.

Burke, Peter. *Popular Culture in Early Modern Europe*. Revised ed. London, 1994.

Cressy, David. *Birth, Marriage, and Death: Ritual, Religion, and the Life-Cycle in Tudor and Stuart England*. Oxford, 1997.

Da Matta, Roberto. *Carnivals, Rogues, and Heroes: An Interpretation of the Brazilian Dilemma*. Translated by John Drury. Notre Dame, Ind., 1991.

Davis, Natalie Zemon. "Women on Top." In her *Society and Culture in Early Modern France*. Stanford, Calif., 1975. Pages 124–151.

Gennep, Arnold van. *Manuel du folklore français contemporain*. Vol. 1, parts 1–8. Paris, 1937.

Hutton, Ronald. *The Rise and Fall of Merry England: The Ritual Year, 1400–1700*. Oxford, 1994.

Kaplan, Steven Laurence. *Farewell, Revolution: Disputed Legacies, France, 1789/1989*. Ithaca, N.Y., 1995.

Kinser, Samuel. *Carnival, American Style: Mardi Gras at New Orleans and Mobile*. Chicago, 1990.

Le Roy Ladurie, Emmanuel. *Carnival in Romans*. Translated by Mary Feeney. New York, 1979.

Muir, Edward. *Ritual in Early Modern Europe*. Cambridge, U.K., and New York, 1997.

Ozouf, Mona. *Festivals and the French Revolution*. Translated by Alan Sheridan. Cambridge, Mass., 1988.

Underdown, David. *Revel, Riot, and Rebellion: Popular Politics and Culture in England, 1603–1660*. Oxford, 1985.

THE REFORMATION OF POPULAR CULTURE

Ann W. Ramsey

In the 1960s and 1970s, through efforts to understand "social history from below," historians began to focus on communal rituals and festivities, which from the late Middle Ages forward also became targets of reform or abolition. It appears that early modern secular elites intensified or coopted preexisting clerical campaigns to regulate the sacred and to separate it from popular entertainments. Targets included the Feast of Fools; charivari; confraternal processions; mystery plays; carnivalesque behaviors like feasting, drinking, and masking; and the physical license and magical rites that celebrated saints' days, holy days, agricultural cycles, and rites of passage like birth, baptism, marriage, and death.

DIFFICULTIES OF DEFINITIONS

No universal definition either of popular culture or of its reformation applies equally satisfactorily to all time periods or regions of Europe. Most broadly the reformation of popular culture refers to the combination of social, political, economic, technological, cultural, and psychological changes that established the disciplining of the body, emotions, and cognition as a desired social norm. From the Renaissance forward new models for piety, manners, sexual modesty, hygiene, and work discipline transformed authority relations between elites and the popular classes. Popular culture is one of the most important domains in which elites and the common people developed and contested new technologies of power.

The concept of a reformation of popular culture is best adapted to the early modern period, for which it was first developed. Within the context of that period historians emphasize that elites increasingly regarded communal festivities as impious, socially and politically subversive, superstitious, and backward. Humanism, new attitudes toward the sacred, increasing social conflict stemming from economically uneven recovery from the Black Death (1347), and the growth

of princely sovereignty created a volatile and socially competitive atmosphere. In the fifteenth through the seventeenth centuries the amount of festival license that ruling elites were willing to grant the common people declined. The potential of festival and popular gatherings to lead to revolt was the most important factor in their repression in the late Middle Ages and the early modern period. Sustained periods of warfare, including the wars of religion in France, 1563–1598; the Thirty Years' War in Germany, 1618–1648; and the Time of Troubles in Russia, 1604–1613, and periods of economic depression throughout the seventeenth century helped destroy the fabric of traditional communities and led to the abandonment of many popular traditions.

In the sixteenth century the conflicts between Catholics and Protestants intensified societal scrutiny and regulation of all ritual behaviors. This occurred because the meanings of ritual and the sacred were subject to unprecedented doctrinal and social debate. Popular public rituals, such as confraternal processions and the bonfires of Saint John's Eve, mixed the sacred and the profane. Because Catholics and Protestants disagreed about the correct boundaries between the sacred and the profane and about the nature of the sacred itself, popular celebrations of holy days led to civil violence in the streets between Protestants and Catholics. The uses of public space came under increasing scrutiny by officials responsible for public order. In Paris, for example, the Parlement banned masking in 1514 and in 1524 condemned mystery plays because their burlesque admixture of religion and theater appeared newly dangerous and irreverent.

Early modern sovereign princes developed new disciplinary techniques and claimed new rights of taxation and justice. Armed with the new moral authority invested in them by both the Catholic and the Protestant Reformations, governments intervened in the ritual lives of once-isolated rural communities more systematically. Princely and centralized dominance over towns also grew with the increase in trained

Regulation of Drinking. A protest against Sunday closing laws in England, 1641.

officials. In cities the spontaneity of popular celebrations gave way to highly organized spectacles representing princely authority and hierarchical norms of morality.

This first phase of the early modern reformation of popular culture lasted through the seventeenth century or later in eastern Europe and Russia. It was largely prescriptive in that legislation proliferated, replacing custom with government demands for uniformity in language, such as the Edict of Villers-Cotterêts in France in 1539; urban construction; and compliance with tax officials. It was repressive in that it limited the behaviors tolerated both in public spaces, including theater, prostitution, gambling, and drinking, and inside churches, including dancing, banquets, and rowdy processions. In addition it established more patriarchal norms of authority within households and throughout society. The reformation of behaviors added discipline because it created new institutions to reshape the thought and behavior of both elites and the popular classes through schooling, stricter norms for poor relief, and more enforced periods of labor.

Changes in elite attitudes that sparked reforms of popular culture are better documented than the local circumstances explaining the disappearance or transformation of particular rites of popular culture.

A hallmark of the reform process may be the gradual withdrawal of elites from their former participation in rites of popular culture, sharing or supporting carnival, for example. Local studies necessary to measure and date popular adaptation, resistance, or compliance are incomplete and are subject to differing interpretations.

A second and more complex process, better termed the transformation of popular culture, is often considered part of the reformation of popular culture. It is both a second phase and a second type of reformation of popular culture. Although its roots lie in the sixteenth century as well, it is most evident from the eighteenth century forward, when more capitalist relations of production, a decline of the Christian monopoly of cultural values, and political upheavals such as the French Revolution further transformed authority relations. More long-term structural processes of change, including the shift from oral to print culture, industrialization, and the emergence of a class society, were involved. Such changes made culture a commodity, and this altered the possibilities for making meaning, that is, the production of culture itself. Structural changes, through the advent of bourgeois cultural hegemony, working-class political movements, consumer society, and mass culture, thus changed the nature of popular culture in the modern period.

The concept of elite cultural hegemony. Social historians have found the concept of cultural hegemony particularly useful in discussing both phases of the reformation of popular culture. Developed by the Italian revisionist marxist sociologist Antonio Gramsci (1891–1937), cultural hegemony is the power to define the norms of public order, to determine the content of what constitutes knowledge and rational behavior, and the ability to control the dominant symbols and ritual practices of a society. Hence, one definition of the reformation of popular culture is elites' ongoing efforts to assert and maintain their cultural hegemony. This points to popular culture as a changing set of practices rather than a static repertoire of proscribed behaviors. Accordingly some social historians see popular culture as a "force field of relations," the site of changing power relationships between shifting dominants, subordinates, and subcultures.

Interdisciplinary approaches to the reform of popular culture. Adaptations of Gramsci's approach accord well with tendencies to focus on the cultural dimensions of social conflict. The approaches from semiotics and textual criticism have influenced analysis of discursive practices and the changing meaning of "the popular." Cultural anthropology, ethnography, ritual studies, and comparative religion have contributed to analyses of nonverbal sources, such as the symbolic forms and behaviors in popular festivities and the cultural artifacts and material culture of the popular classes.

EXPLAINING WHEN, HOW, AND WHY CULTURAL NORMS CHANGE

Regardless of the approaches taken, the dominant issue in analyzing the reformation of popular culture is an explanation of how and why cultural norms change. Four dynamics recur in the reformation of popular culture:

1. the social, psychological, and cultural transformation and acculturation of an elite who legitimate their power by adopting distinctive behaviors that display purportedly superior and more dignified aesthetic or moral values;
2. the subsequent elite pursuit of cultural hegemony, which entails some control of the state or earlier a monopoly of violence in society or aspirations to determine the forms of violence in society;
3. intensified ruling-class control of the socialization of the young, manifested especially in disciplining the behavior of young males and defining gender roles for females that enforce the authority of adult males; and
4. the changing ability of social subordinates to fashion a different culture of their own and thus shape the production of elite cultural hegemony and the meanings within popular culture.

CHRISTIANIZATION AND THE REFORMATION OF POPULAR CULTURE

A persistent Christian moralizing ethic, which condemned so-called pagan superstitions and all undisciplined pleasures of the body and senses, has played a significant and ongoing role in the reformation of popular culture. Nonconformist religious movements, Christian revival movements such as the evangelical movement in England from the 1820s, and Catholic action among the working classes are important examples of the enduring role of the Christian critique of popular culture. At different times secular elites and the state successfully adapted this religiously motivated critique.

The abolition of the Feast of Fools in the twelfth through the sixteenth centuries. Christians had always inveighed against pagan practices, and Saint Augustine (354–430) left an enduring critique of popular pleasures and human sinfulness. The best documented medieval reform of popular culture that displays all of the four dynamics mentioned above began in the cathedrals of newly urbanized, twelfth-century Europe. The growing differentiation between town and country, first visible in the twelfth century, is an ongoing prerequisite for reformation of popular culture. Hence examining the twelfth-century context of the reformation of popular culture is fundamental.

In 1198 and 1199 Eudes de Sully, bishop of Paris, successfully banished the Feast of Fools from Notre Dame Cathedral although not from all of Paris. His eagerness to enforce a distinctive disciplined behavior among his younger clergy stemmed in part from the eleventh-century church reform movement. That movement enjoined clerical celibacy and, following Pope Gregory VII (c. 1020–1085) in 1077, emphasized the the church's unique right to lead all of society.

In 1445 Eustache de Mesnil, dean of the Paris Theology Faculty, tried to enforce the ban on the Feast of Fools throughout France. The letter he addressed to all French bishops provides a landmark description of the carnivalesque and demonstrates the extent to which the lower clergy did not yet conform to norms for superior clerical morals and conduct:

> Priests and clerks may be seen wearing masks and monstrous visages. . . . They dance in the choir dressed as women, panders, and minstrels. They sing wanton songs. They eat black puddings at the horn of the altar while the celebrant is saying mass. They play at dice there. They cense with stinking smoke from the soles of old shoes. They leap through the church without a blush at their own shame. Finally they drive about the town and its theatres in shabby traps and carts; and rouse the laughter of their fellows and the bystanders in infamous performances with indecent gestures and verses scurrilous and unchaste. (Chambers, 1954, vol. 1, p. 294)

Carnival and late-medieval civic consciousness. Throughout urban Europe in the late Middle Ages, lay elites embraced prohibited carnival behaviors to protest clerical cultural dominance and because they resented the growing success of campaigns against the Feast of Fools. Lay carnival thus could express urban distinctiveness from the clergy, from the rural nobility, and from the peasantry and promote a competition against the theoretical clerical monopoly of the sacred.

In the fragile social peace of the late Middle Ages confraternities, guilds, youth abbeys, and neighborhood and parish associations celebrated particular loyalties. At the local level they simultaneously fostered social integration and competition, and they frequently led to violence between groups. In Lille in 1382 parish processions and street assemblies were prohibited because marches into neighboring parishes or streets led to riots. The so-called evil carnival (*Böse Fastnach*) in Basel in 1376 led to large-scale bloodshed and was known throughout Europe. In 1378 a famous revolt of Florentine wool carders known as the Ciompi reinforced elite fears of the subversive potential of popular assemblies and festivals. The consolidation of the princely Medici regime followed in Florence in 1433. The church council that gathered in Basel in 1438 issued the most sweeping ban on the Feast of Fools. The juxtaposition of these events strongly suggests the intense competitions for cultural hegemony and political power in Renaissance Europe.

By the sixteenth century municipal officials had a distinct preference for spectacles offered to the city under official auspices. In Arras, France, the joyous companies (youth abbeys) were no longer communal associations of unmarried men as they had been in the countryside, and they were increasingly subject to municipal supervision. At the last-known meeting of the Pleasure Abbey (*Abbaye de Liesse*) of Arras, members marched with their neighbors from Cambrai to hear mass on the Monday of carnival week. The association's functions had shifted from organizing popular festivals to enforcing religious discipline and fostering good economic relations with neighboring cities such as Cambrai.

As the opportunities for venting local rivalries decreased and as more spontaneous processions, play-acting, feasting, and drinking were circumscribed, emergent market relations and state sovereignty transformed the structures of authority in communities. The nature of the popular was altered by destruction of the social and cultural context in which local common people could control the production of culture. Vertical loyalties and bonds of obedience replaced horizontal, traditional loyalties of kinship and locality.

The proliferation of festivals and competition to control the sacred carnival.

In 1404 the chancellor of the University of Paris, Jean Charlier de Gerson (1363–1429), appealed to the French king to enforce a reduction of all festival days so artisans would not squander their resources and lead immoral lives. Well before Martin Luther (1483–1546) rejected the sacramental structure of Roman Catholicism in 1520, lay Christians and clerical elites expressed a growing reserve about the nature and workings of the sacred in the world.

German religious reformers, such as Nicholas of Cusa (1401–1464), and preachers, such as Johann Geiler von Kaysersberg (1445–1510) in Strasbourg, increasingly sought to separate the sacred from the profane and to limit carnival. Objections to carnival increased in part because the number of days of revelry had grown and encroached on the Lenten season. The Flemish painter Pieter Brueghel (c. 1525–1569) captured this clash of worldviews in his painting *The Battle between Carnival and Lent* (1559).

In Florence the Dominican penitential preacher Girolamo Savonarola (1452–1498) controlled the public life of the city from 1490 to 1498 and organized young boys (*fanciulli*), who were the most active participants in carnival, to perform moralizing religious theater. Instead of electing carnival "kings" and "queens," young boys under Savonarola's direction chose Jesus Christ as their king. Savonarola urged them to avoid all spectacles through frequent confession and communion. Bishop Carlo Borromeo (1538–1584) helped transform the public life of Milan through a more sober and institutionalized form of antitheater. The Forty Hours Eucharist Devotion in churches attracted crowds away from carnival with displays of lights accompanying the penitential rituals of fasting, confession, and extended prayer. The policing of eucharistic devotion through reform of Corpus Christi festivals was a powerful instrument of reform of popular culture, as were reforms in the veneration of saints and the Virgin Mary.

In Florence the popular and participatory nature of carnival declined when festivities began to celebrate the glory of Medici princely authority and patronage of the fine arts. The Florentine carnival of 1513 was organized with floats of classical Roman motifs in honor of the election of Giovanni de' Medici (1475–1521) to the papacy. This secular cooptation of carnival was more effective than the moralizing reforms of Savonarola. In Venice the growing commercialization of carnival and its staging for the benefit of tourism also transformed the popular character of the event.

THE INTELLECTUAL REVOLUTION OF HUMANISM

The social and cultural role of humanists begins to explain how the burlesque spontaneity of popular carnival was reformed into a stylized, intellectualized, and moralizing spectacle. In the sixteenth century the written word acquired an authority it had not previously possessed. The more spontaneous secular and religious popular culture of the late Middle Ages and Renaissance became vulnerable to written critique and written rules that took precedence over customs and oral traditions.

Carnival and Lent. *The Battle between Carnival and Lent,* painting (1559) by Pieter Brueghel the Elder (1530–1569). KUNSTHISTORICHES MUSEUM, VIENNA/ART RESOURCE, NY

As humanist scholars such as Lorenzo Valla (1407–1457) collected and compared ancient classical and early Christian manuscripts to accepted church texts, they challenged the authenticity of documents that had supported the traditional authority of the papacy within Latin Christendom. Language analysis (historical etymology) became the basis for a new approach to historical and sacred truth. A new form of authority developed that prioritized ratiocination, critical inquiry, and self-observation as well as norms of standardization, uniformity, and disciplining the self.

Besides the humanist approach to language, the advent of the printing press created a new community of scholars who could debate the meaning of words based on standardized texts in a way that had been impossible in the world of manuscript culture. Printing elevated standardization to a new cultural norm and made books a commodity. Liturgical standardization, enjoined at the Council of Trent (1545–1563) and in the campaign against the Old Believers in Rus-

sia, indicates the similar paths reform of popular culture might take in highly varied settings.

New attitudes toward standardization and critical observation also played a role in the scientific revolution and in industrialization. Standardization and uniformity as cultural norms stood in direct conflict with the concepts of time, rationality, work, leisure, and consumption characteristic of late-medieval popular culture.

The "civilizing process." In Italy in the early sixteenth century republican regimes gave way to principalities in Milan, Genoa, and Florence. As service at a princely court became the path for social mobility, ambitious individuals vied for the favor of the prince. People distinguished themselves by training both body and intellect in skills of politeness, eloquence, physical grace, and the appreciation of beauty in varied art forms. A more formal, refined court aristocracy replaced the increasingly archaic warrior nobility of the

Middle Ages. Sociologists like Norbert Elias have argued that the distinctiveness of Western civilization derives from a special "courtly rationality" that accompanied princely state formation with its ethics of self-discipline and control of affect.

The number of printed editions of books of manners and conduct, such as *The Book of the Courtier* (c. 1518) by Baldassare Castiglione (1478–1529), provides some of the best evidence for this "civilizing process" (Elias, 1982). The Latin writings of Desiderius Erasmus (1466?–1536), including *De civilitate morum puerillum,* (Civilizing the manners of boys, 1529), introduced schoolboys to the conscious cultivation of manners by stressing the importance of subtle observations of the behavior of oneself and others.

As the authority of a multiplicity of lesser and greater regional nobles was rationalized by the consolidation of effective sovereignty in emerging territorial states and a few urban republics, the social circulation of ascending and descending groups and individuals increased. Elias observed:

> Slowly, in the course of the sixteenth century, earlier here and later there and almost everywhere with numerous reverses until well into the seventeenth century, a more rigid social hierarchy [began] to establish itself once more, and from elements of diverse social origins a new upper class, a new aristocracy [formed]. For this reason the question of uniform good behavior [became] increasingly acute, particularly as the changed structure of the upper class [exposed] each individual member to an unprecedented extent to the pressure of others and of social control. (Elias, 1982, vol. 1)

Complexities in the transition from oral to print culture. The radical effects of the humanists' way of thinking about language and the sacred had many unintended consequences. Luther used Erasmus's 1516 translation of the Greek New Testament to challenge the authority of the church's only authorized version of the Bible, the Latin Vulgate prepared by Saint Jerome (c. 347–419 or 420). Comparing the texts, Luther argued that Jerome's rendering of "inward change" (Greek *metanoia*) into the Latin "to do penance" (*poenitentiam agere*) created a false foundation for proper relations between humans and God. Luther's belief in the incontrovertible truth of original texts and confidence in his power to interpret these texts impelled him ultimately to challenge the entire edifice of Roman Catholicism. The Protestant Reformations, building on the epochal change in the way humanists read texts, increased the authority attributed to sacred Scripture and increased lay Bible reading among Protestants. In this way the Protestant Reformations added to the authority of the written word

over popular custom. Luther was more tolerant of some carnival practices than was Lutheranism. In Nürnberg the Lutheran reformer Andreas Osiander (1498–1552) abolished the traditional parades of wild men (*Schembartlaüfer*) in the city's carnival in 1539. These hairy figures who ran through the streets during carnival celebrated animals' emergence from winter hibernation and thus the return of spring and light. Reformers throughout the sixteenth century sought to eliminate such popular pagan substructures in carnival. This was a tool of Christianization and a limitation on ritual violence as the run of wild men frequently led to fighting.

REFORM OF POPULAR CULTURE AND THE REFORMATION AS A SOCIAL MOVEMENT

Throughout most of the sixteenth century, however, literacy remained a minority phenomenon in the general population. The ideas of Protestant reformers were transmitted to the popular classes in printed images and broadsheets that combined satiric depictions of the traditional church with simple texts that could be read aloud.

In the early stages of the Lutheran Reformation broadsheets presented the pope as an Antichrist and depicted priests wearing masks to hide their true iniquity. In its popular phase the Reformation drew on the conventions of carnival, carnivalesque "antirituals" that permitted the popular classes and youths to enact the truth of Luther's written criticisms. Rituals of popular culture thus transformed the larger culture and shaped the Reformation as a movement of popular protest.

The popular enactment of new doctrinal truths produced new forms of highly ritualized violence in the sixteenth century. In Germany on Maundy Thursday, when altars were usually washed with holy water, youths instead broke into the church and scrubbed the altars with lye. The scale of the challenge to established authority grew in popular iconoclastic riots throughout the German-speaking lands, the Netherlands, Switzerland, and France, and the ritualized violence gave antirituals a heightened ideological content that made popular violence and all popular festivities even more threatening to authorities.

The conflict of worldviews about the sacred during the Reformation introduced an ideological content in sixteenth-century popular and ritualized violence. This increased the elites' fears of the potentially subversive character of festivities. Ritual inversions create alternate states of mind that can release participants from the constraints of ordinary time and place. The resulting license is not so much disorder as the defense of alternative visions of order. This enduring characteristic of ritual means that radical efforts to transform power relations and cultural norms return to ritual practices that once supported the traditional ways of life among the popular classes, for example, celebrations of the summer solstice, Saint John's Eve, by ecological groups in Europe.

The disciplining of enactment: confessionalization.
The first phase of the Reformation in the 1520s was a popular movement. In a second phase of the Reformation associated with confessionalization, Protestant reformers increasingly looked askance at the carnivalesque images and behaviors that had initially fueled popular critique of the Roman church. In the 1530s and especially in the 1540s church reformers needed to instill adherence to standardized, written confessions of faith and distinctive patterns of worship and behavior that would set them off from traditional ritual practices. This creation, by Catholics and Protestants alike, of unmistakable confessional identities is termed "confessionalization." In the era of confessionalization the revolution of the written word, set in motion by humanists, bore fruit in the intensified use of printed catechisms. Church and state also cooperated in suppressing wedding and baptismal feasting. For example, detailed Lutheran regulation of wedding and baptismal feasting in Brandenburg Ansbach limited the number of participants allowed to assemble in the peasant countryside in the 1570s. Such measures not only eliminated occasions for waste and license but eroded the ties of kinship celebrated in popular festivities by godparents, confraternities, relatives. Such measures in Lutheran Scandinavia as well eroded horizontal and local bonds of loyalties that stood between subjects and their pastors, priests, and rulers.

Calvinism and the reform of morals.
Of all the Protestant reformers John Calvin (1509–1564) expressed the strongest critique of popular culture, including dancing, drinking, sexual indulgence, and of traditional Catholic religious practices, including relics, shrines, pilgrimages, and the mass. Explanations of the resulting Protestant work ethic focus on Calvinism's emphasis on individual responsibility for a clean, healthy, and cognitively controlled body freed of all sensuality and devoted only to scripturally justifiable activities. Calvinist hostility to ritual body movements, witchcraft, magic, miracles, and altered states of consciousness derived from a fundamental

anxiety about bodily movement and accompanying emotional release. This anxiety created a fundamental hostility to traditional popular culture.

The puritan revolution of popular culture.
Calvinism contributed to the reform of popular culture wherever its consistory system for policing social morals functioned, including Geneva, southern France, Scotland, and the Netherlands. No form of Protestantism, however, was more hostile to popular rituals than English Puritanism. The interregnum of 1649–1660 was a watershed for abolition of the rituals of popular culture in England. Under the government of Oliver Cromwell (1599–1658), Puritans outlawed public ceremonies, such as maypoles, dancing, and drinking matches. A popular ballad of 1648 lamented, "Christmas was killed at Naseby fight" along with "charity" and "good fellowship." The Battle of Naseby, 14 June 1645, marked Cromwell's decisive defeat of King Charles I (1600–1649) of England. While Christmas recovered, the fires of Saint John's Eve vanished along with a culture of sociability and a treatment of marginality perceived as generous and less criminalizing.

THE INDUSTRIAL ERA

The culture of working class associations.
The ability of church, state, and social elites to dominate working-class culture should not be overemphasized. Sixteenth-century royal legislation to outlaw guilds was not highly effective. Guilds and journeymen's associations were neither simple stepping-stones to modern democracy nor disorderly defenders of traditionalism or local backwaters of resistance to market competition. Journeymen especially perpetuated rituals of worker solidarity and sociability that fostered organizing skills and sustained the emotional bonds necessary to nineteenth-century collective action. This occurred despite policing of work sites by proponents of industrialization, such as Josiah Wedgwood (1730–1795) and Samuel Bentham (1757–1831) in England and Joseph Montgolfier (1740–1810) and Étienne Montgolfier (1745–1799) in France. The workers of the *faubourg* (suburb) Saint-Antoine in Paris and young journeymen (*compagnons*) had traditions of violent behaviors that were interwoven with associational rituals. As Victor Hugo (1802–1885), however, wrote of worker protest in *Les Misérables* (1862), the men "terrible, half-naked, cudgel in fist . . . were savages . . . but the savages of civilization" in their violent efforts to end oppression. While such views validate the goals of working-class political ac-

tion, they ignore the workers' cultural traditions that adapted to the industrial world.

The rise of bourgeois cultural norms. The timing and ultimate success of middle-class and upper-middle-class efforts to create a social identity distinct from that of both the traditional landed elites and the growing working class was closely allied with the pace of industrialization and the ability of the middle classes to control the terms of political participation in their respective national contexts. Most advanced in England and in France from the 1830s onward and clearly less successful in areas of slowed national unification, delayed industrialization, and persistent autocratic political regimes, the elevation of middle-class notions of order and morality had decisive effects on the reformation of popular culture in the nineteenth century. At the same time the ability of the working classes to develop a culture of their own in the process of organizing social and political movements must be taken into account.

Revolutions in the means of communication and the growing commercialization of culture mean that the simple schema of repressed practices and required new behaviors become even less useful in analyzing the reformation of popular culture. From the eighteenth century forward the impact of printing and the mass production of illustrated material for audiences that cut across class lines was quantitatively and qualitatively different from the effects seen in the Reformation. The way historians evaluate the maturing of "mass culture" and its relation to "popular culture" and class conflict adds more complexity to discussions of the reformation of popular culture in the nineteenth and twentieth centuries.

POLITICAL APPROPRIATIONS OF CARNIVAL AS TRANSFORMATIONS OF POPULAR CULTURE

In the nascent political activism that led to the revolutions of 1848, the German middle classes, especially in the Rhineland, appropriated and transformed the carnival celebrations that, in Catholic regions, had survived the Reformation only to be banned during the Napoleonic invasion of central Europe in the early nineteenth century. After their incorporation into the Prussian state in 1815, carnival festivities provided the middle classes of the Rhineland with opportunities for assembly, use of public space, printed self-expression, and commerce that were otherwise suppressed by the Prussian regime. Political appropriation of carnival tradition continued into the twentieth century. In

France, for example, in the 1920s and 1930s socialists revived festival practices in many localities to assert a populist political identity and to attempt mass political organizing.

Early industrialization in England. The most informative studies of the reformation of popular culture in nineteenth-century Britain differentiate clearly between ongoing reforms of the remnants of traditional popular festive practices in the countryside and the new set of forces affecting the growing urban populations. In treating the reformation of popular culture in urban industrial society, three factors come to the forefront:

1. the growing effect of a new concept of time emphasizing worker productivity and the control of workers' bodies and workers' use of public space,
2. "the culture that working people were making for themselves in their organized social movements" (Yeo and Yeo, 1981), and
3. "the rise of respectable society" (F. M. K. Thompson, 1988), a theme that organizes the social history of Victorian Britain, 1830–1900.

Ongoing cultural reforms in the countryside. In Great Britain attacks on traditional holidays intensified from the 1760s onward as the capitalist revolution in agriculture brought about the enclosure movement, engrossing, and increasing proletarianization of the rural workforce. The case study "The Taming of Whitsun" in Oxfordshire, England, from 1800 to 1900 by Alun Howkins (in Yeo and Yeo, 1988, pp. 187–208) elucidates a new stage in the reformation of popular culture.

Before 1830 the celebration of Whitsun began with the erecting of maypoles, an ancient gesture marking agricultural fertility. Evergreen-bedecked bowers served as a "court" for "my lord and my lady" of the feast. Often called Whit Ales, up to thirteen days of drinking, hunting (the Whit Hunt), morris dancing, cockfighting, bullbaiting, badger baiting, revelry, and fistfighting followed, with local variations. A combination of factors gradually extinguished Whitsun celebrations and replaced them with the one-day bank holiday of the 1900s. The development of scientific farming, including the use of artificial fertilizers from the 1820s, undercut the quasi-magical attempts to procure fertility through the raising of maypoles. Further rationalization of the agricultural process created regular monthly cattle sales, and the more spontaneous sale of livestock at Whitsun fairs lost significance. The collapse of the paternalistic ethic of the gentry,

60

Recreation in "Respectable Society." *A Summer Day in Hyde Park,* painting (1858) by John Ritchie. MUSEUM OF LONDON/THE BRIDGEMAN ART LIBRARY

who had supported the celebrations and the Whit Hunt in the spirit of traditional elites' obligation occasionally to entertain the poor, providing a source of cheer and outlet for frustrations, collapsed. Finally a "reformation of manners" affected the poor and the gentry alike.

REFORMATION OF MANNERS AND THE RATIONALIZATION OF LEISURE

A refinement of manners was sparked by the effects of science on quasi-magical practices and beliefs. Heightened class conflict increased the distance between masters and servants, and the informal violence of Whitsuntide became less attractive to the gentry. At the same time the evangelical revival encouraged sectarian preaching among the poor. The chief target of this religious moral reform was drink. Methodism took the lead, followed by evangelical bishops from the Established (Anglican) Church, such as Samuel Wilberforce (1805–1873) who was appointed bishop of Oxford in the 1840s.

Historians have debated how to view the rationalization of entertainment that was a major part of the overall reformation of popular culture. Malcomson (1973) argued that growing class divisions caused the gentry to withdraw themselves and their material support from traditional revelry. Howkins's study of Whitsuntide suggests a different dynamic of growing involvement by the gentry in the leisure of the poor after 1840, albeit in a changed role of informal policing and moral mentoring that paralleled the

formal government intervention in sanitary reforms in cities in the 1840s. The outlawing of cockfighting, bullbaiting, and badger baiting in the 1830s did not end those blood sports. Real change came not by legal prohibition but by the process Raymond Williams (1973) called "incorporation." Throughout Europe the repression of working-class blood sports reflected fundamentally new attitudes toward animals and animal cruelty. This change in elite consciousness about the natural world is a complex modern phenomenon with relevance to animal rights movements. The changing attitudes toward nature and animals as factors in the reformation of popular culture deserve more investigation.

The rise of respectable society. The success of the middle-class and upper-middle-class demands for political participation, especially from the 1830s onward, expressed a social and cultural identity distinct from that of traditional landed elites and that of the growing working class. The success of these demands promoted middle-class cultural hegemony and increased supervision of the morality of the growing working class. Attention focused on regulation of behaviors in public. With the further growth of urbanization and the concentration of working-class populations, the middle-class perception that industrial laboring classes were necessarily dangerous classes grew.

Modern gender roles: separate spheres as a norm not a reality. The paradoxes and class conflicts inherent in the reformation of popular culture are especially evident in the transformations of women's social roles and particular subcultures. Women were a special repository of oral traditions and specialized forms of knowledge in midwifery, popular medicine, magic, witchcraft, gossip, and informal networks of information, such as spinning bees or *veillés* (vigils) in France. The policing of bodies and the pursuit of hygiene, both central to the reformation and transformation of popular culture, brought multiple systems of domination to bear on the lives of women. Upper-middle-class and upper-class women often found their spheres of public influence extended as they attempted to impose their religious and behavioral norms on working-class women. At the same time the acquisition of literacy by women, the appearance of female writers, and the creation of new professions and new patterns of consumption for women eventually cut across class lines and further expanded spheres of influence. The creation of "separate spheres" applies to both American and European experiences, but as a norm it is always contested in reality.

CONCLUSION

The reformation of popular culture has not been a purely repressive process. Discipline and empowerment affect all social classes and women as well as men, as the transformation of popular culture shows. It is also deceptive to view the reformation and transformation of popular culture simply as an evolutionary process facilitating the integration of localized social units into more universal social structures. While the suppression of popular festival life transformed traditional communities in the early modern period, the rituals of popular culture, altered in their meanings, in the modern period can serve as the basis for a radical critique of the centralized bureaucratic state. In Europe the revival of popular rituals has served ethnic autonomy movements in areas as diverse as Spain, France, the Netherlands, and the former Soviet Union.

The influence of the Green political movement in Europe also has led to the renewal of rites associated with the peasant agricultural cycle. Such protest against the pervasive destruction of the environment by contemporary modes of production and consumption links ancient forms of popular culture with a redefined notion of universal values, that is, planetary health. It may be questionable whether or not such appropriations represent any effective historical agency by the popular classes. Radical ecological movements have not forged effective ties with labor movements, but the joint demonstrations against the development programs of the World Bank in 2000 suggested efforts to build such coalitions of workers and intellectual activists. This presents possibilities for the transformation of popular culture in the twenty-first century.

Reappropriations of popular celebrations call the values and rationality of mass culture and narcissistic individualism into question. The ideal of the village as the core unit for human socialization can be viewed as an attempt to learn from what social historians have discovered about the human costs involved in the reformation of popular culture. However, a potential exists to distort what has been learned in studying the reformation of popular culture through idealization of a lost golden age of popular culture in which body and emotions were unfettered and human expression and creativity were more authentic. Such a view in part implies that a once-autonomous popular culture existed but ignores the social construction of all realities.

See also other articles in this section.

BIBLIOGRAPHY

Anderson, Patricia J. *The Printed Image and the Transformation of Popular Culture, 1790–1860.* New York, 1991. Includes debates on the nature of mass culture.

Barnes, Andrew E., and Peter N. Stearns, eds. *Social History and Issues in Human Consciousness: Some Interdisciplinary Connections.* New York, 1989. Innovative historical and natural science perspectives on how psychological and emotional changes occur.

Becker, Marvin B. *Civility and Society in Western Europe, 1300–1600.* Bloomington, Ind., 1988.

Bennett, Tony, Colin Mercer, and Janet Woollacott, eds. *Popular Culture and Social Relations.* Milton Keynes, U.K., and Philadelphia, 1986. Useful on Gramsci and the relations of power.

Bercé, Yves-Marie. *Fête et révolte: Des mentalités populaires du XVIe au XVIIIe siècle: Essai.* Paris, 1976. Fundamental attention to the local context in France.

Brophy, James M. "Carnival and Citizenship: The Politics of Carnival Culture in the Prussian Rhineland, 1823–1848." *Journal of Social History* 30, no. 4 (1997): 873–904.

Burke, Peter. *The Historical Anthropology of Early Modern Italy: Essays on Perception and Communication.* Cambridge, U.K., 1987. Venetian carnival and other case studies.

Burke, Peter. *Popular Culture in Early Modern Europe.* London, 1978. Essential starting point that is much debated and includes wide geographical coverage and a bibliography.

Chambers, E. K. *The Mediaeval Stage.* Oxford, 1903. Invaluable broader treatment of popular rituals than the title suggests.

Chevalier, Louis. *Laboring Classes and Dangerous Classes in Paris during the First Half of the Nineteenth Century.* Translated by Frank Jellinek. New York, 1973. Originally published in French in 1958. Fundamental but with a heavy reliance on police records.

Cox, Harvey. *The Feast of Fools: A Theological Essay on Festivity and Fantasy.* Cambridge, Mass., 1969. Best example of the ethical stakes in the 1960s reappropriation of popular culture's enduring challenges to elite norms of rationality with a cultural critique.

Cressy, David. *Bonfires and Bells: National Memory and the Protestant Calendar in Elizabethan and Stuart England.* London, 1989. Corrects past studies and further documents the reformation and suppression of popular culture in early modern England.

Decroisette, Françoise, and Michel Plaisance, comps. *Les fêtes urbaines en Italie à l'époque de la Renaissance: Verone, Florence, Sienne, Naples.* Paris, 1993. Case studies of the reform of popular rituals in Italy.

Dixon, C. Scott. *The Reformation and Rural Society: The Parishes of Brandenburg-Ansbach-Kulmbach, 1528–1603.* Cambridge, U.K., 1996. Excellent documentation of the reformation of popular culture in Lutheran Germany and a case study of confessionalization.

Eire, Carlos M. N. *War against the Idols: The Reformation of Worship from Erasmus to Calvin.* New York, 1986. Fundamental on new attitudes to the sacred and on the meaning of Calvinist iconoclasm.

Elias, Norbert. *The Civilizing Process.* Translated by Edmund Jephcott. 2 vols. New York, 1982. Originally published in German in 1939. Fundamental on the relationship between changes in social structure and changes in personality structure with a concept of civility.

Foucault, Michel. *Discipline and Punish: The Birth of the Prison.* New York, 1979. Fundamental on new technologies of power.

Foucault, Michel. *Folie et déraison: Histoire de la folie à l'âge classique.* Paris, 1961. The foundations of early modern rationality and its differences from medieval values.

Gilhus, Ingvild Sealid. "Carnival in Religion: The Feast of Fools in France." *Numen* 37 (June 1990): 24–52.

Greyerz, Kaspar von, ed. *Religion and Society in Early Modern Europe, 1500–1800.* London, 1984. Collection of provocative essays, especially Peter Burke on the reformation of the cult of saints, Jean Wirth on the concept of acculturation, and Richard C. Trexler on popular and elite culture.

63

Heers, Jacques. *Fêtes des fous et carnivals.* Paris, 1983. Fundamental.

Hsia, R. Po-Chia. *Social Discipline in the Reformation: Central Europe, 1550–1750.* New York, 1989.

Hsia, R. Po-chia, ed. *The German People and the Reformation.* Ithaca, N.Y., 1988. Innovative essays, including an excellent bibliographic essay on core topics in the reformation of popular culture, such as women, the "other."

Ingram, Martin. "Ridings, Rough Music, and the Reform of Popular Culture." *Past and Present* 105 (1984).

Jones, Gareth Stedman. "Working Class Culture and Working Class Politics in London, 1870–1900." *Journal of Social History* 7 (1974): 460–501.

Kinser, Samuel. "Presentation and Representation: Carnival at Nuremberg, 1450–1550." *Representations* 13 (1986): 1–41. Emphasizes the cultural shift from "presentation" or the participatory mode in carnival to formalized "representation" as a way of understanding the changing content of the "popular" in carnival.

Mellor, Philip A., and Chris Shilling. *Re-Forming the Body: Religion, Community, and Modernity.* Thousand Oaks, Calif., 1997. The reformation of popular culture seen from the perspective of a history of the body; stimulating on the differences between the Catholic and Protestant Reformations and the culture of athletic bodies.

Mentzer, Raymond A., ed. *Sin and the Calvinists: Morals Control and the Consistory in the Reformed Tradition.* Kirksville, Mo., 1994. Case studies of the institution of the consistory in Calvinist communities across Europe.

Miller, Pavla. *Transformations of Patriarchy in the West, 1500–1900.* Bloomington, Ind., 1998.

Muchembled, Robert. *Popular Culture and Elite Culture in France, 1400–1750.* Translated by Lydia Cochrane. Baton Rouge, La., 1985. An original paradigm of elite repression or cooperation between absolutism and the Catholic Reformation that is much debated.

Muir, Edward. *Ritual in Early Modern Europe.* Cambridge, U.K., 1997. The Reformations of the sixteenth century as a revolution in ritual behaviors.

Raeff, Marc. *The Well-Ordered Police State: Social and Institutional Change through Law in the Germanies and Russia, 1600–1800.* New Haven, Conn., 1983. Documents the policing legislation of the early modern state.

Ramsey, Ann W. *Liturgy, Politics, and Salvation: The Catholic League in Paris and the Nature of Catholic Reform, 1540–1630.* Rochester, N.Y., 1999. Early modern anxieties over expressive ritual gestures and the problems of performances as factors in the reformation of popular culture.

Robisheaux, Thomas. "Peasants and Pastors: Rural Youth Control and the Reformation in Hohenlohe, 1540–1680." *Social History* 6, no. 3 (1981): 281–300. Case study of the consolidation of patriarchy in the reform of youth culture.

Rosenband, Leonard N. "Social Capital in the Early Industrial Revolution." *Journal of Interdisciplinary History* 29, no. 3 (Winter 1999): 435–457. Revisionist perspectives on guilds and journeymen in late medieval and nineteenth-century protoindustrialization; important for understanding long-term transformations.

Sabean, David Warren. *Power in the Blood: Popular Culture and Village Discourse in Early Modern Germany.* New York, 1984. Fundamental on the early modern state, confessionalism, the reformation of popular culture, the creation of new forms of power, and the psychological foundation of individualism and state authority.

Scribner, R. W. *Popular Culture and Popular Movements in Reformation Germany.* London, 1987. Fundamental work that transformed the field.

Smoller, L. "Defining the Boundaries of the Natural in Fifteenth-Century Brittany: The Inquest into the Miracles of Saint Vincent Ferrer." *Viator* 28 (1997): 333–359.

Spencer, Elaine Glovka. "Custom, Commerce, and Contention: Rhenish Carnival Celebrations, 1890–1914." *German Studies Review* 20, no. 3 (1997): 323–341. Cooptation of carnival for the political development of the German bourgeoisie and its economic values.

Spencer, Elaine Glovka. "Regimenting Revelry: Rhenish Carnival in the Early Nineteenth Century." *Central European History* 28, no. 4 (1995): 457–481. Discussion of carnival in the context of commercialization.

Strauss, Gerald. *Luther's House of Learning: Indoctrination of the Young in the German Reformation.* Baltimore, 1978. Fundamental and much-debated study of the effects of Lutheran schooling on popular culture.

Tellenbach, Gerd. *Church, State, and Christian Society at the Time of the Investiture Contest.* Translated by R. F. Bennett. Oxford, 1940.

Thompson, E. P. "Time, Work Discipline, and Industrial Capitalism." *Past and Present* 29 (1964): 50–62.

Thompson, F. M. K. *The Rise of Respectable Society, 1830–1900.* Cambridge, Mass., 1988.

Underdown, David. *Revel, Riot, and Rebellion: Popular Politics and Culture in England, 1603–1660.* Oxford, 1985.

Von Geldern, James, and Louise McReynolds, eds. *Entertaining Tsarist Russia: Tales, Songs, Plays, Movies, Jokes, Ads, and Images from Russian Urban Life, 1779–1917.* Bloomington, Ind., 1998.

Watt, Tessa. *Cheap Print and Popular Piety, 1550–1640.* Cambridge, 1991.

Yeo, Eileen, and Stephen Yeo, eds. *Popular Culture and Class Conflict, 1590–1914: Explorations in the History of Labour and Leisure.* Brighton, U.K., 1981. Essential case studies for Britian, especially Keith Wrightson on alehouses and Alun Howkins on the combination of forces transforming rural popular culture.

Zika, Charles. "Hosts, Processions, and Pilgrimages: Controlling the Sacred in Fifteenth Century Germany" *Past and Present* 118 (1988): 25–64. Struggles to control the sacred and eliminate popular superstitions in eucharistic worship.

LANGUAGE

Peter Burke

If social history is defined to include the history of everyday practices as well as social structures, the history of language is necessarily an important part of the enterprise. It is no accident that the shift toward the history of the everyday and the history of practices in the 1970s and 1980s—not to mention the so-called linguistic turn—was accompanied by a growing interest in what some of its practitioners described as the "social history of language." Such topics as gossip, proverbs, conversation, and public speaking, once considered peripheral to social history if not impervious to change, began to attract the attention of historians. Some scholars analyzed the uses of language in the shaping of political movements such as the French Revolution and English Chartism, emphasizing the connections between the invention of a new vocabulary or a new type of discourse and a new political culture, a new political consciousness, or a more acute awareness of possible alternatives to old regimes.

In their pursuit of a social history of language, some historians turned to the linguists, especially the sociolinguists, for assistance, often adopting their vocabulary ("speech community," "speech domain," "code-switching," and so on), and sometimes collaborating with them, as in the case of Geraint Jenkins's *Social History of Welsh.* Linguists had of course long been interested in history—indeed, an international conference on historical linguistics took place in 1973—but not so much in social history, preferring to produce either an extremely precise and self-contained account of linguistic changes over time or an extremely general discussion of the relation between language and national history. As for the sociolinguists, for whom the relation between language and society was of paramount importance, with few exceptions (Dell Hymes, for instance), they focused on the present and neglected history. A few historians of earlier generations, among them Lucien Febvre, had taken more than a passing interest in linguistic forms, writing essays on language and nationality in eighteenth-century France, for example, or the language of the law in England, or the language of diplomacy in Sweden. However,

the new social history of language differs from the scattered studies that preceded it by being more systematic, more self-conscious, and concerned with "society" in a more precise sense of that ambiguous term.

One obvious focus for the new interest was the language of class, or more generally the ways in which differences in social status were expressed or constructed in everyday language. Another was the slang, jargon, or semiprivate languages of particular social groups, from beggars to bureaucrats. A third was the study of the forms of language considered appropriate for particular social situations or contexts, the language of insult, the language of compliment, and so on. A fourth was the study of changes in language over the long term considered in relation to changes in a given society—nation-building, the spread of literacy, and so on. These four themes will be considered in order in the following pages, in which it should become clear how much linguistic territory still awaits exploration by historians.

LANGUAGE AND STATUS

Throughout the history of postmedieval Europe, if not before, differences in language at the level of grammar, vocabulary, or accent have been associated with differences in social status. Some scholars in sixteenth-century Italy were already aware of this point and drew attention, for instance, to the archaic language of the peasants of Tuscany. These linguistic differences are sometimes unconscious, but they have often served as a means for certain individuals and groups to distinguish themselves from others. In some parts of Europe, the upper classes or status groups have literally spoken a different language from their social inferiors. Thanks to Tolstoy's *War and Peace,* it is easy to remember that Russian nobles of the early nineteenth century often spoke to one another in French. So did the upper classes in the Dutch Republic in the seventeenth century and in parts of the

Bluestocking. A *précieuse,* or woman intellectual. Engraving by I. Gole, eighteenth century. BIBLIOTHÈQUE NATIONALE, PARIS

German-speaking world in the eighteenth, while the Danes of the period used German as a status symbol and the Norwegians used Danish. French in Languedoc, Provence, and Brittany, like English in Scotland, Wales, and Ireland, and Castilian in Catalonia, served a similar function.

More common as a means of distinction was the adoption by the upper classes of what they considered to be a "purer" or more rational form of speech, a form closer to the written language. They showed their civilization and their connections with the wider world by abandoning the local dialect, or patois, a symbol of the popular culture from which they were gradually distancing themselves (in the sixteenth and seventeenth centuries in western Europe, in the eighteenth and nineteenth centuries farther east). In similar fashion, the habit of speaking in proverbs was gradually abandoned by the upper classes at this time. Proverbs became associated with the archaic world of the peasantry, while the employment of a pure form of language was taken as a sign that the speaker too was refined and rational. In 1690 the dictionary-maker Antoine Furetière defined patois as "corrupt and crude language, such as that of the lower orders" *(langage corrompu et grossier, tel que celui du menu peuple).* In the mid-eighteenth century, the *Encyclopédie* offered a similar definition, "a corrupted language which is spoken in almost all the provinces."

Some speakers went still farther in this direction and adopted a vocabulary so refined that it was scarcely intelligible outside their own circle, like the seventeenth-century French bluestockings, or *précieuses,* ridiculed in the plays of Molière, who distanced themselves from ordinary language by employing euphemisms and other circumlocutions such as *un nécessaire* for a servant. The language of the *précieuses* was an aspect of the culture of the salons in which women led the way in polishing the language of upper-class males, while the Académie Française, with its famous dictionary, continued and institutionalized the process. In Italy the Florentine Accademia della Crusca had a similar function, compiling a dictionary of acceptable words as a way of sorting the wheat from the "chaff" *(crusca).* In Spain the motto of the eighteenth-century Royal Academy, which had a similar function, was "it purifies, it fixes, and it dignifies" *(limpia, fija y da esplendor).* Generally speaking, the criterion of acceptability was that words or phrases should not be associated with the common people, with the provinces, or with particular occupations. The rejection of technical terms is a reminder that the upper classes defined themselves as ladies and gentlemen of leisure.

In England in the late seventeenth century, where there was no academy, a sense of distance from common speech was produced in fashionable circles by introducing French phrases into ordinary conversation. John Dryden's *Marriage à la Mode* (1673) mocked fashionable people who peppered their English with French terms such as *grande monde, risque, épuisée,* or *à la mode* itself. In similar fashion, Germans with social pretensions introduced such words as *galanterie, goût,* and *politesse* into their everyday speech.

Accent too carried a social message. In the Jesuit college of Milan, teachers were already trying in the 1590s to eliminate provincial accents from the language of their pupils. In France in the early eighteenth century, a duke criticized a duchess for speaking with the accent *(ton)* as well the vocabulary of the common people. In England the accent of the southeast was becoming associated with the court in the time of Queen Elizabeth, although Sir Walter Raleigh apparently never lost his West Country accent. The painter Sir Joshua Reynolds also spoke with a Devonshire accent, although it had become more of an embarrassment by his time, when a "Yorkshire tone," for example, was condemned in handbooks on good English. The rise of what would be known as "received pronunciation," and the habit of using accent to place acquaintances socially was already noticeable at that time. By the nineteenth century, schools in England, France, and elsewhere were inculcating standard forms of speech as well as writing and stigmatizing dialect as an inferior form of language.

As some of these examples suggest, the concern with the linguistic signs of social class is not—as it is often thought to be—a peculiarly English obsession. All the same, England in the nineteenth and twentieth centuries does offer a particularly rich field of observation in this respect. The English novel of the period is also a wonderful source, provided that representations of speech in novels are used with caution, in other words, that novels are not assumed to be a simple reflection of linguistic practice but are read with awareness of the process of literary stylization. Like the guides used to correct language, they illustrate contemporary concern with avoiding a provincial ac-

'Bus Conductor. "EMMERSMITH! EMMERSMITH! 'ERE YE ARE! EMMERSMITH!"
'Liza Ann. "OO ER YER CALLIN' EMMER SMITH? SORCY 'OUND!"

Dropping One's Aitches and Shifting One's Rs. Cartoon from *Punch,* 7 April 1896. PUNCH LTD.

cent, as well as vulgarisms such as "I had no call" or "I'll tell you for why," the use of proverbs, and above all, "dropping one's Hs" and speaking of "ouse," "appen," and so on.

Certain forms of language were also associated with gender. "Talking like a lady," as the nineteenth-century phrase went, meant distinguishing oneself at once from men and from "common" women, who were supposed to speak and especially to swear like men. Talking like a lady meant using a particular vocabulary, including modes of address such as "Papa" and, in the mid-nineteenth century, euphemisms such as "bosom" for breast and "limbs" for legs. These turns of speech are so often described as Victorian that it may be worth emphasizing that they had their equivalents in other European languages, as the example of the *précieuses* has already suggested.

JARGONS

The language of the *précieuses* might be described as a kind of jargon, a pejorative term rescued by linguists and used to refer to a virtually private language used by a particular social group. The classic case of jargon in modern Europe is the language of beggars and thieves, whether it was adopted as a way of keeping their affairs hidden from prying outsiders, as a way of creating solidarity, or both. This language was not exactly international, but there were significant features in common between the German *Rotwelsch,* as it was called, the French *argot,* the Italian *gergo* or *furbesco,* the Spanish *gringo,* and the English cant. These secret languages became much better known from the sixteenth century onward because they attracted the attention of both magistrates and professional writers, and dictionaries of various jargons became available in print. Less well known, but equally widespread, were the technical or semiprivate languages of other occupational groups such as students, soldiers, and masons—itinerant occupations all three, giving their jargons an international flavor.

Awareness of these jargons encouraged some men of letters to stigmatize the language of professors, lawyers, physicians, and officials in similar terms. In England from the late seventeenth century, for instance, the phrase "the jargon of the schools" came into use to refer to academic language, which was still laced with technical terms of medieval Scholastic philosophy such as "quiddity" and "entity." In France, Italy, Spain, and elsewhere there was a similar rejection of pedantic language, which was increasingly considered to be out of place in polite discourse, a speech genre that the writers of the many books on "the art of conversation" (especially common in France and England in the eighteenth century) attempted to regulate.

A similar point might be made about the "lawyer's dialect" or "court gibberish," as nonlawyers called it. Doctors too liked to blind their clients with science or at least with "hard words," whether in Latin or the vernacular. We should not forget the language of bureaucracy, a jargon that appears to have been particularly elaborate and formidable in Vienna and Berlin from the eighteenth century. The jargon of the clergy should not be forgotten either. Still more striking, however, is the special language of religious movements or sects, including German and Scandinavian Pietists, English Quakers, and French Jansenists. The Society of Friends, for example, expressed their spiritual egalitarianism by their rejection of deferential forms of speech, replacing them with what they called the "plain" language of "Thee," "Thou," "Friend," and so on. They were also distinctive in their rejection of oaths in their vocabulary (in which "church," for example, was replaced by "steeple-house"), and in their emphasis on the religious value of silence.

The particular speech forms of religious groups should not be confused with religion as a special domain in which ordinary speakers of ordinary language "switch codes," as the linguists say, to a higher or more formal variety of speech, the linguistic equivalent of wearing their Sunday best to church.

SPEECH DOMAINS

After they had distanced themselves from ordinary people in the ways described above, the upper classes in Italy, France, and elsewhere continued to use dialect in certain situations, or "domains." That they needed to do so in order to speak to their servants or their tenants will be obvious enough. More significant culturally, because it is less utilitarian in motive, is the upper-class use of dialect on festive occasions as a symbol or marker of relaxation. They did this at Carnival, for example (a practice that continues in Switzerland to this day), or during the proceedings of festive societies such as the Accademia della Valle di Bregno in sixteenth-century Milan, a group of townspeople who imitated the language of the local peasants for fun. In similar fashion, or perhaps to distance himself from what he was saying, the poet Alfred Tennyson adopted a rustic Lincolnshire accent whenever he told bawdy stories. Conversely, a peasant in nineteenth-century France might use standard language as a sign of formality or emphasis, to invite a girl to dance, to talk about national politics, or even to swear.

These examples illustrate the way in which the same people often use different varieties of language—and sometimes completely different languages—according to the situation they find themselves in. The use of Latin in the Catholic liturgy before Vatican II is an obvious example, while the use of German on the Stock Exchange at St. Petersburg until the end of the nineteenth century is a striking one.

In the sixteenth century, King John III of Sweden is said to have rebuked a fellow ruler who had written to him in French by replying in Finnish. However, French gradually became established as the language of diplomacy in the course of the eighteenth century, replacing Latin, Italian, and German (although the chancery of the Holy Roman Empire insisted on Latin until the early 1700s). Frederick the Great was supposed to have spoken French everywhere except in the stables, a story that surely refers to the celebrated if apocryphal saying of the polyglot emperor Charles V that one should speak French to ladies, German to horses, and Spanish to God. In contrast, the French Renaissance princess Margaret of Navarre considered Spanish the language of love.

One of the most distinctive linguistic domains all over Europe was that of the law. What was sometimes described by contemporaries as the jargon of lawyers might be more objectively described as the language of the law courts, full of Latinisms, pleonasms, and technical terms. In England the lawyers quite literally spoke and wrote a different language, "law French." Archbishop Thomas Cranmer remarked that he had "heard suitors murmur at the bar because their attornies pleaded their causes in the French tongue, which they understood not." The standard work on landholding was known as *Les tenures de Monsieur Littleton,* written, according to the title page of a seventeenth-century edition, "al request des Gentilhommes, Students en la ley Dangleterre." Not until the eighteenth century did the vernacular become the exclusive language of the English law. Even when lawyers spoke English, contemporary critics suggested that the function of their jargon was to exclude the client and thus make them more dependent on professionals.

Linked to the language of the courts, but increasingly distinct from it, was the language of public administration in chanceries and elsewhere. In the case of German, for example, a distinctive "chancery language" *(Kanzleisprache)* developed relatively early, in the later Middle Ages, in order to make imperial decrees intelligible to the laity all over the empire, whatever dialect they spoke. This administrative language, or *Curialstyl,* developed characteristics of its own. It was pompous, probably deliberately so, and drew on Latin and on the languages of the law and sometimes of finance for terms that were lacking in everyday forms of the vernacular. Sometimes assumed to be a German peculiarity, this "bureaucratese" had its equivalents in other parts of Europe: in Italy (where Spanish rule encouraged the adoption of Hispanisms), in the Swedish empire (where Germanisms as well as Latinisms are noticeable), and in Russia, where it was known as *prikazni jazyk* ("departmental language"). Common characteristics of these official languages are circumlocutions and euphemisms, for example, the notorious euphemism of the Third Reich "special handling" *(Sonderbehandlung)* as a way of describing official violence.

One speech domain that has attracted a good deal of interest from social historians in the last few years is that of insult. There are several reasons for this interest. Judicial records offer rich sources, while the confrontations leading to insult make latent tensions manifest and reveal something of the attitudes and prejudices of ordinary people whom other sources do not reach. For example, insult is gendered. Women are most often attacked through their supposed sexual behavior and described as whores, while insults to males are more various, ranging from "spy" through "cuckold" to "idler" or "bankrupt." Forms of politeness, on the other hand, have attracted less attention and are sometimes thought to be essentially unchanging. However, recent work on Britain in the seventeenth and eighteenth centuries emphasizes changing ideas of politeness, or "civility," linking them to political and social changes such as the rise of the middle classes or the reaction against the bitterness of the conflicts between the Whig and Tory parties.

Writing is a domain of its own, and in many cultures there is a difference, lesser or greater, between spoken and written forms of language. However, the written language like the spoken may be subdivided into smaller domains in some of which a foreign language might be thought appropriate for a variety of reasons. In nineteenth-century Finland, for example, the language of bookkeeping was German, probably because German had long been in use as a commercial lingua franca in the multilingual Baltic region in which the German merchants of the Hanse played an important role. In eighteenth-century Germany, some of the bourgeoisie (including the fiancée of the writer Johann Christoph Gottsched) thought it "plebeian" to write letters in German, preferring to use French for the purpose. For the last five hundred years or so, however, this linguistic separation of spheres has been gradually but steadily undermined by the rise of many vernaculars, a process closely linked to the processes of state- and nation-building.

LANGUAGES, STATES, AND NATIONS

One of the major long-term trends in the history of the languages of Europe since the end of the Middle Ages is the decline of Latin, particularly as a written language, and its replacement by vernaculars. The decline of Latin must not be dated too early. Translations from vernacular into Latin were common, and they reached their peak in the first half of the seventeenth century. All the same, the increasing importance of written Italian, French, Spanish, English, German, Dutch, Portuguese, Czech, Polish, and Hungarian is particularly obvious by the sixteenth century, and it was accompanied by statements of the "dignity" of those vernaculars as well as by decrees like that of 1539 in which the king of France ordered legal documents to be drawn up in French. The increasing employment of vernacular for literary purposes was accompanied by their standardization and codification, making them distinct from spoken languages as well as from Latin. The trend to standardization was assisted by the spread of printing, especially when the new medium was consciously exploited for this purpose, as it was, for example, by Martin Luther.

Luther's problem was he wanted to appeal to ordinary people as well as scholars, so that he could not confine himself to Latin. For the same reason, both in his own writings and in his translation of the Bible, he needed to employ a form of German that would be intelligible from Alsace to Saxony. Luther based his German to some extent on the chancery language that, as we have seen, was already current throughout the empire, but in order to reach as many people as possible, he simplified it. In turn, Luther's Bible helped create literary German, just as the Kralice Bible (1579–1594) contributed to the development of literary Czech and the Authorized Version of 1611 contributed to the development of literary English.

In Catholic countries in particular, an alternative to the Bible as a means of linguistic codification was the academy. Academies were discussion groups of men of letters, some of which acquired official status and prepared dictionaries from which inappropriate words were carefully excluded, whether the selection was made on moral or social grounds. The Florentines had their Accademia della Crusca, the French their Académie Française, which had the task of cleaning up the language (nettoyer la langue des ordures), and the Spaniards their Real Academia Española. In Russia the first important linguistic reformer was the polymath academician Mikhail Lomonosov (1711–1765), whose Russian grammar played an important role in the secularization of Russian culture, helping to create a new written language that could compete with the traditional one, church Slavonic, the function of which in the Eastern or Orthodox Church had been comparable to that of Latin in the West.

Language and politics. Governments not infrequently lent their support to these enterprises. In the sixteenth century the grand duke of Tuscany, Cosimo de' Medici, tried to turn Florentine cultural capital into political capital by associating himself with dictionary-making and the Accademia Fiorentina. In the seventeenth century Cardinal Richelieu was involved in the foundation of the Académie Française. There were good pragmatic reasons for statesmen to concern themselves with language. The political theorist Giovanni Botero noted in his *Reason of State* (1589) that conquerors "will do well to introduce their own tongue into the countries they have conquered." As if following his advice, the emperor Ferdinand II made German the official language of Bohemia at the expense of Czech in 1627, six years after his victory at the Battle of White Mountain. Continuing this policy of linguistic centralization, the emperor Joseph II attempted to replace Latin with German in the Hungarian Diet (1784) and made German obligatory in the schools of the empire in 1790. In the Swedish empire, the government encouraged the spread of the Swedish language at the expense of Finnish.

For a dramatic and well-documented case study of the relation between language and politics, we may turn to the French Revolution. The revolutionaries faced a problem not unlike that of Martin Luther in the early years of the Reformation. They needed to broadcast their message as widely as possible in a country in which the majority of the population did not speak standard French, while minorities—Occitan, Breton, German, Flemish, and Basque—did not speak French at all. An early solution to the problem, reached in 1790, was to translate government decrees into patois. However, it was argued that French was the language of the revolution and that speakers of patois, let alone speakers of other languages, were at best unenlightened and at worst counterrevolutionary. The revolution's specialist on language, the abbé Henri Grégoire, claimed that it was necessary "to destroy patois" (anéantir les patois) and make French universal (universaliser l'usage de la langue française). The language policy followed by the French government from 1794 onward thus resembled that of Joseph II discussed above. The Third Republic took that policy a stage further, through the educational reforms of 1880 and the prohibition of Breton in the religious domain (sermons and catechism classes) in 1902.

Language Protest. Troops disperse demonstrators in front of the Parliament building in Vienna protesting the Language Ordinances of 1897, which established equality between German and non-German languages in Austria. From a sketch by Franz Schlegel. ÖSTERREICHISCHE NATIONALBIBLIOTHEK, VIENNA

Linguistic revivals. Competition between languages ensured that the emergence of the vernacular languages of Europe was no simple success story. We should not forget the losers, especially in the domain of writing. The decline of written Czech after the Battle of White Mountain is one well-known example, a decline lamented later in the century in a treatise by the Jesuit Bohuslav Balbín. Literary Catalan was declining at much the same time, as Madrid tightened its grasp on the rest of Spain. In the British Isles, Scottish, Irish, and Welsh were all retreating as English was advancing in the seventeenth and eighteenth centuries, first as a written language and later as a spoken one. In France, Occitan and Breton were in retreat. No wonder that in the eighteenth century the less literate half of the hexagon (southwest of an imaginary diagonal line from Saint-Malo to Geneva) included not only the poorer part of the country but also the principal regions (Brittany, Languedoc, and Provence) in which French was not the mother tongue. The competition between dominant and dominated languages is not a new phenomenon.

In all these regions, the choice whether to speak the local or the metropolitan language both expressed and contributed to the increasing cultural distance between different social groups. In Scotland, Gaelic became, in the words of the eighteenth-entury social theorist Adam Ferguson, "a language spoken in the cottage, but not in the parlour." In Wales the gentry of Glamorgan switched to English in their everyday speech in the eighteenth century, thus expressing their identification with the values of the metropolis and their withdrawal from local popular culture. By the nineteenth century, Scottish, Irish and Welsh parents who wanted their children to rise socially were encouraging them to express themselves in English, while Breton parents were taking a similar attitude toward French. In the nineteenth century, the great agent of linguistic acculturation was the school. In late nineteenth century France, for example, it was forbidden to speak Breton in the schools of the region, although the teachers themselves often spoke Breton at home. Whether the teachers were aware of this or not, a major function of the school at this time was to undermine dominated languages and replace them with dominant ones.

By the end of the eighteenth century, the decline and even extinction of the minority languages already appeared virtually inevitable. All the same, the nineteenth century was to be an age not only of the spread of dominant languages in official domains but also of revivals of dominated languages in unofficial or informal settings. In the Austrian Empire, for instance, as if in reaction against the germanization favored by Joseph II, four Slav languages were revived from the late eighteenth century onward, Czech, Slovak, Serbo-Croatian, and Slovene. In the case of Czech, there was a conscious return to the usage of the sixteenth-century "golden age," while in the other cases a new written language was shaped by standardizing spoken forms. In all these cases, a linguistic movement, complete with societies, journals, meetings, and so on became associated with a movement for political autonomy. Modern Greek developed in a similar way at the time of the independence movement of the early nineteenth century. In similar fashion in Provence, the poet Frédéric Mistral (1830–1914) was one of the leaders of the Félibrige, a movement founded in 1854 to revive literary Occitan. There was a similar movement in Catalonia at about the same time. The two groups were in contact, and both revived the medieval poetry competitions known as the floral games (jocs florals).

Gaelic too enjoyed a revival. Welsh, which had declined least, was also the first to be revived. The Eisteddfod, a poetry competition associated with the days of the Druids, increased in popularity during the late eighteenth century and was held on a national basis from 1858 onward. Dictionaries of Welsh were compiled and an attempt was made (as was the case with Czech) to return to a sixteenth-century golden age. In Ireland, on the other hand, it was only in 1876 that the Society for the Preservation of the Irish Language was founded, followed in 1893 by the Gaelic League. Children were taught Irish in school from 1878 in small doses and from 1922 onward in larger ones. A demand for the preservation of the Breton language was demanded by one wing of the Breton national movement.

In England and Italy, by contrast, there was competition not between languages but between varieties, between the standard form of the language and dialects. In Italy the dialect tradition was of course much stronger; it has been calculated that only 2.5 percent of the population spoke Italian at the time of the unification of Italy in 1861. However, urbanization and emigration weakened the hold of dialect, and the rise of Italian in the twentieth century, like that of other standard national languages, was assisted by a variety of institutions, notably the school, newspapers, the cinema, radio, television, and (thanks to compulsory military service) the army. In England this process of linguistic unification took place much earlier. Even in England, however, it is possible to discern a revival of dialect in the nineteenth century, notably the rise of printed poetry in the Yorkshire and Lancashire dialects from the 1840s onward. Once the agent of linguistic standardization, by the nineteenth century the printing press was also serving the causes of regional resistance and revival.

Linguistic purification. Dominant and dominated languages alike were subjected to purification from foreign words, especially in the nineteenth and twentieth centuries. In France postwar governments struggled against franglais, the contamination of the French language by contact with English, especially American English. In Greece and Germany, purification also became a political issue. In Greece the movement for pure speech (katharevousa) aimed at deleting foreign words and restoring classical elements to the Greek language. The reformer Adamantios Koraïs, for example, denounced "borrowing from strangers . . . words and phrases amply available in one's own language." In place of the foreign, the reformers suggested learnèd, archaic, and pseudo-archaic words. Thus the potato, traditionally *patata*, became *gêomêlon,* a rendering into classical Greek of *pomme de terre.* The new Greek state founded in 1830 officially adopted *katharevousa.* In the late nineteenth century, however, there was what might be called an antipurist campaign in favor of the language of the people, demotic Greek (demotike). In the twentieth century the Left has championed *demotike,* while right-wing governments in 1921–1923, 1935–1936, and 1967–1974 all restored *katharevousa.*

In Germany following unification, there was a movement to remove French, English, and other alien terms from the language, a movement linked to the return to the Gothic script, another symbol of national identity, and institutionalized in the form of a society, the Allgemein Deutsche Sprachverein (founded in 1885), and a journal, *Muttersprache.* The 1930s were the high point of the society's attempts to hunt down and replace foreign words, the so-called *Fremdwortjagd.* Thus *Universität* became "Althochschule," *Student* "Hochschuler," *Rationalismus* "Vernunftum," and so on. The Nazis supported the movement at first but put an official end to the hunt in 1940 after Hitler's speeches were criticized by purists.

The links between linguistic revivals and politics are well known, particularly for their place in a more general reaction against centralization. On the other hand, the social composition of these movements remains to be studied. In the precise sense of the term "social," the social history of linguistic nationalism remains largely unexplored territory. Much work also remains to be done on the place of language in the construction or presentation of the self and of the emotions in letters and other personal documents in different places, periods, and social groups.

BIBLIOGRAPHY

Auty, Richard. "The Linguistic Revival among the Slavs of the Austrian Empire, 1780–1850." *Modern Language Review* 53 (1958): 392–404.

Bauman, Richard. *Let Your Words Be Few: The Symbolism of Speaking and Silence among Seventeenth-Century Quakers.* Cambridge, U.K., 1983.

Browning, Robert. "Greek Diglossia Yesterday and Today." *International Journal of the Sociology of Language* 35 (1982): 49–68.

Burke, Peter. *The Art of Conversation.* Cambridge, U.K., 1993.

Burke, Peter, and Roy Porter, eds. *The Social History of Language.* Cambridge, U.K., 1987.

Corfield, Penelope J. "Historians and Language." In *Language, History, and Class.* Edited by Penelope J. Corfield. Oxford, 1991. Pages 1–29.

Durkacz, Victor. *The Decline of the Celtic Languages.* Edinburgh, 1983.

Grillo, Ralph. *Dominant Languages: Language and Hierarchy in Britain and France.* Cambridge, U.K., 1989.

Higonnet, Patrice. "The Politics of Linguistic Terrorism." *Social History* 5 (1980): 41–69.

Jenkins, Geraint, ed. *The Social History of Welsh.* Cardiff, Wales, forthcoming.

Jones, Gareth Stedman. *Languages of Class: Studies in English Working Class History, 1832–1982.* Cambridge, U.K., 1983.

Kirkness, Alan. *Zur Sprachreinigung im Deutschen: Eine historische Dokumentation 1789–1871.* Tübingen, Germany, 1975.

Klein, Lawrence E. *Shaftesbury and the Culture of Politeness.* Cambridge, U.K., 1994.

Lartichaux, J.-Y. "Linguistic Politics during the French Revolution." *Diogenes* 97 (1977): 65–84.

Leith, Dick. *A Social History of English.* 2d ed. London, 1997.

MacDonagh, Oliver. "The Politics of Gaelic." In his *States of Mind: A Study of Anglo-Irish Conflict 1780–1980.* London, 1983. Pages 104–125.

Mugglestone, Lynda. *"Talking Proper": The Rise of Accent as Social Symbol.* Oxford, 1995.

Obelkevich, James. "Proverbs and Social History." In *The Social History of Language.* Edited by Peter Burke and Roy Porter. Cambridge, U.K., 1987. Pages 43–72.

O'Cuiv, Brian, ed. *A View of the Irish Language.* Dublin, 1969.

Phillips, Kenneth C. *Language and Class in Victorian England.* Oxford, 1984.

Phillipson, Nicholas. "Politics and Politeness in the Reign of Anne and the Early Hanoverians." In *Varieties of British Political Thought 1500–1800.* Edited by John G. A. Pocock. Cambridge, U.K., 1993. Pages 211–245.

Scaglione, Aldo, ed. *The Emergence of National Languages.* Ravenna, Italy, 1984.

Townson, Michael. *Mother-Tongue and Fatherland: Language and Politics in German History.* Manchester, U.K., 1992.

Weber, Eugen. "A Wealth of Tongues." In his *Peasants into Frenchmen: The Modernization of Rural France, 1870–1914.* Stanford, Calif., 1976. Pages 67–94.

CONSUMERISM

Gary Cross

Consumerism commonly refers to the unlimited and general desire for purchased goods and services that define self and social position in advanced market societies. Consumerism can also refer to a movement in the defense of the economic and personal needs of buyers of goods and services against dishonest, manipulative, or overly powerful manufacturing, retailing, and financial interests. This second meaning of the word emerged early in the twentieth century and was often associated with the cooperative movement that attempted in Europe to challenge the economic power of conservative retail chains and banks. This essay will concern itself with the first definition.

PRECURSORS OF MODERN CONSUMERISM

Europeans have tended to identify consumerism with the Americanization of European economies and culture (for example, the penetration of American soft drink and fast food companies since World War II). This perspective, however, tends to overlook the roots of consumerist attitudes in the longer history of European capitalism and culture. Some modern cultural critics influenced by Theodor Adorno and other members of the Frankfurt School of Social Research understand consumerism as a product of twentieth-century mass production capitalism. According to this theory, manufacturers and retailers with a surfeit of goods in inventory due to new mass production techniques created consumer demand for their wares by manipulating the masses through advertising and display. Insecurities, originating in feelings of cultural inferiority or the traumas of increasingly intense and meaningless work, made the working and lower middle classes especially susceptible to these merchandising appeals.

Increasingly, this view is challenged by historical analysis of earlier expressions of consumerism. While a tiny minority of the rich and powerful have pursued comforts and pleasures and hoarded luxury goods for millennia, the advent of consumerism required sustained and eventually widespread economic growth that occurred only in modern history. The aristocracy in Renaissance Italy and France congregated in the bustling life of urban centers such as Florence, Milan, Lyon, and Paris, where they abandoned warrior values. Following, for example, the dictates of Baldassare Castiglione's *Book of the Courtier* (1528), some cultivated reputation through the purchase and use of luxuries in the fine arts, dress, and household furnishings. Castiglione's model for "polite society" fit an age when the military prowess of the nobility was growing irrelevant with the development of modern military monarchies and the new gunpowder weapons of cannon and musket. Castiglione's *Courtier* taught aristocrats and aspiring bourgeois how dress and appearance could define and display individuality within socially acceptable norms. Moreover, close and frequent interaction in court and urban life led to imitation or emulation in the display of wealth and status.

Fashion in clothing and domestic furnishings played a key role. Whereas garment styles were relatively static in the Middle Ages and often marked the social function of the wearer, Renaissance fashion changed more quickly and gave vent to individual expression. Fashion stimulated the clothing industries in Italy and the Low Countries in the fifteenth and sixteenth centuries and later encouraged the fur trade in North America. While comfort, even in the dwellings of the aristocracy, was minimal and even discouraged by the ascetic tradition in the medieval Catholic Church, Renaissance upper-class home furnishings included such innovations as upholstered chairs, wallpaper, and carpets. Stimulating this new taste for innovative goods was the widening contact of Europeans with the luxuries and products of Asia and the Americas through exploration and trade. European collection of this exotica in "wonder cabinets" and reading about it in "wonder books" helped to create a taste for novelty.

In late-seventeenth-century Netherlands, wealth created by overseas trade, agricultural innovation, and

Elite Consumerism. Portrait of Duchess Madeleine of Bavaria by Pieter de Witte (1548–1628). ALTE PINAKOTHEK, MUNICH/ARTOTHEK

a culture that favored self-restraint and investment led to an "embarrassment of riches" in the words of Simon Schama. Dutch burghers cultivated not only the arts (a form of elite consumerism) but also refined and fashionable domestic furnishings that displayed their social position and wealth. Another preindustrial center for nascent consumerism was in eighteenth-century London. The English capital was noted for its extraordinary size and wealth as a major center for trade and crafts. A "consumer revolution" in fashionable clothing and home furnishings preceded and paralleled the better-known industrial revolution in England. Indeed, demand for status goods stimulated industrialization at least as much as increased output encouraged new consumption.

A nascent consumerism resulted from the trickling down of a wide range of consumer goods and services from the aristocracy to the middle class. Some even touched the upper ranks of working people. Fashion and social emulation moved out of court society and into coffeehouses and pleasure gardens. There, money rather than birth gave the individual an opportunity to participate. Mass distribution of tea and fashionable crockery (through Wedgwood and

others) redefined family life, and the cultivation of fashion in women's clothing created an identification of the feminine with the fashionable. Modern ideas about the desirability of the new and the attraction to the "star" performer, which many associate with modern mass marketing, were established in seventeenth- and eighteenth-century commercial cities. Actors, lion tamers, and even healers became well known because they worked in a socially open market like London where information flowed freely. In this context, honor and fame could be obtained by the lowborn, earned by turning themselves into a commodity. The English pleasure gardens located in the London suburbs offered an aspiring middle class access (for a fee) to an experience similar to the private aristocratic gardens. In addition, aristocratic traditions of traveling to inland spas and seaside resorts trickled down to the middle, and eventually working, classes, beginning in the late eighteenth century. These watering places, like the pleasure gardens, offered those with the price of admission a packaged experience and an opportunity to interact with others, discover innovative fashions and products, and emulate trendsetters. Cost and rules of dress and decorum segregated the wealthy from plebeians, but many of the basic features of upper-class seaside resorts filtered down to the less respectable sea spots, like Blackpool, by 1860. A pattern was repeated: aristocratic pleasures and social practices formed a core of a broader consumer culture characterized by personal display and social emulation.

The British cultural historian Colin Campbell has argued that the social origins of consumerism in social imitation and emulation have been overstressed. He finds instead that new romantic attitudes emerged in the late eighteenth century that encouraged an imaginative anticipation of the pleasures and enhancements that new goods would bring the individual. When a new coat or hat, for example, did not produce the expected personal happiness, this disappointment did not temper desire, but only created the need for still more and different goods. For Campbell, a central factor in the development of consumerism is the transition from the desire for more necessities (food and drink, especially) and physical sensation (as in the gluttonous or avaricious sinner of medieval Europe) to the longing for emotional fulfillment in the symbolic meanings of goods.

Probably most important to the explanation of consumerism was simply increased wealth and its distribution. Constraint made sense in a time when the unlimited desire of the rich and powerful led to the exploitation of the many and the horrors of war and conquest. But even a partial and temporary liberation from the fears of food shortages and uncertain hous-

Pleasure Garden. *Montpelier Promenade, Cheltenham,* by J. R. Cockling, c. 1835.
CHELTENHAM ART GALLERY AND MUSEUMS, GLOUCESTER, U.K./THE BRIDGEMAN ART
LIBRARY

ing quickly removed this limit on desire, as can be
seen in the often-noted attraction of the poor for luxury—be it in ostentatious clothing or in the form of
the new consumer pleasures like tea or chocolate that
the London poor adopted instead of more nutritious
food or healthful lodgings.

The history of sumptuary laws is particularly
revealing. Political and religious authorities found
many of the nascent forms of consumerism a threat
to social stability and traditional values. Indeed,
sumptuary laws restricting luxurious spending peaked
during upsurges in fashion in the sixteenth century,
when, for example, Venetians and Genoans were prohibited from having extravagant weddings or ordering
lavish clothing. The French were allowed only three
courses at meals. These laws were intended to rein in
desire and display among the rich. Other sumptuary
laws were designed to dictate what each social class or
occupational group could wear (for example, finding
tailors who made lavish dresses for commoners or restricting the use of fur and velvet to the elite). Such
laws were supposed to impede another purpose of
consumerism—the use of goods to define the social
position of their owners (in this case illegitimately, as
when the commoner tried to "look" like the aristocracy). Inevitably, consumers circumvented these laws
through such tactics as wearing outlawed fabrics in
linings or embroidering plain cloth to make it look
elegant. The decline of sumptuary laws in the eigh-

teenth century coincided with the softening of religious scruples against luxury, a rejection of privilege
(as in the abolition of these laws during the French
Revolution), and more positive views of the impact of
luxury and consumption upon economic growth.

CONSUMERISM AND ITS CRITIQUES, 1700–1850

The nascent consumerism that emerged in the eighteenth and nineteenth centuries in the richest and socially most open corners of Europe produced a wide
variety of responses. Bernard de Mandeville's notorious *Fable of the Bees* (1714) argued that pursuit of
luxury was essential to the creation of wealth. Far from
condemning materialist desire, Mandeville maintained
that individuals should be encouraged to want things
so as to create demand and thus expand the work of
craftspeople and merchants. This frank embrace of the
selfish pursuit of material goods was certainly consistent with an emerging doctrine of unimpeded markets
and was, in more subdued terms, embraced by Adam
Smith's *Wealth of Nations,* published in 1776. The linkage between the demand for luxury and the expansion
of markets, on the one hand, and the growth of capitalist production, on the other, was identified as the
foundation of modern capitalism by the twentieth-
century German historian Werner Sombart.

Yet Mandeville's ideas contradicted long-held concerns that stimulating desire undermined social stability, economic prudence, and traditional ascetic religious values. Eighteenth-century political economists Arthur Young and Restif de la Bretonne assumed that increased wealth reduced the motivation to work. In particular, when employers paid more than subsistence wages, working people would toil less. In their view, the desire for leisure was greater than the longing for more goods. Moreover, the stoic distinction between natural needs and unnatural wants remained powerful, especially because luxurious consumption seemed to undermine community and rational use of free time. Jean-Jacques Rousseau was only the best known of eighteenth-century thinkers fearful of releasing materialist desire. Misery and inequality, he claimed, came not from deprivation but from the need for things. His ideal republic was an alternative to the endless expansion of the market, offering a timeless community of self-sufficiency and self-imposed simplicity.

By the mid-nineteenth century, after the first wave of industrialization was well underway, a longer view of the problem of expanding needs and economic development was developed. John Stuart Mill anticipated a "stationary state," when economic growth and striving would culminate in a new leisure society. Then a learned class of educators could counteract the egoistic commercial spirit, and time could be devoted to noneconomic pursuits and social solidarity. Karl Marx, like Mill, rejected the utopian primitivism of Rousseau and dreamed of a society of abundance created by industrialization. The revolutionary movement that would end capitalism would also eliminate the profit-driven creation of false needs. It would guarantee instead a rational allocation of material goods for life and the social conditions for self-development. Marx shared with Mill's liberalism a dream of a society of limited and realizable material needs.

PRACTICE AND THEORY OF MASS CONSUMERISM, 1860–1930

The rise of consumerism was not a steady upward climb. Especially in the troubling years of the 1840s, food supplies failed to keep up with population increases, and wages lagged behind productivity in new industries, thus slowing the expansion of consumer demand. Especially during frequent economic crises, the standard of living of the European wage-earning and farming masses declined. However, from the 1860s, consumer desire became more a practical than a theoretical issue as rural incomes rose. Decreasing cost and increased variety of goods introduced a broader population to the attractions of spending. New venues of consumption emerged in shopping districts and department stores in major cities. These retail spaces created crowds and a new intensity of consumer emulation. Shops made goods more accessible by placing them on open shelves and displays (abandoning the need for an appointment to enter a shop or the requirement to seek a clerk's assistance to see and touch goods that formerly were kept out of sight). Department stores, like Bon Marché in Paris (opened in 1852), used visual appeals in display windows and especially luxurious presentations and store furnishings to create longings for new and exciting goods that approximated sexual desire, especially for women.

Like the department store, the great exhibitions also legitimized novelty and desire. London's Crystal Palace Exhibition of 1851 pulled together the world's luxuries and technological innovations in a magnificent, often theatrical display that drew millions in a kind of consumerist pilgrimage. The 1851 fair was followed by many others in the nineteenth and twentieth centuries in Paris, Barcelona, and Brussels (as well as New York, Chicago, and San Francisco). New consumer products and brand names were introduced at these fairs, teaching the crowd to associate progress and the future with consumer goods like bicycles, cars, and domestic appliances.

As important were emerging entertainment centers in the form of music and dance halls. From the 1850s, music halls in the major cities of Europe sold drinks to large crowds while entertaining them with well-advertised singing and dancing acts. London music halls accommodated fifteen hundred customers, and chains of music halls signed popular troupes of can-can dancers, comedians, and singers to tour. In the 1870s the modern spectator sport emerged with the enclosed stadium and turnstile (1871) for paying customers. Although only 2,000 watched the English football (or soccer) Cup Finals in 1872, by 1885 the crowd reached 10,000; it increased to nearly 101,000 by 1901 and at least 200,000 at the Wembley Cup Final in 1923. Cheap excursion trains made seaside resorts accessible to wage earners by the 1860s, especially in England. More affluent holiday makers withdrew to exclusive resorts like Eastbourne or found refuge from "day trippers" in hotels distinctly separated from the crowd; still more wealthy English went to the pricier seaside towns on the French and Italian Riviera to join the continental elite.

Even if affluence replicated in consumption the class structure of Europe, it still created a dynamic mass entertainment audience. By the 1890s mechanized amusement parks and films captured the coins of the common crowds. Such parks appeared almost simultaneously in Copenhagen, Vienna, and Blackpool. Vastly easing the flow of the plebeian crowd was the introduction of the cheap electric streetcar in the 1890s. The tram freed working-class consumers from exclusive reliance on the neighborhood pub or ethnic fraternal society for leisure and opened their lives to the anonymous pleasures of mass entertainments.

In this context, the endless expansion of mass consumption had become problematic. Did growing affluence mean an endlessly widening desire? What would be the consequences of pleasure "trickling down" to the masses? Neoclassical economic (marginalist) theory was highly ambivalent about the idea of unlimited consumer desire. Developed in the 1870s by William Stanley Jevons of Britain and Léon Walras of France, marginalism shifted the focus of economics from production to consumption. It defined economic value as subjective utility with no necessary ceilings on the quantity of goods that could be desired by anyone. Still, utility shifted from basic biological needs to higher, less immediate ones when primary needs were satisfied. Jevons and others also retained the old idea that higher wages led to new desires not only for goods but also for freedom from work. Even John Maynard Keynes, the economist who taught the twentieth century to stimulate consumer demand in order to create economic growth, also reasserted Mill's vision when he predicted that affluence would bring the satisfaction of absolute needs and thus allow the full flowering of noneconomic interests and passions in leisure.

If late-nineteenth- and early-twentieth-century educated elites resisted the consumerist notion of limitless material desire, they also were reluctant to accept consumer goods as defining social relationships and personal aspirations. Conservatives were especially concerned about the impact of mass markets on high culture and social stability. Fears of the unrestrained mob had intensified after the French Revolution. Gustave Le Bon's *The Crowd* (1895) perpetuated these anxieties by insisting that the masses were suggestible and thus susceptible to the manipulation of would-be dictators. While Le Bon anticipated fascism, he also expressed a common fear that mass consumption would unleash undisciplined and frustrating desire. The French sociologist Émile Durkheim believed that ordinary people were incapable of sorting through choices and controlling their longings when tempted by the growing array of goods so tantalizingly showcased in stores. Moral confusion was the inevitable result. For Durkheim, the only solution was to impose

constraint on the masses by organizing the consuming crowd into occupational groups and religious communities. The Spanish intellectual José Ortega y Gasset's *Revolt of the Masses* (1930) argued that new shopping and amusement sections of cities amassed crowds of uneducated but no longer impoverished people. Uprooted from their traditional folk cultures and the control of village clergy and gentry, and yet unprepared to embrace the high culture of the urban elite, these crowds were supposedly lured by the promise of immediate pleasure onto the street. The crowd's economic power swamped cultivated values and institutions, leading to a general decline of the arts and learning. Ortega y Gasset and others, like the English critic F. R. Leavis in his *Mass Civilisation and Minority Culture* (1930), saw consumer culture as ephemeral, rooted neither in the permanence and conservatism of folk culture nor in the timeless value of high culture.

Early twentieth-century Marxists often shared these conservative understandings of consumerism. The leftist concept of "false consciousness" was similar to the notion of false needs. The Left saw false consciousness as originating in the traumas of industrial work rather than in the cultural inferiority of the masses. But both Left and Right agreed that the wage earner could not resist the passive if sometimes exciting entertainments mass produced by the "culture industry" in movie houses, dance halls, and amusement parks. With theories developed by the Frankfurt school and other Marxist cultural critics from the 1920s, the Left saw the mass consumer market as undermining the potential of individuals and society. It destroyed class consciousness by luring workers into the pursuit of personal comforts and pleasures and by tying them emotionally to bourgeois and nationalist values. One example is the English embrace of chauvinistic themes promoted in popular newspapers and music halls between 1900 and 1914. To the Left, the essential passivity of consumer culture also seemed to eliminate the will of workers to organize and fight for socialism. The direct authority and discipline of the rural lord or industrial employer was no longer necessary in a consumer culture to keep workers subdued. Bourgeois control was maintained indirectly over consciousness through the appeals of consumption. Finally, according to this view, the need to work for the capitalist in order to gain a "false" freedom in consumption disciplined the wage earner to accept the status quo and alienating work.

A few early commentators on mass consumption offered more positive assessments of the emerging age of affluence, even if they continued to recognize a distinction between natural needs and unnatural wants. The French economist Charles Gide (1847–

1932) argued that abundance would bring cultural refinement. But he also stressed the need for consumer education and cooperative control over distribution. In sharp contrast to Durkheim, the French sociologist Jean Gabriel Tarde (1843–1904) believed that when working people purchased fashionable clothes or home furnishings, they were expanding their cultural horizons. Tarde agreed with the American economist Thorstein Veblen (1857–1929) that mass consumption originated in common envy and the desire to buy into the lifestyle of trendsetting elites. But this was more than simple emulation, for it gave the masses a feeling of personal freedom. More important still, this spending resulted in the gradual reduction of the social distance between elites and the common people. Eventually, the rich would even imitate the taste and culture of the masses, leading to a society of shared values. In the long run, the exchange of fashions between social classes and regions would decrease social tensions. The localized and rare pleasures of the traditional village festival would be replaced by the widespread and frequent enjoyment of the night on the town or the Sunday excursion. The new dynamic world of mass consumption might be chaotic, but over time Tarde expected that it would lead to a new, higher civilization.

The German sociologist Georg Simmel (1858–1918) acknowledged that money and the things that it could buy increased personal freedom because consumption freed the individual from constant dependence on employers and an often oppressive folk culture. Keeping up with shifting styles of adornment, display, and entertainment did more than fill empty lives with fleeting pleasures. Such spending met the social as well as ego needs of the individual. Fashion, Simmel argued, combined individuality and conformity, maximizing one's membership in a group while distinguishing oneself from others. Still, Simmel saw a price for this freedom in that consumer society created impersonal social relationships and encouraged egotistical and calculating attitudes toward others, reducing them to what they owned. The only way that one could preserve individuality was to participate in fashion. In this system, the individual could never catch up and never find a stable identity. The quest for individuality was always frustrating in the fashionable crowd. The only solution for Simmel was to cultivate personal friendship and to develop individualistic taste.

For many Europeans in the interwar years, consumerism was identical with American culture and its threat to European values and economic life. America was the barbarian future of democratic and mechanical conformity and rootless superficiality, a worry reinforced by American dominance of phonograph music and film. Particularly influential was Aldous Huxley's *Brave New World* (1932), an attack on American mass culture with its passive amusements. Even Henry Ford's promise of inexpensive cars seemed to many Europeans to threaten native craft traditions and standards of quality.

CONSUMERISM AND ALTERNATIVES IN THE TWENTIETH CENTURY

In the interwar years, many Europeans believed that mass production would eventually liberate humanity from the scarcity of "necessities," leading not to the endless expansion of symbolic or luxury consumption but rather to the reduction of work time. One seeming sign of this trend was the introduction of the eight-hour day in 1919. For many this prospect was worrisome. Conservatives feared that the assembly line undermined work incentives by diminishing the necessity of long hours to meet basic needs. Moreover, cheap mass-produced goods and pleasures seemed to threaten the value of hard work. This thinking created a seemingly insurmountable dilemma: how to stimulate and profit from mass consumption while also maintaining and fostering work discipline.

At the same time, conservatives feared that increased affluence eroded cultural standards by providing the masses the free time and money that gave them access to cultural goods. This thinking suggested that cultural standards had to be protected from mass consumption through elite domination of the mass media (as in the founding of the British Broadcasting Corporation in 1927) or through adopting educational standards that imposed a canon of literary, musical, and artistic classics on students. Conservatives were concerned about the impact of consumerism on the young, especially insofar as the influence of parents seemed to have declined and, with it, family solidarities and respect for authority. One common solution to the threat of the temptations of public amusements was industry and church sponsorship of youth camps, sports clubs, and playground centers. Throughout Europe, these organized youth activities provided pleasurable alternatives to commercial leisure in a controlled setting that also encouraged loyalty to the company or religious body. A striking example of this paternalism was the Duke of York's Camp, which brought together equal numbers of public (elite) school and industrial boys in shared games and bonfires in the interwar years. Italian and German fascists also found that noncommercial leisure was an excellent vehicle for fostering political loyalty. The *dopo*

The Tavern. *Scène de cabaret* by Louis-Léopold Bouilly (1761–1845). MUSÉE DU LOUVRE, PARIS/ERICH LESSING/ART RESOURCE

lavaro and *Kraft durch Freude* organized tours and youth summer camps, using methods that were scarcely distinguishable from those employed by company and church organizations to instill a "politics of consent."

Much of the Left shared a similar disapproval of consumerism in the interwar years. And thus labor and leftist political groups tried to organize their own noncommercial leisure to foster loyalty to union and party. Since the 1880s in Britain, organized workers' leisure had been built around cooperative societies, trade unions, socialist Sunday schools, and leftist hiking and bicycle clubs. In the 1920s European socialist sports leagues won support from sympathetic local governments and competed openly with conservative nationalist and church sports organizations. Workers' Olympic Games were played in Frankfurt (1925) and Vienna (1931). Communists and their trade unions often used sports and cultural groups to create loyalty to union and party beyond the workplace. Especially important were efforts to link the whole family and not just the union member to the cause. In the 1920s and 1930s British adult educationists encouraged pleasurable hobbies rather than didactic lessons in high culture as an alternative to the crowd pleasures of drinking, gambling, dance halls, and amusement parks. Nonprofit groups like the Holiday Fellowship

and Workers' Travel Association built guesthouses and organized vacation tours. The French Popular Front of 1936 continued the effort of the Left to organize loyalty through noncommercial leisure. Communist youth festivals and sports and leisure clubs were common. Large unions even had camps in an attempt to channel members away from consumer culture. French teachers' and other unions organized youth hostels and inexpensive vacation packages for members. The Popular Front official Léo Lagrange encouraged these noncommercial leisure and vacation programs both to foster political solidarity and to provide uplifting and healthy uses of free time by countering the allures of consumerism.

WHY CONSUMERISM WON

In the interwar years, both the Right and Left shared two assumptions—that mass production meant a shift from work to leisure values and that leisure time absorbed by consumer goods and services was a threat to social and political goals. The belief that affluence meant an expansion of leisure time (and for conservatives an undermining of the work ethic) assumed that consumer needs were satiable and that people preferred time to more goods. This essential assumption was wrong. Expanding opportunities to consume proved to be a more effective way of disciplining labor than long hours of toil. The key was the realization that psychological needs were not finite, as were most physiological needs. Higher wages could not only stimulate mass consumption but also create an open-ended desire for new goods and thus motivate wage earners to seek work rather than leisure. While the economist Lujo Brentano introduced this idea into his analysis in 1894, only in the 1920s did even a small group of industrial employers embrace this doctrine. This seemingly counterintuitive idea that expanding desire disciplined workforces has often been identified with Fordism, named after Henry Ford, the American automaker who introduced a high wage in 1914 to create a market for his cars and a disciplined consumer workforce.

The labor movement generally reinforced this idea of limitless consumption when unions tried to link productivity to wage increases. For example, the French socialist and head of the International Labor Organization Albert Thomas argued in the 1920s that workers should accept more of the intense and mechanized work of scientific management for higher wages. Labor embraced the "Fordist" ideal of mass production as a solution to the traditional dual economy divided between luxury and subsistence and as an opening to a consumer's democracy. This attitude reflects a shift from an emotional and social focus on the workplace to an embrace of the social and personal meanings of consumption off the job. It was simultaneously a recognition that conditions of mechanized industry made irrelevant the older ideals of workers' control over the job and a vision of the possibilities raised by a mass consumption economy for individual freedom to make consumer choices. Although this trade-off was rarely embraced by European industry between the world wars, it did become the implicit basis for economic growth in the postwar era.

The Great Depression experience of joblessness also encouraged this trend. Especially because unemployment was uneven across regions and occupations, sociologists and observers like George Orwell found that those without sufficient work often felt left out and humiliated. The jobless dreamed of the respect and freedom that came from the ability to consume. Even in hard times, European workers tended to hold on to luxuries. While labor leaders favored shortening the workday as a job-sharing measure in the depression, free time became relatively less important than higher income and freedom to consume for those with "time on their hands." Even when the system did not deliver the goods during the depression and World War II, the response was not massive resentment or revolution but quiet personal humiliation at being excluded from the consumers' feast and a longing to rejoin it when the opportunity came again after 1945.

Also during the depression of the 1930s, economists and politically active business leaders in France and England, especially, began to recognize that an expanding consumer economy was a politically feasible alternative to what they saw as the "stagnation" of reduced work weeks (as in the proposal for the forty-hour week). Eventually, the tapping of new and unlimited needs (through Keynesianism especially) not only would overcome the threat to the work ethic but guaranteed growth. Growth through mass consumption also meant more jobs (in new sectors like services rather than mining and basic industry), rather than a sharing of work through the reduction of work time. This new thinking had a profound impact on public policy that continues to the present.

A consumerist consensus emerged after 1945. It was built upon mass production and balanced with high wages, but it was also buttressed by governmental management of demand and business manipulation of needs through advertising. Neither work sharing nor expanded noncommercial leisure (based on a theory of limited consumer desire) had any serious role in the postwar recovery. The obvious explanation is that pressing demand for reconstruction and fulfilling pent-up material needs had long been deferred by the depression and war and that this precluded any choice but expanded production and consumption. A political consensus quickly emerged around expectations of "full employment" and unlimited consumption. The nearly universal commitment to higher levels of personal consumption was broadly shared by the left-wing British welfare statists and French economic planners, as well as more conservative Italian and German Christian Democrats. The American model of mass consumption was an alternative to the social rigidity of European culture, which still showed sharp distinctions between the lifestyles of the working and middle classes. Pro-American politicians favored "growth" rather than "protest" over the shares of the economic pie. The identification of liberty with consumer choice and democracy with mass access to goods became the ideal if not always the reality.

Despite critiques of consumerism as a threat to social stability and cultural values, consumption became the principal means of defining self and social relationships for many Europeans in the second half of the twentieth century. Although thinkers, social organizers, and even at times politicians struggled against it, none produced effective alternatives.

Consumer-culture critics like Simmel or Durkheim set up an illusory contrast between the acquiescent and impulsive consumption of the street crowd, on the one hand, and the sober and uplifting cultivation of self and family in the home, on the other. The twentieth century has shown that crowd pleasures were not nearly so self-destructive as once presumed. Critics of modern consumer desire failed to recognize how commodities met psychological and social needs in a transient and increasingly impersonal social world. Goods and purchased experiences provided ways of marking time throughout the year. This became a major role of developments such as the commercialization of Christmas and the packaged vacation that became an important part of European consumer culture after World War II. Consumer products helped identify stages in personal life and communicate status, aspirations, and complaints to others. The distinctive clothing, music, and social pleasures of youth that emerged after the war illustrate this kind of personal expression. Consumption was much more about reading and being read through the goods that one drove, wore, and ate than about unleashing dangerous desires. Rather than creating a frustrated, aggressive crowd that sought unattainable fulfillment in unrestrained longing, mass consumption fostered a relatively passive population quite easily satisfied with the latest fashions, novelties, and "new and improved" gadgets. Anthropologists like Mary Douglas have shown how mass consumption allowed the fulfillment of contradictory longings, the wearing of many roles, and endless experimenting—even if experiences were manufactured to meet consumer expectations and business profitability. Far from developing obsessions and addictions or slipping into the confusion of overchoice as predicted by Durkheim, modern Europeans generally have responded quickly and often happily to the latest display window. What is striking about consumer society is how well adjusted to affluence modern Europeans have become.

Moreover, home and individual "integrity" were not nearly so free of consumerist allures as expected by critics of consumerism. Instead, much of the social meaning of goods was organized around domesticity and the sexual division of labor. A middle-class ideal of male providing and female domestic spending had emerged in the nineteenth century and became in varying degrees an ideal of working families early in the twentieth century. For many, the depression solidified the gender order by revealing its stress points: the wife's domain of domestic spending and the husband's role of provider were undermined during the crisis. The slump showed that neither women nor men wished to abandon these roles, which after the war were reconfirmed (at least for another generation) in the male ideal of breadwinner and the female status as domestic consumer. By the 1960s this sexual division of labor was being replaced by a two-income household, but this too was an adaptation to the economic demands of rising standards of domestic consumption.

Moreover, reinforcing the trend toward domestic and private consumption was the coming of the radio (and later television) and the access of the working classes to cars. Although these goods were slower to penetrate European households than in the United States, in the 1960s and 1970s much of that gap was overcome. For example, in the 1960s television sets in British households increased from 66 percent to 90 percent, and a BBC study in 1974 found that half of leisure time was spent watching the screen. Even more dramatic was the coming of cars: ownership in France rose from 10 percent of households in 1950 to 75 percent by 1980.

A further sign of privatized consumerism was the rise in the share of family income devoted to housing costs. While planners in 1945 hoped for a more open community based on new public housing, Britons largely rejected the tower blocks. Instead, they longed for the suburban comforts of the semidetached houses that provided such opportunities for self-expressive and private consumption. While the French and other continental Europeans had long favored urban apartment living and had been indifferent to Anglo-American lawn and garden culture, during the 1970s new housing was increasingly suburban and detached, and home ownership rose also. Modern consumerism was less a social or cultural challenge to social stability than an affirmation of domestic and intrafamily values.

Consumer society has become a substitute for civil society. The disappointing results of nonprofit religious, political, or simply voluntary leisure organizations are one illustration of this claim. Consumerism met real needs of personal identity and individual distinction from the group in a society where primary groups had largely disappeared. The utopian idea of a culture of free time beyond the market could not satisfy those needs nearly as effectively as could the consumer culture. Ironically, social groups organized around ideas or even leisure activities may be less flexible and more threatening to members than consumer markets. Because noncommercial holiday clubs that appeared early in the twentieth century were dominated by their members, they often unintentionally excluded others, became fractionalized, and were slow to adapt to change. It has been much easier for commercial impresarios like the Butlin Holiday

85

Camps of the 1930s or the Club Meds from the 1950s, which stand outside the markets they organize, to get people to join in. There was less personal risk in disclosing oneself as a "member" of a society of Porsche owners than to risk humiliation by joining a group that demanded personal interaction. It was relatively easy to buy one's way into a community of shoppers, and there were so many from which to choose.

The collapse of European communism in 1989 is a good example of the success of consumerism. For all of its claims of producing full employment and meeting everyone's basic needs for health, education, food, and other necessities, the Marxist system in the 1970s and 1980s was unable either to increase productivity or to meet the widening horizons of desire. The lack of consumer incentives for hard work created a society in permanent slow motion, which consequently could never meet the demand for consumer goods. In the West, the simultaneous discipline and freedom built into the consumer economy was able to do both.

However, consumerism did not eliminate frustration as Jean Gabriel Tarde and other optimists predicted. Through emulative spending, the poor and marginal population might have become more like the rich. But then the elite moved on to new "inventions," creating a new social distance from the masses. When the people had cars, the rich needed second homes. Frustration was inevitable and unrelenting even when the majority enjoyed material security and participated in the consumer culture directed by the rich. They could never catch up, and the closer they seemed to get to the prize, the more humiliating was their inability to grasp it. Resentment hardly declined because of greater material security. The significance of goods that define status (cars, education, vacations, and houses) increased as basic needs were met and with them the increased frustrations of status seeking.

LIMITS AND CHALLENGES TO MODERN CONSUMERISM

Diversity in the history, society, and economic development of European countries produced somewhat different degrees and varieties of consumerism in the second half of the twentieth century. Relative to the more mobile and market-oriented United States, European bonds to community and family have countered consumerist predilections. In countries like Spain, relatively slower rates of economic development limited discretionary spending, at least until the 1990s. Political traditions restricting markets (like prohibit-

ing Sunday shopping) have impeded the spread of consumption as a leisure time activity. Attempts in the 1990s to extend shopping hours in Germany and England, for example, were rebuffed by social conservatives as well as labor unions. Allocations of economic surpluses to public culture (for example, municipal orchestras) and other nonmarket leisure and recreational purposes have also countered the growth of consumerism. Moreover, cultural and historical differences have channeled consumer desire in western Europe in somewhat different directions than in the United States. One prominent example is the greater emphasis on vacation spending, due to four or more weeks of holiday time in most European countries as compared with the common two-week or less vacation of Americans. This difference has its roots in the paid holiday that came to many European countries in the 1920s and especially the 1930s. Another example is the still greater tendency of Europeans to spend discretionary income on public leisure like social dining and drinking.

Since the 1960s European opponents of consumerism have rallied around movements for environmental protection, noncommercial leisure, reduction of work time, and consumer education. According to the political scientist Ronald Inglehart, in the 1960s a "postmaterialist" cohort began to emerge in Europe. The gradual disappearance of those age groups which had been shaped by the economic insecurity of the depression signaled a "cultural shift" toward the post-scarcity values. In the 1960s and 1970s New Left advocates of postmaterialist values expected a political shift from questions of distribution, growth, and security and toward quality of life and consumer rights issues. These groups attacked the compromise of the traditional Left (Labor, Communist, and Social Democratic parties) for its support of the unrestrained growth of a consumer culture.

In particular, the environmental, or green, movement opposed the impact that unrestrained consumption had upon land use (for roads, for example) and pollution of the ecosphere. In the 1970s new leftists associated with the labor movement argued that the linkage between economic growth and jobs was no longer valid. Technological and business change would no longer create sufficient jobs for full employment (as had previous economic upheavals). The computer was eliminating both white collar and blue collar jobs even as it increased productivity, and the older pattern of technological advance, shifting jobs from one sector (like industry) into another (like service), no longer applied. An expanding mass consumption economy would not produce sufficient jobs. For this group, the solution was reduced work time rather than simply increased output and demand for goods. As important, these advocates of reduced work time saw expanded time away from market work as an alternative to the spread of consumerist values.

Still others supported noncommercial uses of leisure time, perpetuating activities dating from before the commercialization of free time and actually expanding alternatives to consumerism. Surveys found that up to 39 percent of Britons participated in a sport in 1977, and in 1980 there were roughly thirty-six thousand football clubs and fifty thousand other sporting clubs. Numbers of sports clubs rose 3.6 times in France in the 1960s and 1970s. During the same period, cultural clubs increased even more dramatically from 600 to 4,116. An active cultural education policy, encouraged first by André Malraux's famous tenure as cultural minister from 1959 to 1969, bore fruit in rising attendance at artistic and educational events. French promoters of popular arts and recreation may have sought to perpetuate loyalty to church or political party, but all stressed wide participation and many eventually lost their political or religious character. Government facilities and educators have contributed to the growth of amateurism in music and the other arts. Sociologists found in the mid-1980s that middle-class people especially still readily joined groups around a wide variety of enthusiasms (caving, morris dancing, lace making, and lapidary, for example). Such organizations stressed their distinction from others but also their solidarity within, and often did so with a militant opposition to commercialization as if in protest of the profit motive of sellers and the passivity of buyers.

Despite these protests against consumerism, there does not appear to be any systematic alternative to its value of limitless material innovation and social and self-definition in and through goods. While many Europeans question the long-term viability of the consumerist ethic for the environment and the seemingly corrosive effect of consumerism on social relations and political commitments, few have seriously questioned the benefits of growth or have found ways of effectively articulating a form of postmaterialism.

See also **America, Americanization, and Anti-Americanism** *(volume 1);* **Capitalism and Commercialization; Communications, the Media and Propaganda; Shops and Stores** *(volume 2);* **Sports; Consumer Leisure; Vacations; Travel and Tourism;** *the section* **Everyday Life** *(all in this volume); and other articles in this section.*

BIBLIOGRAPHY

Adorno, Theodor W., and Max Horkheimer. *Dialectic of Enlightenment.* 1944. Reprint, New York, 1972.

Adshead, Samuel Adrian M. *Material Culture in Europe and China, 1400–1800: The Rise of Consumerism.* New York, 1997.

Auslander, Leora. *Taste and Power: Furnishing Modern France.* Berkeley, Calif., 1996.

Bailey, Peter. *Leisure and Class in Victorian England: Rational Recreation and the Contest for Control, 1830–1885.* London, 1978.

Brantlinger, Patrick. *Bread and Circuses. Theories of Mass Culture as Social Decay.* Ithaca, N.Y., 1983.

Brentano, Lujo. *Hours and Wages in Relation to Production.* Translated by Mrs. William Arnold. London, 1894.

Brewer, John, and Roy Porter, eds. *Consumption and the World of Goods.* London, 1993.

Campbell, Colin. *The Romantic Ethic and the Spirit of Modern Consumerism.* Oxford, 1989.

Cross, Gary. *Time and Money: The Making of Consumer Culture.* New York and London, 1993.

De Grazia, Victoria. *Culture of Consent: Mass Organization of Leisure in Fascist Italy.* Cambridge, U.K., 1981.

Douglas, Mary, and Baron Isherwood. *The World of Goods.* New York, 1979.

Dumazedier, Joffre. *Révolution culturelle du temps libre: 1968–1988.* Paris, 1968.

Furlough, Ellen. *Consumer Cooperation in France: The Politics of Consumption, 1834–1930.* Ithaca, N.Y., 1991.

Gorz, André. *Critique of Economic Reason.* London, 1989.

Hirsch, Fred. *The Social Limits to Growth.* Cambridge, Mass., 1976

Hoggett, Paul, and Jeff Bishop. *Organizing around Enthusiasms: Patterns of Mutual Aid in Leisure.* London, 1986.

Inglehart, Ronald. *Culture Shift in Advanced Industrial Society.* Princeton, N.J., 1990.

Kenseth, Joy, ed. *The Age of the Marvelous.* Hanover, N.H., 1991.

Kuisel, Richard F. *Seducing the French: The Dilemma of Americanization.* Berkeley, Calif., 1993.

Le Bon, Gustave. *The Crowd.* 1896. Reprint, New Brunswick, N.J., 1995.

LeMahieu, D. I. *Culture for Democracy: Mass Communications and the Cultivated Mind in Britain between the Wars.* New York and Oxford, 1988.

Mckendrick, Neil, John Brewer, and J. H. Plumb. *The Birth of Consumer Society: The Commercialization of Eighteenth-Century England.* Bloomington, Ind., 1982.

Miller, Michael B. *The Bon Marché: Bourgeois Culture and the Department Store, 1869–1920.* Princeton, N.J., 1981.

Mukerji, Chandra. *From Graven Images: Patterns of Modern Materialism.* New York, 1983.

Richards, Thomas. *The Commodity Culture of Victorian England.* Stanford, Calif., 1990.

Schama, Simon. *The Embarrassment of Riches: An Interpretation of Dutch Culture in the Golden Age.* New York, 1987.

Walton, Whitney. *France at the Crystal Palace.* Berkeley, Calif., 1992.

Williams, Rosalind. *Dream Worlds: Mass Consumption in Late-Nineteenth-Century France.* Berkeley, Calif., 1982.

DRINKING AND DRUGS

Thomas Brennan

The history of drink since the Renaissance consists of profound continuities and abrupt changes. The consumption of alcohol is as old as civilization and has provided a reliable backdrop in every age to ritual, festival, commensality, and sociability. Every European culture has long-standing drinking customs. In addition each culture has had its own traditional drinks, determined by climate and reinforced by prejudice, that remained remarkably unchanged despite the new kinds of alcohol made available through the commercial and industrial revolutions of the last two centuries. Public drinking places have enhanced the social impact of drinking, even as they have focused much of the opposition to drinking. At the same time the details of what, where, when, and how people drank could change a good deal, and the consideration of drugs introduces a further element of innovation. Both continuity and change demand attention, for they are equally essential to understanding the roles of alcohol and drugs.

Historians study drink as a food, a commodity, a social ritual, and a social problem. As an aseptic beverage delivering crucial vitamins and calories, alcohol in some form has long been a dietary staple. Thus alcohol was an important commodity—probably the single most important commercial item in medieval and early modern France, for example—and contributes to the growing interest in the history of trade and markets. The economics of producing and distributing wine, beer, or spirits put alcohol at the forefront of commercial and financial innovations in the eighteenth and nineteenth centuries. Above and beyond its dietary significance, alcohol teaches us about taste and fashion, about self-expression and social identity through consumption.

Although historians study drink as an important element in the history of diet, it is the cultural significance of drink that draws most interest. Whether people drink champagne at celebrations, the right wine with foods, a beer with buddies, brandy to warm up, a cocktail to relax, or gin to drown their sorrows, the alcohol consumed has always been laden with symbolism. Alcohol conveys precise messages about mood, intention, and expectations both to ourselves and to others. Alcohol sanctions specific behavior, including revel, riot, and altercation, of course, but also trust and reconciliation. As such alcohol has been a fundamental element in popular culture, but as popular culture came under increasing criticism in early modern history, alcohol was condemned. With the rise of living standards and the increasing access to markets in the nineteenth century, the lower classes consumed more alcohol, and the authorities became increasingly concerned about the alcohol "problem."

EARLY PRODUCTION AND CONSUMPTION

Europe inherited an economy of local alcohol production and consumption from the Middle Ages. Most medieval communities produced some form of alcohol by fermenting grapes, fruit, or grain and drank the results themselves. Brewing was a domestic task throughout northern Europe, often performed by housewives. Historians of medieval England argue for large consumption levels of a weakly alcoholic ale. As a drink or a soup, it was a staple. In northern Germany and, more gradually, across the Netherlands and England, wholesale brewers in the late Middle Ages made a beer with hops that contained more alcohol and stood up to storage and travel better than the ale it increasingly replaced. Beer making, an essentially artisanal and male occupation, replaced the largely feminine ale making with a more commercial product and more commercial consumption.

Vineyards proliferated throughout medieval France, Italy, and southern Germany, though in most cases their wine was quite mediocre and was meant for local consumption. Widespread demand and inadequate transportation encouraged communities to produce for themselves. But wine was also a commercial commodity where it had access to waterborne transportation, and it supplied a large market of urban

In the Pub. Dock workers relax in a pub near the Port of London's King George V Dock. Photograph by Charles Hewitt, 28 February 1948. ©HULTON GETTY/LIASON AGENCY

and rural elites in the northern countries. England's control of southwestern France helped establish a massive export of wine through Bordeaux in the Middle Ages. After losing France in the Hundred Years' War, England helped create new supplies in Spain and the Canaries. The Dutch replaced English merchants looking for wine along the west coast of France in the sixteenth century and shipped the wine throughout northern Europe. Improvements in commercial practices and transportation by 1600 led many areas, particularly in the north, to give up their vineyards. Wine production became specialized, and a sophisticated wine trade made wine available for elite consumption and supplied towns throughout Europe.

The evidence for consumption levels is not readily available before the modern era except occasionally for some towns. Levels of consumption in beer-drinking countries may have reached as much as a liter a day by the sixteenth and seventeenth centuries; the estimates for England and Germany are 250 to 400 liters per year. The inhabitants of certain medieval towns in France, Spain, and the Netherlands may have already reached that level, consuming nearly as much alcohol in one hundred liters of wine, but residents of towns generally drank more than people living in the countryside. Residents of Hamburg in the sixteenth century are credited with drinking seven hundred liters of beer annually. By the eighteenth century many towns in France were consuming as much as two hundred liters of wine per year. Drinking habits in the countryside are much debated, but clearly rural people

drank less than people in towns. English and German peasants continued to brew much of their own beer until the nineteenth century, and those in the vine-growing regions of France drank their own wine or a mildly alcoholic *piquette* (thin wine) made by adding water to pressed grapes. Peasants elsewhere in France are routinely described as drinking nothing but water.

Of course, the overall amounts of alcohol consumed tell only a part of the story. The manner of consumption is equally important to understanding the cultural significance of alcohol. In many societies alcohol joined other foods as a regular part of meals. Drinking often punctuated the rhythms of work in shops and at work sites, and employers frequently provided drink to agricultural workers. Drink also had ritual significance as a "social marker" that set festive times apart from daily rhythms and united drinkers in fellowship. Many villages maintained the custom of church ales into the seventeenth century, and urban revelries of carnival or formal entries always featured alcohol. In many northern cultures a common practice was toasting or pledging *(zutrinken)* then draining glasses in round after round, which encouraged binge drinking. A culture of binge drinking usually consumes less alcohol overall than a culture that consumes alcohol frequently in modest quantities, yet binge drinking is more obvious and troubling to observers. The Germans and to a lesser extent the English gained a bad reputation for their drinking customs.

Attacks on intemperance have a long and distinguished place in European literature, but they took on a sharper tone in the Reformation with religious efforts to instill moral and social discipline. Writers like Martin Luther, Desiderius Erasmus, and Michel Eyquem de Montaigne in the sixteenth century condemned drunkenness while praising wine taken in moderation. The critics at this stage made little distinction between the excesses of upper or lower classes, though Germans as a culture were generally singled out for particular opprobrium. The Germans themselves produced an elaborate and extensive literature of censure, denouncing the drinking that led to violence, loss of self-control, suffering for the wife and children, and a variety of excesses in their efforts to impose moral discipline. Criticism in following centuries became increasingly class based, as much of the popular culture was subjected to growing condemnation and criminalization. An additional theme in this literature directed particular disapproval at taverns as the focus of dissolute behavior.

The place in which alcohol is consumed is even more important to its cultural impact than the manner of its consumption. Thus the spread of public drinking places in the Renaissance shaped and magnified the social impact of alcohol. Although inns and taverns existed in medieval England, mostly selling wine and catering to an elite clientele, ale was generally sold off the premises, usually by small-scale brewers who produced only intermittently. The simple drink sellers of the Middle Ages, whether an alewife selling out of her home or a vine grower with a bush over his door, were increasingly replaced with more elaborate retail shops by the Renaissance. Most obvious in towns, change was in part due to the growing commercialization of beer making and the wine trade. But alehouses and taverns also provided a particular kind of public space and the sociability of public drinking. Thus even in villages a tavern offered a room and some chairs for those assembling to drink. Although public drinking places came in many different forms, all played important social and cultural roles.

Public drinking places are the best though not the only setting for studying the culture of drink. Drinking in taverns and alehouses was particularly ritualized, and public drinking places established an identity that transcended the mere fact of drink. Across Europe they became a haven for masculine sociability, an extension as well as an alternative to work, and a theater of honor and competition. Drinking rituals emphasized belonging and sharing; drinks offered and reciprocated conveyed important information about social relations. The money spent on drinking in groups has been identified as a form of investment in sociocultural reproduction, the creation of social capital in the bonds of work and neighbor-

hood. The drinking group formed around tavern tables, whose appearance in taverns during the Renaissance was thus crucial to expressing and maintaining this dynamic. Some historians have identified tavern sociability as more "fragmented" than traditional village festivals and community because it formed around small groups. Yet towns offered little alternative to such groups, which could grow quite large when guild members assembled.

Studies of public drinking across time and cultures find numerous similarities in the basic patterns of sociability and reciprocity. People drank in groups, mostly of men who knew each other and shared the identities of work or neighborhood. Women in taverns were rare. The drinking group was carefully defined, and admission or rejection from the group was often the most important currency of tavern society. A drink offered was repaid, though the redistribution of drink was sometimes accomplished by games of chance. Gaming, eating, occasionally dancing—though less often in the cramped space of a neighborhood tavern than in the holiday atmosphere of a country *guinguette* or large tavern—might accompany drinking, but the essence of public drinking was communication. The drink offered or refused spoke volumes, but around all the drinking, although rarely preserved, was the talking. Complaints to the police immortalized some of the talk. The insults, slanders, and verbal aggression that violated norms of *honnêteté* (honesty and decency) were public offenses that had to be protested for the sake of one's reputation.

Insults were not uncommon, for the tavern encouraged competitive, even violent behavior. The disinhibiting effects of alcohol, inspired by a combination of chemistry and cultural expectations, clearly

Sixteenth-Century Drinkers. Detail from a choir stall in the church at Montreal-sur-Serein (Yonne), France, by the Rigoley brothers, 1526. LAUROS-GIRAUDON/ART RESOURCE

contributed to the "disorderly" behavior that figures prominently in both contemporary depictions and modern studies of taverns. The conundrum of masculine violence transcended the tavern, of course, but public drinking was repeatedly connected to this violence. Yet it is important to recognize the fundamental order that shaped violence and contestation; over and over the sources reveal the obsessive challenges to and defense of masculine honor. As a public commodity given shape and substance by public reputation and recognition, honor had particular urgency in a public forum. Whether honor represented the sexual features of patriarchal authority and control of womenfolk or the economic imperatives of paying debts and keeping one's word, it depended on the demonstration and approbation of the community. The rituals of drinking leant themselves to the communication of honor endorsed or undercut. The ironic toasts, the "drunken" if quite deliberate slanders, and the refusals to recognize or extend an invitation were more likely to be conscious expressions of social and communal relations than accidents of the drink. If fights escalated more rapidly into murderous rages under the influence of alcohol, they obeyed careful rules of primitive duels.

It is not hard to see why the authorities harbored deep reservations about public drinking places. In addition to the violence that erupted in masculine assemblies, public drinking places were semantically linked to the "public women" and floating poor who lacked private, domestic space. Every society attempted to regulate access, setting a curfew and closing drink shops during the Sabbath. French ordinances from the Middle Ages through the sixteenth century attempted, with obvious lack of success, to exclude local residents from using taverns. They finally gave up the effort in the seventeenth century. Owners were pressured to exclude criminals, prostitutes, drunkards, and other undesirables. Police records contain little evidence of the underworld tavern or its criminal denizens, yet the tavern still enjoyed a poor reputation. Even its respectable clients threatened the social order with their expenditures on leisure and consumption. Religious institutions castigated taverns as counterchurches, "devil's altars" that took men from their Sunday obligations, deprived them of their sense of decorum, and exposed them to lewd behavior. Church and state were not alone in distrusting public drinking; even popular culture demanded a careful balance in the use of taverns. Honor and basic sociability required the laboring classes to spend some time in taverns with their peers, yet wives and artisans alike joined the police in condemning those who wasted their time and money there.

At the same time the revenue brought in from taxing alcohol sold wholesale to merchants or retailed in taverns represented a major part of a community's budget. For that reason towns rarely matched practice to rhetoric and did nothing significant to reduce drinking in taverns. Similarly in early modern France taxes on the sale of wine at every stage of the wine trade made up a significant proportion of the state's income, a fact that ultimately persuaded the state to accept a surprisingly laissez-faire attitude toward wine merchants. Throughout modern Europe the economic interests of beer, wine, and spirits producers resisted attempts to regulate drinking. The official and elite rhetoric condemning drinking and taverns, which has remained the staple of so many histories of alcohol, must be balanced by the far more complex realities of competing interests.

TRANSFORMATIONS

The culture of drinking underwent an abrupt transformation in the seventeenth century with the rapid proliferation of different drinking options. In a startling coincidence of innovations, the range of drink choices suddenly multiplied and with it the places in which one could drink. The newcomers included new types of wine, such as sparkling champagne and aged or fortified wines, and a new type of alcohol, that is, distilled alcohol, or spirits. The most popular of these new drinks, coffee, tea, and chocolate, were neither alcoholic nor indigenous. Indeed they are not usually considered under the rubric of "drinking," and writers concerned about temperance often suggested them as alternatives to alcohol. Each is a mild drug with effects identified variously as sobering, desiccating, destimulating, and eroticizing. To their number should be added that most successful drug of all, tobacco. In England the consumption of tobacco rose rapidly to a level of two pounds per person by the end of the seventeenth century, a rate at which most people could smoke a pipeful a day. It remained at that level through most of the eighteenth century. Tea and coffee became items of daily consumption in much of Europe during the eighteenth century.

The reasons for this bonanza are not too complicated. The late seventeenth century was also a period of commercial revival and the spread of commercial wealth. Countries like England, Holland, and France began to draw upon the goods available in non-European markets. Just as important, their societies experienced an influx of commercial wealth that helped create a powerful, self-conscious mercantile class that defined itself in part through its consumption patterns. Coffee and chocolate became the drinks of the middle and upper classes, who were equally eager to consume the expensive paraphernalia that went with domestic preparation. Many contemporaries saw the contrast between the sobriety of the new commodities and the drunkenness produced by alcohol as metaphors for the growing gap between the elite and popular cultures. Yet the same elites helped to transform the wine trade. Their desire for luxuries propelled the creation of sparkling champagne and the development of aging in bottles. The British elites played a disproportionate role in stimulating the development of port and madeira in Iberian markets as well as brandy in France.

Along with new kinds of drink came new places to drink them. Cafés and coffeehouses appearing throughout Europe in the second half of the seventeenth century served many of these new drinks. Presenting themselves through their furnishings as more refined and sedate than taverns, these establishments consciously appealed to a more respectable clientele. In England, France, and Holland they became assemblies for discussing news and business; the English turned some of them into semiofficial business addresses. The English coffeehouses in particular have been identified by historians as the epicenter of a "public sphere," where the communication and identity necessary for civil society found its roots. The Parisian café developed its business and political identity rather more timidly. Cafés certainly had a more elite, literate clientele than did taverns, and the Parisian police spent some energy spying on the political sedition and subversive speech heard in them. But civil society in Old Regime France remained tied largely to domestic salons and to a "public" that existed more in the imaginations of writers than in any public places.

The premodern history of these new substances repeats and reinforces certain interesting patterns. As exotic and originally quite expensive commodities, they appealed to elite consumers who were aware of a wider world of goods and wished to demonstrate their refinement. The new stimulants were initially controversial but soon enjoyed strong support as healthful and medically useful agents. They were rapidly incorporated into domestic consumption and spread from there to public places and public consumption, at which point they began to undergo a process of gendering. Coffee and tobacco became largely male stimulants associated with public drinking places and male sociability, whereas chocolate remained domestic and largely feminine. Men smoked in taverns and coffeehouses; in elite houses men and some women gathered in smoking rooms. The rituals

of snuff taking that emerged in the eighteenth century were even more elaborate, with expensive paraphernalia that allowed the elites to turn snuff into an upper-class alternative to smoking. Through much of the eighteenth century coffee was identified by the male, bourgeois qualities of reason and sobriety and chocolate by the female, aristocratic qualities of indolence and sensuality. Tea ultimately transcended gender and class and became in England a commodity of universal demand.

Among the popular classes the experience of drinking began to change at more or less the same time. The urban populace, particularly in the major cities, was not far behind the elites in adopting coffee, tea, and tobacco and probably preceded them in the widespread use of spirits. Spirits had been distilled from wine and grain since the Middle Ages and were consumed as medicinal treatments for a variety of physical and emotional ills. In addition to warming and fortifying, spirits served as an anesthetic. It is impossible to determine the amount of spirits consumed before the modern era, but the history of opium in England indicates that drugs were a regular part of popular medicine yet were limited to the purpose of self-medication. Spirits apparently were not drunk socially in the Middle Ages.

Opium had been known and used in Europe since antiquity but never in much quantity. Identified overwhelmingly with its medicinal qualities, the drug offered little more than analgesic aid until almost the nineteenth century. In various forms, but most often as laudanum, opium dulled pain, quieted coughs and children, calmed nerves, and improved digestion. Cheap and easily accessible through the early modern period, it became a staple of popular self-medication. Seemingly it was rarely taken recreationally and was not thought of as addictive. Some evidence indicates that opium consumption was increasing during the first half of the nineteenth century in England, but only a small core of bohemian society used the drug recreationally and articulated a new aesthetic of drug taking.

Clear evidence exists, however, that the medicinal model of spirit consumption was breaking down in sixteenth-century Germany and was replaced by recreational use. The growing number of distilleries in many German and later Dutch towns was matched by increasing complaints of alcohol abuse—less an indication of quantities consumed than of cognitive dissonance over the manner of its use. The process was gradual, and for a long time spirits were consumed in different places and in different ways than was beer or wine. People bought brandy in the morning from sellers who offered no seating, and they did

Hogarthian Horror. "The Tavern Scene," plate 3 from *The Rake's Progress* by William Hogarth (1697–1764). ©BURSTEIN COLLECTION/CORBIS

not drink it socially. By the late seventeenth century, however, the populations of northern Europe were consuming spirits on a regular basis and, perhaps more important, they were drinking it in taverns and treating it like other drinks. Yet as spirits were assimilated into the culture of public drinking, they threatened to disrupt it.

The first sign of crisis came in England with the phenomenon known as "mother gin." The statistics for alcohol consumption reveal a clear surge in the consumption of gin through the first half of the eighteenth century from less than a liter per capita to nearly five liters, much of it concentrated in London. Yet the meaning of this occurrence has been wrapped in polemics since it was first observed. Famous prints by William Hogarth capture the horror induced among the elite by the spread of gin drinking among the London poor. His images of infanticide, debauchery, and decay summarize all too effectively the respectable view of popular drinking. Yet the historian of drink learns quickly to question the perceptions of drinking behavior. Although some historians point to the elevated levels of gin consumption to support Hogarth's depiction, others suggest that the new liquor's novelty, its appearance in new forms of drink shops, and its

popularity among the lowest classes because it was cheap account for much of the opprobrium.

Mother Gin offers a useful example of changes in drink culture, many of whose elements were repeated in the following century. The increasing consumption of gin apparently was tied to rising income rather than misery. Gin retailers, many of them women, belonged to a lower class of sellers, who were unable to set up an alehouse with its increasingly expensive license, furnishings, and commercial requirements. Gin shops, differing from alehouses or taverns, seem a throwback in some ways to the medieval drink shop with little or no interior, sociable space. Some evidence suggests that women figured prominently among gin drinkers, a function both of gin's origins in popular self-medication and of the sex of so many retailers. Thus gin made alcohol consumption available to a wider clientele; even women and the poor could drink alcohol for a modest outlay. But a new beverage drunk in a new setting without familiar rituals by women and a social level that enjoyed little but contempt was a recipe for the elites' moral panic as well as perhaps the immoral behavior of the populace.

Elsewhere the changes in popular drinking patterns were more subtle and less threatening. Within

Paris new shops selling spirits to a popular clientele slowly appeared, but the amount of spirits brought into Paris during the eighteenth century was still quite modest. Wine overwhelmingly remained the drink of the populace. In the late seventeenth century many Parisian wine merchants moved outside of the city's boundaries and created the *guinguette*—a large, boisterous country tavern where city people came to play on holidays. Guinguettes aimed at a popular clientele but provided a more commercialized, anonymous form of entertainment than did the neighborhood tavern. In France, as in Britain and the German states, the increasing variegation of drinking places accompanied a growing segregation of classes and cultures and soon led to conflict over drinking culture.

Industrialization in the nineteenth century brought new and sometimes disturbing changes to drinking patterns, but to exaggerate the impact of modernization is dangerous. Some of the changes were largely a matter of perception, many of them built on continuities with the past. The consumption of alcohol, particularly of spirits, increased, in some cases dramatically, due to more disposable income, the prevalence of cheaper "industrial" spirits, and the modernization of the countryside. Patterns of drinking in public may also have changed with the introduction of "bar" counters and the spread of solitary drinking. Some argued that such changes in quantity and manners of drinking spelled the death of tradi-

tional forms and the rise of a new and brutal sort of alcohol consumption. The idea of "alcoholism," invented in the middle of the nineteenth century, became a specter haunting Europe. With the concurrent criminalization and medicalization of drinking abuses came the emergence of temperance movements to combat the new evil. The recreational use of other drugs also increased, but this phenomenon could hardly compete with alcohol for the attention of social reformers and critics.

Alcohol became readily available to all as a revolution in transportation, beginning with canals at the turn of the century and rapidly augmented by railroads, created national markets across the Continent. Wine produced in the south of France was shipped north and sold for less than many of the local wines, like those of lower Burgundy, which rapidly disappeared in the face of competition. Regions that never before produced or consumed wine could buy it cheaply, and wine became as much a part of peasants' diets as of city dwellers'. At the same time, the industrial revolution made newer forms of alcohol vastly cheaper and more available. The price of grain declined steadily through the century, driving farmers to look for alternative uses. They distilled their grain or planted their grain fields with potatoes and sugar beets, which they also distilled. The prices of such "industrial" spirits, in the form of schnapps, gin, vodka, or whiskey dropped sharply through the cen-

Kvass Seller. Kvass, an alcoholic beverage made from fermented cereal grains and bread, is sold from a container on a Moscow street, August 1964. Customers bring their own mugs.
L. Porter, Fotokhronika, TASS/Sovfoto

tury, making a powerful alcohol available to the working classes.

Industrial spirits became remarkably popular within a short time. Workers found warmth, stimulation, and calories from an affordable luxury at a time, in the early nineteenth century, when their diets were poor and even deteriorating. When standards of living improved, the producers found ways to give their spirits interesting flavors and spent equal energy creating an interesting aura through advertising. They mixed alcohol made from grain or sugar beets with various herbs like juniper, gentian, quinine, anise, and mint and fruits like orange and cherry, and sugar. To the distinctive flavors producers added a distinctive look and elaborate claims of health-giving properties. Advertising insisted on the "digestive" and "tonic" effects of these drinks and suggested the time, place, and style of their consumption.

One of the most successful examples of the marketing of new spirits is the infamous case of absinthe. A green liquid with flavors of anise and wormwood, absinthe became the favorite drink of the bohemian middle class in the mid-nineteenth century. The drink, known as the "green fairy," was quickly surrounded with rituals and a whole culture of consumption. Only with the worst of the phylloxera crisis in the 1880s, when wine was rare and expensive, did absinthe become a drink for the working class, and its sales tripled within a decade. Suddenly the middle class became alarmed at "absinthism." Once in the hands of the lower classes, the drink was seen as a pernicious and poisonous substance capable of unbalancing the weaker constitutions and morals of an already degenerate populace. That absinthe was particularly popular among women only enhanced the fear of its attractions and ravages. But absinthe and the response to absinthism are simply a model, somewhat exaggerated, of the nineteenth-century careers of alcohol and alcoholism.

The usual assumption is that the century that invented alcoholism was a time of historically high rates of consumption, and the statistics in many European countries seem to show an increase in the consumption of alcohol through most of the nineteenth century. The French offer a dramatic example of this trend. Between the 1830s and the end of the century, they doubled the amount of wine and beer they drank per year from roughly 80 and 12 liters, respectively, to 160 and 28 liters. In the same period, their consumption of spirits more than doubled to the equivalent of four liters of pure (proof) alcohol. Total consumption of pure alcohol reached a peak of some twenty-one liters in the first decade of the twentieth century. The British and Germans peaked in their al-

cohol consumption earlier, in the 1870s, and at lower levels, perhaps fourteen liters of total alcohol in Britain and ten liters in Germany, but roughly half of that was in the form of spirits. Yet the trends in these two countries suggest that their nineteenth-century drinking levels were less of a break with their own histories than is often assumed.

Beer drinking in Germany and Britain rose in the second half of the century but had already declined through the first half. In Britain the high point of some 150 liters per capita was probably no higher than at the beginning of the century and well below the estimates for early-eighteenth-century consumption of three or four hundred liters. Germans, too, probably consumed less beer at the height of the nineteenth century than they had in earlier centuries, though the consumption of spirits, which reached a peak in the 1870s, may have made up for it. The per capita consumption of spirits in Britain rose in the first half of the century to more than five liters (proof), but this merely returned consumption to what it had been in the middle of the eighteenth century before the authorities clamped down on the gin "epidemic." Moreover the trend in British drinking was distorted by the impact of Scottish and Irish drinking. Irish and Scottish production of spirits, which must have reflected local consumption, nearly doubled and tripled through the first half of the century to six and eleven liters per capita respectively, though much of this increase was probably due to illicit stills that agreed to pay a more moderate tax. In contrast, per capita production of spirits in England and Wales rose slowly through the century from roughly two liters to three.

Even the figures for France, which seem to indicate a spectacular rise in per capita consumption of alcohol through the nineteenth century, hide a more complicated reality and, when examined in greater detail, reveal continuity with the past. Urban consumption in France, for example, had increased relatively little since the seventeenth and eighteenth centuries. In particular the consumption of wine remained at roughly two hundred liters per person until the late nineteenth century. If urban consumption remained relatively unchanged, urbanization and a basic shift in the consumption patterns in the countryside apparently drove the growth in per capita drinking of the nation as a whole. People in towns had long imbibed far more wine than those in the countryside. As peasants left the villages for the cities, they learned to drink like city dwellers. Those peasants who remained in the villages became part of an increasingly commercial economy that gave them easier access to alcohol, though the level of rural consumption was still roughly half the urban level by the end of the century.

Although urban consumption of traditional fermented drink remained largely unchanged between the eighteenth and nineteenth centuries, the consumption of spirits in French cities rose dramatically in the nineteenth century. Parisians consumed only 1.5 liters (proof) of brandy at the time of the Revolution but reached 5 liters by mid-century and more than 7 liters by the end of the century. The other major cities of France lagged behind this trend only slightly. Here, then, is most of the increase in urban consumption of alcohol, though even with the increased consumption of spirits, the total alcohol drunk by the average adult city dweller rose by little more than a third between the 1820s and 1890s. The consumption of spirits was largely confined to the north of France, which neither produced nor generally consumed wine. Northern France drank three and four times more than the rest of the country throughout the nineteenth century. The same disparity between wine-making regions and those that consumed spirits existed in Britain and in the northern regions of Germany, areas too cold to grow wine grapes, that accounted for the bulk of spirits consumption.

TEMPERANCE

In the end the changes in drinking patterns were to a large extent more apparent than real. But what was apparent to much of respectable society was the sharp increase in the consumption of spirits. Spirits became the source of much consternation and provided the primary impetus to most of the temperance agitation throughout the century. The gin panic was repeated across Europe with the same visions of depravity, family breakdown, and physical and social deterioration, particularly among the working class. The loudest cries of alarm were initially religious. In many Protestant countries religious groups formed movements in the 1830s and 1840s to combat the rise of spirits consumption and to rescue the working classes from what was seen as a particularly noxious evil. The movement against alcohol in France came later and, initially, from medical practitioners. With these movements the discourse about alcohol shifted from that of the premodern period. Drunkenness had always been condemned, of course, but public drunkenness and, even more, public drinking places drew the greatest ire. By the nineteenth century spirits—and in some eyes any alcohol—had become a poison regardless of when or where they were taken. Drink was destroying the moral fiber, the health, and the house-

hold economy of the working class. It also seemed to harm the work process now that employers revered a more regular pace and workers operated more dangerous machinery. The workers' private vices turned out to have very public disadvantages.

The rhetoric of physical and moral toxicity found an echo in the labeling of drug abuse as a medical problem. That reaction occurred nearly simultaneously with the invention of alcoholism and for similar reasons. Although opiates had not become a serious problem among the working classes, the same combination of medicalization and moral crusade that produced a temperance movement yielded a movement against drugs in the second half of the nineteenth century. The moral crusade drew much of its fervor from the recognition of the injustices of the opium trade with China. But the language of the movement expressed the same condemnation of working-class culture—of its lack of thrift, self-discipline, and sobriety—that shaped temperance movements. The mid-century proliferation of morphine, a stronger derivative of opium, provoked medical concerns regarding toxicity and addiction, much as the rise of spirits consumption gave birth to the idea of alcoholism, even though morphine was particularly associated with an elite and feminine clientele. The model of drug addiction, once employed to characterize morphine use, was then gradually extended to all drugs.

Temperance movements aimed first at abstention from spirits, sometimes by promoting traditional forms of alcohol in their stead. Indeed the French understood alcoholism as a problem of "alcohol," which for them meant only spirits, whereas Germany and Britain wrestled with the question of whether to extend abstention to all forms of alcohol or just spirits. Britain moved wholeheartedly beyond an antispirits position in the mid-nineteenth century. After a brief phase of antispirits agitation, the temperance movement swung sharply toward teetotalism and prohibition.

All these movements aimed at an alcohol problem whose dimensions in the nineteenth century are still much debated. The temperance movements founded in the 1830s in Germany and Britain coincided with a period of considerable misery for the working class. But that misery was caused more by industrialization and urbanization than by alcohol consumption, which was actually stagnating or even declining. The evidence cited by temperance movements for growing public drunkenness and alcohol-induced madness were largely artifacts of greater police repression and medical attention. Their objections to popular drinking practices reflected the fundamental clash between respectable middle-class values of

Anti-Liquor Demonstration. Children carry anti-alcohol posters in Moscow, October 1930. ©BETTMANN/CORBIS

thrift and discipline and the demands of popular sociability. Undoubtedly elevated alcohol consumption had health consequences, particularly cirrhosis of the liver, and some lives were ruined by drink in a complex interaction with economic and cultural deprivation. But drink was demonized in so systematic and pervasive a fashion and it so rapidly came to represent all society's ills that clearly more drove the temperance movements than simply the unhappy fate of alcohol abusers.

Controversies over where people drank continued to fuel the urgency of the drink question. In Britain public drinking places became the targets of the temperance movements when they shifted toward prohibition. After an early surge of enthusiasm, the temperance movements reached a plateau of popular support and turned, in the second half of the century, to legal means of restricting access to drink. The number of drinking places grew considerably through the middle of the century, though that increase did not keep pace with the population's growth. Therefore, proportionately fewer pubs operated than had in the seventeenth century. Nationally and locally teetotal agitation focused on efforts to close drink sellers on Sundays and to reduce the number of licensed sellers altogether. The declining social status of the average pub patron certainly made this strategy more attractive.

In the early modern world religious criticism depicted public drinking places as opposed to churches and the Sabbath and distinguishing the saints and the

sinners. Public drinking places became a symbol of class divisions in the modern world. The number of French drink sellers quintupled during the nineteenth century, and the number in Paris rose tenfold. The proliferation of public drinking places and of the exuberant, sometimes drunken behavior of the working classes who drank there heightened the concerns of the social elite about an alcoholic populace. The fact that women were more likely to drink in public in the nineteenth century than in earlier centuries added to the scandal. Drinking in public was also increasingly politicized during the nineteenth century as drinking places became a focus and rallying point for popular political activity.

Cafés inherited the mantle of Enlightenment dissent but were gradually democratized in their decor, their clientele, and their politics. Now workers came there to read newspapers and draft petitions, and workers formed political clubs in the back rooms of cafés. In the French cafés called *goguettes,* workers found a place to sing radical songs. Many German taverns offered meeting space to Socialist groups who had few alternative places to congregate. Tavern keepers were prominent in the elected leadership of the Socialist Party. Through a succession of revolutions, cafés served as rallying points, field stations, and headquarters. Not surprisingly, a succession of regimes took measures against cafés.

The state's traditional distrust of public drinking places was vindicated, and the state responded harshly. Police units devoted specifically to keeping a close eye on cafés looked not only for drunken and disreputable behavior but also for signs of political radicalism. Granted power to shut down subversive cafés by Napoleon III and again following the Commune, the French police duly closed tens of thousands of establishments. Their reports of cafés closed for "bad morals," for being "frequented by drunkards," or as a "meeting place of radicals" reveal the layering and ultimate blending of the traditional language of drink and debauchery with the language of political dissent.

The failure or at best very limited success of the temperance movements reveals the complexity of the social challenge they faced. Their greatest successes usually came early, when they preached temperance to private, usually religious forums. There they found middle-class and some working-class enthusiasm for a message of personal discipline and reform, but the message had little impact on the society or the drink problem as a whole. As each temperance movement turned toward legislative reform, it ran into the political resistance of wealthy, often aristocratic distillers, small shopkeepers and retailers, and the working-class parties. In the crisis atmosphere of World War I, French reformers achieved a few notable successes against absinthe and the proliferation of drink sellers. But the impact of temperance movements throughout Europe was more gradual, less through legislation than through example. Slowly the discussion of the drink question raised people's awareness and promoted at least a more moderate use of alcohol if not abstinence.

In much of Europe alcohol consumption fell sharply in the first half of the twentieth century. Spirits had reached a peak in the 1870s in Britain and Germany, and they filled fewer glasses in France as well after the turn of the century. British and German beer consumption had increased toward the end of the nineteenth century but declined in the first half of the twentieth. By the 1970s, however, Germans had essentially doubled the amount of beer they drank and were consuming unprecedented amounts of wine. In the second half of the twentieth century the British, too, reversed the decline, though levels remained below those of the eighteenth and nineteenth centuries. By historical standards, this was still moderate drinking. At the same time the French drank ever more wine, except when they were at war or recovering from it. They continued to drink at elevated levels until the 1970s, when they began to taper off. But in France as elsewhere a more momentous change in the culture of drink was the decline of the public drinking place. Facing increasing competition from home entertainment, pubs and cafés began closing. Whether public drinking places were a public nuisance or a prop of popular culture, Europe ended the twentieth century with fewer of them.

See also **Alcohol and Temperance** *(volume 3);* **Food and Diet** *(in this volume); and other articles in this section.*

BIBLIOGRAPHY

Albrecht, Peter. "Coffee-Drinking as a Symbol of Change in the Seventeenth and Eighteenth Centuries." *Studies in Eighteenth-Century Culture* 18 (1988): 91–103.

Austin, Gregory A. *Alcohol in Western Society from Antiquity to 1800.* Santa Barbara, Calif., 1985.

Barrows, Susanna, and Robin Room, eds. *Drinking: Behavior and Belief in Modern History.* Berkeley, Calif., 1991.

Bennett, Judith M. *Ale, Beer, and Brewsters in England: Women's Work in a Changing World, 1300–1600.* New York, 1996.

Berridge, Virginia, and Griffith Edwards. *Opium and the People: Opiate Use in Nineteenth-Century England.* London and New York, 1981.

Brennan, Thomas. *Public Drinking and Popular Culture in Eighteenth-Century Paris.* Princeton, N.J., 1988.

Brennan, Thomas. "Towards the Cultural History of Alcohol in France." *Journal of Social History* 23 (1989): 71–92.

Brennan, Thomas. *Burgundy to Champagne: The Wine Trade in Early Modern France.* Baltimore, 1997.

Butel, Paul. *L'opium: Histoire d'une fascination.* Paris, 1995.

Clark, Peter. *The English Alehouse: A Social History, 1200–1830.* London, 1983.

Clark, Peter. "The 'Mother Gin' Controversy in the Early Eighteenth Century." *Transactions of the Royal Historical Society* 38 (1988): 63–84.

Cottino, Amadeo. "Class Structure, Politics, and Science: Toward the Formation of the Italian Alcohol Question." Paper presented at the Social History of Alcohol Conference, Berkeley, Calif., 1984.

Cullen, L. M. *The Brandy Trade under the Ancien Régime.* Cambridge, U.K., and New York, 1998.

Goodman, Jordan. *Tobacco in History: The Cultures of Dependence.* London, 1994.

Haine, W. Scott. *The World of the Paris Café.* Baltimore, 1996.

Harrison, Brian. *Drink and the Victorians: The Temperance Question in England, 1815–1872.* Pittsburgh, Pa., 1971.

Matthee, Rudi. "Exotic Substances: The Introduction and Global Spread of Tobacco, Coffee, Cocoa, Tea, and Distilled Liquor, Sixteenth to Eighteenth Centuries." In *Drugs and Narcotics in History.* Edited by Roy Porter and Mikulás Teich. Cambridge, U.K., and New York, 1995. Pages 24–51.

Medick, Hans. "Plebeian Culture in the Transition to Capitalism." In *Culture, Ideology, and Politics.* Edited by Raphael Samuel and Gareth Stedman Jones. London, 1982. Pages 84–112.

Monckton, H. A. *A History of the English Public House.* London, 1969.

Nourrisson, Didier. *Alcoolisme et antialcoolisme en France sous la Troisième République.* Paris, 1988.

Nourrisson, Didier. *Le buveur du XIXe siècle.* Paris, 1990.

Parssinen, Terry M. *Secret Passions, Secret Remedies: Narcotic Drugs in British Society, 1820–1930.* Philadelphia, 1983.

Pincus, Steve. " 'Coffee Politicians Does Create': Coffeehouses and Restoration Political Culture." *Journal of Modern History* 67 (1995): 807–834.

Prestwich, Patricia E. *Drink and the Politics of Social Reform: Antialcoholism in France since 1870.* Palo Alto, Calif., 1988.

Roberts, James S. *Drink, Temperance, and the Working Class in Nineteenth-Century Germany.* Boston, 1984.

Schivelbusch, Wolfgang. *Tastes of Paradise: A Social History of Spices, Stimulants, and Intoxicants.* Translated by David Jacobson. New York, 1992.

Shammas, Carole. "Consumption from 1550 to 1800." In *Consumption and the World of Goods.* Edited by John Brewer and Roy Porter. London, 1993. Pages 177–205.

Spode, Hasso. *Alkohol und Zivilisation.* Berlin, 1991.

Spode, Hasso. "The First Step toward Sobriety: The 'Boozing Devil' in Sixteenth-Century Germany." *Contemporary Drug Problems* 21 (1994): 453–483.

Spring, Josephine, and David Buss. "Three Centuries of Alcohol in the British Diet." *Nature* 270 (1977): 567–572.

Tlusty, Beverly Ann. "The Devil's Altar: The Tavern and Society in Early Modern Augsburg (Germany)." Ph.D. diss., University of Maryland at College Park, 1994.

Tlusty, B. Ann. "Water of Life, Water of Death: The Controversy over Brandy and Gin in Early Modern Augsberg." *Central European History* 31 (1998): 1–30.

Warner, Jessica. "In Another City, in Another Time: Rhetoric and the Creation of a Drug Scare in Eighteenth-Century London." *Contemporary Drug Problems* 21 (1994): 485–511.

HONOR AND SHAME

Robert A. Nye

Honor and shame have been typically yoked together in a binary form by ethnologists, anthropologists, and other students of so-called "honor cultures" in which much of public behavior is determined by considerations of personal or collective honor. In modern usage shame is a sentiment one feels following disgrace, while honor is a distinction that is conferred on individuals for actions that bring renown or that somehow adheres to groups as a kind of pride in collective achievements. Although it might thus appear that shame is the opposite or inverse of honor, in fact the old French etymology reveals that honor *(honneur)* and shame *(honte)* come from the same root, a usage preserved in the motto of the Order of the Garter, "*honi soit qui mal y pense*" (shame on him who thinks badly of it).

INTRODUCTION

Even in the Mediterranean cultures, where honor flourished as nowhere else, shame has become detached discursively and practically from its connection to honor. One might feel shame, or attribute it to persons, in instances where honor never appeared to be in question: financial embarrassment, a bad case of acne, an unkempt lawn, or a tastelessly dressed relative. But we should not be encouraged by the apparent atrophying of honor in modern social practice and usage to forget the original and historic connections of honor and shame in Western societies. In these societies, honor and shame were essentially different sentiments or social assessments made about action (or inaction) in particular instances relating to kin, marriage, wealth, military reputation, and precedence in public life. Such judgments and feelings were made and felt on the same continuum: shame was not so much the opposite of honor as its lack.

Shame, therefore, was the experience, or the fate, of someone who had suffered dishonor by failing adequately to protect honor. For the social historian or the anthropologist, it is of far greater interest to investigate the behavior and the values that motivated the quest for honor. The effort to attain and retain honor was invariably a salient and persistent aspect of masculine comportment; while shaming rituals are sometimes poignant, dramatic, or violent, the shamed individual experiences the full weight of his shame in relative isolation. Ironically, though honor has no ontological status apart from the unceasing efforts to retain it, in honor cultures shame exists as a menacingly permanent threat.

In the earliest definitions of honor, a man's honor consisted of his land, possessions, and family. In western Europe in the early medieval period, only aristocratic men met these criteria. Eventually, as land and goods were held by a larger and more diverse population, honor became a quality that inhered in individuals. Honorability became a quality of persons that was natural to them but that required continuous assertion and demonstration; ultimately, no man of honor could rest on his laurels without danger of derogation. Moral goodness or other forms of virtue like chastity, asceticism, or a reputation for wisdom might maintain themselves in the absence of action. Honor, however, was born within a military service class that lived in an atmosphere of constant warfare where demonstrations of personal courage or bravery possessed a certain selective advantage for the group. Honor was therefore also a collective ethos of groups of fighting men for whom honorability was a judgment about the reliability and the skill of fellow warriors. From the beginning of its long history, honor was thus both individual and corporate.

The close association with the military virtues of loyalty, prowess in weaponry, and physical courage did not mean that honor lacked a spiritual dimension. Indeed, though it has always had a certain intangible quality, honor has been asserted as an ideal, which, depending on the time and the place, has assumed various mythic forms. The examples of certain "mirrors of chivalry," such as King Arthur or Richard the Lionheart, or the heroic behavior of particular battle units whose valor "won the day" have always served

Defending Honor. Encounter between King Arthur and Sir Mordred. Illumination from St. Alban's Chronicle, late fifteenth century. LAMBETH PALACE LIBRARY, LONDON/THE BRIDGEMAN ART LIBRARY

to encourage emulation and sacrifice. There is a sense, in other words, in which the discourses of honor may become collective representations against which honorable actions are measured in all matters great and small.

In historical investigations of the role of honor in society, the social historian must not expect to find the discourses of honor inscribed openly as rules or easily to identify the honorable standards to which individuals were held. The effort to attain and retain honor may be traced in social practices of various

sorts, but such transactions were not calculated with some preconceived ideal in mind. One of the foremost students of honor, the French sociologist Pierre Bourdieu, has likened the pursuit of honor to the accumulation of symbolic capital that is measured only approximately by individuals and their peers. Honor, he says, is a game played by players with a tacit "feel" for the game that allows them to build their own capital and assess the capital of others. Indeed, the metaphor of the game is appropriate for the history of honor in that games have no transcendent aim except winning or performance but may evolve into rule-bound activities in which an officious legalism replaces creative spontaneity.

Bourdieu also suggests that the participants in the game of honor do not precisely calculate their behavior so much as strategize in choosing among a range of possibilities. In his work on marital and kinship strategies in the Béarn region of France and among the Kabyle people in North Africa, Bourdieu studied the way in which matrimonial strategies could be understood as part of the larger game of the accumulation of honor. An individual hoped to add to his assets by marrying well, endowing his children, and thus "reproducing" himself transgenerationally, handing down his wealth and honor to his heirs. In making particular decisions (whom to marry, how many children to have, how to endow them), the patriarch certainly made calculations, but always as part of a larger, more tacit "feel" for how honor might best be gained and preserved for himself and his family.

Historically, honor is essentially a masculine phenomenon. Even outside the West only men could win and defend their honor or that of their family or group. The sphere of a man's honor included the minors, women, or dependents who were under his protection. Women and children thus possessed no honor of their own, though they could share the shame of a dishonor that befell the kinship unit. Women did have a kind of sexual honor that consisted of their purity or their sexual loyalty to the patriarch; they forfeited it as a result of both rape and consensual relations and were powerless to regain it. Only the patriarch, through an act of vengeance or confrontation in a *point d'honneur* (point of honor), could remove the stain. In the classical systems of honor, women and children were like pawns in chess games played by patriarchs, assets that could be lost or gained, sacrificed or "crowned" in strategies of honor. A wife who produced another man's bastard exposed a man to outside claims on his property; a wayward daughter was damaged goods as a player in her father's strategies for marital alliances; a son's indiscretions might dishonor his father and call into question his own ability as a future manager of the family's assets.

In attempting to understand the role honor and shame have played in certain historical societies, the historian must consider various social practices. These can be grouped into four categories: marriage and inheritance strategies; class and the evolution of honor; the duel and the *point d'honneur;* and honor and sociability. There is nothing sacred about these categories; they illuminate the terrain of honor unusually well but are by no means exhaustive.

MARRIAGE AND INHERITANCE STRATEGIES

Marriage and the production of children was the only way a man could be assured that the assets he himself had inherited and defended would survive him. His honor was subsumed both in his property and his children and in his actions as a manager of these assets. A man's marriage was the foundation of his own stake in the game of honor. The number and sex of his children and his marital strategies for them could either augment or disperse his fortune. Customs respecting exogamy and endogamy, and other issues of time, place, and circumstance are the things that a man had to consider before beginning marriage negotiations for a male or female child. Local dowry customs and the liquidity of land and other forms of family property had to be considered, and these decisions were always made after considering the number and sex of children who had survived the first five years of life.

Inheritance laws and customs varied widely throughout Europe. The partitive inheritance that settled a man's wealth proportionately on all his children prevailed in much of northern Europe; it required strategies that minimized fragmentation of his resources such as a child's voluntary disinheritance and celibacy. In the parts of Europe governed by Roman law, and in Britain, primogeniture was the rule, giving title and most assets typically to the eldest son. There were threats to the honor and wealth of the patriarch in both systems, but he could minimize them by managing the size of his family and exercising as much control as possible over the education and movements of his children, even from the grave. It seems likely that child-rearing practices, courtship practices, and family history in general were marked by these strategic considerations of patriarchal honor in Europe and elsewhere until relatively recent times.

In light of the way the patriarch attempted to control all his assets, it is easy to see how the techniques and restraints he and his wife initiated to control the number of births became incorporated into the domain of honor and shame. Much less is known about what those techniques actually were, but it seems logical to assume that if a large number of children would fragment the inheritance while giving none of them an adequate start in life, couples might employ various forms of birth control, resort to abortion, or practice celibacy. Having children out of wedlock, or having too many in wedlock, could possibly be regarded as a shameful surrender to lust; popular attitudes toward birth control might thus have been favorable. By contrast, in certain parts of Europe until modern times, pregnancy constituted a definitive proof of fertility that brought many a girl to the altar, fostering a relaxed attitude toward premarital sex in general. The threshold of shame with respect to pregnancy, abortion, contraception, and the frequenting of prostitutes has certainly varied depending on inheritance customs, family size, and ages of marriage and conception.

HONOR AND SOCIAL CLASS

One of the most fruitful and largely unexplored aspects of the history of honor and shame cultures concerns the way they differ according to class. We know more about honor within the aristocracy than in any other class. As we have seen, the rituals and values of honor cultures evolved first in noble milieus. However, there is reason to think that wherever forms of individual landownership developed, or where there were strong bonds of corporate loyalty in urban craft guilds or in military fellowships such as the Knights of Malta, mechanisms arose in which the use of masculine and family honor bore a definite resemblance to the principal forms of noble honor. In addition to the independent genesis of honor cultures, social mimesis became an increasingly important explanation for the spread of honor and shame to aristocratizing bourgeois engaged in upward mobility, especially after the seventeenth century.

For the European aristocracy, honor was synonymous with personal courage and reputation for valor. Social derogation for cowardice—the avoidance of military service or evasiveness on the *point d'honneur*—was ruthless, devaluing a man's property and reputation simultaneously. The slightest suspicion that a nobleman was hiding behind his wife's skirts, some higher moral or religious injunction, or even a monarch's ban on dueling was enough to taint his reputation. Throughout the sixteenth and seventeenth centuries, the public comportment of noblemen was attuned to a verbal culture where insults, vows of loyalty, oaths, and other forms of personal alliance provided an unstable foundation for political life. In the absence of specific contractual agreements, appearances, assertions, bluff, and counter-bluff were the chief elements of political discourse.

In England, Spain, and France, state-building monarchs followed a strategy of reducing the fractiousness of honor-hungry noblemen by reducing their independence, tying them closer to court culture, and transforming the sometimes violent and disruptive rituals of shame avoidance into brilliant competitive rituals of courtiership. Demonstrations of rage or prowess at weapons were converted into spectacles of style, wit, and elegance without, after all, abandoning an ultimate resort to the point of honor. As Norbert Elias has theorized in his great study of the civilizing process, the phrase "shame at his estate" originates in a court culture that had substituted censorious standards of refinement for the crude ruses of combat.

In the parts of western Europe where economic development had produced a wealthy and ambitious bourgeoisie, a strategy of marital alliances with aristocratic families and the purchase of offices and titles testified to a widespread middle-class desire to assimilate the most attractive aspects of the noble ethos, including the wearing of the sword and the right to engage in the *point d'honneur*. But middle-class men had also cultivated forms of honor and honorability that were unique to them, particularly forms of behavior that had ensured the survival or prosperity of their ancestors. These included the virtues of thrift and financial independence, sexual self-restraint, and the capacity to work productively, all of which stood apart from noble values. Like the noble traits of courage, loyalty, and prowess at arms, which were *naturalized* as qualities innate to the noble man of honor, sexual "respectability" and the drive to work and save became natural qualities of bourgeois honorability. A middle-class man felt shame at the prospect of financial failure or at accusations of sexual impropriety and strove to live his life honorably according to the values of his class.

It is accepted that the forms of upper-class honor that emerged at the end of the eighteenth century throughout Europe were a synthesis of noble and bourgeois varieties. Aristocratic men found they could serve bourgeois regimes as administrators or diplomats without dishonor, and middle-class men assimilated the reflexive temerity and the readiness to defend a reputation for courage that had once been a wholly noble trait. On the frontiers of Europe, cultural and social cleavages other than those of class determined which men would be stimulated to action from a dread of shame. In Ireland, Protestant gentlemen enthusiastically embraced the ethos of the duel as a way of asserting their identity as a political and religious elite. The usual distinctions between noble and commoner were overlooked in a development that expressed its solidarity behind a screen of chivalric querulousness. Likewise, in the course of the Napoleonic Wars and subsequent military occupations, French, Italian, German, and Russian officers were moved by national cleavages far more than by class distinctions in a veritable epidemic of nationalistic affairs of honor.

Scholars have shown that important forms of honor and honorability were also a part of rural and

Non-elite Honor. *The Musicians' Brawl,* painting (1620) by Georges de La Tour (1593–1652). J. PAUL GETTY MUSEUM, MALIBU, CALIF./THE BRIDGEMAN ART LIBRARY

urban milieus in the old regime. The forms and usages of honor were different, but it seems certain that honor and shame worked in similar ways in nonelite strata of society. In parts of the rural southern Mediterranean, affronts to a man's honor might range from physical confrontation, to insults to or even attacks on his womenfolk, to simple rudeness. Rich peasants, small-town merchants, or other local notables might find it suddenly necessary to defend their honor with force. This was often done by direct violence against the offender or his family, for which the genteel rituals of upper-class duels provided no inspiration whatever. On the contrary, there was a tendency for such affairs of honor to enlist all the members of a clan and for bitterness to carry on for more than a generation.

In late-eighteenth-century Paris, skilled craftsmen might be provoked by other members of the popular classes to defend the honor of their guild or that of their family. In some of these conflicts, brawls broke out almost immediately after an insult was delivered, and bottles, fists, or whatever came to hand were used in self-defense. Occasionally more refined forms were followed that at least resembled upper-class duels. In such cases an interval was observed to allow tempers to cool, and the subsequent fight observed an equality of weaponry and conditions. Conflicts of this sort almost invariably occurred in public places, most generally in cafes or places of recreation, and arose from direct verbal exchange involving real or imagined slights. It is likely that the notorious rivalries that existed between urban guilds throughout Europe were, in their essence, expressions of corporate honor and solidarity in which men felt obliged to defend the territory or the reputation of their craft.

Other historians have found compelling evidence for the existence of honor conflicts among the popular classes in early modern and modern cities. We know that in both Amsterdam and Rome knife fighting enjoyed a ritual status as a way of resolving conflicts between lower-class men. Most men carried knives, and these became the weapon of choice when fights resulted from barroom arguments. There was a standard pattern to such encounters. The men left the premises and fought outside in the presence of their friends, who did not intervene. The conflict usually ended when one of the combatants was disabled, though death was the occasional result. Men prided themselves on their scars or fighting reputations, and especially skilled knife fighters were given a wide berth. Certainly the masculinity of these men, if not some more refined sense of honor, was at stake in such conflicts. Middle-class men in Amsterdam did not carry knives and would not "duel" with men from the popular classes, thinking this beneath them. Instead they wielded sticks or clubs in self-defense, testifying to a desire to indicate that their antagonist did not possess the quality of honor of a man of their stamp.

A class analysis of honor reveals that individuals and groups from all levels of society possessed some rudimentary notion of honor and were capable of experiencing shame at its loss. The constituent elements of honor varied according to class: reputations for courage, generosity, financial probity, sexual respectability, physical strength, or corporate or clan loyalty were central features of class conceptions of honor. These differential values appear to have evolved within classes and met the sense of pride or reputation particular to the group. At the same time, at least at the upper levels of honor cultures, there appears to have been a percolation of honor downward that was the product of social diversification and mobility. By the end of the nineteenth century, the values of an eclectic upper-class system of honor had spread throughout middle-class society, qualifying a man of property or education to participate in affairs of honor and to feel himself slighted or insulted as a result of a number of potential offenses against his person, his family, or his group.

THE DUEL AND THE *POINT D'HONNEUR*

The duel evolved from various medieval forms of knightly encounters and from the judicial duel that determined, until the fifteenth century, certain cases of guilt or innocence. At some point in the sixteenth century the duel became a private matter to be decided between two gentlemen and their friends. The private duel flourished throughout early modern Europe, despite the efforts of state-building monarchs to outlaw it. Although the events that precipitated an affair of honor might have seemed trivial or incidental, differences between men of honor were always potentially dangerous because the courage and determination of each man was immediately engaged and put in question. A man or his friends could make a disproportionately vigorous effort to resolve these differences at the risk of appearing afraid to risk his life. In the long and hoary traditions of the *point d'honneur,* life without honor was not worth living; a public retreat from an affair of honor was usually an instantaneous sentence of social death.

The *point d'honneur* was thus the final court of appeal in a series of potential differences that could erupt between men. In the largely verbal culture of early modern Europe, a gentleman could react to even mildly worded insults or accusations by "giving the lie" to his antagonist, accusing him in effect of lying, which was an imputation on his personal honor and a *casus belli* for a duel. The man so accused had the right to choose weapons and conditions in the subsequent duel. By the late eighteenth century, higher rates of literacy among gentlemen of honor meant that written insults, slanders, or simply unfriendly characterizations could appear in print and serve as grounds for duels. These occasions were greatly magnified in the course of the nineteenth century with the rise of a mass newspaper culture, modern political culture, and a genuine public sphere.

It is difficult to generalize beyond this point. National and regional variations in the sensitivity to the *point d'honneur* varied from place to place and over time; the national and temporal variations of the duel and its rituals provide an anatomy of honor that is more accurate and more revealing than any other documentary source. It is a public record of the depth and the limits of private and personal sentiments and the judgments made about them. These sentiments were probably not experienced by the principals in every affair of honor until the event actually transpired. Dueling narratives may be found in personal memoirs, in the transcripts of trials, in compendia of duels gathered by enthusiasts of the practice, and particularly in newspaper accounts published from the summaries of witnesses. These latter accounts are likely at least to contain no grave exaggerations owing to the fact that they were drawn up by each man's seconds in a version agreed upon by all.

The variations are worth summarizing briefly. The duel was violent though infrequent in Great Britain and consisted mostly of pistol duels, usually by members of the gentry who had military experience or a sporting familiarity with weapons; serious wounds and even death were frequent. However, the duel disappeared rather suddenly in the 1850s thanks to initiatives from the crown, a refusal to pay pension benefits to the widows of military men deceased in a duel, and the existence of libel and slander laws with some teeth.

In France the duel was far more frequent, more bourgeois and civilian in nature, and since the preferred weapon was the *épée* (rapier), wounds and death were far less frequent. The duel increased in popularity in France throughout the 1870s and 1880s, cresting with the political turmoil of the Boulanger affair in the late 1880s and the Dreyfus affair between 1894

Dueling. Engraving of dueling positions from an eighteenth-century manual. ©Bettmann/Corbis

and 1899 and subsiding only slightly thereafter. There may have been as many as three hundred duels in any year at the high-water mark of the practice. Although the duel ebbed and flowed with the conflicts of political life, attracting politicians and journalists in particular, personal and family honor were also frequent causes of affairs. It was common for a cuckold to attempt to repair his wounded vanity (and perhaps exact some revenge) by issuing a challenge to his rival; fathers, sons, and brothers regularly called out men who had insulted their womenfolk or other relatives, living or dead, who could not defend themselves. The duel was discouraged by the police but was not illegal in France, and weak slander laws often obliged men to obtain satisfaction in person that they could not obtain at law or did not want to publicly reveal.

The German Duel. A German-style duel fought in Russia. *The Duel,* painting (1901) by Ilya Efimovich Repin (1844–1930). Pushkin Museum, Moscow/The Bridgeman Art Library

The Italian duel was probably more frequent than anywhere else, though, as in France, not particularly dangerous. The journalist Iacopo Gelli chronicled most of the duels that took place between the 1860s until after World War I. He found evidence of over 3,500 duels for the period 1879–1894 alone; if one considers the many duels that were not reported for reasons of privacy, there may have been as many as nine hundred duels in some years prior to 1914. Unlike the French version, the Italian duel was heavily influenced by military forms and participation. The saber was the overwhelming weapon of choice, and even men with no prior experience were obliged to learn the appropriate techniques of the saber duel. The duel in Austria-Hungary was also overwhelmingly military in participation and form, though far less frequent and somewhat more dangerous. Widespread political and journalistic participation was common to both the French and the Italian duel; the latter was driven in greater measure by matters of personal (read sexual) honor.

The German duel was unique in its deadliness. German duelers favored the dueling pistol, a smoothbore version of the old single-shot flintlock, and particularly dangerous conditions of combat: in a "bar-

rier" duel two men approached one another until they reached a barrier at murderously close range, at which point they both discharged their pistols. Bourgeois men who had passed as reserve officers through the regular army felt themselves the equals of even exalted Junker officers and therefore *satisfaktionfähig* (capable of giving satisfaction). Thus in a large number of interclass duels both bourgeois and aristocratic participants had something particular to prove about the quality of their honor and the extent of their courage. Since the German duel was illegal (despite a high level of official tolerance), it was often conducted in private; duels that came to trial often did so because one of the participants was either seriously wounded or killed, so that the legal record is replete with evidence of the seriousness of Teutonic affairs of honor. Historians of the German duel differ as to whether this surviving relic of the medieval past is an instance of the continuing influence of the old military aristocracy in German life or, given the widespread evidence of nonaristocratic duelers, confirms the similarity of Germany to the other western European powers.

In Europe as a whole, the duel, despite its illegality and its ultimately violent nature, reflected the complexities of masculine honor to a degree that was in fact sometimes excruciatingly legalistic. A case reported by Ute Frevert in her *Men of Honour: A Social and Cultural History of the Duel* (pp. 182–183) from Germany in 1904 illustrates this point. A married army officer, Captain Levetzow, had a brief affair with an unmarried young woman that ended with her subsequent marriage. The affair was discovered soon after, and both her brother and her husband considered their honor to have been affronted. The brother's sense of family honor was outraged by the theft of his sister's virginity by a man who had no intention of marrying her, and the personal honor of the husband was affronted by the fact that the woman who became his wife had been seduced by a third party. Because the liaison took place *before* the marriage, only after which the husband assumed responsibility for her conduct, it was the brother who ultimately demanded satisfaction. This incident also points to how the honor system refused to women (and minors and other outsiders) the possibility of full and independent participation in public life. If someone could not defend with force a conviction they expressed in public, how could they demonstrate the sincerity or defend the accuracy of their remarks?

Excepting brief efflorescences in Fascist Italy and Nazi Germany, the duel died in the bloody trench fighting of World War I. The high mortality rates and the grievous injuries of many of the survivors made the relatively safer risks of the duel seem absurd and empty. After such a war who was not *satisfaktionfähig?* Dueling techniques live on in the German fraternity *Mensur,* a highly stylized ritual whose aim is to scar but not hurt and where courage but no longer honor is at stake.

HONOR AND SOCIABILITY

In the modern era honor and shame assumed gentler forms. Corporate or collective honor had provided an important part of the solidarity of craft guilds and the liberal professions from the late Middle Ages. The motto "All for one and one for all" ensured such groups' independence, trade secrets, and reputation for integrity. Good intracorporate relations were assured among men if they managed to observe a common unwritten code of frank intercourse that respected individual sensibilities and yet allowed each man to express his independence. Differences sometimes arose between colleagues, and these could erupt into full-scale affairs of honor, to the shame of the individuals involved and the collective reputation of the group. In the course of the modern period, forms of politeness gradually evolved that permitted guilds and professional groups and later clubs and voluntary organizations of all sorts to police their members and assure their good order and reputation.

The forms of etiquette or civility that evolved to maintain good relations between men were modeled in their essence on the elaborate dueling handbooks that had circulated in gentlemanly society since the seventeenth century. These forms defined in a progressively legalistic way levels of offense, modes of negotiation and reconciliation, and, by the mid-nineteenth century, "honor courts" that heard and decided on differences between members. It is important to understand that even in scientific and scholarly societies, the personal reputations of individuals counted heavily in discussions about the facts or interpretations they advanced. An honorable man could be assured that the sincerity if not the truth of his utterances would be taken seriously; a man whose honor was in doubt could expect contradiction and resistance at every step. In these settings, as in other public venues in the nineteenth century, the use of arms was still the court of last resort for a man whose honor or integrity was openly doubted.

The wholly masculine nature of club, professional, and political life persisted into the late twentieth century. The social, cultural, or religious exclusiveness of such groups has been due in no small part to the effort to keep out the "wrong kind of man," whether Catholics, Jews, or ethnic or racial minorities who were not believed to possess by nature or breeding the requisite qualities of honor. Although not designed to exclude women in particular, the honor test effectively excluded women for decades from professional, civic, or social groups for which they were in every other way fully qualified. The wholly masculine nature of the culture, discourse, and modes of conflict resolutions in such groups seemed alien to female pioneers on these social frontiers, who often decided to form all-female auxiliary organizations instead.

The gender integration of public life has meant the progressive dismantling of the masculine honor culture that once served as the chief guarantor of civility in the public sphere. It is an open question whether historians will find evidence of forms of honor particular to women and to female sociability over the last few hundred years that have served to guide and regulate social interaction. Women's gossip networks, labor organizations, and clubs might have been guided by rules of conduct that differed from parallel groups of men in important ways. The same might be said for women who fought in national and civil wars or were prominent in resistance movements, particularly in the twentieth century. It may be, in other words, that women took their cues from a distinctly female form of honor that transcended the

Honor and Sociability. A men's club portrayed in *The Bagman's Toast "Sweethearts and Wives,"* painting by Walter Dendy Sadler (1854–1923). PRIVATE COLLECTION/THE BRIDGEMAN ART LIBRARY

mere safeguarding of their sexual honor, which was their sole duty under the aegis of masculine honorability.

The decline of honor has followed apace the gender integration of all-male organizations in the late twentieth century: the military, clubs, the professions, sports teams, government agencies, and the diplomatic corps. Though it is still possible to speak of a "man of honor" in public life, or for a former German chancellor to defend secret financial arrangements ac-

cording to a personal honor code, these forms of discourse are increasingly infrequent in modern societies. All-male bastions still persist in various places, and, where women have colonized occupations and activities formerly reserved for men, they occasionally make use of the masculine forms of honorific titles and procedures. Laws punishing personal and corporate insult—modeled on affronts to honor—are still on the books in France, Germany, and other European countries, but are seldom enforced.

See also **Social Class; The Military** *(volume 3);* **Men and Masculinity; Gestures; Manners** *(volume 4); and other articles in this section.*

BIBLIOGRAPHY

Billacois, François. *Le duel dans la société française des XVIe–XVIIe siècles: Essai de psychosociologie historique.* Paris, 1986.

Bourdieu, Pierre. *Distinction: A Social Critique of the Judgement of Taste.* Translated by Richard Nice. Cambridge, Mass., 1984.

Bourdieu, Pierre. *The Logic of Practice.* Stanford, Calif., 1990.

Brennan, Thomas. *Public Drinking and Popular Culture in Eighteenth-Century Paris.* Princeton, N.J., 1988.

Castan, Yves. *Honnêteté et relations sociales en Languedoc (1715–1780).* Paris, 1974.

Connell, Robert W. *Masculinities.* Cambridge, U.K., and Berkeley, Calif., 1995.

Deák, István. *Beyond Nationalism: A Social and Political History of the Habsburg Officer Corps, 1848–1918.* New York, 1990.

Elias, Norbert. *The Civilizing Process.* Translated by Edmund Jephcott. 3 vols. New York, 1983.

Frevert, Ute. *Men of Honour: A Social and Cultural History of the Duel.* Translated by Anthony Williams. Cambridge, U.K., 1995.

Gilmore, David. *Manhood in the Making: Cultural Concepts of Masculinity.* New Haven, Conn., 1990.

Kelly, James. *'That Damn'd Thing Called Honour: Duelling in Ireland, 1570–1860.* Cork, Ireland, 1995.

McAleer, Kevin. *Dueling: The Cult of Honor in Fin-de-siècle Germany.* Princeton, N.J., 1994.

Mosse, George L. *The Image of Man: The Creation of Modern Masculinity.* New York, 1996.

Nye, Robert A. *Masculinity and Male Codes of Honor in Modern France.* New ed. Berkeley, Calif., 1998.

Nye, Robert A. "Medicine and Science as Masculine 'Fields of Honor.'" *Osiris* 12 (1997): 60–79.

Pitt-Rivers, Julian. *The Fate of Schechem: Essays in the Anthropology of the Mediterranean.* Cambridge, U.K., 1977.

Reddy, William M. *The Invisible Code: Honor and Sentiment in Postrevolutionary France, 1814–1848.* Berkeley, Calif., 1997.

Simpson, Antony. "Dandelions on the Field of Honor: Dueling, the Middle Classes and the Law in Nineteenth-Century England." *Criminal Justice History* 9 (1988): 99–155.

Spierenburg, Pieter, ed. *Men and Violence: Gender, Honor, and Rituals in Modern Europe and America.* Columbus, Ohio, 1998.

Todd, Emmanuel. *The Explanation of Ideology: Family Structures and Social Systems.* New York, 1985.

MEMORY AND THE INVENTION OF TRADITIONS

Tamara L. Hunt and Scott Hughes Myerly

The study of memory can take several forms. This essay begins with the impressive intellectual history of ideas about memory. The social history of memory focuses more on ways that memory has been used to bolster loyalties, to the state and to a religion, and to identify outsiders. In the late twentieth century social and cultural historians devoted a great deal of attention to the uses of memory in the nineteenth and twentieth centuries, particularly around conservative and nationalist causes amid rapid change and new forms of protest. Memory in these uses might be selective but also might be invented outright, surrounded with the trappings of age and ceremony while in fact quite new. Invented traditions included governments and political units as well as ideas about the family, which often mixed desires for family stability with myths about family cohesion and ritual in the past. Finally, historical memory and invention were further tested with reactions to the great wars of twentieth-century Europe that called forth a variety of ceremonies of commemoration but also some efforts at deliberate forgetting.

THEORIES OF MEMORY

For the ancient Greeks memory was the precondition of human thought. Mnemosyne, the goddess of both wisdom and memory, was mother to the Muses, among them Clio, the muse of history. Despite mythological explanations, the Greeks disagreed about what memory actually was, how it functioned, and its role in understanding human history, a debate that has continued ever since. Plato (c. 428–348 or 347 B.C.) argued that memory reveals eternal truth, while Aristotle (384–322 B.C.) thought that it is the way humans understand reality through consciously arranging sensory impressions into a coherent order. Nevertheless, both agreed it is a vital component of human understanding, as did the Roman writers Marcus Tullius Cicero (106–43 B.C.) and St. Augustine (A.D. 354–430), who believed that memory underlies all thought and education.

In the early modern period (c. 1500–1750) the memory debate focused on questioning human understanding but continued along the division between Plato and Aristotle. René Descartes (1596–1650) asserted that knowledge is independent of sensory information and comes from immortal, pure truths, innate to human reason. Memory, the recollection of past sensory events, could never bring true knowledge. Similarly Gottfried Wilhelm Leibniz (1646–1716) argued that memories do not actually reflect events, which come to the mind through the senses and can be confused, but rather are innate, inborn ideas. Conversely, John Locke (1632–1704) argued that the human mind at birth is a tabula rasa, a "blank slate," that receives sense impressions. These sensations not only allow people to understand their present reality but form the basis for both memory and personal identity, which he defined as a present consciousness of thought and experience that extend back in time.

By the eighteenth century the debate broadened to include the relationship between memory, history, and tradition. David Hume (1711–1776) argued that the human mind creates causality. When certain events are seen to go together frequently or uniformly, the mind forges links not extant in reality that connect thoughts. This suggests that memory and tradition, as based almost entirely on recollections of past events, are not necessarily rooted in what actually happened but in what people perceived to have happened.

This emphasis on human memory's unreliability brought both memory and tradition into disrepute among some of the philosophes, who believed that the medieval world was guided by superstition rather than reason. They concluded that, as "tradition," its culture, events, and ideas were backward, negative, and inhibited "progress," which they considered positive, innovative, and superior. This bias influenced concepts of memory and history, as many scholars argued in favor of a more rational historical approach purged of superstition and myth. One exception was the great Neopolitan historian Giambattista Vico (1668–1744), who suggested that historical analysis should be based on "the history of human ideas" or a society's commonly held assumptions, whether factual or not, that were vital to understanding its history.

The reaction of the romantic era (c. 1760–1840) against the rational historical approach generated modern concepts of memory, particularly through works that attempted to incorporate folk speech and folkways into historical works, for example, those of the Scottish author Sir Walter Scott (1771–1832) and the French historian Jules Michelet (1798–1874). Many scholars and folklorists celebrated the concept of "nation" as expressed in popular culture and vernacular speech, and they also thought national memories and traditions improved understandings of nineteenth-century problems, including urbanization, industrialization, population migration and displacement, and intensifying political centralization. While many such scholars focused on the creation and use of history, their work also theoretically addressed memory and the invention of tradition.

Karl Marx (1818–1883) distrusted "official" histories and most traditions, customs, and institutions, viewing them as legitimizing a social "superstructure" of mentalities that serve elites by justifying and legitimizing their domination over the masses and promoting the latter's compliance with elite rule, the fundamental aim of which is to maximize elite wealth and power. Any society's beliefs, customs, and traditions are thus actually founded on the particular economic relations that exist in any time or place and are essentially determined by how work is organized and how property is distributed or owned.

Marx took only limited interest in individuals' memories, but scholarship informed by nationalism took a different view. The Swiss historian Jakob Burckhardt (1818–1897) believed that individual human choice, not impersonal economic or political forces, causes historical change. He viewed tradition as cultural history's central focus and felt that peoples' views of the world are shaped by meaningful historical "fictions" that help them cope with the chaos of modern life. This spiritual cultural history, *Bildung* (civilization or culture), differs substantially from more static political history, *Wissenschaft*, which is based strictly on factual evidence.

The French philosopher Ernest Renan (1823–1892) went further and declared that memory and tradition are the basis for the nation that society attempts to pass on unchanged to future generations. Renan believed that the idea of the nation could transcend divisions based on race, religion, or language by forcing people to abdicate their individual goals and adopt a collective moral conscience. Although Renan suggested that national unification through memory

and tradition is deliberate, his idea resembles the "collective memory" concept introduced by the art historian Aby Warburg (1866–1929). Warburg's concept involves a process far more subtle than the one outlined by Renan. Collective memory is transmitted through cultural artifacts bearing symbols that can be traced back through time, and Warburg proposed that scholars not only study these memory symbols but also the larger *mentalité* (mentality) of the culture that produces them.

Some scholars, however, wondered whether it is possible to recapture fully the *mentalité* of past cultures. Sigmund Freud (1856–1939) proposed that, since elements of memories appear in dreams, memories are actually fragmented and recollection and perception are given structure only by the emotions. This suggests an enormous difference between individual memories and academic history, a view explored by the French philosopher Henri Bergson (1859–1941) and the sociologist Maurice Halbwachs (1877–1945). Bergson believed that "duration," or lifespan, is the essence of the human condition and that memory allows a true understanding of reality through subjective, intuitive understanding of the past. He differentiated duration based on intuitive memory from spatialized and institutionalized concepts of time (as in academic history) that is created for specific public or scholarly purposes. Similarly Halbwachs argued that individual and collective memory is subjective and multilayered because it was formed through membership in a variety of groups (family, profession, community, church, nation) that remember from different perspectives and whose views of the past are transformed as the groups change. These "social frames" *(cadres sociaux)* use memory to reconfigure the present, not to reclaim or reconstruct the past. By contrast, Halbwachs argued that academic history presents a more standardized periodization, focusing on subjects not directly experienced by people of an era, and is often linear and teleological (having a distinct purpose).

Thus by the early twentieth century scholars recognized that memory and tradition could play significant roles in how humans understand history, but scepticism about memory's ability to provide an accurate understanding of the past was increasing. The German philosopher Hans Georg Gadamer (b. 1900), who transformed hermeneutics from a study of biblical texts into a philosophical approach to human understanding and knowledge, argued that individuals attempt to understand the unfamiliar by placing it within their own "horizon" of reality. Thus all new phenomena and ideas—including traditions and historical data that differ from present experience—are

Remembering the Fallen. Civic officials at a war memorial, Lodève, France. MICHAEL H. BLACK/ROBERT HARDING PICTURE LIBRARY

constantly subject to reinterpretation, a process that keeps tradition alive. According to Gadamer, "The historical life of a tradition depends on constantly new assimilation and interpretation" (Gadamer, 1989, p. 358).

The social anthropologist Ernest Gellner argued that in modern mass society, collective amnesia is as important as collective memory and that "both memory and forgetfulness have deep social roots; neither springs from historical accident." He believed that industrial societies create a "shared, homogeneous, literacy-carried, and school-inculcated culture" (Gellner, 1987, p. 68), meaning that people have to possess knowledge of the dominant culture to succeed, for instance in knowing which fork to use at a formal dinner or understanding the allusions made by coworkers. But in addition to such formal learning, people also have to forget their origins in the "other"— those suspect or unacceptable traditions that deviate from the dominant culture.

To some degree the historian Benedict Anderson's work on "imagined communities" is related to Gellner's thesis. Even though it does not address collective memory or amnesia, Anderson's concept of the nation as an imagined community reflects on both. According to Anderson, although a nation's citizens will never meet or know the vast majority of their fellow citizens, they nonetheless feel bonded with them. This makes community possible, by encouraging people to overlook such inequalities, divisions, and oppressions as actually beset a nation in their de-

sire to embrace the ideal of a "deep, horizontal comradeship" (Anderson, 1991, p. 7).

The influential Pierre Nora argued that history and memory are "in fundamental opposition" and introduced the concept of *lieux de mémoires* or "sites of memory." He claimed these sites are "resting places" of memory that can be geographical locations, events, or ideas and that such memories are necessarily selective, rather than complete records of what occurred (Nora, 1989, p. 8). Modern society's relationship with the past is inherently different from that of earlier societies. While past societies lived in memory and saw no significant difference between the present and past, modern societies are self-consciously separated from that past, which is perceived to no longer exist. Nora also differentiated between official memory promoted by the state or establishment historians and popular memory, which is virtually an organic part of the present that is constantly changing through the process of remembering and forgetting.

Other scholars, such as Natalie Zemon Davis, Randoph Starn, and Raphael Samuel, agreed that history and memory differ but suggested that they exist in a beneficial relationship to each other, not in opposition. Davis and Starn concluded that history and memory are actually interdependent and that tensions and conflicts between them constitute a productive force for generating useful knowledge as scholars attempt to "adjust the fit" between them. Similarly Samuel argued that social memories reflected in contemporary media show that collective memory is dynamic, specifically remembering and forgetting elements of the past, and is also historically conditioned, changing with immediate needs. Therefore those collective memories that claim to hand down "traditions" from past generations have been shaped by the crises and evolving perspectives of intervening generations. Nevertheless, Samuel viewed memory and history in a dialectical (interactive) relationship—both are eternally revisionist, each borrowing from the other to fill in gaps or to forge new meanings.

USES OF MEMORY

These twentieth-century theories on the relationship between history and memory are somewhat abstract, but the concepts of tradition and the invention of tradition are rooted in historical analysis. Eric Hobsbawm defined the invention of tradition as "a set of practices, normally governed by overtly or tacitly accepted rules and of a ritual or symbolic nature, which seek to inculcate certain values and norms of behavior by repetition, which automatically implies continuity with the past" (Hobsbawm and Ranger, 1983, p. 1). Certainly not all forms of memory are purposely and consciously invented to influence the present, but the invention of tradition cannot exist without a real or implied link with past memories.

Implied in the concept is that the purpose, conscious or not, of invented traditions is to reinforce a desirable sense of continuity with a real or mythical past whenever a real cohesion does not exist in the present or appears to be threatened or faltering. Thus tradition is most likely to be invented in periods of upheaval or uncertainty, when individuals and groups are searching for stability or legitimacy amid troubling religious, ideological, economic, political, or social changes. The Renaissance in Europe was such a period, as new ideas about art, literature, religion, and science challenged established traditions and concepts.

Central to the Renaissance was an awareness of links with the past, as artists, authors, and architects attempted to emulate the classical world. The beginning of modern European historical thought was also affected by the classics. Leonardo Bruni (1370–1444) modeled his history of Florence on that of Titus Livy (59 B.C.–A.D. 17) and other Roman historians. He criticized earlier scholars for failing to write adequate histories of their times, a failure which he believed had contributed to the ignorance he saw in his own era. Bruni's criticism reflects Renaissance historians' utilitarian goal of drawing practical lessons from the past about politics, ethics, and law. History likewise became important for the resolution of religious contro-

versies; the establishment of the first history university professorships was spurred by the need to investigate troubling, fundamental questions about the Catholic church's origins. In 1440 Lorenzo Valla (1407–1457) used textual analysis to prove that the *Donation of Constantine,* a document reputedly written by the fourth-century emperor Constantine (d. A.D. 337) that gave the bishops of Rome temporal and spiritual control over western Europe and was used to legitimize papal authority, was a forgery. Such investigations continued and spread dramatically after Martin Luther's 1517 challenge to the church, as Catholic and Protestant scholars searched for documentation that legitimized their claims.

Martin Luther (1483–1546) and Philip Melanchthon (1497–1560), in their thirteen-volume study *Magdeburg Centuries,* used historical analysis to argue that the Catholic church had perverted Christianity. The church responded with Cesare Baronio's *Ecclesiastical Annals,* which argued that the seeming innovations introduced by the postapostolic church were not changes but simply interpretations and clarifications inspired by the Holy Spirit to "purify" it, an approach often used to strengthen tradition and the establishment. Protestants likewise used research to charge that many saints' days, rituals, and festivals were actually adopted Roman pagan cults. Protestants also made substitutions, however, inventing new rituals to replace those they had denounced as heretical innovations. After 1560 the Kirk leadership in Calvinist Scotland tried to repress all public festivals and displays as popish and undesirable, but the rituals they introduced were suspiciously close to earlier Catholic ones in timing if not in format. While the days of fasting and humiliation regularly called during the Catholic season of Lent did not include the same rituals, they nevertheless continued the tradition of providing a holy day of relaxation that broke up the cycle of agricultural labor. The Catholic Counter-Reformation also modified some rituals and introduced new ones in an effort to keep followers loyal and to reform the church. New seventeenth-century saints' cults, including those of St. Ignatius Loyola (1491–1556) and St. Teresa of Ávila (1515–1582), emphasized personal devotion while retaining secular features, including processions, bonfires, and playacting. Both sides attempted to reform popular culture and produced ideological pamphlets, rewrote or adapted popular ballads into hymns, censored popular works by removing suspect references, and attacked all plays, bonfires, and festivals that were not sanctioned by church authorities.

But even the threat of force could not eradicate or change such observances overnight, and many pro-

REINVENTING POPULAR RELIGIOUS TRADITION UNDER HENRY VIII

Henry VIII (1491–1547) was central to the establishment of the Church of England. Initiating the break from Rome, he then named himself supreme head of the church, dissolved religious foundations, authorized the printing of an English Bible, and turned his church into a hybrid of Catholicism and Protestant doctrine. His role in changing popular religious tradition has not been acknowledged often, but it was part of his larger policy to secure the throne by emphasizing the Crown's commanding political power.

Inventing religious tradition was one way that Henry VIII and other secular leaders secured their sovereignty during the Reformation. When the king became supreme head of the newly created Church of England in the 1530s, his advisers used new biblical interpretations to justify his political position. They claimed that since he was both prince and father to his people, the commandment that ordered Christians to obey and honor their parents included the monarch as well. This implied that Henry's claim to be the head of the English church was based on the holy word of God through the Ten Commandments, which was a return to the original meaning, through a wondrous rediscovery of a text "lost for centuries," and therefore not some arrogant, greedy pretension to despotism.

In addition to learned argument, some suggested that the monarchy also emphasize its position through more popular means. One adviser suggested that Henry create a new annual holiday, complete with bonfires and processions, that would commemorate his break with Rome, while another proposed replacing traditional Robin Hood plays with new ones that condemned the pope rather than celebrated an outlaw. While neither of these proposals was adopted, the king did make changes that emphasized the national character of the church and his own authority over it, such as combining all festivals celebrating the founding of local churches into a national holiday to be celebrated on the first Sunday in October. Such changes that distorted local festivals aroused resentment that increased when the king declared that saints were only to be respected, not venerated, and ordered the destruction of all images and relics of saints, especially those of Thomas à Becket (1118–1170), who was martyred for opposing his king. Local officials in Canterbury had to quickly find a substitute figure as the centerpiece for their local celebration, since even their statue of St. George, patron saint of England, was destroyed.

Henry VIII was not opposed to Catholic traditions if he could interpret them in a useful way. Thus in 1539, against the advice of some counselors, he declared his support for a variety of Catholic traditions, including Ash Wednesday ashes, Palm Sunday palms, and festivals that included "creeping to the cross" on Good Friday, not because they were sacred but because they either honored Christ directly or were educational for illustrating the scriptures. He later specifically ordered that Rogation ceremonies (the blessing of the fields) be held with special care that year because of ongoing drought and disease. Near the end of Henry's reign Archbishop Thomas Cranmer attempted to convince the king to ban several of the more important church rituals, including creeping to the cross, but the king refused. His grounds were apparently political rather than religious, as that action would have undermined his efforts to reach political agreements with the Catholic states of France and the Holy Roman Empire.

When Henry VIII died in 1547 his church remained a hybrid, somewhere between Catholic and Protestant. The reform of tradition that had taken place under its first supreme head had not defined it as either one, and both traditions continued into the twenty-first century.

hibited festivals and rites continued beyond the seventeenth century. In eighteenth-century Languedoc clergy still complained about boisterous local festivals, plays, and other events formally condemned more than a century earlier by the Catholic Church. In Wales, despite Anglican prohibitions, villagers continued to celebrate saints' days by carrying relics in processions and held fairs with sporting contests, folk healers, plays, and other officially proscribed acts and events. In some cases repressed or supplanted traditions helped generate challenges to local or national authority. In 1744 Romanian peasants in Transylvania rebelled when Orthodox customs were replaced by Catholic ones in local parishes. This was not a rejection of the new doctrines but rather a defense of traditions and cultural heritage, which the peasants saw as under attack by ecclesiastical innovations. Thus peasant societies in early modern Europe guarded their traditions jealously, not out of attachment to abstract, remote ideologies that supposedly structured their beliefs but because change was itself viewed as dangerous from their rigidly conservative mentality. Hence, "tradition" as a principle of opposition to change was regarded by the majority of Europeans as a fundamental ethical principle.

Monarchs might also face substantial opposition when attempting to alter long-held customs or beliefs. Some Protestant princes turned to reinterpreting old traditions to strengthen their interests but with additional elements that seemed, like invented church traditions, to reaffirm a venerable past and to revitalize it in new, appealing ways. Swedes asserted a glorious past by claiming that their Gothic ancestors were heroes who respected knowledge, challenging antiquity's view that they were merely destructive barbarians. When Karl IX (r. 1604–1611) toured the country, he constantly told subjects that their Gothic forebears had conquered Rome. His successor Gustav II Adolph (r. 1611–1632) appeared at a jousting tournament dressed as Berik, the legendary conqueror of southern Europe, and later reminded members of the Swedish estates that their forefathers had once ruled the world.

Other monarchs also used tradition to enhance royal glory and claim more political power. The ceremony of touching for the "king's evil" (that is, scrofula)—an old rite whereby sufferers were believed cured when touched by the monarch—emphasized the status of the king as regal and as a magical, semidivinity as well. This medieval custom was renewed in seventeenth-century England and France. Whereas Louis XII (1462–1515) touched about five hundred people per year in the early sixteenth century, Louis XIV (r. 1643–1715) touched almost six times that number following his coronation. The Sun King also invented a number of royal traditions by which virtually every aspect of his daily life was rigidly structured and solemnized into weighty ritual. The daily repetition of ceremonies, such as the *lever* (rising in each morning) and *coucher* (retiring at night), made the smallest details of Louis's life the court's focus, suggesting that ancient, time-honored rites were being faithfully maintained. The venerability of such rituals enhanced the monarchy's status at a time when its increased political power was still challenged by the nobility.

But some rulers discovered that traditions connected with a previous monarch could be used against them. Throughout the early modern period Norwegian peasants opposed unwelcome innovations and ordinances from their overlord Danish kings by declaring that the laws of the celebrated eleventh-century Norwegian martyr-king St. Olaf (r. 1016–1028) were being violated. In England, although James I (1566–1625) and Charles I (1600–1649) introduced their own holidays celebrating everything from royal birthdays and christenings to the government's escape from Guy Fawkes' attempt to blow up the king and Parliament, some churches revived the anniversary of Elizabeth I's accession day. Through this unauthorized holiday for the Protestant queen who saved the nation from Catholicism, participants thus implicitly criticized the court's flirtation with Catholicism.

But monarchs and churches were not alone in using history to invent traditions to attain their goals. The nobility, lesser gentry, and rich commoners likewise sought to glorify their lineages to enhance family status. In early modern England the College of Heralds began registering pedigrees, but the length and luster of the family tree usually depended on the fee paid. Wealthy commoners who wanted to establish a stake in the rapidly changing aristocracy of Tudor and Stuart England could pay for "research" by the heralds, who to collect the fee had to "find" eminent ancestors, which in many cases included lineages stretching back to he Norman conquerors of 1066. Such "discoveries" entitled the holder to a coat of arms or, for nobles, a better one. Sometimes people fabricated their own evidence to support such claims. The eighteenth-century Italian scholar Carlo Garibaldi forged inscriptions on stone tablets to prove that his ancestor was a seventh-century Lombard king.

In late-eighteenth-century France aristocrats also claimed long traditions, but one instance emphasized innocence and pastoral simplicity rather than nobility and elite culture. Nobles were charmed by the discovery of a local peasant festival, the *fête de la rose* (festival of the rose) in Salency, whose rural simplicity and virtue contrasted greatly with the jaded, artificial world of the court and salon. Allegedly begun by a sixth-century local bishop who was later canonized, the festival centered on a village maiden as the *rosière*, or queen of virtue, with a procession, mass, and banquet. After the festival was publicized by the countess of Genlis, nobles who liked its virtuous associations established imitations throughout France. New elements allowed nobles direct participation, For example, the local lord presented the *rosière* with a small dowry and gave the banquet, or aristocratic children wore peasant dress and marched in the procession.

On a much larger scale, minorities that were long subject to discrimination were also dignified with invented histories of phony "rediscovered" works of literature. In the late eighteenth century James Macpherson (1736–1796) and the Reverend John Macpherson (1710–1765) fabricated ancient Highland Scottish history. The former wrote an epic history of Celtic Scotland, based mostly from Irish history, and attributed it to "Ossian," a "Celtic Homer." John Macpherson then wrote a spurious Highland history that validated this text and explained away its discrepancies. So convincing was their work that it was accepted by such eminent authors as Edward Gibbon (1737–1794) and Sir Walter Scott, and it was over a century before new scholarship discredited these fabrications. Likewise, Scottish noblemen forged a more famous "ancient tradition" for Scottish history by claiming that natives wore a forerunner of the modern tartan kilt in the third century A.D. But this costume seems to have been invented in 1770 by an English iron founder who needed a less-dangerous dress for his Highland workers while tending sawmills in the Western Highlands. In other instances long-ignored but genuine works fostered new identities for minorities. In late-eighteenth-century Bohemia, Czech national identity was supported by new histories based on documents linked to the medieval religious reformer Jan Hus (1372 or 1373–1415) that showed the Czech people were historically anti-German, anti-Catholic, and anti-absolutist. This Czech identity challenged official interpretations based on Catholic Counter-Reformation portrayals of the rebel Hussites as an evil memory.

Religious traditions in rapidly industrializing, commercial Britain took a different form. Puritans emphasized order and rational behavior, which influenced the outlook of the commercial and trading classes. Ministers used phrases such as "casting up accounts" to God or asking whether an action was "profitable to the soul," and the "middling ranks" saw no contradiction between faith and commerce. By the late eighteenth century the middle classes asserted that the virtues common to both were actually the essence of the English character, which included sobriety, thrift, duty, hard work, self-denial, and Christian belief. Thus they distrusted aristocrats' luxurious, licentious ways, and scorned the boisterous festivals, games, and pastimes of "inferiors" as irrational and self-indulgent. Instead, the middle classes developed new traditions about home, family, and work. They concluded that women's supposed greater sexuality meant that they were irrational and unsuited to work outside the home or to make important decisions on their own. This strengthened patriarchy in the family and society, which was justified with biblical and historical examples, and created stereotypes about home life, gender, status, and work that became firmly embedded in Western society.

These traditions were further encouraged by British fears about the spread of the French Revolution after 1789, which seemed to challenge established traditions, beliefs, and order. The revolutionary regime swept away ceremonies, such as royal birthdays and formal entrances into Paris, as well as the customary, local saints' days, Corpus Christi festivals, and May Day celebrations, replacing them with a host of new festivals to commemorate important days in the revolution and to remind people of their progress against an oppressive monarchy. The fall of the Bastille, the establishment of the National Assembly, and revolutionary military victories were commemorated along with new festivals celebrating such revolutionary ideals as "the Supreme Being," Youth, Old Age, Spouses, Agriculture, the Law, Liberty, Virtue, and Reason.

European conservatives and moderates in turn appealed to an idealized past to counter French egalitarian ideology. In Russia, Catherine the Great (1729–1796) increased her support for authors who praised rural village life as the historical basis of the Russian character and condemned towns as the breeding ground for unstable thinking that created unrest. In Britain the monarchy was the focus of public celebrations that emphasized its connections to a glorious past. Newspapers stressed that George III's fiftieth jubilee in 1809 fell on the anniversary of Agincourt, and in 1814 London's chief peace celebration following Napoleon's defeat was specifically planned for 1 August, the centenary of the Hanoverian dynasty's succession.

Appealing to an idealized past was also a means of building morale in the face of losses. After their crushing defeat by Britain in the Napoleonic Wars, Danes rediscovered the ancient Icelandic sagas, *Beowulf,* and other works that they saw as the true basis for the Danish character. In the German states romantic authors built on distrust of French influence expressed in the earlier Sturm und Drang movement of the 1770s, when authors such as Johann von Goethe (1749–1832) and Johann Herder (1744–1803) contemptuously rejected the elites who had been strongly influenced by French literature. Herder encouraged the development of a specifically German literature based on folktales, ballads, and other traditional lore. Later romantics built on this idea, publishing collections of folksongs, chapbooks, ballads, folktales, and fairy stories. The most famous, *Kinder-und Hausmärchen* (1812–1815) by Jakob Grimm and Wilhelm Grimm, emphasizes the timeless nature of the nation's spirit. All of this morale building occurred in the context of Napoleon's stunning conquest of Germany and the later Wars of Liberation that pushed the French out by 1814.

THE LIBERTY TREE

The Liberty Tree is an enduring symbol of the French Revolution, a tradition that developed as the amalgamation of this revolutionary symbol with the much older tradition of the maypole and with an ancient celebration of the birth of spring. Ceremonial Liberty Tree plantings often incorporated familiar folk elements drawn from May Day, which helped make the notion of revolution more appealing to conservative peasants. Both rites emphasized village solidarity and corporate action, as young men selected and planted the tree and young women decorated it with ribbons and other emblems.

The Liberty Tree's popularity continued in post-1815 France but with new twists. Immediately after the 1830 revolution Liberty Trees were planted by a number of newly elected, hard-line revolutionary officials specifically to replace crosses erected by priests who were thought to support the monarchy. Anticlericalism was so strongly associated with Liberty Trees that they were an embarrassment for the moderate constitutional monarchy of the 1830s. But by 1848 the tradition had further evolved with the changing times, and many Liberty Trees planted throughout France were openly associated with reconciling the church and the republican state. Clergymen were honored guests at many planting ceremonies, and in one instance, after the local priest referred to parishioners as ''citizens and brothers,'' he told them that the Liberty Tree symbolized the cross with Christ's hands outstretched seeking liberty, a compromise that illustrates how much traditions can change in just sixty years.

The French Revolution and Napoleonic memories and symbols were also later shaped to support many political perspectives and ideologies. This provides a striking example of Halbwachs' theory that "history begins where memory ends," for while many in 1830 and 1848 personally remembered the 1789 revolution, the historians created memories and countermemories about revolutionary traditions and their meanings that served various agendas. While the restored monarchy sought legitimacy by building an antirepublican collective memory through histories emphasizing the bloodshed and destruction of the 1790s, a small group of historians defied this approach with an alternative interpretation or countermemory of republicanism as the embodiment of political liberty. The historians Jules Michelet and Alphonse de Lamartine (1790–1869) attempted to infuse the zeal of 1789 into the new generation of republicans in 1830 and 1848. Many symbols of 1789 were revived. In addition to the widespread appeal of the Liberty Tree, old songs, slogans, and names reappeared. In 1848 radicals in Nîmes held celebrations that invoked Robespierre, the Jacobins, and the sansculottes. In 1871 these traditions were still empowering. Because both the collective memory and the countermemories of 1789 lauded male contributions almost exclusively, Parisian women's groups legitimized their political participation by invoking the 1789 women's March to Versailles.

Yet despite such historical and popular references to the past, some contemporaries charged that they undermined any real understanding of the revolution and simply continued empty traditions that had no real meaning. Alexis de Tocqueville (1805–1859), who wrote a history of the 1848 revolution that stressed continuities with the past, noted in dismay that republicans "were engaged in acting the French Revolution rather than in continuing it" (Tocqueville, 1949, p. 54). In *The Eighteenth Brumaire of Louis Bonaparte* (1852), Karl Marx (1818–1883) pointedly condemned the revolutionaries, declaring, "Precisely in such periods of revolutionary crisis they anxiously conjure up the spirits of the past to their service, and borrow from them names, battle-cries and costumes in order to present the new scene of world history in this time-honoured disguise and this borrowed language" (Marx, 1977, p. 300).

The spread of literacy and the development of a mass reading public made it easier for political groups and governments to create and foster traditions for the collective memory. In Britain the increasingly anachronistic London government successfully fought off challenges by democratic reformers through the promotion of ceremonies and rituals—some traditional, some invented—that linked it with an idealized past, and while Oxford University defended its classical education against charges of anachronism by reemphasizing its colleges' long hallowed traditions. After German unification in 1871, the state likewise encouraged the concept of *Heimat* (homeland) that stressed the supposedly unified history of all Germans in a distant, rural past through nationalist literature, plays, and histories. In Austria-Hungary, as internal strife proliferated between subject nationalities, the fiftieth jubilee anniversary of the Habsburg emperor Francis Joseph (r. 1848–1916) in 1898 emphasized traditions that portrayed the Habsburg dynasty as divinely ordained and more specifically showed Francis

Revolutionary Festival. Mountain and column erected in Paris for the feast of the Supreme Being, 1794. MUSÉE CARNAVALET, PARIS/PHOTO ©RMN-BULLOZ

Joseph as a redeemerlike figure who overcame ethnic and national divisions.

Although increasing literacy, national educational systems, and mass media facilitated efforts to promote the status quo by creating channels for the dissemination of official ideologies and traditions, by the same token these developments also served the new ideologies of socialism, nationalism, feminism, and ethnic identity. With improved access to an increasingly literate and uniformly educated public, proponents of opposing views were able to mount a stiff challenge to the existing order. By 1875 British and French socialists and trade unionists used the media to reject many aspects of middle-class culture. The French socialist Paul Lafargue (1842–1911) argued that bourgeois education and literature should be replaced by an alternative workers' culture that would be inculcated through pamphlets, articles, and lectures. Socialist organizations and trade unions created alternative traditions of worker solidarity by organizing dances, benefits, and other social events in union halls decorated with symbolic banners and regalia and ultimately by organizing political parties.

Yet one aspect of bourgeois culture many workers approved was the idea that women should stay in the home. Workingmen plainly saw workingwomen as a threat to their jobs, a situation that became more acute during a deep recession in the last quarter of the nineteenth century. Since women legally could be paid less than men, industries used them to cut costs.

For many feminists this situation simply reflected their inequality. Using rhetoric and traditions drawn from women's earlier participation in antislavery movements, socialist organizing, and social reform campaigns, women's movements emerged, most notably in Britain. Just like the trade unions, women organized petition drives, fund-raising campaigns, and educational programs. They founded newspapers, women's schools and colleges, and developed their own rituals, banners, and insignias to promote solidarity within their cause.

Oppressed ethnic minorities also used media and education to campaign against imperialism. In late-nineteenth-century Ireland nationalist leaders pushed for Home Rule and to restore Ireland's own Parliament. Yet in addition to political organizing, the newly founded Gaelic League encouraged the recovery of Irish culture by promoting Gaelic language instruction, literature, and drama. Ethnic minorities elsewhere also sought to revive their cultures through language and folklore. This was particularly a problem in the Austria-Hungarian Empire. Emperor Francis Joseph agreed to allow the use of Czech as well as German in the imperial bureaucracy of Bohemia as a measure of appeasement to Czech nationalism, but Bohemian Germans were outraged at what they viewed as an attack on their national identity. By 1898 this conflict paralyzed Parliament and fueled pan-German attacks on the Habsburg state and the Catholic Church, further destabilizing the empire.

INVENTED TRADITION AS MODERNIZATION IN THE OTTOMAN TURKISH EMPIRE

In the sixteenth century the Ottoman Turkish state was at the pinnacle of its prestige, as the greatest, most illustrious power in both Europe and the Middle East. But by the mid- to late nineteenth century its luster had faded, and a series of humiliating military defeats by Austria-Hungary and imperial Russia raised the threat of conquest and overthrow. The need for the Ottoman state to prop up its prestige at home and abroad resulted in the creation of "neotraditions" with a number of significant innovations.

To give the state a more modern and Western image, an Italian artist was hired to devise a coat of arms, previously unknown in the empire, for Sultan Mahmud II (r. 1808–1839). It included both old and new symbols balancing each other. An arrow and quiver set off a modern rifle and bayonet, and a scimitar appeared opposite a modern cavalry saber, arranged to emphasize the continuity of the old and the new. Likewise the apparently Moroccan-derived *fes* (fez), which was subsequently understood as a distinctly Turkish symbol by Westerners, was adopted as the official headgear for male subjects because it looked more European than the old turban, being similar to the top hat and military shako, minus the brim or bill. The state also commissioned an official national anthem (a Western creation) from the Italian composer Gaetano Donizetti (1797–1848), as well as military marches from famous European composers such as Franz Liszt (1811–1886) and Johann Strauss (1804–1849). This is an even greater irony, since the military marching band had originally been borrowed by Euro-

peans from the Ottoman Janissary army in the early eighteenth century.

These changes were accompanied by an increased emphasis on martial spectacle, which was further enhanced by the sultan's personal appearance before the people (another innovation). Military elements also became a part of new ceremonies, sometimes forced upon minorities, of "conversion" to Islam. These ceremonies were staged to compete with the activities of aggressive European missionaries, who occasionally paid money to converts' families. Also to counter the missionaries, a new Islamic religious office, the *misyoner,* was created in another neotradition.

Some of these actions reflected the monarchs' desires for their subjects to acquire more discipline and to compete better with the West. In addition neotraditions attracted the political loyalty of the empire's numerous minorities. The historian Selim Deringil noted, "What the Ottoman elite . . . were trying to foster from the mid-nineteenth century onwards was . . . [a] transition from passive obedience [by subjects] to active and conscious subscription to the new normative order" (Deringil, 1993, p. 29). The Ottomans even tried to enhance the sanctity of their six-century tradition by officially claiming in 1885 that experts had discovered that they actually originated from Adam and Eve and that the dynasty was "one of the oldest in the world, and will live forever." The fact that it lasted only thirty-four years more underscores the importance the Ottoman state placed on the invention of tradition as a political tactic.

WAR AND MEMORY

Although conflicts between states, aggravated by nationalism, helped fuel the outbreak of World War I, the war created divisions within countries that by 1918 were still unresolved. Consequently many governments encouraged collective memories that served to heal this division and support their regimes, but they often were challenged by alternative interpretations. When France's Tomb of the Unknown soldier was dedicated in 1920, the official memorial committee used religious symbolism to imply that France had redeemed its honor by taking back Alsace-Lorraine, which had been lost to Germany in 1871.

French Socialists, however, argued that this was not the monument of a hero but the grave of an unfortunate soldier who died in a conflict fought to benefit industrialists and government officials.

Circumstances were far more difficult in postwar Germany. The Weimar government and some of its nationalist rivals attempted to forge a heroic picture of the struggle. Stressing the soldiers' faithfulness to Germany and willingness to sacrifice themselves, they emphasized the positive aspects of the wartime experience, such as camaraderie in the trenches, adherence to military virtues, and in particular dutiful loyalty. This official attempt to deal with the defeat and humiliating peace did not accurately reflect the memories of most

INVENTING MILITARY TRADITION

The military invention of tradition is essentially about managing armies. It is important for the state to keep this instrument of violence under firm control, lest it be used to overthrow the state, as has often happened in history. Much of martial tradition concerns the regiment, and this form of tradition is most developed in the British army, which benefits from the state having avoided political rupture with the past since the Glorious Revolution of 1688.

In the military subculture memorable incidents often generate appealing customs that frequently develop over time into a venerable encrustation of tradition. These customs are often based on fact, but sometimes are invented, as is the case with the traditions associated with Royal Horse Artillery full-dress uniform, a Hungarian-derived, light cavalry hussar uniform with lavish amounts of yellow braid (gold bullion for officers), worn on special occasions. Recruits are taught that the reason for this gaudy dress was that, if the artillery caisson reins break, the braid can be used as a makeshift substitute. This suggests that the dress was deliberately designed for a practical reason in a modern sense of combat utility rather than as gaudy decoration, which has long been banished from the battlefield. The history and evolution of this dress, however, has nothing to do with harnesses. It was adopted in the late eighteenth century, when this "flying" artillery was developed, to link the image of the gunner with the speed of light cavalry, swiftness being its primary tactical advantage. That the braid was ever used as substitute reins is possible, but the notion that this was the reason for the design is nonsense, since the overwhelming priority in late-eighteenth-century British military design was how the uniform looked, not modern practicality. But

the story is useful to discourage soldiers from thinking that the fancy outfit is absurd, which would diminish the glorious and venerable associations the uniform must embody.

Other purely decorative uniform elements have also been embellished with meanings invented later. The tradition of a black stripe running through the lace of officers' uniforms in some regiments is asserted to be a mark of mourning for a general killed in battle, most often one who had commanded the unit. This custom is especially associated with General James Wolfe's death at Quebec in 1759. Yet the old Forty-first Regiment wore such lace without such an association, as did other late-eighteenth-century units.

Rich traditions mystify regimental memories, which are most useful for recruiting, morale, and discipline. The idea of mutiny is also rendered to some degree more unthinkable, because it runs counter to the service's sublime traditions. Regimental tradition, like the duty, is not voluntary but enforced, and it permeates every aspect of army life. The psychological effect of such richness is thus a means of mind control that is both obvious and subtle. Even a soldier who hated the army could not help but feel the deep, emotional glow of pride and belonging when the band played stirring martial music as he and his comrades marched through cheering crowds on some venerable anniversary of victory. Any allusions to cowardice, officer incompetence, or the army's inadequate provisions of weapons, food, or shelter (as sometimes happened) seem most inappropriate and in bad taste. Tradition as a martial management principle thus maximizes an army's utility for the state.

soldiers and ignored the desertions, absenteeism, and voluntary surrenders that brought the army to the verge of collapse. Most published personal accounts, including those of private soldiers, omitted such details to avoid harming their comrades' memories.

Growing fascist organizations also played on memories of the "good" things about the war, such as camaraderie and unity, a sense of purpose and power, and the freedom from responsibility for decision making inherent in armies, in their creation of political paramilitary organizations. After attaining power fascist leaders forged new traditions that allegedly came

from a glorious national past. Benito Mussolini's government drew on imperial Rome as an inspiration for Italian glory. For example, he proclaimed 21 April a national holiday in honor of the birth of ancient Rome as part of the new regime's ideology.

Adolf Hitler's German fascists also used history to promote their concept of an organic German people, or *Volk.* This concept transcended nationalism by embodying a mystical historical racism intended to bind people together, and Nazi political and social inventions affected everything from family life to public service. To increase the birthrate the Nazis emphasized

Anachronistic Celebration. Bewhiskered Victorians in early-nineteenth-century uniforms lead the Lord Mayor's Procession past the Royal Exchange *(right)* on the way to the Royal Courts of Justice, where the lord mayor of London is sworn in. *The Ninth of November—Sir James Whitehead's Procession, 1888* painting (1890) by William Logsdail (1859–1944). GUILDHALL ART GALLERY, CORPORATION OF LONDON/THE BRIDGEMAN ART LIBRARY

the "traditional" domestic role of wife and mother, publicly discouraging women from working outside the home. The Nazis encouraged rural festivals and folk costumes to emphasize links with the mystical past. But primary emphasis went to traditions that legitimized Nazi power and the central role of Hitler as leader. Nowhere was this more clearly reflected than in the massive party rallies at Nürnberg. Begun in the 1920s, these party days were annual events from 1933 to 1938 with speeches, torchlight parades, fireworks, martial songs, flags, and a host of ceremonies.

The National Socialists also defined the concept of Germanic-Aryan *Volk* by contrasting it with "degenerate" Jewish culture. Posters, news accounts, literature, films, and radio programs proclaimed that Jews were responsible for a variety of ills, including the humiliating Versailles peace treaty, the Bolshevik revolution, oppression of German factory workers, and the 1929 economic collapse. By the mid-1930s the regime had already stripped German Jews of most rights, including citizenship. This was followed by the industrialized mass extermination of Jews and other "undesirables," such as Sinti and Roma (Gypsies), homosexuals, and political enemies.

The Nazis enforced these racist and genocidal policies in conquered territories and encouraged their allies to adopt them. Later media reports on Nazi genocide were reinforced at the Nürnberg trials, where German leaders were tried for "crimes against humanity." Yet after the war ended many attempted to obliterate its memory. To distance themselves from the Holocaust and to justify their wartime actions, collaborators across Europe cultivated "collective amnesia," claiming either to have been in the resistance or avoiding the subject altogether. Austrians quickly embraced the myth that their nation was Hitler's earliest victim, a distortion that even allowed the country to build memorials to Austrian soldiers who had fought in the *Wehrmacht,* claiming they had defended the homeland from further oppression. Liberated countries adopted a similar national amnesia. In Norway memories of World War II formed an important source of national identity for decades to come. Some Norwegian Nazis later claimed they were not really collaborators but had offered subtle resistance. Only one Norwegian out of thousands of traitors, Vidkun Quisling (1887–1945), was executed for high treason, while the many light sentences for collaboration were later reduced or commuted. In France after 1945 the government tried to obliterate the collaboration of Vichy government officials by literally banning these memories, passing legislation making it illegal to mention that anyone collaborated. In Italy the Christian Democrats attempted to reforge a Catholic democratic state linking the church to the resistance. This position ignored the Vatican's complicity with the fascists and its refusal to criticize the Nazi regime as Jews were rounded up on its very doorstep.

Jewish Holocaust survivors made perhaps the greatest effort to build a collective memory with the publication of numerous memorial books and autobiographies. David Patterson argued that the recovery of memory played an important role in their lives, allowing them to rediscover traditions nearly obliter-ated by Hitler's "Final Solution" and providing a means of coming to terms with the world's seeming indifference to their fate. Finally, reliving the memories through memorials, ceremonies, and other rituals contributed to the ongoing process of recovery from the horrors they suffered. Ironically, Hitler's victimization of Europe's Jews forged stronger feelings of Jewish unity, as even non-European Jews personally un-

Resuscitation of Classical Rome. Benito Mussolini (uniformed figure in center) reviewing young Fascists, 1938. POPPERFOTO/ARCHIVE PHOTOS

touched by the Holocaust incorporated it as a part of their cultural heritage.

Inside Germany the problem was not one of remembering but rather of forgetting. Suffering another devastating defeat that left the country in ruins, Germans came face-to-face with the crimes committed by their state. Allied troops forced civilians and officials to witness the death camp horrors by making them walk past the piles of corpses and bury the bodies. In the face of overwhelming condemnation, many Germans intentionally "forgot." East Germans denied all responsibility and blamed West Germans. West Germans adopted the concept of *Stunde Null*, or zero hour, in which their remembered history began only with the end of the war, and tried to break completely with the past. Such obliterations let West Germany as well as the United States, France, and Britain employ former Nazi officials in high positions in the new regimes. As militant anticommunists, they were considered politically safe. For more than twenty years this collective amnesia predominated. Even by the 1980s, when publications and films began to discuss modern German history more, schools, museums, and events celebrating the reunion of West Germany and East Germany in 1989 avoided reminders of this past, focusing almost solely on the cold war.

In the twenty-first century political and social traditions appear easier to invent than at any time in the past. Modern currency and coinage regularly depict political and cultural heroes, sporting events glorify nationalism, and advertising regularly draws on real or mythic memories to sell products. Even more pervasive are those media that purport to tell the "truth," such as television documentaries, newscasts, radio commentaries, newspaper and magazine articles. Yet they are all products that must suit the audience as well as the owners of these business operations. While historical films have potentially an even greater appeal, they do not re-create the past but do forge a new version of it. They must necessarily include invented dialogue and situations within story-line structures that omit much in order to work. In a different way Internet sites artificially display an equality among images of the past. Anyone with access to the Internet can create a web page that may appear to have as much validity as any other. This aspect of Internet technology plays a particularly important role in conflicts such as that in Northern Ireland, where sites that seek to promote republican or loyalist traditions based on differing interpretations have multiplied. Amid so many electronic options, the use and manipulation of memory and the invention of tradition are thus even more prevalent than ever.

See also other articles in this section.

BIBLIOGRAPHY

Anderson, Benedict. *Imagined Communities: Reflections on the Origin and Spread of Nationalism.* Rev. ed. London, 1991.

Burke, Peter. *Popular Culture in Early Modern Europe.* New York, 1978.

Clinton, Alan. "The Continuities of Counter-Memory: French Republicanism and the Revolutionary Tradition." *European Review of History* 1, no. 1 (1994): 29–42.

Confino, Alon. "The Nation as a Local Metaphor: Heimat, National Memory, and the German Empire, 1871–1918." *Memory and History* 5, no. 1 (1993): 42–86.

Davis, Natalie Zemon, and Randolph Starn. "Introduction [to Special Issue on Memory and History]." *Representations* 26 (spring 1989): 1–6.

Deringil, Selim. "The Invention of Tradition as Public Image in the Late Ottoman Empire, 1808 to 1908." *Comparative Studies in Society and History* 35, no. 1 (1993): 3–29.

Gadamer, Hans-Georg. *Truth and Method.* 2d rev. ed. New York, 1989.

Gellner, Ernest. *Culture, Identity, and Politics.* New York, 1987.

Grever, Maria. "The Pantheon of Feminist Culture: Women's Movements and the Organization of Memory." *Gender and History* 9, no. 2 (1997): 364–374.

Halbwachs, Maurice. *The Collective Memory.* Reprint ed. Leuven, Belgium, and Amersfoort, Netherlands, 1991.

Halbwachs, Maurice. "La mémoire collective et le temps." *Cahiers internationaux de sociologie* 101 (July–December 1996): 45–65.

Hobsbawm, Eric, and Terence Ranger, eds. *The Invention of Tradition.* New York, 1983.

Hutton, Patrick H. "The Role of Memory in the Historiography of the French Revolution." *History and Theory* 30, no. 1 (1991): 56–69.

Hutton, Ronald. *The Rise and Fall of Merry England: The Ritual Year, 1400–1700.* Oxford, 1994.

Johnson, Martin P. "Memory and the Cult of the Revolution in the 1871 Paris Commune." *Journal of Women's History* 9, no. 1 (1997): 39–57.

Marrocu, Luciano. "Gli artifici della memoria: Storiografia e tradizione nella Sardegna dell 1800." *Dimensioni e problemi della ricerca Storica* 1 (1988): 25–39.

Marx, Karl. "The Eighteenth Brumaire of Louis Bonaparte." In *Karl Marx: Selected Writings.* Edited by David McLellan. Oxford, 1977. Pages 300–325.

Nora, Pierre. "Between Memory and History: *Les lieux de mémoire.*" *Representations* 26 (1989): 7–25.

Nora, Pierre, ed. *Realms of Memory: Rethinking the French Past.* 3 vols. English-language editor Lawrence D. Kritzman. Translated from the French by Arthur Goldhammer. New York, 1996–1998.

Olick, Jeffrey K., and Daniel Levy. "Collective Memory and Cultural Constraint: Holocaust Myth and Rationality in German Politics." *American Sociological Review* 62, no. 6 (1997): 921–936.

Passerini, Luisa. *Fascism in Popular Memory: The Cultural Experience of the Turin Working Class.* Translated by Robert Lumley and Jude Bloomfield. New York, 1987.

Patterson, David. *Sun Turned to Darkness: Memory and Recovery in the Holocaust Memoir.* New York, 1998.

Peitsch, Helmut, Charles Burdett, and Claire Gorrara, eds. *European Memories of the Second World War.* New York and Oxford, 1999.

Roudometof, Victor. "Invented Traditions, Symbolic Boundaries, and National Identity in Southeastern Europe: Greece and Serbia in Comparative Historical Perspective (1830–1880)." *East European Quarterly* 32, no. 4 (1998): 429–468.

Rubin, David C. *Memory in Oral Traditions: The Cognitive Psychology of Epic, Ballads, and Counting-out Rhymes.* New York, 1995.

Samuel, Raphael. *Theatres of Memory.* Vol. 1: *Past and Present in Contemporary Culture.* London, 1994.

Tocqueville, Alexis de. *The Recollections of Alexis de Tocqueville.* Translated by Alexander Teixeira de Mattos. Edited by J. P. Mayer. New York, 1949.

Urry, John. "How Societies Remember the Past." *Sociological Review Monograph* (1996): 45–65.

Waldman, Marilyn Robinson. "Tradition as a Modality of Change: Islamic Examples." *History of Religions* 25, no. 4 (1986): 318–340.

HUMOR

Benjamin Roberts

While boating on the Rhine River near Leiden in the seventeenth century, a man on board notices a young woman in a garden house along the banks watching the river. He walks to the stern of the ship, starts to urinate in full view of the woman, and yells, " 'You don't have this.' " Without giving much thought to the matter she snaps back, " 'I've seen better' " (Roodenburg, 1997, p. 120). This is one of the many humorous anecdotes recorded in a book of jokes by the Dutch lawyer Aernout van Overbeke (1632–1674). The humor of the past reveals much about society, culture, sexuality, and male-female relations. Overbeke's anecdote suggests that Dutch women in the seventeenth century were quick-witted, that the young man (who like Overbeke belonged to the urban elite of the Dutch Republic) exposing himself was not ashamed of his jest, and that the Dutch of the seventeenth century apparently enjoyed a good dirty joke. This joke was probably told only in the company of men but in all social groups; as humor is not appropriate in all circumstances, the teller of this joke, like any modern counterpart, most likely saved it for the proper occasion. Although humor is just as much a part of human life as eating and drinking, it has constantly been influenced by religious, pedagogical, and political factors in Europe since the beginning of the Renaissance. Examination of a wide range of sources—iconographic images, literary works, moralistic writings, personal documents, satires, film, and television—reveals the development of European humor.

THE MEDIEVAL BACKGROUND

Humor as a social phenomenon is as old as the hills, but studying it is a relatively new research terrain for social and cultural historians. For the history of humor, the Russian medievalist Mikhail Bakhtin fulfilled a role comparable to that of Philippe Ariès in the history of childhood. Bakhtin's *Rabelais and His World,* published in 1965 after a twenty-five year ban in Russia, was the first study in which humor was illumi-

nated as an essential element of the culture of carnival: carnival, which ritualized winter turning into spring, was celebrated by turning the world upside down, the pauper becoming a prince, the king a jester for a day. The culture of the Middle Ages, as Bakhtin saw it, was distinctly polarized: the official culture of the church and the educated spurned laughter, whereas the popular culture was dominated by the tradition of carnival and laughter. Aaron Gurevich, a cultural historian of the Middle Ages, found this view of medieval society an inadequate simplification of its complex cultural levels, arguing that the church and the educated were not against laughter. In his novel *The Name of the Rose* (1982), the Italian author Umberto Eco portrays a polarization within the medieval church. In Eco's book the monk of the Benedictine order, Jorge de Burgos, is appalled by laughter, whereas William of Baskerville, of the Franciscan order, is more mundane. As the medievalist Jacques Le Goff argues, ecclesiastical writers in the Middle Ages struggled with two viewpoints: that laughter was natural and idiosyncratic to man, and that laughter was unnatural. The latter view derived from the belief that if "Jesus, the great model for humanity, . . . never once laughed in his human life, then laughter becomes alien to man, at least to a Christian man" (Le Goff, 1997, p. 43). Petrus Cantor, a twelfth-century scholar, argued that, since Christ was born a human and was capable of laughing, his refusal to laugh must be a virtue (Verberckmoes, 1998, p. 80). Throughout the Middle Ages and early modern period, this debate was a recurrent theme for theologians and moralists.

Le Goff divides the Middle Ages into two broad periods, one of repressed laughter and one of tolerance of laughter. From the fourth century to the tenth century, for monks especially, laughter was a vice akin to idleness. To laugh was a particularly abrupt way of breaking an almost celestial silence. With the second half of the Middle Ages came greater freedom to laugh, but the church tried to control it. A parallel development was an increase in vernacular literature, an element of which was self-reflection; this self-reflection partly consisted of satire and parody. The royal courts were the first to embrace and domesticate new modes of laughter.

MODERN PERIODS: RENAISSANCE AND REFORMATION

A lack of sources limits the theoretical debate among historians on laughter in the Middle Ages. This is not true of the Renaissance and early modern period. A prominent source and character in the history of humor in the late Middle Ages and early modern period is the court jester. One might say that this "stand-up comedian" in his silly attire was the court's substitute for Prozac. During carnival even friars, monks, and nuns liked to imitate these clowns. Some Italian fools at the time received interregional and international fame, such as Dolcibene, the two Gonellas, Beatrice d'Este's Diodato in Milan, Isabella d'Este's Fritella at Mantua, and Borso d'Este's Scocola at Ferrara, the last immortalized in the frescoes at Schifanoia. A primary source for humor, in addition to the many literary and iconographic references to court jesters in the late Middle Ages and the Renaissance are the numerous *beffa* or jest books. These trick or practical joke books were especially popular around the Mediterranean region, with Florence "*la capitale de la beffa*" (Burke, 1997, p. 64). Some of these books included plays in which a character was made a fool of, such as Niccolò Machiavelli's *La mandragola* (1518) and Pietro Aretino's *Il marescalco*. A common setting was at the court of the duke of Mantua, where the duke requests that the master of the horse get married. The master of the horse is not attracted to women, but he pursues the wedding anyway, only to find out that his bride is a page. The *beffe* also included instructions for pranks, "such as making someone fall asleep at the dining table, . . . recipes for dyeing one's hair or cures for impotence" (Burke, 1997, p. 64).

Laughter came under religious scrutiny during the Counter-Reformation, when reformers tried to change the Catholic Church from within rather than break with it as the Protestants had. Many clergy and writers of conduct books criticized the *beffes* on moral grounds. New printed *beffes* became embedded in a moral story, using metaphors signifying cures, lessons, and punishments, and lost their practical-joke quality. Children had to be taught to control their laughter; the elderly often lost their control. Writers of conduct books preferred verbal jokes to pranks, as did the upper echelons in society. Peter Burke detects at the end of the sixteenth century a general restriction from partaking in humor by the clergy, women, and gentle-

Court Jesters. "Car of Fools and Jesters," drawing from *The Triumph of the Emperor Maximilian I* by Hans Burgkmair (1478–1553). FINE ARTS MUSEUM OF SAN FRANCISCO, ACHENBACH FOUNDATION FOR GRAPHIC ARTS, 1963.30.34824

men, which corroborates Bakhtin's idea of the polarization of humor, as does northern European art of the sixteenth century. Depictions of laughing faces on people of lower means often served as examples of unacceptable behavior. "Jesters, satyrs, peasants, drunks, bagpipe-players were all presumed to be the opposite of what a civilized person was supposed to be" (Verberckmoes, 1998, p. 47).

Northern European moralist writers of the Counter-Reformation also participated in suppressing verbal humor. During the sixteenth and seventeenth centuries, the pedagogical and moralistic writings by the humanists Desiderius Erasmus (1466?–1536), Laurent Joubert, and Juan Luis Vives (1492–1540) were influential in determining how laughter was regarded for the rest of the early modern period. Especially for Erasmus, laughter was no laughing matter. It had serious purposes, such as relieving pain caused by sickness, and he advised that it was good to laugh occasionally while in the company of others. But for other than medicinal uses, laughter was denounced. Humanistic writers understood that laughter is an exceptional form of human expression, yet at the same time were pressured to restrain it by pedagogical means. Faced with this dilemma, they tried to distinguish the real laugh from the false by categorizing the various forms of laughter. Vives described the unstoppable laugh of the Greek philosopher Democritus (c. 460–370 B.C.) as fake and unreal, a forced sardonic laugh, and Erasmus labeled it false, bitter, and foolish. Erasmus classified laughter as follows: the ionic laugh, that of the bon vivant with a taste for luxury and pleasure-seeking; the megaric laugh, or laughter at the wrong moment; the chrionic laugh, or laughter that bursts forth; and the syncronousic laugh, a laughter expressing shock that is difficult for the body to control. According to Erasmus these laughs were inappropriate for respectable people because they implied a wild spirit.

In *De anima et vita* (1538), Vives theorized about the effects of laughter on the body, drawing on the humor theory developed by Galen, the second-century Greek physician. According to that theory, bodily fluids—the humors—determine a person's health and temperament. Vives wrote that those with yellow bile were inclined to laugh more easily because their hearts gave off warmth, whereas those having a phlegmatic temperament and thus troubled with black bile laughed less due to their slow circulation. For Vives laughter was a natural human condition that nevertheless people should not give into easily. Conduct books advised a controlled laugh and only in appropriate situations. Laughter had a social dimension: the naive, such as peasants, children, and women, were likely to lose their self-control if laughter caught them off guard, whereas intelligent people could control themselves and not burst into laughter.

In *Traité du ris* (Treatise on laughter, 1579), Joubert studied the physical aspects of laughter, distinguishing real laughs from fake ones. According to Joubert's anthropological description, laughter manifested itself physically: "The face goes into motion, the mouth and lips widened, the chin extended, the eyes glistened and teared, the cheeks blushed, the chest shuck, the voice trembled." The situation became worse as the laugh continued:

> The throat widens, the lips stretch even further, the face wrinkles especially the cheeks and corner of the eyes, the teeth become exposed, the eyes tear and swell as if they are going to jump out of their sockets, the veins in the forehead and neck swell, the arms, shoulders, and buttocks tremble, and one starts to stamp with their feet . . . so that one begins to cough, throw up, and the nose spits out what someone has drank, one starts to piss, shit, and to sweat. (Verberckmoes, 1998, p. 61)

In some cases, he noted, a laugh could last so long that a person must lean on something to brace himself or herself or fall down. According to Joubert, in the worst-case scenario a person could faint but not die. Damasceno, an Italian priest and astrologer in the seventeenth century, wrote a pamphlet in which he drew an interesting conclusion from humoral theory: a person's temperament could be determined by the way that person laughed. A hee-hee-hee laugh indicated a melancholic temperament, a heh-heh-heh laugh a choleric temperament, a ha-ha-ha laugh a phlegmatic temperament, and a ho-ho-ho laugh a sanguine temperament. Of course, this view of temperament was not taken too seriously, although humoral theory retained medical currency into the nineteenth century.

During the religious and political upheavals in the northern and southern Netherlands in the sixteenth century, moralistic writers of the Counter-Reformation tried to constrain laughter. Pieter Croon of Mechelen (in present-day Belgium) echoed the church's old conviction regarding laughter, writing, " 'Now is the time for weeping and in heaven will be the time for laughter' " (Verberckmoes, 1997, p. 80). Despite this stern disapproval of laughter, Croon's contemporaries were aware that laughing was part of human nature, thus it was important to restrain and control laughter as much as possible. Spiritual writers consoled their audiences with the assurance that "earthly tears would be followed by heavenly laughter" (Verberckmoes, 1997, p. 81). Reformers distinguished between sacred and profane humor, creating a whole new comic terrain. Those who made fun and folly of the church, such as "the puppet players Jacob Cobbeniers and his wife Elisabeth Lauwers, who around 1600 in a puppet play let St Peter and St Paul kiss and feel a woman, Margite, and even let the two saints embrace each other," could be tried before an ecclesiastic or secular court (Verberckmoes, 1997, pp. 84–85). Mockery of the Catholic Church was not taken lightly.

Early modern society was also aware of the psychological effects of laughter. Depressive bouts known as melancholy were a common plight of the wealthy and the idle. Toward the end of the sixteenth century melancholy was a household term. In *The Anatomy of Melancholy* (1621) the Oxford clergyman and scholar Robert Burton (1577–1640) made a scientific study of the causes and effects of melancholy, and laughter as an important remedy. Various reports claimed people died of melancholy, and numerous pamphlets were published on how to cure it. The physician known as Paracelsus (1493–1541) advised the victims of melancholy to battle it with its opposite. A melancholy patient should be treated with laughter, while a clown, on the other hand, should be handled with melancholy. The idea behind both therapies was to normalize the person's temperament. For those with severe cases of melancholy, some cures called for such unusual remedies as liquid gold or venereal ecstasy (Verberckmoes, 1998, p. 68). More commonly, doctors and others concerned were apt to recommend a good laugh now and then. The letters of the prominent Amsterdam lawyer Willem Backer (1656–1731) urged his daughter, who was plagued with melancholy, to read, paint, take walks, and see a comedy at the theater.

THE SEVENTEENTH CENTURY

Not surprisingly the elites, who were likely to fall prey to melancholy, were also the first to abide by the numerous domestic conduct books and theological treatises restraining laughter. In the seventeenth-century Dutch Republic, the humor of the urban elite shifted to a more cultivated wit and punning. In Amsterdam in the late seventeenth century, for example, the society for the reform of theater rewrote comedies, purging them of their vulgar elements. This was a stark contrast to the scenes depicted by the painter Jan Steen (1626–1679), a keen observer of the human comedy. Steen's themes were everyday situations, such as seduction, lovesickness, marriage, and childbirth, as well as historical episodes from which he culled humor and wit. About *Doctor's Visit* (c. 1667–1670), which portrays a young, lovesick girl, the art historian Mariët Westermann writes:

> The young woman perks up at the sight of the lover entering. Her accelerating pulse confounds the doctor, who signals his incompetence with his costume, outmoded for the 1660s, and with his bewildered expression. The smiling girl at the virginals and the grinning character at far right, who sports Steen's features, enhance the comic flavour. Letting us in on the joke, Steen suspends a herring [a phallic metaphor] and two onions in a farcical simile for the cure. (Westermann, 1997, p. 143)

How could Steen hope to sell his canvases, candidly depicting smoking, drinking, disorderly behavior, and sexual illicitness, to the urban elite with their high moral standards? According to Westermann, the elites saw no resemblance between themselves and Steen's round-bodied characters, nor between their own moral lifestyles and the situations he represented. Thus they could enjoy the humor without feeling morally implicated.

The sense of humor of the seventeenth-century urban elite is more clearly revealed by Overbeke's *Anecdota,* his book of jokes. Overbeke, who was well educated and friends with many prominent people in the Dutch Republic, recorded some 2,440 jokes and anecdotes, whose subjects included physical handicaps, women, permissive parenting, capital punishment, sex, and bathroom humor. In contrast with the late Middle Ages and the early modern period, it was acceptable to laugh at those who were physically impaired. Many jokes popular among all strata of Dutch society were childlike, with their emphasis on bodily excretions and sexual attributes. The comical situation

was also popular, and some jokes along these lines were circulated into the twentieth century. For example, a dimwit ties a rope around his waist. When someone asks why, he replies, "I want to hang myself." The other remarks, "Then you have to tie the rope around your neck and not your waist." The dimwit retorts, "I already tried that but it makes me choke."

Punishment of adults in the early modern period took place in public (juveniles were often spared public humiliation) and was a form of entertainment for the masses. Overbeke's collection includes a joke about a public execution. The sentenced man has to climb the ladder to the gallows backward, to the delight of the spectators, who roar with laughter. The condemned man pardons himself to the executioner, saying, "Excuse me, this is my first time." In another, a man condemned to death by the courts is given the choice of death by hanging or by beheading. (Death by hanging was less honorable.) The man replies, "Hanging, I can't stand the sight of blood."

Many jokes Overbeke recorded were about sex, impotence, and the sex organs. People of his day freely discussed sexuality; such discussions were more restricted later in the seventeenth century. He alluded to the female genitals as "c . . . ," "stocking," or "slit," and to the penis as "clown," "glodhopper," "finch," "instrument," and "middle knee." Lusting women figured in many jokes. For example, after returning home following an absence a woman complains that her dog was more polite to her than her husband. When asked what she means, she replies, "At least my dog jumped on top of me." Overbeke's contemporaries were not surprised that many women became prostitutes, reasoning that such women longed for sex.

What motivated Overbeke to record the jokes of his day? His father had died from "morbo melancholico" or depression, for which humor was a well-known remedy. Another reason might have been his social background. His forefathers were from the southern Netherlands and had fled to the Dutch Republic during the revolt against Spain. Although they worked themselves up to the higher strata of Dutch society in the seventeenth century, they never belonged to the very top. Overbeke studied law at the University of Leiden, went on the grand tour, and became a lawyer in the Hague, where he was close to many high officials and members of the stadtholder's court. With his sense of humor and love of writing poetry, Overbeke was somewhat of a bohemian. He probably benefited from his sense of humor especially in high circles, where humor had an important social function. As everybody enjoys a good joke, humor serves as a good social lubricant, enlivening all sorts of gatherings. Civilized people released their physical fury through humor. Instead of fighting duels, urban society solved differences in a sophisticated fashion, replacing the sword with the tongue in contests of wit. Lawyers such as Overbeke were especially suitable for this type of linguistic warfare because they honed their wit and dry humor at trials.

In early modern France humor played an important part in the shift from physical violence to verbal retort in the civilization process. Norbert Elias (1897–1990), the father of the theory of the civilization process, never said a word about humor; nevertheless it is a fact that physical violence decreased throughout the early modern period, replaced by sophisticated humor. According to the Dutch historian Rudolf Dekker, who stumbled upon Overbeke's *Anecdota* in the Dutch national archives, Overbeke's record of humor and anecdotes endorses the image of the seventeenth-century Dutch as a humorous folk and illustrates a shift in the national character by the nineteenth century, when the Dutch no longer were known for their boisterous humor but rather for their sedate soberness. What happened to the image of the boisterous Dutchman slapping his knee? Beginning in the late seventeenth and continuing into the eighteenth, conduct book writers, moralists, and theologians, all influential in the Dutch bourgeois culture, condemned immoderate laughter, especially laughing at the expense of another person. In the course of two centuries the Dutch became heavy-handed Calvinists.

For early modern England Burton's *The Anatomy of Melancholy* (1621) and the diary of Samuel Pepys (1633–1703) are important sources. Both men owned large collections of jest books, a genre popular among Italian humanists in the Renaissance; as they were translated they became popular throughout the rest of Europe. Stories in these books depicted a scene of daily life, ending with a smart reply intended to make the listener burst out laughing. Indeed, telling jokes was an amusing pastime. On 9 October 1660 Pepys wrote that he and his friends "were very merry at table, telling of tales," and a month later he wrote, "And did tell many merry stories, and in good humours were we all." Many times the affair of telling jokes was accompanied by drinking. Pepys recorded many practical jokes he played, even on William Penn. He noted ludicrous accounts, such as on 1 July 1663, "Sir Charles Sedley stripping himself naked on the balcony of a cook's shop in Covent Garden, before 1000 people, then engaging in various obscene acts, 'abusing scripture', and preaching an obscene 'Mountebank sermon'" (Brewer, 1997, p. 95). In general the educated frowned upon jest books, but apparently Pepys did not. He classified his "merry books" as "vulgaria." Because reprints were often cheaply produced, jest books were literally read to pieces by his contemporaries.

In the seventeenth century little difference existed between the humor of the gentry and of the populace. As elsewhere in Europe this changed in the eighteenth century, mainly because humanist thinkers embraced the French classicism manifested in conduct books. In 1748 Lord Chesterfield (1694–1773) condemned laughter in a letter to his son: "Loud laughter is the mirth of the mob, who are only pleased with silly things; for true wit or good sense never excited a laugh" (Brewer, 1997, p. 103). Apparently Lord Chesterfield was not one to invite to a party. Toward the end of the seventeenth century the court jester died out as well. The English king William III of Orange (1650–1702) was the last king to appoint a jester to the court in 1694. During the eighteenth century humor joined French culture, literature, language, fashion, and court in the esteem of the European elites. Especially in urban areas, people came to prefer sophisticated humor over the traditional boorish humor of rural society with its practical jokes and pranks.

THE NINETEENTH AND TWENTIETH CENTURIES

In the early nineteenth century Berliners were well known for their wit. The city was acclaimed by guidebooks as the "mother city of wit," and its inhabitants were applauded for their "mockery, ridicule, bluntness and cheek." Dry wit was reputedly "natural phenomenon, an inborn characteristic of Berlin's lower classes" (Townsend, 1997, pp. 200–201). In 1844 the German author Theodor Mundt noted that Berlin's popular humor had two qualities: it could either ignite or still the frustrations of the people regarding Prussia's political situation in the 1830s and 1840s. Apparently it had a soothing effect on the populace until 1848.

According to the historian Mary Lee Townsend, Berlin humor of the early nineteenth century profoundly influenced the establishment of a public sphere with a sense of community. In that sphere laughter was an important ingredient of public debate. A comic strip figure, Eckensteher Nante, was a significant symbol. *Eckensteher,* literally one who stands on a street corner, first appeared in the Berlin press in 1832 to denote a lower-class worker, and by the 1848 revolution the character by that name was a major political icon. On some occasions he was even suggested as a candidate for emperor of a united Germany. Eckensteher's popularity can be credited to his wide circulation through an inexpensive medium. His social background as a menial laborer in Berlin ap-

A Cartoon from *Punch*, c. 1860. "The police wear beards and moustaches. Panic among the street boys." ©HULTON-GETTY/LIAISON AGENCY

pealed to many of the other Berliners who were drawn to the city for work. The strip addressed and satirized many social issues of early nineteenth-century society, such as poverty, drinking, and the political repression of Prussian citizens. A recurring theme concerned the Prussian state's poor care of veterans of the Napoleonic Wars. In a strip in an 1845 booklet, "an ex-soldier remarks to his friend, 'It is nice to die for the Fatherland . . . because then you don't have to live as a disabled veteran' " (Townsend, 1997, p. 212). All social strata read the strip, but each group probably found something different in it. The bourgeoisie most likely laughed at the stupidity, passiveness, and harshness displayed, while the poor probably laughed at the situations with which they identified. The strip's effect on politics was probably marginal in the long run, but it kept the political groups of Berlin on their toes up to the 1848 revolution.

During the second half of the nineteenth century, caricatures became popular in the English magazine *Punch,* which first appeared in 1841. The editors marketed humor that the English bourgeois middle class could appreciate. During the first nineteen years of *Punch*'s publication, its satire poked fun at the government, the propertied classes, the Catholic Church, and the English royal family. In 1860 the editor Mark Lemon (1809–1870) decided it would be more lucrative to humor than to offend the bourgeoisie, and *Punch* became a polite weekly that exhibited many characteristics of the English temperament. From 1860 to after the World War II the jokes in *Punch* fit

into a typically English pattern. In his penetrating look at English humor, Harold Nicolson describes the jokes in *Punch* as childish (with a naive delight in the play on words) and self-protective (ridiculing the unfamiliar, foreigners, surprising events, and intellectual superiority); they required minimal mental effort (whether appreciation of the unfamiliar, of poking fun at knowledge, or of inspired nonsense), aiming instead to comfort (by comparing dilemmas of the present with the past and thus rationalizing them). Nicolson argues that the English are not less sensitive than other nationalities when its comes to making fun of their "institutions, climate, cooking, habits and foibles" (Nicolson, 1956, p. 43). Rather, the core of the English sense of humor is a high self-regard masquerading as self-ridicule: for example, if the English were truly ashamed of their cuisine, they would not be inclined to poke fun at it.

While *Punch* catered to the English bourgeoisie, Oscar Wilde (1854–1900) constantly made fun of them from above. His plays, such as *The Importance of Being Earnest* (1895), mocked middle-class norms and values and therefore Victorian society. All the prized merits of the English bourgeoisie, such as hard work, honesty, marriage, good morals, and proper behavior, faced ridicule in Wilde's one-liners. To wit: "Any preoccupation with ideas of what is right or wrong in conduct shows an arrested intellectual development" (Wilde, 1987, p. 1113). In fact self-ridicule became the main ingredient for humor in the film industry and later for television in twentieth-century America. Classics such as Charlie Chaplin's *Modern Times* (1936), which derided industrial society, and *The Great Dictator* (1940), which ridiculed Hitler, who had risen to power in Nazi Germany, made audiences on both sides of the Atlantic roar with laughter. Hitler, however, failed to see the humor and banned Chaplin's films. By the 1950s American situation comedies such as *I Love Lucy* brought American culture and the American sense of humor into European households. Europeans produced their own sitcoms, incorporating their own national identities and jokes. Most American sitcoms more or less portrayed American family values with a moralistic message and dealt with matters like sex in an indirect Victorian fashion. The popular 1990s British sitcom *Absolutely Fabulous* had viewers in Britain and on the Continent gasping for air at the quick-witted humor of its stars, Jennifer Saunders and Joanna Lumley. The duo portrayed two forty-something women of the baby boom still living in a version of the hedonistic 1960s world of sex, drugs, and rock and roll. The candor fired off in high-speed dialogue was a refreshing element in British humor. While most viewers laughed at the mockery of the 1960s, the real butt of the humor was the no-nonsense 1990s and its New Age overtones.

CONCLUSION

From the Middle Ages to the nineteenth century, moralists, theologians, and the church attempted to restrain laughter. During the seventeenth and eighteenth centuries attitudes toward laughter shifted. By replacing physical violence with verbal wit, the elites first initiated this social intercourse, and the bourgeoisie and the lower strata of society adopted it. Propelled by humanist pedagogical writers of the sixteenth and seventeenth centuries, such as Erasmus, Vives, and Joubert, the change was more apparent during the eighteenth century, when the bourgeoisie incorporated humor in their lives on a broad scale. However, the personal documents of Overbeke and Pepys, both of high social status, are closer to the humor of daily life in the seventeenth century and illustrate that people continued to laugh about commonplace matters despite finger-pointing by moralists. Sources from the Renaissance and the early modern period demonstrate that the history of humor is a dichotomy between the humor portrayed in secondary sources and the humor of daily life in personal sources. In the nineteenth and twentieth centuries the influence of moralists and theologians on the suppressing of humor declined. By the end of the twentieth cen-

Charlie Chaplin. Chaplin *(holding bowl)* and Jack Oakey *(holding spaghetti)* in *The Great Dictator*, 1940. BETTMANN/CORBIS

tury, a sense of humor was considered a particular asset, with employers seeking not only skills and commitment in their prospective workers but also the ability to laugh. The old adage, "Laugh and the world laughs with you, cry and you cry alone," survived. Another modern variable involved political regimes and uses of humor to release political tension amid censorship, a key theme for many communist countries in the twentieth century.

The social and cultural history of European humor remains a fertile topic. Specific explorations, such as examinations of early modern Holland, have been revealing and suggest important adjustments of established views. But many periods and regions have not been studied, and systematic accounts have not been developed. The difficulty of the topic lies not in discussing written efforts at humor but in deciphering what humor meant to different people and how it was used. Many studies, such as those concerning the role of political humor and satire amid censorship efforts in the nineteenth and twentieth centuries, are specific. Analysis of new forms of popular theater, such as music halls, in the late nineteenth century inevitably deal with earthy humor and how it was received when the middle class patronized working-class establishments. Other studies refer to humor in passing. Works on changing European manners in the eighteenth century—among them Lord Chesterfield's popular treatise—note a hostility to humor, perceived as suggesting poor breeding and lack of self-control. How much this attitude actually affected humor is another question. Clearly, ample room exists for additional research in a branch of social-historical inquiry fed by the growing interest in cultural evidence and issues.

See also other articles in this section.

BIBLIOGRAPHY

Bakhtin, Mikhail. *Rabelais and His World.* Bloomington, Ind., 1984. Originally published in 1965.

Brewer, Derek. "Prose and Jest-books Mainly in the Sixteenth to Eighteenth Centuries in England." In *A Cultural History of Humour: From Antiquity to the Present Day.* Edited by Jan Bremmer and Herman Roodenburg. Cambridge, U.K., 1997. Pages 90–111.

Burke, Peter. "Frontiers of Comic in Early Modern Italy c. 1350–1750." In *A Cultural History of Humour: From Antiquity to the Present Day.* Edited by Jan Bremmer and Herman Roodenburg. Cambridge, U.K., 1997. Pages 61–75.

Burton, Robert. *The Anatomy of Melancholy.* Oxford, 1989. Originally published in 1621.

Dekker, Rudolf. *Lachen in de Gouden Eeuw: Een geschiedenis van de Nederlandse humor.* Amsterdam, 1997.

Eco, Umberto. *The Name of the Rose.* London, 1982.

Gurevich, Aaron. "Bakhtin and His Theory of Carnival." In *A Cultural History of Humour: From Antiquity to the Present Day.* Edited by Jan Bremmer and Herman Roodenburg. Cambridge, U.K., 1997. Pages 54–60.

Le Goff, Jacques. "Laughter in the Middle Ages." In *A Cultural History of Humour: From Antiquity to the Present Day.* Edited by Jan Bremmer and Herman Roodenburg. Cambridge, U.K., 1997. Pages 40–53.

Muchembled, Robert. *De uitvinding van de moderne mens: Collectief gedrag, zeden, gewoonten en gevoelsleven van de middeleeuwen tot de Franse revolutie.* Amsterdam, 1991. Translation of *L'invention de l'homme moderne: Sensibilités, moeurs et comportements collectifs sous l'Ancien Regime.* Paris, 1988.

Nicolson, Harold George. *The English Sense of Humour, and Other Essays.* London, 1956.

Roberts, B. "Dutch Affective Parent-Child Relations in the Eighteenth Century: Catharina Backer and Her Parents." *History of Education Society Bulletin* 56 (autumn 1995): 17–26.

Roodenburg, Herman. "To Converse Agreeably: Civility and the Telling of Jokes in Seventeenth-Century Holland." In *A Cultural History of Humour: From Antiquity to the Present Day.* Edited by Jan Bremmer and Herman Roodenburg. Cambridge, U.K., 1997. Pages 112–133.

Spierenburg, Pieter. *The Spectacle of Suffering: Executions and the Evolution of Repression: From a Preindustrial Metropolis to the European Experience.* Cambridge, U.K., 1984.

Townsend, Mary Lee. "Humour and the Public Sphere in Nineteenth-Century Germany." In *A Cultural History of Humour: From Antiquity to the Present Day.* Edited by Jan Bremmer and Herman Roodenburg. Cambridge, U.K., 1997. Pages 200–221.

Verberckmoes, Johan. "The Comic and the Counter-Reformation in the Spanish Netherlands." In *A Cultural History of Humour: From Antiquity to the Present Day.* Edited by Jan Bremmer and Herman Roodenburg. Cambridge, U.K., 1997. Pages 76–89.

Verberckmoes, Johan. *Schertsen, schimpen en schateren: Geschiedenis van het lachen in de zuidelijke Nederlanden, zestiende en zeventiende eeuw.* Nijmegen, Netherlands, 1998.

Westermann, Mariët. "How Was Jan Steen Funny? Strategies and Functions of Comic Painting in the Seventeenth Century." In *A Cultural History of Humour: From Antiquity to the Present Day.* Edited by Jan Bremmer and Herman Roodenburg. Cambridge, U.K., 1997. Pages 134–178.

Wilde, Oscar. *The Complete Works of Oscar Wilde.* Leicester, U.K., 1987.

MUSIC AND DANCE

William Weber

History books usually place music among the sister arts, incorporating its history into style periods such as the baroque, the romantic, or the realist. Yet an argument can be made that music has been related much more closely with politics and the social life of its publics than with painting, poetry, or the novel. While broad artistic communities existed in the late nineteenth and early twentieth centuries, for the most part a European musician had far more to do with his patron than with painters or writers. Much the same can be said of the dance, for it evolved in close relationship to music in the grand festivals put on at courts to honor births, marriages, or visiting dignitaries. In such contexts we can profitably study the history of music, dance, and indeed society itself.

Music is the most social of the arts. As a performing art governed by ritual, it is much less an individual experience than reading books or viewing artworks. Music is involved in a great variety of social contexts: the home and the school; the tavern and clubs; public institutions such as the church and municipalities; and events in parks and arenas. Most important of all, musical performance has been central to the social life of middle and upper classes, and in some places the working classes as well. Music therefore offers the historian an unusually good context within which to study some of the most important social groups and movements in modern European history. It also helps us understand European politics from what the British call "out of doors," outside formal institutions. Commentators have often discussed musical life in civic terms—Charles Burney, for example, spoke of the "Republic of Music" in his music history published in 1776.

Scholars from both history and musicology have viewed the musical life as an integral community with its own traditions and discourse, which also contributed significantly to the functioning of larger society and politics. To see how music related to larger social or cultural frameworks, we do best to start not with categories such as the Enlightenment or the middle class, but rather with musical practices and the social framework with which they were linked. Musicologists are very much attuned to this problem; in many cases their interests bear a much closer relationship to the methods of Roger Chartier, a leader in French thinking on mentalities, than to those of traditional intellectual historians. They start from social contexts in attempting to re-create musical practices in the musical life of a cathedral, court, or city. Jeffrey Kallberg has contributed the most important ideas about how musician and public worked within a contract that laid down both musical and social expectations for a musical genre, and within which they negotiated change in both composition and performance. Neal Zaslaw has shown that we cannot understand fully how W. A. Mozart approached writing a work unless we know precisely for whom and in what context he intended it. Jane Fulcher has demonstrated how deeply politics, as it is broadly conceived today, interpenetrated musical life in discourse and in musicians' careers. The social history of music, in other words, involves more than audience studies: it goes to the heart of music itself as an interactive art.

It is important to see that music had a distant and ambiguous relationship with the mainstream of European intellectual and cultural life from the sixteenth to the late eighteenth century. The learned tradition of scientific and philosophical theory on music—notions of the "harmony of the spheres," specifically—became much less important in the universities and in European thought generally, and written discourse on composition or performance of music remained limited, usually appearing only in pedagogical form. Polyphonic music, based chiefly in the church, served as the main area of higher learning among musicians but had weaks links with literary life; indeed, humanistic thinkers tended to be hostile to it as a scholastic exercise. It was only during the middle of the eighteenth century that commentary on music shifted from aural into printed form and became part of a larger cultural discourse—philosophy, history, criticism, and journalism. The arrival of music within these spheres marked a major milestone in the art's history, giving it a lofty role in secular cultural life such as it had not possessed before.

Music historians studying the later Middle Ages and the Renaissance have contributed a particular amount to social historians, most importantly on the nature of patronage and court life. Iain Fenlon has argued for discontinuity in patronage, showing how the dukes of Mantua reshaped the music of their court, both sacred and secular, in idiosyncratic ways. By contrast, Kristine Forney has stressed long-standing traditions in the ways music was performed and works commissioned within confraternities of sixteenth-century Antwerp. Study of musical performances at court can tell us a great deal about the larger nature of sociability, gender roles, and political meanings, and about how people listened. Christopher Page has done such a study on the late medieval *trouvères,* and Tess Knighton, on the court of Castile in the fifteenth century; they show how textual, musical, and social needs interacted in the ways music was presented. Musicologists and historians have raised questions about the validity of speaking about the Renaissance as an epoch in the sweeping terms that are so common. Nino Pirrotta has argued that Claudio Monteverdi was not directly influenced by the intellectual life of Florence; rather, he took advantage of its interest in drama in order to explore new ways to set music and dramatic text. Honey Meconi has likewise asked musicologists to reconsider the extent to which humanism affected the sixteenth-century practice of *imitatio.*

The very roles musicians played within the courts of the fifteenth through the eighteenth century can help us see that the old society was not as bound to a rigid corporate structure as is often claimed. High-level musicians were extremely mobile and independent in their careers, moving frequently from one place to another as opportunities presented themselves. New genres and styles in fact spread around Europe in large part through the journeys of monarchs and their agents. The career moves made by Josquin des Prez, Monteverdi, or G. F. Handel, who reshaped musical practices significantly as they went, illustrate the individualism that Jonathan Dewald has shown among aristocrats of the time. Many musicians of this sort served as secretaries and political advisers to monarchs or noblemen. Handel, for example, took his first trip to London in 1708 chiefly to send back reports on the unsteady condition of English politics as the King of Hanover awaited the succession. Thus, let us not say that musicians were always banished to eat with the kitchen staff.

The rise of opera in the seventeenth century offers a useful perspective on the varieties of absolutism and society. Lorenzo Bianconi and Thomas Walker demonstrate that operas grew up variously in courts and cities, and as court institutions within cities. In some cases one could find larger audiences in courts than in urban theaters. Bianconi and Walker see opera emerging within a small elite that served the political and social purposes of monarchs or of the patriciate. Robert Isherwood likewise shows that the operas Jean-Baptiste Lully produced for Louis XIV brought a new scale to the traditional festivals for visiting dignitaries and interacted textually with court gossip and politics. Opera then shifted from court to municipal contexts, at a time when the cosmopolitan public began to take on political authority, forming what is usually called the "public sphere." The Académie Royale de Musique, for example, became established in Paris well before the death of Louis XIV and demonstrated how the public had succeeded the king as the principal source of authority over taste. By the middle of the eighteenth century such a shift away from royal courts and into city centers had taken place in the great majority of countries.

MUSICAL CULTURE WITHIN EIGHTEENTH-CENTURY PUBLIC LIFE

Musical culture provides an excellent context within which to study the emergence of the new forms of public life that related closely to development of the public sphere during the eighteenth century. Between about 1700 and 1870, London, Paris, and to varying extents the capital cities of Europe generally played host to a particular elite social life, bringing together wealthy and influential people, generally in greater numbers than had been the case at the courts. The cities indeed robbed the courts of their former central role in politics and culture. The social world of the new urban elites was not as intimate as that of the courtiers; nonetheless, individuals did not experience nearly the degree of anonymity that was to characterize urban life by the end of the nineteenth century, as a result of population growth and the rise of mass politics. The urban elites most commonly referred to themselves as part of the *beau monde,* or simply as "the World." Musical, theatrical, and political issues—*querelles,* as the French termed them—were debated within a tightly knit network of institutions and personal relationships. Letters of the period move back and forth between personal gossip, party politics, and opera news with a naturalness that seems quaint in our day. One can argue that members of the *beau monde* learned how to participate in a political community by participating in opera disputes. The best-known of these disputes arose over the Italian style in London and Paris shortly after the turn of the century,

Courtly Dance. Italian *bassadanza* accompanied by two shawms and slide trumpet, fifteenth century. BIBLIOTHÈQUE NATIONALE, PARIS, MS. 5073, FOL.117V

and again in Paris in the late 1730s, early 1750s, and late 1770s. Jean-Jacques Rousseau put himself on the public stage through musical discourse, first publishing an extravagant treatise on musical notation and then denouncing the French language as an operatic vehicle—in effect, an attack on the court, coming as it did in the midst of the intense constitutional crisis of the 1750s.

London led Europe in establishing public musical activities during the eighteenth century. Public spaces became central to the capital city and its cultural life. Concerts held in York Buildings—the first public room in London designed specially for music—have a history leading up to the construction of the Royal Festival Hall in the South Bank arts complex in 1951. The growing concentration of the elites, together with the professionals and artisans who worked for them, reshaped both the institutions and the discourse of musical life in profound ways. Indeed, the modern concert originated in early-eighteenth-century London. Professional musicians became unusually independent in their relationships with wealthy families, establishing fee-for-service relationships much more consistently than was done elsewhere. Public concerts became far more numerous and specialized there than anywhere else in Europe partly because the loose, postrevolutionary state of political authority in Britain

meant that licenses were not required for such events, as they were almost everywhere else. The petty capitalism that evolved among musicians was nonetheless still based upon patronal relationships within a tiny elite. As Simon McVeigh has shown in *London Concert Life from Mozart to Haydn,* few concerts were held outside the West End, and musicians did not widely develop publics among the middle classes until the 1830s.

London's Italian opera company, established in 1708, was the only example in a monarchical system of an opera founded on a commercial basis, legally independent of the court. The high fees given to singers there came to set the standard throughout Europe. The King's Theatre became the most important meeting place for the peerage and indeed the British elite as a whole; it in effect became its main resort outside Parliament. Though opera librettos made only muted political implications, the theater made a powerful statement about the unity and consolidation of the Hanoverian succession.

Throughout Europe public theaters, especially opera, stood at the center of the elite public world. Going in order "to be seen" should not be construed necessarily as an opportunistic act of attempted upward mobility; since being in public was so basic to elite life, attendance was assumed to be a normal social act for anyone presumed part of the *beau monde*. Opera became considerably more of an obligation than the spoken theater, since it was linked to international elites. Many of the manners and mores of the *beau monde* seem quite foreign and sometimes downright offensive to us today. The etiquette of the *beau monde* in theaters was rather more multifaceted and tolerant than ours today. Attendance at a theater was a social act; to go was by definition to mingle with the assembled company as much as to see a production, and as a result a diarist usually saw no need to mention what he or she saw on a given night.

In fact, an individual would often attend several theaters in an evening, arranging to see favorite scenes, players, or singers, or meeting with people in different halls and boxes. The idea that musical pieces might comprise integral, permanent works of art was weak as yet; most operas were patchworks—*pasticcii*—of arias from different works by various composers. But that should not impugn the seriousness of the public. Since many people saw an opera production often within a season, it was not thought obligatory to sit through it all. Social behaviors—talking, moving about, some sources say playing cards—were tolerated to an extent not normally seen today, but that does not mean that no one cared about what went on stage. People liked to say that nobody listened to the opera, or that nobody knew much about it, but such a statement was a trope, a gentlemanly irony. The English man of letters Horace Walpole, one of the leading connoisseurs of singers in his time, several times said in his letters that he was not going to listen that night at the King's Theatre, since nothing interested him about the production. Least of all should we think that composers such as Mozart, J.-B. Rameau, or C. W. Gluck were not respected in their time; the controversies that broke out over their music were testimony to their great significance in public life.

Public display of sexual license was another trait basic to the *beau monde* and, by that token, to the musical world of the cosmopolitan elite. While freedom from moral codes had long been something of a privilege of the uppermost social orders, sexual intrigue became far more open and more competitive within this milieu than it had been before. The opera was the focal point for sexual gossip; Lady Mary Coke, a divorcée from the Argylle family, always kept her Paris-based sister well informed on such matters in her letters. The French playwright P.-A. Beaumarchais became famous all over Europe for the critique of the new elite mores in his legendary dramatic triad, which librettists then toned down for the less adventurous audiences in other capitals. Lorenzo da Ponte, for instance, made the Count in Mozart's *Marriage of Figaro* much less licentious than in the play. People read Beaumarchais avidly in Vienna but were not ready to see discourse on sexual morality approached so bluntly on stage. Indeed, in Vienna the public took on cultural authority more slowly than in London or Paris. Emperor Joseph II severely limited the role of ballet at the opera—an act that would have risked an aristocratic uprising in the two other cities.

Musical culture is invaluable as a context within which to think about the evolving relations between areas of what we call high and popular culture. In the eighteenth century there was much less stratification than we may presume among listeners by levels of learning and taste. Songs based on well-known popular tunes were thought mundane and were distinguished from works done with greater craftsmanship and called artful, but it would not be unusual to perform them together. *Opera seria* was not thought "serious" in anything like the sense in which we use the term and by the 1780s *opera buffa* rivaled the other genre for leadership in musical style. Indeed, the best-known melodies from Lully's *tragédies lyriques* were soon set as hymns and drinking songs. Opera was assumed to be accessible, indeed attractive, to all members of the elites and to the people from other social levels who formed part of the elites' world; both aficionados and less serious listeners went to the same productions in the same halls. From the founding of public opera halls in Venice in the 1630s such productions were for what one might call "general taste."

Concerts also followed practices that seem foreign to the musical world of today, in which popular and classical tastes are carefully segregated. Programs were often called "miscellaneous" in the sense that had originated in poetry—meaning that a variety of idioms and tastes would be provided. One would almost always hear both vocal and instrumental music: after opening with an overture, a program might offer an operatic number, a solo virtuosic piece, an Irish melody set to a sentimental text, and it might close the first half with an opera finale. In the provinces one might in fact see a juggling act or a trained dog. The norm at most concerts was an experience comparable to what we might hear at a pops concert today: a program that included works thought to demand quite different levels of learning. Connoisseurs accepted such practices; they themselves wrote the texts of the popular songs and were the main judges of vocal talent.

Yet musical life began to develop a much more learned avenue of taste during the eighteenth century: the performance of revered "ancient" music. By tradition it had been unusual, though not unknown, for works more than a generation old to remain in performance. Britain led in the performance of old music, and by 1780 one could hear concerts all over Britain that offered music by such composers as William Byrd, Henry Purcell, Arcangelo Corelli, and Handel. Charles Burney and John Hawkins published the first music histories in 1776, and the Concert of Antient Music was established in London that same year under aristocratic auspices. France saw an even more remarkable innovation: the continuing performance of works by Lully and some of his successors, yielding an operatic repertory far older than that found anywhere else in Europe. While these works were all dropped from the repertory by the early 1780s, the idea of a French canon—Lully, Rameau, and the frenchified Gluck—was firmly established.

Germany and Austria also began to take leadership within musical life at this time. While only a few old works remained in performance there (chiefly ones on religious texts by Carl Heinrich Graun and Handel), a field of highly learned musicians and amateurs emerged to lead Europe in the redefinition of musical taste in the nineteenth century. The first major such figure was Johann Forkel, the music director at the University of Göttingen. A music historian as well as performer and journalist, Forkel was the first to focus university musical training upon historical study. Honoring Johann Sebastian Bach with the greatest reverence, he and his successors mounted a moral critique of contemporary musical taste, arguing that it suited parlor conversation more than serious listening, bringing what we now might call the "commodification" of music. Their idealism can be seen to have had roots in the new discourse on freedom and equality in late-eighteenth-century Germany. Ironically, while their thinking grew up within bourgeois emancipation, it early on developed an ideology antagonistic to the music business.

THE EXPANSION OF PUBLICS AND CLASSICAL REPERTORIES IN THE NINETEENTH CENTURY

Musical life of the nineteenth century offers an important context within which to study the leadership of different social classes and the interaction among them. One central change in class structure in the period was the agglomeration of aristocracy and high bourgeoisie into a new upper class; another came in the growing social and cultural leadership of the middle classes. The first change was reflected early within musical life, as members of the two elites began to mingle more closely than had been the custom before. If in the eighteenth century articles on high-ranking concerts spoke of the *beau monde* being in attendance,

now they told repeatedly how the aristocracies of birth, wealth, and talent were represented, elites that were beginning to have a common, if quite loose, identity. Leadership came from each of these groups in different ways: in France, for example, noblemen formed societies to present music before Haydn, while bankers such as the Rothschilds served as patrons of the most famous virtuosos, and intellectuals turned out in force at the concerts of the orchestra that played the classical repertory at the Conservatoire. Ultimately, however, leadership came mostly from the upper middle class through its links with an expanding middle-class public. The foundation for the new musical world of the nineteenth century lay in emergence of musical training for both children and adults, represented by a piano in every parlor and the performance of music there at family gatherings. The economic power of the domestic market transformed the musical world fundamentally, stimulating the sale of sheet music with new marketing techniques and the rise of what the British called "popular music" by the end of the century. This does not mean, however, that the middle classes had a more or a less serious musical taste than other classes. As Nicholas Temperley argued in the introduction to *The Romantic Age* (1981), it is impossible to discern significant differences on the whole between them and the nobility.

With the disappearance of the *beau monde* around 1850, musical life began to separate out into a diverse set of publics and activities. In demographic terms there simply had become too many people within the upper classes for a unitary elite world to exist, and the opening of politics to new groups made the upper classes feel threatened and wary of public life. In London, for example, by about 1860 significantly fewer members of the peerage took boxes at the opera, and its performances clearly had become less central to their social life. The public life of the World, formerly focused on the opera, now became much more private than it had been before. Politico-musical *querelles* of the sort that had been the highlight of public life all but disappeared. The last major such affair in England was the attempt to found a competing theater at Covent Garden in 1847; in France it was the visit of Richard Wagner for a production of *Tannhäuser* in 1859.

After the middle of the nineteenth century concerts began separating out into separate locales for different kinds of tastes. The diversified ("miscellaneous") programs that had been standard since the early eighteenth century gave way to a separation between what were thought to be lighter or more serious repertories. Canonically defined "classical" works moved into the forefront of concert life, as symphony or-

Serenade. Serenade in the Graben, Vienna, on the eve of the feast of St. Anne, 1805.
©MUSEEN DER STADT WIEN, VIENNA

chestras and string quartets came to rival the opera, and levels of artistic worth established a new aesthetic and ideological frame of reference. Listening habits became much more strict at such concerts than had been the case before, with talking or moving about condemned as disrespectful to the great works. Still, new kinds of informal "promenade" concerts became just as prominent in public life as those of symphony orchestras. The players at such events—either as bands or orchestras—were often just as good as those at the serious concerts, and sometimes in fact were the same people.

The rise of classical-music concerts came in large part as a reaction to what came to be called popular music. We can find its origins in virtuosic and vocal music dominant in the 1830s that was termed "salon music." While music had been published for amateurs for performance since the sixteenth century, the sale of music increased dramatically with the invention of lithography and the expansion of marketing techniques. The main products, medleys of tunes from the best-known operas, were usually composed by famous virtuosos and then rewritten to be played by amateur singers, pianists, and instrumentalists. A wide-ranging commercial world evolved linking domestic music, the opera, the concert hall, and outdoor performances, with publics ranging from bands in poor mining towns to the most aristocratic salons. Thus, the term "popular" is appropriate by at least 1850: everyone was presumed to know this music, and its dissemination lay in a mass-market industry.

The market for this music expanded many times over what it had been in the eighteenth century. It came about as a joint effort of piano companies, publishers, virtuosos, periodicals, and most of all entrepreneurial musicians such as the Paris-based Henri Herz, who started companies to do these things.

During the second half of the century another major component of popular music emerged in performances of songs in music halls and cabarets. While a good deal of singing had gone on in taverns, it had not developed far at all commercially and in many cases might still be called folk music. By 1900 this kind of music, having developed a broadly inclusive public, rivaled formal concerts in prominence and in the size of the public, even though such taste was condemned ideologically by the traditional musical community that had emerged out of the court. Indeed, the rise first of salon music and then of music halls helped pressure that older world into an increasing focus upon a classical repertory and self-consciously serious, learned taste. By the end of the nineteenth century it had become difficult for composers to write for both worlds. A new aesthetic hierarchy had emerged that posed an overarching dichotomy between "light" and "serious" music, of a sort that had not existed in the eighteenth century.

Women took on important new roles within musical life during this period, most strikingly as composers. During the early nineteenth century female singers increasingly composed songs or did virtuosic improvisations upon well-known arias. Clara Schumann emerged as the most prominent woman composer, as well as serving as a powerful performer and teacher; Augusta Holmès had operas produced in Paris, and Ethel Smyth in London. The musical conservatories founded all over Europe were attended chiefly by women and offered what amounted to education on the secondary to graduate levels, leading to employment in a wide variety of contexts. Women were particularly successful in publishing songs for both domestic and concert performance, writing in a variety of light and serious idioms. Still, by World War I the division in taste between popular and serious music made it difficult to compose for both markets, and that hurt women much more than men. And there is evidence that during most of the twentieth century women were excluded from the composing profession as it underwent fundamental changes in both the popular and classical areas.

Equally remarkable was the growth in concert life among the lower middle and working classes. During the eighteenth century a few members of these groups had participated in local music societies, but they had to play a highly deferential role to the gentlemen in charge. Beginning in the 1830s entrepreneurial musicians began to set up choral societies for a broad spectrum of social groups, constituted variously in public and private contexts. Mass concerts by organizations such as the Orphéon in France and the Tonic Sol Fa organization in Britain brought the larger population into public musical life in unprecedented ways. With the development of cheap brass instruments, bands proliferated in Britain, Germany, and France among poor miners and industrial workers, and such ensembles competed for prizes and concert performances on a national basis. Though in some cases an owner might use such activities to blunt the influence of unions, the musical societies contributed significantly to the unity and pride of workers' communities.

MUSICAL LIFE SINCE 1945

A period of particular greatness in concert life arose between the revolutions of 1848 and World War II. During this time there was a relative continuity in repertory, taste, and social locales within which some remarkable music-making occurred in a context of public vitality. Geography helped: cities tended to be close-knit and easily accessible, integral communities within which musical life served as one of the citizens' main pleasures. The vital links between domestic and public music undergirded all this; many people played at home what they had heard in halls. And new music, though beginning to be controversial, was found on most programs and entered into creative relationships with the classics. Much of this changed after 1945. Air travel, television, motorways, and the opening up of new cultural distractions dispersed urban social and cultural life in ways harmful to music. Many of the small communities that had sustained bands, choruses, and orchestras disappeared or lost their unity and the focus of their lives upon music. Indeed, fewer people learned to play or to sing; the piano ceased to be a universal domestic object in middle- or upper-class households. If working-class amateur participation weakened to a particular extent, so did classical-music institutions, hurt by the decline of the amateur public and by competition from popular music.

Yet musical life benefited from some of these same changes. New technology made it possible for far more people to hear music performed on a professional level, which, also thanks to better pay earned by unionized musicians, led to higher levels of performing standards overall. Governments and foundations replaced the individual patron in the support of ensembles, a development which particularly benefited repertories with a limited commercial base such as avant-garde music and early music. In fact, in some areas music became one of the more learned of the arts, a vast change compared to its nature in the seventeenth century. Music history became a standard discipline in most universities. While early conservatories served chiefly to educate local players and teachers, after 1945 they became the places where the most important performers were trained.

One of the most significant changes dating from the start of the twentieth century was the separation of new and classical music into increasingly separate performing contexts. Before that time most programs offered a relatively balanced fare of new and old works, with pianists and violinists playing their own works alongside the classics. But by World War I orchestras and chamber-music ensembles had become musical museums, and the public found itself suspicious of anything new, whether conservative or avant-garde. Repertories of classical music that began with Handel and Bach ended with Wagner and Johannes Brahms; the musical clock stopped, and Richard Strauss and Claude Debussy were honored on a wholly new basis. At the same time composers, publishers, and patrons began staging concerts and establishing organizations devoted specifically to the performance of new music. This can be seen as early as the 1860s in the concerts put on by supporters of Wagner; it culminated in the founding of the International Society for Contemporary Music in 1922. After 1945 funding by governments, radio stations, and universities established the world of new music on a firm

and social practices. But by the 1960s jazz had developed a sophisticated public that grew large enough for concerts. Rock went much further in that direction soon after its rise in the early 1950s, since early stars such as the Beatles became so popular that they began putting on concerts not only in large halls but also in sports stadiums. In the 1970s new sound systems made possible new theatrical dimensions to the rock concert. And in the 1980s "crossover" composers and performing groups began to present combinations of jazz, classical, and avant-garde works in interesting new ways. Some concert series also began attempting to lighten their social atmosphere in order to attract a younger public. Avant-garde musicians influenced by Karlheinz Stockhausen and John Cage formulated new ideas of the concert independent of tradition, devising music performed in a space rather than a formal hall, usually with performers given improvisatory roles.

Popular Music. The Beatles. JOHN ZIMMERMAN/CAMERA PRESS/RETNA LTD.

DANCE

The history of dance poses the intricate task of analyzing how related segments of social structure have interacted—that is, how dance functioned within opera but became a separate artistic world during the twentieth century. In the early modern period the same performers served, depending on the context, as singers, dancers, and actors, but these several roles eventually grew increasingly separate. Dance history is now its own field, whose publications historians of music must get to know. Music historians likewise need to recognize how important dance was for the opera-going public during the eighteenth and nineteenth centuries, and not simply treat it as a distraction from the music. As we saw above, variety served as the central principle behind performance of almost all kinds prior to the late nineteenth century. To deride dance unless it plays an organic or dramatic role within an opera is to impose anachronistic assumptions upon an earlier and very different culture. A dance number could variously emphasize an operatic mood, advance the plot or drama, or offer a quite different artistic experience. What made a good theatrical director was his ability to splice segments together to form a sequence that would prove pleasing and perhaps provocative to his audience.

basis. The major concert centers that emerged were the Darmstadt Festival in the Rhineland, the Donaueschingen Festival in Baden Baden, the Domaine Musicale in Paris, and the League of Composers in New York.

Popular music in its increasingly diverse forms inspired the chief public interest in new musical trends after 1945. Young people increasingly left classical-music concerts to their elders. In France the *chanson* took a distinctive path independent of American pop. In Britain the Beatles and other groups established a new area of sophisticated music with large publics. In Germany rock groups contributed significantly to the evolution of new sonorities and the use of electrified instruments. Jazz became a powerful movement throughout Europe, in many ways independent of its American origins. In all these countries popular music moved from the cabaret into the concert hall. While both jazz and rock began in dance halls, neither seemed at first appropriate to the concert hall due to the seemingly functional role of the music and the casual manner of popular musicians' musical

The competitive nature of Renaissance states brought a new scale and intellectual focus to the tradition of holding grand festivals involving a variety of arts. In 1489, for example, the duke of Milan gave a dinner in which the entrées were accompanied by performers acting out the mythological meanings of the food—characters danced as either the fruits of Pomona or the lamb of Jason was brought in. By the early sixteenth century these dances were called *balletti*, meaning a figured dance understood as a composition of sequential movements. These works were semistaged versions of the social dances of the time, originating in the protocol of court etiquette or in practices of a more popular nature. Treatises appeared to instruct dancers how best to perform these numbers; those of Fabritio Caroso and Cesare Negri at the turn of the seventeenth century specified movements of the feet in detail. Dance was still principally done by members of a court, an amateur activity performed under the instruction of a choreographer. Emphasis was less upon difficult movements than upon the spelling out of elaborate patterns throughout a space, with the audience usually looking down from galleries. The shows were imbued with allusions to individuals and events; sources exist to tell us who danced which parts, and that can have major implications for a political climate. It was conventional for the head of state—Louis XIV himself at the start of his personal reign, for example—to perform before his or her court. The events took different forms in France, where figured dancing was most prominent; in Italy, where the masquerade served as the context for dance; and in Britain, where the masque merged the two traditions with the audience dancing in the "revels."

The focus in dance upon professionals had already begun when Louis XIV last danced in 1670. The Académie Royale de Musique developed the most important company of both male and female dancers to perform in public in Paris. The individual dancer, increasingly women more than men, now came to the fore. The hall was larger and the audience at a somewhat greater distance than at court, though boxes looked down directly upon the stage and at some performances women of the high nobility sat on stage in a semicircle. Basic aspects of ballet technique evolved at this time, most important of all the "turnout" to form a right angle. Marie Carmargo, who made her Paris debut in 1726, then shortened her skirt, to gain freedom for the jump with quick beating of the feet called the *entrechat quatre,* and danced in heelless slippers to gain greater elevation from the *plié* done upon the floor. Commentary on dance evolved separately from that on music; Louis Cahusac, for example, became a leading interpreter of how dancers expressed a great variety of emotions. Jean Georges Noverre, the best-known choreographer of the eighteenth century, made a critique of ballet done simply for show and called for dancers to speak to the heart, representing character and feeling. Noverre changed dance composition at the Opéra from formal symmetry to evolving dramatic movements, and he had a powerful in-

fluence in London as well as Paris, partly through his work with David Garrick. At the same time, dance became a major accomplishment among the upper classes. Musicians often taught it as well, and dance schools became attached to many universities, especially in Germany.

Ballet as we know it came into place around the 1830s, chiefly in the systemization of dance instruction and the increasing focus on dancing *en pointe.* The ballet class, best seen in the *Code of Terpsichore* by Carlo Blasis (1830), became codified into a set of exercises helping a dancer progress from the simpler to the more difficult movements. A whole new way of moving evolved at this time, based upon extension of the back leg and the use of short running steps featuring speed and lightness. Marie Taglioni presented it most prominently in 1831–1832 in the opera *Robert le Diable* and the dance work *La Sylphide.* Plot and set design of romantic opera played an important role in the new manner of dancing. Neoclassical mythology gave way to historical plots, focused on richly exotic moods and sets. Popular theaters on the boulevards of Paris led in this change, offering

Ballerina. *Prima Ballerina,* painting (c. 1876) by Edgar Degas (1834–1917). MUSÉE DU LOUVRE, PARIS/CORBIS

productions on the Incas in Peru and Captain Cook in Tahiti that were made into successful ballets. The ability to lower lighting thanks to the use of gas brought a new sense of mystery and an unearthly quality to the drama. A star system evolved, even larger in scale than had been the case in the eighteenth century.

The social historian needs to pay close attention to the process by which dance began to move away from opera in this period. During the seventeenth century a single act of dance occurred between the acts of an opera, and in the eighteenth it became less common and less important under the influence of the librettists Apostolo Zeno and Pietro Metastasio. But in France it took on increasing importance within the *tragédies lyriques,* especially those of Jean-Philippe Rameau, and within the growing number of two-act *opéras-ballets,* which themselves might have vocal music. An evening at the Paris Opéra would usually have two or three parts, one or two of them focused on ballet. Noverre's leadership brought ballet's role to the fore, making some commentators complain that dance was replacing opera in the public's attention. But in the middle decades of the century the best-known dance works took on a life of their own—*Sylphide,* then *Giselle* (1842) and *Copéllia* (1870)—even though they were still produced under the auspices of the opera company.

It was in Russia that ballet first became functionally independent of opera. Not only did the tsars give far more funding to dance than any other court or municipal theater, but also from early in the nineteenth century the state theater in St. Petersburg put on full-length works of dance alone. Everywhere else in Europe prior to around 1900 a ballet was rarely given without an opera on the same program. The French dancer Marius Petipa, who arrived in St. Petersburg as *premier danseur* in 1847, was the chief leader in building the quality of the dance company to rival that of Paris. The works of Peter Ilyich Tchaikovsky, from *Swan Lake* in 1877 to the *Nutcracker* in 1892, were the culmination of Petipa's work in making ballet equal if not greater in prominence compared to opera.

The powerful impact of modernism brought dance to the fore as a separate art just after the turn of the twentieth century. No other movement has cut across the arts as rapidly and deeply as this one. Sergey Diaghilev, born in a highly cultured gentry family, first had interests chiefly in music and art, but went on to direct Europe's leading dance company between 1909 and 1929 and in so doing reshaped the field fundamentally. Under his influence and that of Michel Fokine, character dancing in folk idioms took on a new intellectual stature, and a new manner of dancing arose, most prominently in Diaghilev's productions of *Firebird, Petroushka,* and *Rite of Spring* with the music of Igor Stravinksy. Diaghilev and Fokine turned ballet away from female leadership, not only with a focus on male dancers but also with the primacy of the male choreographer as *auteur.* Though overshadowed within the writing of cultural history, women dancers—chiefly Isadora Duncan, Ruth St. Denis, Loie Fuller, and Maud Allen—were pioneers in the field of modern dance. Duncan rejected balletic tradition directly at the start of her career, abandoning tights, shoes, and classical technique, and built a new kind of solo dance aimed at expression and the pursuit of a new philosophical direction. This became a highly international movement, gaining leaders from the United States, strong public support from Britain, and the support of a variety of movements concerned with rethinking the body in Germany. One could argue that modern dance seriously rivaled modern music within the public, for it was more successful in overcoming the weight of tradition and attracting audiences to new kinds of performing contexts. While musicians, dancers, and painters worked together in establishing the principle of the self-defining artist, in the course of the twentieth century the latter two groups put their works on public display much more successfully than the former.

See also other articles in this section.

BIBLIOGRAPHY

Bianconi, Lorenzo, and Thomas Walker. "Production, Consumption, and Political Function of Seventeenth-Century Italian Opera." *Early Music History* 4 (1984): 209–296.

Botstein, Leon. "Listening through Reading: Musical Literacy and the Concert Audience." *Nineteenth-Century Music* 16 (1992): 129–145.

Citron, Marcia J. *Gender and the Musical Canon.* Cambridge, U.K., 1993.

Ehrlich, Cyril. *The Music Profession in Britain since the Eighteenth Century: A Social History.* Oxford, 1985.

Fenlon, Iain. *The Renaissance: From the 1470s to the End of the Sixteenth Century.* London, 1989.

Fulcher, Jane F. *French Cultural Politics and Music from the Dreyfus Affair to the First World War.* New York, 1999.

Fulcher, Jane F. *The Nation's Image: French Grand Opera as Politics and Politicized Art.* New York, 1987.

Goehr, Lydia. *The Imaginary Museum of Musical Works: An Essay in the Philosophy of Music.* Oxford, 1992.

Guest, Ivor, *The Dancer's Heritage: A Short History of Ballet.* 6th ed. London, 1988.

Johnson, James H. *Listening in Paris: A Cultural History.* Berkeley, Calif., 1995.

Knighton, Tess. "Spaces and Contexts for Listening in Fifteenth-Century Castile." *Early Music* 25 (1997): 661–677.

Large, David C., and William Weber, eds. *Wagnerism in European Culture and Politics.* Ithaca, N.Y., 1984.

Little, Meredith. "Recent Research in European Dance, 1400–1800." *Early Music* 14 (1986): 4–14.

McVeigh, Simon. *Concert Life in London from Mozart to Haydn.* Cambridge, U.K., 1993.

Meconi, Honey. "Did *Imitatio* Exist?" *Journal of Musicology* 12 (1994): 152–178.

Page, Christopher. "Listening to the *Trouvères.*" *Early Music* 25 (1997): 638–660.

Pirrotta, Nino. "Monteverdi and the Problem of Opera." In his *Music and Culture in Italy from the Middle Ages to the Baroque.* Cambridge, Mass., 1984. Pages 248–253.

Raynor, Henry. *A Social History of Music from the Middle Ages to Beethoven: Music and Society since 1815.* New York, 1978.

Rosselli, John. *Singers of Italian Opera: The History of a Profession.* Cambridge, U.K., 1992.

Russell, Dave. *Popular Music in England, 1840–1914: A Social History.* Montreal, 1987.

Salmen, Walter, ed. *The Social Status of the Professional Musician from the Middle Ages to the Nineteenth Century.* New York, 1983.

Taruskin, Richard, and Piero Weiss. *Music in the Western World: A History in Documents.* New York, 1984.

Weber, William. "Beyond *Zeitgeist:* Recent Work in Music History." *Journal of Modern History* 66 (1994): 321–345. Review essay.

Weber, William. "Did People Listen in the Eighteenth Century?" *Early Music* 25 (1997): 678–691.

Weber, William. "L'institution et son public: L'opéra à Paris et à Londres au XVIIIe siècle." *Annales E.S.C.* 48, no. 6 (1993): 1519–1540.

Weber, William. *Music and the Middle Class: The Social Structure of Concert Life in London, Paris, and Vienna, 1830–1848.* London, 1975.

Weber, William. *The Rise of Musical Classics in Eighteenth-Century England.* Oxford, 1992.

Zaslaw, Neal, ed. *The Classical Era: From the 1740s to the End of the Eighteenth Century.* London, 1989.

Section 20

❧ ❧

MODERN RECREATION AND LEISURE

Policing Leisure   155
John K. Walton

Sports   167
Allen Guttmann

Holidays and Public Rituals   185
Scott Hughes Myerly and Tamara L. Hunt

Consumer Leisure   201
Charles Rearick

Vacations   219
John K. Walton

Travel and Tourism   229
Stephen L. Harp

POLICING LEISURE

John K. Walton

Leisure is a problem for governments and employers because the time and space it occupies and the activities or idleness it entails exist beyond the disciplines imposed by the need to make a living. Leisure activities are capable of invading or otherwise affecting the workplace in ways that disrupt production and threaten output. In addition they can take on guises that threaten basic aspects of state power, breaking or challenging the law by attacking property, attacking a person or the official version of consensual morality, and disturbing the peace or outraging the sensibilities of influential citizens. But leisure is also capable of shoring up the established order, whether by distracting people from grievances that might otherwise politicize them in radical ways or at least give rise to riot and disorder or by promoting thrift, domesticity, the respectable pursuit of approved knowledge (put another way, the acquisition of "cultural capital" of acceptable kinds), attachment to unthreatening religious organizations, or patriotism, discipline, and other acceptable qualities. Leisure can also provide investment outlets and returns on capital for entrepreneurs and investors whose interests are bound up with meeting popular demand in ways acceptable to authority and consensual state-endorsed morality. This last point, in particular, draws attention to important conflicts and paradoxes inherent in the relationship between the modern state and the development of leisure. As leisure provision is drawn into the marketplace, it develops its own propertied interests, who have a stake in what is provided and whose efforts to allure or satisfy customers may lead them into conflict with the state (national or local) as guardian of order, morality, and other kinds of property. Their attempts to meet the state's conditions for continuing operation, for example, by accepting censorship, may affect the nature of their own output. This theme is particularly evident and contentious when sex and intoxicating substances are at issue or when popular commercial entertainment also has radical political content. The theme recurs throughout this article alongside questions relating to class, gender, ethnicity, and the construction of identities.

These themes worked themselves out in contrasting ways in different parts of Europe, with differing patterns of change over time. The pretensions of the state to intervene in the private sphere, the role of religion and its relationship with the state, the extent of governmental tolerance of organized oppositional culture, the level of urbanization and the pace and nature of industrial development and agrarian change, the timing and nature of the emergence of leisure industries, and the extent of governmental willingness to expend resources on the policing of leisure all affected outcomes. Moreover patterns varied in different kinds of places within countries or economic regions. Leisure was policed in different ways according to the degree of threat activities posed to the lifestyles and property of the influential, to the dignity and ceremony of centers of government, and to the productivity of industrial workforces. Some popular or disreputable districts were just too difficult to police from without in direct, formal ways that might seem oppressive and provoke resistance. There surveillance might be confined to policing boundaries and keeping incompatible lifestyles apart. As specialized resort towns emerged, conflicts over appropriate or preferred uses of desirable spaces became particularly pressing. Residential suburbs had to be guarded more straightforwardly against plebeian incursion. Account has to be taken of these differences and developments.

ORGANS OF POLICING LEISURE

Who might be said to have policed leisure, how, on whose behalf, and with what success? Police forces, in the sense of bodies of men and later women charged with the duty of maintaining order in public and some private places and with power to inflict penalties on those who defy or ignore the laws they enforce, are only part of this story. They are far from a simple or straightforward part, even when the extent of their ambitions or those of their paymasters has been so extensive as to attract the label "police state," whether retrospectively or at the time. Consider, for example, the elaborate structures of control that already existed in the eighteenth-century Grand Duchy of Württemberg, now in Germany. Parallel local hierarchies existed, the Lutheran Church and the state, with the pastor, schoolmaster, and church consistory ranged alongside local court, council, bailiff and *Bürgermeister* (mayor) in each village. The district ducal commissioner or *Amtmann* held regular courts of heads of households in every settlement. Church pastors were required to appoint "secret censores" to report moral failings, and they offered rewards for prosecuting neighbors for "immorality, laziness, idleness or general disorderliness," under which headings much disreputable leisure activity could be gathered. But despite all efforts to encourage Württemberg villagers in self-control and mutual denunciation and to persuade them to internalize "official" values, a whole range of proscribed leisure activities and illicit beliefs flourished, helped by the tensions between the different arms of the surveillance machinery. For example, pastors and schoolmasters fell out, and mutual denunciations canceled each other out.

Ambitious aspirations to control also flourished in the contrasting setting of eighteenth-century Paris. François Jacques Guillauté remarked in 1750, "The policing of a city . . . is the surveillance of an infinite accumulation of little items." Guillauté's efforts to supervise work, leisure, and supplies led him to a proto-Benthamite or Foucauldian plan to divide the city into "twenty districts, of twenty sections, of twenty houses numbered street by street, each storey designated by a number, each lodging by a letter," an apparatus of *commissaires* (commissioners), *inspecteurs* (inspectors), and syndics, and an identification card system with a view to setting up a complete regulatory system to record all comings and goings. Such aspirations generated wonderful archives but understandably fell far short of their goal. One failing was the propensity of the police to be corruptible by gamblers and brothel-keepers. Policing leisure in the eighteenth-century metropolis was even more difficult than in the countryside.

At the other end of this period the better-known totalitarianism of Eastern Europe under Stalinism and its successor regimes similarly had its limitations, despite fearsomely holistic aspirations and an extensive commitment of resources. Even during the 1930s, after the militants of the cultural revolution had "destroyed the mechanisms of commercial culture" (Stites, 1992) and tried to impose a state-sponsored culture of high-minded improvement whose populist rhetoric failed to disguise its prescriptive puritanical aspirations, Soviet citizens still had a measure of agency and choice within a mass culture that found room for "what some people would call simple, common or vulgar entertainments." The state had to adjust its goals to take account of popular tastes and preferences. In the post-Stalin era this became increasingly obvious, as the Houses of Culture, which were supposed to provide culture and entertainment for all and socialize them into an approved socialist frame of mind, were infiltrated by hobbyists, interest groups, and enthusiasts who might pay lip service to orthodoxy but derived their satisfactions elsewhere, regarding their particular pleasures as ends in themselves rather than means toward what the authorities called "cultural enlightenment." After 1953 consumer needs received growing attention, and Western fashions increasingly infiltrated. Leisure reverted overtly to the private sphere, and the state cultural apparatus became depoliticized. State bureaucrats' ambitions to impose a unified set of officially approved leisure and cultural preferences were frustrated, and popular culture never lost its pluralism. This held good in Hungary and Poland as well as the USSR.

This was the case even in states with ambitions to police leisure by suppressing alternatives and winning hearts and minds through active provision of approved facilities and activities while backing their efforts up with coercion and terror and warrening society with informers. Other European settings established much narrower limits to the successful policing of pleasures. Leisure aspirations could be repressed, discouraged, channeled, or controlled in many ways. But as some historians' successful challenges to the simplistic social control literature of the 1970s demonstrated, the play (in both senses) in social systems kept the technologies of control, formal or informal, from making the desired or posited impact. This was especially the case where, as in Britain, the direct role of the state in policing leisure was limited to banning specific activities that shocked influential sensibilities, licensing and surveillance of commercially run gathering places that involved the consumption of intoxicants and perceived threats to order and morality, and preservation of a sense of security in the streets and other public places. Levels of involvement in these spheres changed over time, especially in an interventionist direction in response to novel levels of urbanization and social dislocation, most obviously associated with the industrial revolution and the two world wars.

A strong de facto economic dimension of the most basic kind figured in the policing of leisure. The spread of industrial work discipline from the late eighteenth century accentuated the demarcation between work and leisure time. Working hours expanded and were policed more effectively until the mid- or late nineteenth century. In the twentieth century the rise of Fordism and Taylorism tightened the screws on industrial workforces again. The increasing importance of precise clock time as opposed to more traditional, less precise measurements contributed to these changes. However, in rural France and some other rural areas the working day had long been punctuated by the bells of the parish church announcing meal breaks and the conventional times for starting and ending work. In many industrial settings, too, leisure was smuggled into the workplace, often lubricated by drink. The successful importing of drink was an important part of an apprentice's skills in engineering as late as the 1870s. When workers took pride in craft and workforces lived in close proximity, the skills and techniques of work might be discussed sociably afterward over a few drinks. This pattern apparently declined in late-nineteenth-century London but persisted long afterward in other settings, especially those associated with coal mining. The pressures and de-skilling of "machinofacture," assembly lines, and other routinized workplaces brought about the separation of work and leisure, which entailed the effective policing of leisure at the workplace.

Real wage levels exerted their own policing function regarding what kind of leisure and how much could be afforded, especially if defiance of labor discipline might prejudice future employment. Underemployment and unemployment generated unwanted leisure for those who lacked the resources to enjoy it. At higher social levels middle-class orthodoxy believed that the work-leisure boundary was patrolled by a work ethic that required long, committed hours of managing resources and markets. But the extensive evidence of high spending and pleasure preferences among the industrial and commercial middle classes, even in the mid-nineteenth century, undermines the moral force of such pretensions outside the ranks of a few well-documented eccentrics. The aristocracy and its associates in the so-called "leisure class" had to work at their leisure because they were required to follow a strict timetable of formal events, where they displayed themselves with all the formality of a rigid system of etiquette. These issues defy easy categorization.

INDIRECT REGULATION

Much of the regulation of popular leisure arose indirectly, through school and religious influences, through voluntary organizations acting as pressure groups, and elusively but importantly through the restraining influence of widely shared values that were not necessarily those fostered by the government or churches, though they might look like them from a distance. Formal schooling, whatever the relationship between voluntary bodies (usually religious) and the state in its provision, entailed the imposition of discipline in punctuality, cleanliness, and classroom behavior. These values were expected to have an impact on both work and leisure. Bodies like the English Sunday Schools were among the organizers of counter attractions to lure children and adults away from the temptations of fairs, festivals, and drinking places. Churches, temperance organizations, mutual insurance societies, and other voluntary bodies also offered alternatives, which might involve tea parties, picnics, or excursions to the countryside or the coast. These options, particularly evident from the 1830s onward, survived strongly through the nineteenth century before beginning to decay in the twentieth century. Such provisions often failed to meet the expectations of promoters, as the recipients took the opportunities and rejected aspects of the message, going to the picnic in the afternoon, to the fairground in the evening, or on railway excursions organized by the temperance movement and getting drunk at the seaside.

Churches and moral reform organizations also formed pressure groups to change the laws regarding leisure activities in more restrictive directions. In the nineteenth century and early twentieth century they worked toward tighter regulation of, for example, Sunday observance, permitted drinking hours, gambling in public places, and sexual immorality in various guises. In the twentieth century, especially after World War I, the external influences on government worked in the opposite direction. Pressure groups fought rearguard actions against liberated social practices. Sunday observance became less widely enforced, even in Protestant northern Europe. The Catholic "continental Sunday" had long been a source of complaint among English advocates of restriction. Constraints on the open hours of drinking and dancing establishments fell away sharply across Western Europe in the last quarter of the twentieth century. In the industrial Ruhr district of Germany, for example, where Catholics and Protestants lived side by side, the spread of commercially run Sunday dancing was such a strong trend in the late nineteenth century that the police, despite ineffectual aspirations, were quite unable to control it.

Everywhere most of the intervention was directed at the working class, as in the ineffectual prohibition of street betting on horse races in England between 1853 and the legalization of betting shops in 1961. Yet the leisure practices of the comfortable were not immune from censure and legislative interference.

Casino gambling, especially roulette and baccarat, was the object of periodic moral panics and campaigns for intervention across most of Europe. In Britain, significantly, its legal existence was unthinkable between the mid-eighteenth century and the late twentieth century. Gambling was banned successively but temporarily in France, the German states, and Belgium at various points in the nineteenth and early twentieth centuries and in Spain definitively in 1924 after many years of de facto toleration while the law was ignored. The fashion for tanning, which spread across the European beach haunts of the wealthy after World War I, called forth outraged campaigns about the immorality of bodily exposure in several Catholic countries. It reached a climax of outrage with efforts at legislative intervention in Belgium and Spain in the mid-1930s, and the Spanish Civil War settled the outcome in that country in favor of extreme restrictions for more than a generation.

These interventions were only part of the story and rarely the most important or effective part. More important was the policing that operated hegemonically, as people restricted their own leisure choices according to versions of propriety and suitability that became enshrined as common sense. Submission to prescribed regimes of exercise or self-presentation might fall into this broad category, as leisure was adjusted to meet the dictates of fashion or the medical prescriptions that governed when and how to bathe at a spa or the seaside.

Generally more significant was the tyranny of respectability in its various guises, restraining leisure behavior on the basis of concern for what peers, workmates, neighbors, and employers might think. This was the most pervasive and diffuse vector for policing leisure, all the more effective when it was genuinely self-policing. But these constraints had to come from within, and Peter Bailey rightly emphasized that for many people respectable behavior was contingent on external circumstances. Not only might the boundaries of acceptability vary for individuals according to context and company, but claims to respectability might be proffered or abandoned at will. Consequently for most people it was more like a garment that was donned or discarded according to circumstances than like a consistent, articulated, internalized identity. Shani D'Cruze's work on women, leisure, and the circumstances of sexual assault in the Lancashire cotton manufacturing district in the late nineteenth century shows that working-class communities and different groups within them had their own ideas about what constituted acceptable or reprehensible behavior, and the lines between them shaded according to circumstances. The ideas were no less real to

the actors involved than the stricter definitions that prevailed among those who made or enforced the law. The "rough" working class, so labeled by outsiders, had its own internalized respectabilities that amounted to a significant degree of self-policing.

The external policing of leisure by the national or local state, featuring laws to legitimize the coercive restraint of controversial activities, was nevertheless important. However, its impact never matched its aspirations or those of the moral reform pressure groups who tried to extend and tighten its grasp. Over much of Europe the changes associated with industrialization, urbanization, and swelling migration flows coincided with an evangelical religious revival in the late eighteenth and early nineteenth centuries. The fears of authority facing novel agglomerations of people with an obvious potential for subversion of all kinds were augmented by influential pressures for control from well-connected religious groups. This applied in Catholic as well as Protestant Europe. In the late nineteenth century, as these voices became somewhat less clamorous and carried less conviction, their place was taken by a social Darwinist and eugenicist agenda concerned that overindulgence in popular pleasures would not only plunge families into the secondary poverty that arose from the misuse of otherwise adequate resources but would also further the degeneration of the race. Both the religious and the eugenicist concerns still made impacts in the 1920s and 1930s, and their voices were far from stilled in the late twentieth century.

In the interwar years, however, it was increasingly acceptable for even the working classes to enjoy pleasure for its own sake, without the overt addition of a legitimizing agenda of moral or physical recreation. The leisure revolution of the 1960s and 1970s, when a new generation of hedonistic working- and middle-class consumers began to break the bounds that had constrained their forebears, definitively changed these expectations, as, for example, restrictions on open hours began to crumble and licensing hours were relaxed. Even then, however, policing leisure remained important or even more so, as problems associated with newly popular drugs, with hooliganism at spectator sporting events, and with urban violence attained a higher profile in the eyes of the media and the government.

POLICING FESTIVALS

What kinds of leisure were perceived to need policing, and how did this perception change over time? Above all, large-scale popular festive gatherings of any kind

Popular Festive Gathering. A village festival in Russia, nineteenth century. The church is visible through the trees to the left.
MARY EVANS PICTURE LIBRARY

attracted the paternal and disciplinary attention of authority, whether their ostensible bases were religious or secular. So did all activities involving the consumption of alcohol, gambling, violence, close contact between the sexes, or any rowdy liveliness that encroached on the public street, disrupted traffic and trade, or appeared to threaten the property, security, and dignity of the comfortable. Under the first heading came, most obviously, fairs, carnival, wakes, or other local feast days. Fairs, as trading events with entertainments grafted on to reap the opportunities offered by large crowds with money in their pockets, were already boisterous and potentially dangerous events in the London of Ben Jonson's *Bartholomew Fair* (1614). Over time the balance between commerce and amusement steadily tilted to the latter, even in the provinces. These were calendar customs, mark-

ing out the passage of the year and underpinned by custom. When the calendar changed in 1752, the English had to make decisions about whether to observe the new date or the old.

Over much of Catholic Europe religious observances gathered crowds for traditional, evolving ceremonies. Carnival, a feast of excess and misrule at the approach to the lean times prescribed by Lent, was overtly an occasion for the subversion of authority, disguises involving challenges to status and gender boundaries, excess, and the upending, temporarily and symbolically, of the usual social and moral order. Even England had its petty carnivals. On 5 November the saving of a Protestant Parliament through the discovery of the Gunpowder Plot of 1605 was commemorated with bonfires, blazing tar barrels, and sometimes the burning in effigy of unpopular contemporary figures. In a minor echo of carnival, too, Shrove Tuesday celebrations often included mass football games involving most of the male inhabitants of a parish, following conventions rather than rules and entailing systematic horseplay and conventionalized violence. Right across Europe, too, local festivals commemorating the patron saint of the parish were celebrated with drinking and dancing as well as formal religious services, drawing in people from surrounding settlements along with the locals.

These big traditional gatherings were policed mainly by convention and consent during the eighteenth century. The local festivals suffered increasingly from the withdrawal of elite patronage, as landed society withdrew into its own select institutions, disappeared for long periods to the new leisure towns or to the metropolis, and lost touch with local popular culture. Festivals did not come under direct attack until the beginning of the nineteenth century, and then the criticisms were usually the economic disruptions of industrialization and a widespread decline of rural laborers' incomes rather than directly coercive. Much the same applied to the fairs, which gradually came under pressure from the rise of new patterns of trade, especially through the growth of fixed-site retailing alongside the regular weekly markets. As fairs lost the commercial functions that gave them legitimacy, they were more vulnerable to suppression at the behest of the upholders of order and morality. Hiring fairs for farm servants, where young people who had been confined in service for several months might enjoy a few liberated days of drinking and dancing while they looked for a new employer, were particularly worrying in the eyes of reformers. But in the parts of England where this mode of employment remained strong the fairs survived well beyond World War I.

Carnival, with a much stronger purchase among the urban elites of Catholic Europe, was more resilient. These large-scale annual events were difficult to police in the formal, bureaucratic manner that emerged, at least on paper, in much of Europe by the early nineteenth century. The scale of carnival's turbulence was beyond the intervention of small numbers of ill-paid police forces, whose members were part of the culture they were policing. The only way to control carnival in the short run was to suppress it. This became an option, as the fairs and parish feasts came under economic pressure anyway. Attempts at closure were invariably resisted in urban settings, and the pattern of suppression in England before 1870 was overwhelmingly weighted toward small agricultural villages in the south and east. In many urban settings and settings that were becoming urban, local festivals adapted to new economic circumstances and some-

times gained a new vitality by attracting commercial patronage from publicans and other entertainment entrepreneurs. Pleasure fairs circulated with increasingly sophisticated amusement technology. This in turn brought renewed pressure for suppression from religious interests with allies among local residents and property owners whose lives were disrupted, whose sensibilities were affronted, and who did not benefit from the extra trade generated. When attempts were made to ban urban fairgrounds from municipal property, fairs merely migrated to new sites on private land and continued to flourish. The urban pleasure fair was tamed in the late nineteenth century more by regulating the properted interests associated with it through licensing and associated surveillance than from coercive suppression, which was rarely practical politics. Especially in parts of northern England, local popular holidays were increasingly associated with excursions to the seaside and the countryside, leaving the local festivities increasingly etiolated.

POLICING SPECIFIC PRACTICES

Those who sought to police popular morality along the lines of the evangelical revival of the late eighteenth and early nineteenth centuries, echoing the moral panic evoked by the rise of the urban working class, were more successful in intervening against specific practices than in suppressing whole festivals. In this role formal, disciplined police forces eventually came into their own. Some specific intervention came earlier with attempts to police prostitution in eighteenth-century London and Paris. Aspirations to suppress foundered on the ubiquity of the services and the market for them and the impossibility of preventing the police from being seduced into protecting many they were supposed to be arresting. In England it was easier to target popular blood sports, which were more disruptive, less consensual, and more appealing to a masculine cult of violence and cruelty that attracted censure both from evangelicals and from secular advocates of gentlemanly civility and moderation. In the early nineteenth century cockfighting, bull-baiting, and the Stamford custom of bull running were abolished officially. The last Stamford bull-running ended in a celebrated standoff between troops, police, and traditionalist locals during the late 1820s. Cockfighting survived as a disreputable clandestine activity, along with dogfighting and human pugilism. These pursuits were targets for the new police forces. Peel's Metropolitan Police of 1829 provided a model that rapidly disseminated through the counties and boroughs in the 1830s. Success in dealing with pugilism

Human Pugilism. *The Great Fight,* the boxing match between Broome and Hannan at New Park Farm, near Bicester, England, 26 January 1841. Aquatint by C. Hunt after H. Heath. ©HULTON GETTY/LIAISON AGENCY

was limited by promoters, who chose sites on county boundaries, where fights could easily be relocated out of reach of interfering local policemen. Significantly foxhunting and hare coursing, which retained not only aristocratic and genteel patronage but were also rural activities with a strong following among farmers, remained unscathed. The rural police did become active in conjunction with the gamekeepers who acted as the landowners' private estate police forces in pursuing poachers. The status of pheasants and similar creatures as property was disputable because they were reared by estate owners but were wild in their freedom to roam. Efforts to catch pheasants clearly combined pleasure with profit and an element of challenge to the rural social order. This theme runs right through the period. Even among blood sports in England, what was policed and how it was policed depended on whose leisure was at issue in explicitly class terms.

Something similar applied to the popular village and small town football games, many of which survived into the late eighteenth and early nineteenth centuries in England. Survivals were confined to small, stagnating towns and villages that were slow to develop formal local government institutions and the corresponding local police presence and whose commercial interests were neither assertive nor influential enough to require intervention to protect their property and trade. Workington, the largest town to keep a mass football game, an Easter calendar custom in

this case, did so after losing it for several years. In Workington survival was assisted when the game became a curiosity that attracted trainloads of lucrative spectators from the surrounding area. The outcome may also have been affected by the town's distance from higher-order centers of government. Usually this kind of activity was a prime candidate for police intervention and suppression, as were other popular sports that used public spaces, such as roadracing, proscribed because of the competitors' preferred state of undress and because the crowds blocked the streets, and stone bowling, a Lancashire pastime suppressed in the 1860s as a hazard to other road users.

Football in England was policed by another route. The public schools and their associated cult of "muscular Christianity" imposed rules limiting time, space, numbers, and acceptable behavior, which were available nationally from 1863. Rules formed part of a wider pattern of taming popular sports through the formal codification of regulations imposed on the competitors, thereby making games more acceptable in the new, more disciplined urban societies. Football's expansion on this new basis as soccer and rugby meant that aspects of it were self-policing through the voluntary organizations that oversaw its development and disciplined offenders and recalcitrants. This became the norm elsewhere in Europe. Where clubs remained amateur, their finances were policed, often ineffectively, by the ruling bodies. Even where the

Football Hooliganism. Ajax Amsterdam soccer fans clash with police in Eindhoven, the Netherlands, 10 September 1989. GREG BOS/REUTERS/CORBIS-BETTMANN

professional game came in, travel expenses and wage payments were limited and regulated. In Britain professional soccer players were subjected to a maximum wage until the early 1960s, and illegal payments to players were severely punished. As the varieties of football developed into spectator sports across Europe, the formal police forces of town, county, and province also needed to keep order among the watching throng. Debates continue about the origins of football hooliganism and when crowd misbehavior reached a level to deserve that label. While disorder was not absent in the early days of large-scale spec-

tatorship in the late nineteenth century, the sheer scale and violence of the last quarter of the twentieth century was completely unprecedented and all the more alarming for that.

Policing by regimes of rule and administration imposed and enforced by the voluntary bodies, which ran the sports and could cast dissenters into a sporting wilderness, was echoed in other sports that emerged or were remodeled in the late nineteenth century. Many ruling bodies, as in athletics and rowing, cleaved to an amateur ideal that excluded, marginalized, or disadvantaged the working class, which was developing its

162

own separate sports federations by the interwar years. Other sports also followed football in excluding women. Women's bodies at leisure were policed by rule and convention in the sporting sphere as in others, as expectations about passivity and the dangers of vigorous exercise continued to dominate medical orthodoxies until well after World War II.

POLICING PRIVATE BEHAVIOR

Formal intervention by the policing regimes of national and local government was particularly associated with the regulation of relations between the sexes, especially where alcohol was also involved. This was central to the concerns over fairs and other calendar customs, but it was increasingly sustained regarding the daily and weekly routines of popular pleasure, where along with the regulation of gambling pastimes, the intervention of police forces in everyday life was perhaps most resented and controversial. Attempts to corral commercial sex into licensed brothels were unthinkable in Britain but were common over long periods in southern Europe. In Spain at the beginning of the twentieth century it was an acknowledged but seldom discussed reality. Prostitutes walking the streets, where their importunities annoyed passersby and their presence might create embarrassing situations for "respectable" women, posed problems of police regulation everywhere, especially in resorts and the developing shopping and theater districts of larger towns.

Working-class courting customs in the public street also aroused complaint in England, although it proved impossible to suppress the so-called "monkey parades" on Sunday evenings, in which young women and young men made contact and arranged assignations. Elsewhere in Europe, for example, in the Spanish institution of the *paseo* (walk), this seems to have been less worrisome. Outdoor courting customs in urban back alleys and entries, well documented in autobiographies and by the Mass-Observation team who investigated working-class life in Bolton, England, in the late 1930s, apparently were passively tolerated by authorities. What mattered was to keep the main public thoroughfares clear and comfortable for "respectable" passersby. Obvious prostitutes apart, this was more a matter of the police breaking up groups of men who gathered to gossip on street corners, especially when they abused or even committed minor assaults on their "betters." This was a major function of the British police from their introduction, especially in London and in the manufacturing towns of the 1840s.

Private leisure premises were even more difficult to regulate through formal policing. Licensing proved an effective tool up to a point, as establishments became more elaborate and entrepreneurs had more to lose if their activities were legally suppressed. Commercialization of leisure outlets carried its own commitment to self-policing in pursuing an extensive consumer market. Providers could not afford to alienate potential customers by shocking their sensibilities. Eighteenth-century spa resorts employed masters of ceremonies to police "the company," imposing dress codes and shared expectations of politeness and etiquette on potentially overbearing aristocrats as well as on their socially insecure inferiors from the new middle ranks. When an external regulatory regime also had to be satisfied, a certain amount of self-censorship crept in to anticipate and evade problems. Thus by licensing public houses, where beer and spirits were retailed in a sociable atmosphere, English justices of the peace discouraged working-class radical political organizations and trade unions from using them as meeting places because it threatened the livelihoods of the licensees. The Beer Act of 1830 put free trade principles before regulation and allowed beer houses to proliferate outside the magistrates' control, generating moral fears of prostitution, gambling, uncontrolled drunkenness, and political subversion.

Small establishments served well-defined local clienteles, however, and the bigger pleasure palaces that developed in the second half of the nineteenth century were more vulnerable to external pressures. Thus the London music halls of the late nineteenth and early twentieth centuries were inspected for audience composition, with special attention to evidence of prostitution, and program content, with a view to excising sexual innuendos, the undermining of constituted authority, or the ridiculing of clergymen. If they transgressed, the proprietors might suffer indirectly through particularly expensive and demanding interpretations of the fire regulations, for example.

CENSORSHIP OF MEDIA

Performers were difficult to police, especially when they departed from their submitted scripts or when they used idioms impenetrable to would-be censors. The contents of cinema, radio, and eventually television programs were also subjected to censorship. The British cinema in particular faced absurdly specific and restrictive codes that reflected the anxieties of authorities in the interwar years. While the British Broadcasting Corporation exercised monopoly powers over broadcasts, seeking to reconstruct a common

In the Pub. Colliers drinking in a South Wales pub during the coal strike of 1912. ©HULTON GETTY/LIAISON AGENCY

culture according to what later became known as "establishment" values, censorship occurred effectively within the organization. World War II precipitated a more populist and inclusive broadcasting culture, and the popularity of rival stations like Radio Luxembourg grew. Breaking out, the radio series *Round the Horne,* broadcast during the 1960s on the *Light Programme* to families enjoying Sunday lunch, might include a range of camp homosexual references that the management either failed to understand or gleefully allowed to go through.

Rarely did censorship block up all potential loopholes, and in practice it included negotiations. In Munich, for example, the folk singers who performed on a host of little stages, often in Bavarian dialect and with a strong propensity toward caustic political comment, had long been subjected to censorship of both the political and moral content of their work. In response to protests against censorship in the early twentieth century, the Munich police in 1908 formed an advisory committee of established writers, at one time including Thomas Mann, to pronounce on the artistic merit of controversial items. Nevertheless, comments critical of the regime still had to be couched in coded language. In Belgium and Spain public decency leagues restrained what could be said explicitly, but as elsewhere unscripted innuendos conveyed much. Even after the Weimar Republic abolished censorship, performers still had to carefully consider their output. At this time the effective censors were the ascendant National Socialists, whose reputation for power through direct action was more threatening than were the previous official governments.

DIFFICULTIES IN POLICING LEISURE

Official censorship was equally difficult to enforce in eighteenth-century Paris. Censorship before the French Revolution was erratic, and a great deal of scurrilous and "indecent" material was disseminated through vaudevilles or the extensive market in cheap street literature. Robert Isherwood pointed out, "No doubt, censorship was lax because the police had no desire to stifle a form of entertainment that kept the public diverted" (Isherwood, 1986, pp. 254–255). He cited Alexandre-Jacques Du Coudray's writing in 1775 as an explicit justification for loosely policing popular entertainments, which distract the populace from factionalism and revolt. The relationship between the need to restrain and control and the need to allow a measure of self-expression on the safety valve principle, was always difficult to negotiate.

The perception was, however, that the leisure of the populace above all needed policing. Within that broad category, specific groups or locations aroused disproportionate attention, among them the young of both sexes; sexual nonconformists, including homosexuals as well as prostitutes; concentrated areas identified with poverty and crime, like slums and rookeries; and stigmatized ethnic and religious minorities, for example, the Irish, Jews, or gypsies. The organized public order and defense forces of the state sometimes provided cause for alarm, as when soldiers' training camps or sailors on leave detached from the forces of order. In England during the 1860s, panic about the spread of venereal disease among the armed forces led to passage of the controversial Contagious Diseases Acts, which identified the prostitutes rather than their customers as the source of the problem but still put garrison districts under a distinctive form of martial law for several years.

Above all the leisure subjected to the most sustained policing was that of the lower orders and later the working class, especially when they concentrated in public spaces in large cities. This was particularly true of the centers of government, where disorder of any kind might and sometimes did take on political and revolutionary overtones. The pleasures of the poor constituted one of the most significant specters that haunted the national and the local authorities throughout the period under review, and the official technologies of surveillance were never sufficient. Police methods had to interact with economic, cultural, and psychological systems of control. From the eighteenth century to the twentieth self-policing was at least as important as external restraints in controlling popular leisure in modern Europe.

See also other articles in this section.

BIBLIOGRAPHY

Abrams, Lynn. *Workers' Culture in Imperial Germany.* London, 1992.

Bailey, Peter. *Leisure and Class in Victorian England.* London, 1978. Reprinted 1987.

Bailey, Peter. "The Politics and Poetics of Modern British Leisure." *Rethinking History* 3 (1999): 131–175.

Bailey, Peter. *Popular Culture and Performance in the Victorian City.* Cambridge, U.K., 1998.

Bennett, Tony. *The Birth of the Museum: History, Theory, Politics.* London, 1995.

Chinn, Carl. *Better Betting with a Decent Feller: Bookmaking, Betting, and the British Working Class, 1750–1990.* London, 1991.

Clark, Peter. *The English Alehouse: A Social History, 1200–1830.* London, 1983.

Corbin, Alain. *Village Bells.* New York, 1998.

D'Cruze, Shani. *Crimes of Outrage: Sex, Violence, and Victorian Working Women.* London, 1998.

Henderson, Tony. *Disorderly Women in Eighteenth-Century London: Prostitution and Control in the Metropolis, 1730–1830.* London, 1999.

Isherwood, Robert M. *Farce and Fantasy: Popular Entertainment in Eighteenth-Century Paris.* New York, 1986.

Malcolmson, Robert W. *Popular Recreations in English Society, 1700–1850.* Cambridge, U.K., 1973.

Meller, H. E. *Leisure and the Changing City, 1870–1914.* London, 1976.

Murfin, Lyn. *Popular Leisure in the Lake Counties.* Manchester, U.K., 1990.

Roche, Daniel. *Le peuple de Paris: Essai sur la culture populaire au XVIIIe siècle.* Paris, 1981.

Russell, D. *Football and the English.* Preston, Lancashire, U.K., 1997.

Sackett, Robert Eben. *Popular Entertainment, Class, and Politics in Munich, 1900–1923.* Cambridge, Mass., 1982.

Stites, Richard. *Russian Popular Culture: Entertainment and Society since 1900.* New York, 1992.

Storch, Robert D., ed. *Popular Culture and Custom in Nineteenth-Century England.* London, 1982.

Thompson, E. P. *Customs in Common.* London, 1991.

Turrado Vidal, Martín. *La policía en la historia contemporánea de España (1766–1986).* Madrid, 1995.

Walkowitz, Judith R. *City of Dreadful Delight: Narratives of Sexual Danger in Late-Victorian London.* Chicago, 1992.

Walton, John K. *The English Seaside Resort: A Social History, 1750–1914.* Leicester, U.K., 1983.

Wegert, Karl. *Popular Culture, Crime, and Social Control in 18th-Century Württemberg.* Stuttgart, Germany, 1994.

White, Anne. *De-Stalinization and the House of Culture: Declining State Control over Leisure in the USSR, Poland, and Hungary, 1953–89.* London, 1990.

SPORTS

Allen Guttmann

Sports had a place during the Renaissance, but a relatively small one compared to their place at the end of the twentieth century. Sports are so important a part of modernity that more than one Marxist scholar has glumly concluded that they, and not religion, are "the opiate of the masses."

Modern sports are, however, vastly different from those of the Renaissance. In theory, if not always in practice, they are national and international rather than local. They are open to all on the basis of athletic ability rather than restricted to a few on the basis of social class. In their formal-structural characteristics, modern sports differ from those of the Renaissance in a number of ways. They are highly specialized, in that many of them (like rugby and soccer) have evolved from earlier, less differentiated games; it is increasingly rare for anyone to excel at more than one sport. Modern sports are rationalized, in that the rules are constantly revised from a means-ends point of view; the equipment and facilities are standardized; and the players train scientifically, employ technologically advanced equipment, and strive for the most efficient use of their skills. They are quantified, in that achievement is defined by points scored or by the precise measurement of times and distances. Finally, they are characterized by the quest for an unsurpassed quantified achievement, which is what we mean by the "sports record" in this uniquely modern usage. A number of traditional sports have survived into the twenty-first century, but they have been pushed to the margins of modernity. While the Frenchman of the *pays Nantais* still enjoys his traditional game of *boule,* tens of millions of Europeans play soccer football and hundreds of millions watch the World Cup on television.

THE RENAISSANCE

For the Renaissance aristocrat celebrated by Baldassare Castiglione in *The Courtier* (1528), a much-mocked adage might actually have been true: it was not whether one won or lost but how one played the game. There has rarely been as much emphasis on decorum and good form in the practice of sports.

Tournaments. This attitude can be seen in the evolution of the tournament from the bloody melee of twelfth-century armed combat to the allegorical pageantry of sixteenth-century spectacle. Early tournaments involved a crowd of knights energetically engaged in a free-for-all the purpose of which was to capture and to avoid captivity. Spectators were rare, rules were minimal, and bloodshed was an accepted part of the game. At a tournament held near the German town of Neuss, in 1240, scores of knights were killed. Deadly violence was so characteristic of medieval tournaments that the Roman Catholic Church attempted in vain to ban them.

In contrast to medieval mayhem, the tournament held by René d'Anjou at Tarascon in 1449 was a model of chivalry, a symbolic statement of political authority rather than a visible proof of martial prowess. René's account of the event is a compulsively detailed etiquette book regulating exits and entrances, proper verbal formulas, and appropriate dress. The jousting pairs that replaced the mob of medieval combatants are scarcely mentioned.

The tournament staged by Henry VIII in 1511 to mark the birth of his son by Katharine of Aragon was an occasion for Henry and his court to appear as *Ceur loyall* (Loyal Heart) and other allegorical characters. Of the thirty-six vellum membranes of the Great Tournament Roll of Westminster, only three show Henry tilting before the pavilion from which his queen observes and admires him. Thirty membranes picture the gorgeously colorful entry and exit processions.

Despite the shift of emphasis from combat to spectacle, there was always the possibility of mishap. At a tournament held in Paris in 1559, Henry II carelessly failed to close the visor of his helmet and was killed by a splintered lance. To eliminate totally the possibility of accident, "ring tournaments" were introduced. Galloping knights aimed their lances not at

THE COURTIER

If [the courtier] happens to engage in arms in some public show—such as jousts, tourneys, stick-throwing, or in any other bodily exercises—mindful of the place where he is and in whose presence, he will strive to be as elegant and handsome in the exercise of arms as he is adroit, and to feed his spectators' eyes with all those things that he thinks may give him added grace; and he will take care to have a horse gaily caparisoned, to wear a becoming attire, to have appropriate mottoes and ingenious devices that will attract the eyes of the spectators even as the lodestone attracts iron.

— *Baldassare Castiglione,* Il cortegiano *(1528), translated by Charles Singleton (New York, 1959), pp. 99–100.* —

one another but at a set of rings dangling from cords. The symbolism, sexual rather than martial, was appropriate for an age in which wars were no longer decided by knights on horseback.

Fencing. By the sixteenth century swordplay had become a prized sport in its own right. The substitution of the rapier for the heavy two-handed sword signaled a shift from brute strength to agility and finesse. Ambitious fencing masters perfected their art in Italy and France and then gave lessons to the young nobleman of England, Germany, and Poland.

Fencing became highly rationalized, with rules to govern every aspect of the sport. Treatises on the sport emphasized its aesthetic appeal. At the court of Louis XIV, correct performance of the ceremonial bow, the *révérence,* seemed as important as the proper way to execute a thrust. Fencers' manuals like Camillo Agrippa's *Trattato di scientia d'arme* (Treatise on the science of arms; 1553) and Girard Thibault's *L'académie de l'espée* (The academy of the foil; 1628) were illustrated by diagrams of the appropriate positions to take before, during, and after the match. Such manuals resembled textbooks in geometry.

Football. Renaissance gentlemen were not content just to refine the sports traditionally associated with a bellicose nobility; they also borrowed from the peasantry. While various versions of folk football, which European serfs had played for centuries, continued to be popular in the countryside, young Italian noblemen transformed rustic play into urbane entertainment.

Folk football was typically a violent confrontation in which men, women, and children struggled furiously to kick, throw, or carry a ball across fields and streams and through the streets of their neighbors' village. The final goal was the portal of the parish church, but rival parishioners were seldom treated with Christian charity. Writing in *The Boke Named the Governour* (1531), Sir Thomas Elyot condemned—to no avail—the "beastly fury, and extreme violence" of the game.

Folk football had little resemblance to its descendant, the game played on the Piazza di Santa Croce in Florence and depicted by Jacques Callot in a set of prints dedicated to Lorenzo de' Medici in 1617. This sport was particularly popular in the sixteenth century, when Giovanni Bardi wrote his *Discorso sopra il gioco del calcio fiorentino* (Discourse on the game of Florentine football; 1580). In its classic form, the game was a highly regulated contest played by teams of twenty-seven on a rectangular field exactly twice as long as it was wide.

The contestants, wrote Bardi, should be "gentlemen from eighteen years of age to forty-five, beautiful and vigorous, of gallant bearing and of good report." He urged also that every gentleman player should wear "goodly raiment and seemly, well fitting and handsome." The emphasis upon the aesthetic aspect of the game is precisely what one expects of Renaissance sports, but there were also political ramifications. The ball was associated with the six golden balls of the Medici coat of arms and the game was frequently staged as a symbolic statement of that family's political power. There were, for instance, two games of *calcio* played in the summer of 1558 to celebrate the marriage of Lucrezia de' Medici and Alfonso II d'Este.

Archery. In Gubbio and other Italian cities, the middle class competed in crossbow contests, but archery's center of gravity lay north of the Alps, in France, Germany, and the Netherlands. Crossbow guilds, whose patron was frequently St. George, recruited members of relatively high status. They were government officials, wealthy merchants, and occasionally members of the nobility. Under the dubious patronage of St. Sebastian, whom Roman archers martyred, the longbowmen tended to come from somewhat less affluent circumstances.

Crossbow guilds spread in the fourteenth century from Artois, Brabant, Flanders, and Picardy to

Tournament. Knights practicing in the tilting ring, woodcut, 1592. ©BETTMANN/CORBIS

northern France and to all of German-speaking Europe. Entry into an archery guild was usually restricted. Abbeville's guild was typical. The bourgeoisie of that French town limited membership to fifty. Women were generally excluded from archery guilds, but there were exceptions to the rule. The guild of St. Sebastian at Kappelen in Flanders had guild sisters who competed for the title of queen.

The annual archery meet, the *Schützenfest,* was a major civic festival, scheduled many months in advance, that might last a week or longer. Contestants were attracted from hundreds of miles away and matches like that held in Augsburg in 1509 attracted thousands of spectators. With a complicated instrument like the crossbow, it was unlikely that many of these spectators really understood the fine points of the sport, but the difference between a hit and a miss was obvious to everyone. When the mimetic target (a bird, a deer) evolved into an abstract configuration of concentric rings, each with a different quantified value, everyone was able to tell the winners from the losers.

If spectators flocked to archery contests, it was not simply to admire toxophilic prowess. Annual festivals were accompanied by pageantry and revelry. There were banquets with rich food and high-minded speeches; there was also drunkenness, buffoonery, and sexual promiscuity.

"Blood sports." Football games and archery matches were not the only sports events to threaten Renaissance notions of measure and decorum. Joseph Strutt, an early-nineteenth-century historian of British sports, asserted that "blood sports" attracted only "the lowest and most despicable part of the people," but, in fact, lords and ladies were passionate foxhunters and Tudor royalty led the way to the bear pits. Elizabeth I was so fond of animal baiting that she prohibited London's theaters from performing plays on Thursdays because they interfered with "the game of bear-baiting, and like pastimes, which are maintained for her Majesty's pleasure." Henry VIII was fond enough of cockfights to add a pit to Whitehall. More than a century later, on 13 March 1683, *The Loyal Protestant* reported that Charles II had taken most of the court "to see the sport of cock-fighting; where they received great satisfaction."

Renaissance Italy, too, had its share of violent sport. While dandies in silken uniforms entertained the Medici court with exhibitions of skill at *calcio,* hardier Italians pummeled one another while playing *gioco della pugna* (game of the fist). In the Venetian version of the sport, hundreds of men, representing different sections of the city, fought pitched battles for the control of the bridges that linked their neighborhoods. After witnessing the *gioco della pugna* in 1574,

Henry III of France remarked that the event was "too small to be a real war and too cruel to be a game." In Florence in 1611 twenty-six men were killed in a grand *gioco*.

EARLY MODERN TIMES

At the risk of simplification, one can say that the cultural difference between the Renaissance and modern times can be read from the changing meaning of a single word: "measure." To the readers of Henry Peacham's popular handbook, *The Compleat Gentleman* (1622), measure implied balance and moderation. A century later, the same term implied quantified measurement. It was clearly associated more with arithmetic than with geometry. This semantic shift can be observed in the ways that Europeans conceptualized their sports. The vocabulary of aesthetic response gave way, although never completely, to the language of quantified achievement. This conceptual transition took place in England much earlier than in the rest of Europe.

The passion for quantified results seems to have been driven as much by the gambler's desire for clarity as by the empirical scientist's demand for exactitude. Gambling was, in fact, the impetus for a great deal of early modern sport. As Robert Burton noted in the 1621 edition of *The Anatomy of Melancholy,* the impulse to wager impelled men to "gallop quite out of their fortunes."

Races. Foot races are probably a human universal, but the English seem to have developed a mania for them after 1660 when Charles II returned from exile. *The Loyal Protestant* of 3 March 1683 reported the king's presence when a hardy citizen managed to walk five times around St. James's Park in two hours. James Pellor Malcolm's compendium of odd events included a mention of a poulterer who walked 202 times around Upper Moorfields "to the infinite improvement of his business, and great edification of hundreds of spectators." The passion for contests of this sort grew to the point where *The Sporting Magazine* for April 1822 reported that some fifteen thousand spectators had come to cheer fifty-six-year-old George Wilson as he successfully walked ninety miles in twenty-four hours.

These races, which foreign travelers like Jean-Bernard Le Blanc and Zacharias Konrad von Uffenbach saw as typically English, were not limited to men. In 1667 Samuel Pepys watched girls race across a bowling green. In May 1749 an eighteen-month-old girl earned her backers a considerable sum of

---

A BOXER OF BILLINGSGATE

I, Elisabeth Stokes, of the City of London, have not fought . . . since I fought the famous boxing woman of Billingsgate 9 minutes, and gained a complete victory, which is six years ago; but as the famous Stoke Newington ass woman (that is, ass-driver) dares me to fight her for 10 pounds, I do assure her I will not fail meeting her for the said sum, and doubt not that the blows which I shall present her with will be more difficult for her to digest than any she ever gave her asses.

— London Daily Post, *7 October 1728* —

---

money when she toddled the half-mile length of Pall Mall in twenty-three minutes, seven minutes faster than required.

When sportsmen turned their attention from humans to horses, times measured to the minute were not good enough. In 1731, stopwatches were used to time winners to the second. The "sport of kings" was modernized in other ways as well. In 1750 gentlemen meeting informally at Richard Tattersall's tavern began to think of themselves as the Jockey Club. They set about rationalizing England's horse races. In 1769 the first racing calendar appeared. A little more than a decade later, the English had established a series of annual events that are still high points of the sporting season: the St. Leger (1778), the Oaks (1779), and the Derby at Epsom (1780). A few years later, in an effort to rationalize breeding, the first stud book was published (1791). During the Renaissance, English sports were likely to imitate French sports, but now it was upper-class anglophile Frenchmen who established Le Jockey-Club (1833) and inaugurated thoroughbred races like the Derby at Chantilly (1836).

Pugilism. Illegal but nonetheless cherished as a convincing manifestation of John Bull's envied virility, pugilism flourished in eighteenth-century London. The *True Protestant Mercury* for 12 January 1681 reported a bout between a butcher and a footman in service to the duke of Albemarle, but it was not until after 1743, when Jack Broughton's rules were published, that London newspapers paid serious attention to "the manly art" (and not until 1822 that *Bell's Life*

Boxers. A prize fight in England, 1788. ©BBC HULTON/ LIAISON AGENCY

in London began its run as the world's first sports weekly—with pugilism as a feature). Visitors from the continent expressed amazement that noblemen stripped to the waist and avenged insults with their fists instead of with their swords, and the British responded with scorn for the effeminate foreigners who relied on metal instead of mettle. Champion boxers like Broughton in the 1740s and Daniel Mendoza in the 1790s were patronized by the aristocracy, lionized by the masses, and immortalized by Thomas Rowlandson and other artists. In 1810 Tom Cribb became something of a national hero when he defeated Tom Molineaux, an African American challenger. That pugilists were shunned by the respectable middle classes mattered little to the "fancy."

Throughout the eighteenth century lower-class women flocked to ringside to see the fights at popular venues like James Figg's Amphitheatre, which opened in 1743. Women were relatively rare *in* the ring, but Uffenbach encountered a rowdy female spectator who claimed that she herself "had fought another female in this play without stays and in nothing but a shift."

Golf and cricket. At the other end of the social scale, golf was played by Scottish royalty as early as the sixteenth century. (Queen Mary was a noted enthusiast.) The game began to assume its modern form after the founding of the Royal and Ancient Golf Club of St. Andrews in 1754. The Royal Musselburgh Golf Club offered prizes to female golfers in 1810, but it was not until the end of the nineteenth century that a significant number of women took to the links.

Although the game of cricket can be traced with certainty as far back as the sixteenth century—when John Derrick of Guildford recalled that "he and diverse of his fellowes [at school] did runne and play there at creckett"—cricket, too, attained its modern form in the mid-eighteenth century. The first complete set of rules was published in 1744, a year after Broughton's rules brought a modicum of order to the prize ring. Cricket's first recorded gate money, collected at the Finsbury Artillery Ground, also dates from 1744. In 1787 Thomas Lord and a number of other enthusiasts formed the Marylebone Cricket Club, the game's most authoritative institution.

Cricket was popular among eighteenth-century Englishmen of every social class. The game was played on country estates, where the squire bowled and his tenants batted, and on village greens, where parsons bowled to peasants. Cricket was also popular at the public schools to which noblemen and wealthy merchants sent their sons. The women's game has never been as widely played as the men's, but its history is nearly as long. On 14 July 1743 the *London General Advertiser* referred to a tournament at the Finsbury Artillery Ground to which women's teams from several Sussex villages were invited. Two years later, in Surrey, eleven maids from Bramley, with blue ribbons in their hair, succumbed to the superior play of eleven red-ribboned maids from Hambleton.

By the end of the nineteenth century, cricket was everywhere perceived as the archetypical English game. For many Englishmen, spring meant not the resurrection of Jesus Christ but the return to action of the game's greatest player, William Gilbert Grace. He was probably the century's most famous (and richest) amateur athlete. Between 1870 and 1910, benefit matches and reimbursements for expenses brought him approximately 120,000 pounds.

Cricket was played in colonial Virginia as early as 1710, but eighteenth-century Europeans resisted imports from the British Isles. From Abruzzi in the south of Italy to the Polish forest of Bialowieza, hunting was the favored pastime of the aristocracy (and draconian game laws were passed in an attempt to preserve their monopoly). The length and breadth of Europe, every region had its own distinctive way to wrestle and to play folk football. Ubiquitous also was some form of bowling—*boule* in France, *Kegeln* in Germany, *trou-madame* in Flanders.

Traditional sport. Just as cricket came gradually to be perceived as characteristically English, the bullfight—the *corrida de toros*—was thought to represent the Spanish soul. The eighteenth-century matador was not yet a national icon, but a number of men (and a handful of women) won a modicum of fame with cape and *spada*. Germans were known for their passion for shooting clubs; every town from Königsberg in the east to Freiburg in the west had at least one *Schützenverein* where burghers gathered to shoot, drink the local beer, and play a game of cards. The winter scenes painted by Henrik Averkamp document Dutch hibernal enthusiasm for ice skating, sledding, and playing *kolf* (the ancestor of golf). At the other end of the continent, Russian peasants played *gorodki,* a game in which wooden balls were thrown at small wooden figures.

None of these traditional sports has entirely disappeared, and there are now several European organizations devoted to their preservation, but all of them, even bullfighting, have been supplanted in popularity by modern sports invented, for the most part, in Great Britain or the United States.

MODERN TIMES: INVENTION AND DIFFUSION

From the eighteenth century until the middle of the twentieth, Great Britain's role in the development and diffusion of modern sports was more important than that of any other nation. Even the French, who can claim credit for the Tour de France (1903) and its many imitations, acknowledge that the British led the way to modern sports. Although basketball (1891) and volleyball (1895) were American inventions, it was not until after World War II that the United States finally supplanted Great Britain as the primary agents in the invention and diffusion of modern sports.

Through most of the nineteenth century rowing, which is now perceived as a relatively minor sport, attracted huge crowds of spectators. There were boat races at Eton as early as 1793, but the modern version of the sport received its strongest impetus on 10 June 1829 when students from Oxford and Cambridge competed against one another on the Thames. The Henley Regatta began ten years later. In 1845 its course was fixed at 4 miles, 374 yards—the distance from Putney Bridge to Chiswick Bridge. The rationalization of the sport can be dated from 1828 when Anthony Brown of Ouseburn-on-Tyne designed a pair of iron outriggers to increase the oarsman's leverage. In 1865 Robert Chambers, champion of the Tyne, used a sliding seat when he rowed against Harry Kelley, champion of the Thames. By the 1870s the clumsy boats of the previous century had been lightened and streamlined to the point where they were useless for any purpose other than racing.

In 1879 the Henley Regatta promulgated an amateur rule that revealed its purpose in the crassest terms. The definition of an amateur excluded not only anyone who rowed for money but also anyone who had ever been employed in manual labor of any sort whatsoever. The *Times* of London approved: "The outsiders, artisans, mechanics, and such like troublesome persons can have no place found for them [in amateur sports]" (26 April 1880). Four years later, the upper-middle-class oarsmen who founded the Amateur Rowing Association (1882) adopted a similar set of exclusionary rules designed to restrict the sport to men (and women) of the leisure class. Although challenged by other national organizations with more egalitarian principles, the leaders of the Amateur Rowing Association insisted that the lower orders had no sense of fair play.

On the continent, the Germans were the first to show real enthusiasm for amateur rowing. In 1836 six years after Britons resident in Hamburg had formed a rowing club, German merchants founded the Hamburger Ruderclub. They held their first regatta on the Alster in 1844. The Deutscher Ruderverband (German Rowing Federation) was born at Cologne in 1883. Emulation of the English included adoption of the amateur rule and the fairly unproblematical acceptance of female rowers. Berlin's women formed their first rowing club in 1901.

In 1869 four intrepid women competed in a bicycle race from Paris to Rouen. In the 1880s and 1890s, millions more took to the road on chain-driven safety bicycles, which had front and rear wheels of the same size (unlike the dangerous penny-farthing model with a huge front wheel). Unescorted (and uncorseted) female cyclists became a symbol of women's emancipation.

Women were also among the first players of lawn tennis. Apart from the fact that both games require the players to propel a ball across a net by means of a strung racket, modern lawn tennis has very little in common with royal or court tennis, an indoor game popular among Renaissance aristocrats. Credit for the invention of lawn tennis can be given to Major Walter Wingfield, who received a patent for his portable hourglass-shaped court on 23 February 1874. A mere three years later the All-England Croquet Club of Wimbledon staged its first tennis tournament (men only). Spencer Gore won. Seven years later, Maud Watson defeated her sister Lilian to become the first women's champion.

In 1877 Britons in Paris began to play tennis at Le Decimal-Club. In the 1880s the game became immensely popular in Bad Homburg, in Deauville, and in other venues frequented by the European leisure

Rowing. Spectators watching the Henley Regatta, c. 1931. HULTON-DEUTSCH COLLECTION/
CORBIS

class. In the 1920s the French displaced the British as the leading players. Between 1924 and 1929, Jean Borotra, René Lacoste, and Henri Cochet dominated the men's game as Suzanne Lenglen did the women's. Lenglen, famed for exotic attire and flamboyant behavior as well as for athletic skill, was the first sportswoman to become an international celebrity.

Lawn tennis began as an upper-class sport and has never quite lost the aura of exclusivity. Runners, on the other hand, have had their social ups and downs. Early in the nineteenth century, runners like the famed Robert Barclay Allerdice ran or walked incredible distances to win equally incredible sums of money, but the presence of gamblers and the circuslike atmosphere of pedestrianism probably inhibited rather than encouraged the evolution of modern track-and-field sports. It was not until 1864 that Oxford met Cambridge in "athletics" (the preferred British term for track-and-field sports), a full generation after the collegiate rowers met at Henley. The collegiate runners, jumpers, and throwers shared the amateur status and the social prestige of the rowers. The Mincing Lane Athletic Club (1863), which became the London AC (1866), and the Amateur Athletic Association (1880) were both dominated by graduates of the two great universities.

Continental Europeans certainly did not need anyone to teach them how to run and jump, but British influence determined which of a thousand different kinds of athletic contests became standard. This can be seen quite clearly in the units of measurement.

For decades, runners who lived in an otherwise metric world ran 100-yard dashes and set records for the mile. Pierre de Coubertin, founder of the modern Olympic Games (1896), was French and Sigfrid Edström, the force behind the creation of the International Amateur Athletic Federation (1913), was Swedish, but the track-and-field disciplines sanctioned by the International Olympic Committee and by the IAAF were based—with the exception of the discus and the javelin—on British custom.

Soccer football. The stamp of British culture can be seen even more clearly in soccer football. The first set of rules for soccer, which is by far the most widely played of the many games derived from folk football, was devised by fourteen English collegians in 1848 on the basis of the various rules for a number of different games played at Eton, Harrow, Rugby, Winchester, and several other public schools. The first football club was founded in Sheffield in 1855 by graduates of Sheffield Collegiate School. The Old Harrovians, who established their club in 1860, were obviously another group with public-school ties. The name "soccer" (from "association") derives from the fact that the sport was nationally organized by the Football Association (FA) founded in London on 26 October 1863, a day that must rank as the most important in the modern history of the game. The FA became the model for the national organization of innumerable other sports throughout Europe and beyond.

173

THE FOUR-MINUTE MILE

My body had long since exhausted all its energy, but it went on running just the same. . . . With five yards to go the tape seemed almost to recede. Would I ever reach it?

Those last few seconds seemed never-ending. The faint line of the finishing tape stood ahead as a haven of peace, after the struggle. . . . I leapt at the tape like a man taking his last spring to save himself from the chasm that threatens to engulf him.

My effort was over and I collapsed almost unconscious, with an arm on either side of me. It was only then that real pain overtook me. I felt like an exploded flashlight with no will to live. . . . It was as if all my limbs were caught in an ever-tightening vice. I knew that I had done it before I even heard the time. . . . The stopwatches held the answer. The announcement came— ''Result of the one mile . . . time, 3 minutes''—the rest lost in the roar of excitement. I grabbed [Christopher] Brasher and [Christopher] Chataway, and together we scampered round the track in a burst of spontaneous joy. We had done it—the three of us!

— *Roger Bannister on the 3:59.4 mile run on 6 May 1954.* The Four Minute Mile *(New York, 1955), pp. 214–215.* —

The "old boys" wanted to keep the game for themselves, but soccer was quickly diffused downward through the social strata. Aston Villa Football Club and the Bolton Wanderers, both founded in 1874, were typical of the many clubs that recruited their first members from the congregations of churches and chapels. Within a few years other clubs destined to figure grandly in the annals of English sports were organized by the employees of industrial enterprises. Manchester United, for instance, was begun by a group of railroad workers and Coventry City had its start as a club for the workers at Singer's bicycle factory. In most cases the initiative came from the workers; it was not until the twentieth century that companies like Rowntree's (chocolates) and Peugeot (automobiles) began to sponsor sports clubs.

Soccer spread rapidly. Birmingham had its first club in 1874; six years later it had 155. Delighted by the game's popularity, the FA in 1872 inaugurated an annual tournament, the Football Association Cup. The day of the cup final quickly became for working-class Britons the equivalent of Derby Day at Epsom for the nation's ruling class. When a team of Lancashire workmen—Blackburn Olympic Football Club— defeated the Old Etonians in the cup final of 1883, it was clear that soccer was destined to become "the people's game."

By the late nineteenth century, there was an economic basis for soccer's working-class popularity. The second half of the nineteenth century saw a significant rise in real wages. The Factory Act (1850) and subsequent legislation shortened Saturday hours for industrial workers. There was more time and more money for soccer and other forms of amusement and recreation. In time, workers elsewhere demanded and received similar relief from the onerous conditions of early industrialization.

The creation of Britain's railroad network made it possible for teams to play distant opponents, but games away from home raised financial problems for clubs with working-class players. The Football Association agreed that clubs might reimburse needy players for their travel expenses, but believers in amateurism drew the line at payments for "broken-time" (time lost from work). In 1888, however, the FA's middle-class directors reluctantly accepted the establishment of openly professional teams. The strongest teams of the Football League came from the Midlands or the north of England, the country's most industrialized areas. By the early twentieth century, the connection between "the people's game" and the British working class was so strong that the football grounds of England and Scotland were said to host "the Labour Party at prayer." The religious metaphor was applied to the increasingly capacious stadia erected in the early twentieth century; they were dubbed "modernity's cathedrals."

The first continental football club seems to have been established by British schoolboys at Geneva's La Châtelaine school in 1869, but the first game was played in 1863 at the Maison de Melle near Ghent. The ball and the rules were introduced by an Irish pupil, Cyril Bernard Morrogh. Boys with British connections were among the principal diffusers of the game. Eighteen-year-old Konrad Koch, who learned the game at Rugby, brought soccer to Braunschweig's Gymnasium Martino-Katharineum in 1874. Fourteen-year-old Pim Mulier, who had also studied at an English boarding school, formed the Haarlemsche Football Club (1879). Although Britons resident in Le Havre had played soccer as early as 1872, the game's takeoff can be dated from 1888, when boys from l'École Monge returned from a visit to Eton.

Sports Enthusiasts. West Ham supporters arrive for the Cup Final between West Ham and Bolton Wanderers at Wembley, near London, 1923. ©HULTON GETTY/LIAISON AGENCY

The date of soccer's arrival, soon or late, depended on the strength or weakness of commercial ties with Britain and on an area's geographical distance from the British Isles. Edoardo Bosio, a businessman in the industrial city of Turin, is considered to be the father of Italian football. Returning from an 1887 visit to England, he recruited a team from the employees of his firm. In 1893 British engineers working in Spain introduced the game in Bilbao. The following year British engineers working in Russia brought soccer to the employees of the Morozov textile mill. Hungarians did not play their first game until 1896, when Charles Löwenrosen, a schoolboy whose parents had migrated to England, returned to Budapest for a visit. That year, Scots employed in Sweden organized a team in Göteburg.

Between 1889 and 1901, Denmark, Switzerland, Belgium, Italy, the Netherlands, Germany, Czechoslovakia, and Hungary all established national football federations (in that order). Between 1924 and 1932, openly professional leagues began to operate in Austria, Hungary, Czechoslovakia, Italy, Spain, and France. The French were relatively slow because soccer had to vie for popularity with rugby, especially in southwest France. When the Fédération Française de Football (1919) finally accepted professional soccer, in 1932, many of the sport's star players were recruited from eastern Europe. The belated establishment of Ger-

many's Bundesliga (1963) can be explained by a nationalistic commitment to *Turnen* (German-style gymnastics) and by the Nazi regime's abolition of professional soccer.

Modern skiers pay homage to the Norwegians as well as to the English. Races on skis certainly predate recorded history, but the oldest known organized ski competition occurred among Norwegian soldiers in 1767 and the famed Holmenkollen ski jump can be traced back to 1879. Cross-country skiing became popular throughout northern Europe in the 1890s, after the Norwegian explorer Fridtjof Nansen published a dramatic account of his 1888 trek across Greenland. In 1901 Norwegian and Swedish skiers met in Stockholm for the first Nordic Games. The evolution of downhill skiing owes more to the English than to the Scandinavians. Arnold Lunn, an Englishman living in Mürren, Switzerland, invented the slalom on 6 January 1922 and promoted downhill skiing at the famed Kandahar Ski Club, which he founded in 1924. That same winter, the first Winter Olympics were celebrated at Chamonix in France. The skiers' *Wunderjahr* also saw the foundation of the Fédération Internationale de Ski, in which Lunn played a major role.

While the French lagged far behind the British in the invention and diffusion of modern sports, they were unquestionably the leaders when it came to the creation of international sports organizations. One reason for the French lead in this matter was the British assumption that *their* national federations were all that modern sports needed in the way of bureaucratic organization. When the French formed the Fédération Internationale de Football Association (FIFA) in 1904, the Football Association initially hesitated to join. The FA joined but then dropped its membership in FIFA in 1920 to protest the readmission of Germany. The British rejoined in 1924 and withdrew again in 1928 to protest what the FA saw as FIFA's violations of strict amateurism. The FA's quarrels with FIFA meant that the English boycotted the first three World Cup competitions sponsored by FIFA. When the European Cup was begun in 1955, the FA refused to allow Chelsea, the English champion, to enter the competition.

RESISTANCE TO MODERNITY

Devotees of traditional games, such as Basque pelota and Swiss *Hornuss,* have spurned the appeals of modern sports. In 1884 Thomas Croke condemned the Irish penchant for cricket and tennis and defended "hurling, football kicking according to the Irish rules, 'casting,' leaping various ways, wrestling, handygrips," and other Hibernian sports. That year Michael Cusack and Maurice Davin founded the Gaelic Athletic Association, which counted Charles Stewart Parnell among its patriotic sponsors. The most vigorous and sustained resistance to modernity, however, was mounted by the German gymnastics movement.

German gymnastics had its immediate origins in the innovative forms of physical education devised in the late eighteenth century by schoolmasters such as Johann Friedrich GutsMuths. Putting into practice some of the thoughts articulated by Jean-Jacques Rousseau in *Émile* (1762), German pedagogues allowed their pupils an unprecedented freedom to do sports, but—they were, after all, German—they carefully measured and recorded the children's athletic achievements. A generation later, Friedrich Ludwig Jahn transformed the program for health and hygiene into a nationalistic political movement. Inspired by Johann Gottfried von Herder and Ernst Moritz Arndt, Jahn replaced the Greek term *Gymnastik* with a suitably German word of his own invention: *Turnen.* The essence of *Turnen* was the combination of noncompetitive physical exercises and patriotic sentiment. The *Turnplatz* that Jahn built for his pupils on the outskirts of Berlin in the spring of 1811 soon began to attract students from the university. Students and other young middle-class men formed *Turnvereine*

(gymnastics clubs) and within a few years, the *Turnbewegung* (gymnastics movement) had spread throughout Germany, inspiring such nationalistic fervor that thousands of gymnasts volunteered to fight against the Napoleonic army that then occupied most of their fatherland.

Jahn was an anti-Semitic xenophobe, but most of his followers were liberals and many played an important role in the failed revolution of 1848, after which thousands of them emigrated to the United States and Latin America. Those who remained became increasingly conservative. After the formation of the Reich in 1871, the members of the Deutsche Turnerschaft (1868) proclaimed themselves to be Kaiser Wilhelm's most loyal subjects.

Adolf Spiess and other German educators transformed Jahn's gymnastic exercises, which had included running, jumping, vaulting, tumbling, climbing, and swinging from ropes, into a series of formalized, rationalized, repetitive drills. Physical-education classes, where rows and columns of children moved in synchronized response to barked commands, became a means for the authorities to inculcate the virtues of discipline and unquestioning obedience.

Working-class gymnasts who found the chauvinism and authoritarianism of the *Turner* movement unpalatable formed the Arbeiter Turnerbund (Workers' Gymnastics Union) in 1893. The ATB had close ties to Germany's socialist party. Similar organizations, with similar links to socialism, were established throughout western Europe. By 1920, when these organizations joined to create the Socialist Workers Sports International, all of them had accepted modern sports (played, they proclaimed, with fraternal goodwill). In the 1920s and 1930s, the SWSI sponsored a series of highly successful Workers' Olympics. It is noteworthy, however, that nearly 90 percent of the SWSI's membership of 1.3 million came from German-speaking areas.

Early in the nineteenth century, Scandinavian educators like Per Henryk Ling created an alternative gymnastic tradition which they maintained was more scientific (and less xenophobic) than *Turnen.* In 1814 he established his Central Institute in Stockholm as a place to train proponents of his system. Although they were rivals, the *Turner* and the Lingians both saw themselves as proponents of an alternative to modern sports.

In opposition to competition and the "egoistic" individualism of sports, the *Turner* dedicated themselves to the creation of a *Volksgemeinschaft* (national community). The instrumental rationality of sports was judged to be no better than "Taylorism" (a reference to the American efficiency expert Frederick W.

Mass Exercise. *Turnfest* in Leipzig, 1913. BUNDESARCHIV, KOBLENZ

Taylor). The quantification characteristic of modern sports enticed athletes to quest for records and this, too, was an occasion for ire. Writing in 1897, Ferdinand Schmidt condemned "records made possible by one-sided . . . preparation aimed exclusively at lowering times by fractions of a second or lengthening distances by a centimeter." Soccer football was described as a barbaric pastime whose most characteristic physical motion resembled *der Hundstritt* (kicking the dog). When Pierre de Coubertin invited German athletes to compete in the Olympic Games of 1896, the Deutsche Turnerschaft ordered its members to decline the invitation. The strength of the DT can been seen in the numbers. In 1910 it had over a million members while the Deutscher Fussballbund (German Soccer Federation) had a mere 82,000.

From the 1860s to the outbreak of World War I, German gymnastics flourished throughout eastern Europe as a vehicle for nationalism and as an alternative to modern sports. In Prague, in February 1862, two middle-class Czechs, Jindrich Fügner and Miroslav Tyrs, founded the first Sokol ("Falcon") club. By the end of the century, the movement had won the fealty of the Czech working class. By 1914 the Prague "nest," which had begun with seventy-three members, had 128,000 "falcons," one of whom, Tomás Masaryk, became president of Czechoslovakia when liberation from Austrian rule was finally achieved in the aftermath of the war.

By the turn of the century, the Slovenes of Ljubljana, the Croats of Zagreb, the Serbs of Belgrade, and the Bosnians of Sarajevo had all founded Sokol clubs that combined gymnastic exercises with a fervent demand for independence from Austrian rule. On the whole, Slavic gymnasts were less likely than the *Turner* to fight tooth and nail against modern sports, but Budapest's first athletic club, founded in 1875 by Miksa Esterházy, split apart in a bitter quarrel over the two modes of physical culture.

In the long run, the gymnasts lost their struggle against modern sports. By the 1930s Hungary was known more for its soccer players than for its gymnasts and Germany's *Turner* had to admit that they were far outnumbered by enthusiasts for football and other British imports. Gymnasts were, of course, included in the Olympic Games, but by the 1940s the quantified individual contests of modern gymnastics bore little resemblance to the activities promoted by Jahn.

Gymnastics was not the only alternative to modern sports. During the early 1920s, there was a movement within the Soviet Union to create a socialist alternative to modern sports, which were seen by many as the product of "bourgeois" capitalism. This drive for some kind of noncompetitive physical education appropriate to "proletarian culture" more or less ended in 1925, when A. A. Zigmund was removed from his post at Moscow's State Institute of Physical Culture (and subsequently executed). Three years later, the USSR staged the first of its Spartakiads. These quadrennial competitions, whose preliminary rounds were meant to involve the entire able-bodied adult population of the Soviet Union, were originally conceived as a socialist response to the "bourgeois" challenge of the Olympic Games, but they continued even after the USSR decided to participate in the international system of "bourgeois" sports.

TRANSFORMATIONS

The early history of modern sports is closely linked to the history of private sports clubs because most European sports participants—unlike their counterparts in the United States—were (and still are) club members. Europeans who yearn to participate in sports join clubs, which form the basis of national sports federations that are joined together in international sports federations, most of which are recognized by the International Olympic Committee. In 1921, when Alice Milliat, a member of the Parisian club Fémina Sport, decided that the IOC had done too little to promote women's sports, she used her position as president of the Fédération des Sociétés Féminines Sportives de France to organize the Fédération Sportive Féminine Internationale. A year later the FSFI sponsored the first of its quadrennial Women's Olympics.

Nineteenth-century liberalism was the ideology behind the IOC, the FSFI, and other nongovernmental sports organizations. Sports are thought to be a matter of individual choice free from interference by the state. In 1920s and 1930s, communist and fascist dictatorships rejected this liberal-democratic ideology and replaced the existing networks of independent sports organizations with a rigid system of centralized state control.

In the Soviet Union, in line with Marxist principles, local branches of national sports clubs were created at the workplace. Railway workers, for instance, were expected to join Lokomotiv while members of the secret police competed for Dynamo. Bureaucratic structures changed frequently, but the system established in 1936 was typical. An All-Union Committee on Physical Culture and Sport Affairs, attached to the Central Executive Committee of the USSR, was charged with the administration of Soviet sports. One of its first actions was to establish a soccer league.

The system created by Italy's Fascist regime was quite similar except that the state-run organizations established were differentiated by the age of their members rather than by the nature of their work. Adults, for instance, were expected to enroll in the Opera Nazionale Dopolavoro (The National After-Work Association). During most of the Fascist era, administration of the sports system was entrusted either to the National Olympic Committee or to the Ministry of Education.

When Adolf Hitler came to power in 1933, the leaders of many of Germany's sports federations welcomed Nazi rule. (Edmund Neuendorff, head of the Deutsche Turnerschaft was particularly enthusiastic.) Despite their many avowals of fealty and allegiance, the leaders of the various sports federations were ousted and the entire system was reorganized and placed under the rigid control of Reichssportführer Hans von Tschammer und Osten. In addition to reorganizing the existing sports federations, the regime included sports programs in its organizations for children (the Hitler Youth and the League of German Maidens) and for workers (Strength through Health).

Throughout the 1920s and 1930s, liberal-democratic governments remained relatively indifferent to the success or failure of their athletes in international competition, but fascist regimes instrumentalized sports as a means of demonstrating national revitalization and to symbolize ideological superiority. Benito Mussolini, who was often depicted as an athlete, made sports an instrument of foreign policy. Large sums of money were invested in training elite athletes. Fascist Italy came in second to the United States at the 1932 Olympics in Los Angeles; the Italian soccer team won the 1934 World Cup and the 1936 Olympic gold medal; in 1938, Gino Bartali won the Tour de France.

Nazi Germany was even more successful, hosting and winning the 1936 Olympics. The "Nazi Olympics," brilliantly documented in Leni Riefenstahl's film, *Olympia,* were such an organizational triumph that Pierre de Coubertin marveled at their "Hitlerian efficiency." The prestige acquired by such triumphs was the lure that enticed the Soviet Union to join the Olympic movement in 1952.

Berlin Olympics. Presentation of medals for gymnastic events to *(left to right)* Konrad Frey (Germany; bronze), Karl Schwarzmann (Germany; gold), and Eugene Mack (Switzerland; silver), August 1936. AKG LONDON

Motivated by eugenics as well as by the desire for national prestige, Italy's Fascists brushed aside the objections of the Roman Catholic Church and extended the benefits and pleasures of sports to female as well as to male youth. Similarly, the Nazi regime was willing to compromise its belief that women should devote themselves to *Kinder, Küche, Kirche* (children, the kitchen, and church.) Sports were seen after 1933 as a prerequisite if women were to bear healthy sons. In addition, Olympic gold medals won by outstanding female athletes like Gisela Mauermayer, in the discus, enhanced the myth of Aryan superiority.

In the latter half of the twentieth century, the sports policies of Europe's liberal democracies began in some respects to resemble those of the totalitarian powers. In one form or another, a ministry of sport was established. The number of medals won (or not won) at the Olympics became a vital matter of national prestige and, therefore, of governmental concern. Elite athletes were subsidized, training centers were constructed, coaches were hired, institutes for the scientific study of sports were founded.

Concerned about fitness and health as well as world-class achievement, governments also invested in facilities designed to promote Sport for All. Western European critics complained, often with justice, that the funds spent on elite athletes were disproportionately large. Ironically, however, the disproportion was far greater in the communist societies of eastern Europe, where the rhetoric of equality masked enormous investments in the production of a tiny cohort of world champions. While athletes from the German Democratic Republic trounced those from the United States (with a population roughly sixteen times as large as the GDR's), the recreational needs of ordinary citizens were neglected.

SPECTATORSHIP AND THE MASS MEDIA

Throughout European history, from antiquity to the present, sports spectators have tended to boisterous behavior and acts of violence. Disasters like that which occurred at Brussels' Heysal Stadium in 1985, when English hooligans supporting Liverpool attacked Italian fans of Turin's Juventus club, seem minor when compared to the catastrophe that occurred in 532 when thirty thousand people perished in one of Constantinople's sports-related riots. Renaissance tournaments were grand occasions for pomp and pageantry, but they too were liable to disruption by what Henry Goldwel in 1581 called "the too forward unruliness of many disordered people."

Between the 1890s and the 1950s, crowd disorders like those characteristic of nineteenth-century soccer matches became less frequent as working-class sports fans internalized middle-class notions of proper decorum. Although the average crowd for the Football Association's Cup Finals in the decade before World War I was 79,300, there were very few disturbances of any magnitude. In the 1920s and 1930s even larger crowds displayed remarkable self-restraint. In the 1960s, however, a segment of young working-class male fans began to use soccer pitches as a site where they were able to indulge in "aggro" (aggression) and act out their alienation from British society. In the

1980s the Germans and Dutch became almost as notorious as the British. The 1990s brought a kind of convergence in spectator behavior in which working-class soccer fans became somewhat less disorderly while upper-middle-class tennis and cricket spectators became more boisterous and verbally aggressive. Whether or not the decline in football hooliganism can be attributed to governmental countermeasures, such as the drastic increase in the extent and the celerity of police intervention, is uncertain.

In any event, Italian rather than British fans may have established the pattern for the future. In regional rivalries like those between wealthy Milan and impoverished Naples, Italian *tifosi* ("those infected with typhoid") have created a relatively nonviolent secular carnival in which physically nonviolent supporters vie in chanting comic insults and displaying colorful (and frequently obscene) banners and placards.

The sports fans who paint their faces orange for Holland or parade about in kilts to demonstrate their Scottish loyalties perform as much for the television cameras as for the morale of the players. The evolution of the mass media has drastically altered the world of sports. Sports journalism, which began in the eighteenth century with periodicals like *The Sporting Magazine* (1792), now offers thousands of specialized publications. The *London Morning Herald* introduced a regular sports page in 1817 and conventional newspapers now devote some 15 percent of their space to sports coverage, but they cannot sate the demand for statistics and trivia. Sports dailies like the *Gazzetto dello Sport* (Milano) and *L'Équipe* (Paris) sell millions of copies. Moscow's *Sovetsky Sport* and *Futbol* (and a host of similar journals published in Warsaw, Budapest, and other capitals of the now-defunct Warsaw Pact) were replaced by an active sports press driven by economic rather than ideological motives.

Radio sportscasting began in the 1920s. German radio broadcast coverage of the Münster Regatta in 1925. In 1927, when Britons owned some two million radios, the British Broadcasting Corporation covered the Oxford-Cambridge boat race, the Grand National Steeplechase, Wimbledon, and the Football Association's Cup Final. Radio reinforced the public perception of these fixtures as annual celebrations of nationhood. In 1929 French fans were able to follow the Tour de France on radio.

The boom in televised sports did not occur until the 1950s, but the Olympic Games of 1936 were televised in twenty-seven television locales scattered throughout Berlin and the BBC carried the 1938 Cup Final. Eurovision began in 1954. Forty-five stations in eight countries telecast the 1954 World Cup. Satellite transmission, which began in the 1960s, eventually transformed the Olympic Games and the World Cup into spectacles witnessed "live" by more than a billion viewers. The spread of cable television in the 1980s and 1990s intensified the competition among media magnates like Rupert Murdoch, Silvio Berlusconi, and Bernard Tapie to control the transmission of sports throughout Europe.

By the 1990s competition for the right to telecast sports events had completely transformed European sports. In 1980 television provided French soccer teams with 1 percent of their income; in 1990, the figure was 23 percent. While a handful of successful soccer clubs focus on international matches and vie for huge sums of television-generated money, thousands of smaller clubs have been deserted by fans who prefer to watch Real Madrid or Bayern München on television rather than support the local team.

Lucrative television contracts have also contributed to the Europeanization of European sports in the sense that teams like Olympique Marseilles can win a national title by acquiring stars from less wealthy foreign clubs. The collapse of communism was followed by a mass westward migration of soccer players. In 1990, for instance, seventeen of the twenty-two players on the Czech national team departed for greener fields. The process of Europeanization was accelerated in December 1995 when the European Court ruled that professional athletes like Belgium's Jean-Luc Bosman were workers who had a right to unrestricted movement within the European Union.

Europeanization is, in fact, too narrow a term to describe the social changes in sports. Most sports sociologists now speak of "globalization." Easy access to telecasts of the United States' National Basketball Association games contributed to basketball's unprecedented popularity in Europe. By the early 1990s, for instance, Michael Jordan of the Chicago Bulls was a hero to Roman boys (and girls) and basketball was Italy's second most popular spectator sport. Britain's Channel 4 began to telecast National Football League games in 1982. One reason that American sports appeared on European television in the late 1990s is that the American Broadcasting Company owned a major share of Canal Plus (UK), Sport Kanal (Germany), TV Sport (France), and Sportnet (Netherlands).

Globalization has had other effects. Americans now play in Italy's thirty-two-team professional basketball league and American gridiron football has made gains even in the homeland of soccer and rugby. A thirty-eight-team British American Football League was created in 1985. Six years later, the NFL launched a World Football League with teams in Barcelona, Frankfurt, London, and seven North American cities.

Another result of globalization has been a change in the racial mix of European sports. Initially, the appearance of black athletes on European teams incited outbursts of racist rhetoric. In 1987, when Jamaican-born John Barnes became Liverpool FC's first black player, fans from nearby Everton taunted their rivals with cries of "Niggerpool, niggerpool!" Although athletes of African descent are no longer an oddity on European teams, including those sent to the Olympic Games, an undercurrent of racism continues to flow. Many observers of the 1998 World Cup saw the victorious French team as a symbol of French multiculturalism, but it is certainly too early to celebrate the demise of racism.

POSTMODERN SPORTS?

Although modern sports like soccer have attracted unprecedented numbers of participants and spectators, many young Europeans prefer what the French refer to as *les sports californiens*. Tourists traversing the square between Cologne's cathedral and its Römisch-Germanisches Museum are imperiled by teenage Germans on skateboards. Austrian skiers have to share Alpine slopes with snowboarders and windsurfers have flocked to Baltic beaches. If hang gliders have not yet been spotted in the vicinity of Mount Olympus, they can probably be expected early in the twenty-first century.

What all these sports have in common is that they rely on new technologies, attract young people of both sexes, offer an element of risk, and resist formal organization in clubs and national and international federations. Will these sports continue to symbolize "the postmodern pastiche" or will they eventually, like others before them, become "modern"? Will they remain largely informal activities practiced in a natural or an urban landscape or will they be rationalized to the point where they too have elaborate rules and regulations, specialized venues, bureaucratic organizations, world championships, and a plethora of quantified records? To both questions, history suggests the latter alternative.

See also other articles in this section.

BIBLIOGRAPHY

Ariès, Philippe, and Jean-Claude Margolin, eds. *Les jeux à la Renaissance*. Paris, 1982.

Arnaud, Pierre, ed. *Les origines du sport ouvrier en europe*. Paris, 1994.

Arnaud, Pierre, and Thierry Terret, eds. *Histoire du sport féminin*. 2 vols. Paris, 1996.

Bernett, Hajo. *Die pädagogische Neugestaltung der bürgerlichen Leibesübungen durch die Philanthropen*. Schorndorf, Germany, 1960.

Bernett, Hajo. *Der Weg des Sports in die nationalsozialistische Diktatur: Die Entstehung des Deutschen (Nationalsozialistischen) Reichsbundes für Leibesübungen*. Schorndorf, Germany, 1983.

Bianda, Renato, Giuseppe Leone, Gianni Rossi, and Adolfo Urso. *Atleti in camicia nera: Lo sport nell'Italia di Mussolini*. Rome, 1983.

Birley, Derek. *Land of Sport and Glory: Sport in British Society, 1887–1910*. Manchester, U.K., 1995.

Birley, Derek. *Sport and the Making of Britain*. Manchester, U.K., 1993.

Blecking, Diethelm, ed. *Die slawische Sokolbewegung*. Dortmund, Germany, 1991.

Bottenburg, Maarten van. *Verborgen Competite*. Amsterdam, 1994.

Brailsford, Dennis. *Bare Knuckles: A Social History of Prize-fighting*. Cambridge, U.K., 1988.

Brailsford, Dennis. *Sport and Society: Elizabeth to Anne*. London, 1969.

Brailsford, Dennis. *Sport, Time, and Society: The British at Play*. London, 1991.

Bredekamp, Horst. *Florentiner Fussball: Der Renaissance der Spiele*. New York, 1993.

Bromberger, Christian. *Le match de football: Ethnologie d'une passion partisane à Marseille, Naples, et Turin*. Paris, 1995.

Brookes, Christopher. *English Cricket: The Game and Its Players through the Ages*. London, 1978.

Davis, Robert C. *The War of the Fists: Popular Culture and Public Violence in Late Renaissance Venice*. New York, 1994.

Delaunay, L. A. *Étude sur les anciennes compagnies d'archers, d'arbalétriers, et d'arquebusiers*. Paris, 1879.

Dunning, Eric, and Kenneth Sheard. *Barbarians, Gentlemen, and Players: A Sociological Study of the Development of Rugby Football*. Oxford, 1979.

Dunning, Eric, Patrick Murphy, and John Williams. *The Roots of Football Hooliganism: An Historical and Sociological Study*. London, 1988.

Eichberg, Henning. *Leistung, Spannung, Geschwindigkeit: Sport und Tanz im gesellschaftlichen Wandels des 18./19. Jahrhunderts*. Stuttgart, Germany, 1978.

Eichberg, Henning. *Der Weg des Sports in die industrielle Zivilisation*. Baden-Baden, Germany, 1973.

Eisenberg, Christiane, ed. *Fussball, Soccer, Calcio*. Munich, 1997.

Elias, Norbert, and Eric Dunning. *Quest for Excitement: Sports and Leisure in the Civilizing Process*. Oxford, 1986.

Errais, Borhane, Daniel Mathieu, and Jean Praicheux. *Géopolitique du sport*. Besançon, France, 1990.

Fabrizio, Felice. *Sport e fascismo: La politica sportiva del regime, 1924–1936*. Rimini and Florence, 1976.

Fabrizio, Felice. *Storia dello sport in Italia*. Rimini and Florence, 1977.

Gaboriau, Philippe. *Le Tour de France et le vélo: Histoire sociale d'une épopée contemporaine.* Paris, 1995.

Ghirelli, Antonio. *Storia del calcio in Italia.* Turin, 1990.

Gillmeister, Heiner. *Tennis: A Cultural History.* London, 1997.

Goja, Hermann. *Die österreichischen Schützengilden und ihre Feste, 1500–1750.* Vienna, 1963.

Goksøyr, Matti, Gerd von der Lippe, and Kristen Mo, eds. *Winter Games, Warm Traditions.* Oslo, 1997.

Gori, Gigliola. *L'atleta e la nazione.* Rimini, Italy, 1996.

Guttmann, Allen. *From Ritual to Record: The Nature of Modern Sports.* New York, 1978.

Guttmann, Allen. *Games and Empires: Modern Sports and Cultural Imperialism.* New York, 1994.

Guttmann, Allen. *Sports Spectators.* New York, 1986.

Guttmann, Allen. *Women's Sports: A History.* New York, 1991.

Halladay, Eric. *Rowing in England: A Social History, the Amateur Debate.* Manchester, U.K., 1990.

Hargreaves, Jennifer. *Sporting Females: Critical Issues in the History and Sociology of Women's Sports.* London and New York, 1994.

Hargreaves, John. *Sport, Power, and Culture.* Oxford, 1986.

Heywood, William. *Palio and Ponte: An Account of the Sports of Central Italy from the Age of Dante to the Twentieth Century.* London, 1904. Reprint, London, 1979.

Holt, Richard. *Sport and Society in Modern France.* London, 1981.

Holt, Richard, ed. *Sport and the Working Class in Modern Britain.* Manchester, U.K., 1990.

Horak, Roman, and Wolfgang Reiter, eds. *Die Kanten des runden Leders.* Vienna, 1991.

Hubscher, Ronald, Bernard Jeu, and Jean Durry. *Le sport dans la société française (XIXe–XXe siècle).* Paris, 1992.

Itzkowitz, David C. *Peculiar Privilege: A Social History of English Foxhunting, 1753–1885.* Hassocks, U.K., 1977.

Jarvie, Grant, ed. *Sport, Racism, and Ethnicity.* London, 1991.

Jarvie, Grant, and Graham Walker, eds. *Scottish Sport in the Making of the Nation: Ninety-Minute Patriots?* London, 1994.

Jones, Stephen G. *Sport, Politics, and the Working Class: Organised Labour and Sport in Inter-war Britain.* Manchester, U.K., 1988.

Kloeren, Marie. *Sport und Rekord.* Cologne, 1935.

Körbs, Werner. *Vom Sinn der Leibesübungen zur Zeit der italienischen Renaissance.* Berlin, 1938.

Krüger, Arnd, and John McClelland, eds. *Die Anfänge des modernen Sports in der Renaissance.* London, 1984.

Krüger, Arnd, and James Riordan, eds. *The Story of Worker Sport.* Champaign, Ill., 1996.

Krüger, Arnd and Angela Teja, eds. *La commune eredita dello sport in Europa.* Rome, 1997.

Krüger, Michael. *Körperkultur und Nationsbildung.* Schorndorf, Germany, 1996.

Lanfranchi, Pierre, ed. *Il calcio e il suo pubblico.* Naples, 1992.

Lowerson, John. *Sport and the English Middle Classes, 1870–1914.* Manchester, U.K., 1993.

McCrone, Kathleen E. *Playing the Game: Sport and the Physical Emancipation of English Women, 1870–1914.* Lexington, Ky., 1988.

Malcolmson, Robert W. *Popular Recreations in English Society.* Cambridge, U.K., 1973.

Mangan, J. A. *Athleticism in the Victorian and Edwardian Public School.* Cambridge, U.K., 1981.

Marsh, Peter, Elisabeth Rosser, and Rom Harré. *The Rules of Disorder.* London, 1978.

Mason, Tony. *Association Football and English Society.* London and Boston, 1978.

Mason, Tony. *Sport in Britain.* London, 1988.

Messing, Manfred, and Martin Lames, eds. *Zur Sozialfigur des Sportzuschauers.* Niedernhausen, Austria, 1996.

Murray, W. J. *The World's Game: A History of Soccer.* Urbana, Ill., 1996.

Pfister, Gertrud, ed. *Frau und Sport.* Frankfurt, 1980.

Pieth, Fritz. *Sport in der Schweiz.* Olten, Switzerland, 1979.

Riordan, James. *Sport in Soviet Society: Development of Sport and Physical Education in Russia and the USSR.* Cambridge, U.K., 1977.

Schaufelberger, Walter. *Der Wettkampf in der Alten Eidgenossenschaft: Zur Kulturgeschichte des Sports vom 13. bis ins 18. Jahrhundert.* Bern, 1972.

Tischler, Steven. *Footballers and Businessmen.* New York, 1981.

Tranter, Neil. *Sport, Economy, and Society in Britain, 1750–1914.* New York, 1998.

Ueberhorst, Horst. *Frisch, Frei, Stark, und Treu: Die Arbeitersportbewegung in Deutschland 1893–1933.* Düsseldorf, 1973.

Vale, Marcia. *The Gentleman's Recreations: Accomplishments and Pastimes of the English Gentleman, 1580–1630.* Totowa, N.J., 1977.

Vamplew, Wray. *Pay Up and Play the Game.* Cambridge, U.K., 1988.

Vamplew, Wray. *The Turf: A Social and Economic History of Horse Racing.* London, 1976.

Veto, József, ed. *Sports in Hungary.* Budapest, 1965.

Wagg, Stephen. *The Football World: A Contemporary Social History.* Brighton, U.K., 1984.

Wahl, Alfred, and Pierre Lanfranchi. *Les footballeurs professionnels: Des années trente à nos jours.* Paris, 1995.

Weischenberg, Siegfried. *Die Aussenseiter der Redaktion.* Bochum, Germany, 1976.

Whannel, Garry. *Fields in Vision: Television Sport and Cultural Transformation.* London, 1992.

Zieschang, Klaus. *Vom Schützenfest zum Turnfest.* Ahrensburg, Germany, 1977.

HOLIDAYS AND PUBLIC RITUALS

Scott Hughes Myerly and Tamara L. Hunt

Rituals are easy to recognize. Some are performed alone or by a private group, such as family and friends or members of social clubs. These rituals include meditation and prayer; rites of passage, such as baptisms, weddings, and funerals; or club initiations and commemorations. But public rituals, such as royal coronations, protest demonstrations, the Olympics' opening ceremonies, or mass rallies, are meant to be seen by everyone, and as such they are essentially a form of theater. Just what social and cultural purposes or functions do public rituals have? For more than one hundred years scholars have disagreed about defining ritual, what it is, and what it does.

THEORIES AND DEFINITIONS

Ritual first became a scholarly issue in the nineteenth-century debate over the origins of religion. William Robertson Smith (1846–1894) believed that pre-ancient religions consisted of beliefs (dogma) and ritual (practices) and that, of the two, ritual developed first. He thought religion cemented community bonds and that ritual was actually a way of venerating the social order through worship of divine representations that the community had itself collectively created. Similarly Jane Ellen Harrison (1850–1928) argued that primitive humans reenact whatever moves them spiritually and that ritual magically dramatizes everyday life. For her ritual was the origin of drama, and theater emerged as a secular variation of ritual. The sociologist Émile Durkheim (1858–1917) believed that reality is divided between two domains, the sacred (religion) and the profane (everything else). Religious practices, or rites, were rules of correct conduct in the presence of symbolic sacred objects, and conversely, negative rites were observances commonly viewed as taboo.

Somewhat later Arnold van Gennep (1873–1957) characterized ritual as a means of coping with crises and critical life transitions, such as birth, death, puberty, or marriage. All of these, as well as special

days, such as New Year's Day or Easter, he termed "rites of passage." The pioneer psychologist Sigmund Freud (1856–1939) also believed that ritual is a powerful yet subconscious factor shaping social behavior. His analysis of human behavior stresses the central role of repressed, forbidden sexual desires and suggests that ritual has hidden functions and larger social purposes of which its participants are normally unaware. Religious ritual helps people cope with distressing inner conflicts of which they are not conscious, so they can continue to function in society. Thus early scholars viewed ritual as forging social bonds that unified communities through shared practices and beliefs.

Functionalism and other models. Influenced by these debates, the anthropologists A. R. Radcliffe-Brown (1881–1955) and Bronislaw Malinowski (1884–1942) combined insights from sociology, theology, and theater to advocate "functionalism," in which ritual is viewed as a social mechanism that stabilizes and regulates societies' interactions. They agreed with their predecessors that ritual essentially maintains the bonds of community. However, they preferred anthropological fieldwork as a means to garner solid data about ritual rather than earlier approaches that relied heavily on conjecture and inference.

But functionalism's drawback is that it views societies as static and unchanging, and in the tumultuous post–World War II era scholars looked for a model of ritual that would account for the social changes they were witnessing. Many had difficulty accepting the functionalist model that seemed to overlook or downplay the importance of individuals and dissidents. For example, the anthropologist Clifford Geertz agreed that rituals were part of "cultural performances" that shaped the "spiritual consciousness of a people," but he disagreed with earlier scholars, such as Malinowski and Durkheim, who argued that rituals symbolized underlying shared values in society. Geertz pointed out that their approach inherently favors those aspects of ritual that promote harmony over

185

RITUAL AND THE SYMBOLIC BODY

A fundamental shift in European ritual emphasis occurred with the transformation from medieval to modern society. Earlier ritual concentrated on emotional fulfillment and on the sensual, the gratification of the emotions associated with the symbolic "lower body" (that is, the physical and emotional side) in Catholic ritual and in the sensual release of carnival. However, during the Reformation, Protestantism led the way in emphasizing the symbolic "upper body" (that is, the intellectual and rational side), as intellect, self-regulation, and restraint were stressed and the churches tried to repress carnival. Strict rules and rationality became the focus of mentality, and a new personality type emerged that was emotionally repressed and disciplined. Individuals internalized the external coercive regulations of the church and the state. In the twentieth century the symbolic lower body experienced a renewal in ritual, as people sought greater gratification and spiritual fulfillment. This trend generated greater interest in ritualized public entertainment events, such as celebrations, festivals, televised religious services, and mass spectator sports, usually managed by professional promoters and image consultants. Emotionally satisfying versions of Christianity, including the evangelical and charismatic movements, accented a personal relationship with its supreme deity. The quest also led many Christians toward Buddhism, Islam, and the renewal of the neo-pagan religion of Wicca, which revered the female deities, mainly symbolized by Nature or Mother Earth, of pre-ancient European societies.

those that suggest conflict. He further argued that functionalism could not be used to explain social change since it emphasizes stability and group consensus. Geertz developed a model that could be used by anthropologists and social historians to understand the role of cultural-religious drama in social change, arguing that three forces are at work in ritual: (1) "social structure," or the framework and context in which ritual takes place; (2) "culture," or the fabric of meaning within which humans interpret their experience; and (3) "personality systems" of participants, or the personal motivational patterns with which participants approach the ritual. An alteration in any one of these is a harbinger of social change, even if the other elements remain the same.

Social and cultural historians were also attracted by the model proposed by Victor Turner, one of Geertz's contemporaries. Turner's model explained ritual as an element in social change that takes place within a conflict-resolution setting he called the "social drama." According to Turner, these dramas occur within a group that shares a similar history and social values, and they begin when a dissident individual or group makes a deliberate breach with the norm to challenge authority. Tension rises as other individuals choose sides, and the resulting division reveals the fragility of the existing social consensus. At this point, according to Turner, leaders of the dissident group step in to keep the crisis from spreading uncontrollably, and their intervention may take the form of public rituals, such as parades or ceremonies, that symbolically promote a resolution of the conflict through castigation of a scapegoat or praise of an individual or idea honored by both sides. Once the crisis is defused, a reintegration of the disaffected occurs, but only after social changes have been adopted as a part of the new status quo.

Both of these models emphasize the importance of the actions of individuals or groups in ritual as a part of social change, but for some social historians these concepts did not go far enough. Despite their critiques of earlier scholars, both Geertz and Turner implicitly advocated the notion that a dominant ideology exists in society and is shared by its vast majority. Those who dissent will ultimately be reincorporated into the mainstream through "cultural performances" or "social dramas." But this seemed to ignore the power relationships often revealed in the rituals adopted by oppressed or dissident groups, and many social historians of the 1960s and 1970s turned to the ideas of Karl Marx (1818–1883), who interpreted ritual as expressing the relations of economic power. He argued that ritual operated to maintain elites in power to the disadvantage of working people. Most rituals, especially those of church and state, thus help delude people with nonrational, mystical charismatic flimflam designed to aid the powerful at the expense of the masses by instilling values and notions within the latter that keep them passive and compliant to the politico-economic system while being abused by its very operations.

Eric Hobsbawm was perhaps the most notable of the historians who took this view of public holiday and ritual, arguing that such manipulation was at the heart of both colonial and nationalistic ceremonies and holidays in the late nineteenth century. He posited that the emergence of mass society encouraged the development of powerful political forces that demanded more democracy, while the traditional elite and other conservatives resisted such demands. Thus European regimes faced conflicting political, economic, and social claims that had to be placated, but they also had to maintain and promote the state's power. One way to achieve these goals was through the creation of national holidays that used symbols and allegories to promote unity of the people under the supremacy of the state.

Still other historians portrayed ritual as a means by which otherwise voiceless Europeans in marginal groups were able to express and empower themselves, albeit in a limited and brief manner. As E. P. Thompson demonstrated in his study of English charivari (shivaree), or public shaming processions, public rituals often have different and frequently inconsistent layers of meaning. Throughout the early modern period and into the early nineteenth century in France, the British Isles, Scandinavia, Hungary, Portugal, Italy, and elsewhere, traditional community standards, especially in regard to marriage, were expressed and enforced through charivari, targeting anyone who dared to violate local values. This traditional ritual especially targeted adulterers, those who abused or neglected their spouses, or outsiders who married local wealthy widows. Villagers who staged charivaris sometimes dressed up in fantastic costumes at night and "serenaded" offenders by banging on pots and making obnoxious noises. These were not just adolescent pranks but often included sober, respectable people. They had no legal sanction, and similar dress-up and noisemaking activities sometimes were used to challenge injustice by the authorities. In this way the collective values of ordinary people were demonstrated by proving that the law is not always sovereign and that perceived wrongs the law did not address could be successfully opposed through group action when the majority so desired.

Specific groups could also be empowered by ritualized public behavior. Robert Darnton's examination of the "great cat massacre" in eighteenth-century France shows that apprentices used public ritual to protest their working conditions and to ridicule the existing legal and social system by staging mock trials of cats belonging to their bourgeois employers to express discontent. Yet not all groups that used ritual to their advantage were disaffected. Leonore Davidoff has shown that middle- and upper-class women in Victorian England used the rituals surrounding the "rites of passage"—birth, coming of age, marriage, and death—as well as those governing social interactions to enforce the clear distinctions between the classes. These social rituals were an effective barrier that limited the entry of individuals and families into the higher social circles that enjoyed exclusive access to greater economic, political, and marriage opportunities. Ignorance of these rituals of "proper" behavior often resulted in social disaster and disgrace.

Refining the definitions. Social history's approach to the study of ritual and public holidays emphasizes the role of individuals, dissidents, and subcultures in such ceremonies, and it highlights the view that ritual is not only used by the powerful to regulate the masses but also can empower and unify for the disaffected and those excluded from power. While many scholars contributed to a larger understanding of ritual, subsequent work followed along the lines of the basic approaches described above, combining, developing, and refining them in various ways and prompting in more complicated debates.

One factor is that rituals are often ambiguous or their meanings change over time while retaining the same outward ceremonial forms. It is most significant that few languages have a single word that equates to "ritual" in English. This is partly because rituals are laden with symbols and trappings whose various meanings are not clear. For example, a piece of cloth—a nation's flag—can symbolize pride or oppression, depending on one's perspective and identity, and it can thus simultaneously symbolize both unity and exclusion. But symbolic ritual is also powerfully appealing because it functions as a shorthand version of reality, a quick, easy means to identify and categorize life's endless complexities.

Ritual's intricate, multifaceted meanings render a complete and thorough definition most difficult. When approaching this subject, each person's understanding highlights priorities and perspectives that reflect their economic interests and social status and thus their fundamental assumptions about the nature of the social order. Ritual can thus become an intellectual labyrinth in which analysis actually leads away from a comprehensive definition. Nevertheless, ritual may be broadly defined as any scripted (often rigidly) program of stylized performance that seeks to render appealing and often compelling those values and beliefs that it overtly represents or that constitute its underlying theme, and it normally marks some sort of transition, such as commemorations, institutional transitions, or a change in status, age, or occupation for individuals. Rituals are thus a medium of communication and are usually aimed at reaffirming values and beliefs or, within their context of meanings, addressing and solving some problem, such as absolving someone of his or her sins (ritual purification). In either case rituals benefit the interests of their spon-

Procession in Siena. *Procession of the Town-Districts* through the Piazza del Campo in front of the Palazzo Publico. Painting (1550) by Vicenzo Rustici (1556–1632). Banca Monte dei Paschi, Siena, Italy/Erich Lessing/Art Resource, N.Y.

sors, who are oftentimes associated with an institution or institutionalized beliefs that are deemed true and even sovereign by a majority associated with that society or subculture. Ritual is emblematic of power relationships, even when they express sharply conflicting values and beliefs.

Rituals have particular psychological and emotional effects on the participants, both performers and observers, by evoking, consciously or subconsciously, an underlying cultural story or theme that is more complex or deep-seated than the performance itself. Ritual is often rendered more venerable through formality or more potent as a form of mockery through comedy. It is frequently sanctioned through tradition by invoking the past, especially when its staging is periodically or regularly repeated, and it thus appears to be normal, natural, and authoritative. Ritual can also mediate between tradition and change to ease transitions into the unknown.

Rituals may be brief, as with a formal greeting, or may last for days, marking a symbolically meaningful occasion. They may require distinctive or unique locations, such as a church or other symbolic

place, and special trappings, such as costumes, particular objects used in the show, and accompanying sounds (aside from spoken words), such as music, singing, chanting, or poetry. Frequently an essential aspect is that a suitably theatrical atmosphere be created from all these elements to evoke the proper setting, akin to the special effects of the lights, sounds, and sets in video productions. An occult magic ritual, such as a séance, performed in bright sunshine amid crowds dressed in swimsuits at the beach with a background of pop music seems incongruous.

Ritual is akin to routine and custom, but it normally has a substantially more profound wealth of meaning and emotional content than either routine or custom. It is akin to theater or drama but in an abridged form. Like commercial theater it can be entertaining and even riveting, but it can also exert a control over conduct and belief that is both obvious and subtle. Because ritual defines how something can be expressed, it controls what can be expressed and promotes acquiescence to its fundamental meanings while eliminating alternative perspectives. In a discussion someone may challenge specific ideas or values, but that person is far less likely to question a ritual formula. Anyone who mars a ritual performance seems rude or ignorant.

Nevertheless, a ritual must seem appropriate to its audience, which ultimately decides by acceptance or rejection if it will take the performance seriously. When the majority of participants or spectators either ignore or mock a ritual, the result is worse than a failure, since it shows a loss of prestige and authority for those who stage it. Thus a delicate balance often exists between manipulation and integration, between those sponsoring a ritual and its wider audience. The elements that constitute a ritual at any given time can represent a consensus of the cultural opinion and mentality of its voluntary participants, although rituals staged by dominant elites may be contrary to the wishes of the majority.

RITUAL IN EARLY MODERN EUROPE

Public rituals exist in all societies, and in Europe they long predate written records. In the Middle Ages ritual was extremely important for religion, which was itself fundamental to each community's sense of unity. But scholars disagree about whether rituals functioned primarily to buttress feudalism's power hierarchy or to cement community bonds. By the sixteenth century Roman Catholic Christianity and Eastern Orthodox Christianity were the primary European faiths. Islam in southeastern Europe, Judaism, and the remnants of ancient, prehistoric Nature religions, are important exceptions. The rarity of literacy, even among the rich and powerful, was a decisive factor that encouraged a heavy emphasis on the dramatic, emotionally laden special effects of church ritual to sanctify religious belief. This was especially significant for the Catholic Church, with its quasi-monopoly as the dominant faith and as the wealthiest and most politically powerful state in Europe. Its rituals were usually staged in richly decorated churches, which served as awe-inspiring settings for these medieval rites.

The most important religious rituals for ordinary people were the sacraments. These had a specific criteria, combining matter, such as the "host," or the bread of the Eucharist, with verbal forms recited according to an exact Latin formula. Receivers of the sacraments must also have the correct intentions, which means to truly repent their sins, and in return they receive renewed grace. The seven sacraments, fixed in 1439, included infant baptism, communion (eating the host, or the wafer, which has mysteriously been transformed by the priest into the body of Christ), confirmation (attaining adult status), mar-

riage (not a sacrament in the early medieval period), penance (confession of sins), the ordination of priests, and extreme unction (essential last rites preparing the soul for death).

These rites punctuated the life cycles of believers, but time was marked in other ritual ways. The "holy day," from which derives the word "holiday," was of three sorts. The Easter cycle of feasts, "movable" because their lunar calendar basis gave them different dates from year to year, celebrated the crucifixion and ascension of Jesus Christ into heaven. The Christmas cycle of fixed feasts celebrated events in the life of Christ. Based on the solar calendar, it lasted from November to March. By 1500 hundreds of fixed saints' days were also noted. Each village or district had a local patron saint whom it particularly honored, but additional saints' days were also kept with a reduced emphasis.

Momentous holy days meant a rest from normal work routines, preparation of a special meal, and other distinctive activities, including a mass, festivities, and processions. Saints were ranked according to their overall importance. Among the most significant were Matthew, Mark, Luke, John, Anthony, Patrick, Olav, Anne, Paul, Joan, and Francis. Saints' days fell mainly during winter, when the agricultural work cycle was reduced.

Holy days often overlay special days observed long before Christianity existed, and they stressed the need to reaffirm the wisdom that was embedded in the collectively derived meanings of noteworthy events. They also marked the passage of the work year, which was vital for regulating the work rhythms of traditional agricultural societies. The closer Catholic rituals resembled the practices of beliefs already held, the easier it was for the church to encourage conversion, the leap of faith from one belief system to another. In such borrowings the trappings of ritual are important, since they are easily copied but always with the requirement that they be appropriate in the new role.

Easter began as rites marking the return of spring, Christmas was originally the winter solstice in Europe and later the birthdate of the Indo-Persian god Mithras, and St. John's Eve replaced Midsummer Day, the year's longest day. Such occasions were observed with bonfires or ritual bathing, fire and water symbolizing purification. In agricultural communities the planting season often began with a procession bearing the local saint's image followed by a blessing of the fields.

While holy days are ranked according to their importance, the observance of any form of special day or holiday is distinctive, and holidays exert subtle ef-

Marriage Celebration. *The Wedding Dance,* painting (c. 1566) by Pieter Brueghel the Elder (c. 1515–1569). THE DETROIT INSTITUTE OF ARTS/THE BRIDGEMAN LIBRARY

fects on belief and mentality. People subscribe to a holiday whose saint or other focus they might not even honor simply to enjoy a day of rest from the normal work routine. This enhances the symbolic importance of a holiday for all of a society, and its oftentimes multiple meanings obscure its promotion of an agenda.

But as a critique and modification of Catholicism, saints' days were largely eliminated in those countries that embraced Protestantism in the sixteenth century. Some traditional saints' days continued, however, evolving into more modern forms. In England, Saint George survived while other saints disappeared, partly because he was not actually associated with any particular place in that country. Apparently this symbol of one of Europe's earliest nationalisms was thus easier to elevate into a modern, national symbol.

Protestantism also stressed that each believer must read the Bible, a mandate aided by the invention

of the printing press, which made books cheaper. The former Catholic emphasis upon elaborate rites was modified by eliminating some rituals and simplifying others in a more austere approach to faith intended to restore early Christian practices. "Ritual" thus came to be used as an abusive term by Protestants, but only in the sense that their rites were fewer and less elaborate than Catholic ones, not that they rejected them entirely.

SECULAR RITUALS IN EARLY MODERN EUROPE

As religious ritual diminished in importance from the sixteenth century onward, secular rituals proliferated, a trend that illuminated major shifts in the centers of power and in group identity. Some rituals had social functions for certain elites, such as of table manners and related forms of courtly etiquette. The decline of crude behavior among the medieval nobility was seen as virtuous by most, but it also instilled self-control and tamed the traditionally independent, elite warrior class. This aided the growth of royal state power and benefited the growing merchant class, whose interests frequently were allied with those of the monarchs, by turning the aristocracy away from seeking wealth through predatory violence to cultivating "courtly" behavior that would secure royal favor.

For centuries monarchs' and noblemen's courts had required a heavily ritualistic style of proceedings to sanctify and solemnize their weighty powers in the eyes of the masses they wished to dominate. Law courts came somewhat later, with similarly heavy responsibilities to settle serious conflicts. Judges and to a lesser extent lawyers wore special clothes that evoked dignity and wisdom—a practice that continued through the twentieth century. Judges constituted the central focus of the courtroom, seated above those who pleaded their cases.

By the seventeenth century more European monarchs held powerful sway over increasingly centralized states, and spectacular rituals underscored their greater power. These might dramatize important transitions in monarchs' lives by celebrating or marking events such as coronations, marriages, funerals, birthdays, and the birth of an heir. Nobles were mere supporting players. Such state-sponsored display

reached its pinnacle in seventeenth-century absolutist regimes, in which monarchs held unprecedented power. The most vivid example was the French "Sun King," Louis XIV, whose court was Europe's most brilliant. He literally made his entire daily routine into an endless series of elaborate rituals, and to seek the royal favor, nobles vied with each other for such lofty honors as holding the king's coat when he got dressed each morning. These rituals kept the aristocrats busy at the royal palace of Versailles, with their attentions safely focused on the ceremonial glories of Louis's domestic life. The nobles were thus kept away from their provincial strongholds, where they might plot rebellion as their ancestors had done, and they came more to resemble trained poodles than men of the sword.

Despite this subordination to monarchs, the ritual of the duel symbolized continued noble pretensions to private feuding, an unofficial right to settle disputes among themselves outside the law with ritualized combat. Duels reaffirmed their claims to monopolize bravery and honor, while holding themselves aloof and apart from wealthy merchants who might try to imitate their betters.

But the growing power of merchants and cities was also marked by ritual, which emphasized the commercial methods of self-enrichment by celebrating urban prosperity, often in conjunction with local defense, trade guilds, transitions in urban government

Christmas. Christmas in the royal household of the Empress Maria Theresa of Austria (1717–1780) with her husband, Francis I, and children, Maria Christine, Ferdinand I (later duke of Modena), Marie-Antoinette (later queen of France), and the infant Maximillian (later Elector of Cologne). Painting (1763) by Maria Christine, archduchess of Austria.
KUNSTHISTORISCHES MUSEUM, VIENNA/THE BRIDGEMAN ART LIBRARY

THE MOCK MAYOR OF GARRAT

Over time people's attitudes toward holidays and festivals change, which challenges the historians who study rituals. A case in point is the mock mayoral elections of Garrat. An eighteenth-century burlesque pageant held in a hamlet south of London on the occasion of local or national elections, the event was originally a parody of English electoral politics that embraced many elements of carnival, including satirizing religious authority, electing a man of low standing as "mayor" to preside over the festivities, parodies of social customs, drinking, dancing, and other boisterous activities. John Brewer interpreted this seeming disorder as both a "safety valve" for defusing social tensions and a reinforcement of the existing social order by emphasizing its importance. He noted that gentry and aristocrats patronized the celebration and regularly attended it as spectators.

However, like Clifford Geertz, Brewer emphasized the importance of the way spectators and participants view public holidays. If either the plebeians or the patricians perceive it as something other than a licensed festival, the significance of the event is transformed, and this is what happened to the mock mayoral elections of Garrat. In 1763 the playwright Samuel Foote wrote and produced a comedy entitled *The Mayor of Garret* [sic], which turned the tables on the festival and savagely mocked plebeians who claimed to have political knowledge or power. Staged 167 times between 1763 and 1776, the play was enormously popular not only because of its quality but also because it provided a view of plebeian political action that London audiences found comforting in light of the ongoing popular discontent surrounding John Wilkes, whose defiance of the government in the 1760s in the name of British liberty stirred volatile public conflict about the nature of power, citizenship, and civil rights.

While Foote depicted popular politics as ridiculous to his patrician audiences, thereby defusing its threat, he also suggested to political radicals that the real mock mayoral elections at Garrat could be rendered useful for their political agenda. Consequently, although the festival continued to use many of the same forms and rituals, it came to have disparate meanings to its various audiences. To radicals and working-class supporters the Garrat processions were a desirable allegory for political change, but for patricians they were a burlesque that portrayed the aspirations of plebeian politicians as ridiculous. Moreover, many local people continued to view the event simply as a festive occasion that provided an opportunity for revelry and free food and drink.

The mock mayor spectacle at Garrat disappeared in the 1790s, and Brewer speculated that the adoption of French revolutionary ideology by British artisans and workers made it impossible for the patrician sponsors to ridicule the danger of plebeian politics any longer. Radicals probably withdrew their support from the festival as well, as its reputation for riotous behavior was not in keeping with the emerging emphasis on plebeian education, self-restraint, and order. The changing political backdrop to the festival imbued it with new meanings, even while it kept much of the same outward show. Those meanings rather than the rituals themselves led to the demise of this popular holiday.

officials, and occasions when rulers made elaborate, symbolic entries into a city. The entertainment of such events was enhanced by exotic elements that celebrated trade. According to Johann Deitz, "militia revels" in late-seventeenth-century Lübeck, Germany, included characters costumed as "Indians, Moors, and Turks," thus emphasizing the city's exotic, far-flung trade connections and its prestige as an economic power.

Such ritualistic holiday celebrations were often significant sources of knowledge about a country's or a city's history for most commoners. They stressed the venerable antiquity, whether real, exaggerated, or imagined, of the political establishment and portrayed its rule as both just and impossible to oppose. This was especially true when monarchs faced an uncertain succession. In England, as part of their coronation processions, both Elizabeth I and Charles II displayed painted arches or *tableaux vivant* (striking poses to form living pictures) that depicted their venerable heritage. Likewise, when states' armed forces (now state-paid armies and navies) won major victories in battle, celebrations and thanksgiving rituals encouraged subjects to feel that they had a vital stake in the outcome, which promoted the emergence of nationalism.

But public rituals were not only shaped by the powerful; ordinary people also created and observed rituals that reflected their immediate concerns. For example, carnival was a traditional, popular event that included ritualized rebellion. It was strongest in southern Europe, but aspects also appeared in Scandinavia, Britain, and elsewhere. Held in cities, carnival was an interval of indulgence during the days preceding the penitence and fasting of Catholic Lent. Everyone participated in this "world turned upside down" festival, when the status quo was mocked. The poor in particular indulged in normally restricted pleasures. They ate richer food than usual, and sexual prohibitions were loosened. Revelers wore bizarre costumes, humiliated pompous people, and ridiculed the church and the state. They selected a "king" and "queen," who symbolically reigned over this celebration of disorder and inversion. Conservative, rigid people often abhorred carnival as threatening the social order, and in times of severe economic stress—always most destructive for the poor—the festivities could develop into rebellion. Such ritualized ventings of hostility normally made the establishment more stable in the long run, yet the simple fact that the masses could take over the streets showed their latent power to seriously challenge the status quo.

RITUAL IN MODERN EUROPE

By the late eighteenth century ritual challenges to authority developed into more modern modes of political opposition, especially for those who expressed solidarity by resisting what they considered injustices. Proposing toasts and taking oaths at meetings were typical of western European ritual political expression in the late eighteenth century and the early nineteenth century. These were dramatic declarations of commitment, especially early on, when such activities were deemed as borderline treason. Related forms of political visual symbolism with significant ritual overtones were also especially important in this era. Symbolic dress and hairstyles publicly proclaimed political opinions. Militant radical signs, such as trousers; "round hats," forerunners of modern brimmed hats; and short hair fundamentally changed the trend of European male fashion and opened a new era.

These fashions coincided with the French Revolution of the late 1780s, which heralded the eventual transformation of old regime Europe. Festivals with processions became a major means of asserting political legitimacy, and both counterrevolutionaries and revolutionaries sponsored them to promote their respective agendas. Revolutionary rituals emphasized the idealized notions of "liberty, equality, and fraternity," and participation by all classes reduced social barriers and promoted a sense of solidarity. These rituals borrowed their forms from the old saints' days, and other Catholic ritual practices were likewise adapted because people were used to them. Maximilien Robespierre's *Fête de l'Unité* (festival of unity) borrowed heavily from church rituals to commemorate the monarchy's fall, including baptizing the ground in the name of liberty. Mona Ozouf, one of the foremost scholars of French revolutionary festivals, argued that these rituals involved a "transfer of sacrality" (Ozouf, 1988, p. 267) from the church to the revolution, which claimed to embody a more righteous ideology than either the corrupt church or the decadent monarchy. As a part of this transfer, the revolutionaries set about changing societal elements related to religion, including the marking of time. They introduced a calendar with ten days per week, new names for the months, and renumbered years, starting with the year one in 1792 to show that history had begun anew. Yet old ways of thinking persisted, and Napoleon scrapped this calendar in 1806.

NINETEENTH-CENTURY NATIONALISM AND PUBLIC RITUAL

As the festivals of the French Revolution suggest, politicized public holidays were one means by which new political regimes attempted to assert their legitimacy. During the nineteenth century this became a standard tool of governments that sought to promote unity through nationalistic fervor. Yet these ceremonies had to be managed in such a way that only the state's message was promoted, leaving no room for political opponents to turn the occasion to their own purposes. This was a constant concern during the reign of Napoleon III. For example, in 1849, early in his presidency, he banned celebrations in Lille commemorating the beginning of the revolution of 1848, which ultimately had brought him to power, due to worker unrest and criticism of the government. In addition he criminalized singing the revolutionary song, the "Marseillaise," even though Louis Napoleon's electoral campaign had courted people's identification of him with the first French Revolution.

The potential for dissidents to use French history to justify their opposition to government was so great that Napoleon III and later the Third Republic avoided holidays connected with France's revolutionary past. The notable exception was Bastille Day, which was made a formal holiday in 1880. Although this festival ran the risk of giving workers, socialists, and other dissidents a public platform, the emphasis on state pomp and popular holiday defused the event's inherent radicalism. As in virtually every other European state, French celebrations became larger and more grandiose throughout the nineteenth century, reminding their audiences of the grandeur of the nation and the power of the state. Thus nationalistic holidays functioned on a number of different levels, as entertainment, as a unifying force, and as a threat.

The newly unified German state faced similar problems in creating a national identity, given the disparate religions, histories, and interests of Germans scattered across central and eastern Europe. Because war was central to the forging of modern Germany, many of the new state ceremonies introduced after 1871 commemorated battles and events connected with the Franco-Prussian War. The kaiser also became a focus of national unity, and as in other monarchical states, such as Britain, the royal birthday was a national holiday, celebrated with elaborate state and military pomp.

The enthusiasm people exhibited at such celebrations highlights the close similarity between the awe and veneration people feel for religion and what they feel for the modern state as a sacred entity—as a secular religion. This development was due to changing conditions. Industrialization and urbanization eroded the ancient supporting and sustaining bonds of family, extended family, and community. Powerful institutions and states displayed in appealing ways appear as safe and even fascinating havens of power and strength to those who feel insecure. The sense of unity and belonging that a state or political party offers may provide such a feeling, for which allegiance is an intrinsic aspect.

Yet leaders tend to use state power to their own best advantage. They serve those interests within the polity that wield the most political influence, often while treating individual citizens high-handedly or with brutality, directly in proportion to a person's wealth. States vary widely in the degree to which ordinary people are protected from government abuse, but the more oppressive the government, the greater its need to convince the public that it actually serves them. Ritual and related trappings can work as a form of advertising by partially masking oppression, and they manufacture consent and popular approval by overwhelming and obliterating all negative impressions to the maximum extent. Mass communications elevated ancient techniques of political flimflam to a sophisticated level as images and sounds began broadcasting daily into hundreds of millions of homes throughout the world.

One tactic for achieving a public goal is to enhance the scale, duration, and quantity of ritual to impress and overawe the public with charismatic, entertaining ceremonies. This is not done solely to encourage people to feel that the state is the only true protector that always serves their best interests. Its purpose is to convince the public that it is vital and essential to their very existence, and without the state they would perish or be enslaved by malevolent enemies. Not everyone is persuaded by such means, but if the senses and emotions are manipulated skillfully enough, a high percentage of the public will be influenced, swayed, or convinced by these shows. Ritual can be a critical factor in modern politics, for an oppressive state can continue to hold power only when it enjoys the support of enough people, of a "critical mass" of the population, which may be only a minority.

Yet states were not the only entities that created new holidays in the nineteenth century. Politicized religious groups, such as the Protestant Orange Order in Ireland, regularly used parades and ceremonials to symbolically assert their domination over Catholics by marching through their neighborhoods. Those parades often commemorated seventeenth-century Protestant military victories over Catholics and provoked unrest or riots. On a larger scale socialists were responsible for the founding of an international May Day holiday when the Socialist International of 1889 called for a one-day strike on 1 May 1890 to press for an eight-hour workday. Although they specifically denied that this was a worker's holiday or celebration, socialist leaders did not take into account the appeal to the rank and file of the long-standing, widespread folk celebrations traditionally associated with May Day. While the political content of the event survived in the slogans, banners, speeches, and the abstention from work, May Day celebrations became popular family holidays for workers, replete with parades, parties, and goodwill.

Nevertheless, May Day's appeal to workers as an expression of symbolic unity was great, so much so that in 1917 the Russian revolutionaries adopted the Western calendar so they would celebrate May Day on the same day as the rest of the world. But to appeal to a broader public, the Bolsheviks also adapted traditional rituals drawn primarily from the Russian Orthodox Church. Leon Trotsky believed that rational appeals to the masses were not sufficient to emotionally attach their loyalty to the state. Therefore church saints became the model for revolutionary martyrs, and the icon, so culturally significant in the

Nazi Rally. Nazi mass rally at Nürnberg, 1936. AP/WIDE WORLD PHOTOS

Orthodox Church, reemerged in a new form. On the death of Vladimir Lenin, his preserved body was put on public display in a mausoleum-monument, and this shrine was visited by millions of pilgrims. Joseph Stalin's portrait was later displayed everywhere to keep him in the public eye, compensating for his dislike of public appearances.

RITUAL AND FASCISM

The foregoing examples illustrate a prominent feature of ritual: in dramatic changes of a regime or faith, familiar figures are often retained in a modified form or with new meanings because people prefer what they know and mistrust change. Among the most vivid examples of state ceremony as quasi-religious ritual are those of the German Nazis, who never won a national election but built a powerful regime that delicately balanced coercion and consensus. Their rituals and to a lesser extent those of similar fascist parties in Italy, Spain, Finland, and elsewhere promoted various messages of national, racial, and ethnic unity and superiority. The Nazis were particularly adept at this game. Their rituals borrowed heavily from Christianity, refurbished with new symbols and ideologies and starring Adolf Hitler as a protective, wise, powerful father figure.

The Nazis probably staged more sensational rituals than any other twentieth-century European state. They were on a grander scale with longer parades, some over four hours, and extremely eye-catching uniforms. The Nürenberg nighttime rallies were staged with a breathtaking theatricality. These elaborate, colorful, dramatically torchlit displays included enormous masses of participants, a backdrop of monumental civic buildings, hundreds of swastika banners, and sensational lighting effects, and they were filmed to reach a wider public. No detail was overlooked in instilling the desired sensations of unity and unquestioned loyalty within the participants and audience while advertising the Nazi virtues of mass unity, bravery, and aggression. The emotions were further reinforced by omnipresent trappings, such as the formation of uniformed, regimented organizations; the use of birds of prey, especially eagles, on badges and other symbols; and the frequent, ornamental display of weaponry, including some that were traditionally venerable but obsolete, such as swords and daggers.

Nazi displays emphasized an irrational, emotional, and mystical content to conceal fundamental social, political, and economic conflicts between the rich (wealthy businesspeople who backed Hitler's rise to power) and ordinary Germans. The emphasis on powerful emotional impressions also was intended to

195

SPORTS AND RITUAL

Pleasure and entertainment became increasingly vital aspects of modern European life, and sports were noteworthy for ritual. Traditional peasant games in western Europe involved rites of local significance, displaying honor, pride, and solidarity among village men. With ever-expanding urbanization and wealth, these games acquired an institutional emphasis on obedience to regulations, such as rigid boundaries, precise measurements, and codified rules strictly enforced by officials. A greater degree of hierarchy, specialist players, team captains, coaches, winners and losers, and the idolizing of elites harmonized with and reflected integral values of industrial capitalism, and victory was analogous to the almost sacred goal of profits in business.

The largest supposedly nonprofit sports event, the International Olympic Games, emerged in Athens, Greece, in 1896, and its ritual aspects continually proliferated. Victory award ceremonies were enhanced, and gold medals were first awarded in 1904. The parade of nations was introduced at the opening ceremonies of the 1912 games in Stockholm, Sweden, and the five interlocking rings logo appeared in 1920 along with the first "Olympic oath."

In 1936 Adolf Hitler further enhanced Olympic ceremonials, using the games to promote Nazism at home and German prestige abroad. With no ancient nor modern precedent, the Olympic Torch run was added, a dramatic event with runners dressed as ancient Greeks bearing the torch from Athens to Berlin, and concluding with an attractive, blond German runner followed by six black-clad runners who lit the Olympic flame brazier. The winter games likewise included torchlight ski runs, which like similar rites recalled a glorious, pagan Germanic past that the Nazis freely invented as a racist and nationalist self-promotion. All this advertised the idea that the Nazis were capable, respectable, tolerant (black athletes were allowed to compete), and peace-loving, and widespread media coverage made the Olympics more popular than ever. Subsequent games included more events and ceremonies and larger expenditures as corporate sponsors competed for profits through the idealized games.

Twentieth-century sports included strong ritual elements, especially in the spectator sports that were outlets for national or local pride, such as football (soccer) or rugby. Singing team songs or national anthems before or during the match was a standard feature of organized sports, and victories in national or international championships prompted parades and organized celebrations. Other ritual trappings included team colors, flags, and pennants that reinforced identification with the team and allowed people from different social and economic backgrounds, even those living in cities or countries other than where the team was based, to feel a sense of unity by rooting for a team. Widely diverse events, such as rock concerts, cult film events, and New Year's Eve celebrations shared similar elements. Some corporations adopted some of the ritual of sports, organizing "teams" of workers, dressing them in special uniforms, and staging "competitions" to achieve greater profits.

Sports rituals, like all other rituals, play a variety of roles in society. Sports provide entertainment, forge a feeling of unity and belonging among the participants, and embody cultural values and social ideologies dominant in society.

obscure the fact that they offered no genuinely comprehensive explanatory narrative or "myth." Germans increasingly were expected to believe in Nazi symbols as such, though they lacked a deeper content beyond vague, shallow simplicities. Perhaps at no other time in human history were so many expected to accept an ideology founded on a purely symbolic and impressionistic content with little actual substance. One ideologue wrote: "Flag! Führer! Volk [folk]! Eternal Germany! Who can interpret their meaning? . . . We sense it, and therefore we believe it and trust in the word of our fellow believers" (Taylor, 1981, p. 518).

The scripting and staging of the Nazi shows functioned, like many rituals, as a psychological conditioning by carefully excluding any other perspective or viewpoint. In this appeal to religious emotions, human existence was simplified into an eternal struggle between good and evil, somewhat analogous to that between the Christian deity and devil. The swastika flag replaced the Christian cross as a holy symbol, and

Olympic Games, 1912. Swedish gymnasts enter the Old Stadium in Stockholm.
C. Vioujard/Gamma/©Hulton Getty/Liaison Agency

words like "holy," "sacred," and "eternal" were end-lessly repeated.

These shows were designed to satisfy, reassure, entertain, and make people feel good about a regime that destroyed both individual rights and anyone who dared to question orders. Ritual offered a sense of belonging and security to people who felt alone, weak, or lost, especially after the twenty years of World War I, its harsh peace settlement, and the worst inflation followed by the most destructive economic depression in German history. As with revolutionary France and Russia, traditional holidays were pressed into Nazi state service, including those associated with the harvest and labor, Mother's Day, Easter, and Christmas, which were recast as "authentic" German folk traditions.

MILITARY RITUAL

Nazi ritual constantly celebrated war, strength, and aggression and was saturated with militarism. But martial ritual is notable in virtually every modern state. Military life is an intensely ritualized modern subculture. It is rooted in the absolute necessity to effectively coordinate and command masses of young men, whose duty is to fight and risk death when many would rather be anywhere else than on a battlefield. Military ritual developed as a technique of control in battle, especially through military drill, but also from the simple need to efficiently move large numbers of men from one place to another.

Military daily routines are punctuated with on-going rituals, such as changing the guard and inspections. Rules ritualize a host of ordinary, mundane activities, including the manner of addressing others and the body's motions and movements. All this conditions soldiers, rendering them into efficient tools for enforcing the will of the state on its enemies, foreign and domestic. Compulsory participation in military ceremonies establishes esprit de corps, even when it is directly contrary to the soldiers' own desires. As "whole" institutions that rigidly manage all aspects of the soldiers' lives, armies can forge literally anyone into cannon fodder.

Ritual powerfully reinforces discipline, but it is a major component of a larger military management process, for which the psychological conditioning of strict rules, wearing uniforms, and drills are basic components. Military life exerts a particular form of mind control, in ways that are both subtle and obvious, over young men who as civilians never seriously considered killing anyone. The military ideals of power, honor, bravery, national defense, brotherhood, solidarity, self-sacrifice, harmony, and efficiency are communicated through virtually every aspect of martial display. "Our troops" exert a strong emotional appeal to civilians, who are often fascinated by this sublime vision. Martial ritual display has served as an idealized, inspirational model for the civilian world in a wide variety of organizational and personal contexts, where such values are deemed important, useful, or profitable.

TWENTIETH-CENTURY RITUALS AND HOLIDAYS

By the twentieth century, independence days, often with a military component, became a focus for nationalism, especially in those smaller countries long subservient to foreign rule. The phenomenon evolved in eastern Europe in the nineteenth century, starting with Greece. Later a host of new nations emerged, including Bulgaria, Yugoslavia, Hungary, Czechoslovakia, Romania, Poland, Albania, Finland, and the Baltic states, Estonia, Latvia, and Lithuania. National independence days were celebrated with the solemn rituals of parades, speeches and wreath laying. Only Iceland, which received its independence from Denmark in 1944, did not fit the pattern of a ceremonial connection between the military and independence since it had no military institutions and it alone among European countries had not been involved in major warfare since the Middle Ages.

Holidays and rituals have played a vital role in building a national community in lands that had not existed previously as independent states and that included people from different linguistic, ethnic, or religious groups. In Germany after 1871 ceremonies frequently emphasized the defeat of France rather than praising any qualities of the new state or its people.

What happens to national holidays when the perceived threat from external enemies fades and unity is asserted through education, legislation, economic ties, or other social and cultural interactions? Norway's national holiday, 17 May, while asserting local and national pride, became an occasion for family outings and pleasure. The other four holidays in May were revived saints' days. Since Norway was predominantly Lutheran, these spring holidays were not a return to Catholicism but additional days of springtime leisure immediately following the end of the long, severe Norwegian winter. Norway boasted more legal holidays in May than any other country.

One holiday with a self-indulgent emphasis is Christmas, which declined as a Christian celebration and became an American-style occasion for consumers. Even Communist Russia generated a version of Santa Claus as a distributor of gifts. Easter was especially important in eastern and southern Europe. While these commercialized holidays were viewed increasingly as time off from work rather than religious celebrations, they maintained many traditional ritual elements attached to them in past centuries. Those examples reflect what social historians have discovered about earlier rituals and holidays. While the ceremonies appear unchanged over time, participants attach different meanings to them to serve other purposes or to meet new needs. Ritual in modern Europe became more secular than ever. Europeans considered themselves far more sophisticated than their medieval ancestors, but they continued to adopt rituals and modify them to meet the changing needs and desires of states, corporations, religions, and ordinary people. This form of communication and social bonding appeared no less fundamental to human expression than in the past.

Se also other articles in this section.

BIBLIOGRAPHY

Books

Bell, Catherine. *Ritual: Perspectives and Dimensions.* New York, 1997.

Bocock, Robert. *Ritual in Industrial Society: A Sociological Analysis of Ritualism in Modern England.* London, 1974.

Bushaway, Bob. *By Rite: Custom, Ceremony, and Community in England, 1700–1880.* London, 1982.

Darnton, Robert. *The Great Cat Massacre and Other Episodes in French Cultural History.* New York, 1985.

Davidoff, Leonore. *The Best Circles: Society, Etiquette, and the Season.* London, 1973.

Elias, Norbert. *The Civilizing Process.* Vol. 1: *The History of Manners.* Translated by Edmund Jephcott. New York, 1978.

Elias, Norbert. *The Civilizing Process.* Vol. 2: *State Formation and Civilization.* Translated by Edmund Jephcott. New York, 1982.

Epstein, James A. *Radical Expression: Political Language, Ritual, and Symbol in England, 1790–1850.* New York, 1994.

Falassi, Alessandro, ed. *Time out of Time: Essays on the Festival.* Albuquerque, N.Mex., 1987.

Firth, Raymond. *Symbols: Public and Private.* Ithaca, N.Y., 1973.

Geertz, Clifford. *The Interpretation of Cultures.* New York, 1973.

Hobsbawm, Eric, and Terence Ranger, eds. *The Invention of Tradition.* New York, 1983.

Hutton, Ronald. *The Rise and Fall of Merry England: The Ritual Year, 1400–1700.* New York, 1994.

Hutton, Ronald. *Stations of the Sun: A History of the Ritual Year in Britain.* Oxford, 1996.

Kertzer, David I. *Ritual, Politics, and Power.* New Haven, Conn., 1988.

Kiernan, V. G. *The Duel in European History: Honour and the Reign of the Aristocracy.* Oxford, 1988.

Lane, Christel. *The Rites of Rulers: Ritual in Industrial Society—The Soviet Case.* Cambridge, U.K., 1981.

MacAloon, John J., ed. *Rite, Drama, Festival, Spectacle.* Philadelphia, 1984.

Mandell, Richard D. *Sport: A Cultural History.* New York, 1984.

Mosse, George L. *The Nationalization of the Masses: Political Symbolism and Mass Movements in Germany from the Napoleonic Wars through the Third Reich.* New York, 1975.

Muir, Edward. *Ritual in Early Modern Europe.* Cambridge, U.K., 1997.

Ozouf, Mona. *Festivals and the French Revolution.* Translated by Alan Sheridan. Cambridge, Mass., 1988.

Schama, Simon. *Citizens: A Chronicle of the French Revolution.* New York, 1989.

Thompson, E. P. *Customs in Common.* New York, 1991.

Tilly, Charles. *The Contentious French.* Cambridge, Mass., 1986.

Turner, Victor. *From Ritual to Theatre: The Human Seriousness of Play.* New York, 1982.

Wortman, Richard S. *Scenarios of Power: Myth and Ceremony in the Russian Monarchy.* Vol. 1: *From Peter the Great to the Death of Nicholas I.* Princeton, N.J., 1995.

Articles

Baecque, Antoine de. "From Royal Dignity to Republican Austerity: The Ritual for the Reception of Louis XVI in the French National Assembly (1789–1792)." Translated by Colleen P. Donagher. *Journal of Modern History* 66 (1994): 671–696.

Baxter, Douglas Clark. "First Encounters: Bourbon Princes Meet Their Brides: Ceremony, Gender, and Monarchy." *Proceedings of the Annual Meeting of the Western Society for French History* 22 (1995): 23–31.

Borsay, Peter. " 'All the Town's a Stage': Urban Ritual and Ceremony, 1600–1800." In *The Transformation of English Provincial Towns, 1600–1800.* Edited by Peter Clark. London, 1984. Pages 228–258.

Brewer, John. "Theater and Counter-Theater in Georgian Politics: The Mock Elections at Garrat." *Radical History Review* 22 (winter 1979–1980): 7–40.

Bucholz, R. O. "Nothing but Ceremony: Queen Anne and the Limitations of Royal Ritual." *Journal of British Studies* 30 (1991): 288–323.

Cremona, Vicki Ann. "Carnival in Gozo: Waning Traditions and Thriving Celebrations." *Journal of Mediterranean Studies* 5 (1995): 68–95.

Finley-Croswhite, Annette. "Ceremonial Reconciliation: Henry IV's Royal Entry into Abbeville 18 December 1594." *Proceedings of the Annual Meeting of the Western Society for French History* 17 (1990): 96–105.

Goody, Jack. "Knots in May: Continuities, Contradictions, and Change in European Rituals." *Journal of Mediterranean Studies* 3 (1993): 30–45.

Howkins, Alun, and Linda Merricks. "'Wee Be Black as Hell': Ritual, Disguise, and Rebellion." *Rural History* 4 (1993): 41–53.

Inglis, K. S. "Entombing Unknown Soldiers: From London and Paris to Bagdad." *History and Memory* 5 (1993): 7–31.

Koneski, Blazhé. "Animal Sacrifice in Macedonia." Translated by Ljubica Arsovska. *Macedonian Review* 22 (1992): 192–194.

McClendon, Muriel C. "A Moveable Feast: Saint George's Day Celebrations and Religious Change in Early Modern England." *Journal of British Studies* 38 (1999): 1–27.

O'Gorman, Frank. "Campaign Rituals and Ceremonies: The Social Meaning of Elections in England, 1780–1860." *Past and Present* 135 (1992): 79–115.

Taylor, Simon. "Symbol and Ritual under National Socialism." *British Journal of Sociology* 32 (1981): 504–520.

CONSUMER LEISURE

Charles Rearick

Until the beginning of the eighteenth century, Europeans did not conceive of a portion of their time as leisure; they had neither our modern concept nor the kind of experience it denotes. The word itself existed in English and French *(loisir)* in the medieval and the Renaissance eras, but it meant "opportunity" or "occasion." Monks and nobles might appear leisured to a modern eye—they abstained from common labors and business—but they did not view their lives that way. For monks the absence of work meant time for contemplation and prayer. For nobles daily life was filled with honorable activities—hunting, fencing, and jousting, for example. Common people's lives included some playful periods of festivity and rest scattered through the year, but their ordinary days lacked set times that were distinct from work. People routinely mixed singing, conversing, drinking, and rest into their workdays, varying the proportions of the mix according to their own inclinations at and the demands of their tasks.

RHYTHMS OF EARLY MODERN LIFE

For ordinary people especially, what we would call leisure was missing. When spring plowing and summer harvesting had to be done, peasants toiled to exhaustion with virtually no time left over. In other periods of the year, principally in winter, they experienced dead time, more than a hundred days of it; but still they worked, making tools and household goods. And they participated in fairs, festivals (mostly holy days) or saint's day celebrations, and occasional pilgrimages (the only socially sanctioned travel for ordinary women). On feast days, common people engaged in the same kinds of collective play that they enjoyed whenever they found time for respite: various ball games, card games, and dancing. Those times of revelry took place at irregular intervals closely tied to nature and weather—the pattern not only for the farming population but also for miners, sailors, shipping workers, and many others.

Although people did not pay admission to participate in customary festivals and recreations, often they did spend some money—the beginnings of consumer leisure are visible as early as the blossoming of market economies in Renaissance Europe. On almost every festive occasion, people paid small sums to see entertainments offered by traveling showmen: acrobats and jugglers, dancing bears and learned pigs, puppets, magicians, ventriloquists, fire-eaters, dwarfs and giants, singers, dancers, and actors. During religious feast days and pilgrimages, celebrants found occasions for pleasure and purchases of wine, sweets, and images, for example, from peddlers and local shopkeepers. From the sixteenth century on, ordinary Europeans increasingly consumed recreation and entertainment along with goods, and commercial recreation occupied a growing place in the early modern economies and in daily life—particularly of urban dwellers.

The possibilities for consumption proliferated in each successive century. From the sixteenth through the eighteenth centuries, more and more entrepreneurs ventured into business as theater and opera impresarios, booksellers, painting and print dealers, and proprietors of taverns and coffeehouses. Fundamentally, what the leisure merchants provided was pleasure, or at least the possibilities for fun, unburdened by moral or political ideals and purposes. Their establishments made powerful appeals to common desires and appetites—for drink, food, sex, sociability, dreams and illusions. In contrast to the traditional cycle of periodic festivities, the new establishments invited people to indulge and to enjoy themselves on a regular basis. They served up whatever the entrepreneurs thought pleased the audience—with little regard for discriminating dictates of good taste. The distinction between popular and high culture was not yet clear or firmly established. On the same London stage in the seventeenth century, spectators could find juggling and ballet, high tragedy and low comedy. Theatrical and fairground spectacles catered to all manner of dreams and fantasies; they merchandised the imaginary, giving customers a chance to see the marvelous and the magical, to experience life in distant times and places, and to share in the joys and sorrows of bigger-than-life characters.

The core public for the emergent leisure was an urban population that did not have access to court and noble entertainments yet did have some disposable income; these were principally middle-class people at first, especially men, who had more opportunity to spend time and money in public places than did women. The working people of towns and villages were a large potential clientele whose participation was held back by a relative lack of time and money. Some entertainers and businessmen even in the early modern era, however, began to tap that potential. Street and fairground performers, such as the Italian *commedia dell'arte* players, lived off small coins collected from assembled commoners. To partake of coffeehouse or café life, customers had to pay only the price of a drink. Entry to pleasure gardens was often free. For poor people who were minimally literate, publishers offered small, cheap booklets—almanacs, devotional tracts, and entertaining tales—of miracles, spectacular crimes, and great deeds.

As the country with the most advanced market economy and largest urban population, England was a leader in developing consumer leisure from the sixteenth through the eighteenth century. Many societies on the continent approached England's level of commercialization only much later. As late as the nineteenth century, such eastern European countries as Poland and Russia were still predominantly agrarian and attached to traditional patterns of leisure. By then in western Europe, entertainments and pastimes that were once the preserve of the patrician elite had opened up to a more diverse public. The royal courts still served as patrons to theater and opera companies, musicians, and painters, but a paying public was also supporting performances outside the palaces and noble mansions. Commercial entertainment halls and theaters were in the forefront of an expanding public sphere, open to all those who could pay.

SOCIAL DISTINCTION AND CONFLICT

As customers bought admission to new entertainments and pastimes, they made choices about their own self-images. In their leisure activities more than in work time, people found opportunities to adopt and assert social identities that they themselves chose. To participate in the emergent consumer culture was to engage in a social performance. The well-to-do middle classes, for example, displayed their status and wealth publicly by sitting prominently in the best seats in the theaters. They also enhanced their prestige by using their money to engage in leisure activities that were traditionally associated with established elites. And they did all that choosing and self-fashioning as individuals, now acting independently of community customs.

The pastimes and recreation preferences of Renaissance elites exercised a profound long-term influence on others in European society. Renaissance nobles in urban centers (Florence, Venice, and Mantua, for example) had conspicuously devoted much of their time to self-cultivation and the arts along with more basic enjoyments such as drinking and feasting. Their tastes marked certain recreations with the cachet of high status, which guided many marketers of leisure in subsequent centuries. Entrepreneurs grasping the dynamics of social emulation produced innumerable commercial imitations of the elite's pleasures. Merchants, for example, provided moneyed but common-born men and women with the opportunity to buy and collect art and expensive curiosities. Other businessmen created public pleasure gardens (Vauxhall in the mid-seventeenth century and Ranelagh in the eighteenth century) reminiscent of noble gardens. More fundamentally, the nobles served as models for middle-class people wanting to break away, at least part of the time, from the work ethic and the stigmas attached to pleasure seeking.

The middle strata of society also kept an eye on the pastimes of people below, and most often they disapproved of what they saw. Opponents of common people's recreations were numerous and powerful long before commercial offerings expanded. They had barely tolerated the excesses of popular festivals, during which participants threw over the normal rules and constraints. What too often ensued, critics charged, was unbridled indecency, sexual license, and blasphemy. Critics had also long condemned the drunkenness and brawling associated with taverns and alehouses. The expanding commercial establishments of the seventeenth and eighteenth centuries aroused the same alarms as those most pastimes had. Thus clergy and reforming middle-class leaders condemned new places of drink and recreation as dens of immorality and idleness and associated them with all manner of debauchery. In fact, they assailed everything popular in which they found coarseness and brutality—from blood sports to drunken unruliness. These moral spokesmen, enemies of popular culture, were champions of politeness, manners, refinement, and self-improvement. Some simply advocated work. The rising valuation of work, particularly among the middle classes, left leisure activities more suspect than ever. In the advanced commercial society of seventeenth- and

The Audience. *The Laughing Audience,* engraving (1733) by William Hogarth (1697–1764). PRIVATE COLLECTION/
BRIDGEMAN ART LIBRARY

eighteenth-century England, Puritan spokesmen took
the lead in the campaigns against play, fighting especially hard against all Sunday recreations, judged to
be violations of the sanctity of the Sabbath. In Poland
in the sixteenth and seventeenth centuries, where the
Reformation had only a weak impact and where the

middle class was small, some Roman Catholic preachers and writers took a similar stand. They decried the
large number of holidays (altogether about a third of
the year) as openings to sin, while also attacking lords
who forced peasants to work on holidays. For them,
as for the Puritans, leisure was to be devoted primarily

to religious practices. Other objections to popular recreations came from educational advocates—especially those following classical and noble models of honorable or superior activities.

Despite such opposition, the supply of commercial recreations increased through the early modern era with only an occasional setback—like the one in Puritan England, for example, from 1642 to 1660. The theater became one of the most important entertainments for all levels of society. A flourishing commercial theater developed particularly early—in the sixteenth century—in Italy, Spain, and England. In Elizabethan England, for example, companies of actors that had long performed for noble patrons increasingly played in public venues for anyone willing to pay admission. Those early professionals, traveling from town to town, were men and boys, as women were not allowed to act in England (unlike Italy, Spain, and France); female roles were played by boys until the mid-seventeenth century. All across Europe the social status of the actor was low, as it was for vagabonds and others not fixed in the established social order. Actresses were placed on virtually the same level as prostitutes.

Playwrights and performers in England enjoyed greater political freedom than in France or Italy, but the London city fathers nonetheless maintained restrictions on the theater, allowing only a small number of plays to be performed and those only in certain places such as open-air inn yards. In the last decades of the sixteenth century, new theaters—notably, the Rose, the Swan, and the Globe—were built outside the city walls, thus escaping the control of the London councilors. Besides the relative freedom, other favorable conditions in England were the strong commercial economy and the large population of London (more than 160,000 inhabitants in 1600), many of whom were ready and willing to pay for professional drama. By 1600 the city boasted five theaters offering plays every day of the week and a dozen notable dramatists who were able to earn their living from playwriting. Professional playwrights such as William Shakespeare and Ben Jonson delved into distant history and literature for stories of political power struggles and family life, subjects untouched in the medieval mystery plays. The lines and plots they crafted were vigorous and rich yet entertaining to largely uneducated popular audiences. London's theater took on great importance for England's national identity and social life, and it exercised strong long-term influence abroad. In the late sixteenth century, for example, troupes of English actors traveled to Germany and introduced a new level of professional acting skill and stage effects, bringing new vitality to German theater.

Public performances took place on stages surrounded by audiences of socially diverse men and women—wealthy and poor, masters and servants, merchants, artisans, and apprentices. The show onstage was not the only one taking place. Spectators watched others in the audience and engaged in social performances, putting themselves on display and interacting with others—in prominent seats and in the foyers. The public space of the theater (as of other new leisure establishments) brought together a mix of people, strangers who responded to the actors on stage and to each other. And like commercial venues of all sorts, theaters served as a meeting ground for prostitutes and clients.

The plays themselves interest social historians not primarily as literary texts but as mirrors held up to society, reflecting not simply an author's views but also audience tastes and values as organized and filtered through a culture's systems of representation. The shows over time also registered changes in the social composition of audiences. In seventeenth-century France, for example, the classical theater of high tragedies and public formalities was tailored to aristocratic milieus. As the bourgeoisie grew and strengthened in the eighteenth century, domestic comedies became prominent, and critiques of the traditional order began to appear. The status of actors also changed. As theaters became a more accepted part of social life and organized on a more permanent and financially stable basis, actors, both men and women, gained better pay and respect—the beginnings of their ascent to the special prestigious status that some stars of the stage attained in the nineteenth century.

Church authorities attacked and opposed the theater for centuries, viewing it as a public source of immorality. Protestants, from English Puritans to German Pietists, were particularly hostile, and when they gained access to civil power, they were often effectively repressive. Civil authorities harbored their own fears of the stage with its enactments of deception and impersonation, satirical and subversive texts, and footloose performers, and governments restricted the theater in cities across Europe. In Old Regime Paris, only two companies of actors obtained the king's authorization to perform: the *Comédiens-Français* and the *Comédiens-Italiens,* forcing other theatrical companies to establish themselves outside the city limits. To be as close as possible to their urban patrons, numerous theaters were established outside the old city boundary on the boulevards extending west from the Bastille. At the same time, performers in fairground theaters were not allowed to speak, sing, or dance onstage, so they mimed, performed on tightropes, and presented marionettes and big visual spectacles—to the delight of large popular audiences.

In the summertime, city people often preferred the outdoor diversions offered by pleasure gardens, suburban parks chock-full of commercial amusements. At London's Vauxhall (1660–1859) and Ranelagh (1742–1803), for example, patrons dined and drank and attended performances of songs, overtures, and concertos; they also watched juggling, dancing, and fireworks. Renovations of Vauxhall Gardens in 1732 turned the simple park into an elegant resort filled with buildings ranging from Gothic to Chinese, fountains, waterfalls, domed pavilions, statuary, concert platforms, tea shops, and restaurants. Access to all those attractions cost a modest one shilling in the eighteenth century, allowing the lowly to enter and mingle with the upper classes—servants and soldiers relaxing alongside rich merchants and the nobility. Similar pleasure gardens sprang up around continental cities. In nineteenth-century Vienna, the Prater (formerly a hunting preserve for the emperor) developed into a lively amusement park and exhibition ground for people from all over the capital.

NEW LEISURE INSTITUTIONS

An important new place of leisure in the seventeenth century was the coffeehouse or café, a relatively sedate alternative (despite the caffeine) to the traditional alehouse and tavern. Shops offering the new beverage spread from the Middle East to Europe early in the century, appearing, first in Italy and after mid-century in France, Germany, and England. They quickly became important centers of conversation, politics, business, journalism, and literature in the cities. In the early decades their patrons were mostly of the middle classes, men who were prosperous enough to afford the relatively costly drink and just beginning to develop social institutions of their own. Over coffee customers exchanged the latest information about business and politics. In the early eighteenth century, they also read newspapers that enterprising writers created for the coffeehouses, weekly and then daily papers reflecting the interests, critical moral tone, and literary tastes of the gentlemanly clientele. By making periodicals available, coffeehouses served as a special kind of public reading room, one where the private act of individual reading was accompanied by ongoing discussion of literature and politics.

By the early 1700s London's coffeehouses, now numbering over two thousand, became more socially segregated, as patrons congregated according to their occupational, cultural, and political interests. Some

regulars concentrated on business, bought and sold stock, and created new commercial ventures (Lloyd's of London insurance company was one). Other customers came together in pursuit of shared literary interests. Some of the social groups that coalesced there eventually moved away from the public premises to form private clubs—for men only. Also by the eighteenth century, coffeehouses and cafes were attracting consumers who were less well-off; some clients were drinking not coffee but alcoholic drinks that were sold on the same premises. Critics escalated their attacks, saying such places were the haunts of riffraff (rakes, robbers, and idlers) and dens of excessive smoking, arguing, and subversive politicking. Not long after the first café opened in Paris, Louis XIV ordered the police to monitor discussions there, and police reports confirmed the presence of malcontents discussing politics. In France and England of the eighteenth century, coffeehouses did become prime centers of political dissent. Parisian cafés in the last decades of the century were indeed places where revolutionaries gathered to discuss radical ideas and organize political action.

In England the heyday of coffeehouses stretched over more than a century—from 1652 to 1780. They then went into relative decline, while tea, imported by the British East India Company, became more plentiful and popular than coffee. Many coffeehouses converted or reconverted to taverns and alehouses.

In continental cities cafés served the middle classes and, increasingly, the working classes. They also became the haunts of the alienated and marginal—writers and artists, Bohemians of all sorts, and revolutionaries of many stripes. In the capitals they flourished as cultural and social havens for artists and intellectuals through the nineteenth century. In Berlin, where the first café opened in 1818, and in cities of the Habsburg Empire, critics of the conservative regimes met in coffeehouses to exchange ideas and give mutual support in the years leading to the revolutions of 1848. Through the rest of the century, the coffeehouses of Vienna, Berlin, and Paris were vital centers of sociability and discussion for the middle and upper classes who wanted to see and be seen in the most fashionable places of leisure.

But many cafés also drew the poor and working people whose lodgings lacked adequate heat and light. For workers the café was a precious semipublic space, outside the private space of the cramped, uncomfortable apartment but also away from the public openness of the street. Women and children were often habitués alongside men in Vienna, Paris, and other continental cities, and in the late nineteenth century the family café was commonplace. Parisian cafés, so famous as sites of sociability and conversation, also

Reading the Papers. *The Newspapers,* engraving (c. 1795) by Louis-Léopold Boilly (1761–1845). Bibliothèque Nationale, Paris/Giraudon/Art Resource, NY

harbored the lonely and the isolated—silent, sad, detached spectators, as we can see in paintings by Edgar Degas and Henri Toulouse-Lautrec. In the twentieth century that kind of customer was still in evidence, but many were no longer habitués. As housing for the working class improved, people tended to spend more of their free time at home, and the cafés steadily declined in number.

Consumer leisure grew most dramatically in Europe's biggest cities of the eighteenth century, London and Paris, where fashions were set for other places. There the ways of spending time and money proliferated. Many entertainments were now more formally organized than before and housed in facilities that required greater investment. Public billiard rooms, cafés, concert halls, assembly rooms, and theaters multiplied. The world's first permanent circus, installed in its own building, appeared in London in 1770, organizing in one big show an array of traditional acts—clowns, acrobats, and equestrian routines. Professional sporting events emerged as regular spectacles—boxing matches in London and horse races, for example. Gambling reached new heights of popularity—bets were placed on card games in men's clubs, on cockfights, boxers, and horses. Shopping for fashionable

clothing, prints, and paintings occupied a growing place in the leisure of the well-off—shopping as entertainment, distinct from basic provisioning in neighborhood markets that even the poor frequented. Middle-class women in particular became shoppers in luxury boutiques, following a path blazed earlier by aristocratic males. Buying and reading novels, attending ballad operas, and viewing exhibitions of all sorts were new recreations for many. Crowds in search of curiosities paid to see collections of natural history specimens, paintings (public art museums did not yet exist), waxworks, menageries, various magic lanterns, peepshows, and shadow plays (*Schattenspiel,* Italian shows, and *ombres chinoises*), automaton figures, trained-flea circuses, and freak shows. The uneducated lower ranks and the most cultivated alike shared an insatiable curiosity and appetite for novelty—for wonder-inspiring displays of the unusual not yet cleanly categorized as magical or scientific, instructional or entertaining.

Spending on commercial amusements increased even though many free spectacles were still available—attending public hangings, for example, and looking at lunatics in insane asylums. Rising quantities of advertising raised consumer consciousness of all the entertainment choices. From the seventeenth century on, guidebooks to the available bounty found a steady market among city visitors and natives alike. In late-eighteenth-century Paris, for example, an inexpensive, regularly updated *Almanach des Loisirs* provided information about places of pleasure, including their hours and prices.

THE RISE OF FREE TIME

In the eighteenth century factory owners seeking higher productivity adopted the practice of imposing precisely measured work hours on their employees, leaving small periods of the day and week (principally Sunday) to be called "free time." That sense of leftover time is the core of the modern concept of leisure, defined in opposition to work and to the clocked hours spent working. English manufacturers took the lead in imposing steady work regulated by strict clock time—even before the invention of steam engines and the creation of steam-powered mills and factories. In the early stages of industrialization, the time that was free was scant indeed, but it was distinctly separate from work and workplace. Workers in the new industrial conditions were not members of long-established communities with time-honored celebrations. Hence they were open to new opportunities for ease and pleasure, but they had little disposable income or time.

In the process of imposing, a steadier rhythm on labor time, employers fought against leisure traditions that workers still practiced—taking off Monday ("Saint Monday") after a Sunday of hard drinking, for example, and skipping work during parish holidays. Factory owners in the textile trades worked their employees—children as well as adults, at least until factory reform acts of the 1830s and 1840s—unremittingly twelve or more hours a day, Monday through Saturday. By 1834 the English manufacturers had succeeded in reducing the year's legal holidays to four—down from eighteen in 1830 and forty-seven in the mid-eighteenth century. With the spread of industrialization across Europe through the rest of the century, the English pattern of long intense labor and little free time became an international model for factory workers. In late-nineteenth-century Russia, for example, the work schedule in factories was twelve hours or more, 308 days a year.

The new labor intensity and loss of autonomy seem to have had an impact that carried over even into the realm of leisure. Workers subject to the new industrial conditions showed preferences for recreations that allowed for a large measure of passivity and a lack of solidarity. Industrial-era leisure became merely time for the most minimal and functional physical and psychological renewal so as again to meet the demands of work.

Workers and their unions agitated for shorter working hours—or more free time—and made gains in the second half of the nineteenth century. As workers gained that time, middle-class reformers—first in England—worked to establish "rational recreation," meaning self-improving kinds of leisure, mostly noncommercial—brass bands and choral societies, for example, and especially the singing of religious music. Employers, whom some would characterize as philanthropic and others as paternalistic, often served as sponsors. From about 1830 to 1900 the reform forces succeeded in suppressing most animal blood sports (inexpensive commercial entertainment such as cockfighting, bear-baiting, and ratting), and municipal authorities in London (as in Paris and other cities) suppressed many urban fairs, now deemed too noisy and rowdy.

NEW COMMERCIAL LEISURE, 1850–1914

While some favorite amusements of long standing were being, eliminated, entertainment overall mushroomed and became almost omnipresent in the fast-growing cities of the second half of the nineteenth century. A multitude of new cafés and restaurants, theaters, concert and music halls, opera houses, cabarets, wax museums, panoramas, skating rinks, and dance halls sprang up and flourished. Leisure-time shopping was raised to a new level by innovative emporia now known as department stores, which featured abundant displays of merchandise, cafés and tearooms, concerts and other entertainment (early movies, for example). In the last years of the century, a technologically new spectacle of moving pictures appeared in the crowded marketplace of amusements and drew a fast-growing clientele. Outside the capitals, traveling theaters and circuses periodically added to the usual local offerings.

Demand for entertainment was strong from all classes, but the greatest rise in leisure consumption is traceable to workers and a new lower-middle class—people in clerical and other service-sector jobs who led lives outside work-based and religious organizations and customary community recreations. These customers eager for leisure businesses were city dwellers who now enjoyed greater disposable income and more free time than before. In the decades after 1848, commercial forms of leisure became the dominant ones in many people's lives, eclipsing recreations under noble, church, and municipal patronage.

The most common place of popular leisure was still the café, pub, cabaret, or tavern. Nowhere were they more numerous than in Paris. Drinking establishments there increased from some three thousand in 1789 to about twenty-two thousand in 1870. Then in the following decades under the Third Republic, especially after restrictions on café commerce were eased in 1885, the number of cafés soared to thirty thousand. In 1909, when London had 5,860 drinking places, Paris still had thirty thousand. No other city had more cafés than the French capital, or more in relation to its population—11.5 per thousand inhabitants in Paris compared with one per thousand in London.

Some drinking, places provided space for dancing and drew customers primarily for that activity; these evolved into dance halls. Some charged admission at the door; others charged each time a customer danced. Now a form of play that had been a part of almost every popular festivity was merchandised in a specialized place of business on a nightly basis. Usually a particular dance hall was associated with certain strata of society—high, middling, or low—but some crossover and mixing occurred. Upper-class people in nineteenth-century Paris, for example, enjoyed going to the *bals* of poor and working people, slumming or mixing with the rabble for frissons of adventure, sexual excitement, and even dancer. All across Europe the upper layers of society regularly picked up dances from the people below. The waltz, for example, began as a German peasant dance. Nobles and the middle classes adopted it at the end of the eighteenth century. Other dances of the lower classes became spectacles for the rest of society. A prime example is the cancan, which brazen lowborn Parisian women danced in popular *bals* for decades before it became a stage act for elite spectators at expensive night spots like the Moulin Rouge.

Participation in public dancing is difficult for historians to measure, but contemporary testimony and the number of dance halls in business from period to period give some indication of its extent. In general the number of dance halls and size of the clientele appear to have been greater in the nineteenth century than in the twentieth, with some notable exceptions. One exception is the period between the two world wars; another is the flourishing; of night spots catering to youth in the second half of the twentieth century.

Theater in the nineteenth century continued to be a major entertainment for all classes and developed some new forms that had special appeal for the fastest-growing parts of the urban population. Some of those forms were particularly suited to patrons from the middle classes, who composed the majority of the audiences in large commercial theaters (the boulevard theaters of Paris, for example). Such spectators favored amusing plays featuring vaguely middle-class characters and conventional values. The same prospering classes also patronized and enjoyed a new kind of light musical play, the operetta, a cheery entertainment with catchy melodies, dance, and a comic or sentimental plot. Meanwhile the aristocratic elite maintained a conspicuous presence at traditional grand operas.

In the late nineteenth century, writers such as Émile Zola, Gerhart Hauptmann, and Henrik Ibsen broke with the century's theatrical conventions, challenged bourgeois values, and put the spotlight on workers, the poor, and social rebels. Their naturalist dramas disturbed the satisfied or insecure middle classes with such provocative subjects as class conflict, urban squalor, and the oppression of women. Depictions of strong, norm-defying women were particularly provocative, coming at the end of a century marked by strict gender divisions and an ethos directing; women to remain subordinate and quiet in the domestic and private sphere. It was also an era in which almost all public entertainment was fashioned with men in mind as the primary spectators.

Plebeian theatergoers, meanwhile, flocked to see melodrama—sentimental, tear-provoking tales of good ultimately triumphing over evil (popular ideals and hopes realized, at least onstage). Commoners also enjoyed seeing big spectacles featuring thundering horses, elephants, and a large cast of human performers—forerunners of blockbuster action movies. Also popular were sensationalist, gory tales—theatrical versions of eighteenth-century Gothic novels and even older broadsides depicting bloody crimes. Murder and mayhem were the specialties of the house at Le Grand Guignol in Paris, which opened in 1897. There spectators watched realistic blood-drenched scenes of slashing stabbing, torture, rape, and killing. Audiences for such dramas not only played out their fears and fantasies but also took pleasure in seeing taboos shattered and good taste flouted—all under the controlled conditions of the stage. This theatrical genre did not spread widely across Europe, but it did endure in popular literature and prospered in film a few decades later.

Drinking-cum-entertainment places featuring singers and variety acts emerged before the middle of the nineteenth century as music halls in England and *cafés-concerts* in France. They grew in the decades after 1850 to be a leading form of commercial popular entertainment in London, Paris, and other cities great and small. Some leading music halls, like the Folies-Bergère, charged a steep admission price and catered

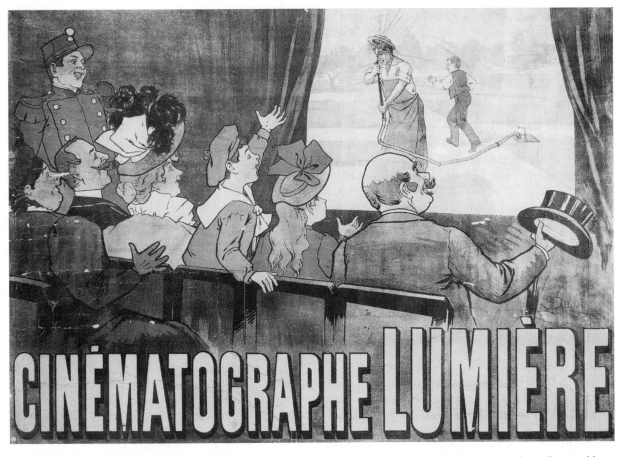

At the Movies. A Cinématographie Lumière poster advertises the film *Arroseur et arrosé* (Waterer and watered, or The sprinkler sprinkled), 1896. LAURIE PLATT WINFREY, INC.

to customers wanting to be part of a social elite. Others appealed to large, socially diverse audiences by charging little or no admission and making money simply from selling drinks and food.

The music hall played important roles in the social life of its public and in the cultural formation of class—roles that social historians are still working to clarify. The leisure experience there fell somewhere between that of the theater and that of the coffeehouse—between spectatorship and performance on the one hand and participatory socializing on the other. Music hall customers often chatted during the show while smoking and drinking, and they shouted out to the performers and joined in singing favorite songs. The acts onstage did not require the audience's full attention nor did they proceed according to any narrative or logical sequence; spectators came and went informally.

Music hall song and humor, it seems clear, played mostly to males and particularly those of the working classes—or rather, to workers as conceived by performers playing to socially mixed audiences. A favorite genre of the usual crowds was comic songs about everyday life—especially about drinking and romantic pursuits. Sung by singers who seemingly personified the little guy, those songs expressed clichéd views of common life that nourished a sense of shared identity and experience in the audience. That is, spectators and performers assumed the perspective of modest working-class people or, more vaguely, a populist spirit. Audience members who were not workers joined in as good-natured sympathizers. Enjoying a convivial social atmosphere, they played along with the pretense that everyone present constituted a popular collectivity or class. Many of the most applauded performers, for their part, projected a plebeian identity through their lyrics, jokes, and accents.

In the early decades of their existence, music hall songs and stories often expressed working people's grievances. A playful show of social antagonism, the mocking of authority figures, and the flouting of social norms had long been a part of customary revels—Guy Fawkes' Night in England, charivari, and carnival—and the *commedia dell'arte* as well. Such prac-

209

tices served as safety valves for traditional society. The music hall carried on some of that same function through ritualized joking and songs, venting, common people's resentments of landlords, tax collectors, the rich and haughty, and meddlesome mothers-in-law. Turn-of-the-century cabaret performances in Paris, Vienna. and Berlin offered even more political and social satire and mocking than did the music halls, but the audiences there were small by comparison, limited to artistic circles and the well-off.

By the late nineteenth century, the edgy political and social material was toned down or eliminated from the large popular halls. Censorship was not the main reason. As the music hall evolved and spread, it was not simply an amusement attuned to its popular audience; it was also a commercial enterprise increasingly under the control of big businessmen who were conservative, socially and politically. Music hall entertainment became less critical of established society and less "vulgar" as the owners of the halls and performers alike aspired to respectability and reached out to larger audiences, including whole families. Performers under that new regime passed over social antagonisms lightly and cleansed away vulgar language and gestures. These changes were particularly marked in England, an influential leader in variety entertainment. By the turn of the century control of most major English music halls had passed into the hands of large syndicates. Among, them was the largest syndicate in the world, Moss Empires, whose centralized management oversaw nearly forty "theatres of variety," dictating their programming and performers and even the time allotted to each act.

After 1895 the music halls had to compete with a new entertainment—moving pictures, shown on a new kind of projector invented by the Lumière brothers of Lyon. Their invention was the latest in a string of magic lanterns reproducing sights and movement for viewers who enjoyed seeing the illusion of real-life scenes and stories. The Lumières' new device enjoyed several advantages over its predecessors. It used images that were not laboriously crafted by hand but were mechanically reproduced by a photographic process. And unlike Thomas Edison's Kinetoscope (a kind of peep box), the Lumières' machine was a projector that allowed not just one viewer but many, assembled as an audience, to watch the moving images and to share the storytelling.

Movies immediately attracted audiences who relished the novel visual sensations that the early short comic films and news clips provided. The new spectacle moved into city music halls, wax museums, and department stores. For about the first decade after its invention, cinema was a cheap amusement largely for working-class spectators in city centers and on fairgrounds. Then over the next decade, with the construction of new halls built for the cinema and the production of longer, high-toned films, spectators from the middle classes embraced the new entertainment. Cinema became so popular with urban audiences that it drove numerous older competitors out of business in the years before World War I; notable casualties included music halls and *cafés-concerts,* wax museums, and panoramas.

Even with all the new kinds of entertainment available, the city was a crowded, dirty, and noisy place for the many. Getting away from it was a pleasure, and in the second half of the nineteenth century, new public transport systems gave the masses the opportunity to do so. Working people toward the end of the century enjoyed day trips by railroad to seaside resorts, versions of New York's Coney Island such as Blackpool in England. On Sundays city people took tramways and railways for an outing to the country. Parisians, for example, made excursions to riverside cafés and restaurants along the Marne and the Seine. From the 1880s on, growing numbers of city dwellers (even of modest circumstances) bought bicycles and pedaled out to explore the countryside, to fish, and to picnic alongside streams and rivers.

THE AGE OF MASS MEDIA

In the late nineteenth century, cinema joined a series of new inventions—the phonograph and the cheap illustrated newspaper and magazine—that made possible the mechanical mass reproduction of sights, voice, and music for the entertainment of the masses. These centrally produced, one-way means of communication afforded to a relatively few business and entertainment leaders the power to influence or manipulate masses of ordinary people by selected messages about life at that time and about commodities for sale. The new media also extended a democratization of culture already under way. The new technology of cinema, for example, brought reproductions of performances to many places simultaneously at low cost to the consumer. People of modest means, scattered rural inhabitants, and residents of small towns were now able to see the same stars and productions that moneyed spectators in big city venues did.

After World War I, companies that had developed the "wireless" for military and maritime uses extended it into broadcasting for everyday civilian audiences. Radio stations sprang; up in major cities in the early 1920s, transmitting news, music, and some advertising (though nowhere as much as in the United

Listening to the Radio. Scotland, 1955. BERT HARDY, PICTURE POST/LIAISON AGENCY

States). State-run, university, and religious stations (for example, Radio catholique belge) came into being in the same decade. One leader in noncommercial radio was the British Broadcasting Company (BBC), which was funded by the sale of radio licenses. The BBC provided entertainment—including popular music and plays—but above all it made itself a force bespeaking social distinction with its serious, high-culture offerings as well as the elite accent of its announcers. Although it was state controlled and enjoyed a monopoly from its origins in 1922, it maintained independent self-governance in programming and news reporting. Meanwhile, radio in Fascist Italy and Nazi Germany served as a prime medium of political propaganda.

In the 1930s radio became a common household fixture, delivering mass-produced entertainment and news in the home. Radio was a watershed in the shift of leisure from public space to the private domain. By early 1936 there were 27.5 million receivers in Europe (56.7 million in the entire world; 22.9 million in the United States). Men, women, and children separately followed programs addressing their distinct interests, but at times entire families came together to hear entertainment with broad appeal. Neighbors and friends who did not own a set joined the audience by paying social visits to someone who did. Silent listening usually prevailed during the programs, in contrast to the lively talk that marked pub and church gatherings. But this new leisure practice, unlike movie-going, was often not wholly free from work—women, for example, sewed, knitted, or cooked while giving some attention to the wireless.

Through the new medium, distant celebrities became intimates of the audience at home, or so it seemed, as the relationship was decidedly one-sided.

The disembodied voices often conveyed the sense of being family members reaching out to include the unseen listener. For many the radio served as a connection to a larger world of information and entertainment, a function perhaps particularly important to women who were homemakers. Radio was also a new instrument of political persuasion and propaganda, and it was a powerful advertising tool and promoter of consumption.

Governments in Europe limited the number of stations, the kind of programming, and advertising for many decades. The state monopoly on radio broadcasting lasted in France until reforms permitting the licensing of private radio were carried out under the Fifth Republic's first Socialist president, François Mitterrand, in the early 1980s. Hundreds of new stations then emerged, giving listeners an unprecedented range of political opinion and advertising along with heavy doses of American and English popular music.

Radios became smaller and more portable after World War II with the development of transistors, and listeners stayed tuned to their favorite programs in their cars and on beaches. In 1979 Sony introduced the Walkman, and in the 1980s this new type of small radio and cassette player became extremely popular. Listeners could now take their favorite music almost everywhere—on subways, buses, and trains and in streets and parks. Youth especially took to the new earphones, entertaining themselves in solitude even amid crowds. Here was one more step taken in the long historical shift toward private, individualistic, more technologically mediated leisure.

Despite the entertainment available at home, masses of Europeans still went out to the movies regularly—once a week or even more frequently—in the 1920s and 1930s. In fact the practice of moviegoing grew steadily, while attendance at plays and musical performances declined except among a classically cultivated minority. Factory workers and clerical employees commonly went to cinemas more frequently than other social groups. In the 1930s children also went weekly to see productions specially designed for them. Increasing numbers from the middle classes, too, joined movie audiences over the decade. Husbands and wives usually attended together, a leisure practice in contrast to the customary one of males going out alone to pubs and taverns.

Movie theaters were commonplace in urban working-class neighborhoods and were particularly numerous in industrial workers' quarters of cities like Birmingham, England. Many of the cinemas were converted former theaters and music halls, but in city centers between the world wars, lavish new movie halls were built in the style of vast dream palaces with

Egyptian, Assyrian, and Moorish decors. Yet even these showy places provided cheap seats that permitted the lowly of society to enjoy access alongside the better-off.

Some people were willing to pay to see only newsreels and documentary films; for them there were city-center halls specializing in such programs. But the biggest draws were films of fiction—the mainstay of most movie theaters. Throughout Europe, Hollywood movies became audience favorites from World War I on. So many American exports moved onto European screens and won such favor that many French, British, and other film companies found it difficult to survive. Appealing to nationalist sentiments, European film-makers turned to their governments for legislative protection and financial aid, measures that were almost always inadequate.

The images and stories shown by the movies not only entertained but also conveyed new styles, attitudes, and ways of living. Ordinary women across Europe styled their hair as Greta Garbo did, for example, and tried to smoke cigarettes and kiss as the stars did on the big screen. Many screenplays conveyed a franker acceptance of sex than the norms in most European (and American) societies authorized. Hollywood productions after World War I established the vamp as a familiar feminine type and generalized what even the French quickly came to call sex appeal (using the English phrase). Reinforcing these anti-Victorian models were movie magazines, with their accounts of the glamorous off-screen lives of the stars—lives of romance, luxurious ease, and seaside vacations. Movies also depicted class differences: they especially showed to the masses the lifestyles of the rich and the social elite. Yet story lines in mainstream films almost always ended with social reconciliation. Socialist and communist militants perceived the cinema as an opiate, while censors and conservatives worried about its power of moral subversion. Cinema has had a strong impact on cultural values and morals; the nature and extent of it have been the subjects of unending debate.

AT HOME WITH THE SMALL SCREEN

In the 1950s television took root in European everyday life. Although television broadcasting had begun with the BBC in 1936, TV did not become a part of most households until after 1945. For several decades as television spread across Europe, one or two government-run channels provided limited programming with little or no advertising; plays, concerts, variety shows, and news filled out the schedule. These were produced and controlled by the public service companies, which

pursued a mission of safeguarding cultural standards from pressures of low, popular tastes. National systems beamed programs to all citizens simultaneously. Small countries went further, moving into the airwaves well beyond their national boundaries. Luxembourg's television station, like Radio-Luxembourg from its outset in 1933, reached out to large audiences in neighboring states with programs that catered more to popular tastes than government-controlled channels generally did. Luxembourg radio and television also mixed in profitable commercial advertising before the national stations of large countries did. In Britain it was not until 1955 that a commercial TV channel began to operate, ending the BBC monopoly. Responding to the appeal of commercial programming, the BBC's directors introduced some more popular, more current music and comedy—including the widely watched satirical program *That Was the Week That Was* in the 1960s.

The social rebellions that peaked in 1968 led to new openings for independent TV producers and film-makers, who chafed at the old elite conceptions of culture. Private, for-profit stations took off in the 1980s in France, Germany, Norway, and elsewhere. Their hallmark was programming that derived from many old forms of entertainment—variety shows rooted in music hall traditions, drama and comedy adapted from theater, and soap operas and newscasts carried over from radio. In the communist-bloc countries, government-run television served as an important vehicle of political propaganda, as radio had been for fascist states of the 1930s. The result, however, was far from a brainwashing of the society. Many viewers found the ideological programming heavy-handed and sought news and entertainment from nonofficial sources, mostly from Western Europe.

When the small screen entered the home, it commonly altered family life, first by becoming a new center of attention and the main source of entertainment. TV viewing quickly took over many of the hours hitherto spent listening to radio, moviegoing, and reading, although it did not supplant those older practices. Viewers spending the highest number of hours in front of the tube were the very young, the old, and the unemployed. Surveys in Britain revealed that lower-income people watched more hours than did those with higher incomes. Children have been among the most assiduous and regular of viewers, choosing programs designed for them as well as general programming.

What effects has TV watching had on society? From a historical point of view, it seems clear that the medium itself has been a prime instrument for the promotion of consumption—not just through commercial spots but also through the images of attractive automobiles and kitchens shown in program after program. Further, as critics have emphasized, the medium seems to foster passivity (even addiction) in its viewers. Observers also worry that children who spend many hours watching TV come to accept the programmers' version of what the world is and should be. The possible influence of violent scenes on viewers' behavior has been of particular concern. Some studies suggest that the effects depend on whether the young viewers watch alone or watch and interact with their parents and others. While research on these matters has been inconclusive, public opinion about violence, sex, and foul language on TV has long been strong and polarized.

For historians the question of how media representations of life relate to real life in society has been particularly important. Some TV fare seems at first glance to be purely escapist or divorced from everyday life—game shows, for example, though many of them play on consumer desires. Much on the small screen, however, clearly reflects social questions and anxieties and is an articulation of them. Comedy is especially attuned to such issues. Situation comedies and satire have often mocked and questioned dominant values and authority figures, from fathers to politicians. Yet often they have also reinforced stereotypes and well-entrenched views about class, gender, and nationalist identity, for example. Serialized shows portraying families, which have always been among the most popular programs, have presented media versions of ideals and social realities marking a period of history. They have served up what producers thought would please large audiences—often idealizing and seldom departing from well-established systems of social representation, including dominant constructions of gender. Most domestic sitcoms in the early decades of TV depicted middle-class, nuclear, patriarchal families in a sentimental and humorous way; in the 1960s and 1970s they began to depict less conventionally mainstream households, breaking with some taboos—showing prejudice, for example, in working-class British males. Viewers following the TV family's problems and resolutions derive a sense of sharing in the familial life unfolding in the programs, as fans of soap operas vicariously live the enacted moments of passion and disappointment. Compared with the sociability known to theater and music hall audiences in previous eras, television viewing seems to resemble isolated voyeurism, though it provides some compensatory experience for the lonely.

Live reporting worldwide also results in a kind of shared experience for far-flung individuals—viewers everywhere receive instant information and vicariously participate in events or happenings as they are still occurring. Viewers in every corner of Europe also share a familiarity with images of one highly developed consumerist culture—that is, images of American society, its consumer goods, and its leisure. Since the end of World War II, American programs have not only been staples on European TV, they have also been viewers' favorites. In the 1960s and 1970s, the shows drawing the biggest audiences in Europe were the same ones that were hits with Americans of the time: *Bonanza, Hawaii Five-O,* and *Kojak.* In the 1980s it was *Dallas,* in the 1990s *Baywatch* (which beat the record set by *Dallas*).

By the 1990s television sets were in about 98 percent of homes in the industrialized world. At the end of the twentieth century, the introduction of satellite and cable transmission greatly expanded the programming to dozens or even hundreds of channels. Audiences became more segmented into discrete groups formed around shared interests, tastes, and age. The specter of state control was drastically reduced, and the threat of the media's homogenizing effects diminished, even though commercial advertisers still enjoyed plenty of opportunity to influence sensibilities and minds. Entertainment and shopping possibilities in the home continue to expand with the integration of television and computer and the development of more interactive media.

PROBLEMATIC LEISURE IN CONTEMPORARY SOCIETY

For much of the later nineteenth century and the twentieth, social theorists and labor leaders anticipated an increase of free time, continuing a pattern known after the early stages of industrialization. Yet a sense of ease taking and plentiful free time seems to have eluded many people in the late twentieth century. With all their labor-saving devices and officially limited work hours, they were left with a nagging question: where did all the leisure go? Even in their hours away from work, people felt harried, in need of renewal and too infrequently finding it. One reason for this trend is that much so-called free time went into buying and maintaining leisure goods. The far-reaching leisure industry of the late-twentieth-century world both stimulated as well as catered to consumer desires. Increased free time was accompanied by increased consumption of such leisure products as sports equipment, televisions, VCRs, computers, and the services of tourism and travel personnel. Those with higher incomes spent a greater part of their household budget and greater sums of money on such items, but they did not necessarily have more leisure. In the second half of the twentieth century, high-salary earners (business executives and professionals, for example) typically worked longer hours than did service and manufacturing workers, whose workdays tended to be more strictly set by clock time.

The market extended into the leisure of virtually every social group, developing forms appealing to just about every desire and interest. After 1945 a commercialized leisure identified with youth emerged as an important part of society and the economy. One distinctive part of that youth culture took shape around 1960 when European teenagers discovered rock music imported from the United States. By the late 1950s and 1960s, young people were not only more numerous than ever, they were also wielders of unprecedented consumer power in large part stemming from their parents' prosperity. Embracing rock with relish, many young Europeans bought records, listened to the new tunes on the radio and television, and paid admission to rock concerts, participating in sometimes frenzied celebrations led by new young stars radiating youthful energy, rebellious high spirits, and sexuality. This vigorous subculture was also a counterculture, reacting against norms and conventions set by adult authorities and the respectable. Youthful protesters in the late 1960s denounced the mind-numbing conformist entertainment and government-controlled news of mainstream media, and they disparaged the soulless consumerism of the modernizing and prosperous Western European societies. Yet much of that very same counterculture was soon harnessed by commercial forces and transformed into commodities—records, big-ticket concerts, clothing—marketed to the young.

Leisure-business giants consolidated their economic power on a world scale in the late twentieth century. In the 1980s and 1990s international media corporations bought up entertainment conglomerates and built vast empires dominating the diversified communications industry—newspapers and magazines, film companies, television channels, and recording companies. Rupert Murdoch's British Sky Broadcasting, Luxembourg CLT, and Silvio Berlusconi's Fininvest, to name a few, spread their operations across Europe. Their products and the marketing, of them pervaded contemporary European societies. Giants of the industry fashioned extensive webs of related products and commercial tie-ins, linking the marketing of a movie, for example, to the selling of the same as a video, book, and soundtrack music CD. Cartoon characters on television or in movies reappeared in stores as toys, games, books, and clothing. Large amusement parks, where customers would spend an entire day or more, recreated the characters and stories already popularized in the entertainment media.

Walt Disney's theme parks led the way. The hugely successful Disneyland in California (1955) and Disney World in Florida (1971) and in Tokyo (1983) offered pop-culture themes that most people knew to be preeminently American, but the models and predecessors included European attractions that had developed in nineteenth-century world's fairs (the Paris Universal Expositions of 1889 and 1900, for example) and Copenhagen's Tivoli Garden, which pioneered the genteel, whole-family atmosphere that Disney was after. A Disneyland in Europe opened in 1992 twenty miles outside Paris, offering a mix of American and European fantasy—Mickey Mouse and the German Snow White, Star Wars and the British Peter Pan. Initially Europeans did not flock to the place as expected, and the first three years were financially disastrous, with losses of $1.5 billion. After making accommodations to European culture (allowing the sale of wine and beer, adding more European-themed attractions, and reducing admission prices), Disneyland Paris began to flourish. In fact, it has become France's top tourist attraction with 11.8 million visitors in 1997 (compared with 5.6 million for the Eiffel Tower). Before Euro Disney (later renamed Disneyland Paris), European competitors had already entered the market, most of them with success. The Danish manufacturers of toy building blocks opened a Legoland theme park (featuring toy building blocks) in 1968, and in 1989 Parc Asterix in Senlis near Paris began offering customers a visit to the illusory world of the French historical hero of comic-strip fame. Other parks in Europe feature still other European cartoon characters, visits to the future, an entire country in miniature, or the Wild West, along with roller coasters and other rides and strolling performers.

A lament heard at the end of the twentieth century was that free time had been colonized by powerful commercial forces inimical to true leisure, the essence of which is playfulness. Social manipulation—even control—by mass media supplants fantasy and individual freedom. Consuming overrides creativity. Media entertainment, overwhelmingly popular and pervasive, relentlessly sells commodities and promotes consuming as the key to a good life. In a consumer culture built on commodities and exchange values, free time becomes something that is spent shopping in malls or on the Internet. The culturewide promotion of consumption blights the potential of leisure as a time for rest, personal renewal, and self-development.

Many critics lambasted the entertainment industry, too, for pumping out formulaic, standardized, and often sensationalist fare that catered to the lowest common denominator. To attract audiences and promote consumption, TV producers tended to make everything entertainment—including real-life conflicts among intimates ("reality" TV) and news reports. Media representations themselves became real life for many, particularly the young, who spent a substantial part of the evening or day tuned in. Corporate power in the realm of leisure was all the more worrisome to those who saw it as one piece in a growing system of conditioning, surveillance, and control made possible by omnipresent computerized record keeping, surveys, polls, reportage, and advertising.

Ownership of the media by international corporations and cartels only heightened concern about the effects of such power. Among Europeans, that concern centered on the powerful appeal of American mass culture. American productions occupied such a large place in late-twentieth-century European leisure that they seemed to threaten the vitality of Europeans' own popular music, movies, and television programs. In the view of alarmed critics, a global homogenization of popular culture and leisure threatened the very survival of national and regional cultures.

Other observers took the brighter view that the media's role has been to carry forward a long-running process of democratization of—or increasing access to—the means of communication and sources of information. In this view community television and local radio provide some expression from below, and local and regional identities and media coexist with media voices from the national and international level. In addition, the Internet made possible the free exchange of news and information from the many to the many. Cultural studies scholars noted that not all mass-media viewers necessarily take in the same message from a given program; the spectators' readings or decodings can be quite varied and multiple, though they can generally be correlated with such social parameters as occupational or class status, gender, and ethnicity. The receiver of media messages is not just passive or manipulated; each person selects and molds meanings (each has some agency).

Going beyond aesthetic judgments, social historians of the end of the century looked especially into consumer leisure's effects on social life and individual potential. Was the merchandised leisure stultifying and repressive or emancipatory and fulfilling? How did the impact differ for different social groups? Employing a historical perspective, observers debated whether contemporary practices were more or less liberating than what went before. Understanding the historical richness of possibilities might itself have a liberating effect on notions of free time.

While observers and historians carried on their debates, ordinary people voted with their money and time. Demand for commercially produced leisure was strong and growing almost everywhere in western Europe. Historically, the market for consumer leisure has expanded as disposable income has increased and work hours have decreased. Technology, too, played a part, yielding ever more novel diversions and spectacular simulations. Entrepreneurs pressed forward almost everywhere, expanding operations that proved profitable and taking them to less-developed areas. Continuing long-term patterns, millions in formerly communist eastern Europe have become consumers of the commercialized forms of leisure already flourishing in the West.

See also **America, Americanization, and Anti-Americanism** *(volume 1);* **Consumerism; Festivals; Popular Culture; The Reformation of Popular Culture** *(in this volume); and other articles in this section.*

BIBLIOGRAPHY

Abrams, Lynn. *Workers' Culture in Imperial Germany: Leisure and Recreation in the Rhineland and Westphalia.* London and New York, 1992.

Altick, Richard D. *The Shows of London: A Panoramic History of Exhibitions, 1600–1862.* Cambridge, Mass., 1978.

Bailey Peter. *Leisure and Class in Victorian England: Rational Recreation and the Contest for Control, 1830–1885.* London, 1978.

Bailey, Peter. *Popular Culture and Peformance in the Victorian City.* Cambridge, U.K., 1998.

Bailey, Peter, ed. *Music Hall: The Business of Pleasure.* Philadelphia, 1986.

Barrows, Susanna. "Nineteenth-Century Cafés: Arenas of Everyday Life." In *Pleasures of Paris: Daumier to Picasso*. Edited by Barbara Stern Shapiro. Boston, 1991. Pages 17–26.

Benson, John. *The Rise of Consumer Society in Britain, 1880–1980*. London and New York, 1994.

Bentley, G. E. *The Profession of Player in Shakespeare's Time*. Princeton, N.J., 1984.

Bermingham, Ann, and John Brewer, eds. *The Consumption of Culture, 1600–1800: Image, Object, Text*. New York, 1995.

Blanchard, Ian, ed., *Labour and Leisure in Historical Perspective, Thirteenth to Twentieth Centuries: Papers Presented at Session B-3A of the Eleventh International History Congress*. Stuttgart, Germany, 1994.

Bradby, David, Louis James, and Bernard Sharratt, eds. *Performance and Politics in Popular Drama: Aspects of Popular Entertainment in Theatre, Film, and Television, 1800–1976*. New York, 1980.

Bratton, J. S., Jim Cook, and Christine Gledhill, eds. *Melodrama: Stage, Picture, Screen*. London, 1994.

Bratton, J. S., ed. *Music Hall: Performance and Style*. Philadelphia, 1986.

Brennan, Thomas. *Public Drinking and Popular Culture in Eighteenth-Century Paris*. Princeton, N.J., 1988.

Brewer, John, and Roy Porter, eds. *Consumption and the World of Goods*. London and New York, 1993.

Burke, Peter. "The Invention of Leisure in Early Modern Europe." *Past and Present* 146 (1995): 136–150.

Burke, Peter. *Popular Culture in Early Modem Europe*. London and New York, 1978.

Camera Obscura, nos. 20–21 (May-September 1989). Special issue entitled "The Spectatrix." Includes articles on British and Italian research and theory.

Charney, Leo, and Vanessa Schwartz, eds. *Cinema and the Invention of Modem Life*. Berkeley, Calif., 1995.

Condemi, Concetta. *Les Cafés-concerts: Histoire d'un divertissement*. Paris, 1992.

Cross, Gary. *A Social History of Leisure Since 1600*. State College, Pa., 1990.

Cross, Gary. *Time and Money: The Making of Consumer Culture*. London and New York, 1993.

Cunningham, Hugh. *Leisure in the Industrial Revolution c. 1780–c. 1880*. New York, 1980.

De Grazia, Sebastian. *Of Time, Work, and Leisure*. New York, 1962.

De Grazia, Victoria, and Ellen Furlough, eds. *The Sex of Things: Gender and Consumption in Historical Perspective*. Berkeley, Calif., 1996. A collection of specialized articles and an excellent bibliography.

Frith, Simon. *Sound Effects: Youth, Leisure, and the Politics of Rock*. London, 1983.

Golby, J. M., and A. W. Purdue. *The Civilisation of the Crowd: Popular Culture in England, 1750–1900*. London, 1984.

Gurr, Andrew. *The Shakespearean Stage, 1574–1642*. 3d ed. Cambridge, U.K., and New York, 1992.

Haine, W. Scott. *The World of the Paris Café: Sociability among the French Working Class, 1789–1914*. Baltimore, 1996.

Isherwood, Robert M. *Farce and Fantasy: Popular Entertainment in Eighteenth-Century Paris*. New York, 1986.

Jones, G. S. "Working-Class Culture and Working-Class Politics in London, 1870–1900." *Journal of Social History* 7 (1974): 460–508.

Jones, Stephen G. *Workers at Play: A Social and Economic History of Leisure 1918–1939*. London, 1986.

Linder, Staffan Burenstam. *The Harried Leisure Classes*. New York, 1970.

Lough, John. *Paris Theater Audiences in the Seventeenth and Eighteenth Centuries*. London, 1957.

Lury, Celia. *Consumer Culture*. New Brunswick, N.J., 1996.

Malcolmson, Robert W. *Popular Recreations in English Society*. Cambridge, U.K., 1973.

Marrus, Michael R., ed. *The Emergence of Leisure*. New York, 1974.

McKendrick, Neil, John Brewer, and J. H. Plumb. *The Birth of a Consumer Society: The Commercialization of Eighteenth-Century England*. Bloomington, Ind., 1982.

Modleski, Tania, ed. *Studies in Entertainment: Critical Approaches to Mass Culture*. Bloomington, Ind., 1986.

Peter, Matthias. "Time for Work, Time for Play: Relations between Work and Leisure in the Early Modern Period." *Vierteljahrschrift für Sozial- und Wirtschaftsgeschichte* 81, no. 3 (1994): 305–323.

Quarterly Review of Film and Video 11, no. 1 (1989). Special issue entitled "Female Representation and Consumer Culture," edited by Jane Gaines and Michael Renov. See, for example, Mary Ann Doan, "The Economy of Desire: The Commodity Form in/of the Cinema," pp. 23–33.

Rearick, Charles. *The French in Love and War: Popular Culture in the Era of the World Wars*. New Haven, Conn., and London, 1997.

Rearick, Charles. *Pleasures of the Belle Époque: Entertainment & Festivity in Turn-of-the-Century France*. New Haven, Conn., and London, 1985.

Scannell, Paddy, and David Cardiff. *A Social History of British Broadcasting*. Oxford, 1991.

Schama, Simon. *The Embarrassment of Riches: An Interpretation of Dutch Culture in the Golden Age*. London and New York, 1987.

Segel, Harold B. *Turn-of-the-Century Cabaret: Paris. Barcelona, Berlin. Munich. Vienna, Cracow, Moscow, St. Petersburg, Zurich*. New York, 1987.

Silj, Alessandro. *East of Dallas: The European Challenge to American Television*. London, 1988.

Skovmand, Michael, and Kim Christian Schroder, eds. *Media Cultures: Reappraising Transnational Media*. London, 1992.

Smith, Anthony, ed. *Television: An International History*. New York, 1995.

Sorlin, Pierre. *European Cinemas, European Societies, 1939–1990*. London and New York, 1991.

Sorlin, Pierre. *Mass Media*. London and New York, 1994.

Thomas, Keith. "Work and Leisure in Pre-industrial Society." *Past and Present* 29 (1964): 98–115.

Thompson, E. P. "Time, Work-Discipline, and Industrial Capitalism." *Past and Present* 38 (1967): 56–97.

Walton, John K., and James Walvin, eds. *Leisure in Britain, 1780–1939*. Manchester, U.K., 1983.

Yeo, Eileen, and Stephen Yeo, eds. *Popular Culture and Class Conflict 1590–1914: Explorations in the History of Labour and Leisure*. Brighton, U.K., 1981.

VACATIONS

John K. Walton

In British English the word "vacation" normally has a restricted and rather technical sense, applying to the periods when the universities are closed or the law courts out of session. The word "holiday" occupies the space that "vacation" occupies in North America, although it does not necessarily involve geographical mobility in search of health, recreation, or sheer enjoyment: the same word is used for a work-free day or days spent at home as for a period of rest, recuperation, or fun in a different environment. The notion of taking a holiday overlaps with that of tourism, although this latter word, more respectable administratively and academically—television programs advertise or evaluate holidays while local governments provide tourist offices and universities offer degrees in Tourism Studies but never Holiday Studies—tends now to have more up-market connotations involving longer, more ambitious journeys and a less sedentary holiday experience. It was not always thus, however, and in some circles (especially up-market literary ones) the nineteenth-century contempt for the mere "tourist," led by the nose by mentors and guidebooks and incapable of independent cultural judgment, remains as a contrast to the more adventurous, culturally aware "traveller," willing to "rough it" off the "beaten track" and eager to sample other cultures on their own terms.

By the 1840s complaints were proliferating in England about the contamination, expedited by the new railways and steamers, of the chosen destinations of elite travelers by the presence of inferior tourists. This social distinction justified itself in cultural and even moral terms. In John Urry's terminology, the "romantic gaze," which emphasized solitary individuals in direct, sensitized, and informed exchanges with landscape and culture, was being threatened by the "collective gaze," which derived satisfaction from experiencing sites and sensations in company according to shared values that were communicated by mass media and were therefore inferior in the eyes of romantics. Worst of all from this elevated perspective is the "package tourist," perceived as incapable of escaping from the values and practices imposed by the provider of holiday services and as preferring to be insulated from all troubling contact with the host culture—wanting, in fact, all the reassuring cultural landmarks of home in a setting that guarantees sunshine, bathing amenities, and cheap drink. From the 1960s on, working-class holidaymakers in Mediterranean resorts have inherited all the opprobrium that was heaped on Thomas Cook's original package tourists of a century earlier. Those who fancied themselves cultured travelers decried the interruption of their solitary contemplation of cathedrals or Roman amphitheaters by bands of lower-middle-class Cook's Tourists, Baedeker in hand and shepherded by guides.

Elsewhere in Europe similar problems of terminology crop up. The word in Spanish is *vacaciones;* but an older variant, the verb *veranear* (to pass the summer), conjures up a more leisured style of holidaymaking in which aristocratic or bourgeois families would spend two or three months at a spa or seaside resort. *Turismo* is also in use there, with a similar shade of meaning to "tourism" in English. In French, holidays are *vacances,* but *congé* overlaps with this concept, meaning "leave from work" and extending to the idea of a holiday away from home; in practice the words are used almost interchangeably. The kind of holiday taken by an *estivant* (summer visitor), is similar to that of a Spanish *veraneante.* There are also *hivernants,* passing the winter in favored climatic locations, above all the Riviera. The slipperiness of the terminology is obvious, as is the sense that the differing shades of meaning can also carry connotations of status and claims to cultural capital.

The notion of a holiday in the sense implied by "vacations" entails an extended trip, more than just an excursion to a local beauty spot or even a day's outing involving a journey of several hours. The holidaymaker makes more of an investment of time and money than the "excursionist" or "day-tripper," those particular bogeys of self-consciously respectable middle-class families looking for sedate pleasures. The emergent discipline of Tourism Studies has prompted extensive but sterile discussion over how long a stay away from home is necessary for the perpetrator to qualify as a tourist; but these efforts notwithstanding, the statistical computations that a standard definition is intended to facilitate remain visibly flawed and approximate and become less plausible the farther back in time inquiry goes. The statistics of holidaymaking are notoriously "soft," and for present purposes it matters little if a vacation is said to be anything from a long weekend to an extended stay of several months.

Here, however, a problem arises in that the notion of holiday depends on an "other," the idea of necessary work. Those privileged people whose life entailed a circuit of high-class resorts in their fashionable seasons were members (or hangers-on) of a leisure class for whom the concept of a vacation was scarcely relevant. Indeed, the observance of the dictates of international fashion was at the core of their construction and presentation of self, and thus resort life might almost be regarded as work rather than leisure, the remuneration being psychic and coming as the reward for suitably directed expenditure of time, money, and expertise, but no less important for that. Crucial to the idea of a vacation, anyway, is that it involves physical displacement, whether to a single destination or to several: change of scene, if not of culture, in pursuit of pleasure and (in some sense) relaxation. Recreational travel can also be in the mind, of course, and travel books have long provided for the armchair tourist. Across Europe in the nineteenth century, shows and spectacles represented the exotic through giant pictures, transparencies, models, and magic lanterns at fairgrounds and theaters before the cinema, television, and then the computer made their own contributions in the twentieth. But over the nineteenth and twentieth centuries, the desirability of a physical break from quotidian routine became broadly generalized across industrial societies in Europe, though at differing rates in different countries and regions, and with varying and changing destinations and degrees of commercialization. What are the roots of this important set of developments?

ORIGINS OF THE EUROPEAN VACATION

It is tempting to regard medieval pilgrims as the first European tourists, though we might find a more directly commercialized ancestry for the phenomenon in ancient Rome, at Baiae (especially, and for several centuries), Ostia, and around Naples, as extensive tracts of shoreline were thickly sown with the villas of the wealthy. Pilgrims ostensibly traveled for spiritual reasons, rather than pursuing pleasure and reinvigoration through change of scene and break from rou-

tine in the style of a modern vacationer; but they followed recognized routes with commercial infrastructures of guides and services, whether their goal was Canterbury, Compostela, or Rome. Geoffrey Chaucer in the fourteenth century shows us that individual participants' concerns might be decidedly worldly, even hedonistic. But the roots of the modern vacation can be more securely traced to two other phenomena: the rise of the Grand Tour and of the European spa system from the later sixteenth century.

In its mid-sixteenth-century origins, the Grand Tour was a device for encouraging young aristocrats to experience life and culture at courts and in cities throughout Europe, broadening its horizons in the late eighteenth century under the spur of romantic fashion to include mountain scenery and natural curiosities such as glaciers. The practice came into wider vogue during the seventeenth and eighteenth centuries, extending its social range through the gentry to the middle ranks of professionals and merchants (who might take the Tour later in life) and including growing numbers of Americans in the nineteenth century, before new time pressures and means of transport made the old leisurely patterns obsolete. The goal of the Tour was the cultural centers of northern and central Italy, with their classical remains and treasures of art and architecture. The seventeenth-century tendency to pass through various German states in a roundabout journey had given way by the early nineteenth century to a more single-minded direct route through Paris, Dijon, and Switzerland. Perhaps 15,000 to 20,000 people at a time followed the Tour in any year of the later eighteenth century, and, as befitted this small (but not numerically insignificant) elite, the tourist infrastructure was limited and exclusive, featuring special road transport arrangements, lodgings, guides, vendors of works of art (and manufacturers of fakes), and a growing volume of travel advice literature. What these pioneer tourists sought can be summed up, in the sociologist Pierre Bourdieu's telling phrase, as cultural capital: in this case, an ability to claim first-hand knowledge of places, cultures, scenes, languages, and classical allusions that was supposed to mark out the cultivated gentleman and set him and his circle apart from those who did not share his experiences. Individuals might follow their own bent, in pursuit of anything from diplomatic and political expertise to sexual adventures; but above all the Grand Tour gave a valued distinction to participants, setting them apart from social inferiors. This is a recurring theme in the history of tourism and vacations.

The other precursor of modern tourism was the spa resort, which came to offer something more closely resembling a modern vacation. Across Europe the rise of the spa followed a similar trajectory to that of the Grand Tour; but the ostensible motive for spending time taking the waters was, in the first instance, health, as the doctors took over the holy wells and elaborate medical discourses crystallized around the ascribed curative qualities of chalybeate, ferruginous, or sulfurous springs. Spa itself, in Belgium, was one of the first such resorts to attract an international clientele, including a visit from Tsar Peter the Great, while Bath and Wiesbaden were among the substantial towns that grew up around mineral springs. Sociable attractions and fashionable amenities developed in the larger spas to entertain the invalids and their relatives, and to attract the hale and hearty to what were often attractive little upland settlements. The band, the assembly rooms, the public walks, and in some cases the brothel and the roulette wheel provided a range of diversions for those who could afford them, while in many cases inferior accommodation catered to a regional clientele and to paupers sent in hopes of revitalization. The elite social institutions of the spa were easily policed, by subscriptions and dress codes, although masters of ceremonies intervened to preserve politeness in the exchanges between the nobility and the marginal middle ranks. This polite holiday regime, with its daily routines and rituals, reached its heyday in the early nineteenth century over much of Europe. In England the larger spa towns evolved from vacation destinations into retirement and commuter centers, mainly in the second half of the nineteenth century. In Germany and eastern Europe, and over much of Spain and Italy, the spa sustained its popularity through the nineteenth and into the twentieth centuries, although individual resorts generally remained small and their social amenities exclusive.

THE SEASIDE AESTHETIC

From the late eighteenth century, however, new destinations came to the fore. The vogue for the seaside was the most enduringly important across Europe, mutating over time with the growing popularity of the Mediterranean and of sunbathing, but, except where transport problems and limited disposable incomes sustained the dominance of spas with local clienteles, coming to hold sway as the dominant holiday form. The seaside holiday was boosted by two eighteenth-century developments. First, the medical fashion for sea bathing in cold, boisterous northern waters helped turn something dangerous, forbidding, and frightening into a healthy activity. The medical vogue for sea bathing is an example of cultural preferences rising through the social strata rather than trickling down through emulation, for the doctors who began to prescribe cold bathing and (in some cases) seawater drinking regimes, in England in the first half of the eighteenth century and then across western Europe, were giving a "scientific" veneer to already popular practices. Right across western Europe, from northwest England through the Netherlands, France, and the Iberian Peninsula to Corsica, there is evidence of popular sea-bathing rituals that celebrate the health-giving properties of the sea at certain times of year. The medical profession recast and formalized these beliefs, imposing its own medical rituals that prescribed the number and duration of baths to be taken for specific ailments and the precautions that had to be adopted. This in turn necessitated a prolonged stay at the seaside to fulfill the requirements of the "cure," just as in the case of the spas. Thus the health seekers and their friends created a critical mass of demand that encouraged speculation in accommodation, entertainment, and amenities, promoting the rise of that distinctive but versatile kind of town, the seaside resort.

The second development was the new aesthetic of the maritime landscape and of the sea itself. The romantic revaluation of the later eighteenth century brought the untamed sea and the untidy shoreline within the canons of the picturesque and the sublime, rendering maritime landscapes fit subjects for the painter and enabling wind, tempest, storm-surge, and wreck to be appreciated and enjoyed as noble spectacles and with a suitable frisson of horror. The sea was fecund and full of reminders of creation and its vestiges. Those who braved its perils were also ennobled and romanticized, and they and their boats gradually became fitting additions to the composition of marine paintings. All this made the seaside an attractive destination and encouraged the building of houses for visitors facing the waves, in contrast with seafaring settlements that tried to shelter from their fury. A similar cultural reassessment of mountain scenery made upland areas from the English Lake District to the Alps into tourist destinations in their own right, with evangelical dimensions of proximity to God and romantic anthropologies of the stalwart and unassuming virtues of mountain peasantries (though these might coexist with fears of brigands, just as brave fishermen might otherwise be presented as lazy, untrustworthy, and of doubtful morals).

On these twin foundations the seaside holiday based itself, beginning in England in the 1730s, spreading to France, the Low Countries, and north Germany toward the end of the century, and gravitating outward to (for example) Sweden by the early nineteenth century and Spain by the 1820s. The resorts soon

Taking the Waters. The Pump Room at Bath, 1789. ©HULTON GETTY/LIAISON AGENCY

attracted pleasure seekers who required the amenities of polite society, just as at the spas; and such visitors soon turned the vocabularies of the picturesque and sublime into lazy cliché in ways that caught the satirical ear of Jane Austen. In Britain especially the seaside competed effectively with the spa to become the dominant vacation destination by the early nineteenth century. In northern Spain the two kinds of resort were often complementary, with wealthy health seekers taking a cure in an upland spa and following up with a stint of sea bathing, while in Germany most of the North Sea and Baltic resorts were distant from population centers, enduringly hard to reach, and less dynamic in their growth. But everywhere the seaside, like the spa, became a bourgeois as well as an aristocratic destination. It was, however, open to a wider range of people, as it was more difficult to regulate access to and use of the beach, which lent itself to a wider range of activities than the pump room and assembly rooms; it also provided a much more child-friendly environment, thus ensuring the growing popularity of the family holiday, complete with buckets and spades, in the early nineteenth century.

THE RAILWAY AGE

The special status of the seaside, especially in England, was confirmed in the railway age. For a century from the 1840s the railway journey became an almost inevitable introduction and conclusion to a vacation, as well as linking the different stages of a tour and making possible day excursions from the holiday base.

Railway companies might also provide steamboats, piers, and hotel services. The railways built on existing patterns of holidaymaking, extending them to new social groups and broadening their geographical range rather than starting something entirely new, in England at least. Brighton had attained an off-season population of 40,000 using road transport before the railway arrived from London in September 1841, and Margate's visiting season had prospered in the eighteenth century using sailing vessels to carry Londoners down the Thames estuary. By the same token railways to the French Riviera and in parts of the Swiss Alps augmented established tourist flows rather than initiating them, while San Sebastian, which became Spain's premier seaside resort in the later nineteenth century, was already attracting visitors by road from Madrid (despite the strenuous nature of the two-day journey) before it began to benefit from its strategic position on the Madrid-Paris rail route after 1864. But the journey was emphatically part of even the most sedentary holiday, as the process of packing and booking tickets conjured up anticipations of the pleasures that awaited at the other end, and a whole literature of travel nostalgia emerged later to celebrate first the stagecoach and the diligence, then the steam railway itself.

The economies in time and money that the railways and steamers brought, and their greater convenience and (eventually) safety, opened vacations out to a widening public in the second half of the nineteenth century, especially in England; and demand was channeled disproportionately into the seaside. New resorts

222

blossomed on hitherto neglected shores, although the railways that fed them had almost always been constructed for other purposes, and larger resorts spread and subdivided, developing distinctive areas for different social groups as the working classes began to join their social betters at the beach. On the European mainland this came much later than in England, where brief but conspicuous working-class seaside holidays within London's orbit or wherever industrial areas had easy access to the coast were older than railways. A full-scale working-class holiday season emerged in the northwest in the 1870s, fueled by the rising family incomes of (especially) the cotton factory workers and the attractions of Blackpool, the first working-class seaside resort. The petty bourgeoisie might have their week at the seaside, traveling from Madrid to San Sebastian by special cheap trains and economizing on everything except the basics of a presentable turnout; small farmers from the Castilian plains might travel to Santander by the mixed train to follow a medically prescribed bathing regime, sleeping in fifth-rate *fondas* and gawking obtrusively at sea, ships, and city sights. Parisian shopkeepers and small traders might find their way to Normandy outside the fashionable season; but there as in Germany the working class proper was excluded. The scale of French middle-class outrage when the Popular Front government introduced paid holidays in 1936, promising a wage earners' ex-

odus to coast and country, indicated the limited nature of what had gone before; and even then, most beneficiaries of the new legislation stayed at home and relaxed rather than invading the holiday preserves of their betters.

It was not just a matter of resources; people had to *want* vacations away from home, and to be prepared to save for them rather than spending spare cash locally on daily or weekly pleasures, or insisting on accumulating savings as a hedge against disaster or a route to property ownership or a small business. Seekers after health, tranquillity, scenic beauty, spiritual uplift (associated especially with mountains), status and cultural capital, in varying mixtures and combinations, were joined in growing numbers by those who wanted commercial pleasures in a setting that offered relief from the constraints of everyday life. The seaside came to cater to this preference very effectively, alongside the others. The abundance of coastal sites ensured that all tastes could be satisfied, from those who wanted exclusive quiet in ruggedly romantic surroundings to those who preferred formal classical architecture and fashionable promenades, to those in turn who wanted cheap amusements, from Punch and Judy to the music hall, and someone else to cook and clean up. The seaside resorts of the railway age offered a distinctive range of entertainments for those who wanted them. The pleasure pier was an English in-

At the Seashore. The beach of Sanlucar, Spain, painting by German Alvarez Algeciras. Archivo Iconografico, S.A./ ©Corbis

novation (seldom exported) that linked land and sea, provided access to steamer excursions, and offered promenades and bands above the waves in surroundings enlivened by wrought-iron Gothic and Oriental architecture. It was also one of the homes of the minstrel show (which involved putting on blackface and singing "plantation" songs to the banjo) and the Pierrots (comedians and songsters with whitened faces). These entertainers also accompanied the Punch-and-Judy puppet show on the beach, alongside, in the more popular English resorts, a variety of stallholders who might use a knife to remove corns, sell medical recipes or horoscopes, or read character from the bumps on the head, a popular version of phrenology that long outlasted its pretensions to medical science. Fringe and officially discredited beliefs flourished alongside donkey rides and later fairground amusements, which offered strange sensations and threatened dignity and seemliness by exposing hidden parts of the body in unpredictable ways.

From the 1870s the larger English resorts also acquired Winter Gardens, which provided indoor promenades and decorous music but soon moved down-market wherever working-class demand pressed strongly. As the seaside vacation market became visibly lucrative and attracted investors in syndicates and limited companies, a range of other entertainment complexes were built that offered dancing, shows, exhibitions, and even zoos and circuses. As in the United States, the popular resorts (and more pretentious ones such as Southport and even Spain's San Sebastian) found room for large-scale fairgrounds on dedicated sites, and these introduced their customers to an exciting range of up-to-the-minute technologies, stirring the senses in novel ways. Resorts on the western European mainland experienced fewer pressures to go down-market, and the casino (whether privately or municipally owned) tended to be the main entertainment center, sometimes offering roulette, chemin de fer and the full gambling menu, but more usually—and more noticeably—presenting innocuous fare of concerts, dancing, and special events for children. At the French resorts in Biarritz and Deauville, and in Monte Carlo and San Sebastian, casino nightlife carried an atmosphere of the demimonde, and resort entertainment for the elite was distinctively daring.

These distinctive forms of seaside entertainment augmented the peculiar attractions of the beach itself, where children played in the sand and all ages bathed according to regulations that were strict on paper but often loosely interpreted in practice. This was especially the case in England, where into the twentieth century the lumbering, wooden bathing machine, which provided changing space and protection for

modesty, and was backed into the water by a horse, demanded substantial sums from would-be bathers, segregating the sexes and imposing body-concealing costumes. The regulations were often flouted by those who preferred the freedom of recreational nude bathing, or, more respectably, wanted to bathe in costume *en famille*. In the new century disrobing in public on the beach became more widely tolerated; the practice was controversial, however, because it offended the prudish and those with vested interests in controls. Elsewhere in Europe customs varied: the French beaches were carefully monitored for safety but permitted mixed bathing and revealing costumes that shocked some English visitors; the Spanish used bathing machines and policed morality in almost English style; the northern Europeans were much more relaxed by the early twentieth century.

The growing popularity of sunbathing, alongside the continuing transition from the medicinal and regulated to the recreational and liberated use of the sea, brought conflicts over the morality of bodily exposure further to the fore. The myth that the fashion designer Coco Chanel invented sunbathing, making a tanned skin chic and enabling the French Riviera to develop a summer season in the mid-1920s, survives tenaciously. In fact the fashion for what was now seen as a healthy brown skin was well established before World War I in places as far apart as San Sebastian and the Baltic, although the prevailing nudity that amazed and delighted the British trade unionist Harry Pollitt at Libau in 1921 was confined to northern European beaches. As with sea bathing earlier, the vogue for sunshine and fresh air as prescriptions for good health was promoted by a rising tide of medical opinion. Likewise, fashionable cures for tuberculosis had called for mountain air and beginning in the 1860s had helped to boost the Swiss Alps as a destination. This trend coincided with a fashion for the freedom of the open air and the abandonment of restrictive clothing conventions. The Mediterranean, hitherto shunned as enervating and malarial, was now seen as a potential destination for beach holidays, although the international popularity of its shores, the French and Italian Rivieras apart, was a phenomenon of the 1950s onward. In Spain a backlash was beginning on the eve of the civil war in the mid-1930s, as Catholic campaigners against bodily exposure and sexual temptation claimed a connection (at that point speculative) between sunburn and skin cancer; but this was swimming against a very powerful tide.

By the interwar years the seaside holiday was well established as an annual institution across Europe, from the Irish Sea to the Black Sea (in Romania and the Crimea) and from Norway to Andalucía in

Allier — 206 - VICHY, le Gargarisme

Health Resort. Gargling room at a spa at Vichy, France. ©COLLECTION VIOLLET

Spain. The English working class most especially adopted the practice, helped by cheap transport and the development of specialized, popular resort districts on accessible coastlines. Its social range (and the number and variety of bathing resorts) decreased as an observer moved from west to east, but a spell at the seaside, from a weekend to a full summer, was the dominant mode of vacationing.

BETWEEN THE WARS AND AFTER

The interwar years also saw the proliferation of new types of holidays, whether developed for profit or by voluntary organizations. Some of them intended to provide cheaper, healthier, less pretentious alternatives to the commercialized formality of the urban seaside resort. As part of the interwar trend toward relaxation and informality, the holiday camp made headway. In reaction against the restrictions of boardinghouses and lodgings, with their curfews and regulations, the holiday camp offered cheap accommodation in tents or chalets, with self-made entertainment on site (in contrast with the urban commercial theaters and music halls of established resorts), and celebrated freedom and the outdoor life. It had ancestors in turn-of-the-century England, both in the clusters of shacks and converted tramcars that colonized cheap seaside land and offered bohemian escape from convention for people of limited means, creating an alternative aesthetic scandalizing to the planners of the 1940s, and in the tented encampments that provided cheap, mor-

ally regulated, alcohol-free seaside accommodation for young men. The camps of the 1930s, and especially those of the more commercialized 1950s, gained a reputation for sexual adventure but also (increasingly) for a new kind of mass-market regimentation. Their French counterparts remained less commercial in their organization, usually run by voluntary bodies aiming to make unpretentious, natural holidays accessible to workers who were entitled to them as citizens; but Club Méditerranée, which started life in 1950, attracted a more up-market clientele and a reputation for sensual pleasures in simple surroundings whose essential artificiality was carefully masked. Hitler's enormous holiday barracks on the Baltic Coast in the late 1930s offered a very different vision of the purpose of vacations, precisely targeted at industrial efficiency and the physical development of the "master race."

Another strong interwar trend across western Europe was the outdoor holiday in a mountain or forest setting, which emphasized the virtues of walking and climbing in groups in terms of health, fitness, and closeness to nature and sometimes God. Again, this type of holiday built on earlier developments like England's Holiday Fellowship, which sought to divert working people from the fleshpots of the popular resorts, where holiday savings were said to be dissipated in a debilitating round of commercial pleasures, and to encourage them to improve body, mind, and spirit in healthy and uplifting communal endeavor. Such initiatives were undertaken by socialists and religious

225

Resort Advertising. Poster advertising the ski resort of Chamonix, France. PRIVATE COLLECTION/BARBARA SINGER/THE BRIDGEMAN ART LIBRARY

life while providing brief, controlled contact with prescribed sights and experiences at ports of call. Other enjoyments included the winter sports holiday, especially in Switzerland. The great city as tourist destination, as exemplified especially by Paris with its shops, museums, and nightlife, combined three major holiday priorities in varying proportions according to individual preference and amply allowed for the ubiquitous anthropological tourism of people-watching. At the other end of the spectrum was the rustic holiday, with a tent or farmhouse for accommodations and its celebration of the simple life. In this last, especially, the traveler-tourist distinction came into play, and in the 1930s, even more so than a century earlier, there was a lively market for travelers' tales describing voyages on foot and by local transport to places off the beaten track in Europe as well as farther afield. Contempt for mere tourists was often explicit in this literature.

Such contempt, as has been noted, had a long history and did not abate as travel agencies proliferated and incomes and aspirations rose from the second half of the nineteenth century. In the 1950s and 1960s it reached a sustained peak of vitriol with the rise of a new kind of airborne package holiday industry, which increasingly took working-class people from northern Europe to the sunny beaches of the Mediterranean. The package tour put together by a travel company that contracted to provide transport, hotels, food, and guidance was well-established before World War II. By the 1930s many British firms were producing thick books (no mere brochures these) describing tours down the Rhine or single-destination holidays at the Belgian seaside, priced in guineas. Many postwar offerings followed this pattern, with travel by coach (tour bus) initially more common than by air.

Then international tour operators began booking acres of bed space in new purpose-built hotels on Mediterranean coastlines, offering lowest-common-denominator catering (but with much better facilities than prevailed in the popular British resorts), and focusing on beaches, sunshine, and relaxation while striving to insulate holidaymakers from the shock of parachuting straight into novel cultures. This seemed to some observers to add up to a new form of "mass tourism" that exploited its customers, creating a narrow range of holiday experiences that met existing expectations without broadening horizons. This was a patronizing view, denying the agency of holidaymakers, who were reduced to mere ciphers and whose preferences, as expressed in spectacular growth in demand, were discounted. It rested on more than a century of prejudice, which embraced (for example) the ways in which working-class holidaymakers in England's Black-

enthusiasts alike, with overlapping agendas. In Germany the antagonisms between young Nazis and socialists were fought out in youth hostels and through hiking songs. As was indicated by the controversy over paid holidays in France, it is an error to imagine that vacations are necessarily detached from politics.

Building on developments from the later nineteenth century, growth areas in interwar vacationing included visits to historic and literary landscapes; these entailed pretensions to deploying and enhancing cultural capital and might be regarded as a legacy of the Grand Tour, extending its range to hitherto neglected areas such as southern Spain. The motor tour took advantage of the flexibility of a new mode of transport and diversified demand away from existing "honeypots" while necessitating interaction with host cultures, if only in seeking directions, refueling, and repairs. The cruise offered an insulated, on-board social

pool created their own vacation culture by shaping the supply of entertainment to their preferences. What it increasingly ignored was the proliferation of niche markets within the complex world of the travel trade, the variety of uses to which the package holiday might be put, and the access it gave to new commodities and cultural practices. Meanwhile, the state as entrepreneur was setting up resorts of a similar kind in eastern Europe, especially on Romania's Black Sea coast, which attracted East German visitors in growing numbers, and also in France at Languedoc, where Gaullist technocrats promoted futuristic complexes aimed at diverting demand from the Riviera. Moreover, the advent of mass car ownership across Europe opened up the prospect of increasing flexibility through touring holidays while disrupting the routines of older resorts accustomed to captive, sedentary families using amenities clustered around railway stations, and generating all the new problems of parking and traffic management. The older form of mass tourism, the railborne seaside holiday in one's home country with children, fell into decline but not yet terminal collapse, except in the case of ill-endowed provincial resorts that had grown only for want of accessible alternatives.

Overall, the explosion of vacations in Europe after World War II, though prepared by developments between the wars, was a major social phenomenon. The time set aside for vacations increased dramatically, rising to five to six weeks in places like Germany. Class differences remained. Many working-class people did not in fact travel during vacations. The wealthier middle classes sought steadily more exotic destinations. But the importance of the vacation took on unprecedented contours, and also differentiated Western Europe from other advanced industrial societies such as the United States and Japan, where vacation time remained more limited.

The historiography of these phenomena has developed in interesting ways. As the content of this essay suggests, historians have focused more on destinations, technologies, and processes in the tourist industry than on vacations themselves. Serious narratives of the vacation experience, grounding theories in evidence, are in short supply, although Alain Cor-

bin's work on changing ideas about desirable environments to visit has been helpful as an approach to eighteenth-century developments, particularly in France. As the inventor of the seaside holiday and of many aspects of tourism in the modern world, England has been the focus of the most developed historiography. Pimlott's *The Englishman's Holiday,* a remarkable book by a civil servant first published in 1946, eventually helped to encourage studies of seaside resorts from an urban history perspective, comparing and contrasting towns and coastlines as holiday destinations. The other dominant genre in Britain has been the study of elite tourism in relation to perceptions of landscape and literature, with a strong bias toward the eighteenth and nineteenth centuries. France is the other European country with a developed historiography, with more emphasis on the social and political values surrounding the development of vacations and the perceptions and expectations of holidaymakers, themes that are not neglected in the excellent regional studies of holiday destinations by Gabriel Désert and Michel Chadefaud.

As for twentieth-century topics, retrospective glances by sociologists, anthropologists, geographers, and planners have been more influential than the scant work by historians, with conspicuous exceptions like Ellen Furlough on France and Nigel Morgan on England. The vacation as a historical theme in its own right would benefit by borrowing and testing insights from the work of John Urry, Jean-Didier Urbain, Rob Shields, and others in sociology, cultural studies, and related disciplines. A social and cultural history of the vacation and its meanings for the vacationers themselves must take due account of race, class, gender, and the sense of self. Vacation genres, such as the honeymoon, cry out for historical analysis, as work on Niagara Falls has shown in the United States, and the themes of liminality and carnival need further exploration in relation to vacations, particularly for eastern and southern Europe. John Pemble's *The Mediterranean Passion* has shown how subtly and accessibly they might be pursued even within a conventional historical methodology. A strong platform has been built for the vacation as a theme of social history.

See also other articles in this section.

BIBLIOGRAPHY

Barke, M., J. Towner, and M. T. Newton, eds. *Tourism in Spain: Critical Issues.* Wallingford, U.K., and Tucson, Ariz., 1996.

Battilani, P. *Vacanze di pochi, vacanze di tutti: Breve storia del turismo.* Bologna, Italy, 1998.

Chadefaud, Michel. *Aux origines du tourisme dans les pays de l'Adour, du mythe à l'espace: Un essai de géographie historique.* Pau, France, 1987.

Constandt, M. *Een eeuw vakantie: 100 jaar toerisme in West-Vlaanderen.* Tielt, Netherlands, 1986.

Corbin, Alain. *The Lure of the Sea: The Discovery of the Seaside in the Western World, 1750–1840.* Berkeley, Calif., 1994.

Désert, Gabriel. *La vie quotidienne sur les plages normandes du Second Empire aux Années folles.* Paris, 1983.

Fisher, Stephen. *Recreation and the Sea.* Exeter, U.K., 1997.

Furlough, Ellen. "Making Mass Vacations: Tourism and Consumer Culture in France, 1930s to 1970s" *Comparative Studies in Society and History* 40 (1998): 247–286.

Galerie CGER. *Histoire d'eaux: Stations thermales et balnéaires en Belgique, XVIe–XX siècle.* Exhibition catalog. Brussels, 1987.

Hardy, Dennis, and Colin Ward. *Arcadia for All: The Legacy of a Makeshift Landscape.* London and New York, 1984.

Marshall, J. D., and John K. Walton. *The Lake Counties from 1830 to the Mid-Twentieth Century: A Study in Regional Change.* Manchester, U.K., 1981.

Morgan, Nigel J., and Annette Pritchard. *Power and Politics at the Seaside.* Exeter, U.K., 1999.

Pemble, John. *The Mediterranean Passion: Victorians and Edwardians in the South.* Oxford and New York, 1987.

Pimlott, J. A. R. *The Englishman's Holiday: A Social History.* London, 1957.

Shaw, Gareth, and Allan Williams, eds. *The Rise and Fall of British Coastal Resorts: Cultural and Economic Perspectives.* London and New York, 1997.

Shields, Rob. *Places on the Margin: Alternative Geographies of Modernity.* London, 1991.

Towner, John. *An Historical Geography of Recreation and Tourism in the Western World, 1540–1940.* Chichester, U.K., and New York, 1996.

Travis, John F. *The Rise of the Devon Seaside Resorts 1750–1900.* Exeter, U.K., 1993.

Urbain, Jean-Didier. *Sur la plage: Moeurs et coutumes balnéaires (XIXe–XXe siècles).* Paris, 1996.

Urry, John. *The Tourist Gaze: Leisure and Travel in Contemporary Societies.* London, 1990.

Walton, John K. *Blackpool.* Edinburgh and Lancaster, Pa., 1998.

Walton, John K. *The Blackpool Landlady: A Social History.* Manchester, U.K., 1978.

Walton, John K. *The British Seaside: Holidays and Resorts in the Twentieth Century.* Manchester, U.K., and New York, 2000.

Walton, John K. *The English Seaside Resort: A Social History, 1750–1914.* Leicester, U.K., and New York, 1983.

Walvin, James. *Beside the Seaside: A Social History of the Popular Seaside Holiday.* London, 1978.

Ward, Colin, and Dennis Hardy. *Goodnight Campers!: The History of the British Holiday Camp.* London and New York, 1986.

Wilson, C. *Benidorm: The Truth.* Benidorm, Spain, 1999.

TRAVEL AND TOURISM

Stephen L. Harp

Until the late twentieth century the history of travel and tourism was not a serious subject for historical inquiry. Before the advent of social history, political historians duly noted where decisions and pronouncements were made, and the place of leisure travel became obvious in retrospect. King William of Prussia had, of course, been taking the waters and enjoying the social scene at Ems when the Ems dispatch was issued in 1870, provoking the French to declare war. General Philippe Pétain's World War II government, Vichy, is named for the southern French spa town that possessed abundant hotel rooms to accommodate a government forced out of Paris. Even the emergent field of social history initially left the study of tourism at the margins. Gradually, the careful analysis of workers, peasants, the bourgeoisie, and eventually women, that is, specific social groups, was extended to cover cultural practices besides work. The neglect of travel and tourism has been an unfortunate missed opportunity. The history of travel and the increasing participation in leisure travel of various social groups reveals the degree to which those groups used it to set themselves off from others and thus to construct, mentally and materially, differences of class and gender as "natural" social divides. In modern Europe travel was as much a defining characteristic of social position as the work with which it was so often contrasted.

EMERGENCE OF THE GRAND TOUR

Europeans, particularly but not exclusively social and political elites, had long traveled for purposes of trade, migration, and warfare. In the Middle Ages religious pilgrimage, such as the physical journey to Santiago de Compostela in Spain and other sites, mirrored the spiritual journey of the pilgrim. During the Renaissance, as artists and writers in northern Europe placed yet more emphasis on their classical forebears, trips to the sites of ancient Rome were in many respects a secular form of this ongoing cultural enrichment. Although such travel affected a very small number of

Europeans, it served as an important precedent in that it gave excursions to Italy a certain cultural imprimatur useful within upper circles of northern European society.

In the seventeenth and especially eighteenth centuries, aristocratic and wealthy British families increasingly sent their sons on a Grand Tour of Europe. Experiencing a Grand Tour set a young Englishman apart from his contemporaries, not to mention his social inferiors. For the growing upper-middle class, a tour of classical ruins was construed as cultural training not unlike attending university. Lasting for several months, a tour usually included Paris and other major European capitals and was almost always dominated by the Italian cities. Despite intermittent political conflict and religious differences between France and Britain in the eighteenth century, the political and military importance of France, a cause of its linguistic and cultural importance in ancien régime Europe, made Paris and Versailles necessary stops. On the Italian Peninsula, Venice, Florence, Rome (including the digs at Pompei), and sometimes Naples were must-sees, and Genoa and Turin usually figured as stopping points en route from the Alpine crossing to the south. Although young and sometimes older men, and more rarely women, from other European countries also made the journey to Italy—among them Johann Wolfgang von Goethe—contemporary reports point out that the British, bankrolled by profits from growing trade, were the most likely to go on tour. Art collections, architecture, classical ruins, and brothels apparently were the main attractions.

Dominated by the wealthy and the noble, the Grand Tour in the eighteenth century was in many respects personal, and connections governed access. Before the French Revolution collections of European paintings were in private residences, not museums, so letters of introduction were often necessary to gain admittance. The opportunity to meet the leading writers of the eighteenth century depended as well on admittance to a salon or the granting of a private audience. As a young man on tour, James Boswell, a

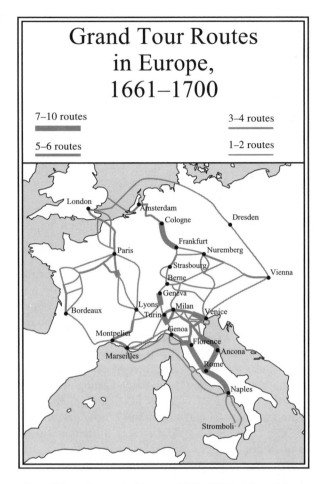

Grand Tour Routes in Europe, 1661–1700

7–10 routes

5–6 routes

3–4 routes

1–2 routes

London
Amsterdam
Cologne
Dresden
Frankfurt
Paris
Nuremberg
Strasbourg
Berne
Vienna
Geneva
Lyons
Milan
Bordeaux
Turin
Venice
Genoa
Montpelier
Florence
Marseilles
Ancona
Rome
Naples
Stromboli

Grand Tour Routes in Europe, 1661–1700. Adapted from John Towner, *An Historical Geography of Recreation and Tourism in the Western World, 1540–1940* (Chichester and New York: John Wiley, 1996), page 108.

the Grand Tour bestowed a relatively exclusive social distinction on travelers when they returned home.

The French Revolution and the Napoleonic Wars interrupted travel, particularly by the British, until 1815. In the nineteenth century the idea of the Grand Tour remained an important image as the numbers of Europeans with the time and financial resources to travel grew. Napoleon's road building across France and through the Alps facilitated access and reduced travel times. Following the example of the Louvre, which became public during the French Revolution, museums opened their doors. The populations that could afford to tour grew. The number of traveling women, escorted by family members, servants, and friends in addition to husbands and fathers, steadily increased. In fact the growing ranks of the bourgeoisie coincided with longer tours by women, sometimes joined for parts of the trip by husbands, fathers, and brothers otherwise practicing their trades.

Both evolving aesthetics and accessibility changed the destinations and the perceptions of early-nineteenth-century tourists. Whereas the agricultural productivity of plains had been of some interest to earlier tourists, who considered their trips an education in economics as well as art, in the late eighteenth and early nineteenth centuries literary and artistic interest in romanticism brought seascapes and mountains into the

The Grand Tour. *Englishmen Viewing Pictures on the Grand Tour* by Thomas Rowlandson (1756–1827); ink on paper, c. 1790. PRIVATE COLLECTION/THE BRIDGEMAN ART LIBRARY

lawyer and later the biographer of Samuel Johnson, obtained audiences with leading European literary lights, including Jean-Jacques Rousseau and Voltaire, as well as the royalty and nobility of Europe by judiciously using letters of introduction from other important personages (Withey, 1997).

Logistical difficulties precluded large numbers of people from going on tour in the eighteenth century. Even the aristocracy and the emerging upper middle class had estates to manage and professions to practice. While it is true that in the eighteenth century well-developed roads and reliable coach service were available, particularly in France, a Grand Tour still required months of travel. The costs in transportation, accommodation, and time were substantial. The highest estimates are that at most 15,000 to 20,000 Britons—less than 1 percent of the total population—went abroad each year in the mid-eighteenth century (Towner, 1996). Never involving many Europeans,

forefront of interesting sights in many tourists' estimations. The Alps, long considered a mere untamed obstacle en route to Italy, became a destination in their own right and an important stop on many a Grand Tour. Mountain climbing for the few and hiking for the many became primary attractions. In Italy romantic sensibilities led to interest in Gothic cathedrals along with the classical monuments. Gothic cathedrals in France and the German states became destinations rather than examples of medieval backwardness before the Renaissance. In the nineteenth century the few travelers to Greece, which became more accessible after its independence from the Ottoman Empire, were in search of classical ruins overrun by vegetation and partially destroyed by time. Lord Byron's poetry was an obvious inspiration. During the period 1792–1815, the heyday of early romanticism, the British Lake District so dear to William Wordsworth became a primary alternative for wealthy British tourists unable to tour the Continent. With a volume of Wordsworth in hand, visitors sought the uncontrolled nature he described. Ironically, in a pattern that became familiar to twentieth-century tourism. Wordsworth's descriptions of such places led to their exploitation as tourist sights; travelers in search of a wild nature undisturbed by human presence were met with people just like themselves.

TAKING THE WATERS: SPAS AND SEASIDES

In the seventeenth and eighteenth centuries, the British and then the continental European aristocracy and bourgeoisie "discovered" both the spa and the seaside. In both cases the relatively unfettered access to and use of the waters in the old regime ended abruptly as middle-class usage grew in the early nineteenth century. Bourgeois notions of social propriety and medical doctors' attempts to assert their professional credentials led to the strict regulation of bathing in both spas and at seaside resorts.

Named for Spa, a well-known spring of mineral water in what came to be known as Belgium after 1830, spas had long existed in Europe. The Romans established baths filled with spring water, and some of those same baths remained in operation throughout the Middle Ages. They attracted local inhabitants and the infirm from farther away long before the aristocracy and then the bourgeoisie began to patronize them in larger numbers in the seventeenth and eighteenth centuries. In Hungary the Roman baths experienced a boom in the eighteenth century (Towner, 1996). Improved roads and coach service made baths across

Europe more accessible, and towns such as Bath in western England, Vichy in south-central France, and Baden-Baden in the southwestern German state of Baden became important destinations.

Into the eighteenth century baths remained large pools in the open air, situated within the towns and open without charge to all who wished to bathe. Although only scattered evidence has survived, it appears that in the early modern period bathers of both sexes and from all social groups wore little clothing while frolicking in the baths. Doctors directed patients to take the waters either by drinking from the spring or by bathing, but the amount imbibed and length of bathing time varied greatly, left above all to the discretion of the patient. By the early nineteenth century, however, as bourgeois usage grew dramatically, so too did the expectations for regulation of access. In France the open-air pools largely disappeared, replaced by individual bathing compartments in which a bather

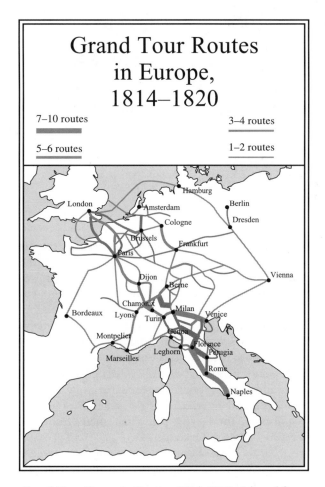

Grand Tour Routes in Europe, 1814–1820. Adapted from John Towner, *An Historical Geography of Recreation and Tourism in the Western World, 1540–1940* (Chichester and New York: John Wiley, 1996), page 109.

Tourist Advertising. Travel poster for the spa at Baden-Baden, Germany. BADEN-BADEN MARKETING GMBH

for the body, and individualized boxes for prescribed steam baths. During an average three-week course of treatment, only a minor portion of a patient's time was spent in the bathing pools. Even when patients were in the baths, the length of daily treatments was closely controlled by the spa's staff (Mackaman, 1998).

Social stratification was a defining characteristic of spa towns. Locals worked in the baths, hotels, and the newly organized casinos. In towns such as Vichy and Aix-les-Bains (in the Savoy), service to wealthy travelers was the primary employment for local residents. Those travelers registered their names, addresses, professions, and the number of accompanying servants—all markers of social station in the nineteenth century—before going to the baths for their cures; meanwhile locals lost their earlier, nonmedical access to the baths. Spa employees and larger municipal police forces kept the homeless and begging poor out of the casinos and off the important promenades, where their presence was assumed to damage the appeal of the spa town (Towner, 1996).

After 1750, first in Britain and then on the Continent, the aristocracy and increasingly the bourgeoisie began to flock to the seaside also, spurring the development of resorts. In many parts of Europe, though sources are comparatively scarce, evidence indicates that people swam or played in the waters of the Atlantic and the Mediterranean. Fishermen and local peasants of both sexes apparently took to the water, often without the benefit of clothing. As bourgeois interest in the seaside grew, so too did municipal regulations governing use of the beaches. By the early nineteenth century nude bathing, apparently practiced more by men than women, was banned on most beaches, which also were usually segregated by sex (Corbin, 1994). Although access to the sea remained open to people of all social classes, the primary beachfronts connected to resort towns were largely reserved for wealthy travelers, whose expenditures supported local economies.

Although romantic interest in the sea as untamed nature was not unlike the "discovery" of the Alps, the motivation for travel to the seaside, as in the case of spas, was also medical. For skin and pulmonary ailments, especially tuberculosis, doctors often advised an extended stay on the coast. By the early nineteenth century doctors also began to regulate immersion in seawater, offering careful instructions as to the preparation, duration, and necessary movements during daily bathing sessions.

Doctors and bathers made an important distinction between men and women. While women in particular were prescribed strict guidelines, carried out by attendants at the individual bathing boxes who os-

would not come into contact with anyone but the spa staff. At least in France, the strict separation of the sexes and careful attention to appropriate attire resulted in part from women's complaints of men's behavior at the baths; the institution of new norms of propriety may have resulted as much from women's increased presence as from a desire for social control on the part of the bourgeoisie in general. Nevertheless, segmentation by social class was clearly instituted. The poor and working poor were excluded from many of the baths, and an array of new hospitals for the poor requiring hydrotherapy segregated them from the wealthy bathers (Mackaman, 1998).

In the first half of the eighteenth century, doctors largely controlled access to the baths. In France a patient needed a medical certificate issued by a doctor to enter the waters. Doctors also quickly developed a complement of hydrotherapeutic techniques, including hot and cold pressurized showers, hot mud packs

tensibly preserved female modesty, doctors exercised comparatively little control over men, who customarily treated jumping into the waves as a sort of male rite of passage, a proof of virility. The medical control at the seaside was thus inseparable from a broader social control of women's movements and their bodies in the nineteenth century (Corbin, 1994).

THE RAILROADS AND MIDDLE-CLASS TOURISM IN THE NINETEENTH CENTURY

Although the network of European roads and coach services improved steadily, facilitating tourism among wealthy Europeans in the eighteenth and early nineteenth centuries, railroads allowed faster, considerably cheaper transportation and dramatically increased the number of people who could afford to travel. By the middle of the nineteenth century, middle-class professionals, such as doctors and lawyers, and moderately successful businesspeople could take or send their families on vacation. The middle class could thus enjoy a holiday of travel and use it for social distinction, much as the wealthy bourgeoisie had before the advent of the railroad. Interestingly the greater accessibility made possible by the railroad did not erase social distinctions but rather altered their contours. Just as the railroad had first-class, second-class, third-class, and occasionally fourth-class carriage, tourist destinations changed to accommodate greater social diversity and to satisfy the desire of those who could afford better for social differentiation.

The railroad thus had an ironic effect on established tourist destinations. For example, on the southern coast of England, Brighton had been a favored destination of the English nobility and royalty in the eighteenth century. However, when the railroad connected Brighton to nearby London, the middle and lower middle classes of the city began to make day trips to the seaside town. The royal family and the

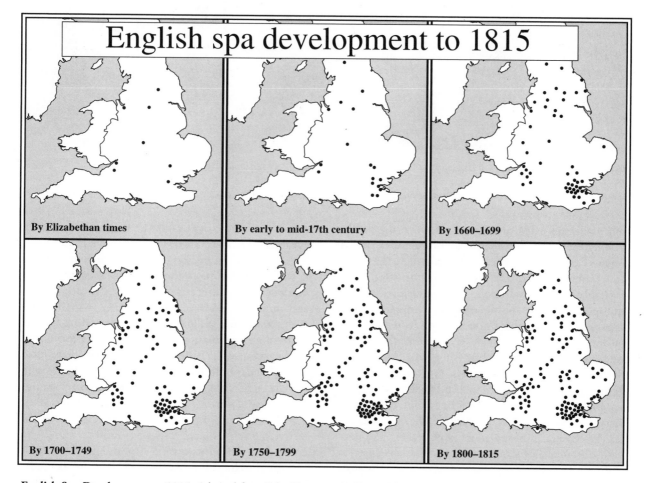

English Spa Development to 1815. Adapted from John Towner, *An Historical Geography of Recreation and Tourism in the Western World, 1540–1940* (Chichester and New York: John Wiley, 1996), page 63.

Bathing Machine. *Bathing at Ramsgate,* engraving (1788) by William Birch after Benjamin West.

social elite relocated their social season to the north, placing themselves outside the logistical and financial reach of these new tourists. In France, where the warm and more desirable seasides were in the south, the railroad made it easy for the wealthy of Paris and of Europe to make a journey that was impractical for those of limited means. Empress Eugénie, wife of Napoleon III of France, made Biarritz on the southwestern French coast a sought-after resort town once the railroad line was established. On the Riviera the French annexation of Nice in 1860 facilitated the development of a French railway line from Paris. Nice expanded rapidly, and in wintertime, the social season on the Riviera, its population exploded as the international social elite swarmed in. The British expatriot community installed a *promenade des Anglais* (English boardwalk), and the Russian nobles in nearby Villefranche successfully argued for improvements in the municipal infrastructure for their use (Haug, 1982). Wealthy Americans also went to Europe in droves.

The convenience and speed of the railroad made it possible for tourists to visit an array of provincial destinations in addition to the northern capital cities and important Italian cities of the Grand Tour and the established spas and seaside resorts. More tourists with more destinations sought information about where to go, what to see, and how to get there most easily. Guidebooks became increasingly widespread in the late eighteenth and early nineteenth centuries. But whereas early guidebooks were very personal accounts, guidebooks in the age of the railroad emphasized objectivity, eventually eliminating authors' subjective comments. Because tourists on land were by midcentury traveling almost exclusively by railroad, guidebooks adopted railway itineraries as their organizational framework. In Britain, John Murray published little red guides to sights and hotels of Europe in a format quickly adopted by Karl Baedeker in Germany (Buzard, 1993). Publishing guides in several European languages covering western, northern, and southern Europe by 1914, Baedeker and his successors built a veritable empire of guidebooks that told tourists where to go and what to see (Koshar, 1998; Hinrichsen, 1988). In France, Adolphe Joanne launched a similar series, published by Hachette, that had a monopolistic control of bookstores in French rail stations. The importance of railway lines in the *Guides-Joanne* was obvious; several guidebooks traced a single line across France, with the first portion covering the journey outward from Paris and the second the trip back to the French capital (Nordman, 1997).

The Murray, Baedeker, and Joanne guidebooks, like their eventual competitors, offered practical information about the quality and prices of hotels, admission prices to museums, train schedules, details about the sights a dutiful tourist should not miss, and even advice about appropriate behavior. In short, the guidebooks attempted to instruct the novice tourist in how to travel. By providing abundant information updated in successive editions, guidebooks took some of the uncertainty out of travel. But arrangements remained entirely in the hands of individual tourists, who needed to negotiate not only with hotels but also with the multitude of train companies within a given country.

For the lower middle class and skilled workers with limited means, less time, and little familiarity with the profusion of train schedules and fares, Thomas Cook offered both greater certainty and moderate prices. A British cabinetmaker and minister, Cook organized his first tour by railroad for workingmen and workingwomen attending a temperance meeting in 1841. In 1851 he negotiated prices with the railroads and lined up accommodations for some 165,000 British men and women who traveled to the see the Great Exhibition in London, accounting for some 3 percent of the visitors (Withey, 1997). By the 1860s, as railroad fares declined within Britain, often obviating the need for his services, Cook focused on tours of the Continent, beginning with Paris (1861), Switzerland (1863), Italy (1864), and Spain (1872) (Towner, 1996; Withey, 1997). Even more visitors used Cook's coupon books for railway travel and hotels, accepting his itinerary but seeing the sights on their own. Travelers' checks, a further reduction of the risks of travel, eventually evolved out of this practice.

In several respects Cook and his competitors opened up touring to social groups that had not traveled in the past. Without abandoning his initial base—usually skilled artisans or lower-middle-class

At the Shore. Bathers at Brighton, England, late nineteenth or early twentieth century.
©BETTMANN/CORBIS

tradespeople on day trips—as the destination increasingly became the Continent, Cook also served a broad spectrum of the middle class, including doctors, lawyers, salaried employees, teachers, and ministers. The last two groups, who had time but limited incomes, were a primary constituency. Although Cook had less luck organizing tours of Britons to the United States, he successfully recruited wealthier Americans seeking the cultural cachet and the social capital that a tour conferred (Levenstein, 1998).

Cook's tour came to embody the increased access to travel in nineteenth-century Europe. As a result those travelers who could afford longer, slower, and more costly trips ridiculed Cook's month-long tours to Europe as offering no time for a real appreciation of the monuments, museums, and landscapes seen in a blur. The perceptions of social distinction shifted. For those of modest means, touring offered status, but for the wealthy, the fact of touring the Continent became less important than in what manner and in whose company (Withey, 1997; Levenstein, 1998).

The most obvious social change among travelers in the nineteenth century was the increased presence of women. Although a few women had done the Grand Tour or taken the waters in the eighteenth century, in the course of the nineteenth century tourism by women unaccompanied by men became standard. The railroads and guidebooks (which were often, as in the case of the Baedeker, downright sexist, even by nineteenth-century standards) facilitated travel and hence travel by women not in the company of men. In Cook's tours both single women and women traveling in groups were more heavily represented than men (Withey, 1997). One reason for this was clearly ease of transport, but another was the broader cultural changes in nineteenth-century Europe. Whereas men had been the primary collectors of art early in the century, women increasingly became connoisseurs of art, music, and culture generally, though the remunerated professions of artist, curator, or academic remained the preserve of men. Bourgeois women's predominance in the church was also a factor. In largely Protestant Britain women took an important role in the temperance movement, sometimes necessitating travel by train, and in Catholic areas women were proportionately better represented in the organized group tours to pilgrimage sites, such as the spring at Lourdes in the Pyrenees Mountains.

By the end of the nineteenth century, growing nationalist and imperialist sentiment, laced with social Darwinism, was also reflected in well-off Europeans' travel. Guidebooks could be quite nationalistic. In the 1860s the Baedeker guides in the German language fervently claimed that the French-held Alsace-Lorraine should in fact be part of united Germany. British guides frequently deplored the supposedly inadequate hygiene on the Continent, especially the absence of toilets flushed with water. In countries with expanding empires, most notably Britain and France, trips to the colonies gained in popularity among the wealthy. Although the numbers remained small, Britons and to a lesser extent other Europeans, very often under the auspices of a Cook's tour down the Nile, traveled to Egypt in search of cultural exoticism. By the 1880s they were reassured by the British protectorate. Britons also went to Palestine to visit the Holy Land. The colonies of Algeria and Morocco were sometimes destinations for the French. While traveling outside Europe, Europeans could congratulate themselves on their own national superiority in having a grander empire than other Europeans and their racial superiority, presumably manifest in the vast material divide between themselves and indigenous peoples.

BICYCLE AND AUTOMOBILE TOURISM IN THE EARLY TWENTIETH CENTURY

While the overwhelming majority of travelers in the early twentieth century continued to use the railroad, technological innovations of the late nineteenth and early twentieth centuries renewed the emphasis on traveling by road as well. In the 1890s the "safety" bicycle with two wheels of the same size became the sporting rage for those rich enough to buy one. In an era when male doctors and commentators attacked the bicycle as a potential agent of the moral corruption and of the loss of virginity among women, with few exceptions these early cyclists were above all wealthy, usually bourgeois men.

In the first decade of the century, the automobile began to rival the bicycle as a sport vehicle, and it quickly became a means of tourist transportation for aristocrats and bourgeois Europeans. The automobile's price and extremely high maintenance costs made it a socially exclusive mode of transportation. (In France in 1901 a single automobile tire, with a projected life of no more than a thousand miles, cost ninety-nine francs. At that time a provincial male laborer earned approximately three francs daily.) An automobile allowed wealthy men, accompanied by women and usually a mechanic-driver, to make long trips, veritable adventures given the unreliability of automobiles as compared to trains.

Both bicycle and especially automobile tourism necessitated an infrastructure eventually provided by local and national authorities. Well-maintained, eventually paved roads with road signs became the subject

Religious Tourism. Pilgrims at Lourdes, France, 1876. ©Bettmann/Corbis

of important lobbying efforts by tourists enamored of the new forms of transport. An array of nonprofit organizations emerged across Europe to advocate the interests of cyclists and then motorists. Inspired by the British Cyclist Touring Club, "touring clubs" funded by members' contributions and often public subsidies worked with local and national governments to provide an infrastructure for all forms of tourism. Cycling received pride of place in the 1890s, when touring clubs frequently organized one-way cycling excursions on Sunday mornings capped off with a large noon dinner; wives and less athletic members joined the group for the meal, and all returned home by train. After 1900 touring clubs, working alongside the more

socially exclusive automobile clubs, also argued for roadway improvements necessary for automobiles.

In several countries the touring clubs, while overwhelmingly bourgeois, were among the largest of associations. The Touring Club de France, founded in 1890, had nearly 100,000 members in 1914 and 400,000 in 1939 (Rauch, 1996). The Touring Club Ciclistico Italiano, founded in 1894, dropped "cycling" from its name in 1900 and grew to 450,000 members in the interwar years (Bosworth, 1997). In various countries the groups fervently embraced a positive notion of progress arguing for greater expenditure of state monies to benefit their bourgeois members' interests in travel by road; they often used strong

Bicyclists. A group of American bicyclists riding through an English village. Illustration from the *Illustrated London News,* 1898. ©HULTON-GETTY/LIAISON AGENCY

nationalist language that became downright virulent during World War I.

Automobile and tire companies also promoted tourism by car. The example of the Michelin Tire Company in France and across Europe is instructive. Beginning in 1900 Michelin produced guidebooks offering advice about tires and a list of mechanics, Mich-

elin dealers, and hotels, first for France but by 1914 for central and western Europe generally. In 1908 Michelin established its own tourist office to provide precise itineraries of the most passable and scenic roads. In 1910 the company began to offer a series of maps of the road network designed for the needs of motorists and provided French towns with free signs so that tourists could figure out which town they were entering. Michelin also joined forces with the Touring Club de France to pressure the French government to number all French roads and place signs along them directing motorists. By the interwar years Michelin produced an array of guidebooks to French regions that assumed readers were traveling by car. Baedeker and other guides altered their own guides to make them useful to motorists as well as to train travelers. While Michelin and other companies catered solely to the bourgeoisie before World War II, after the war their efforts on behalf of the wealthy created an infrastructure for automobile tourism open to the European masses.

MASS TOURISM IN THE TWENTIETH CENTURY

Before the twentieth century workers and peasants, the overwhelming majority of Europeans, traveled very little for pleasure as opposed to work, migration, or army service. Employers, particularly in Britain, began to give lower-level white-collar workers paid vacations in the middle and late nineteenth century. However, the first documented touring by blue-collar workers dates from the 1880s, when textile workers from Lancashire and Yorkshire took the train for day trips to the western coast of England. Blackpool became a favored beach destination as the numbers of both day-trippers and longer-term travelers grew; in 1937 some 7 million tourists visited the town (Cross, 1993).

Across Europe the interwar years saw a significant expansion of working-class tourism, even, in the eyes of some historians, the emergence of mass tourism. In Weimar Germany, paid vacations of up to two weeks slowly expanded to include some industrial workers, and at least some of those workers traveled. The German Social Democratic Party sponsored a series of subsidized tours designed as political and cultural education, and meant to be socialist alternatives to the commercial trips offered by and for the capitalist bourgeoisie. Yet clearly most German workers

---

BATTLEFIELD TOURISM AFTER WORLD WAR I

Just as tourism provides an alternative angle for considering social distinctions in modern Europe, so too it reveals the political context in which it took place. The example of World War I is instructive. As early as 1916, while witnessing the wholesale destruction of the battlefields of northeastern France, advocates for tourism envisaged postwar "pilgrimages" to the battlefields that would redress France's balance of payments with the United States. In cooperation with the Touring Club de France, the Michelin Company in the spring of 1917 introduced the first battlefield guidebook, which was followed by twenty-eight additional volumes by 1921. Michelin became the most important interwar producer of such guides, which had a combined circulation of more than 1.5 million copies.

The guidebooks, designed for French people wealthy enough to have a car in the early 1920s, claimed to tell the "whole history" of the war. Interestingly, they told only the history of the western front and offered no analysis of the network of alliances that erupted in war in 1914. That is, Germany was the clear aggressor; the French government or army had no responsibility in causing the war. Moreover, the guidebooks featured leading French generals with abundant photographs and words of praise, even for those, such as Robert-Georges Nivelle, who were not known for their strengths in the field. Ordinary French foot soldiers received credit for following orders; the mutinies of 1917 were conveniently glossed over. Overall, the guidebooks made it clear that World War I was an inevitable, defensive war won by larger-than-life generals (of the social and political elite) who commanded working-class and peasant soldiers with alacrity. The message for the postwar era was clear: not only were socialist and communist interpretations of the war discredited, but the "natural" leaders in France also survived the war with their credibility intact. The French bourgeoisie, in the form of generals and politicians of centrist and right-wing parties, knew how best to govern France. They could do it successfully if the civilian masses managed to follow orders much as the soldiers had.

did not travel as tourists in the 1920s. Similarly "proletarian tourism," organized and subsidized by the Communist Party, emerged in the newly formed Soviet Union. In France the Popular Front government of 1936, a coalition of socialist, communist, and radical parties, implemented paid two-week holidays for all French workers. Before the outbreak of war in 1939 most French workers did not go on vacation, apparently for lack of money, but the legislation created a fundamental social entitlement. As in most of postwar Europe but in direct contrast with the United States, vacation allowing time for travel became a right of French citizens guaranteed by the state rather than a revocable privilege granted by employers. In 1937 the Communist trade union, the CGT, founded a tourism bureau to facilitate workers' travel (Furlough, 1998).

Fascist states, sensing the popularity of tourism for the masses, claimed to sponsor working-class tourism; but historical evidence indicates that, at least on longer tours, the middle classes were better represented numerically. According to Fascist ideologues in Italy, properly packaged tourism for the people would show Italian masses the geographical, cultural, and historical wonders of their country. But Italian workers could afford the longer-distance "popular trains" for tours, such as to Rome, only when they received subsidies from employers. Local day trips, some under the auspices of the national government, became much more frequent in the 1920s and 1930s among both industrial workers and peasants (de Grazia, 1981). In Germany, Hitler's vast *Kraft durch Freude* (strength through joy) program organized an array of tourist options, including extended train trips and cruises. Much as Nazi propaganda trumpeted workers' participation, actual travelers on the train trips were most often lower-level salaried employees from the private sector. On cruises just over 20 percent of those traveling were workers, despite their much larger proportion of society at large (Keitz, 1997). *Kraft durch Freude* vacations were fundamentally tied to the regime's racial ideology. Trips within Germany were supposed to allow German workers to appreciate the superiority of their racial heritage. Cruises with calls in Scandinavia reminded German tourists of their Aryan origins; posters advertising such tours featured young, blond-haired people wondering at fjords and other natural wonders of the north (Baranowski and Furlough, forthcoming).

After World War II and the penury of the early postwar years, tourism grew to include the European masses. Increased standards of living and paid vacations financed travel across the Continent. In the Soviet Union (for which scholarship on travel and tour-

ism is scant), trips, usually by train, to the resorts of the Black Sea became more frequent. In Western Europe the growth of incomes combined with lower costs of production led to the development of a mass market in automobiles. The German Volkswagen, the French Citroën 2CV, and the Italian Fiat were among the best-known small cars within the financial reach of the vast majority of workers and farmers after the war. As had been the case for wealthy Europeans earlier in the century, the expansion of automobile ownership was strongly linked with tourism. Cars allowed more tourists of modest means to go farther, search for inexpensive accommodations, bring along their own camping gear, and access affordable transportation once they reached the desired destination. In 1964, 65 percent of French tourists took a car on vacation, only 25 percent took the train, and 10 percent took an airplane, bus, or other alternative. Within France, however, those most likely to go on vacation were still overwhelmingly urban; in 1964, 73 percent of Parisians left the city on vacation, whereas only 16 percent of the rural population took traveling vacations. Workers from greater Paris may not have had the means of the bourgeoisie, but they took vacations that rural folk could not or would not undertake (Furlough, 1998).

The European masses very often traveled to the same destinations as did the nineteenth-century bourgeoisie. Tour buses hauled people across European borders to visit the cities and other long-standing tourist sights, and the spas of Europe witnessed a huge influx of new users. In Germany, Bad Reichenhall received 11,320 visitors in 1900, 26,880 in 1939, and 75,287 in 1975. The beaches in resort towns, once reserved primarily for the elite, exploded with new bathers. As in the 1920s, when wealthy Americans flocked to the Riviera during the summer to sun themselves, postwar tourists often spent their summer vacations at the beach. Postwar fascination with youth and the body, created or at least fed by the consumer culture developing at the same time, led to significant changes in social comportment at the beach. The nineteenth-century distinction of social class between the clothed and the unclothed quickly transformed into a divide between the young and the old. While social distinctions by no means disappeared, a new cult of the body changed sartorial norms (at least among those other than Scandinavians and northern Germans, for whom nudity had never become taboo in the first place). Men and boys increasingly wore abbreviated, tight-fitting swim trunks, while women often wore bikinis. Topless and nude beaches proliferated. Interestingly the entrance of the masses at the beach as users rather than servants coincided with the

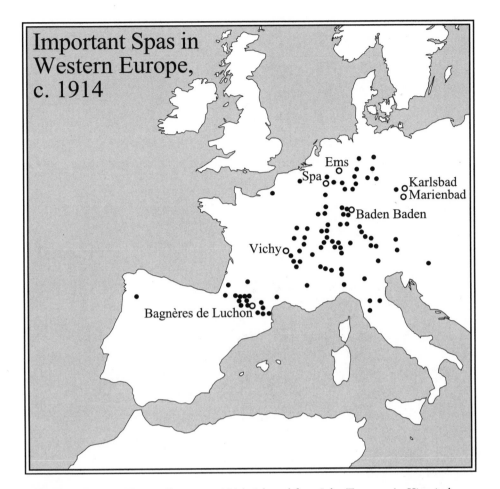

Important Spas in Western Europe, c. 1914. Adapted from John Towner, *An Historical Geography of Recreation and Tourism in the Western World, 1540–1940* (Chichester and New York: John Wiley, 1996), page 55.

erosion of nineteenth-century bourgeois notions of beachfront propriety.

The declining cost of air travel made Europe a popular destination for middle-class Americans and made the world more accessible to middle-class Europeans. For Americans after World War II, as for nineteenth-century Americans on the Grand Tour, a trip to Europe—whatever one actually did there—offered a certain cachet useful at home. Western Europeans traveled less frequently to North America, and a vacation in the United States offered a rather different form of social distinction at home. Although in the late 1950s and 1960s European countries lost many of the colonies that had been elite tourist destinations in the heyday of the empires, resorts in former colonies offered a sort of neocolonialism, in which Europeans could be pampered by non-Europeans while enjoying exotic sights and sounds. The French firm Club Méditerranée was an early sponsor of such non-Western tourism in its creation of exotic villages

in Polynesia and other warm locales. In a sign of the times, Club Med purported to erase social distinctions among participants by mandating the use of first names and the informal second-person *tu* rather than the formal *vous,* as well as by discouraging mention of participants' professions or social standings in "civilization." Paradoxically, the new equal Europeans, almost always white, were served in the villages by local people of color who desperately needed work because of their countries' impoverished economies (Furlough, 1993).

CONCLUSION: TRAVEL, TOURISM, AND SOCIAL DISTINCTIONS

Before the 1790s, when the term "tourist," derived from the French term *tour* (trip), first emerged in the English language, "traveler" was the primary designation for one engaged in leisure travel. In the course

On the Beach. The beach at Odessa, Ukrainian SSR, 1987. JANET WISHNETSKY/©CORBIS

of the nineteenth century, most European languages acquired a term equivalent to the English "tourist," and tourists and social observers since then have often distinguished between "travelers" and "tourists." Late-nineteenth-century "travelers" condemned Cook's "tourists" as superficial. "Travelers" supposedly appreciated what they saw and experienced, whereas "tourists" completed a list of things that needed to be seen.

Until the late twentieth century, historians and other writers often accepted the distinction at face value. Daniel Boorstin, Paul Fussell, and André Siegfried, though by no means isolated examples, have been most articulate in stressing the difference between the old bourgeois, aristocratic, educated travelers and the twentieth-century hordes who supposedly understood little besides how to have a good time.

By using the terms interchangeably, this essay has implicitly argued that no objective difference exists between "travelers" and "tourists." Clearly the wealthy young British men on the Grand Tour of Europe were as interested in pleasure as in art and ideas. The historian Harvey Levenstein showed that many middle-class travelers in the nineteenth century, even Cook's tourists, were far more interested in European art and architecture—which also offered them the possibility of a sort of cultural capital upon returning home—than were the fabulously wealthy who spent much of their time simply enjoying themselves in the company of their compatriots. In short, the distinction between travelers and tourists, like the distinctions that post–World War II tourists often made between themselves and other, presumably less-knowledgeable and culturally sensitive tourists, are not "real," measurable differences. That does not mean, of course, that they were any less important to contemporaries.

From the early modern era on, social distinctions made between those who could and those who could not afford to take the tour, take the waters in a spa, or go to the beach mirrored the social segmentation of European society as a whole. The prescribed roles for women and men further reflected widespread—and from a later perspective erroneous—assumptions about the "natural" differences between the sexes. Consequently the history of tourism, like other aspects of life that may at first appear somewhat superficial, provides an opportunity to consider social history more generally. Moreover, as social history has intertwined with cultural history, historians have maintained that the "real" social distinctions within Europe resulted in large part from their being seen as real by contemporaries. Tourism, one of many means by which people drew distinctions between themselves and others, provides a glimpse at how the hierarchies that long characterized European society evolved over time.

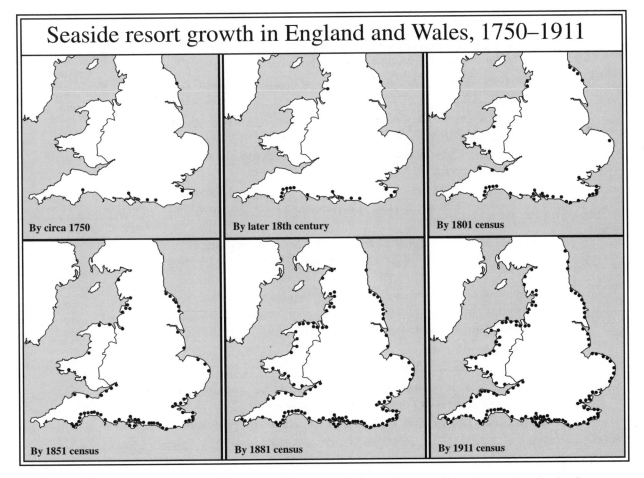

Seaside resort growth in England and Wales, 1750–1911

By circa 1750

By later 18th century

By 1801 census

By 1851 census

By 1881 census

By 1911 census

Seaside Resort Growth in England and Wales, 1750–1911. Adapted from John Towner, *An Historical Geography of Recreation and Tourism in the Western World, 1540–1940* (Chichester and New York: John Wiley, 1996), page 179.

See also **Explorers, Missionaries, Traders** *(volume 1);* **Migration** *(volume 2); and other articles in this section.*

BIBLIOGRAPHY

Baranowski, Shelley O., and Ellen Furlough, eds. *Being Elsewhere: Tourism, Consumer Culture, and Identity in Modern Europe and North America.* Ann Arbor, Mich., forthcoming.

Bernard, Paul P. *Rush to the Alps: The Evolution of Vacationing in Switzerland.* Boulder, Colo., 1978.

Bertho Lavenir, Catherine. "Normes de comportement et contrôle de l'espace: Le Touring Club de Belgique avant 1914." *Mouvement Social* 178 (1997): 69–87.

Bertho Lavenir, Catherine. *La roue et le stylo: Comment nous sommes devenus touristes.* Paris, 1999.

Boorstin, Daniel J. *The Image: A Guide to Pseudo-Events in America.* New York, 1987.

Bosworth, R. J. B. "The Touring Club Italiano and the Nationalization of the Italian Bourgeoisie." *European History Quarterly* 27, no. 3 (July 1997): 371–410.

Buzard, James. *The Beaten Track: European Tourism, Literature, and the Ways to Culture, 1800–1918.* New York, 1993.

Corbin, Alain. *L'avènement des loisirs, 1850–1960.* Paris, 1995.

Corbin, Alain. *The Lure of the Sea: The Discovery of the Seaside in the Western World, 1750–1840.* Translated by Jocelyn Phelps. Berkeley, Calif., 1994.

Cross, Gary. *Time and Money: The Making of Consumer Culture.* London and New York, 1993.

De Grazia, Victoria. *The Culture of Consent: Mass Organization of Leisure in Fascist Italy.* Cambridge, U.K., 1981.

Eisner, Robert. *Travelers to an Antique Land: The History and Literature of Travel to Greece.* Ann Arbor, Mich., 1991.

Furlough, Ellen. "Making Mass Vacations: Tourism and Consumer Culture in France, 1930s to 1970s." *Comparative Studies in Society and History* 40 (1998): 247–286.

Furlough, Ellen. "Packaging Pleasures: Club Méditerranée and French Consumer Culture, 1950–1968." *French Historical Studies* 18, no. 1 (spring 1993): 65–81.

Fussell, Paul. *Abroad: British Literary Traveling between the Wars.* New York, 1980.

Goethe, Johann Wolfgang von. *The Flight to Italy: Diary and Selected Letters.* Edited and translated by T. J. Reed. New York, 1999.

Grewal, Inderpal. *Home and Harem: Nation, Gender, Empire, and Cultures of Travel.* Durham, N.C., 1996.

Harp, Stephen L. *Marketing Michelin: Advertising and National Culture in Twentieth-Century France.* Baltimore, forthcoming.

Harris, Ruth. *Lourdes: Body and Spirit in the Secular Age.* New York, 1999.

Haug, C. James. *Leisure and Urbanism in Nineteenth-Century Nice.* Lawrence, Kans., 1982.

Hinrichsen, Alex W. *Baedeker-Katalog: Verzeichnis aller Baedeker-Reiseführer von 1832–1987.* Holzminden, Germany, 1988.

Keitz, Christine. *Reisen als Leitbild: Die Entstehung des modernen Massentourismus in Deutschland.* Munich, 1997.

Koshar, Rudy. " 'What Ought to Be Seen': Tourists' Guidebooks and National Identities in Modern Germany and Europe." *Journal of Contemporary History* 33, no. 3 (1998): 323–340.

Leed, Eric J. *The Mind of the Traveler: From Gilgamesh to Global Tourism.* New York, 1991.

Levenstein, Harvey. *Seductive Journey: American Tourists in France from Jefferson to the Jazz Age.* Chicago, 1998.

Lloyd, David W. *Battlefield Tourism: Pilgrimage and Commemoration of the Great War in Britain, Australia, and Canada, 1919–1939.* New York, 1998.

Löfgren, Orvar. *On Holiday: A History of Vacationing.* Berkeley, Calif., 1999.

MacCannell, Dean. *The Tourist: A New Theory of the Leisure Class.* New York, 1976.

Mackaman, Douglas Peter. *Leisure Settings: Bourgeois Culture, Medicine, and the Spa in Modern France.* Chicago, 1998.

Nordman, Daniel. "Les *Guides-Joanne.*" In *Lieux de mémoire.* Edited by Pierre Nora. Vol. 2. Paris, 1997. Pages 529–567.

Pemble, John. *The Mediterranean Passion: Victorians and Edwardians in the South.* Oxford, 1987.

Rauch, André. *Vacances en France: De 1830 à nos jours.* Paris, 1996.

Rauch, André. *Vacances et pratiques corporelles: La naissances des morales du dépaysement.* Paris, 1988.

Siegfried, André. *Aspects du XXe siècle.* Paris, 1955.

Swinglehurst, Edmund. *Cook's Tours: The Story of Popular Travel.* Poole, U.K., 1982.

Tissot, Laurent. "How Did the British Conquer Switzerland? Guidebooks, Railways, Travel Agencies, 1850–1914." *Journal of the History of Transport* 8, no. 1 (March 1995): 21–54.

Towner, John. *An Historical Geography of Recreation and Tourism in the Western World, 1540–1940.* Chichester, U.K., and New York, 1996.

Urry, John. *The Tourist Gaze.* London, 1990.

Walton, John K. *The English Seaside Resort: A Social History, 1750–1914.* Leicester, U.K., and New York, 1983.

Walton, John K. "Taking the History of Tourism Seriously." *European History Quarterly* 27, no. 4 (1997): 563–571.

Withey, Lynne. *Grand Tours and Cook's Tours: A History of Leisure Travel, 1750 to 1915.* New York, 1997.

Young, Patrick. "The Consumer as National Subject: Bourgeois Tourism in the French Third Republic, 1890–1914." Ph.D. diss., Columbia University, 1999.

Section 21

RELIGION

Belief and Popular Religion   249
Keith P. Luria

Church and Society   263
Andrew E. Barnes

Judaism   275
Jay R. Berkovitz

Catholicism   287
Keith P. Luria

Protestantism   301
Andrew Pettegree

Eastern Orthodoxy   313
Gregory L. Freeze

BELIEF AND POPULAR RELIGION

Keith P. Luria

Social historians have found their best approach to understanding the cultural lives of Europe's vast majority in the study of popular religion. Their interest in the subject derives from various sources. One was the influence of Durkheimian sociology, which considered religion an inherent part of society's self-perception rather than a spiritual, otherworldly phenomenon. Another was the development beginning in the 1930s of a quantitative sociology of religion, pioneered in France by the work of Gabriel Le Bras. Concerned with the causes and extent of modern dechristianization, sociologists sought to measure the depth and character of religious commitment by counting repetitive, ritual actions. Antonio Gramsci's writings contributed by sparking interest in the culture of subaltern classes, and the impact of marxist historiography and the French *Annales* school of social history focused historians' attention on the activities of people who were not part of the elite. The work of cultural anthropologists on the religious activities of "primitive" peoples also inspired historians, as an ethnographic approach seemed readily applicable to the study of the supposedly "primitive" people of Europe's past. In addition to cultural anthropology and sociology, historians have also borrowed from folklore, literary studies, psychology, and semiotics. Thus the study of popular religion has broadened the methodology of social history as well as its subject material.

While the study of popular religion is a relatively recent concern of social historians, its origins lie in the sixteenth and seventeenth centuries. The religious reformers of that time, such as Desiderius Erasmus or John Calvin, who first singled out the religion of the people for special examination, saw those beliefs and practices as superstition or profanity. They opposed that form of religion to their supposedly more refined or spiritually elevated faith. In so doing early modern Protestant and Catholic critics of customary beliefs and religious practices made a formerly unrecognized distinction between the acceptable and the unacceptable in religious life. They created the realm of religion later called "popular."

Modern social historians have remade the early modern religious reformers' categories. Historians' concerns are not with uprooting superstition but with enlarging the field of religious history beyond the study of church leaders, doctrinal development, or ecclesiastical politics. They study religion as people practiced and understood it, in particular, those people who were not literate and whose beliefs therefore have to be interpreted from their religious behavior. Historians of popular religion have focused on examining rituals, religious organizations, cults of divine figures, and the daily instrumental uses to which people put their religious beliefs.

Even if modern historians have not shared the reforming goals of early modern clerics, all too often they have adopted those reformers' division of religion into that which was elite, official, and focused on spiritual concerns and that which was popular, unofficial, and preoccupied with this-worldly matters, such as illness or poverty. Not all historians have treated popular religion thus defined in a negative manner. For some it represents an organic cultural formation resistant to repressive churches and states, though inevitably fated to disappear under their combined weight. Others, however, have perceived the historical bifurcation in terms that oppose a true elite religion to a popular one based on irrational or essentially non-Christian beliefs.

PROBLEMS WITH THE ELITE-POPULAR MODEL

The bipartite division of religion into elite and popular has shown that the religious past is far richer and more complex than a focus on ecclesiastical institutions and doctrines can reveal. But the dichotomous model also poses problems. For one, it has led European historians to concentrate primarily on popular religion within Catholicism, since, it is assumed, a rationalized or deritualized Protestantism eliminated popular religious customs and practices. Although

Participation in Religious Observances. Procession during a *pardon* (Breton festival in honor of a local saint) at the chapel of Ste.-Anne-la-Palud, Brittany (France). ©J. DUPONT/ EXPLORER, PARIS

Keith Thomas's classic *Religion and the Decline of Magic* (1971) demonstrates the contrary for England and studies of Germany have shown the persistence of popular beliefs among Protestants there, historians of Protestantism generally have been slower than those of Catholicism to realize that Protestant churches also contended with unofficial beliefs and practices, which were not always just Catholic survivals.

Second, the elite-popular schema characterizes popular religion as the cultural expression of only certain social groups—the lower orders, the illiterate, or the unsophisticated. While historical work of the last decades of the twentieth century has shown that social differences are undoubtedly important in understanding religious variety and change, distinct religious styles are not assignable to specific social levels or groups. Much of the European Catholic elite participated in the religious practices later considered popular, such as festivals, confraternities, processions, and pilgrimages. Just like their social inferiors, they flocked to shrines and asked saints for divine protection or miraculous cures. People of all social levels, from royalty to peasants, as well as both clergy and laity participated in such practices. Scholars cannot simply categorize one form of religion as spiritual and the other as instrumental. People of the lower social orders have not seen religion just as a resource for solving mundane problems. For peasants, artisans, and industrial workers religion also has been an expression of their deepest ethical and spiritual concerns. Indeed they often have seen themselves as the guardians of true religion in opposition to a clergy they may mistrust or reformers who seem to be undermining the traditional basis of the faith.

Drawing too strict a line between the religious attitudes of the elite and those of the people risks turning those people into passive observers in the remaking of their religious lives. Religious change has always been a two-way street. People adopted new ideas and practices from the church but adapted them to their own purposes. The church adopted religious innovations from below, for example, in new shrines and saints' cults, and adapted them to its aims. The church was no monolith. Religious orders, for example, could vary in their responses to official policies and popular initiatives. Rather than establish artificial boundaries between artificial groups, it is better to assess religious variation and change by recognizing widespread religious creativity and the multiplicity of meanings that widely shared religious practices could have for those who participated in them.

CLERICAL CONTROL AND LAY AUTONOMY

The elite-popular model has often misconstrued the Catholic Church's attitude toward the people's religion, seeing it from the Counter-Reformation on as only repressive. However, the church has never opposed all the purposes to which people put religion, nor has it ever mounted an all-out attack on popular religion. Catholic reformers wanted to establish more clerical discipline over observances such as confraternity celebrations, processions, pilgrimages, and saints' day festivities, which they felt were too independent of priestly surveillance. They sought to bring greater decorum and uniformity to religious observances, and they wanted to instill in the faithful a greater understanding of doctrine as well as a spirituality that emphasized individualized examination of conscience over collective activities.

Summarizing the church's program in these bold terms, however, can exaggerate the desire of clerics to rid religious observance of many elements that were central to it and not in any way contrary to proper doctrine. It also ignores historical variations in the church's attitude toward popular beliefs. The reform program took shape and bishops first put it into action during the sixteenth and seventeenth centuries. But many of the new rituals and devotions that the church promoted at that time did more to revitalize than to undermine popular religion, as people across Catholic Europe put them to their own uses. The distance between the clergy's attitudes and people's practices probably grew during the eighteenth century, as Enlightenment rationalism found adherents within the church's hierarchy who were more likely than their predecessors to treat popular beliefs as superstition. Following the French Revolution, however, the church came to embrace many aspects of popular practice, notably great pilgrimage centers such as Lourdes, as a means of rallying the faithful against nineteenth-century liberalism, scientific rationalism, and state encroachment. In the aftermath of the Vatican II Council (1962–1965), many of the faithful felt once again that the church was abandoning practices central to their religious lives. But even this gap between institutional program and popular belief has not always been great, as illustrated by Pope John Paul II's devotion, after his survival of an assassination attempt, to the miraculous shrine at Fátima in Portugal.

Just as the church's response to the people's religion is complicated, so too is the people's response to the institution and its clergy. Within the doctrinal framework the church has constructed, people seek to order their religious practice creatively in keeping with their own needs and the circumstances of their lives. To do so they often have carved out a sphere of local religious activity over which they can exercise a control, if necessary, independently from the clergy. They might have resisted a Counter-Reformation bishop's

orders to halt devotion to a local saint of questionable official status by continuing annual processions to that saint's shrine to insure protection of their crops. Or they might have accepted a new cult the bishop was promoting, such as that of a Counter-Reformation saint like Carlo Borromeo, but honored him not as a figure of ascetic spirituality but as a protector against the plague.

The most striking example of the autonomy of local religious life from clerical supervision occurred in revolutionary France. During the government's dechristianization campaigns of 1793–1794 and 1797–1799, churches were closed, and priests were outlawed, arrested, deported, or forced into exile. Catholic religious life was left without the clergy necessary for its functioning. In certain areas, such as the famous Vendée in western France, these policies provoked counterrevolutionary uprisings and efforts to protect priests and continue worship. But Catholic observances did not die out even in progovernment areas. Instead, in between dechristianization campaigns, worship revived, directed by laypeople. The educated, often local schoolteachers, performed marriages and burials. They led "white masses," which followed much of the traditional form but in which the communion elements were not consecrated because no priests were available to preside over transubstantiation. The worshipers invented rituals to take the consecration's place or left time for private veneration of the host. In a display of autonomy from the church as well as from the government, people resuscitated local saints' cults that the Counter-Reformation clergy had thought suppressed a century before. The activities women led also illustrate the extent of people's religious creativity. They organized saints' festivals, directed processions, and conducted female worship services—all unprecedented leadership roles for women. Local activists were not necessarily opposed to the Revolution. They made direct use of its political repertoire to advance their religious revival. They wrote petitions, organized demonstrations, held votes, and if necessary participated in riots to force authorities to reopen churches or to allow religious observances. Indeed their religious style borrowed much from the Revolution's ideology. It was antihierarchical, egalitarian, activist, and anticlerical or at least nonclerical.

LAY ATTITUDES TOWARD THE CLERGY

The French Revolution was an extraordinary circumstance in which people were forced to create new forms or re-create old forms of religion independently of the church. More often popular religion is constructed by means of a negotiation between the laity and clergy. The church may seek to supervise religious practice and belief, but it must contend with the attitudes of people who do not necessarily feel subordinate to their priests. Scholars often refer to such attitudes as anticlericalism, a distrust of if not an outright rebellion against any attempt by the clergy to control the people's religious life. But depicting the laity's perspective with such a term does not do justice to the variety of attitudes possible or to the way cooperation as much as tension can mark lay-clerical relations. It is undeniable that parishioners have often treated their priests with suspicion. But this feeling is not encountered everywhere, and not everyone shares it.

For example, a gender division is often evident. Scholars of modern European popular religion, especially in Mediterranean areas, have repeatedly described formal religious practice as "feminized." The phenomenon has been noticeable since the French Revolution. Attendance at church has increasingly become a form of female sociability, while men have found theirs elsewhere, such as in the café or in other secular leisure activities. The increased availability of lay education, first for men, and differentiation in gendered patterns of labor, have drawn men away from formal religious practice. Men participating in left-wing politics have resented the church's frequent alliance with conservatism.

Clerical celibacy also provokes suspicion. Are priests not men like any others and therefore unlikely to live up to strict standards of sexual renunciation? If they cannot maintain celibacy, can they be trusted to exercise priestly authority over women? Jokes about the sexual behavior of priests reveal another anxiety. Since priests are not "normal" men, what right do they have to subject men to their clerical control?

But anticlericalism cannot simply be equated with irreligion. That men do not participate in regular, formal church worship does not mean they avoid all religious activity. They might, for example, still participate in parish saints' day celebrations but do so to express religious identification with their community rather than with the institution of the church. Moreover those who express anticlerical attitudes do not necessarily spurn the church's teachings. People have often criticized priests for not living up to the ethical or spiritual standards the church has set. When seventeenth-century Counter-Reformation bishops toured dioceses in their efforts to reform religious life, they were often inundated with villagers' complaints about parish priests who were incompetent or neglectful of their duties. Theirs was a pious anticlericalism. The laity saw themselves as better Christians than

their clergy. People did not reject the necessity of the clergy in a proper religious practice; they wanted better priests. In Spain under Francisco Franco or in Portugal under Antonio Salazar, anticlerical criticism of the clergy targeted priests because of the church's close ties to the conservative political regimes. In the wake of the Vatican II reforms of the 1960s, the clergy in Spain and Portugal tried to distance itself from the repressive states. But priests also tried to reform religious life by suppressing religious practices to which many Iberian villagers remained closely attached. They came under fire for repudiating what many of their parishioners considered true religion. In such a case the anticlerical critique extends to the church as a whole. Can the institution, which has rejected pre–Vatican II rituals, provide the means for a proper and true practice of the faith? This attitude is not mere blind traditionalism. It is deeply influenced by its modern political context. The political freedoms of newly democratic societies, even the religious freedom Vatican II fostered, has encouraged a questioning attitude among the faithful. Such a democratization can lead to doubts even about basic doctrinal understandings of sin, confession, and communion. Priests are no longer among the few with access to education, and mass communication has rendered unnecessary their historical role as intermediaries between villages and the outside world. Their traditional status and influence has been undermined. As people negotiate the form of their religious lives with the church, they can treat their local priests not as authority figures but as functionaries whose role is to serve parishioners and their religious requirements.

RELIGIOUS NEGOTIATIONS

The scope of religion as people practiced it is too vast for a comprehensive description. But examples drawn from works on religious change between early modern and twentieth-century Europe can illustrate two central issues in understanding how people lived their religion, that is, their relations with the sacred and their use of religious practices to construct meaningful collective lives in the face of political, economic, and social changes.

The negotiations between religion as the church prescribed it and religion as people practiced it is best witnessed in the transactions of the faithful with the sacred figures from whom they sought protection, healing, and redemption. People asked for divine aid in churches, chapels, and pilgrimage shrines; at sacred fountains or springs; and through relics, images, festivals, processions, and saints' cults. Catholic reformers have not always felt equally comfortable with all these manifestations of sacrality. The church has tried to exercise supervision over them and to rid them of customs deemed profane or superstitious. Meanwhile the faithful have remade their own religious practices by inventing new sources of sacrality and by appropriating the church's reforms for their own purposes.

The cult of saints was central to all of these practices. Saints took on a variety of meanings within Catholicism. They were advocates before God as patrons of communities, groups, and individuals. In the quest for miracles of healing or protection, they served as intermediaries of divine grace. As moral and spiritual exemplars, they taught people how to live properly. Locally they symbolized the historical identity of villages, cities, regions, or nations. Universally they represented the institution of the church that canonized them. It was precisely their malleability that made them important to Catholics of all social and cultural levels.

In certain respects the cult of saints seems to have changed little over time. In the seventeenth-century diocese of Grenoble in France, villagers venerated Saint Anthony the Hermit at pilgrimage shrines and local chapels for a number of reasons. He was called upon to cure ergotism, to safeguard crops, and to preserve people from the plague. But above all Saint Anthony protected livestock, and he was often depicted with his iconographical symbol of a pig. People prayed to him and left offerings at his chapels seeking divine support for their livelihoods. Twentieth-century Cantabrian villagers in Spain would have recognized these concerns immediately because they too asked Saint Anthony to protect their animals. They said prayers to him and made offerings at his chapels, and no one missed mass on his feast day.

The impression of an unchanging form of worship this example provides can be misleading. While certain elements of the cult of saints have remained largely constant over the centuries, the meanings of the cult have changed as a result of negotiations between the church and its faithful. In the early modern period the church faced criticisms of the cult of saints from both Protestants and its own reformers, who felt that many of the practices and beliefs associated with the cult were too superstitious and were based on misunderstandings of doctrine. Catholic reformers tried to disabuse people of the idea that saints worked miracles themselves rather than mediating God's grace for the petitioners. They targeted disorderly festivities on saints' days and processions to shrines not led by priests. Because many figures of local veneration had never been officially canonized, the church insisted on its prerogative over determining true saints from false

by reforming canonization procedures in the 1630s and 1740s. Ecclesiastical authorities also insisted on more stringent verification of miracles, but the church never repudiated the belief that the faithful could receive them by venerating sacred figures.

Indeed the Counter-Reformation church encouraged the cult of saints through promotion of its own heroes, such as Saints Ignatius of Loyola or Teresa of Avila. It championed cults that fostered Counter-Reformation spirituality, such as that of the Blessed Sacrament, focused on the church's central cultic object, or that of the rosary with its meditative prayers. The church encouraged the honoring of sacred figures shared by all Catholics—Christ, Mary, Anne, Joseph, and the Apostles—as a means of both increasing uniformity in devotional practice and emphasizing the church's institutional authority. The attention the church paid to the cult of saints did nothing to undermine it but rather contributed to its immense renewal. The seventeenth century witnessed a "veritable explosion" of sacrality (Sallmann, 1994, pp. 14, 110) as the church beatified and canonized new saints, while people, encouraged by the church's attention to new holy figures, sought out others the institution did not officially recognize.

In many regions, such as the Castilian diocese of Cuenca, people abandoned old, local, and formerly popular saints for more universally known figures. So Saint Quiteria gave way to Saint Anne, but not just because the church promoted Anne as a member of the Holy Family. People expected her healing powers to be superior to those of the discarded Quiteria. In the mountains of the diocese of Grenoble, Anne protected villagers from avalanches, and along the coasts of the Kingdom of Naples, she looked after sailors and fishermen.

THE VIRGIN MARY AND CENTRALIZATION WITHIN POPULAR RELIGION

The same variability of meaning was evident in the veneration of the Virgin Mary, the church's most successful cult. More chapels were dedicated to her and more vows made to her than to any saint. Mary was the perfect vehicle for the forms of spirituality the Catholic Reform encouraged. But she was also the most capable of divine intercessors, one to whom people could turn for help with all sorts of problems. Much devotion to the Virgin was localized, focused on Mary as tied to a particular city, village, chapel, or shrine. In such places she was named not for doctrines of the church but for the local site at which people

Veneration of the Virgin Mary. Pilgrims trying to touch the shrine of the Virgin Mary as it is carried through the streets of Almonte, Spain, on 12 June 2000. ©AFP/CORBIS

venerated her. These places were sanctified by visions or miracles, and people honored Mary at them because they knew that there she would be especially receptive to their pleas. The national and international pilgrimage shrines to which people flocked were overwhelmingly Marian in their dedications, such as those at Altötting in Bavaria, Wagheusel in the Rhineland, Montserrat in Catalonia, or Guadalupe in Mexico. These shrines flourished because of both the peoples' quest for miracles and the church's efforts in encouraging devotion to Mary.

The church promoted forms of Mary's cult that referred to central doctrinal or spiritual concerns, such as Our Lady of the Conception, Assumption, Incarnation, the Rosary, and in the nineteenth century the Immaculate Conception. In the seventeenth century Our Lady of the Rosary was particularly successful. Parish churches throughout southern France, Spain, southern Italy, and elsewhere had more chapels dedicated to Our Lady of the Rosary than to any other devotion, and they were often associated with rosary confraternities. These groups were well suited to the Counter-Reformation's goals. By means of devotion to Mary, the church encouraged a disciplined form of prayer recitation—praying the rosary—that fostered an interiorized and individualized spirituality. Members of the confraternities said the rosary prayers, confessed and took Communion regularly, and submitted themselves to the clergy's direction. In other respects,

however, the new organizations continued to fulfill the time-honored requirements of local religious life. The rosary devotees celebrated Marian festivals together with processions. They took over the funerary duties of the older confraternities they were supplanting, burying their confraternal brothers and sisters and saying masses for their souls.

Thus rosary confraternities were not simply tools of the Catholic Reformation. People who joined them did so for their own reasons of piety, sociability, and social competition. The local elite families, which established the groups, saw them as expressions of their piety but also as a means of building prestige and exercising their control over their communities' religious activities. Women joined them because they were attracted to rosary-style prayer and Marian devotion but also to promote their families' interests and to gain roles in an important communal institution. Poorer members shared in the religious enthusiasm for the rosary and also sought the groups' charitable aid and assistance for funerals. Even the rosary's devotional practices could be put to other uses. In southern Italy rosary beads became miracle-working objects when touched by holy people, like Jesuit missionaries.

The same mixture of the church's institutional goals with the people's religious and social preoccupations occurred in new, urban, Jesuit congregations or sodalities. These associations were first established in the 1560s, and within two decades a network existed in Catholic cities across the Low Countries, Germany, France, and southern Italy. The Jesuits envisioned the sodalities as the vanguard of a hierarchically ordered and Jesuit-guided Catholic society. The congregations were dedicated to the Virgin, and they inculcated in their members new habits of piety based on individual examination of conscience, Ignatius of Loyola's *Spiritual Exercises* (1548), and frequent confessions. The congregants were expected to lead lives of perfect harmony with their fellows and to set moral examples for their neighbors. They practiced good works assiduously, and they acted as pressure groups, coercing local Protestants to convert and pushing civic authorities to ban carnival celebrations. But like the rosary groups the Jesuit sodalities combined a new style of piety with more traditional confraternal activities. The congregants engaged in urban processions, and they undertook pilgrimages to regional shrines. They were devoted to Mary but also to locally important saints, whom they petitioned for traditional needs, such as healing or good weather.

As thousands joined the new sodalities, which at first included members of both sexes and a range of social groups, the Jesuits came face to face with problems they had not initially considered. Segregated congregations for men of different social groups and for women developed quickly. Nobles did not want to associate with bourgeois members, who in turn did not want to worship with artisans. The Jesuit Society did not want its priests ministering directly to women, and women could not be easily accepted with men into congregations that stressed the brotherly equality of their members. The sodalities came to serve not only the Jesuit program but also the goals of the various groups that belonged to them. Rulers saw them as a means of consolidating power; the nobles and bourgeoisie as a means of gaining prestige within their social circles; and craftspeople as a means of combining religious devotion with artisanal sociability. In other words, those manifestations of Marian piety associated with the church's institutional concerns were not separate from those that grew out of the people's creative social and cultural practices.

This interchange between popular piety and the goals of the church is especially apparent in the most spectacular manifestation of the Marian cult, the nineteenth- and twentieth-century apparitions of the Virgin that led to the development of internationally important pilgrimage shrines. After the eighteenth century, during which few apparitions were reported, and after the church's crisis during the French Revolution, Europe experienced a resurgence in apparitions and visions that continued periodically into the twenty-first century. Indeed as David Blackbourn reported in

Marpingen, thousands of cases occurred from the second half of the nineteenth century through the twentieth (Blackbourn, 1995, p. xxiv). That these have been almost exclusively visions of the Virgin Mary suggests that they were the result not just of popular religious sentiment but also of the church's efforts to promote the Marian cult. Devotion to Mary strengthened during the Counter-Reformation, but in the nineteenth century the church preached the arrival of a Marian age that would precede the Second Coming. Some members of the clergy treated these miraculous occurrences with suspicion if not outright disdain, much as had Catholic reformers of previous centuries. But the church as an institution did not. Although most of the reported apparitions failed to pass the test of ecclesiastical investigation, the church promoted heavily those that did. The enthusiasm for Mary and for her new shrines served the church as a means to rally the faithful to a Catholicism that felt embattled by liberal political ideas and scientific rationalism. Workers' movements, secular education systems, and nonreligious pastimes competed with a church formerly accustomed to dominating European cultural life at higher and lower social levels. In the twentieth century the rise of communism provided a new challenge that shrines were called upon to combat.

That the apparitions and shrines were overwhelmingly Marian in character illustrates the influence of the church's institutional preoccupations over popular piety and also the continuation of a centralizing tendency in devotional life that had started with the Counter-Reformation. The church's message found a receptive audience and combined easily with an already fervent popular devotion to the Virgin. For the visionaries and pilgrims Mary's power was tied to particular locations in local landscapes. At the Lourdes grotto in the French Pyrenees or at the Marpingen sacred spring in the German Saarland, Mary's charisma was strong, and the people who came to venerate her at these spots asked for cures or divine protection in much the same way their ancestors had petitioned saints. Thus the church's official piety was infused with the popular enthusiasm of the thousands of pilgrims who flocked to the new shrines.

The church also sought to shape the meaning of the new apparitions and shrines. In 1847 the two shepherd children who witnessed visions of Mary at La Salette (in the French Alps near Grenoble) carried messages from her criticizing, in a thoroughly traditional way, the religious behavior of local people. Mary said that their sinfulness was responsible for crop failures and food shortages, but the Virgin also sent secret messages, revealed in the 1860s, that criticized the French government's religious policies and urged closer relations between Paris and Rome. It is difficult not to see the hand of the French clergy in shaping this part of the Virgin's message at La Salette. At Lourdes the church's doctrinal interests were even clearer. When Mary appeared to the shepherd girl Bernadette Soubirous in 1858, she announced, "I am the Immaculate Conception." The church had promulgated the doctrine of the Immaculate Conception only four years earlier, and support for it within the church was not universal. The Lourdes visions helped greatly in cementing its acceptance. There too, however, official and popular concerns merged, since the declaration of the Immaculate Conception doctrine was an attempt by the church to promote a cult that would fit with traditional, popular religious sentiment (Kselman, 1983, p. 94).

The nineteenth century's cultural, technical, and commercial developments made possible the wide impact of the visions and the success of the new shrines. Increased literacy provided a vast audience for the reports on the Lourdes miracles and those of other shrines published in widely distributed Catholic periodicals. The construction of national railroad networks brought large numbers of pilgrims from distant areas. The developing travel industry insured that the pilgrims were housed and fed, just as it provided for the growing numbers of visitors to secular tourist attractions. The pilgrimage to a miracle-working shrine, that most ancient of popular religious phenomena, became very much a part of the modern age.

Lourdes's success, in particular, made it the model for Marian apparitions and shrines around Europe. In 1876 three village girls told of seeing the Virgin near a spring in Marpingen in Germany. They had likely heard a great deal about Soubirous and Lourdes from their parish priest and their schoolteacher. The first Marpingen apparitions occurred on the same day as a major celebration at Lourdes, the crowning of a statue of the Virgin, which drew 100,000 pilgrims. As the Marpingen visionaries and the village's adults retold their story, it came to resemble that of Lourdes. When the girls saw the vision a second time, they asked Mary, as one of their parents had instructed them to do, if she was the Immaculate Conception. The "woman in white" replied that she was. As at Lourdes and other shrines, the Virgin ordered the building of a chapel, and miraculous healings started to occur, though here the spring rather than a grotto marked the sacred site. Marpingen quickly drew thousands of pilgrims from throughout Germany. Although the church never formally approved the Marpingen miracles as it had those of Lourdes and La Salette, many thousands visited the site during the rest of the nineteenth century and on into the twentieth.

These and the other new Marian pilgrimage sites were also notably different from early modern shrines in that the visionaries who reported the apparitions were poor children or women and more pilgrims were women than men. Women pilgrims often traveled to the new shrines together, independently of their husbands and priests. The gender imbalance is both a sign of and a contributor to the feminization of modern Catholic religious practice. The role of visionary enabled women and poor children to serve as privileged intermediaries in bringing divine aid to their often sorely distressed or impoverished areas. It brought them enormous public attention and established for them a position of prominence and even community leadership that they otherwise rarely enjoyed.

Despite the preponderance of female visionaries and pilgrims, the Marian shrines were not simply a woman's world. The Virgin was an ambivalent symbol of female religious autonomy and leadership. She was a figure of female power but also one of female submission and chastity. Women could approach her for help with reproductive or marital problems, but men too sought her aid. The initial acceptance of the seers' reports in villages depended considerably on the communities' male notables. Their approval of the visionaries' stories made the apparitions credible to the wider world, and building chapels or organizing communities to receive pilgrims was their responsibility. Critics of shrines were quick to point out that these local men acted as much out of commercial interest as piety, but the two motivations were difficult to separate.

The clergy's participation was also essential to the positive reception of visionaries. Although priests were often more skeptical than enthusiastic about the apparitions, unless they played a role the miracles would never have been widely publicized, and the church would never have approved them. Indeed Pope Pius IX's support for La Salette and Lourdes, his granting of privileges to the shrines, and his belief that the Lourdes apparitions vindicated his promulgation of the Immaculate Conception doctrine did much to insure those shrines' success.

It was precisely the malleability of Mary's meanings that made her shrines so attractive a destination for pilgrims of both sexes and of high as well as low social classes. The political tensions of the nineteenth and twentieth centuries added another level of meaning to the Virgin's appearances, as her shrines became identified not only with the popular religious need for miraculous help and with the church's battle against secularization but also with the programs of political groups. Lourdes quickly became associated with the legitimist Bourbon cause against the Second Empire and later against the Third Republic. Marpingen became a weapon in the battle of German Catholic political parties against their liberal rivals and Otto von Bismarck's *Kulturkampf* (cultural struggle). Visions in the northern Spanish town of Limpias in 1919, not of Mary but of a moving statue of Christ, were publicized as supporting right-wing politicians and as a divine warning against the liberal government.

The shrines also quickly became involved in national rivalries. Lourdes came to be seen as the French national shrine, and French Catholics took pride that Mary had appeared in their country to establish the truth of the Immaculate Conception. After the defeat by Prussia and the crisis of the Commune, thousands gathered there proclaiming Mary a symbol of national regeneration. German Catholics hoped that Marpingen would become a rival to Lourdes. They regretted that the Virgin had not previously appeared in their country but had been seen so frequently in their rivals'. Promoters of the Limpias visions sought to make their site a shrine that would attract Spanish pilgrims who were otherwise flocking over the Pyrenees to Lourdes.

The combination of the popular desire for divine aid, the anxiety over political and economic distress, the interest of political elites in divine approbation, and the church's promotion of the Marian cult to mobilize popular support was also evident in the twentieth-century development of Marian apparitions and pilgrimage centers. The most successful twentieth-century European shrines began with a series of apparitions of the Virgin at Fátima in Portugal in 1917, during a time of war shortages and bread riots. The apparitions were interpreted as a divine criticism of the anticlerical Portuguese government. In the 1950s the Catholic-authoritarian leader Salazar identified his regime with the shrine and promoted it as a bulwark against communism. He sponsored a tour of the shrine's image around the country, and in subsequent years it toured the world. Popes, including John Paul II, also expressed their devotion to the Virgin of Fátima. The fervent anti-Communist Pius XII was particularly attached to Fátima and to the Marian cult more generally. In 1950 he proclaimed the dogma of the Assumption, and he declared 1954, the centenary of the proclamation of the Immaculate Conception, a "Marian year." His enthusiasm sparked new apparitions and miracles. As Lourdes did in the nineteenth century, Fátima became a model for shrines in the twentieth. It spawned numerous subsidiaries around the world that took their names from Fátima, and older Marian shrines sponsored "Fátima Day" pil-

The Grotto at Lourdes. Pilgrims entering the grotto at Lourdes, France, site of apparitions of the Virgin Mary in 1858. ©CARLOS REYES-MANZO/ANDES PRESS AGENCY

grimages to share in the devotion to the Portuguese shrine.

Other appearances of the Virgin closely tracked the most difficult periods of twentieth-century European history. The economic problems of the 1930s led to an outburst of apparitions at Ezquioga in the Spanish Pyrenees (1931) and at Beauraing (1932) and Banneux (1933) in Belgium. In economically depressed regions such as these, people sought the Virgin's help, but the local and international political situations also fed Marian devotion at these sites. The apparitions at Ezquioga occurred following a left-wing election victory. It is possible to see (perhaps it is impossible not to see) the Virgin's appearance in 1933 at fifteen different European locations as linked to the rise of nazism in Germany. The difficulties of the immediate postwar years and the tensions of the cold war led to another resurgence in visions of Mary. Between 1947 and 1954, 112 cases were reported, some outside of Europe, such as at Lipa in the Philippines,

Hierarchy and Laity. The bishop of Leira, Portugal, visits the shrine of Fátima in 1951. Fátima was the site of apparitions of the Virgin Mary in 1917. BERT HARDY/©AFP/CORBIS

but most in Italy, Spain, France, Ireland, Austria, Poland, Romania, and Hungary. As previously, these new visions were given a political meaning. Communism was denounced as a punishment for a lack of faith among Catholics, and stories from the shrines told of former communists converted by the Virgin's ministrations.

In 1961 young girls at San Sebastián de Garabandal in northern Spain claimed to have seen the

Virgin, and over two thousand apparitions were recorded there over the next two years. The church, however, did not officially recognize the visions. In 1964 an Italian woman known as Mama Rosa declared that the Virgin had appeared to her in the sun at San Damiano near Piacenza. The apparitions continued for almost two decades, but the church did not authorize Mama Rosa's visions either. In this instance the church's hostility might have come from a particular tension between the institution and the visionary. Among the conservative messages Mama Rosa conveyed from Mary were criticisms of the church's Vatican II liberal reforms. Presumably, however, the eighty thousand pilgrims who, by the 1980s, arrived each year at Mama Rosa's farmhouse were not attracted by disputes within the church (Nolan and Nolan, 1989, p. 308). Water from a well at the sacred site has reportedly worked miracles of healing. Pilgrims brew dried flowers from the site of the visions with the water, and the concoction is said to make an especially effective cure. The same might be said for Fátima or any of the other modern shrines, both those few the church has approved and the many more the church has not. People do not come to them just because the apparitions have been interpreted in ways that offer solace from political strife. Likewise they do not come only because the Virgin assures them of refuge in a world and a church that seem to have left old religious certainties behind. They travel to shrines for much the same reason that Catholics have for centuries, seeking divine help with the perplexing if mundane problems of life.

This mixture of motivations remained true in spectacular manifestations of the Marian cult's popularity in the late twentieth century. In 1981 six youngsters reported visions of the Virgin near the village of Medjugorje in Herzegovina, in an area that Croatia claimed. The apparitions continued into the twenty-first century. In the political context of the former Yugoslavia, the apparitions easily took on an anticommunist connotation. In the ethnically and religiously mixed region, where tensions exploded into war in the 1990s, Medjugorje became a rallying point for the local Croatian Catholic population. Again the clergy's response has been divided, but the heavily publicized apparitions have provoked a popular response similar to that of Lourdes or Fátima. Millions of pilgrims from around the world have visited the site, attracted less by the shrine's role in local political and religious conflicts than by its miracles and the possibility of contact with Mary's divine power.

It is impossible to separate the supposedly "elite" from the supposedly "popular" religious motivations at Medjugorje. The success of shrines and indeed of all collective religious phenomena depends on a combination of impulses shared among a variety of social and cultural groups, including both the laity and the clergy. The meanings of the phenomena are negotiated between the church, with its institutional aims, and the faithful, with their particular purposes. These meanings combine the age-old need for recourse to divine power with more current and often more worldly concerns. It is precisely because of this combination that popular religious belief and practice demand the attention of social historians.

See also other articles in this section.

BIBLIOGRAPHY

Badone, Ellen. "Breton Folklore of Anticlericalism." In *Religious Orthodoxy and Popular Faith in European Society.* Edited by Ellen Badone. Princeton, N.J., 1990. Pages 140–162.

Badone, Ellen, ed. *Religious Orthodoxy and Popular Faith in European Society.* Princeton, N.J., 1990. Useful collection of essays on popular religion in Europe.

Behar, Ruth. "The Struggle for the Church: Popular Anticlericalism and Religiosity in Post-Franco Spain." In *Religious Orthodoxy and Popular Faith in European Society.* Edited by Ellen Badone. Princeton, N.J., 1990. Pages 76–112.

Blackbourn, David. *Marpingen: Apparitions of the Virgin Mary in a Nineteenth-Century German Village.* New York, 1995. Excellent political, cultural, and social study of one Marian shrine and the entire phenomenon of Marian shrines in modern Europe.

Bouland, Fernand. "La religion populaire dans le débat de la pastorale contemporaine." In *La religion populaire dans l'occident chrétien: Approches historiques.* Edited by Bernard Plongeron. Paris, 1976. Pages 27–49.

Brettell, Caroline B. "The Priest and His People: The Contractual Basis for Religious Practice in Rural Portugal." In *Religious Orthodoxy and Popular Faith in*

European Society. Edited by Ellen Badone. Princeton, N.J., 1990. Pages 55–75.

Châtellier, Louis. *The Europe of the Devout: The Catholic Reformation and the Formation of a New Society.* Translated by Jean Birrell. Cambridge, U.K., 1989. Important work on the Counter-Reformation and Jesuit sodalities in early modern Europe.

Christian, William A., Jr. *Apparitions in Late Medieval and Renaissance Spain.* Princeton, N.J., 1981.

Christian, William A., Jr. *Local Religion in Sixteenth-Century Spain.* Princeton, N.J., 1981. Fundamental study of the relation between local religion and centralized Catholicism in early modern Europe.

Christian, William A., Jr. *Moving Crucifixes in Modern Spain.* Princeton, N.J., 1992. A study of apparitions and their political importance in modern Spain.

Davis, Natalie Zemon. "From 'Popular Religion' to Religious Cultures." In *Reformation Europe: A Guide to Research.* Edited by Steven Ozment. St. Louis, Mo., 1982. Pages 321–341.

Davis, Natalie Zemon. "Some Tasks and Themes in the Study of Popular Religion." In *The Pursuit of Holiness in Late Medieval and Renaissance Religion.* Edited by Charles Trinkhaus and Heiko A. Oberman. Leiden, Netherlands, 1974. Pages 307–336. Important critique of the notion of popular religion.

Delumeau, Jean. *Catholicism between Luther and Voltaire: A New View of the Counter-Reformation.* Translated by Jeremy Moiser. London, 1977. Classic but much-challenged work on the triumph of Christianity over an essentially pagan popular religion in early modern Europe.

Delumeau, Jean. *La peur en occident, XIVe–XVIIIe siècles: Une cité assiégée.* Paris, 1978.

Delumeau, Jean. *Sin and Fear: The Emergence of a Western Guilt Culture, 13th–18th Centuries.* Translated by Eric Nicholson. New York, 1990.

Desan, Suzanne. *Reclaiming the Sacred: Lay Religion and Popular Politics in Revolutionary France.* Ithaca, N.Y., 1990. Important account of Catholic religious revival in France during the Revolution.

Durkheim, Émile. *The Elementary Forms of the Religious Life.* Translated by Joseph Ward Swain. New York, 1965.

Forster, Marc R. *The Counter-Reformation in the Villages: Religion and Reform in the Bishopric of Speyer, 1560–1720.* Ithaca, N.Y., 1992.

Gentilcore, David. *From Bishop to Witch: The System of the Sacred in Early Modern Terra d'Otranto.* Manchester, U.K., 1992. A study of saints' cults and healing in southern Italy.

Hsia, R. Po-chia. *The World of Catholic Renewal, 1540–1770.* Cambridge, U.K., 1998. Useful overview of the Counter-Reformation.

http://www.medjugorje.org/medinfo.htm. The Medjugorje pilgrimage information website.

Kselman, Thomas A. *Miracles and Prophecies in Nineteenth-Century France.* New Brunswick, N.J., 1983. A study of the role of pilgrimages in religious and political change in modern France.

Le Bras, Gabriel. *Études de sociologie religieuse.* 2 vols. Paris, 1955–1956. Collection of the work of an important early sociologist of religious practice.

Luria, Keith P. *Territories of Grace: Cultural Change in the Seventeenth-Century Diocese of Grenoble.* Berkeley, Calif., 1991. A study of religious and cultural change in the rural world during the Counter-Reformation.

Muchembled, Robert. *Culture populaire et culture des élites dans la France moderne: XVe–XVIIIe siècles.* Paris, 1978. Argues that elite culture successfully suppressed traditional popular culture during the early modern period.

Nalle, Sara T. *God in La Mancha: Religious Reform and the People of Cuenca, 1500–1650.* Baltimore, 1992. Excellent study of religious change and stagnation in a Spanish diocese.

Nolan, Mary Lee, and Sidney Nolan. *Christian Pilgrimage in Modern Western Europe.* Chapel Hill, N.C., 1989.

Plongeron, Bernard, et al., ed. *La religion populaire dans l'occident chrétien: Approches historiques.* Paris, 1976.

Sallmann, Jean-Michel. *Naples et ses saints à l'âge baroque: 1540–1750.* Paris, 1994. Important study of the cult of saints and changes in the notion of sacrality in early modern Italy.

Soergel, Philip M. *Wondrous in His Saints: Counter-Reformation Propaganda in Bavaria.* Berkeley, Calif., 1993.

Thomas, Keith. *Religion and the Decline of Magic: Studies in Popular Beliefs in Sixteenth and Seventeenth Century England.* London, 1971. Classic study of the disappearance of traditional, magical beliefs and popular culture in Protestant England.

Turner, Victor, and Edith Turner. *Image and Pilgrimage in Christian Culture: Anthropological Perspectives.* New York, 1978.

Vovelle, Michel. *Piété baroque et déchristianisation en Provence au XVIIIe siècle.* Paris, 1973. Study of the process of eighteenth-century dechristianization.

Zimdars-Swartz, Sandra L. *Encountering Mary: From La Salette to Medjugorje.* Princeton, N.J., 1991.

CHURCH AND SOCIETY

Andrew E. Barnes

Change in the relationship between church and society in Europe is best examined by trying to get a sense of why and in what ways the European understanding of the word "church" has changed. From the sixteenth century to the twentieth century, the social face of the Christian church underwent four significant transformations. First, the unitary international church of the Middle Ages gave way to what in the twentieth century was a plurality of national and purely denominational churches. Second, the personality of the clergy became more distinctly pastoral. Third, in most European states religious life came to be centered around the parish church. Fourth, Christian churches implemented and perfected two overlapping strategies for social outreach.

These religious transformations did not take place in a political vacuum. The political face of Europe changed even more radically than did the social face of Christianity during the centuries in question. These political changes in turn shaped the nature of religious change. To recount the transformations in the institutional character of Christian life, it is helpful to think of processes of change that occurred over three time periods, those periods determined by the general thrust of political evolution. During the first period, the Middle Ages (850–1500), national governments were nonexistent or relatively small and weak, with little ability to directly influence the lives of their subjects. The international church was independent of and often antagonistic toward these governments. During the early modern centuries (1500–1800), the centuries of the old regime, national governments grew powerful and successfully asserted their right to regulate every aspect of their subjects' lives. Early modern governments were monarchical and officially Christian, and they used national churches as vehicles through which to monitor and regulate social and cultural behavior. The French Revolution issued in the modern centuries (1800–2000), bringing into existence the "new regime" governments that continued into the twenty-first century. Modern governments were "republican," that is, they were directed by duly elected representative assemblies, and they were "secular," that is, they were officially disassociated from all religious organizations. Modern governments went beyond regulating existing social and cultural behaviors to attempting to instill new ones, an example being patriotic behavior. For this reason modern governments sought to perform many of the functions early modern governments assigned to churches. While national churches no longer received government support, they still functioned as community churches in much the same way that they always had.

THE EMERGENCE OF NATIONAL CHURCHES

Of the four ways in which the social face of Christianity changed, the most important was the multiplication of churches. Until the end of the Middle Ages, Europeans everywhere recognized the authority of the pope in Rome, and in theory if not in practice every church everywhere was understood to be a branch office of a single firm. During the early modern age every European state developed a national church. In the modern era those national churches competed with other Christian denominations as well as other religious creeds for adherents.

The medieval Christian church was recognized by contemporaries as catholic and universal, meaning that they saw it as a single, all-encompassing entity. To a certain extent this image was deceptive. Within the church were many religious orders that had nothing in common except obedience to Rome. Also, as demonstrated in England by the Lollard movement and in Bohemia (Czech Republic) by the Hussite movement, by the end of the Middle Ages it was possible to see, beneath the Latin-speaking hierarchy at the top of the church, the emergence of nationalist clergies concerned with the communication of the gospel in the vernacular.

During the early modern centuries, in the context of the Reformation and the Counter-Reformation,

263

national churches became the order of the day. Protestant churches were explicitly under the authority of territorial rulers, whether the latter were royal, princely, or municipal. These national churches may have followed the reforms of Christian worship mandated by reformers such as Martin Luther, Huldrych Zwingli, or John Calvin, but in every instance, even in Geneva, the city personally reformed by Calvin, eventually ultimate authority in church matters came to rest in the hands of civil governments.

The European states that remained Catholic and went through the Counter-Reformation continued to acknowledge the authority of the pope in Rome, but in these states also control over most aspects of religious life was claimed by state governments. In kingdoms such as France and Spain, royal governments took the initiative in proposing replacements when positions for bishops and abbots became vacant. Royal governments also took over church institutions and made them serve royal purposes. This process is seen most spectacularly in the Spanish monarchy's creation of its own version of the Roman Inquisition. The more important example, however, was the governmental appropriation of parochial institutions discussed below. As for the effort of Rome to direct church reform, this happened on the national level only at the discretion of rulers. The Council of Trent (1545–1563) was the key event of the Counter-Reformation. It produced a series of reform decrees aimed at addressing most of the major complaints about Catholic church practices. Yet these decrees were only officially proclaimed in France, for example, at the discretion of King Louis XIII in 1614.

One legacy of the emergence of national churches was an increase in the readiness of Europeans to demonize their neighbors. The appearance of national churches made the question of spiritual uniformity an important issue for rulers and their peoples, both of which shared two assumptions. One was that social nonconformity was inspired by Satan. The other was that religious beliefs dictated political allegiances; thus subjects who maintained a set of beliefs different from those of the ruler were predisposed toward treason.

The first assumption led to the witch craze of the early modern centuries. During the Middle Ages the Roman Inquisition had been developed to suppress heresy or heterodox religious beliefs, and then had evolved to claim an expertise in the detection and eradication of *maleficarum,* or witchcraft. The medieval Roman Inquisition was an elite, international institution that intervened in local situations with relatively little local support. Still it provided Europeans with a vocabulary for representing those perceived as

The Witch Craze. "Many Poor Women Imprisoned and Hanged for Witches." Anonymous English engraving, seventeenth century. PRIVATE COLLECTION/THE BRIDGEMAN ART LIBRARY

different as a threat to family and state. In early modern Europe local agents both of the government and of the church made use of this vocabulary to explain the threat to the community posed by social deviants. That label might be applied to anyone whose behavior did not conform to communal mores, but sadly it was mostly applied to solitary, poor, and, because of these two conditions, cantankerous old women. The actions of these women, especially when they invoked their rights as members of the community to a share of local charity, triggered social discord, which was understood to anger God. Motivation for such divisive behavior could only come from Satan. In fact the manuals on witch finding that early modern European officials inherited from the Inquisition taught that Satan had launched a campaign to conquer the world and that women were prime recruits for his army. Determined to take the battle to Satan, local officials prosecuted female malcontents with an enthusiasm that occasionally bordered on the maniacal.

The witch craze ended quite abruptly in the second half of the seventeenth century. A variety of developments contributed to its end. Mostly, though, skepticism on the part of government officials about the reality of Satan's conspiracy for world conquest brought the trials to a halt. Beginning in the eighteenth century, belief in witchcraft was dismissed by Europe's educated elite as superstition. Among some of the common folk, however, the belief remained alive into the twenty-first century.

The second shared assumption among the rulers and the ruled led to religious persecution. Just as the medieval Inquisition identified the dangers posed by social diversity, it also identified the dangers posed by cultural diversity. Religious beliefs contrary to those of the state church were heretical. In inquisitorial manuals heresy was a sin of pride that, through its repudiation of the true faith, angered God. For early modern European governments it was equally important that heresy provided a justification for political resistance to authority, even political collaboration with enemy states. The demonization of those who followed another confession or version of Christianity helps explain why, even though from the sixteenth century onward many states had religious minorities who declined to participate in the national church, it took so long for governments to accept or tolerate religious diversity. During the sixteenth and seventeenth centuries most major European states fought wars over religion. Significantly, these wars were treated by contemporaries as both civil wars and wars against foreign aggression. The Peace of Augsburg (1555), which brought an end to the first series of religious wars fought in the Holy Roman Empire (Germany), introduced the political principle that each ruler had the right to dictate the version of Christianity practiced in his or her realm. Wars continued to be fought, but this principle remained the compromise most often adopted at the end of the fighting.

Catholic subjects of Protestant princes could always relocate to a Catholic land, and Protestant subjects of Catholic princes could go to a Protestant land. During the early modern centuries one group of Christians had nowhere to turn. Most early modern Christians accepted the idea that the church and the community were synonymous. Baptism for them was simultaneously the religious act of becoming a Christian and the social act of joining the community. Because it served both these functions, they supported the baptism of babies, even though it was recognized that babies could not consciously embrace Christianity. Believers in adult baptism only, known collectively as Anabaptists, rejected the connection between the church and the community. Anabaptists argued that the only true way to be a Christian was to leave the community and the rest of the world behind, and that only an adult could reach such a decision. Implicit in their arguments was the idea that Christians owed no loyalty to the community or the state. For this reason both Protestant and Catholic governments hunted down Anabaptists and burned them. Anabaptist groups found some refuge in eastern European enclaves. Most, however, found space to thrive and grow only when they moved to North America, where they had a tremendous impact on New World Protestantism.

It was not until most wars over religion ceased, toward the end of the seventeenth century, that the principle of religious toleration, the idea that it was possible for participants in more than one creed to live in the same state, gained political support. It gained support primarily in commercial states, like Britain and the Dutch Republic, where mercantile middle classes exerted real political influence. Even in these states religious toleration was selective. In Britain, for example, Protestant dissenters were permitted to maintain their own churches though they were prohibited from participating in the political process or from attending church schools or national universities. Catholics, or "papists" as they were labeled, continued to suffer persecution.

During the eighteenth century national churches were a favorite target of Enlightenment thinkers, especially French philosophes. They did not so much celebrate toleration as condemn the idea of a national church as chauvinistic. Still they questioned the notion that followers of a creed different from that of the ruler would necessarily be disloyal. In France, during the Revolution, legislation stripped away all civil penalties for worshiping outside the state church. Napoleon and his troops applied the idea of religious toleration implicit in this legislation in all the states they conquered. By the start of the modern age, freedom of religion was regarded by liberal Europeans as a civil liberty that every individual had a right to demand.

Few individuals demanded it, however. The secularization of governments did not prompt religious diversity. Unlike in the New World, where competing Christian churches throve in the same locale, in Europe, with some notable exceptions, the typical pattern of worship remained that of a national church with almost a monopoly of local believers and a group of smaller churches competing on the local social fringe. When national churches were suppressed, such as occurred in states that underwent communist revolutions, all religion was banned. When these communist regimes collapsed at the end of the 1980s, the dominant pattern was reestablished. For the most part government harassment of religious minorities disappeared in Europe in the twentieth century. There were few states, however, where the hold of the national church over the churchgoing population was threatened by competing creeds.

THE TRANSFORMATION OF THE CLERGY

The historian John Bossy has insisted that a distinction be made between "medieval Christianity" on one side of the Reformation and "post-Reformation Protestantism" and "post-Reformation Catholicism" on the other, arguing that the two post-Reformation creeds are discrete religious experiences that emerged from the common core of medieval Christianity. Concerning dogmatic and doctrinal issues, his point is well taken. But from the social, institutional perspective, the involvement of government made the evolutions of both Protestant and Catholic national churches remarkably similar. The Catholic retention of the sacraments and religious orders and the Protestant reliance on the Bible should not camouflage the parallels in institutional development. The national churches created in the sixteenth century were ecclesiastical organizations that were simultaneously government agencies. Their first order of business was ensuring religious orthodoxy; their second was linking local communities with the nation-state; and their third was assisting the state in providing goods and services to local populations. These shared concerns shaped the way both Protestant and Catholic national churches evolved and ensured that they evolved in the same direction.

The similarity is seen most obviously in the second way in which the social, institutional face of Christianity changed. At the close of the Middle Ages, most clerics continued to aspire to the ancient ideals of spiritual athleticism. By the modern age, the clergy had become primarily pastoral in inclination as well as occupation. At the end of the medieval period anger and disillusionment with the behavior of the clergy was widespread in European society. Beginning with the Gregorian reform movement in the eleventh century, the clergy claimed that it was engaged in a spiritual contest from which the laity, that is, all ordinary Christians, were excluded. This idea supported the development of a special set of laws, applicable only to members of the clergy, that placed the clergy outside the authority of royal, princely, and civil courts. Many clerics abused the special status the laws created for them by committing crimes and then invoking clerical privilege to escape punishment. Broad popular skepticism about the commitment of clerics to the spiritual contest in which they were supposedly engaged was fueled by the not uncommon disregard among the clergy for the clerical vow of celibacy.

Medieval Christians recognized two categories of clerics. First was the secular clergy, so called because they lived "in the world" or *saeculum* so as to maintain pastoral care of the laity. Clergy associated with parish churches, such as parish priests and their vicars, and clergy associated with episcopal churches or cathedrals, such as canons, vicar generals, and bishops, were members of the secular clergy. Second was the regular clergy, the clergy who lived according to some rule or order (*regula*). Members of religious orders all lived by a rule and thus were designated as regular clergy. The rule provided followers with a guide or pathway toward spiritual perfection or, to continue the meta-

phor from above, a set of weapons with which to win the spiritual contest in which they were engaged. Monks and nuns all were members of the regular clergy. Friars and members of mendicant or begging orders, such as the Franciscans and the Dominicans, likewise were regulars.

Most of the complaints about clerical behavior were directed at regulars. Members of religious orders made up the majority of the clergy at the end of the Middle Ages. Monasteries dotted the European countryside, and most towns and cities had at least two or three convents. Most of the students who attended universities claimed to be members of religious orders. Many rural monasteries were the major landlords in the vicinity, and their members often maintained a luxurious lifestyle that challenged any notion of sanctity. Inhabitants of urban convents were often notorious for their loose living. Students were perceived by the communities surrounding the universities as overindulged, overprotected hell-raisers, much given to alcohol and prostitution.

Yet many were also disappointed with the secular clergy, particularly the parish clergy who likewise were castigated as immoral and alcoholic but were uneducated. More important, parish clergy were condemned as woefully incompetent and woefully negligent as pastors. The shortcomings of the parish clergy had become obvious as early as the twelfth century, when Europe's first "commercial revolution" had triggered both a rise in population and a clustering of people in towns and cities. These towns and cities needed pastors, but instead of supplying the need with parish clergy, Rome opted instead to create new religious orders such as the Franciscans and the Dominicans.

Both the Protestant Reformation and the Catholic Counter-Reformation sought to regulate the behavior of the regular clergy. Protestant and Catholic reformers differed in their approaches to the problem, however. Protestant reformers responded by suppressing both religious orders and the special set of laws for clerics. Monastic communities were dissolved, and monastic lands were sold. Monks and nuns were sent out into the world to live as ordinary people, and ecclesiastical courts were abolished. Catholic reformers responded in the traditional way of Roman Christianity by supporting the establishment of new religious orders and the reform of old ones. Among the masculine orders the most important new one was the Society of Jesus, better known as the Jesuits, while the most important of the reformed was the Capuchins, who were a reformed branch of the Franciscan order. Among the feminine orders the most important new one was the Daughters of Charity founded by St. Vincent de Paul and St. Louise Marillac, while the most important reformed order was the Carmelites, reformed by the spirituality of St. Teresa of Ávila. These new and reformed religious orders attracted the best and brightest of the individuals drawn to religious life, leaving the older religious orders to decline owing to the lack of new recruits.

More important than the solutions adopted for the problems of decadence among the regular clergy in the long term were the solutions adopted to address the problem of an inadequate supply of pastors. Here Protestant and Catholic reformers followed the same strategy. Seminaries, special schools for training pastors, were set up and made mandatory for men who aspired to the cure of souls, that is, to pastoral authority over laypeople. The training in these seminaries was different. The expectation that Protestant ministers were to marry and live as ordinary citizens oriented Protestant training toward involvement in the civil life of the communities in which Protestant ministers were to serve as pastors. The requirement that Catholic priests remain unmarried and limit their involvement in the personal lives of their parishioners dictated that their training emphasize learning to live in isolation away from social allurements. As the focus of Catholic seminary training suggests, with the insistence that pastors be trained came a determination that they comport themselves in public with probity. In both Protestant and Catholic lands from the sixteenth century onward, clerical social behavior came under greater scrutiny. Church and political officials worked together to identify and remove from office clerics who did not behave according to public expectations.

The reform of the clergy was the greatest and most durable achievement of the sixteenth-century religious reformations. Few significant developments in the evolution of the clergy occurred after that time. In the twentieth century the parish clergy remained the point of contact between the church and the community in both Protestant and Catholic Europe. Other types of clergy did not disappear, but their interactions with the laity declined.

Still a space remained in both Protestantism and Catholicism for clerical evangelists. Pastoral clergy help laypeople maintain and deepen their faith, but they are not as good as evangelists at firing up religious enthusiasm or prompting religious conversions. In both forms of Christianity evangelists stimulated the emergence of fringe movements, sectarian groups among Protestants and new religious orders among Catholics. These groups never succeeded in pulling in more than a minority of the devout laity, but their activities had a ripple effect, enlivening and giving meaning to the faith of ever-broadening circles of laypeople. In Britain this phenomenon was seen in the Methodist break from the Church of England in the eighteenth century and in the Oxford movement in the nineteenth century. An excellent example from the Catholic world is the devotion to the Sacred Heart of Jesus. The devotion first gained a following, primarily among nuns, in the seventeenth century, but it soon became popular among elite women. Initially Rome, skeptical about the theology upon which the devotion was framed, refused the many requests for official acknowledgment of the devotion. In 1720 the future St. Paul of the Cross had a vision in which he saw the Virgin Mary holding a version of the sacred heart. He dedicated his life to preaching the devotion to the Passion of Jesus Christ. In 1741 his male followers were organized into a religious order, the Passionist Fathers, and in 1771 his female followers were organized into a religious order, the Passionist Nuns. In 1765 Pope Clement XIII granted Catholics the right to celebrate the feast of the Sacred Heart.

THE GROWTH OF PARISH-CENTERED CHRISTIANITY

The new pastors needed new churches in which to pastor. The third way in which the social, institutional face of Christianity changed was the vitalization of the parish church and parish life. Medieval Christians did not expect to receive much spiritual edification at their parish churches, and most were not disappointed. The Christian church of the Middle Ages inherited from the Roman Empire an organizational structure that grouped the inhabitants of local communities into parishes and the regional populations in those parishes into dioceses. The official church of the community, the parish church, was where all local Christians were expected to worship and receive spiritual instruction. Even if they worshiped somewhere else, parish members were expected to pay tithes, that is, church dues, at the parish church. Parish priests were responsible for the spiritual salvation of every member of their flocks.

In the Middle Ages parish churches were often decrepit and run down. Behind this sad state of affairs was the economic fact that most of the money from tithes and from land owned by the parish was often claimed by the local landlord, the effective owner and operator of the church, who gave back a portion too small to maintain the church in good repair.

Another factor contributing to the sorry condition of parish churches was that for most medieval Christians the parish church was important solely as

Protestant Worship. Protestant worship service in the Nieuwezijdskapel, Amsterdam, painting (c. 1660) attributed to H. J. van Baden. MUSEUM CARTHARIJINECONVENT, UTRECHT

the location of official rites and rituals. Children were baptized there, families were joined in marriage there, and neighbors were reconciled through the rite of communion there. If they desired a more spiritual religious experience, medieval Christians looked elsewhere, to shrines, to the churches of religious orders, or to the open-air gathering places where revivals were preached.

Both the Reformation and the Counter-Reformation made the renovation of parish churches a top priority, and the involvement of state governments was the key. In Protestant lands churches became explicit extensions of the state. In Catholic lands the connection was more indirect but still present. In both situations the state made parish churches the smallest, most local administrative unit. Thus parish records of births and deaths were a form of census, while government announcements were made from the pulpit on Sunday mornings. Since the church was

an arm of the state, governments measured loyalty by attendance at Sunday services.

The parish church took on more than just political functions. During the early modern centuries it emerged as the first locus of modern Christian communal life. As the strongest, best-constructed local building, the parish church was the place of refuge during war or times of natural disasters. In the moments before or after services on Sunday mornings, official proclamations and news were read out. New devotions and religious ideas usually were introduced locally at the parish. The first schools were usually attached to parish churches, which meant the parish church also was where most people learned to read and write. Paupers came there on feast days to receive handouts, and the plaza or place in front of the church never ceased to be the venue for local markets and festivals. The parish church continued to serve as the locale for rites of passage for parish members.

The high point for the parish church as a social and political institution was probably reached in the eighteenth century, when old regime governments also reached their height. Subsequently the role and influence of the parish church in local communities progressively diminished to the point that the church retained significance only for the faithful. Especially during the nineteenth century, new venues rivaled the place of the parish church in village life. The café appeared, where villagers could get not just coffee, tea, wine, and spirits but information from newspapers and gossip. During the French Revolution the official connection between church and state was dissolved in most nations. Even though the connection was reestablished in most places, in the nineteenth century governments took over more and more of the activities once performed at the parish church. In the twentieth century, most Europeans who still attended church did so at their local parish. The parish remained at the core of the European Christian experience but with minimal impact on the lives of local nonbelievers.

CHRISTIAN SOCIAL OUTREACH

The fourth way in which the institutional face of Christianity changed was less apparent. Two sets of developments progressively shifted the spotlight away from the churches and toward the social and political movements the churches spawned. The social influence of parish churches declined in part because the social services the parishes once provided, that is, health care, education, and poor relief, were taken over by governments. Christian churches perfected these services as vehicles for social outreach. Helping the poor became the preferred way to channel the energies of pious laypeople and also the chief means of keeping the poor within the faith. The government's appropriation of social services forced churches to devise a new strategy for influencing social behavior. The most effective strategy proved to be Christian lobbying organizations.

Social service. During the Middle Ages neither the church nor the state dedicated any funds to social services. Social institutions such as hospitals, schools, and poorhouses existed, but in general they were built by wealthy patrons and maintained by pious lay brotherhoods known as confraternities. As a result the early modern centuries inherited from the Middle Ages a social welfare system based on what would much later be called volunteerism.

The Reformation and Counter-Reformation appropriated the system and changed it in two ways. Both Protestants and Catholics started distinguishing between "deserving" and "undeserving" poor. The deserving were those who demonstrated a willingness to work and fidelity to the local church. In addition both Protestants and Catholics used lay charity to reinforce the authority of the local church. They did so in different ways, but the social impact was the same. Both used funds from lay charity to develop new social service professionals, such as nurses, teachers, and social workers.

Medieval Christians were rewarded with indulgences for their acts of charity. Indulgences were grants from the treasury of spiritual grace maintained by the church that might be applied toward the remission of the spiritual penalties sinners had incurred in the act of sinning, grants popularly misunderstood to offer sinners a way out of spending decades or even centuries in purgatory.

Protestantism rejected the validity of indulgences and shifted the theological focus of acts of charity from the benefit for the soul of the giver to the benefit for the soul of the receiver. Nevertheless, Protestantism integrated the act of giving into parish life. Collections for the parish poor took place after the sermon every Sunday. Church deacons, usually the most prosperous and influential members of the congregation who presumably gave most of the funds for the poor, were entrusted with the task of visiting the houses of the poverty-stricken to distribute the money. Significantly, Protestant congregations also began to pay "visitors of the sick," men with some medical training, to make weekly rounds providing medical advice to the poor. Congregations also came to expect able-bodied poor women to perform nursing duties in exchange for their weekly handouts.

From the point of view of early modern European Christianity, it is difficult to make a distinction between illness and poverty since the two sources of suffering were perceived as different species of the same divine punishment. By the same token it is hard to differentiate between medicine and poor relief. During the early modern age the former had little to do with curing disease. Rather, medicine, like poor relief, was mostly concerned with easing the earthly pain of a heavenly judgment. With these points in mind it is possible to appreciate the office of visitor of the sick as the forerunner to the modern occupation of social worker. "Visitors" did not and could not offer much medical advice, but they could and did serve as intermediaries between the community and the underclass, assessing for the former the poor person's state of health and facilitating for the latter their claims to the goods and services offered by the community. Visitors of the sick investigated and validated claims of illness. Healthy or able-bodied poor people were expected to work to improve their lots. Refusal to work pushed healthy paupers into the undeserving poor category, which cut them off from community charity. Visitors also articulated the needs of those they certified as both poor and sick. Based on their professional expertise, visitors were expected to determine whether the sick poor person needed a greater share of charitable funds, some nursing assistance, or more specialized medical advice. Replace the early modern idea of illness with the twentieth-century notion of indigence and it is possible to view the vistiors' tasks as having become those of the modern social worker.

Catholicism affirmed the validity of indulgences, maintaining charity as an avenue down which sinners might proceed toward spiritual redemption. It also reaffirmed the validity of confraternities as dispensers of social welfare. But the majority of medieval lay confraternities were attached to the churches of the religious orders and thus were extraparochial. The Counter-Reformation confraternities that administered poor relief operated out of parish churches. Further, the funds these confraternities collected went less toward paying for specific acts of charity for specific individuals, such as dowries for local poor girls, and more toward paying for the upkeep of hospitals and schools.

These hospitals and schools were staffed by professionals. While the Protestant churches can be credited with creating the prototype for the social worker, Catholicism provided the models for twentieth-century nurses and teachers. Protestantism offered little spiritual reward for the physically taxing, poorly compensated labors associated with nursing. The Catholic idea of charity, however, imbued such labors with the highest spiritual rewards. Nursing became the vocation of new orders of religious women, of which the Daughters of Charity was the most influential example. While in no way as demanding an occupation as nursing, teaching, especially at the lowest level, was mentally exhausting and rarely well paid. Catholicism made this tedious task a pathway to spiritual perfection. The Society of Jesus was the first and most successful of the teaching orders.

By the middle of the seventeenth century the Christian churches had established intraconnecting networks of social services funded and directed by Christian volunteerism. By the end of that century, however, most governments realized that these networks could not meet the need for social services. Throughout the eighteenth century governments appropriated poor-relief systems, transforming hospitals and workhouses from the hostels and halfway houses they had been under the churches into the forerunners of the modern medical hospital, the modern mental asylum, and the modern prison. The nationalization of school systems occurred in the nineteenth century; governments replaced church schools with state versions of primary and secondary schools. Government control of social work was primarily a twentieth-century development. As governments attempted to provide citizens with social services "from the cradle to the grave," state-trained and state-employed social workers emerged as the point of contact between service providers and service consumers.

Through the twentieth century churches continued to operate their own networks of social services based on the idea of Christian volunteerism. But only practicing Christians used those networks, and they rarely depended on them exclusively. Heirs to the government support that previously went to church hospitals and schools, government institutions provided the bulk of social services in most European states. Their access to the population at large curtailed, churches found themselves battling to retain their social influence. In the struggle to maintain a Christian say over the cultural values communicated in government social institutions, churches discovered that the most effective way to sway government policy was through the mobilization of the Christian portion of the populace. Eventually both Protestant and Catholic churches came to appreciate that lobbying organizations were the most efficient way to mobilize the Christian population.

Lobbying organizations. The Christian lobbying organization had at least two predecessors. Missions—that is, arranged tours of traveling evangelists—were a part of European Christianity from the start. They lost some of their importance during the medieval centuries owing to the sense that the population was already Christianized and thus more in need of pastors than evangelists. Beginning in the early modern centuries, however, missions recaptured much of their importance. Churches depended on itinerant preachers, who moved across the countryside staging revivals, to shore up the faith of portions of the population perceived as leaning toward other confessions or toward religious indifference. Missions also proved the most economical way (in material if not human terms) to introduce Christianity into non-European lands. This last factor further enhanced the importance of missions during the modern centuries. European imperial conquests in Africa and Asia created stiff competition between European churches to promote their version of the creed among the conquered popula-

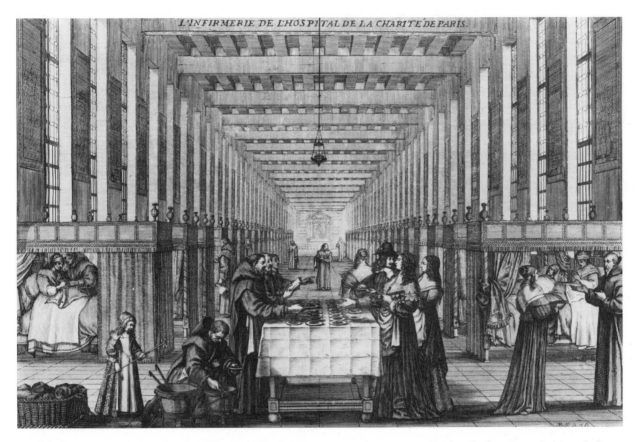

L'INFIRMERIE DE L'HOSPITAL DE LA CHARITE DE PARIS.

Christian Social Outreach. Infirmary of the Daughters of Charity, Paris. Engraving (1635) by Abraham Bosse (1602–1676).

tions. Reliance on missions was not an innovation, however, but a rediscovered means toward an institutional end. The goal of churches in sponsoring missions remained the reinforcement of or creation of a parish church or its equivalent.

The second predecessor was the crusade, a military mobilization of a Christian population with the aim of achieving a religious objective. The Crusades of the eleventh century to the fourteenth century, sponsored by Western Christendom, aimed at freeing Jerusalem from Muslim control. By the start of the thirteenth century crusades also had become a means to force religious change within Europe. In southern France a crusade wiped out a religious heresy. Along the coast of the Baltic Sea a crusade forced the conversion of the non-Christian population. The *reconquista* in Spain, the centuries-long effort to retake the Iberian Peninsula from the Muslims, was a form of crusade. During the sixteenth and seventeenth centuries, the age of religious warfare, many European states witnessed the development of movements that could be characterized as crusades. Masses of armed sectaries moved about, offering their opponents a

choice between (re)conversion to the true faith or death.

The Christian lobbying organizations that emerged from the late eighteenth century onward built on the legacies of these Christian organizational structures, but in one essential way they were different. The earlier organizations were concerned first and foremost with effecting religious change. The new organizations and the political and social movements they fostered sought to realize political agendas through political processes. In a republican age the ambition of these organizations was to influence public opinion, and through public opinion the voting public, and through the voting public government decision making. That these organizations provided practicing Christians with moral vantage points from which to view the secularism of the age is not immaterial. That they made governments reluctant to further curb the activities of Christian social institutions or to place obstacles in the path of Christian evangelical movements is important also. But their prime historical significance was the influence over public policy making they provided to church people.

271

The Company of the Holy Sacrament, a secret network of Catholic elites who promoted the Counter-Reformation in France, may be considered a forerunner of the type of Christian lobbying organization that appeared in the eighteenth century. The actual prototype was the Society for the Abolition of the Slave Trade established at the end of the eighteenth century by the "Clapham sect" of Protestant ministers in London. Using mass meetings, the news media, and church visitations in conjunction with lobbying the British Parliament, the society rallied the Christian population of Britain behind the proposition that slavery was un-Christian. The society persuaded the British government to abolish the slave trade in 1807 and to declare slavery illegal in 1834. It provided a model for cooperation on social issues for Protestant Christians of different denominations. In that sense it was the ancestor of the Protestant ecumenical movement that produced the 1910 World Missionary Conference held in Edinburgh, Scotland, which in turn sired the World Council of Churches, founded in 1948.

Increasingly during the nineteenth century the Catholic Church found itself in conflict with the secular republican governments of the states in which Catholicism was once the state religion. Complicating the conflict was the repudiation by many Catholic clerics of the very idea of a republic. These men and women called for the return of monarchies and rejected the legitimacy of representative government and democratic assemblies. It was only during the pontificate of Pope Leo XIII (1878–1903) that European Catholics embraced the use of lobbying organizations to effect political change. In Germany the Catholic Church fought the *Kulturkampf*, cultural war, with the government of Prince Otto von Bismarck. At issue was the right of government officials to demand expressions of loyalty from members of the clergy. After more than a decade of stalemate, Leo brokered a solution, making significant use of the Catholic Center Party in the German Reichstag as a tool to force favorable terms for the church from the government. Leo pressured French Catholics into acknowledging the legitimacy of republican government, then directed them, through his program of *ralliement* (rallying to the French Third Republic), to the use of lobbying organizations to promote the church's program. These two efforts were only a prelude to his most ambitious initiative, a plan, announced in the papal encyclical *Rerum Novarum* (1891), to build a network of Catholic labor unions and worker's cooperatives to stand as a bulwark against the spread of international socialism. Leo's plan did not yield the desired harvest, but following his pontificate Catholic Europeans used a range of lobbying organizations to influence the political processes in their home societies.

After the end of the early modern age very few of the institutional features of European churches changed. European Christianity remained structured within the context of national churches. The vast majority of Christians experienced their faith at parish churches under the direction of parish priests. Christians wanting to do more than just participate in parish life were directed toward a spectrum of volunteer activities, from helping the poor in Europe to preaching to the unconverted outside Europe to maintaining a Christian influence over government decision making. The social message Christian churches communicated certainly evolved. The language with which the churches communicated their message, like the churches themselves, became nationalized. But the institutional context in which these changes occurred remained constant after the early modern centuries. That the portion of the European population participating in this institutional life was probably lower at the end of the twentieth century than at any other time since the fourth century, when Constantine made Christianity the official religion of the Roman Empire, should not be read as a negative comment upon European churches as institutions. In late-twentieth-century Europe, there were no political penalties and few social and cultural incentives for being a Christian. That so many Europeans continued to embrace that identity is testament to the ongoing appeal of Christianity's doctrines and beliefs and the appeal of the institutional context in which those ideas were shared.

See also **Witchcraft; Charity and Poor Relief: The Modern Period; Charity and Poor Relief: The Early Modern Period** (*volume 3*).

BIBLIOGRAPHY

Bossy, John. *Christianity in the West, 1400–1700.* New York, 1985.

Brady, Thomas A., Jr., Heiko A. Oberman, and James D. Tracy, eds. *Handbook of European History, 1400–1600.* New York, 1994.

Briggs, Robin. *Witches and Neighbors: The Social and Cultural Context of European Witchcraft.* New York, 1996.

Chadwick, Owen. *The Popes and European Revolution.* New York, 1981.

Châtellier, Louis. *The Europe of the Devout.* Translated by Jean Birrell. New York, 1989.

Clasen, Claus Peter. *Anabaptism: A Social History, 1525–1618: Switzerland, Austria, Moravia, South and Central Germany.* Ithaca, N.Y., 1972.

Delumeau, Jean. *Catholicism between Luther and Voltaire: A New View of the Counter-Reformation.* Philadelphia, 1977.

Gibson, Ralph. *A Social History of French Catholicism, 1789–1914.* London and New York, 1989.

Gilchrist, J. *The Church and Economic Activity in the Middle Ages.* New York, 1969.

Grell, Ole Peter, and Andrew Cunningham, eds. *Health Care and Poor Relief in Protestant Europe, 1500–1700.* London and New York, 1997.

Grell, Ole Peter, Andrew Cunningham, and Jon Arrizabalaga, eds. *Health Care and Poor Relief in Counter-Reformation Europe.* London, 1999.

Hilton, Boyd. *The Age of Atonement: The Influence of Evangelicalism on Social and Economic Thought, 1795–1865.* New York, 1988.

Klaits, Joseph. *Servants of Satan: The Age of the Witch Hunts.* Bloomington, Ind., 1985.

Little, Lester K. *Religious Poverty and the Profit Economy in Medieval Europe.* Ithaca, N.Y., 1978.

McLeod, Hugh, ed. *European Religion in the Age of the Great Cities, 1830–1930.* London and New York, 1995.

Monter, William. *Ritual, Myth, and Magic in Early Modern Europe.* Brighton, U.K., 1983.

Oakley, Francis. *The Western Church in the Later Middle Ages.* Ithaca, N.Y., 1979.

Pettegree, Andrew, ed. *The Reformation of the Parishes: The Ministry and the Reformation in Town and Country.* New York, 1993.

Strauss, Gerald. *Luther's House of Learning: Indoctrination of the Young in the German Reformation.* Baltimore, 1978.

Wallace, Lillian Parker. *Leo XIII and the Rise of Socialism.* Durham, N.C., 1966.

JUDAISM

Jay R. Berkovitz

Owing to the rich textual and hermeneutical legacy of Judaism, Jewish historical research has, until the latter part of the twentieth century, been dominated by an overwhelming concern with intellectual development. This emphasis reflects continuity with central elements of the Jewish religious tradition, on the one hand, and a modern cultural-political response to the increasing participation of Jews in European society, on the other. Aiming to enhance the literary and philosophical prestige of Judaism, and thereby advance the cause of civic and social emancipation, nineteenth-century practitioners of *Wissenschaft des Judentums* devoted much of their energies to documenting and highlighting contributions that Jews had made to human civilization. Only since the 1980s has the study of Jewish history expanded to include social institutions and the experiences of ordinary people. Employing quantified data drawn from notarial documents, censuses, tax rolls, and birth, marriage, and death records, the new historiography has been able to reconstruct demographic trends, migration patterns, and occupational distributions of European Jewry. More descriptive accounts furnished by memoirs, personal correspondence, and oral testimonies have also been used to balance the picture that emerged from quantified sources. These methodological approaches, shared both by Jewish and general social historians, have been applied to the dynamics of acculturation, assimilation, and the shaping of modern Jewish political, cultural, and religious identities. However, in contrast to general trends in the field of social history, where the focus has only recently shifted from the working classes, the study of Jewish modernization has included the entire Jewish community.

The modern history of Judaism, with its rich variety of geographical, ethnic, cultural, and religious expressions, traces its foundation to the Hebrew scriptures and the Pharisaic articulation of Israelite traditions. Initially preserved and transmitted orally, the authoritative rabbinic interpretation of biblical Judaism was recorded in the Mishnah, elaborated upon in the Talmud, and expanded further in biblical and tal-mudic commentaries, philosophical tracts, mystical compositions, legal codes, and responsa literature. Medieval interpretations and embellishments of earlier teachings were frequently novel, even far-reaching in character, but remained faithful to the ancient traditions. Even movements that deviated more radically from normative Judaism in the nineteenth and twentieth centuries nonetheless continued to derive much of their authority and core ideas from the very same Jewish tradition from which they diverged, albeit each in accordance with its own reading and emphases. Together, these diverse strands constitute a largely unbroken continuity to the Judaism of today and find expression through the corporate life of the Jewish people. Owing to the interdependence of these elements, this article examines the social impact of modernity on Judaism and Jewish culture, and therefore integrates social and intellectual history.

RELIGIOUS TRADITION AND SOCIAL HISTORY

Public discussions concerning the status of the Jews, occasioned first by the prospect of their readmission into western and central Europe in the seventeenth century and later by the need to ascertain their suitability for citizenship, invariably centered on the social dimension of the Jewish religion. As the likelihood for entrance into modern society improved, the challenges it presented seized the attention of the Jewish community and remained the main topic of internal debate for most of the modern era. At issue was the corpus of social teachings that determined the ethical obligations toward non-Jews and the relationship of Jews to general society, its institutions and culture. Various reformulations of Judaism were a product of the encounter with general culture and were made in direct response to demands for social and political accommodation. Equally significant are modes of piety and ritual behavior that, while governed by internal traditions and hermeneutics, were influenced by larger social and cultural forces as well. Thus historians have discovered that even mystical and pietistic expressions of Judaism, such as Kabbalah and Hasidism, though not a direct product of overtly modernizing trends, offer equally fruitful subjects for social historical analysis.

Traditional Judaism is rooted in a set of beliefs and values that are discernible in its distinctive patterns of social organization, ritual, and religious concepts. Outlined in the Torah (the Pentateuch), its fundamental teachings draw upon an ethical-monotheistic faith that combines religious universalism and particularism. In contrast to other ancient religions, Judaism emphasized that the divine presence is encountered mainly within history rather than in nature. The doctrine of the election of Israel implied a responsibility to live an exceptionally moral and religious life, to serve as "a light unto the nations" by exemplifying a heightened awareness of God's presence, sovereignty, and ultimate purpose in the world. The conviction that Israel's relationship to God is unique has shaped the lifestyle and mode of existence of Jews since ancient times. This special relationship, known by the term *berit* (covenant), required obedience to the ethical, moral, and ritual imperatives of the Torah. Formalized at Sinai, the covenant centered on the attainment of holiness as the ultimate purpose of Judaism and coupled the ideal of faithfulness to the God of Israel with the emphatic denial of the legitimacy of idolatry. Based on the numerous biblical admonitions warning of the harsh consequences that would befall Israel should it fail to live up to the ideals of the Torah, a rabbinic theology of history came to view exile from the land, the destruction of the Jerusalem Temple, and suffering at the hands of other nations as divinely ordained. Ultimately, divine retribution was intended to restore Israel's commitment to the terms of the covenant, to facilitate its spiritual and political redemption, and to pave the way for the establishment of divine sovereignty on earth.

Jewish law and social separation.

The system of law known as halakhah (from the Hebrew root "to go") supplied the essential structure for the pursuit of holiness. It consists of traditions either rooted explicitly in biblical legislation or believed to have been transmitted orally to Moses. Halakhah and aggadah (nonlegal teachings) together constitute the Oral Law, which, according to rabbinic tradition, was revealed with the Written Law. The power of the rabbis to enact legislation beyond the areas set forth in the classical literature rests on their authority as interpreters of the oral tradition. Over the centuries, the detailed norms of halakhah have come to regulate virtually every area of life, including personal status, family relations, ritual, torts, purity laws, and communal affairs. The attainment of holiness has remained a central objective of this massive legal framework and, owing to the interconnectedness of the moral, ritual, and ethical spheres, has had important social implications. Biblically, it entailed both a separation from the immoral influences of idolatrous nations and a dedication to the service of God. Social segregation was mandated by the prohibition against following "in their ways" (Leviticus 18:3) and was amplified in the Talmud and by medieval rabbinic literature to include restrictions on the consumption of food and wine prepared by gentiles, the appropriation of non-Jewish folkways and rituals, and the emulation of gentile dress. The extent to which these laws succeeded in limiting the interaction of Jews and non-Jews has varied considerably over the course of history. How restrictively these limitations were applied normally depended on the intensity of social and economic relations in a particular locale, and frequently corresponded to the concerns of rabbinic and communal leaders about the dangers of extensive social intermingling and acculturation that modernity posed.

Ritual observances have also contributed to the ethos of separation, although this may not have been their intended purpose. The elaborate dietary laws are a case in point. A detailed classification system specifying which quadrupeds, fish, and fowl may be consumed (Leviticus 11:1–47), rigorous requirements concerning ritual slaughter, prohibitions against the consumption of blood and certain kinds of fat, and the strict separation of meat and milk products were legislated for the expressed purpose of establishing Israel as a holy nation. Although in the course of discussions concerning the aim of these laws various medical, philosophical, religious, and psychological benefits have been proposed, the social role of the dietary restrictions as markers of Jewish distinctiveness, and their implications for a separate Jewish economy, have remained paramount. These regulations, like many other ritual requirements such as the observance of the Sabbath and festivals, public prayer, religious education, and care for the dead, not only encouraged the formation of separate Jewish communities but also reveal the common interest shared with ecclesiastical and lay authorities that were intent on keeping Jews socially apart.

Divine service.

No less than its role in distinguishing the Jews as a separate nation, the ritual system of classical Judaism provided a highly structured framework for divine service, falling under three main headings: worship, the study of the Torah, and the performance of acts of kindness. Worship is broadly defined to include a spectrum of divinely ordained rites known as mitzvot that are designed to hallow the mundane aspects of daily life; using symbolism and ceremony, they seek to cultivate human consciousness of the divine presence, and to place human nature, needs, and instincts in a religiously meaningful context. Some assume the form of blessings recited upon the performance of bodily functions in the morning, before eating, and in advance of any obligatory act, such as the affixing of a mezuzah upon the doorpost, recitation of kiddush (sanctification) over wine at the onset of the Sabbath, or the performance of the rite of habdalah (separation) at its close. Each of the aforementioned rites, like most Jewish ceremonies, is performed in the home, the principal arena for the realization of the *vita religiosa* alongside the synagogue. Though from the standpoint of talmudic law women are exempt from most affirmative precepts limited as to time, such as wearing phylacteries (tefilin) and ritual fringes (tzitzit), they traditionally enjoyed a central role in the private rituals of the home.

Public ritual, including formal prayer and rites of passage such as circumcision, bar mitzvah, naming of children, and weddings, were generally conducted in the synagogue, not because of its inherent sanctity but because of its communal character; hence the original Hebrew term *bet-knesset* (house of assembly). Technically, each of the ceremonies marking a life-cycle event could be performed in private, but it became customary to conduct these in a public forum. By its presence the community acknowledged and affirmed the passage to the new status. This was also the case for death and burial rites: beginning with the sixteenth century, preparations of the body for burial were performed by the *Hebra Kadishah* (sacred society) of the community. Even mourning rites, including condolence visitations during the week of intensive bereavement and the gathering of a minyan (a quorum of ten men) in the home, reflected a public dimension of an otherwise private experience. The central elements of synagogue worship included ancient liturgical compositions that positioned the biblical declaration of faith in the God of Israel, the conception of reward and punishment, and the centrality of mitzvot within a framework devoted to the theme of redemptive history; petitional prayers; and the public reading of the Torah. In contrast to the domain of the home, where women were vitally involved in private family rituals, active participation in the public ritual of the synagogue was limited to men. Historically, so long as the home remained central in the ritual life of Judaism, this imbalance only mirrored the generally distinct roles performed by men and women in Jewish life.

Faithful to the Ancient Traditions. The Passover Seder. Miniature in a German Haggadah, c. 1400. ISRAEL MUSEUM, JERUSALEM/GIRAUDON/ART RESOURCE, NY

The annual cycle of major and minor festivals played a crucial role in the life of the community. In addition to the Sabbath, the calendar listed the three pilgrimage holidays (Passover, Shavuot, and Sukkot), the days of repentance (Rosh Hashanah and Yom Kippur), Hannukah, the carnival-style Purim celebration, Rosh Hodesh (new moon), and several fasts marking the destruction of the ancient Temples in Jerusalem or other catastrophes. The pilgrimage holidays were originally agricultural festivals signifying the beginning of spring (Passover), the summer harvest (Shavuot), and the conclusion of the harvest season (Sukkot). In talmudic times they assumed a primarily historical meaning, commemorating crucial moments in Israel's early history: the exodus from Egypt, the giving of the Torah at Mount Sinai, and the divine protection accorded to the Israelites during their sojourn in the desert. The Passover seder and narration of the exodus is a particularly paradigmatic rite of memory. Festivals and fasts provided a framework both for understanding contemporary developments in a national-historical

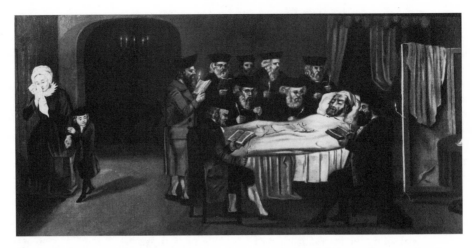

Prayer for the Dying. Saying prayers at a sick person's deathbed. Painting from a cycle of fifteen paintings dedicated to the Prague *Hebra Kadishah,* c. 1772. THE JEWISH MUSEUM, PRAGUE

perspective and for reassessing the significance of earlier events in light of the present. Ritualized remembering forged and sustained the national character of the Jewish people and its religious ideals. At the social level, Jewish festivals fostered shared values and a strong collective identity by bringing ordinary people and elites together regularly in common rituals.

While the study of Jewish ritual can tend to emphasize both separation and timelessness, social historians have contributed some correctives. For example, until the seventeenth century in central Europe, many Jewish rituals were accompanied by considerable spontaneity and even rowdiness, much like popular celebrations by non-Jews in Europe. But religious leaders began to attack these elements, much as their Catholic and Protestant counterparts were doing, and gradually Jewish ceremonies became more consistently somber and serious.

The study of the Torah, according to rabbinic tradition, is a devotional act that stands above all other meritorious activities. Early sources prescribed an equal allotment of time for the study of scripture, Mishnah, and Talmud, but medieval Franco-German practice modified this injunction in favor of the virtually exclusive study of Talmud, said to contain the others. Medieval authorities also debated whether Torah study should be the exclusive preoccupation of the elite and whether it ought to be combined with engagement in either philosophical inquiry or mystical speculation. The debate, which subsequently broadened to include the status of other branches of knowledge such as the natural sciences and humanistic studies, continued into modern times. The ideal of Torah study as a lifelong pursuit was incumbent upon all Jews. According to the majority view among talmudic authorities, however, women were exempt from Torah study. Nevertheless, there is abundant historical evidence of women's involvement in the study of the Bible and those sections of the oral law that applied to them.

Conceived in significantly broader terms than the obligation to give charity, the performance of acts of kindness *(gemilut hasadim)* encompasses the entire range of duties of consideration toward one's fellow human beings. Rabbinic tradition derived its theoretical and practical dimensions from an interpretation of several biblical narrative passages, concluding that one is enjoined to imitate God's moral attributes. Providing clothing for the needy, visiting the sick, and comforting the mourner, for example, are viewed as acts of divine worship, and such acts are understood, especially according to kabbalistic teaching, as a crucial human-divine partnership in the perfection of the world. The mandate to be holy thus expressed itself in efforts devoted to the needy and, at the communal level, in an array of confraternities and societies for free loans, needy brides, visitation of the sick, burial, and consolation of the bereaved. Occasionally, religious and moral idealism was compromised by financial strain, interethnic tensions, and an antialien and antipoor bias that intensified in response to the growing number of beggars in the seventeenth and eighteenth centuries.

TRANSFORMATIONS OF JUDAISM IN MODERN EUROPE

Scholarly opinion remains divided on how the essential feature of modernity ought to be defined and precisely when its impact was first felt in Jewish history. Debate centers on whether the period between the sixteenth and eighteenth centuries, an era of momentous political, economic, social, and cultural transformation, left an enduring mark on Jewish society and culture as well.

Influence of the 1492 expulsion and the Renaissance. The expulsion of the Jews from Spain in 1492, which completed a pattern begun by earlier expulsions from England (1290) and France (1394), offers an example of an event that, according to the standard view, set in motion a monumental rippling effect on Jewish life and culture. By the beginning of the sixteenth century, much of the European Jewish population had shifted eastward to Poland-Lithuania, while centers of Jewish life in the Protestant Netherlands, northwestern Germany, England, and Italy were reinforced by the arrival of the Iberian émigrés. As a result of these migratory patterns, and owing to the pronounced political, social, and cultural dissimilarities between east and west, the Jewish experience of modernity varied widely from region to region. Variability is also reflected in the vastly different patterns of modernization that Ashkenazic and Sephardic Jews experienced, owing to their distinctive cultural traditions and histories. These dichotomies emerged boldly in the early modern period and, owing to their comparative dimension, offer social historians numerous opportunities to study European Jewry's dynamic encounter with modernity.

According to the pioneering view advanced by Gershom Scholem, the expulsion of the Jews from Spain set in motion a three-stage process that unfolded over the ensuing several centuries and precipitated the decline of rabbinic hegemony. Initially, the Spanish expulsion aroused acute messianic longings and produced a novel interest in the kabbalistic (mystical) doctrine of redemption. The central force in this development was the system of Kabbalah devised by Isaac Luria, with its strong emphasis on the myth of primeval catastrophe and the conception of *tikkun* as the mystical essence of salvation. Over the next century, according to Scholem, the revival of Kabbalah produced a wave of ascetic piety, new rituals, liturgical compositions, and mystical meditations that prepared the way for the popular embrace of the pseudomessiah Shabbetai Tzevi in 1666. The expectation of immediate redemption entailed halakhic aberrations, signaling a breakdown of rabbinic authority. The third stage in the process was the emergence of eighteenth-century Hasidism, a movement that attempted to make the world of Kabbalah accessible to the masses. Hasidism preserved those elements of Kabbalah that

were capable of evoking a popular response, but it removed the messianic component in the hope of neutralizing the redemptive theology believed to be the cause of the Shabbetai Tzevi debacle. The implications of Scholem's explanation are very far-reaching, especially in relation to the history and phenomenology of mysticism. In constructing his theory of historical causality, Scholem posited a direct linkage between the expulsion, its imputed theological meaning, and movements that would later break with orthodox tradition. Accordingly, Lurianic Kabbalah and the aftermath of Shabbetai Tzevi's apostasy prepared the way for the modernization of Jewish life and the emergence of modern deviant and reformist movements. This interpretation gained wide acceptance among a full generation of historians.

In the 1990s the Scholem thesis underwent thorough reconsideration. Moshe Idel has shown that Lurianic Kabbalah was not an innovative response to the trauma of expulsion but an extension of older mystical trends, some of which even originated in ancient rabbinic Judaism. He has also demonstrated that Lurianic Kabbalah was not the dominant form of Jewish mysticism in the sixteenth and seventeenth centuries and, further, that it failed to infiltrate the masses as Scholem claimed. Where it was disseminated, as in Italy, it was nonmessianic. This refutation of the Scholem thesis, drawing on modes of analysis used in the fields of religion and intellectual history, has recently received additional substantiation from the realm of social history. The publishing history of early modern kabbalistic conduct literature has shown that Lurianism spread much later than has been assumed and that its influence can be documented only *after* the Shabbetai Tzevi movement. In fact, even the laws and customs contained in the Zohar, the thirteenth-century kabbalistic commentary to the Torah, failed to penetrate ritual life until the emergence of Hasidism. Demonstrating that the eighteenth-century revival of mystical piety did not draw upon Lurianic Kabbalah, which had already weakened by the time the movement appeared, but bore a closer connection to the nonmessianic Cordoveran Kabbalah, Idel has proven that Hasidism was not a reaction to crisis. Far from having become the adversary of rabbinic Judaism, Kabbalah evinced an affinity with patterns of classical rabbinic thought and had firmly permeated normative rabbinic culture before the breakdown of traditional society.

Italy offers an equally instructive case study of vastly differing assessments of the influence of the Renaissance on Jewish life. All agree that the rise of humanism and the emergence of modern science stimulated Jewish scholarly interest in classical philosophy,

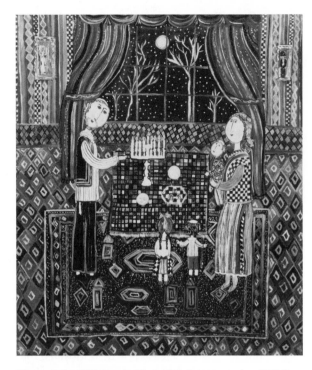

Hannukah. *Lighting the Hannukah Lamp,* painting (1996) by Dora Holzhandler. PRIVATE COLLECTION/THE BRIDGEMAN ART LIBRARY

tian neighbors. Most importantly, there is no evidence of appreciable improvement in the social relations between Jews and non-Jews. The social and political status of the Jews in Renaissance Italy remained virtually unchanged from medieval times.

The example of Italy reveals that the main features of medieval Jewish life—segregation, discriminatory legislation, public assaults on Judaism, and the centrality of rabbinic authority and law—were strongly resistant to the forces that had transformed European society and culture. In fact it was in Venice in 1516 that the term "ghetto" was first used to designate the section of the city where Jews were required to settle; the term was subsequently applied to Jewish quarters in major cities on the continent. European Jewry was largely unaffected by the rise of humanism, the emergence of modern science, and the advent of capitalism, insofar as most could only settle in eastern Europe or in the eastern Mediterranean, far from the centers of economic growth and cultural advancement. As a result, the largest number remained outside the mainstream of society, while medieval social structures and *mentalités* persisted until the late eighteenth century. One exception to this pattern was the converso diaspora, where there was an encounter of Jewish and Western culture in the seventeenth century. We have also seen a connection between attacks on ceremonial spontaneity and wider currents in European popular culture.

Patterns of modernization. Dissimilarities between the Ashkenazic and Sephardic models of transformation in early modern Europe reflect the divergent historical experiences of the two main ethnic branches of the Jewish people. "Ashkenaz" and "Sepharad" are biblical terms identified with Germany and Spain respectively; each subsequently evolved into a religious and cultural tradition connoting distinctive pronunciation of Hebrew, liturgical rites, religious customs, and approaches to general culture. Ashkenazic Jews traced their lineage to the Land of Israel, from there to Italy, and in the High Middle ages were concentrated in the Rhineland. By the beginning of the early modern period, when the largest concentration was in Poland and smaller numbers resided in central Europe, opportunities for contact with Christian society and culture were severely restricted. Their communities, known as *kehillot,* were recognized as legally autonomous by the secular governments, and the lay and rabbinic leadership was empowered to govern in accordance with Jewish law. Rabbinic jurisdiction over civil cases, and the right to punish those who failed to abide by communal regulations, evinced their cultural self-containment. Their literary produc-

science, and rhetoric, as well as participation in the arts. Likewise, works of Hebrew poetry and grammar, biblical commentary, historical writing, and systematization of talmudic and halakhic learning reflected the unmistakable imprint of Italian humanism. David Ruderman, for one, cited collaboration between leading Italian humanists and Jewish scholars as proof of the widespread tolerance enjoyed by Jews. Accordingly, the Renaissance is commonly characterized as an era in which Jewish culture and thought was thoroughly transformed, as evidenced by the emergence of new terms of reference, literary sources, and modes of expression, while Judaism was accepted as intrinsically valid by Christians. Others, led by Robert Bonfil, argue that the various indications of acculturation do not represent adaptation to the majority culture, nor do they suggest that Jews came to view their own religion as inferior to that of others, but only that they maintained an openness toward general culture. In spite of noteworthy instances of scholarly cooperation, the social barriers separating Jews and non-Jews were still in force. Jews continued to be an insecure minority threatened with expulsion and forced conversion, and amidst the penetration of humanist ideals and the considerable evidence of cross-cultural exchange, they nonetheless continued to assert their spiritual superiority and uniqueness over their Chris-tion echoed this social reality, insofar as the language of learned culture was mainly Hebrew and its focus was limited to the religious sphere. With the rapid expansion of printing, rabbinic literature was widely disseminated, and in the seventeenth century numerous communities imposed obligatory participation in a study group or study on one's own. Study assumed its most intensive form in the large concentration of yeshivot of Poland-Lithuania, where professional students were supported by the local community. After the 1648–1649 Chmielnicki massacres, the yeshivot declined, but they were still attended by students from western Europe.

Tracing its religious traditions to Babylonia, Sephardic Jewry was a product of the unique political and cultural forces that shaped Andalusian society of medieval Spain. In contrast to the Ashkenazim, the Sephardim were involved in governmental affairs and in extensive social and intellectual intercourse with the elite of the Muslim population. Their secular poetry and scientific works were inspired by the Arabic literati, and they used Arabic in their prose works. They took keen interest in philosophy, ascribed greater importance to Bible study, and developed systematic approaches to biblical exegesis and the codification of Jewish law. This rich medieval legacy under Islam, as well as the experience of crypto-Judaism engendered by Christian intolerance, predisposed Sephardic Jews historically to successful integration in public life and culture. Moreover, their subsequent resettlement in areas of western Europe where tolerance reigned, and the fact that their reconstituted communities did not possess the range of social and religious controls available to Ashkenazic *kehillot,* accelerated the Sephardic encounter with modernity. Their extensive participation in European society and culture, as well as a variety of modern religious expressions that included voluntary Jewish identity and individualism, were attained without the concomitant breakdown of traditional Jewish society.

In the last quarter of the twentieth century, historians of European Jewry have expanded our understanding of the transformation of traditional Jewish society, some after investigating Levantine Jewry and Sephardic communities of the West, and others on the basis of an examination of individual Ashkenazic communities in western and central Europe. Having detected signs of a break from traditional patterns in the late seventeenth and early eighteenth centuries, they agree that the process of acculturation had begun before the onset of ideological and political efforts to ease the acceptance of Jews in general society. In their view, resettlement in the West, not enlightenment and emancipation, marked the beginning of social and cultural reintegration. Communities of Sephardim in France, Holland, Germany, and England exhibited evidence of advanced acculturation, but their integration into general society did not require emancipation from the patterns of social and cultural segregation typical of Ashkenazic Jews.

The argument that sectors of western Ashkenazic Jewry began departing from the traditional lifestyle at the turn of the eighteenth century rests on evidence of growing laxity in ritual observance, increased social interaction between Jews and Christians, imitation of gentile dress and appearance—including shaving the beard and adopting gentile hairstyles—an increasing preoccupation with luxury, the cultivation of secular branches of knowledge such as philosophy and science, and a decline in sexual morality. Many of these changes found expression in contemporary iconography as well, especially in the depiction of Christian interest in Jewish rites and the harmonious relations between Jews and non-Jews. The new tendencies met with an intensification of efforts on the part of leaders of Ashkenazic communities such as Metz and Frankfurt to regulate public morality in the late seventeenth century. Growing social control in communities of western and central Europe corresponds to Peter Burke's theory that after 1650 the struggle to suppress deviant behavior passed from ecclesiastical to lay powers. Lay leaders sought to delineate the boundaries between the sacred and the profane and keep the two domains distinct in order to prevent the incipient dissolution of traditional society. In some instances, class affiliation determined the type of accommodation made by Jews to modernity. Signs of acculturation among the middle and lower classes in England, for example, resemble those changes that had been limited elsewhere to elites, and suggest that Jews imitated the behavior of their economic peers in gentile society while discarding much of Jewish tradition.

Whether the aforementioned indications of acculturation were elements of a new process or were only variations on the traditional pattern is still fiercely contested. According to Jacob Katz, a genuine break from tradition is indicated when nonnormative acts are justified by a new value system; this occurred in the last third of the eighteenth century when the authority of the rabbinic tradition came under attack and a new vision of the future was first formulated. For Katz, it was the era of Enlightenment and Jewish emancipation that launched the process leading to both acculturation and acceptance within European society as citizens. Gentile advocates of Jewish emancipation expected the bestowal of citizenship to bring the Jews' social and cultural isolation to a close. Liberal thinkers envisioned a society open to all persons, irrespective of class, national origin, or religious affiliation. The Jews were invited to participate in this new undertaking, provided they were willing to accept the conditions set by discussants of the Jewish question in the late eighteenth and early nineteenth centuries. Concretely, this involved the surrender of communal autonomy and rabbinic jurisdiction in civil affairs, and was predicated on the envisioned transformation of Jewish social and economic life.

The Haskalah movement.

A cultural revolution from within accompanied the external forces leading to the curtailment of communal autonomy. The promise of a "neutral society" founded upon secular, humanistic, and rational principles, together with a growing frustration with the cultural limitations imposed by ghetto life, inspired the emergence of the Haskalah movement (from the Hebrew root *sekhel,* which means intellect or reason), a Jewish variant of the European Enlightenment. Its chief proponents, known as *maskilim,* worked mainly as teachers, writers, employees in Hebrew printing presses, and tutors to the rich. As they became acquainted with the major writings of the philosophes, they subjected traditional Jewish society to a critical reevaluation according to new criteria drawn from the Enlightenment, such as the primacy of reason, the aesthetic ideal, the universal brotherhood of man, and economic productivity. In their writings and through their activism on behalf of educational and communal reform, they constructed a new vision of the ideal Jew and of the relationship of Jews to non-Jewish society.

The Haskalah movement undermined the theological, halakhic, and cultural foundations of social separatism. Conscious of the alleged liabilities presented by traditional Judaism, Jewish intellectuals developed strategies to advance the process of cultural and social integration by adjusting Jewish religious and social teachings to the cultural norms of European society. In the realm of education, the *maskilim* distinguished between two categories of knowledge, one pertaining to human affairs and another relating to more narrowly conceived religious subjects. The former, humanistic and scientific studies, was an autonomous sphere that was accessible through human reason and empirical observation. Viewed as absolutely crucial for citizens of the modern state, instruction in secular subjects became the highest educational priority in Jewish schools, while the religious curriculum was recast to reflect an emphasis on Hebrew language and grammar, Bible, ethical obligations, and morality. The new schools that were formed under the influence of the Haskalah aimed to produce a generation of Jews capable of taking their place in the new order

as productive and loyal citizens. To accomplish this goal, a new Judaism was substituted for the old, one that was refashioned to correspond to the social, cultural, and political underpinnings of emancipation. Restrictions on social intercourse with non-Jews were deemed incompatible with the concrete demands of citizenship and its wider implications; halakhic constraints on the consumption of gentile wine and the emulation of gentile customs were cited as the most egregious examples of the outmoded character of traditional Judaism. Emphasizing the central elements of the Sephardic legacy, particularly its rationalist tradition and integrationist ethos, the *maskilim* mounted energetic efforts against the rabbinic establishment, which they viewed as the embodiment of cultural obscurantism and excessive political power. Critical of religious and social traditions that were purportedly the product of superstition and persecution, radical *maskilim* distinguished, as did deism, the divine core of religion from variable customs.

Emancipation and reform.

In contrast to the common core of ideological positions to which *maskilim* in most areas of central and western Europe subscribed, the process of Jewish emancipation varied significantly from state to state, and even from region to region within states. Insofar as emancipation was the product of complex local political forces, the bestowal of civic equality in Europe tended to be uneven. Historically, the era began with the admission of the Sephardic Jews of France to citizenship in 1790 and ended more than a century later with the formal extension of equality in Russia in 1917. Whether granted immediately or only after a prolonged battle, "emancipation" has come to signify the extended process of Jewish acculturation and integration in modern society. The range of its manifold effects is discernible not only in diverse political frameworks but also in various social contexts pertaining to urban or rural populations, class, and gender.

On the basis of these considerations, recent studies have debunked the older view that emancipation led inexorably to rampant assimilation and the rupture of tradition. In the case of the Jews of rural Alsace, occupational patterns, family life, and religious observance were resistant to change because social and economic conditions in the region remained relatively stable for much of the nineteenth century. The conservatism of the rural population is evident in the persistence of folk customs, the use of Yiddish, fertility patterns, opposition to religious reform, use of Jewish names, sentiments of ethnic solidarity, and in the slow pace of assimilation to bourgeois standards of behavior. The city, by contrast, facilitated economic transformation, acculturation to bourgeois lifestyle, and accommodation to the norms of non-Jewish society; as a result, traditional loyalties and affiliations waned, while assimilation accelerated in larger cities such as Paris, Berlin, Prague, and Vienna. Economic and intellectual urban elites active in communal institutions typically labored to "regenerate" the lower classes in accordance with ideals expounded by the Haskalah, and their efforts found expression both in the creation of philanthropic schools for the Jewish urban poor and in broader activities directed at the transformation of Jews in rural areas.

These developments obviously call attention to links between social and religious history in modern Judaism. Divergences emerged within the Jewish community based in part on social class. Many Jews took advantage of opportunities in higher education, and their religious outlook tended to differ from that of other social groups within Judaism. The rural-urban split was pronounced. Patterns of emigration of Jews within Europe by the later nineteenth century added to the complex mix. Many Russian and Polish Jews moved west, interacting with more assimilated coreligionists in places like Britain, and even internal movements, as from Alsace to Paris, had implications for religious outlook and relationships with the wider society.

Barriers to social integration were in the forefront of internal Jewish discussions concerning adaptation to modern society. Concerns about the compatibility of Jewish ritual with the demands of social integration and patriotic loyalty were exacerbated by the acknowledgment that emancipation had shattered the theological assumptions about exile, the return to the Land of Israel, and social separation from non-Jews. For many, citizenship required the removal of problematic aspects of the Jewish religion, and therefore proponents of modernization, including the majority of delegates to the Napoleonic Sanhedrin, repudiated its social and political dimensions. Various factors, including growing indifference to religious observance and the assimilation of bourgeois values, led some to conclude that moderate ritual reform was in order. Typically, efforts to enhance the aesthetic appeal of the synagogue included recitation of prayers in the vernacular, the regularization of the modern sermon, the use of the organ, and the insistence on greater decorum. In Germany, disappointment with the slow progress of legal emancipation, the decline in Jewish observance, the increasing wave of conversion to Christianity, and rising anti-Semitism induced more radical views. As the prospects of civic emancipation grew dimmer, German reformers intensified their efforts to eliminate traces of the political from

Judaism. They removed references to the Land of Israel and the Messiah from the prayer book for fear that these might weaken their claim to equal rights, and sought to blur the ethnic and national features of traditional Judaism by eradicating the dietary laws, traditional Sabbath observance, the prohibition of intermarriage, and circumcision.

Despite the vast differences and bitter struggles between reformers and staunch defenders of the normative tradition, all sectors of the Jewish community acknowledged the debilitating effects of modernity. Strongly rejecting the efforts of radical reformers, Neo-Orthodoxy and Positive-Historical Judaism—later to be known as Modern Orthodoxy and Conservative Judaism—offered solutions to the challenges of rampant assimilation and the erosion of rabbinic authority that reflected their respective conceptions of halakhah and Jewish peoplehood, while upholding an unswerving commitment to emancipation and social integration. Ultra-Orthodox opponents of religious reform, on the other hand, resisted any and all compromises to the integrity of the ancestral faith, urging a greater degree of separation from general society.

As in western and central Europe, growing numbers believed that the Russian Haskalah would facilitate acceptance within general society. Education was regarded as the vehicle that would accelerate the acculturation process by encouraging students to reject patterns of traditional behavior and thought believed to be irrational, retrograde, and divisive. As a result of state involvement in the creation of modern Jewish schools in the 1840s and 1850s, together with the policy of liberalization under Alexander II and the example of modernization in the West, the Russian Haskalah flourished. Although it stressed values similar to those of the German Haskalah, it was less inclined to surrender the distinctive social or religious ideals of traditional Judaism, and the idea of religious reform was only rarely considered. Owing to the stagnant economy, lack of liberalism, and discriminatory legislation, the process of modernization in the East was exceedingly slow. Within this context, the response to modernity in eastern Europe assumed several distinct forms: the creation of communal yeshivot to fight off assimilation; the emergence of the pietistic Musar movement; the Jewish socialist movement; the emergence of secular Jewish culture, particularly through the advocacy of national cultural autonomy in the multiethnic society of Russia and the Austro-Hungarian Empire; and the creation of the Zionist movement.

Zionism. Influenced by nineteenth-century nationalism, Zionist leaders viewed emancipation in the West as an enormous political disappointment

In the Synagogue. *He Cast a Look and Was Hurt,* painting (1910) by the Polish artist Maurycy Minkowski (1881–1930). GIFT OF MRS. ROSE MINTZ JM 14-75/PHOTO ©THE JEWISH MUSEUM, NEW YORK/PHOTO BY JOHN PARNELL/©THE JEWISH MUSEUM, NEW YORK, VISUAL RESOURCES ARCHIVE/ART RESOURCE, NY

and argued that cultural autonomy would ultimately fail to preserve Jewish identity, although the latter claim proved to be exaggerated. Ethnic identity remained strong, as evidenced by continued Hebrew literacy, Jewish folkways, and the vigor of Yiddish literature and theater. Whether Zionism viewed its goal of national resettlement in the Land of Israel as the solution to the problem of anti-Semitism or to the problem of Judaism in the modern world, its program was a positive, though secularized, assertion of the belief in messianic redemption and the historic destiny of the Jewish people. For Zionism, as for other modern Jewish movements, modernity marked the end of the traditional concept of exile and the passive waiting for divine redemption, and signified the beginning of an active pursuit of personal or national fulfillment. Differences between cultural and political Zionism reflected the contrasting historic experiences of east and west European Jews. In the east, where ethnic identity was strong and anti-Semitism physically brutal, Zionism struck deep roots. In the west, Zionism appeared to contradict the social and political premises of emancipation, and therefore remained a largely philanthropic movement until the advent of Nazism. Known as the "Final Solution," the Nazi policy of extermination tragically confirmed Zionism's analysis of the nineteenth-century Jewish question.

Gender. Emphasizing the different ways that Jewish men and women experienced acculturation and assimilation, recent scholarship has shown that emancipation was a highly gendered process. Limited mainly to the domestic scene, women did not have the same opportunities as men to encounter general society and culture in the workplace or in institutions of higher education; this difference would persist as long as the boundaries between domestic and public realms remained in force. Consequently, among most Jewish women the incidence of conversion to Christianity was far less than for men, as long as women's entrance to the workforce was limited. On the positive side, it has been shown that Jewish women in imperial Germany were more traditionally minded than their assimilated husbands. Because bourgeois culture understood religious sentiment as an expression of family values, religion was believed to fall naturally within the private sphere dominated by women. In eastern Europe, where traditional Jewish society did not discourage women from participating in the public realm, Jewish women were more vulnerable to the allure of modern society than men, as evidenced by the fact that more women than men converted to Christianity. It is also noteworthy that in east European Jewish society, where the cult of domesticity was not adopted, responsibility for the inculcation of Jewish religious values was not entrusted to women only. Owing to the progressive relegation of the home and home-based rituals to a less important status, and the concomitant prominence attached to the public sphere, as well as the broad social movement of feminism in the latter decades of the twentieth century, the participation of women in ritual life has increased, even in areas considered halakhically nonobligatory. This has produced numerous new ritual expressions, mainly in the Reform and Conservative movements, and more recently, the proliferation of women's prayer groups and women's Torah institutes, including the rigorous study of Talmud among the Modern Orthodox.

See also **The Jews and Anti-Semitism** *(volume 1) and other articles in this section.*

BIBLIOGRAPHY

Berkovitz, Jay R. *The Shaping of Jewish Identity in Nineteenth-Century France.* Detroit, 1989.

Bonfil, Robert. *Jewish Life in Renaissance Italy.* Translated by Anthony Oldcorn. Berkeley, Calif., 1994.

Cohen, Richard I. *Jewish Icons: Art and Society in Modern Europe.* Berkeley, Calif., 1998.

Dubin, Lois C. *The Port Jews of Habsburg Trieste: Absolutist Politics and Enlightenment Culture.* Stanford, Calif., 1999.

Endelman, Todd M. *The Jews of Georgian England, 1714–1830: Tradition and Change in a Liberal Society.* Philadelphia, 1979.

Frankel, Jonathan, and Steven J. Zipperstein, eds. *Assimilation and Community: The Jews in Nineteenth-Century Europe.* New York, 1991.

Gries, Ze'ev. *Conduct Literature: Its History and Place in the Life of Beshtian Hasidism* [in Hebrew]. Jerusalem, 1989.

Horowitz, Elliott. "Coffee, Coffeehouses, and the Nocturnal Rituals of Early Modern Jewry." *Association for Jewish Studies Review* 14 (1989): 17–46.

Horowitz, Elliott. "The Eve of Circumcision: A Chapter in the History of Jewish Nightlife." *Journal of Social History* 23 (1989): 45–69.

Hyman, Paula E. *The Emancipation of the Jews of Alsace: Acculturation and Tradition in the Nineteenth Century.* New Haven, Conn., 1991.

Hyman, Paula E. *Gender and Assimilation in Modern Jewish History: The Roles and Representation of Women.* Seattle, Wash., 1995.

Idel, Moshe. *Kabbalah: New Perspectives.* New Haven, Conn., 1988.

Israel, Jonathan I. *European Jewry in the Age of Mercantilism, 1550–1750.* 3d ed. London, 1998.

Kaplan, Marion A. *The Making of the Jewish Middle Class: Women, Family, and Identity in Imperial Germany.* New York, 1991.

Katz, Jacob. *Divine Law in Human Hands: Study in Halakhic Flexibility.* Jerusalem, 1998.

Katz, Jacob. *Tradition and Crisis: Jewish Society at the End of the Middle Ages.* Translated by Bernard Dor Cooperman. New York, 1993.

Kieval, Hillel J. *The Making of Czech Jewry.* New York, 1988.

Lowenstein, Steven M. *The Berlin Jewish Community: Enlightenment, Family, and Crisis, 1770–1830.* New York, 1994.

Mendes-Flohr, Paul, and Reinharz, Jehuda. *The Jew in the Modern World.* 2d ed. New York, 1995.

Meyer, Michael A. *Response to Modernity: A History of the Reform Movement in Judaism.* New York, 1988.

Rozenblit, Marsha J. *The Jews of Vienna, 1867—1914: Assimilation and Identity.* Albany, N.Y., 1983.

Ruderman, David. *Jewish Thought and Scientific Discovery in Early Modern Europe.* New Haven, Conn., 1995.

Scholem, Gershom. *Major Trends in Jewish Mysticism.* 3d rev. ed. New York, 1954.

Shulvass, Moses A. *From East to West.* Detroit, 1971.

Tirosh-Rothschild, Hava. "Jewish Culture in Renaissance Italy: A Methodological Survey." *Italia* 9 (1990): 63–96.

Zipperstein, Steven J. *The Jews of Odessa: A Cultural History, 1794–1881.* Stanford, Calif., 1985.

CATHOLICISM

Keith P. Luria

Catholicism's social history cannot be separated from its political or intellectual histories. But social historians have brought to the study of Catholicism questions and methodologies different from those found in older "church history." They are less concerned with the evolution of doctrine and more with the interaction between what the church taught and the way people practiced their faith. And rather than study the internal institutional development of the church, they have turned their attention to its relations with Europe's political entities.

The interest in subjecting Catholicism to social historical analysis has stemmed largely from the growing prestige of social science approaches evident throughout the historical discipline in recent decades. Historians influenced by sociology, such as Gabriel Le Bras and the school of religious sociology he founded in France, assessed people's commitment to Catholicism through quantifying their participation in ritual activities, such as Easter communion or attending mass. Others, drew their inspiration from anthropological theories, such as Émile Durkheim's idea of religion as a reflection of group's self-conception. Scholars like John Bossy and Natalie Zemon Davis have examined how religious rituals and beliefs could bind people together and could set them against those with different conceptions of religion or society.

The sociological and the anthropological do not exhaust the ways social historians study Catholicism. But they do represent two poles: the quantitative, which emphasizes the church and its varying ability to impose practices and beliefs on the faithful, and the ethnographic, which emphasizes the meanings people derive from their religion and the uses to which they put it. Keeping both of these approaches in mind, the social history of Catholicism must assess the impact the church had in shaping society, and it must also be aware of how the church was inevitably shaped by social and political concerns of the laity.

The integration of western European society and Catholicism, both as an institution and as a practiced faith was most complete in premodern Europe,

apparent in the daily lives of families and individuals, the organization of groups and communities, and the functioning of states. The Protestant Reformation challenged this fusion between church and society, but, in Catholic countries, it did not disintegrate. Indeed it was strengthened. Beginning in the eighteenth century and continuing through the twentieth, the pressures of increased secularization and competing beliefs adversely affected the church's dominant role in creating national unity and communal identity. The social history of Catholicism between the early modern period and today traces this long transformation.

CATHOLICISM AND THE "SOCIAL MIRACLE"

Catholic rituals in premodern Europe had a dual purpose. Not only did they fulfill doctrinal requirements enabling the faithful to strive for salvation, they also worked what John Bossy has called the "social miracle" (Bossy, 1985, p. 57). Rituals created social bonds and harmony where rivalries and enmity could otherwise prevail. The sacrament of baptism provides an example of this dual purpose. For the church, baptism incorporated an infant into the community of Christians, washed him or her of original sin, and, through exorcism, protected him or her from diabolical influences. But for the family, baptism also incorporated the child into the earthly community of which he or she was a part. The rite also created a bond of affinity between the child's family and the godparents. Baptism thus satisfied doctrinal concerns and reinforced social bonds. Marriage did the same. The church's blessing of spouses conferred grace upon them and signaled the creation of a new Christian household. But the church also encouraged marriage's role as a means of allying families, ending feuds, and establishing peace.

Religious practices similarly established social bonds in groups such as confraternities. In small villages, confraternities could include all the adult inhabitants. In cities, they brought together members

The Social Miracle. *The Burial of the Count of Orgaz,* painting (1586–1588) by El Greco (1541–1614), summarizes the great themes of premodern and early modern Catholicism: sacramental rituals, intercession of the saints, mediation of the clergy, and the social bonds of a religious confraternity. CHURCH OF S. TOMÉ, TOLEDO, SPAIN/GIRAUDON/ART RESOURCE, NY

of particular neighborhoods, crafts, professions, or social classes. While most were organizations for men, some had both men and women, and others, such as Rosary confraternities in France, became primarily women's organizations. Initiation rituals, common religious observances, and periodic feasting bound the members to each other. The confraternities' rules, moreover, strove to insure brotherhood and charity among the membership. Disputes were submitted to arbitration to prevent lawsuits and ill feeling. Wealthier members helped the poorer through loans or alms. And the group aided its members even in death, arranging funerals, accompanying bodies to burial, and paying for memorial masses.

Rituals also cemented the social bonds of communities. Processions, for instance, were held on important civic and religious holidays—the festival of a city's patron saint or the feast of Corpus Christi. And they were staged at moments of crisis—during military threats or epidemics. Urban processions usually included representatives from the city's clergy, its governing body, and its various craft guilds and/or confraternities. These groups marched in a hierarchical order that reflected their status in the community. Thereby, through Catholic ritual, the social body was created and displayed in pageant form.

The most potent means of creating the "social miracle" was Catholicism's central ritual act, the Mass and its eucharistic service. The Eucharist brought about reconciliation of social conflict through its symbolism of many parts united in a never divisible unity, the body of Christ. Confession, the repenting of sins, and the making of restitution for them, including those committed against one's neighbors, was the necessary preparation for partaking of communion.

Thus Catholic belief and ceremony both mirrored and created the social structure, ensuring citizens a place within a divinely ordained system, and establishing social harmony. However, we should be careful in assuming that religion's role was entirely efficacious. Religious practices could provoke disputes or provide the occasions for them. Members of social elites competed for prestige through their patronage of religious devotions or establishments. A community's poor might use the annual Carnival, the time prior to Lent when normal social rules and order were suspended or inverted, to riot and seek redress for the un-Christian inequities under which they suffered. Therefore, we must not simplify Catholicism's reinforcement of a traditional European social order; its powerful effect could work in quite the opposite direction.

Much the same is evident in Catholicism's role in states. European monarchies were sacral political systems. Catholic teaching legitimated monarchy as a divinely ordained means of maintaining social order and justice. Kings drew authority from ceremonies derived from Catholic ritual, such as the French royal coronation during which new monarchs swore to defend the true faith and took communion in both kinds, the body and the blood, a privilege usually reserved for priests. The ceremony lent rulers a semidivine status, which was evident in the belief that they could cure scrofula by touching the afflicted.

But the political role of Catholic belief and ritual did not function perfectly. We cannot assume that subjects were convinced by the claims kings made in ceremonies and political propaganda. Certainly the sacred character of the French monarchy did not prevent revolts. In another sense also, the fit between Catholicism and royal authority was not seamless. Kings and popes frequently found themselves in conflict. Furthermore, kings could find themselves beset by quarrels within the church that weakened their power. The Jansenist controversy, for example, helped undermine the French monarchy in the decades before the Revolution (see below). Nonetheless, as long as Catholicism remained a country's largely unanimous faith, it would continue to buttress its social and political systems.

THE CATHOLIC REFORMATION

The Protestant Reformation of the sixteenth century challenged this unanimity. Protestant countries broke the web of connections between Catholicism, society, and the state. In Catholic societies these connections were, if anything, renewed and strengthened by the vast Catholic reform movement extending from the sixteenth century into the first half of the eighteenth. The church convened the Council of Trent between 1545 and 1563, to set an agenda for combatting the spread of Protestantism, improving the quality of its clergy, and transforming the religious and social lives of the Catholic faithful. Bishops ensured these goals by frequent episcopal visits to their dioceses' communities to investigate the ritual practices, beliefs, and moral behavior of their flocks. They targeted many customs of traditional local religion and tried to suppress those they found indecent or too independent of clerical control, such as confraternity banquets, nocturnal pilgrimages, or overly enthusiastic devotion to miracle-working relics and images. Reformers sought instead to encourage a piety based on the individual's examination of conscience, proper attention to the church's sacraments, and reverence for approved devotions. On their visits, bishops also investigated illicit sexual behavior, drunkenness, familial conflicts, and a host of other social sins.

Decorum in Popular Religious Practice. Procession to the shrine of Notre-Dame de la Garde, Marseille. Eighteenth-century print. MUSÉE DU VIEUX-MARSEILLE, MARSEILLE, FRANCE

Together governments and the church worked to create confessionalized Catholic states in which people were subjected to more political control and more religious discipline than ever before. With the political appointment of reform-minded bishops in countries like Spain and France, the Catholic Reformation advanced jointly with the extension of government control over autonomous regions and unruly subjects.

So described, the Catholic-Reformation church can easily appear as a modernizing institution in European society, one that rationalized its own internal structure, allied itself with states doing the same, imposed social discipline, and sought conformity and control. But the description exaggerates the repressive tendencies in the Tridentine program. Catholic reformers did seek to establish greater clerical control over religious practices and to focus them on the church's central doctrinal concerns, such as the Eucharist or the cult of Mary. They did insist on greater decorum in festivals, processions, pilgrimages, and confraternal celebrations. And they did want to instruct the faithful in a better understanding of church doctrine. But Catholic reformers never opposed all popular religious practices; they permitted the cult of saints and relics, confraternities, and the belief in miracles. Indeed, many of the church's efforts revitalized religion's traditional local purposes. Authorized saints may have been substituted for unauthorized ones, but the faithful could still seek miraculous intervention to help with life's problems. And even if stern bishops disapproved of what people believed, nothing prevented these people from taking what the bishops offered and adapting it to their own purposes. Hence the widespread Rosary devotion, with its individualized and meditative prayers, may have been a Catholic-Reformation style of worship, but Rosary confraternities also provided a new means to accomplish an old end by establishing bonds of affinity between their members.

The church did not seek to create a modern society based on disciplined, isolated individuals. Such an idea was entirely foreign to its social conceptions and would remain so for a long time to come. Insofar as efforts at increasing social discipline were successful, and success was partial at best, the Catholic Reformation reinforced the sense of a divinely ordained, and church-guided, society of estates or orders. In this way, the church was still congruent with the Catholic society around it. One can see this congruence at work, for example, in new religious groups established for laypeople, most notably Jesuit sodalities, which organized their members into the traditional corporate groups of European society, with separate associations for nobles, bourgeois, and artisans. But as European society changed in the early modern period, these old means of maintaining Christian charity and brotherhood would seem increasingly outmoded.

THE EIGHTEENTH CENTURY

As long as the church maintained the allegiance of rulers and their people, Catholicism would remain the essential unifying principle of social order and monarchical political systems. The first disassociation of Catholicism and society, in what had been heretofore Catholic countries, appeared in the eighteenth century as certain social groups fell away from Catholic observance. Royal governments, which had long seen the church as providing legitimacy for monarchs and stability for the social order, now looked to other ways of justifying their authority and of controlling their subjects. The impact of this development varied from country to country, and its reasons remain in some ways poorly understood. But they included disputes within the church, the impact of Enlightenment attacks on the church, and a process of dechristianization starting to take hold in certain places, notably France.

That the church's clergy had deep socioeconomic divisions was hardly a phenomenon new to the eighteenth century; however, it became at this time a source of growing conflict. In France, high-ranking aristocrats dominated the upper clergy. Parish priests, generally of middling social origins, were better trained and more conscientious in their duties than before the Tridentine reforms. They resented their inferior position in the church more than ever before, and their relations with their superiors became increasingly embittered. One result of the spread of Enlightenment rationality in France was the demand for more socially responsible and useful priests. The Enlightenment *bon curé* (good parish priest) who labored in his parish to provide religious, educational, and welfare services, fit this demand well; the wealthy, worldly, aristocratic upper clergy, who appeared little concerned with pastoral cares, did not. Antagonism between the lower and upper clergy resulted in their split in the 1789 Estates-General, which led to the formation of the revolutionary National Assembly. The priests had in no way sought to undermine the church's position in society, but as the Revolution progressed, their challenge to the institution's hierarchical order would have that effect.

In Spain, Italy, and elsewhere, the upper clergy was less aristocratic than that of France, but the rural clergy was also less well trained and supported. The fall in religious vocations throughout western Europe in the second half of the century left the church seriously understaffed and unable to carry out its spiritual functions in some rural areas—the Alentejo in Portugal, the Mezzogiorno in Italy. And as a large landowner in these regions, it was the target of local resentment. In certain places, such as the Mezzogiorno, the problem was somewhat offset by the missionary work of Jesuits, Redemptorists, and Lazarists. But male orders too suffered from the fall in vocations.

Women's orders, especially those engaged in charitable, hospital, or educational work, survived on much better terms, but in cities more than the countryside.

During the eighteenth century, the church was also beset by doctrinal controversies that embroiled it in political conflicts and contributed further to its loss of public esteem. The most important of these disputes was over Jansenism, especially acute in France, though it had echoes elsewhere. The rigorist theology of the Jansenists found strong support among the French clergy despite its being declared heretical. Efforts to suppress the movement, such as the 1713 papal bull *Unigenitus,* backfired and made Jansenist priests appear the victims of papal and royal despotism. Jansenists set themselves up as opponents of heavy-handed political authority and helped turn public opinion against the royal government and the Jesuits, allies in the persecution of Jansenists. The Jesuit-Jansenist confrontation also furthered a decline in respect for the French church and led to the dissolution of the Jesuits in France in 1764. The Jesuits had problems in other countries as well. Portugal expelled the order from its possessions in 1759, and they were ejected from Spanish possessions in 1767. Finally, in 1773 under pressure from Catholic monarchs, Pope Clement XIV (reigned 1769–1774) dissolved the order.

Contemplative orders that did not seem involved in useful work were also under fire. In 1781 the Austrian Emperor Joseph II (reigned 1765–1790) closed monasteries and convents not engaged in teaching or nursing. Joseph used much of their former property to fund schools and hospitals. The reasons behind these government policies against the Jesuits or contemplative orders were different in each case, but they indicate that the monarchies of Europe were disengaging themselves from their traditional close connections to the church.

Historians of French religious life in the eighteenth century have also explored a wider disaffection with the church that they call "dechristianization." The phenomenon is not well understood and attempts to measure it have been questionable, but in France if not elsewhere it seems undeniable that at least some of the social elite were turning away from religious practices the church had tried to inculcate since the Council of Trent. The quantitative study of wills in Paris and in Provence has shown that after 1730 testators' requests for memorial masses fell dramatically. The evidence suggests that the belief in purgatory, central to the church's scheme of salvation, was exercising less and less hold over Catholic minds. Whether this development means society was becoming dechristianized, or perhaps just turning its reli-

Jansenist Nuns. The refectory of the monastery of Port-Royal-des-Champs, near Versailles, France. The monastery, one of the centers of the Jansenist movement, was destroyed on the orders of Louis XIV in 1711. Anonymous painting, eighteenth century. Musée des Granges de Port-Royal, France/Photo: Gérard Blot/Réunion des Musées Nationaux/Art Resource, NY

gious concerns in other directions, has been a much harder question to answer.

Other indications suggest, however, that adherence to the church's teachings and moral strictures was falling off. One sign was the fall in vocations. Another was the decreasing share of the bookselling market that religious publications commanded. Confraternities were losing members to more secular forms of sociability: the elite to Masonic lodges and others to cafés. Demographic studies of French localities have demonstrated a marked late-eighteenth century increase in prenuptial pregnancies and illegitimate births. In general, however, birthrates fell, suggesting that people were using contraception and thus rejecting the church's rules on sexual activity.

Historians have offered various reasons for dechristianization. One is that the rigorous demands of the Catholic-Reformation church drove people away from strict observance. Another is that politicized and irreconcilable disputes, such as that between the Jansenists and their opponents, called into question Catholic doctrine's absoluteness. Belief began to seem less a matter of truth than of opinion, and thus it could be rejected. Presumably contributing to this development were the secularizing ideas of the Enlightenment, but its role was complex. Throughout Europe, an enlightened Catholicism did not entirely reject the church but called on it to play a more useful role in society, helping to promote social welfare, education, and public morals, all part of enlightened, absolute monarchs' programs in Austria, Prussia, and Portugal, as well as in France. Finally, changing economies were leading to the migration of people from rural areas to rapidly growing cities, disrupting the parish life that the Tridentine church had seen as essential to social and religious discipline. Urbanization and increased literacy also meant the wider circulation of ideas inimical to Catholicism. Beset by internal disputes, a decline in vocations, and a poor distribution of its resources, the church was ill prepared to cope with these changes in European society. Religious conformity and the complete fit between Catholicism and society became impossible to maintain. The revolutionary upheaval of the late-eighteenth century would make this disengagement permanent.

THE FRENCH REVOLUTION AND NAPOLEONIC WARS

In France, criticism of the church as a wealthy and unbeneficial institution, combined with the effects of dechristianization, culminated first in the revolutionary government's takeover of the church and later in its attempt to abolish Christian worship entirely. In November 1789, the Assembly nationalized church property. In July 1790, it passed the Civil Constitution of the Clergy, which made clerics into salaried civil servants and applied the Revolution's democratic ideals to the church's administration. Voters would henceforth elect their parish priests and bishops. The French Catholic church became completely dependent on the state, but Catholicism was no longer the country's single legal religion. Toleration was established and citizenship offered to Protestants and Jews. The refusal of the papacy to respond positively to these developments led to a further and even more fateful decision in November 1790, when the Assembly voted the Ecclesiastical Oath that required each member of the clergy to swear loyalty to the nation and the constitution. The oath split the French church and provoked widespread resentment and resistance. Most bishops refused it, as did about half of the lower clergy. The divisions were deep and lasted far beyond the Revolution. Those regions where oath-taking priests predominated—Paris, the southeast, and parts of the southwest—would later be known for anticlericalism and low rates of Catholic observance. Regions where priests who refused the oath were numerous—the west, the east, northeast, and the Massif Central—would remain areas of strong Catholic piety well into the twentieth century. In such areas opposition to the Revolution was bitter, leading in the Vendée and Brittany to bloody counterrevolutionary revolts.

The Civil Constitution was short-lived; the Revolution's radicalization led to a government-sponsored campaign in 1793 to 1794 in which churches were closed, vandalized, or converted into revolutionary temples. Priests were outlawed, forced into exile, arrested, and sometimes executed. Catholic worship was replaced by revolutionary festivals, such as the cult of reason. Resistance to the campaign was widespread, even in prorevolutionary areas, but open Catholic practice largely ceased until the fall of Maximilien Robespierre (1758–1794) in 1794. Under the Directorial regime after 1795, Catholic worship once again became legal. But with much of the clergy dispersed and now without government financing of the church, Catholicism in France depended largely on lay initiative as townspeople or villagers undertook to lead worship themselves, reopen churches, and reestablish devotional life.

The church's position in France was not regularized until Napoleon (1769–1821) negotiated the Concordat with the papacy in 1801. Although Catholicism was recognized as the "religion of the majority of the French people," the church did not return to its prerevolutionary status as the only established faith (Desan, 1990, p. 24). All religions were legally equal. The church, moreover, was firmly under Napoleon's control. He ensured stipends for the clergy and appointed the bishops. All priests were to swear an oath of loyalty to the state, and prayers for the government were recited in all churches. Former church property would not be returned.

In no other country was the religious upheaval of the revolutionary years as traumatic as it was in France. But in every place touched by warfare, Catholic practice was disrupted and the church's relations with government and society affected. In regions where revolutionary or Napoleonic regimes were established, the church surrendered property; monasteries and convents were closed and parish priests lost positions. Confraternities, previously so important for lay-involvement in religion, declined or disappeared in much of Italy, and in Spain their role in parish life diminished. The Revolution also deeply politicized the question of religious choice. Adherence to Catholicism was no longer universal in nominally Catholic countries. Henceforth, it involved a conscious decision and that decision was not only a matter of faith it was also a statement about one's political stance and outlook on the modernization of Europe in the nineteenth century.

THE NINETEENTH CENTURY

After the revolutionary trauma, the church could no longer assume dominance over the spiritual lives of people in Catholic countries. Catholicism increasingly competed with other religions guaranteed toleration in liberal states. It also competed with the growth of religious indifference and with political ideologies that were suspicious of the church or rejected it altogether. The church saw itself as embattled with rapidly triumphing forces of secularization, materialism, scientific advances, liberalism, and eventually socialism. Historians too have long considered the nineteenth century a time of prevailing secularization. However, recent work in the social history of religion suggests a more complex situation.

The picture of Catholic practice in the nineteenth century presents striking geographic and class differences. Rural areas maintained high levels of compliance with Catholic observances. But in a time of rapid urbanization, fewer and fewer city inhabitants took the church's prescriptions seriously. The evidence for this conclusion comes from quantitative studies of participation in life-cycle rituals, such as baptisms, marriages, and funerals, or other Catholic obligations, such as attendance at mass and the taking of Easter communion. Available statistics show that in Paris almost 90 percent of families sought out priests to perform baptisms for their children in 1865; by 1908 the number had dropped to under 59 percent. Wealthier quarters often had much higher participation rates than working-class districts, where rates were particularly low. In Paris's working-class twentieth arrondissement between 1909 and 1914, only 6 percent of the population took Easter communion (Kselman, 1995, pp. 169–170). In the Spanish city of Logrono, over 90 percent of the inhabitants took Easter communion in 1860, but by 1890 that figure had fallen to 40 percent. Only 6 percent of the eighty thousand people in Madrid's working-class district of San Ramon took Easter communion in the 1930s and only 7 percent attended mass (Callahan, 1995, p. 51).

The numbers reflect a serious decline from the near-universal participation of the early modern period, and they suggest why ecclesiastics viewed cities as cesspools of immorality, political radicalism, and atheism. The Parisian priest François Courtade complained in 1871, that the "laboring population of Paris are without faith and without God. The notion and feeling of the divine seem to have entirely withdrawn from them" (Kselman, 1995, p. 165). Of course, he wrote this in the year of the Commune, but the sentiment was common among the Catholic clergy. In 1855, the Spanish bishop Antonio Palau wrote: "Who can doubt that people from all parts of the world, of all religions . . . flow to the great centers of manufacturing and commerce, and communicate . . . their religious indifference. . . . Faith has grown languid, charity has become cold [and] religious sentiment has grown weak" (Callahan, 1995, p. 43).

But we must be careful in drawing the conclusion that urbanization necessarily led to religious indifference. Research in the later decades of the twentieth century has shown that much depended on where the people flocking to urban centers came from. Cities located in regions with observant rural populations had much higher rates of participation in Catholic ceremonies than those that were not. For example, Quimper in Brittany and Metz in Lorraine—both areas of strong Catholic piety—had relatively high rates of taking Easter communion. Limoges—located in the Limousin, long known for religious indifference—had rates that were much lower.

The overall statistics on observance also hide a large gender imbalance. Women were more observant than men. The trend, already apparent in the eighteenth century, accelerated during the nineteenth and continued into the twentieth. Church attendance increasingly became a form of female sociability; men met in the café or in political groups, often those with strong anticlerical views. Some have suggested that the predominance of women in Catholic worship developed from a particularly feminized Catholic piety, of which popular shrines, such as Lourdes, associated with visions of the Virgin are one example. Such feminized piety is described as sentimental or saccharine with an emphasis on the need for quiet suffering, as found for instance in the cult of Saint Thérèse of Lisieux (1873–1897). Compared with the more austere piety of the Catholic Reformation or the eighteenth century, that of the nineteenth century, especially in its popular devotions, does seem more emotional, if not to say insipid. However, to describe such characteristics as especially feminine is to impose an already heavily gendered language on the phenomenon. Men were also involved in popular religious observances, and priests promoted and led them. It is equally possible that Catholic worship attracted women because it stressed their role, or that of saintly figures like Thérèse of Lisieux and Bernadette Soubirous (1844–1879), the Lourdes visionary, or that of a female sacred figure like Mary in the future of the church and the salvation of countries turning toward secularism. The questions that feminization of religious practice poses remain one of the most pressing areas for future research.

The overall decline in Catholic observance stemmed in part from the church's own shortcomings. The church failed to adapt its network of pastoral care to a rapidly urbanizing society. European cities grew enormously across the nineteenth century and the provision priests and parish churches did not keep pace. The ratio of priests to urban inhabitants declined steadily. In Vienna it was 1 priest to every 1,641 people in 1783, 1 to 4,290 in 1842, and 1 to 5,949 in 1910. Paris had 1 priest for every 3,056 inhabitants in 1861 and 1 for every 4,790 in 1914. Marseilles had 1 for every 2,450 in 1861 and 1 for every 4,550 in 1921. And the shortfall was particularly evident in the working-class areas into which rural immigrants flooded. In Paris in 1906, the priest-to-inhabitant ratio was 1 to 3,681 in the central, wealthy arrondissements and 1 to 5,760 in the working-class surrounding districts (McLeod, 1995, p. 16; Kselman, 1995, p. 170). Presumably some of the strong anticlericalism of urban workers derived from their sense that the clergy had deserted them.

The growth of belief systems hostile to Catholicism also contributed to the decline in religious practice. Middle-class liberals and working-class socialists often saw the church as an enemy. Liberals could, at times, reach accommodations with the church, as did Spanish Moderates in negotiating a concordat with

Rome in 1851. And after the upheaval of the 1848 Revolution, bourgeois Frenchmen found a new appreciation of the church as an instrument of social control. But as heirs to eighteenth-century rationalism, many liberals found themselves at odds with Catholicism. The church opposed certain basic liberal beliefs, for example, religious toleration. Liberals deplored the church's ownership of large amounts of property, its influence within educational systems, and its alliance with right-wing politics. Liberal governments moved to curtail the church's role and power in society. In 1836, the Spanish government suppressed male religious orders, and over the next twenty-five years liberal regimes sold much ecclesiastical property. In Prussia, Otto von Bismarck's *Kulturkampf,* the decade-long campaign against the church in the 1870s, included expulsion of the Jesuits, prohibition of using pulpits for political uses, state approval of clerical appointments, and establishment of state control over religious schools and instructors. Education was also a source of conflict in France, where, in the 1880s, the Third Republic laicized the school system.

The antipathy between the church and political radicals was even stronger. The church saw socialism as godless. Workers were suspicious of the church's alliance with social elites, employers, and political conservatism. Although the church was not an inveterate defender of capitalism—unconstrained economic development seemed egotistical, and unrestrained competition for wealth seemed sinful—its view of society was steeped in an idealized understanding of the past in which rich and poor were tied together by the bonds of Christian charity. Political radicals saw conflict between classes as inevitable, and workers had no use for clerics who preached resignation rather than political action. Mutual hostility erupted in serious outbreaks of violence, most notably during the Paris Commune of 1871, when priests held hostage were killed.

The social and political conflicts in which Catholicism was engaged in the nineteenth century can easily make it appear that the church was in constant retreat before the onslaught of the modern world. And the complaints of clerics, especially Pope Pius IX (reigned 1846–1878), who issued the Syllabus of Errors in 1864 to combat modernity, can give the same impression. However, the church could also make use of what modern life offered. Cities, so often derided as spiritual wastelands, were also places where new Catholic groups could organize. Catholic leaders established schools, youth groups, women's clubs, sports associations, credit unions, cooperatives, and unions in their effort to reclaim the religious loyalty of urban populations. The success of these efforts was limited,

particularly when workers were targeted. In the aftermath of the Commune, the French aristocrat Albert de Mun founded Catholic workers' discussion circles and recreational societies. In Spain, church leaders sponsored associations of workers and employers. Workers were suspicious of such organizations, which were more concerned with regaining them for the faith and fighting socialism than with improving their economic situation. In the spirit of Pope Leo XIII's encyclical *Rerum novarum* (1891), some of the clergy sought to open the church to science, political democracy, and worker's rights. Leo (reigned 1878–1903) had insisted on including in the document the statement that workers had a right to organize independent unions. But the church could not shed its paternalism, and when such ideas were put into practice they still involved clerics leading laypeople whom they expected to be obedient.

The church had more success when it could combine opportunities available in modern society with its more traditional undertakings. The most spectacular development in nineteenth-century Catholic piety were the apparitions of the Virgin Mary that led to the development of popular pilgrimage shrines. The church preached the imminent arrival of a Marian age that would precede the Second Coming, and the message found a receptive audience among a laity with an already fervent popular devotion to the Virgin. Although not all the apparitions and pilgrimages gained ecclesiastical approval, the church promoted those that did energetically, and it used the means the modern world provided to do so.

The most successful of the nineteenth-century shrines was that of Lourdes in the French Pyrénées, where the Virgin appeared to Bernadette Soubirous in 1858. Lourdes quickly became a magnet for pilgrims from all over Europe, who came to the sacred grotto seeking miraculous cures. The church's promotion of such a miracle shrine might seem a retreat from the modern world into the popular religion that the Catholic-Reformation church had tried to discourage. Indeed, the church hierarchy, faced with a European culture it no longer dominated, now found strength in the deep well of popular devotion and practices, which rallied the faithful to an embattled religion.

However, the church's investment in popular shrines did not represent a turning away from the modern world. It was precisely the cultural, technical, and commercial developments of the nineteenth century that made the shrines' success possible. Increased literacy provided a large audience for the reports of miracles published in widely-read Catholic periodicals. *La Croix,* produced by the Assumptionist order

Manifestation of Popular Devotion. Holy Week procession in Seville, Spain, early twentieth century. SCHEUFLER COLLECTION/©CORBIS

in the 1880s and 1890s, was one of France's most popular newspapers. New national railroad networks made it feasible for large numbers of pilgrims to travel to remote locations like Lourdes. The newly developing travel industry saw to the housing and feeding of the pilgrims. These miracle-working shrines were very much a part of the modern world.

The shrines also became embroiled in the modern world's political conflicts. Lourdes served the cause of the Bourbon legitimists against the Second Empire and later against the Third Republic. But eventually it also became identified with French nationalism; French Catholics took pride in Mary's appearance in their country. And after the defeat by Prussia and the crisis of the Commune, the shrine was declared a symbol of national regeneration. Lourdes's success sparked imitations. At Marpingen in the German Saarland in 1876, village girls had visions of the Virgin near a spring. A pilgrimage quickly developed that boosted German Catholic morale in the struggle against Bismarck's *Kulturkampf.* The Marpingen apparitions also raised the possibility that Germany would now have a shrine to rival the French Lourdes.

Thus the church at the end of the nineteenth century was not in complete retreat from the modern world but was painfully coming to grips with it. Catholicism's sources of strength lay no longer in the universality of Catholic practice, but in sometimes spectacular manifestations of popular devotion. Rather than being a primary determinant of European society and culture, the church was and would continue to be subject to problems that divisions in society provoked.

THE TWENTIETH CENTURY

The church's problematic reconciliation with the modern world continued through the first half of the twentieth century. In multiconfessional societies, and in those with growing religious indifference, the church remained on the defensive. In liberal democracies, even in those with nominally Catholic majorities, the church increasingly operated in a self-contained sphere with its own associations, school systems, welfare institutions, and political parties. In Spain and Portugal, the church was closely allied with fascist regimes, which enforced the conservative morality Catholicism condoned. The church's relations with Italian Fascism and Nazism were much more problematic. And under post–World War II communist regimes, the church provided a rallying point for political resistance and was an important component of national identity against Soviet domination. Thus for much of the century, the church's relation to society depended largely on the political system of individual countries. At the end of the twentieth century, however, the trend toward political liberalism and democracy seemed to be leading to the compartmentalization of Catholicism throughout all of Europe.

In France the separation of state and society from the church proceeded the farthest. In the first decade of the century, the anticlerical Third Republic applied harsh laws against Catholic religious orders, and in 1905 it enacted a complete separation of state and church. Relations between the two remained embittered. In 1925, an assembly of French cardinals and archbishops issued a declaration condemning laicity and urging the faithful to disobey the law. This resistance seemed precisely the sort of disloyalty that secularists feared from ultramontane Catholics. The French clergy, as was the case with the church as a whole, was intransigent in the belief that no well-ordered society could exist unless its laws conformed to Catholic teachings. The church's relations with the Vichy government, which enforced a conservative moral regime, were much better. But under the postwar republics the church once again had to contend with governments that disassociated themselves from religious institutions and with a population that was increasingly nonobservant.

In Spain the conflict between the church and liberal governments as well as that between the clergy and left-wing workers provoked great conflict, culminating in the Civil War of 1936–1939, during which seven thousand members of the clergy were executed, churches were sacked, and the bodies of clerics were exhumed from their graves. The Civil War's violence convinced many that it was necessary to organize society around the church's moral, social, and political teachings. Francisco Franco's regime overturned the liberalizing policies of the republican government. It repealed the divorce law and made religious marriages compulsory for all. It also decreed Catholic religious teaching mandatory in schools, and gave ecclesiastical authorities oversight of educational curricula. Hence, the segregation of Catholicism and society was, in principle, reversed; Catholic observance became a sign of social respectability and political orthodoxy. But the church-state alliance also worked to limit Catholicism's impact. Regions and social groups resistant to the regime were also strongly anticlerical.

In Fascist Italy and Nazi Germany, the situations were different. As was the case in Spain and Portugal, a church that had long opposed liberal ideas had no problem at first in seeing authoritarian regimes suppress them. However, in neither country would the church-state alliance endure. The nationalization of the Papal States at the time of Italian unification had set off a long church-state conflict that Benito Mussolini (1883–1945) and Pope Pius XI (reigned 1922–1939) brought to an end with the signing of the Lateran Treaty of 1929. However, conflict arose over church autonomy and fascist ideology. The papal encyclical *Non abbiamo bisogno* ("We have no need") of 1931 denounced the pagan worship of the fascist state and declared its conception of society to be incompatible with Catholic doctrine. In Germany, Cardinal Eugenio Pacelli (the future Pope Pius XII, 1939–1958) signed a concordat with Hitler in 1933. Disputes between the state and the Vatican quickly resumed. In 1937, when the Vatican issued the encyclical *Mit brennender Sorge* ("With burning anguish") condemning racism (though without specifically mentioning Nazism), the regime reacted with a fierce antichurch campaign that sent many priests to concentration camps. Thus although the church and these totalitarian regimes shared common enemies in democratic liberalism and socialism, they were not capable of, nor even inclined to, re-create the integration of Catholicism and European society that had long since disappeared. Nonetheless, the willingness of the church to come to agreements with these regimes disillusioned many, and the disillusionment was accentuated by the sorry and controversial record of Pius XII's refusal to speak out against the Holocaust.

The church's encounter with conservative, totalitarian regimes would finally bring about its long overdue reconciliation with liberal democracy and eventually with religious toleration. But this would occur in a post-World War II Europe in which the church as an institution was increasingly isolated from much of society, and its teachings increasingly out of step with social mores.

Ironically, only where the church was persecuted, as in Poland, would its integration with society remain strong. The Polish church provided political leadership as well as a rallying point during the centuries-long struggle for national unity and independence. Catholic symbols, such as the shrine of the Black Madonna at Czestochowa, were also national symbols. In the twentieth century, the great variety of Catholic educational, cultural, welfare, and labor organizations constituted much of Polish civil society. However, before the war Poland was an ethnically and religiously diverse country; Catholics accounted for 65 percent of the population. It was only after the war, especially with the extermination of the Jewish community, that the church could claim the religious allegiance of 95 percent of Poles. The church's hostility to communism made it the center—and its primate, Cardinal Stefan Wyszyński (1901–1981) the leader—of resistance to the postwar regime. And the church's alliance with Solidarity helped bring about the downfall of that regime. However, since the establishment of the post-communist government, splits between church and society have appeared. Catholic leaders see their faith as central to Polish identity and seek to have the church exercise a tight control over society. The primate Cardinal Józef Glemp encouraged Catholic political candidates to run against those of other religious, specifically Jewish, backgrounds. The church has opposed the liberalization of divorce and abortion laws. The disputes these policies have provoked, even in strongly Catholic Poland, are replaying the sorts of church-society conflicts found throughout Europe as modernization increasingly has marginalized the church's role in European society.

The church has had two very different responses to the problem modernization poses. One has been to continue to draw strength from some of its most ancient practices, for example, miracle-working shrines. Miracles at Fatima in Portugal, which started in 1917, have continued to this day, and Pope John Paul II has expressed his personal attachment to the devotion. Pilgrims also flock to Medjugorje in Croatia where apparitions of the Virgin started in 1981.

The church's major institutional response was the Second Vatican Council, which Pope John XXIII (reigned 1958–1963) convened between 1962 and

Pilgrimage to the Black Madonna. Pilgrims pause to pray during their journey from Warsaw to the shrine of the Virgin Mary at Częstochowa, Poland. CAMERA PRESS, LONDON

1965. The impact of the Council's work on liberalizing Catholic doctrine, ritual practice, and openness to the world, especially the non-European world, has been profound. The Council greatly reduced the church's traditional hostility toward modern society. Henceforth, an ecumenical institution would respect other Christian faiths and promote religious freedom and tolerance. It would devote new energy to improving the earthly lot of the poor as well as their salvation. The laity would gain a greater role in worship, a democratization of traditional clerical-directed devotional life. The Council thus reformed many of the policies that had guided the church since the sixteenth-century Council of Trent.

But manifestations of popular piety and the liberalization begun at Vatican II have not reversed the separation of the church and European society nor the decreasing importance of Catholicism as a source of individual identity. Regular church attendance has continued to fall, especially among the young. According to a survey done in France in the early 1990s, only 12 percent of those who consider themselves Catholic attend mass regularly (down from 20 percent

in the mid-1980s). And only 2.5 percent of those under twenty-five attend (Hervieu-Léger, 1995, p. 155). The church has lost battles over divorce, homosexual rights, and abortion as European electorates have ratified liberal laws on all these issues in most European countries. A more conservative papacy under John Paul II exacerbated some tensions during the 1990s, though the pope roused great popular enthusiasm during his frequent travels, particularly in eastern Europe.

Although Catholicism no longer holds the place it once did in organizing social life and determining social attitudes, it has by no means disappeared from public life in Europe. Fierce political conflicts over such issues as abortion demonstrate the church's continuing ability to interject itself into debates on social morality. And even in France with its long history of secularized public education, attempts by the government to alter the funding of religious schools led to huge protest demonstrations in the 1980s and 1990s. Clearly, even though Catholicism is no longer a dominant element in European society, its impact is still considerable, and social historians will continue to assess its impact.

See also **Secularization** *(volume 2);* **Charity and Poor Relief: The Early Modern Period; Charity and Poor Relief: The Modern Period** *(volume 3);* **Schools and Schooling** *(in this volume); and other articles in this section.*

BIBLIOGRAPHY

Blackbourn, David. *Marpingen: Apparitions of the Virgin Mary in a Nineteenth-Century German Village.* New York, 1995. Excellent political, cultural, and social study of one Marian shrine and the entire phenomenon of Marian shrines in modern Europe.

Bossy, John. *Christianity in the West, 1400–1700.* Oxford, 1985. Important interpretation of the social impact of pre-modern Catholicism.

Callahan, William J. *Church, Politics, and Society in Spain, 1750–1874.* Cambridge, Mass., 1984. Useful analysis of late-eighteenth and nineteenth-century Spanish Catholicism.

Callahan, William J. "An Organizational and Pastoral Failure: Urbanization, Industrialization, and Religion in Spain, 1850–1930." In *European Religion in the Age of Great Cities, 1830–1930.* Edited by Hugh McLeod. London, 1995. Pages 43–60.

Callahan, William J. and David Higgs, eds. *Church and Society in Catholic Europe of the Eighteenth Century.* Cambridge, U.K., 1979. Essays that provide a useful country-by-country overview of Catholicism.

Chadwick, Owen. *A History of the Popes, 1830–1914.* Oxford, 1998.

Chadwick, Owen. *The Popes and European Revolution.* Oxford, 1981.

Chartier, Roger. *The Cultural Origins of the French Revolution.* Translated by Lydia G. Cochrane. Durham, N.C., 1991. Offers a synopsis of eighteenth-century dechristianization.

Chaunu, Pierre. *La mort à Paris. XVIe, XVIIe, XVIIIe siècles.* Paris, 1978. A study of dechristianization through a massive analysis of wills.

Christian, William, A., Jr. *Visionaries: The Spanish Republic and the Reign of Christ.* Berkeley, Calif., 1996. A study of apparitions and their political importance in modern Spain.

Davies, Norman. *Heart of Europe: A Short History of Poland.* Oxford, 1986.

Davis, Natalie Zemon. *Society and Culture in Early Modern France: Eight Essays.* Stanford, Calif., 1975. Contains vital essays on popular religion.

Delzell, Charles F., ed. *The Papacy and Totalitarianism between the Two World Wars.* New York, 1974.

Desan, Suzanne. *Reclaiming the Sacred: Lay Religion and Popular Politics in Revolutionary France.* Ithaca, N.Y., 1990. Important account of Catholic religious revival in France during the Revolution.

Durkheim, Émile. *The Elementary Forms of the Religious Life.* Translated by Joseph Ward Swain. New York, 1965.

Gibson, Ralph. *A Social History of French Catholicism, 1789–1914.* London, 1989. Excellent study of Catholicism in nineteenth-century France.

Hervieu-Léger, Danièle. "The Case of French Catholicism." In *The Post-War Generation and Establishment Religion: Cross-Cultural Perspectives.* Edited by Wade Clark Roof, Jackson W. Carroll, and David A. Roozen. Boulder, Col., 1995. Pages 59–85.

Hsia, R. Po-Chia. *The World of Catholic Renewal, 1540–1770.* Cambridge, U.K., and New York, 1998. Useful overview of the Catholic Reformation.

Kselman, Thomas A. *Miracles and Prophecies in Nineteenth-Century France.* New Brunswick, N.J.: 1983. A study of pilgrimages' role in religious and political change in modern France.

Kselman, Thomas A. "The Varieties of Religious Experience in Urban France." In *European Religion in the Age of Great Cities, 1830–1930.* Edited by Hugh McLeod. London, 1995. Pages 165–190.

Le Bras, Gabriel. *Études de sociologie religieuse.* 2 vols. Paris, 1955–1956. Collection of the work of an important sociologist of religious practice.

McCarthy, Timothy G. *The Catholic Tradition: The Church in the Twentieth Century.* 2d ed. Chicago, 1998.

McLeod, Hugh, ed. *European Religion in the Age of Great Cities, 1830–1930.* London, 1995. Useful collection of essays on religion's confrontation with the modern city.

McLeod, Hugh. *Religion and the People of Western Europe, 1789–1970.* Oxford, 1981. Excellent synthesis of the social history of religion in modern European history.

Rémond, René. *Religion and Society in Modern Europe.* Translated by Antonia Nevill. Oxford, 1999. An interpretative essay on the place of religion in contemporary European integration.

Roof, Wade Clark, Jackson W. Carroll, and David A. Roozen, eds. *The Post-War Generation and Establishment Religion: Cross-Cultural Perspectives.* Boulder, Colo., 1995.

Sperber, Jonathan. *Popular Catholicism in Nineteenth-Century Germany.* Princeton, N.J., 1984.

Tackett, Timothy. *Priest and Parish in Eighteenth-Century France: A Social and Political Study of the Curés in a Diocese of Dauphiné, 1750–1791.* Princeton, N.J., 1977. An analysis of the social conflicts in the eighteenth-century French church.

Tackett, Timothy. *Religion, Revolution, and Regional Culture in Eighteenth-Century France: The Ecclesiastical Oath of 1791.* Princeton, N.J., 1986. Important work on the Revolution's treatment of the church.

Van Kley, Dale K. *The Religious Origins of the French Revolution: From Calvin to the Civil Constitution, 1560–1791.* New Haven, Conn., 1996. A provocative study of Jansenism's contribution to the Revolution's origins.

Vovelle, Michel. *Piété baroque et déchristianisation en Provence au XVIIIe siècle.* Paris, 1973. Study of the process of eighteenth-century dechristianization.

PROTESTANTISM

Andrew Pettegree

Protestantism takes its name from the petition presented by certain German towns and princely states at the Imperial Diet of 1529. It signified their formal adherence to the doctrinal principles of the movement of evangelical protest that had raged in Germany surrounding the controversial teachings of the dissident Catholic monk Martin Luther (1483–1546). In 1529 the Imperial Diet attempted to bring an end to the controversy by reaffirming a strict prohibition of Luther's teaching, first banned by the Edict of Worms in 1521. The evangelical states entered their "protestation." This association was formalized by the presentation the following year of an evangelical confession of faith, the Confession of Augsburg (1530), and the formation in 1531 of a defensive alliance, the Schmalkaldic League, to guard the new faith.

The emergence of formal Protestant churches crowned a decade of evangelical ferment sparked by the teachings of Luther and attempts by the church to silence his followers. The Reformation is traditionally deemed to have begun in 1517, the year Luther published his Ninety-five Theses against indulgences. But the pressure for reform within the Catholic Church was of long standing. Luther, in this sense, followed a long line of distinguished churchmen and thinkers who criticized abuse within the church. Much of this criticism focused on the poor morals and low educational standards of the clergy and the venality and worldliness of the clerical hierarchy. But this dissatisfaction also reflected a fundamental long-term shift in the relationship between clergy and laypeople since the High Middle Ages. By the sixteenth century laypeople were eager to exercise more direct control over parts of civic culture that previously had been largely in the clerical domain, such as schools and hospitals. With the rise of lay literacy, education and even the skills of reading and writing were less wholly a clerical preserve, and laypeople judged their clergy by more demanding standards. The century around the Reformation witnessed a significant increase in the amount of money laypeople were channeling into the church through donations, the re-

modeling of their parish churches, and the founding of chantries, altars, and special masses.

Luther's teaching made such a powerful impact because it effectively provided an outlet for both of these strands of criticism. The first ten years of the Reformation movement were marked by the publication of a steady stream of Luther's writings denouncing clerical abuse and calling for reform. In the process he developed a radical theology of reform that found little place for the mediating role of the priesthood. Luther's criticisms initially found their strongest resonance among intellectuals and fellow members of the clerical orders. Humanists, who had their own criticisms of clerical laxity, were at first broadly supportive, as were many within the clerical estate who shared Luther's disillusionment with the clerical leadership. As his attack on the church broadened, Luther's views found increasing resonance in the German imperial cities, sophisticated communities that allowed a broad scope for the expression of lay opinion.

THEOLOGICAL AND ORGANIZATIONAL FOUNDATIONS

The core of Luther's new theological system was less a critique of clerical morals than a fundamental reevaluation of his understanding of grace and salvation. Justification by faith—by God's grace alone and not through works—was a liberating theological concept for those who, like Luther, had labored under an overwhelming burden of their own sinful natures and the impossibility of conciliating a pitiless God through propitiary works. But quite apart from the emotional release, evidently as powerful for many of Luther's followers as for the reformer himself, the doctrine of justification also had significant implications for the life of the church. If good works were of no effect, then many of the church's institutions and vocations, including memorial masses, monasteries, and purgatory, lost their purpose. Through justification Luther also placed new emphasis on the relationship between God

The Triumph of Truth. A German broadside summarizes the optimism of the early Reformation: as patriarchs, prophets, and apostles lead the triumphal procession of Christ, the knight Ulrich von Hutten on horseback leads the chained representatives of the papal church *(center)*. At the right, Martin Luther walks beside the triumphal chariot bearing the Savior.

and the individual Christian, and this, rather dangerously expressed as "the priesthood of all believers," did much to undermine the spiritual vocation of the priesthood. Luther's confidence in the laity may have been short-lived, but it provided the motivation for his greatest literary achievement, the German vernacular translation of the Bible (New Testament, 1522; complete Bible, 1534).

Vernacular scripture provided the crucial bridge between Luther the theologian and a wider popular movement. Many who could not comprehend the implications of justification could grasp the potency of the reformers' demand for "pure scripture," with its implicit criticism of late medieval theology and the authority of tradition. According to studies of the popular response to Luther, "pure scripture" (*rein evangelium*) became the slogan of the German urban Reformation in the years of its most rapid growth (1521–1524). From this point forward the commitment to vernacular scripture and to a generalized knowledge of the Bible among the Christian population was a leitmotiv of all Protestant churches.

Luther's preaching was characterized by a strong apocalyptical sense. Luther clearly believed that he was a preacher of the last days, and his struggle with the papacy was for him the final climactic battle with the Antichrist. In this respect it is hardly surprising that he at first gave little attention to church building. His whole being was bound up in the call to repentance, not the creation of a counterchurch. But as the new churches took shape, the need for order became obvious. In 1529 Luther responded to this pressure with

two catechisms, one for adults (*Large Catechism*) and one for children (*Small Catechism*), which set the tone for the strong educational impulse that became a leading characteristic of the Protestant movement. Philipp Melanchthon (1497–1560), Luther's friend and disciple, provided a systematic theology for the new movement with his *Loci communes* (1521). Another follower, Johannes Bugenhagen (1485–1558), revealed a talent for church organization reflected in the drafting of published church orders for the new churches of north Germany and Scandinavia.

These developments were a recognition that the movement of reform had become an independent church. Beginning in 1525 a wave of important cities, including Nuremberg, Strasbourg, and Augsburg, formally adhered to the Reformation and were followed by a number of the most important German princely states, including Hesse, Saxony, and Brandenburg. In 1357 Denmark adopted a Protestant church order, followed by Sweden in 1539. In a parallel process, the last efforts at a formal reconciliation with the Catholic Church, the Colloquy of Regensburg in 1540, failed. The establishment of Protestantism was complete.

With the establishment of formal Protestant churches, reformers acknowledged that the gulf between Protestantism and the Catholic hierarchy was now unbridgeable. But church building was also a defense of Protestant orthodoxy against challenge from within. Luther's movement was characterized from the beginning by an emotional contradiction. On the one hand, the movement in its early years was fueled by an enormous sense of release. Liberation from the weight of traditional Catholic devotional practice was the emotional heart of Luther's doctrine of grace. In addition the incautious formulation of the priesthood of all believers seemed to validate a large lay role in the interpretation of scripture but in fact revealed more starkly a fundamental problem of authority. If the power of the church hierarchy to arbitrate on matters of doctrine was denied, who then was to exercise this authority? Luther's response, that scripture was the final source of authority, invited a mass of conflicting interpretations, particularly in a movement that eagerly promoted free access to the words of scripture through vernacular translation.

It was soon apparent that these fundamental problems would not easily be resolved. Luther was alarmed by evidence of radicalism in the Wittenberg movement on the part of colleagues, such as Andreas Bodenstein von Karlstadt (1480–1541), and the self-taught laymen known as the Zwickau prophets. Luther's personal authority was enough to crush these local critics, but he could only watch, powerless, when in 1525 a wide swath of south Germany rose in revolt, claiming Luther's gospel as its inspiration for its program of social reform. The reaction to the Peasants' War (1524–1525) revealed the conservatism of the magisterial reformers. Luther urged the German princes to crush the rebels, and obedience to the established secular authority was henceforth a fundamental cornerstone of the creed of Lutheran churches. But the ending of the Peasants' War did not lead to the destruction of the sectarian instinct. The radical wing of the Reformation reconfigured as Anabaptism, a broad-ranging movement that encompassed a wealth of congregations and prophetic leaders, many of them self-educated laypeople from outside the normal clerical structure. The movement reached its first apogee in their "kingdom of a thousand years" in Münster, a north German city that fell into radical hands through the normal political process. Once in control the Anabaptist leadership declared Münster the new Jerusalem, where the saints might await the imminent end time. The incident attracted huge publicity among both the adepts, who flocked to Münster, and the increasingly appalled mainstream church leaders. In 1535 an army supported by both Catholics and Protestants suppressed the kingdom with great barbarity, a first indication that the established churches might have more in common than divisions over doctrine implied. Anabaptism, in fact, proved surprisingly resilient, particularly in the Netherlands, where the Friesian priest Menno Simons (1496–1561) revived a movement shorn of its more violent apocalypticism. Other groups, such as the Antitrinitarians, found ref-

uge in the more confessionally diverse lands of eastern Europe.

The horror of sectarianism was only one aspect of the disappointment that confronted leaders of the evangelical movement in the decades after the establishment of Protestant churches. Luther endured the progressive alienation of many who had initially welcomed his call for reform. The Peasants' War signaled the limits of the movement's appeal to the rural population, and 1525 also witnessed a decisive break with the Dutch humanist scholar Desiderius Erasmus (1466–1536), though many of the younger humanists remained faithful to Luther. By the end of the decade Luther was also embroiled in a damaging dispute with the leader of the Swiss Reformation, Huldrych Zwingli (1484–1531). In the longer term reformers also were forced to contemplate disappointment on a more fundamental level, a recognition that the Reformation had not achieved the wholesale reform of morals and that the effort to bring laypeople to an informed understanding of faith would be long and arduous. Surveys of the condition of the churches, or visitations, conducted in the Lutheran lands found that in the 1580s most inhabitants lacked even the most rudimentary understanding of the essentials of doctrine. Consideration of this evidence has led some historians to talk of the failure of the Reformation, though this seems overdrawn. The movement for renewal within the Catholic Church experienced similar problems in overcoming ingrained habits of belief and practice.

The real shortcoming of Luther's movement was its failure to put down deep roots outside of the German Empire or neighboring lands susceptible to German cultural influences, such as Scandinavia and parts of eastern Europe like Hungary and Bohemia. Promising beginnings in the lands of western Europe, such as France and the Netherlands, had by the 1540s been erased by determined opposition from the local lay powers, and even in England the Protestant settlement introduced under Henry VIII and Edward VI seemed successfully reversed in the reign of Mary Tudor. By the time of Luther's death in 1546 it was clear that Protestantism would not, as had once seemed possible, carry all before it.

Zwingli was an independent thinker of the first rank. Appointed to the position of people's priest in Zurich in 1518, Zwingli seized the opportunity to introduce root and branch reform. By 1525 Zurich had carried through a civic Reformation, the first city to do so, expelling Catholic priests and abolishing the Mass. The impact of Zurich's radical Reformation was initially profound in Germany as well as in the Swiss Confederation, but it was limited by a damaging

THE SOCIAL IMPACT OF PROTESTANTISM

The question of which groups within society were most attracted to Protestantism and why has long divided scholars. Undoubtedly Luther's movement initially found its most profound resonance among the populations of towns, though precisely which groups embraced the new movement varied according to local circumstances. The urban elites, sensible to the wider political implications of confronting conservative political neighbors or superiors, were not normally the prime movers, though often, when pressure for reform became irresistible, they would assert control of the movement to preserve their own authority. In some German towns the Reformation became a vehicle for prosperous but politically excluded groups within the citizenry to break the power of an entrenched oligarchy.

Much research on different case studies has sought to establish whether the Reformation appealed disproportionately to different trade groups. In aggregate this work has hardly improved on the contemporary verdict of the shrewd sixteenth-century Catholic writer Florimond de Raemond. The first "victims" of the new faith were in his observation "painters, clock-makers, draughtsmen, jewellers, booksellers, printers—all those whose crafts demand a certain degree of superior discernment" (Duke, Lewis, and Pettegree, 1992, p. 35) Printers and booksellers were especially important early converts to Protestantism, and in general the evangelical doctrines made deeper inroads among trades characterized by a high degree of literacy or mobility. Trade groups whose skills were relatively portable, such as goldsmiths or weavers, provided a disproportionate number of converts, whereas those with a low degree of product innovation, such as butchers and others in the food production process or coopers, proved disproportionately resistant to the new doctrines. In this sense the venerable "Weber thesis" may have expressed an essential truth. Max Weber (1864–1920) argued that an essential aspect of Calvinism that he called the Protestant work ethic created a climate particularly conducive to the growth of capitalism. In its purest sense the Weber thesis failed to command support. It may be that Weber indeed identified a real connection but inverted the causal relationship. The Reformation, and perhaps especially Calvinism, proved most alluring to groups that were already socially and economically mobile.

The importance of highly skilled members of new trades in the movement also explains why so many towns and cities were willing to open their gates to large groups of religious refugees and protect them against the resentment of indigenous guilds and tradesmen. The value of such newcomers to the local economy, particularly in towns experiencing stagnation, was widely recognized at the time. Indeed the Reformation, by stimulating an enormous movement of peoples between European lands of different confessions, played as important a role in stimulating protoindustrial development as any other aspect of economic change during the early modern period.

The Reformation also played an important role in recasting social relationships within the community. The role of women in society was drastically reordered, many have argued to their disadvantage. The denigration of the female religious vocation certainly cut independent career opportunities, and the end of the cult of saints removed many female role models. Against these outcomes Protestant societies often successfully articulated a new vision of the dignity of female roles within the family and tenaciously defended the rights of women within this context. Calvinist consistories, for instance, devoted considerable attention to upholding the dignity of marriage and protecting women from brutality, abandonment, or illtreatment. Many women benefited from the legitimation of clerical marriage, which gave clerical families for the first time the legal protections of a legitimate relationship. Indeed, clergy families became a powerful new social force in most Protestant cultures, a phenomenon linked to the increased professionalization of the Protestant ministry. By the end of the sixteenth century an increasing proportion, in many areas a majority, of clergy in post were university educated, and the increased desirability and social prestige attached to their work was reflected in the emergence of recognizable clerical dynasties.

The Protestant emphasis on the family as the natural unit of social organization had a profound and persistent impact on the social culture of Protestant lands. In the first Reformation century Protestantism placed an obligation on the family to function as a sort of small church community, the head of the family instructing both children and servants in the rudiments of the faith. Such an emphasis gave full rein to the puritan instinct, by which families and groups of households dissatisfied with the morals of society practiced a culture of reinforcement and greater austerity within the privacy of their own homes. At its best this was a support to the wider community; applied with too critical an eye to the failings of others, it easily reinforced the sectarian instinct.

Calvinist Communion Service. Engraving by Bernard Picart, 1732. NATIONAL GALLERY OF PRAGUE

quarrel between Zwingli and Luther. The more conservative Luther was appalled by Zurich's radical "cleansing" of the local churches to remove all physical vestiges of Catholicism. The two men soon clashed over eucharistic doctrine, Zwingli again favoring a more radical solution, and after a failed attempt at reconciliation at the Colloquy of Marburg (1529), the gap between the two was unbridgeable. Inside the Swiss Confederation the appeal of the reform movement was retarded by suspicion of Zurich's motives. Although the two most powerful German-speaking urban cantons, Bern and Basel, eventually adopted the reform, the rural mountain cantons decisively rejected Protestantism and with it Zurich's imperial pretensions. Open confrontation in the Battle of Kappel wars left Zurich defeated and Zwingli dead on the field of battle. The Zurich Reformation was ultimately rescued by the leadership of Heinrich Bullinger (1504–1575), but its capacity for expansion was decisively checked.

As Zurich retreated into introspection, a new leadership force emerged from the unlikely quarter of French-speaking Geneva. The small independent city was a late convert to reform, but in the 1530s it was a beacon for evangelical refugees from France, among them the young scholar John Calvin (1509–1564). After an uncertain beginning to a ministry that led to his expulsion and exile from 1538 to 1541, Calvin gradually imposed his personal stamp on the Geneva Reformation. By the time of his death Geneva had become a model Christian commonwealth and the center of a growing international movement.

Even more than Luther, Calvin was the spirit that underpinned the long-term survival of Protestantism. Calvin was a writer and thinker of exceptional clarity. Sharing Luther's gift for excoriating polemic, he also synthesized Reformation thought into a coherent systematic theology. His *Institutes of the Christian Religion* (1536; final expanded version 1560) was a work of genius that functioned equally effectively as a handbook for the individual Christian and for the Christian community. Along with Luther's vernacular translation of the Bible, it was among the most important literary products of the Reformation.

Guided by Calvin's preaching and supervised by the consistory, a joint morals commission staffed by clergy and lay elders, Geneva became the archetypal godly community. In the process the Reformation shed much of the apocalypticism that characterized the first generation. Calvinism, the least apocalyptic of the major Protestant schools, gave much greater attention to building the church in the community.

THE AGE OF RELIGIOUS WAR

The peaceful construction of the church in Geneva contrasted strongly with Calvinism's disruptive influence elsewhere in Europe. Calvin's strong emphasis on the sanctity of suffering together with the movement's sophisticated organizational structure provided the basis for church building even where the state power remained hostile. Calvin's followers (if not Calvin himself) were also far more willing than Luther to contemplate defiance of the state power. Early Calvinist congregations in France and the Netherlands were characterized above all by a remarkable sense of providentialism, which allowed them to survive and even grow despite intense persecution.

A midcentury crisis in the affairs of several northern European states allowed Calvinist congregations the chance to seize power. While a Calvinist church swiftly established supremacy in Scotland—the consequence of a political revolution of which the Calvinist congregations were the beneficiaries rather than the cause—the emergence of churches in France and the Netherlands led to prolonged conflict. The French Wars of Religion (1562–1598) were a sustained struggle to prevent the Calvinist insurrection from undermining the Catholic character of the kingdom. Although Calvinists remained a decided minority, the Edict of Nantes in 1598 nevertheless guaranteed French Calvinist (Huguenot) churches important freedoms. In the Netherlands the Dutch revolt (1566–1609) led to the creation of a free Calvinist state in the northern provinces with the Union of Utrecht in 1579. In England the restoration of a Protestant settlement under Elizabeth I, who ruled from 1558 to 1603, completed a decisive shift in the balance of religious power in northern Europe.

The century of conflict unleashed by Luther's teachings achieved some sort of resolution in the first half of the seventeenth century. In Germany the Religious Peace of Augsburg (1555) permitted local autonomy for Catholic and Protestant principalities and bought the empire a half-century of uneasy peace. But tensions always simmered beneath the surface, not least because Calvinism, which had begun to make inroads into the German lands in the 1560s, was not included in the terms of the peace. A particular element of unpredictability was provided by successive electors of the Rhineland Palatinate, who after converting their lands to Calvinism in 1562 aspired to an aggressive leadership role. Toward the end of the century the Habsburg imperial family embarked upon a more active policy of recatholicization in their patrimony, and conflict loomed. The spark was provided by a rebellion in 1618 in Bohemia, one of the most integral yet most thoroughly protestantized parts of the Habsburg dominions. Fearing that the accession of the new emperor, Ferdinand II, would spell the end of Protestant liberties, Bohemians in 1619 offered

their crown instead to the elector palatine, Frederick V. He foolishly accepted, preparing the way for the Habsburg reconquest of Bohemia and the investiture of his own territories. These events initiated the Thirty Years' War, a conflict that gradually involved most of the powers of Europe. Although the religious configuration was not straightforward—the German Lutheran princes initially refused to support the Palatinate, and France later joined the anti-Habsburg struggle for straightforward political reasons—religious issues underpinned the conflict and made it more bitter, more destructive, and more difficult to resolve. In particular the intervention of the Lutheran king of Sweden, Gustavus II Adolph, was essential in turning back the tide of Habsburg success and preserving the Protestant cause in central Europe.

In 1648 the Peace of Westphalia finally permitted the warring parties to extricate themselves from the conflict and brought to an end the period of European relations primarily governed by religious loyalties. The peace also effectively confirmed the de facto division of Europe between Protestant and Catholic. Henceforth Protestantism was the majority creed of Germany, Scandinavia, Britain, the Dutch Republic, and more isolated outposts in eastern Europe, such as Hungary. Missionary efforts by Protestants and Catholics alike concentrated more on sustaining isolated minorities than on attempts to upset this balance. The focus of conversion also shifted to the non-Christian world opened up by colonial expansion and, nearer home, to the Christianization of populations still mired in ignorance and unbelief among the numerically dominant rural populations and the newly emerging urban proletariat. The challenge these groups posed to formal religion was a constant theme of religious life during the next two hundred years, stimulating repeated attempts to revive the original evangelical fervor of the Reformation era.

THE CHURCH IN THE AGE OF REASON

The move away from religious warfare reinforced other social changes that gradually over the next century would have a profound impact on attitudes toward religion and the place of the church in society. This profound shift in attitudes toward intellectual and scientific questions led historians to dub this period the Age of Reason, though the effect of questioning historic certainties was often uncomfortable for official religion. This was an age characterized above all by new developments in the world of ideas. With the scientific revolution, experimental science came of age as a discipline and seized the imaginations

It is easy to assume that the relationship between Protestantism and artistic culture was antagonistic. Protestants certainly took a highly critical view of the artistic manifestations of Catholic devotional culture. Although Luther reproved the violent removal of images, hostility to pictures and sculptures of saints, particularly when they were the focus of devotion, often led to destruction. Such iconoclastic episodes characterized the first wave of the Reformation in many Lutheran and Swiss cities, such as Wittenberg in 1521 and Basel, with its *Kirchensturm* (church storm), in 1527. Churches influenced by Calvin took a still more radical position. Iconoclasm was a feature of the early stages of the religious conflict in France and the Netherlands, and England and Scotland experienced the violent, unauthorized removal of images.

The cleansing of the churches did allow for the preservation of some masterpieces, such as Jan van Eyck's *Lamb of God* altar in Ghent, which was removed to safety elsewhere. The collapse of the Catholic devotional tradition did not spell the end of religious art in Protestant countries. In Germany Lucas Cranach (1472–1553) gave artistic expression to the new Reformation doctrines. Cranach and his followers designed and produced highly influential images expressing both the polemical and antipapal rhetoric of the Reformation, such as *Passional Christi und Antichristi* (1521), and its new core doctrines, such as *Law and the Gospel* (1529). In the process they developed a wholly new artistic medium, the didactic woodcut, which played an important public role both as a means of book illustration and as single-page broadsheets. Mature Lutheran art also developed a distinctive pictorial form, the memorial picture (fine examples may be seen in the Wittenberg Stadtkirche).

In Calvinist cultures artistic hostility to religious pictorial art was more intense and enduring. Artistic energies were therefore often redeployed into other media, notably music. Calvin himself quickly grasped the value of music. Communal singing became a crucial part of the German service, specifically versions of the psalms set to music and sung unaccompanied in unison. These metrical psalms quickly became an identifying characteristic of Calvinist communities and were sung wherever congregations gathered, in church, in the fields, or even, during the religious wars, as armies went into battle. In more settled times distinguished composers provided harmonized versions for domestic entertainment, and it is in this form that they have continued to be most frequently performed.

The success of the metrical psalms opened the way for the Protestant rediscovery of religious music. Deprived of the Mass, Protestant composers developed the chorale, a musical form that reached its apogee in the music of the German Lutheran Johann Sebastian Bach (1685–1750). Protestantism found its most characteristic musical expression in congregational singing, not least the tradition of hymnody bequeathed by Luther to the German churches. Luther himself wrote hymns and firmly believed in their capacity to instruct and inspire. The tradition was renewed and continued by the English Nonconformist churches, notably the Methodist movement of the Wesleys. Hymn-singing has remained one of the most fondly maintained aspects of the Protestant tradition.

Protestantism also left its mark on the physical appearance of the church. In countries where it was not possible to appropriate former Catholic churches, Protestants erected new structures that reflected architecturally their greater emphasis on preaching and participation. Round, oblong, or hexagonal structures made the pulpit the focal point and eliminated the long choir leading to the high altar. Such structures were common in France, though few survived the destruction that followed the ban on Huguenot churches in 1685. Examples survived in Leiden, in the Netherlands, and Burtisland, Scotland. The rise of Nonconformist churches in the eighteenth century led to a new wave of building that followed these Protestant architectural principles even more rigidly, providing many of the best examples of church structures that make an elevated pulpit the focal point.

One cultural field in which the influence of Protestantism was profound is the novel. Protestants played a significant part in the development of the narrative form. The influence of the puritan conscience, obvious in the religious allegories of John Bunyan (1628–1688) and the poetry and prose works of John Milton (1608–1674), is equally present in Daniel Defoe's *Robinson Crusoe* (1719), whose hero, in the context of an adventure story of enduring appeal, struggles in the thrall of an all-powerful Providence. The power and appeal of nineteenth-century Nonconformity were echoed in the Victorian "industrial novels," notably Elizabeth Gaskell's *Mary Barton* (1848) and the works of George Eliot (1819–1880). Finally, Samuel Butler (1835–1902), in *The Way of All Flesh* (1903), draws an enormously powerful vision of the suffocating respectability of clerical life in the last era during which the church provided a unique path to respectability. Butler's work is infinitely more acute in its psychological perceptions than Anthony Trollope's popular novels of ecclesiastical politics and cathedral life.

The Salzburg Expulsion. *March of the Salzburg Emigrants,* Protestants expelled from the archbishopric of Salzburg between 1731 and 1734. Many emigrated to Prussia. Copper engraving (1734). BILDARCHIV PREUSSISCHER KULTURBESITZ, BERLIN

of the thinkers of all nations. The world of ideas found a newly confident philosophy, leading to the pleasing rational certainties of the Enlightenment.

The effects of these developments on organized religion were not straightforward. Most leading figures in the world of science strongly affirmed the existence of a divine being. Indeed many affirmed that science "proved" the existence of God. In this period the new science, the discoveries of the German Lutheran Johannes Kepler (1571–1630) and of Isaac Newton (1642–1727), was widely regarded as a bulwark against atheism. According to John Locke (1632–1704), the most influential thinker of the day, the conviction that there is a God "is the most obvious truth that reason discovers"; its evidence is "equal to mathematical certainty." The effect on belief was more subtle. The growing understanding of natural phenomena as capable of scientific explanation restricted the areas of the unknown in which God's power was seen to be at work. In the medical field this period experienced a sea change in attitudes toward epidemics from the conviction that plague was a heaven-sent punishment (in Dutch it was known as *de gave Gods,* God's gift) to a search for medical causes. The trial and execution of witches, still ferocious in the early seventeenth century, dwindled away by the end of the century. While most humans continued to believe in God, the belief in the Devil as a ceaselessly active force receded. The growing fixity in religious boundaries in Europe also led to a gradual increase in religious tol-

eration. This was more a matter of fact than principle, a weary acceptance that differences between the religious confessions were too deep-seated to be eliminated. But toleration was also assisted by a more profound revulsion against persecution for religious belief.

This development was certainly halting and not without setbacks. During this period formal toleration was revoked in Hungary, and in Poland the Roman Catholic minority found relief from the frustrations of the country's endemic political turmoil by treating both Lutheran and Orthodox minorities with increasing severity. In England the resolution of the bitter legacy of the Civil War led, after the Restoration in 1660, to a switchback of vindictiveness interspersed by self-serving partial toleration until coexistence was finally embedded in the Toleration Act of 1689. In France, Louis XIV repudiated the privileges formerly granted the Huguenot minority. The Revocation of the Edict of Nantes in 1685 ordered the forcible closure of all Protestant churches and provoked the last major religious emigration of the Reformation era. But Louis's policy was widely perceived by contemporaries as anachronistic, and those countries that opened their doors to the refugees benefited greatly from the injection of the new economic skills brought by the Huguenots.

With the eighteenth century the Protestant churches of Europe were generally entering calmer waters—but at a price. Some of the established churches had reached too comfortable an accommodation with the state. In England the power of preferment created a subservient and venal clerical class, eager for advancement, uncritical of the status quo, while bitterly divided over inequalities of wealth. With curates existing on as little as £20 per year, pluralism was rife. Yet few protested against a system in which the only hope of advancement lay in dutiful and patient obedience to lay patrons. In Germany, too, Lutheran churches had drifted into a relationship of easy and unreflective obedience to the state, initiating a tradition of Erastian complacency that had disastrous results in later centuries.

This increasing ossification of established Protestant churches inevitably provoked a reaction. Within the churches there arose new and challenging movements of spiritual renewal. The frustration of hopes of reform led in turn to the rise of nonconformity and dissent.

Within the Protestant establishment the most serious spiritual challenge was posed by Pietism, which sought to supplement the emphasis on institutions and dogma by promoting the practice of piety. It found its chief inspiration in the writings of Johann Arnd (1555–1621), a Lutheran theologian in whose work mysticism played a profound role. In Pietism the emphasis on inner experience and the life of the spirit was balanced by the insistence that belief should be reflected by a deeper and active commitment to the Christian life. In this respect Pietism drew heavily on the inspiration of the English Puritan movement, many of whose leading writings were at this point translated into other European vernaculars, including German and Hungarian. English Puritans, weary of the partial Reformation of the English church, were also the original inspiration behind a tradition of dissent that had a profound impact on the development of Protestantism in North America. From the time of the first settlers in Massachusetts, the Pilgrims in 1620, a succession of nonconformist groups sought sanctity in separation in the virgin lands of the New World. Among the most successful were the Quakers, who like the German Pietists dedicated themselves to living in accordance with the inner light. Inspired by the preaching of George Fox (1624–1691), the Quakers believed that ordained ministers and consecrated buildings were unnecessary for a church, teachings that brought them into conflict with successive seventeenth-century English governments. In 1682 William Penn (1644–1718) founded Pennsylvania as a holy experiment based on Quaker principles.

THE CHURCH IN THE INDUSTRIAL AGE

The greatest of the dissenting traditions was the Methodist movement founded by John Wesley (1703–

John Wesley. Portrait by Nathaniel Hone (1718–1784) NATIONAL PORTRAIT GALLERY, LONDON

1791). Methodism to some extent grew from the same impatience with established churches that had spawned earlier dissenting movements, but it also tapped into the new frustrations that were a consequence of industrial growth. In particular the English parochial system was slow to adapt to the rapid growth of urban populations that followed the birth of industrialization. As a result large swaths of the urban population were effectively unchurched. Wesley's ministry attempted to reverse what he saw as the inexorable growth of ignorance and atheism.

Wesley, the product of both a conventional Anglican education and a failed colonial venture in Georgia in 1735, began his preaching ministry after a conversion experience led him to embrace practical religion. As the churches were closed to him, Wesley took to the fields, where in an astonishing fifty-year ministry he attracted huge crowds and a growing following. Wesley always opposed separation from the Church of England, which had denied him a pulpit, but the real distinctiveness of his movement was formally recognized soon after his death in the Plan of Pacification of 1795. Methodism was by then a distinct and vital force in English life characterized by a lack of hierarchy and devotion to the inspirational hymns of John Wesley and his brother Charles Wesley

(1707–1788). Evangelical Christianity also made itself felt in the established church and in secular politics through the twenty-year campaign, from 1787 to 1807, led by William Wilberforce for the abolition of the slave trade.

The growth of an industrial proletariat was only one of a number of related challenges posed to Protestantism during the nineteenth century. New systems of belief of a secular nature posed an implicit challenge to organized religion that became a direct challenge with socialism and marxism. The rise of secular concepts of social organization, influenced by the teachings of Voltaire (1694–1778) and Rousseau (1712–1778), was often directly hostile to the power of the church in government. These ideas found their purest echo in the U.S. Constitution and their most violent expression in the French Revolution. Even though the Protestant nations of Europe avoided the worst excesses of revolutionary France, the spirit of the age proved increasingly impatient with the established churches' pretensions to a monopoly of religious truth. In a gradual process governments across Europe enacted formal toleration and thus extended full civil rights to previously marginal groups, including Roman Catholics, Jews, and finally even atheists. The rise of the secular urge in politics also led to considerable conflict in areas where church-state relations had previously been essentially harmonious, such as education and ecclesiastical patronage.

European Protestant churches reacted to these diverse challenges in different ways. In several of the dominant Protestant confessions, state encroachment or the rise of Liberalism—the political insistence on individual freedom and constitutional government and the economic doctrine of laissez-faire—led to painful divisions within the church. In 1843 almost half the ministers of the established Presbyterian Church of Scotland left the church to found a new Free Church in a dispute over ecclesiastical patronage known as the Great Disruption. The new political circumstances prompted two major splits in the dominant Dutch Reformed Church, the *Afscheiding* of 1834 and the *Doleantie* of 1887. In England the Oxford movement (1833–1845) was also largely inspired by a sense of the moral corrosiveness of Liberalism, although there the leading figures eschewed separation, at least until their spokesman John Henry Newman (1801–1890) defected to Roman Catholicism.

In Germany the major challenge was posed by the rise of biblical criticism in an age in which scholarly discoveries for the first time called into question the literal truth of parts of the biblical canon. German universities found an impressively dispassionate response, arguing that reasoned criticism should be met by refutation rather than authority. With the German example, the Protestant churches of the mainstream adapted themselves relatively easily to the advance of science. In time churchmen learned to live with and even embrace the new climate of an age of mass political activism. In the Netherlands the towering figure of Abraham Kuyper (1837–1920) presided over an explicitly confessional political party, the first mass membership party of the Netherlands, committed to upholding orthodox Calvinist values against the secular tide. This, indeed, was the era that saw the emergence of several explicitly religious parties in Europe, usually broadly in the conservative, Christian Democratic tradition.

The nineteenth century also saw a rapid expansion of Protestant missionary activity in Africa and Asia. This was a relatively new interest (compared to Catholicism's), and it had a complex relationship with the problems encountered in Europe itself.

THE CHURCH IN THE TWENTIETH CENTURY

The twentieth century was a period of almost unprecedented political turmoil in Europe. Coupled with social changes of bewildering rapidity, the turmoil confronted Protestant churches with challenges that they struggled, often unsuccessfully, to meet. For the first time large sections of the population repudiated any formal belief. Protestant countries also for the first time faced the challenge of absorbing significant immigrant communities strongly committed to non-Christian belief systems. Even the Protestant confessions in the modern era shifted the balance of influence from Europe to the New World, which accurately reflected the shifting political and economic balance. To some extent this was anticipated in the nineteenth century by the proliferation of new religious movements rooted in a tradition of American revivalism. The Mormons (1830), Seventh-Day Adventists (1863), and Christian Scientists (1879) are the three most prominent examples. The American Great Awakening also transformed the Baptists from a small, rather marginal group into a huge church that by the end of the twentieth century had over 35 million members worldwide (mostly in the United States). In the twentieth century the most important movements of revivalism—Pentecostalism (1901), Fundamentalism, and (closely related to Fundamentalism) Evangelicalism—emerged from an American, conservative tradition.

For the more staid and decidedly uncharismatic European Protestant churches, the twentieth century

Purveyor of the Sacraments. Angela Berners-Wilson presiding at the liturgy of the Church of England. ©PATRICK LANDMANN/LIAISON AGENCY

threw up difficult challenges that often found them wanting. Faced with the discordant but powerful forces of nationalism, socialism, and class conflict, the churches were sometimes driven into positions that left an enduring stain on their reputations. During World War I (1914–1918), established Protestant churches on both sides enrolled as cheerleaders for a rampant militarism that at war's end left millions dead. Twenty years later the German Lutheran Church willingly embraced the nationalism and racial policies of the Nazi movement. The small dissident group that left the church over the issue of Nazi racial policies, the Confessing Church (Bekennende Kirche), has too often served as a fig leaf for the complacency or enthusiasm of the vast majority. Two centuries of Erastian subservience to the power of the state left the German church with few intellectual weapons to resist the lure of a regime antithetical to Christian principles.

The horrors of World War II accelerated the church's retreat from the front line in public affairs. Scarred by the experiences of the war era, European Protestant churches withdrew increasingly from any politically sensitive role in an age when church membership continued on an apparently inexorable decline. The postwar period also saw a significant detachment of Christian values, still generally regarded as a touchstone of decent behavior in most countries of the Protestant tradition, from formal church membership. In this curiously ambivalent yet not unaffectionate relationship, Protestant churches were valued still as a social institution, primarily as a purveyor of the sacraments of passage, such as baptism, marriage, and burial, by a far wider community than those who regularly attended church. The churches were for the most part happy to subsist in this curious netherworld between habit and redundancy. In the parts of Protestant Europe where the faith was still passionately upheld, such as Northern Ireland, sectarian passion was often seen more as an embarrassment than as a vindication of faith.

By the beginning of the twenty-first century, most European Protestant traditions had rejected such a distortion of their role as much as they had by then repulsed the wilder excesses of American Protestant evangelism, a rejection all the more striking given the otherwise all-pervasive influence of American culture on Europe. This movement depended heavily on the new media of television evangelism and on charismatic fundamentalism. These developments find their most significant echo in the nondenominational "house churches," which emerged at the end of the twentieth century as a significant force alongside the mainstream Protestant denominations.

See also **Secularization** *(volume 2); and other articles in this section.*

BIBLIOGRAPHY

Brooke, J. H. *Science and Religion: Some Historical Perspectives.* Cambridge, U.K., 1991.

Chadwick, Owen. *The Secularization of the European Mind in the Nineteenth Century.* Cambridge, U.K., 1975.

Clark, J. C. D. *English Society 1688–1832: Ideology, Social Structure, and Political Practice during the Ancient Regime.* Cambridge, U.K., 1985.

Craig, Gerald R. *The Church and the Age of Reason, 1648–1789.* London, 1960.

Duke, Alastair, Gillian Lewis, and Andrew Pettegree, eds. *Calvinism in Europe, 1540–1610: A Collection of Documents.* New York, 1992.

Edwards, Mark U. *Printing, Propaganda, and Martin Luther.* Berkeley, Calif., 1994.

Erb, Peter C. *Pietists: Selected Writings.* London, 1983.

Fulbrook, Mary. *Piety and Politics: Religion and the Rise of Absolutism in England, Württemberg, and Prussia.* Cambridge, U.K., 1983.

Gilmont, Jean-François, ed. *The Reformation and the Book.* Aldershot, U.K., 1997.

Goertz, Hans Jürgen. *The Anabaptists.* Translated by Trevor Johnson. London, 1996.

Gutteridge, Richard. *Open Thy Mouth for the Dumb!: The German Evangelical Church and the Jews, 1879–1950.* Oxford, 1976.

Hastings, Adrian. *A History of English Christianity, 1920–1985.* London, 1986.

Hastings, Adrian. *A World History of Christianity.* London, 1999.

Karant-Nunn, Susan C. *The Reformation of Ritual: An Interpretation of Early Modern Germany.* London, 1997.

McGrath, Alister E. *Reformation Thought: An Introduction.* Oxford, 1988.

McLeod, Hugh. *Religion and the People of Western Europe, 1789–1970.* Oxford, 1981.

Miller, John. *Religion in the Popular Prints, 1600–1832.* Cambridge, U.K., 1986.

Oberman, Heiko. *Luther: Man between God and the Devil.* Translated by Eileen Walliser-Schwarzbert. New Haven, Conn., 1989.

Pettegree, Andrew, ed. *The Reformation World.* London, 2000.

Stoeffler, F. Ernest. *German Pietism during the Eighteenth Century.* Leiden, 1973.

Wintle, Michael J. *Pillars of Piety: Religion in the Netherlands in the Nineteenth Century, 1813–1901.* Hull, U.K., 1987.

EASTERN ORTHODOXY

Gregory L. Freeze

The Eastern Orthodox Church, distinct from the Roman Catholic Church since the Great Schism of 1054, includes more than a dozen autocephalous churches in Europe, each autonomous in its administrative structure but all united by ecumenical councils, common dogma, and tradition. They range from the Russian Orthodox Church to much smaller churches in east central and southeastern Europe. In modern times these European churches developed along national state lines, as in the Balkans, where the breakup of the Ottoman Empire in the nineteenth century led to the formation of autocephalous churches in Greece (1833), Romania (1864), Bulgaria (1871), and Serbia (1879). Some sees acquired formal independent status still later, as in Poland (1924) and Albania (1937). In precommunist regimes the Orthodox Church was often the dominant if not the official church and had sizable flocks. In 1897 Russia had nearly 87.1 million believers, or 69.4 percent of the population, and majorities also prevailed in Romania (17 million), Greece (9 million), Serbia (8 million), Bulgaria (8 million), and Georgia (5 million). Many other countries, not only former parts of the Russian Empire such as Finland and Poland, had small but devoted contingents of Orthodox observers.

Following the example of European historiography, social historians have given increasing attention to Eastern Orthodoxy, especially in the lands of the former Soviet Union. This research has focused on five main issues. The first concerns the church's status in the political order, from privileged to persecuted—a key determinant of its capacity to act independently with respect to social and political questions. A second issue is institutional development. To what degree did this medieval institution internalize the features of modern social organization, and how did this internal growth affect its role in society and culture? The third question is the clergy—size, distribution, status, role, composition, education, and other characteristics—and its capacity and willingness to join and shape social and national movements. A fourth issue is the church's social mission, that is, its engagement in social problems such as alcoholism, divorce, social justice, and revolution. The final issue is "popular Orthodoxy," the patterns and meanings of lay observance as well as forms of deviance and dissent. Whatever the church might have taught, the central question is how the folk received, modified, or rejected the norms of official institutional Orthodoxy.

This article focuses on the Russian Orthodox Church, by far the largest and most influential see in Europe. It has also been the target of intensive research and scholarship, a windfall of the demise of the USSR, which effectively liberated scholarship from the shackles of Soviet archival restrictions. The Moscow Patriarchate wielded considerable influence in the twentieth century, especially after World War II, playing a salient if not dominating role over Orthodox Churches elsewhere within the Soviet bloc.

CAESAROPAPISM AND AGENCY

In contrast to traditional historiography, which portrayed the Orthodox Churches as docile handmaidens of the state and hence devoid of agency, scholarship has demonstrated a far more complex, even conflicting relationship between the Orthodox Church and the secular state. Most important, as Orthodox canonists have emphasized, Eastern Orthodoxy did not adumbrate any so-called caesaropapism, whereby the emperor, in contrast to the medieval papacy, purportedly "ruled" the church. Rather, the operative conception is "symphony," that is, a harmonious cooperation between the temporal and sacred spheres with clear limits on the ruler's authority over purely spiritual matters.

In Russia and elsewhere individual rulers sometimes transgressed these boundaries. In the Muscovite period (1450–1689), such intrusion was uncommon and personal, primarily directed at an individual prelate. In the subsequent imperial period (1689–1917), the intrusion intensified, especially from the early nineteenth century, when the emperor's official rep-

The Survival of Orthodoxy. Religious procession at Stolobny, Russia, commemorates the 330th anniversary of the discovery of the relics of St. Nil Sorsky. SOVFOTO/EASTFOTO

resentative, the chief procurator, assumed a more active role in church administration. However, traditional accounts tended to exaggerate this role and failed to recognize that intervention—most notoriously by K. P. Pobedonostsev (chief procurator, 1880–1905)—only succeeded in provoking episcopal resentment. Indeed this intrusion, when coupled with

a transparent determination by government officials to act in the interests of the state and not the church, impelled even archconservative prelates to demand a radical change in the status and rights of the church.

Given these tensions and diverging interests, Eastern Orthodoxy played a more important role in nation building than in state building. In Russia, Orthodoxy not only left a deep imprint on the dominant political culture but also provided a primary referent for Russian national identity, especially in the late imperial period. During that period the centripetal forces of a multinational and multiconfessional state impelled Russians and other East Slavs to define ethnicity at least partly in religious terms. The church's role in nation building was still more pronounced in the Balkans, where Orthodox clergy and confession were key factors in nationalist movements against the Ottoman Empire, providing support, legitimacy, and leadership in Greece, Serbia, Romania, and Bulgaria. Precisely because Eastern Orthodoxy admitted a division along nation-state lines, with inevitable if begrudging recognition of autocephaly from the ecumenical patriarch in Constantinople, it tended to provide a critical religious dimension to nationalist identity and to liberation movements.

THE INSTITUTIONAL DEVELOPMENT OF THE RUSSIAN ORTHODOX CHURCH

Given Russia's vast geographical expanse, population dispersion, and marginal resources, both human and material, the medieval Russian Church had only a minimal capacity to exercise control over popular religious practices or even over its own clergy. Armed with only a handful of far-flung dioceses and preoc-

cupied with administering a vast empire of church-owned properties and peasant inhabitants, bishops had neither the means nor the time for more than episodic, nominal supervision of parishes and priests. Not until the Church Council *(Stoglav)* of 1551 did prelates even attempt to adumbrate new norms and regulations. That effort received a further impulse in 1589 with the establishment of the patriarchate, which provided the first foundations for ecclesiastical centralization. Thus the seventeenth-century church, like the state, began to construct a more elaborate administration, primarily to regularize the collection of dues and tithes but also to supervise religious matters, such as the appointment of clergy and other dimensions of spiritual life.

Peter the Great, tsar from 1689 to 1725, introduced far-reaching reforms to improve ecclesiastical administration. Emblematic was his demand that the church establish seminaries to educate candidates for the priesthood. Although bishops had earlier complained about the low educational level of priests, the church did not erect a new system of ecclesiastical education until the eighteenth century, and it took several decades to achieve even modest results. By the 1760s the church operated two academies and 26 seminaries with approximately six thousand students, but growth accelerated thereafter. By 1914 this network consisted of four academies, 57 seminaries, and

Caesaropapism. The statue of Peter the Great (cast in 1782 by É.-M. Falconet) with the headquarters of the Holy Synod of the Russian Orthodox Church in the background. Peter replaced the patriarchate with the Synod. ©HULTON GETTY/ARCHIVE PHOTOS

315

185 elementary schools with more than fifty thousand students. This system revolutionized the educational standards of parish priests; beginning in the early nineteenth century, virtually all new ordinands had seminary diplomas. The academies, though small in size, likewise had a profound impact on the church, supplying the great majority of recruits for the episcopate, the "learned monasticism" that dominated the hierarchy.

No less important was the process of institution building in central and diocesan administration. Although later derided by critics as bureaucratization, this organizational development gave the church a new capacity to exercise influence in rural parishes, not merely elite palaces. The critical impulse again came from the reforms engineered by Peter the Great, who applied the principles of secular governance to the church. His reforms replaced the patriarch, head of the church, with a governing Holy Synod made up of ranking prelates and subject to oversight by a secular official, the chief procurator. He also constructed a regularized diocesan administration with explicit norms to direct the clergy, parishes, and popular religious practices. Peter's prescriptions gradually took effect after his death in 1725, and by the late eighteenth century the church had an elaborate structure that enabled it to establish and enforce uniform policies. For the balance of the imperial period the church continued to expand its administration. For example, it divided dioceses into smaller, more manageable units. It also developed important adjuncts, such as the ecclesiastical press. Although the church had a press earlier, chiefly to publish liturgical books, in the mid–nineteenth century it produced a vast complex of printed literature, including catechisms, sermon collections, official newspapers, academic journals, diocesan gazettes, and popular spiritual literature for the lay reader.

Institutionalization of Orthodoxy was not without negative dimensions. Contemporaries, whether lay or clerical, complained loudly about a bureaucratization that, in the idiom of prerevolutionary Russia, was synonymous with corruption and venality. The lay clerical staffs, underpaid and overworked, routinely succumbed to the temptation of bribes to expedite petitions and to circumvent canons. These problems, while endemic to the ancien régime as a whole, were especially acute in the church, for its minuscule, inelastic budget failed to keep pace with the explosion in the volume of administrative duties. As a further aggravation, hypercentralization mandated synodal review and approval of even the most trivial diocesan matters, from the divorce of individuals to the construction of a new parish church. This episcopal

TABLE 1
PARISHIONER-PARISH RATIOS

Year	Average number of parishioners per church
1740	647
1780	1,030
1840	1,403
1890	1,793
1904	2,305
1914	2,414

preoccupation with compiling vast, often unutilized documentation alienated priests and parishioners, who castigated bishops as bureaucrats, and it distracted the church administration from essential, urgent spiritual matters.

Bureaucratization also had a profound impact on that nuclear unit of church, the parish. In medieval Russia the parish *was* the church. It functioned as a self-governing unit, built and maintained the local church, and selected and supported the parish priest. That autonomy gradually receded in the eighteenth century. One change concerned the appointment of parish clergy. Previously selected by parishioners and subjected to a perfunctory review by the bishop, the local clergy in the eighteenth century were chosen by the bishop, increasingly from select students in the seminary. Diocesan authorities asserted control over parish finances, especially income from the sale of votive candles. Bishops restricted the formation of new parishes and encouraged mergers. Although the purpose was to eliminate a profusion of small, uneconomic parishes, the net effect was to increase the average size of parishes nearly fourfold between 1740 and 1914 (see table 1). As in Western churches, the situation was most acute in cities and industrial areas.

In the mid–nineteenth century, however, the church made a concerted effort to resuscitate parish life as one means to bolster popular piety and observance. In 1864, for example, the church, with state collaboration, promulgated a statute for parish trusteeships (*prikhodskie popechitel'stva*), which were essentially parish committees to raise funds for church repairs, parish schools, charity, and support for the local clergy. That reform was not successful because the funds generated were usually minimal and were used mainly for renovation of church buildings, but it did signal a growing recognition of the need to involve the laity in parish affairs. From the 1890s to 1917 the church considered far-reaching proposals for parish reform, while the laity became increasingly assertive, chiefly with respect to the parish treasury and the appointment of local clergy. This process culminated in the parish revolution of 1917, when the church finally recognized the laity's prerogatives. In January 1918 the Bolshevik decree on the separation of the church from the state, which denied the church juridical status and conferred all operational power on the parish, completed and legitimized the new status quo in Russian Orthodoxy.

THE CLERGY

The clergy has its own social history—origins, training, recruitment, career patterns, and public role. Regardless of the specific national church, Orthodox canon provided for two distinct subgroups: a married parish clergy and a celibate monastic clergy from which all bishops were to come. That universal structure acquired a specific coloration in imperial Russia, where central authorities came increasingly to regu-

late the training, recruitment, and assignment of clergy. In contrast to medieval Muscovy, where monasteries and parishes had chosen new clergy, the church in imperial Russia had a system of diocesan and central controls and a formal table of organization *(shtat)* specifying the number and rank of monks and parish clergy. This centralized regulation, moreover, incorporated an emerging government policy of estate building, whereby the state restricted social movement and endeavored to engineer social composition and identity by aggregating amorphous, complex social groups into larger, more homogeneous estate categories *(sosloviia)*.

Parish clergy. The parish clergy in pre-Petrine Muscovy were a motley group. Elected by the parish and formally ordained by the bishop, they had a modicum of education and remained largely exempt from effective supervision by diocesan superiors. They served at the will and expense of the parishioners, whether serf-owning nobles or communities of peasants and townspeople. In that sense the secular clergy were intimately bound to this world and barely distinguishable in culture or economy from peasant or urban parishioners. Although fathers naturally preferred for sons to follow their crafts and succeed them, neither the church nor the state imposed barriers to

Christianity and Communism. Synod of the Russian Orthodox Church marking the millennium of Christianity in Russia, Moscow, 1988. The patriarch addresses the meeting; at his left sits the representative of the Soviet government, the chairman of the Council for Religious Affairs. LASKI/SIPA PRESS

recruitment of nonclerical young men or to the pursuit of a secular career by the clergy's offspring.

That all changed in the eighteenth century, when several factors coalesced to transform the parish clergy into a hereditary caste estate. One factor was state policy. After Peter the Great in 1718 established a capitation tax, freezing the status and residency of nonprivileged groups, it gradually became virtually impossible for peasants and townsmen, those most likely to seek the lowly status of priest, to enter the clergy. Another factor that steadily gained in importance was the educational requirement. Because the seminaries served only the clergy's offspring, outsiders could not acquire the seminary degree that, after 1800, became a prerequisite for ordination to the priesthood. Finally, the clergy blocked access by outsiders. That natural hereditary instinct gained new momentum when the Petrine table of organization *(shtat)* limited the number of clergy in each parish and left few openings for clerical progeny, let alone outsiders. Moreover, a priest needed to have a kinsman inherit his position. Since the church had no pension system, an "heir," such as a son, son-in-law, or other kinsman, was the priest's only assurance of material support in his old age. As a result, by the late eighteenth century almost all priests came from the clerical estate, a pattern that prevailed until the end of the ancien régime in 1917. That process of social exclusion ran contrary to the democratization tendencies in contemporary European churches, in which Protestant pastors came decreasingly from clergy families and Catholic priests came increasingly from lower-status groups. In the Russian Empire, however, where the nineteenth-century state had belatedly raised new estate barriers, the social exclusivity of the clergy was part of a larger system that sought to ensure sufficient and trained manpower for basic professions and to avoid the mobility and instability characteristic of contemporary western European societies.

But this caste-like system was also fraught with serious dysfunctions. The first, the most obvious by the mid-nineteenth century, was a surfeit of candidates. The clerical caste simply produced too many seminary graduates for an inelastic service structure. In addition they were not necessarily inclined toward church service. Family circumstance and necessity rather than vocation and religious zeal were the main forces channeling clerical progeny to careers in the church. Moreover, by excluding potential recruits from the lower-status groups, this caste order eroded the bonds between the clergy and the laity and reinforced a distinctive, alienating clerical subculture. The caste walls also forced pious laymen to pursue religious ca-

reers outside the church in schismatic and sectarian movements.

To overcome these deficiencies, a reform commission of the 1860s attempted to engineer changes in the church's social and educational policies. The principal goal was to improve the status and service of parish clergy, chiefly by enhancing the opportunities for the clergy's sons to pursue secular careers and for outsiders to gain admittance to the seminary and parish service. The result was a series of reforms adopted between 1867 and 1871 that abolished the "inheritance" of clerical positions, gave the priests' sons a nonclerical social status, and opened the seminary to matriculation by nonclerical children.

Like many of the other great reforms, these well-intentioned changes worked far better on paper than in reality. They mainly facilitated a mass exodus of clerical sons into lay careers without a compensatory influx of candidates from other social groups. In the 1870s the number of candidates for the priesthood dropped sharply, along with their educational qualifications. For the remaining decades of the ancien régime, the church experienced a decline in the educational standards of the parish clergy as bishops were driven to ordain candidates with poor seminary performance and incomplete education. According to data on those ordained between 1906 and 1912, nearly half (49.3 percent) lacked a seminary degree or its equivalent. The reforms did not democratize this contingent of candidates, for the seminaries continued to serve primarily the sons of clergy, not other social groups. In the last seminary class before World War I, for example, 83 percent of the seminarians came from the clerical estate and the rest from sundry social categories.

Monastic clergy. The monastery was traditionally the dominant force in the church, claiming a monopoly over appointments to the hierarchy and possessing enormous wealth in land and church peasants. In medieval Muscovy the proliferation of monasteries reflected the strong monastic, contemplative impulse in Orthodoxy and resulted in the accumulation of much land, estimated at a third of all land, and other resources. Such expansionist power and pretensions reached a zenith after the establishment in 1589 of the patriarchate, as its occupant constructed his own set of administrative and financial institutions to mimic those of the state.

Not surprisingly the resource-starved early modern Russian state became increasingly envious, especially as it struggled to finance its armies and civil service. It therefore attempted to restrict church landholding and, from the mid-seventeenth century, re-

TABLE 2
RUSSIAN MONASTICISM, 1764–1914

| | | Male | | | | Female | | |
| | | | Inhabitants | | | | | Inhabitants | |
Year	Monasteries	Monks	Novices	Total	Convents	Nuns	Novices	Total
1764	319			7,659	68			6,453
1796	307			4,190	81			1,671
1823	336	3,939	1,197	5,136	98	1,950	1,229	3,179
1840	435	5,122	3,259	8,381	112	2,287	4,583	6,870
1850	464	4,978	5,019	9,997	123	2,303	6,230	8,533
1894	511	7,582	6,696	14,278	263	8,319	21,957	30,276
1914	550	11,845	9,485	21,330	475	17,283	56,016	73,299

peatedly sought to divert church resources for its own needs. Peter the Great went much farther, transferring a substantial portion of monastic estates to state control and exploitation, though without formally sequestering the property. His vacillating successors hesitated to take the final step and left it to Catherine the Great to confiscate church estates and peasants in 1764. The prize was indeed immense: 816,736 male peasants, who provided an annual income of 293,848 *rubles* along with vast quantities of dues in kind, including 167,375 bushels of grain. Although in exchange the state provided a budget to support the monasteries and ecclesiastical administration, that budget was exceedingly niggardly, worth far less than the revenues the church received from its lands and peasants before confiscation.

The secularization of church property was fraught with momentous consequences for the church. Most important was the impact on the church's economic independence and its capacity to attend to strictly ecclesiastical needs, let alone undertake a broader social mission. Secularization dramatically and immediately affected monasticism, triggering a contraction in the number of monasteries and those who lived in them. Whereas the church had started the century with 1,201 monasteries, secularization reduced the number to a mere 400, one-quarter of which were convents. The number of monks and nuns decreased as well, falling from about 25,000 in 1724 to 5,861 in 1796.

That contraction was not permanent, however, as the nineteenth century witnessed a renaissance of monastic life, especially for women. Altogether the number of monasteries increased nearly 2.7 times between 1796 and 1914, and the increase in the number of monks, nuns, and novices was even larger (see table 2). Significantly, female monasticism accounted for most of the growth in the number of monasteries (64 percent) and their inhabitants (80.1 percent). Expressed most dramatically, male monastics increased 5.1 times, but nuns and female novices multiplied 43.9 times during this same period. As in the Catholic states of western Europe, Russian monasticism underwent a feminization, and the convent provided an attractive and ever-expanding alternative to marriage and secular careers. In contrast to the men, the majority of whom came from the clerical estate, female monastics came predominantly from the lower social orders of townspeople and peasants. Although secular society regarded monasticism with unveiled hostility, monasteries, often the sites of relics and miracle-working icons, remained a powerful force in popular religion and exercised a considerable influence over the more conservative elements of the educated classes.

POPULAR ORTHODOXY

Although Russia had been nominally Christianized in 988, Christianization remained a slow process that

Public Icon Procession. *Bringing Out the Icon to the People,* painting (1878) by Konstantin Apollonovich Savitskii (1844–1905). TRETYAKOV GALLERY, MOSCOW/THE BRIDGEMAN ART LIBRARY

had to eradicate paganism and overcome the vast dispersion and high mobility of the medieval Russian population. The church, especially through the role of colonizing monasteries, had made substantial progress in converting the populace, but by the sixteenth century Russian Orthodox beliefs and practices remained profoundly local with only a modicum of control and uniformity. At the council of 1551 the church began defining an orthodox Orthodoxy—free of pagan customs, with one standard for the newly and self-consciously Orthodox realm. In the mid-seventeenth century Patriarch Nikon instituted dramatic liturgical reforms, but given the backwardness of the ecclesiastical administration and its preoccupation with the management of huge landholdings and church peasants, attention to purely spiritual, sacramental, and liturgical matters remained marginal and episodic. Hence religious practices, especially in the multitude of dispersed rural parishes, remained localized and diverse, free from external control, and permeated with superstition and magic that had little to do with the norms of hieratic Orthodoxy.

Nevertheless, the church continued its attempts to make popular Orthodoxy "orthodox," most explicitly in the *Spiritual Regulation* (1721) and later in a steady stream of synodal decrees. The goals were to regularize religious practices and to instruct the flock in the rudiments of the faith. Such instruction, however, proved difficult, especially in rural areas, where the seasonality of church attendance, driven by weather conditions and the agrarian production cycle, and

nearly total illiteracy hindered catechization. The church made headway in urban parishes, particularly in the early nineteenth century, and expanded its role by teaching religion in the emerging network of schools. By the late nineteenth century local diocesan authorities generally could boast that many parishioners, chiefly younger ones, had learned to recite the Ten Commandments, the creed, basic prayers, and other rudiments of the faith. Diocesan authorities took strict measures to protect the sanctity of the church by restricting religious processions, combating suspicious miracles, regulating icon production, resisting appeals to canonize local saints, and dissuading laity from observing pagan traditions and rites.

In the mid-nineteenth century, however, the Russian Church, like its peers in the West, began to take a less negative attitude toward popular Orthodoxy. While consistent with the populist ethos current in secular culture, this new posture primarily derived from a desire to rekindle religious fervor and popular commitment to the Orthodoxy. To be sure the church continued its efforts to enlighten the believers through religious instruction in schools and at services, but it began to respond more favorably to manifestations of popular Orthodoxy. For example, whereas it had earlier severely restricted public icon processions, it now perceived them as a valuable demonstration of piety and an effective tool in raising religious consciousness. Church authorities also displayed a greater receptivity toward canonization of local saints. Although still insisting on observance of canonical requirements, namely formal investigations to demonstrate the veracity of purported miracles, the church proceeded with several canonizations and had several others under consideration in the last two decades of the ancien régime.

The willingness to accommodate popular Orthodoxy derived from anxieties about Russian piety. The official statistics appeared to demonstrate an extraordinarily high level of observance. Despite vast social and economic change, official statistics on the proportion of believers who confessed and received communion at Easter did not suggest de-Christianization. Those figures actually rose in the second half of the nineteenth century (see table 3). These data are all the more striking when compared with the far lower rates of communicants reported in contemporary European churches, for example, 43 percent in Prussia and 18 percent in Paris. Nevertheless, these statistics show an overall rise in the number of people who participated in neither communion nor confession, chiefly because of the decline in semicompliance, that is, those who made confession but did not receive communion either because they deemed themselves unworthy or because the priest withheld this rite. Moreover these official data understate the number of noncommunicants, for they often failed to record the large number of migrants to the factories and cities, precisely the areas most affected by religious indifference. The revolution of 1905–1907, in the view of many bishops, had a still more unsettling effect, especially on the younger generation, and bequeathed a new level of religious indifference and immoral conduct.

Significantly, the Orthodox Church experienced a feminization in religious observance and piety as well as in monastic life. The most direct evidence comes from the statistics on Easter Communion. In 1900, for example, the rate of participation was 91 percent for women compared to 87 percent for men, a gap that increased steadily in the last years of the ancien régime. A patriarchal institution, the church increasingly recognized women as its bastion and sought ways to accommodate and tap their piety. The most striking measure was the decision in 1912 to establish a female theological institute, in effect a form of higher theological education, to train women for spiritual and other service in the church. Despite the masculine bias in tradition and canon, the church recruited women for missionary activities, reestablished the ancient office of deaconess, gave women franchise in parish assemblies and councils, and in 1918 permitted them to serve as sacristans and parish elders.

DISSENT: OLD BELIEVERS AND SECTARIANISM

The Orthodox Church's campaigns to purify popular beliefs and practices alienated a large segment of believers, creating a population of "Old Believers," or "Old Ritualists," who repudiated the liturgical reforms of the seventeenth century and the subsequent attempts to impose them on parish religious life. Their rebellion had multiple causes, some purely religious, such as fears of deviating from traditional (therefore "true") Orthodoxy; some broadly cultural, such as a widespread apocalyptical spirit of the seventeenth century; some social, such as reactions to enserfment and the degradation of the popular status; and others political, such as the rise of the secular, absolutist state. Such sentiments found their most dramatic expression in the wave of self-immolations of the late seventeenth century, when resolute Old Believers sought to evade Antichrist and save their souls by committing mass suicide.

Whatever the particular mix of motives for the initial rebellion, the subsequent growth of the Old Belief had other dynamics. One was the imposition of a standardized Orthodoxy in lieu of local, popular religion, a process that removed the immanent sacred and extirpated other icons of popular veneration. Another factor increasingly important in the nineteenth century was the secular meaning of Old Belief. Namely,

TABLE 3
CONFESSION AND COMMUNION
OBSERVANCE AT EASTER:
PERCENTAGE OF THE POPULATION

Year	Both confession and communion	Confession only	Neither confession nor communion
1784	92.80	5.69	1.51
1797	85.80	8.60	2.70
1818	85.96	7.70	5.32
1835	84.98	6.50	8.53
1850	85.04	6.02	8.94
1900	89.06	0.49	10.46

❧ ❧

TABLE 4
OLD BELIEVERS IN RUSSIA, 1740–1897

Year	Males	Females	Total
1740	4,379	5,515	9,894
1797	6,687	7,155	13,842
1802	44,772	47,870	92,642
1815	112,570	128,707	241,277
1835	216,962	262,908	479,870
1860	326,498	384,900	711,398
1897	1,029,030	1,175,573	2,204,603

it provided a transcommunity network, facilitated business dealings, and provided a safety net for fellow believers. The Old Belief protected its adherents from invasive church policies, above all those directed toward the sacrament of marriage, including canonical restrictions on minimum age and kinship.

The result was an incessant growth in the number of registered Old Believers. Because the Old Believers were subjected to various forms of discrimination and disabilities, the official figures were notoriously unreliable. State authorities estimated that their numbers were severalfold higher than those reported by the church. The church's statistics, for all their incompleteness, register a steady increase in Old Believers from fewer than 10,000 in 1740 to 2.2 million in 1897 (see table 4). These impressive numbers still fail to capture the influence and appeal of the Old Belief or the number of Orthodox who in some degree also observed the Old Belief and bore the label of "semischismatics" (poluraskol'niki).

Sectarian movements had deep roots in medieval and early modern Russia but gained momentum only in the late nineteenth century, chiefly because of Western influence and the emergence of more private, individualized religious practices. These movements included a plethora of mystical or rationalist sects, some with ties to Orthodoxy and claiming membership in the church. Many Orthodox prelates regarded them as even more menacing than the Old Belief. As the church convened its first missionary councils in the 1880s, sectarianism loomed as the fastest growing, most menacing threat to its supremacy.

CHURCH AND SOCIETY

The rise of the secular state paralleled a decline in the church's role and status in society. Earlier, in the particularistic society of sixteenth- and seventeenth-century Muscovy, the parish church formed the epicenter of community life. The local church was the site for sacraments and rites of passage and the locus of sociability, official business, and trade. After 1700, however, the parish gradually surrendered this central role, with power devolving from the clergy to the civil service, and the parish failed to acquire legal status as a juridical entity in state law. Although the church retained some secular power, including the authority to impose penance for crimes and sins, its authority gradually receded in the imperial period. The marginalization was in part deliberate. To prevent peasant disorders, the state in 1767 specifically forbade priests to pen petitions for peasants or to become embroiled in serf-squire disputes. Priests did become entangled, especially in borderlands, where non-Orthodox squires were involved, but they did so at their own peril. By the first half of the nineteenth century, in theory if not always in fact, the church and clergy had been confined to the spiritual domain.

However, in one important sphere, marriage and divorce, the church actually expanded its role. The medieval church had claimed exclusive competence over the sacrament of marriage, but its skeletal administration was hardly able to regulate the formation or dissolution of families. Bishops assessed a fee for wedding certificates, but they did not mandate verification of age, kinship, and the like. In fact, before 1700 the church did not even compile parish registers to expose uncanonical marriages, bigamy, or other violations of canon law. Marital dissolution, whether for divorce or for entry into a monastery, was virtually unregulated. At most the laity required a letter of divorce from the local priest.

That all changed after the mid-eighteenth century. As the church developed its new bureaucracy and documentation, including parish registers of births, marriages, and deaths, it could determine and verify such matters as age, kinship, and marital status. Although the initial goal was to combat uncanonical marriages, after 1800 the church was increasingly concerned with preventing marital dissolution, whether through separation or divorce. Responding to the post-Napoleonic restoration's revulsion against the liberal divorces of the French Revolution, considered synonymous with an assault on social and political stability, and reflecting a new sacramentalism in teachings emphasizing the indelibility of sacraments, the church strictly banned separation and made divorce all but impossible. It formally recognized several grounds for annulment and divorce, such as bigamy, exile to Siberia, premarital impotence and insanity, adultery, and disappearance for more than five years, but in practice it made such proceedings extremely protracted and seized every opportunity to cavil, stall, and reject. The church granted no separations whatsoever and approved only 32.8 annulments and 58.3 divorces per year between 1836 and 1860.

In the final decades of the ancien régime, however, the church began to retreat from this strict application of canon law. It did so partly in response to growing criticism from elites, who looked jealously at the more liberal separation and divorce practices in western Europe, but also in response to complaints from the lower social orders, who resisted this modern intrusion into their private lives and envied the relative freedom of sectarians and Old Believers. The church became more liberal and expeditious in processing divorce cases, the number of which rose from a few score at midcentury to nearly four thousand by the eve of World War I. Although the church was much less eager to modify canon law, in 1904 it agreed to allow the guilty party in adultery cases to remarry after a relatively brief penance.

The Orthodox Church reoriented toward greater involvement in worldly matters. The church intensely desired to secure a prominent role in public education, partly to help prepare former serfs for citizenship and also to ensure religious instruction (zakon bozhii) in the curriculum. Although the church had evidenced interest before by participating in schools established for state peasants in the late 1830s, the approach of emancipation in the late 1850s triggered a furious attempt to establish parish schools all across the empire. This effort abated in the 1860s and 1870s, when state and public schools took precedence, but the church intensified its educational activities in the 1880s. The butt of much criticism by professional pedagogues and anticlerical intellectuals, the resulting network of parish schools functioned more effectively than once thought and substantially augmented the network of state and public schools.

The church's social engagement went beyond divorce and education to include a host of other critical social issues. The medieval church had taught the need for charity and alms, especially for the orphaned, and eighteenth-century bishops developed a social theology of mutual reciprocity between husband and wife, elites and commoners, each expected to perform his or her duties toward the other. But in the mid-nineteenth century some clergy adumbrated a new, this-worldly Christology that enjoined the church to enter into the world and its problems as Christ had done and explicitly rejected a one-sided, otherworldly focus and indifference to temporal problems. In addition some clergy believed that, to hold the flock's loyalty, the church had to become meaningful in the people's everyday lives. Such ideas were particularly attractive after midcentury to the seminarians, many of whom had been exposed to the radical subculture of Russia's emerging intelligentsia.

As a result, clerical participation and sometimes leadership in movements to address social issues steadily expanded. Priests preached frequently about various social ills, such as abuse of wives and children and inhumane treatment of animals. But the church did more than just preach. To address poverty, for example, the Russian Empire had little in the way of institutionalized, formal welfare. Although the church had few means to alleviate this evil, it promoted the duty of the rich to aid the indigent and attempted, through the parish trusteeships, to organize parish assistance for the poor, sick, and orphaned. It also gave attention to the problem of alcoholism because of its ruinous effect on the peasant household economy and its pernicious impact on morality and spiritual life. The church addressed other issues, such as prostitution, and played a key role in raising funds (through special collections during the liturgy) for social causes.

This social engagement reached a peak during the revolutionary turbulence of the early twentieth century, when liberal and radical segments of the clergy became deeply embroiled in their parishioners' battle for social justice. In the revolution of 1905–1907 many clergy not only urged reforms to improve their own lot but also expressed support for the "liberation movement" and the demands of peasants and workers. Those sentiments were crushed during the years of reaction (1907–1914), when state authorities and church hierarchs joined forces to eliminate radical aspirations, but social discontent continued to run deep in the ranks of the parish clergy. The February Revolution of 1917 demolished inhibitions entirely, impelling clergy, often in joint assemblies with the laity, to endorse radical programs for ecclesiastical, political, and social reform. Many priests soon had second thoughts about radicalism, however, as it took on new and destructive forms and was sometimes directed against the clergy.

FROM SOVIET DE-CHRISTIANIZATION TO POST-SOVIET RENEWAL

The troubles and travails the clergy experienced in the aftermath of the February Revolution paled in comparison with what ensued after the October Rev-

Destruction of a Church. Destruction of the Chudov Monastery in the Kremlin, Moscow, 1928. THE DAVID KING COLLECTION

olution of 1917. The Bolshevik leadership disestablished the institutional church, expropriating its assets and dismantling its administration, but also sought to avoid antagonizing the country's huge rural population of believers. Local radicals, however, were less circumspect. They attacked the clergy, executing some 5,000 to 10,000 of them, and destroyed monasteries, relics, and icons. The radical leadership engineered a campaign in the early 1920s to seize church valuables to feed the starving during the Volga famine, but in fact they aimed at demolishing the church and its hold on the laity. That campaign resulted in numerous arrests and executions but did not shake the church's influence with the laity. While the regime ruthlessly closed monasteries and removed religious symbols from public spaces, dismantling chapels in schools and icons in railway stations, it remained cautious in its dealings with parishioners. Consequently of the 41,000 parishes that existed in 1914, approximately 37,000 were still operating in the late 1920s. To the consternation of party stal-

warts, in the second half of the 1920s popular piety experienced a revival not only in villages but in some urban and factory districts.

The Bolsheviks perceived the religious revival through a strictly class perspective, claiming that the bourgeoisie, whether rural kulaks or urban entrepreneurs, was using the parish church to mobilize political opposition. Their fears were all the more intense since they coincided with a deepening crisis of the New Economic Policy, perceived as a growing contradiction between the regime's industrialization imperative and the resistance from peasants and workers. By the late 1920s, as the regime grew alarmed over an apparent religious revival, it redoubled the efforts of its propaganda organs and voluntary antireligious associations such as the League of Militant Godless.

These efforts presaged a great turn in religious policy in 1929 and 1930 that inaugurated a decade of de-Christianization by the government. The clergy was persecuted, and many were arrested, imprisoned, and executed. The repressions destroyed the few remnants of the institutional church. In 1937 alone the regime closed seventy dioceses and executed sixty bishops. By 1939 only four bishops remained at large, and the former diocesan administration was effectively gone. No less devastating was the assault on the parishes. In 1937 the regime closed some 8,000 parishes, turning their churches into clubs, theaters, and warehouses or leaving them idle and in disrepair. By 1941 the parish, like the church, had virtually disappeared. Of the 41,000 parishes in operation in 1914, fewer than 400 remained. The repression of the 1930s also pummeled lay believers, now labeled "churchmen" *(tserkovniki)*. Of the 150,000 believers arrested, 60 percent were laymen and laywomen, and 80,000 were executed.

Repression failed, however, to extirpate belief. In the 1937 census 45.1 percent of the population admitted that they were believers, and police reports from the late 1930s confirm the tenacity of belief. The traumas of World War II provided a new impulse for religious revival in occupied territories, where religious repression ceased, and in the Soviet-controlled areas as well. In 1943 the regime accepted a new accommodation with the Orthodox Church that restored the patriarchate. By 1946 Soviet authorities reported the presence of some 10,243 churches, 41 bishops, and 104 monasteries. The great majority of them were in areas newly annexed or previously under German occupation, accounting for approximately seven or eight times as many parishes and clergy as the rest of the USSR. In the waning years of Stalinist rule, the regime made some attempt to combat religious sentiments but made no concerted attacks. It even approved some applications to reopen churches.

Joseph Stalin's death in 1953 hardly meant an end to persecution of the church, clergy, and popular believers. Nikita Khrushchev, despite his innovations and flexibility in other spheres, proved a zealous antireligion activist and launched successive campaigns to tame the church that Stalin had partially rehabilitated in the 1940s. Between 1950 and 1965 the number of monasteries contracted from seventy-five to sixteen, churches from 14,273 to 7,551, and ordained clergy from 11,571 to 6,694. The next two decades of stagnation, between 1965 and 1985, did not bring large-scale antireligious campaigns, but the number of parishes slightly decreased to 6,806.

The end of Communism followed by the dissolution of the USSR enabled the Russian Orthodox Church to recover much property and influence. By 1998, for example, the church had 151 bishops in 121 dioceses overseeing some 478 monasteries and 19,000 parishes. The church asserted a new political and social role, participating in the new Russian parliament and organizing relief for the poor. Nevertheless, the decades of official antireligious campaigns took their toll. Given the decades of repression of religious tradition and belief and the scant resources of a transition economy, the church has encountered great difficulty in resuscitating the Orthodoxy, popular and institutional, that shaped the long prerevolutionary history of Russia.

See also **Russia and the Eastern Slavs** *(volume 1);* **Secularization; Communism** *(volume 2); and other articles in this section.*

BIBLIOGRAPHY

Belliustin, I. S. *Description of the Clergy in Rural Russia.* Translated by Gregory L. Freeze. Ithaca, N.Y., 1985. Account of religious life by a parish priest in the mid–nineteenth century.

Corley, Felix, ed. and trans. *Religion in the Soviet Union: An Archival Reader.* New York, 1996. Collection of recently declassified materials from Russian archives.

Curtiss, John Shelton. *Church and State in Russia: The Last Years of the Empire, 1900–1917.* New York, 1940.

Ellis, Jane. *The Russian Orthodox Church: A Contemporary History.* London: 1986.

Florovsky, Georges. *Ways of Russian Theology.* Translated by Robert L. Nichols. Belmont, Mass., 1977–1987. Translation of a classic, wide-ranging account of the Russian Church from earliest times.

Frazee, Charles A. *The Orthodox Church and Independent Greece, 1821–1852.* London, 1969.

Freeze, Gregory L. "Bringing Order to the Russian Family: Marriage and Divorce in Imperial Russia, 1760–1860." *Journal of Modern History* 62 (1990): 709–746.

Freeze, Gregory L. "Church and Politics in Late Imperial Russia: Crisis and Radicalization of the Clergy." In *Russia under the Last Tsar: Opposition and Subversion, 1894–1917.* Edited by Anna Geifman. Oxford, U.K., and Malden, Mass., 1999. Pages 269–297.

Freeze, Gregory L. "Counter-Reformation in Russian Orthodoxy: Popular Response to Religious Innovation, 1922–1925." *Slavic Review* 54 (1995): 305–339.

Freeze, Gregory L. "Handmaiden of the State? The Church in Imperial Russia Reconsidered." *Journal of Ecclesiastical History* 36 (1985): 82–102.

Freeze, Gregory L. *The Parish Clergy in Nineteenth-Century Russia: Crisis, Reform, Counter-Reform.* Princeton, N.J., 1983.

Freeze, Gregory L. *The Russian Levites: Parish Clergy in the Eighteenth Century.* Cambridge, Mass., 1977.

Freeze, Gregory L. "A Social Mission for Russian Orthodoxy: The Kazan Requiem of 1861 for the Peasants in Bezdna." In *Imperial Russia, 1700–1917: State, Society, Opposition.* Edited by Ezra Mendelsohn and Marshall S. Shatz. DeKalb, Ill., 1988. Pages 115–135.

Freeze, Gregory L. "The Stalinist Assault on the Parish, 1929–1941." In *Stalinismus vor dem Zweiten Weltkrieg: Neue Wege der Forschung.* Edited by Manfred Hildermeier. Munich, 1998. Pages 209–232.

Freeze, Gregory L. "Subversive Piety: Religion and the Political Crisis in Late Imperial Russia." *Journal of Modern History* 68 (1996): 307–350.

Hauptmann, Peter, and Gerd Stricker, eds. *Die Orthodoxe Kirche in Russland: Dokumente ihrer Geschichte (860–1980).* Göttingen, Germany, 1988. A valuable collection of published sources.

Hosking, Geoffrey A., ed. *Church, Nation, and State in Russia and Ukraine.* New York, 1991.

Husband, William B. *"Godless Communists": Atheism and Society in Soviet Russia, 1917–1932.* DeKalb, Ill., 2000.

Nichols, Robert L., and Theofanis George Stavrou, eds. *Russian Orthodoxy under the Old Regime.* Minneapolis, Minn., 1978.

Peris, Daniel. *Storming the Heavens: The Soviet League of the Militant Godless.* Ithaca, N.Y., 1998.

Pokrovskii, N. N., and S. G. Petrov, eds. *Politbiuro i tserkov', 1922–1925 gg.* Moscow, 1997. Publication of top-secret materials from the Kremlin Archive.

Roberson, Ronald G. *The Eastern Christian Churches: A Brief Survey.* 3d ed. Rome, 1990.

Robson, Roy R. *Old Believers in Modern Russia.* DeKalb, Ill., 1995.

Rössler, Roman. *Kirche und Revolution in Russland.* Cologne, 1969.

Savramis, Demosthenes. *Die soziale Stellung des Priesters in Griechenland.* Leiden, Netherlands, 1968.

Schulz, Günther. *Das Landeskonzil der Orthodoxen Kirche in Russland 1917–1918: Ein unbekanntes Reformpotential.* Göttingen, Germany, 1995.

Smolitsch, Igor. *Geschichte der russischen Kirche, 1700–1917.* 2 vols. Leiden, Netherlands, 1964–1991. Also published in Russian as *Istoriia russkoi tserkvi, 1700–1917.* Best inclusive account, with an extensive bibliography on printed sources and secondary literature in Russian and Western languages.

Vasil'eva, Ol'ga IU., ed. *Russkaia pravoslavnaia tserkov' i kommunisticheskoe gosudarstvo 1917–1941: Dokumenty i fotomaterialy.* Moscow, 1996. Archival documents on the early Soviet era.

Ware, Timothy. *Eustratios Argenti: A Study of the Greek Church under Turkish Rule.* Oxford, U.K., 1964.

Ware, Timothy. *The Orthodox Church.* 3d ed. London and New York, 1993. An excellent historical overview and an informed account of theology and dogma.

Section 22

EDUCATION AND LITERACY

Schools and Schooling   329
Paul F. Grendler

Higher Education   353
Charles R. Day

Teachers   365
Scott J. Seregny

Printing and Publishing   377
Thomas Cragin

Literacy   391
R. A. Houston

Reading   407
Daniel P. Resnick and Jason Martinek

Journalism   419
Thomas Cragin

SCHOOLS AND SCHOOLING

Paul F. Grendler

Schools are intimately linked to European society because almost every schooling decision has had social consequences. Schooling divides the population into the educated elite and the unschooled or less-schooled mass. Education also creates new social distinctions. Different groups have received more or less schooling or distinctive schooling according to their economic condition, intended occupation, religion, and gender. Education has enabled a limited number of academically gifted individuals to rise from the ranks of workers, peasants, and the lower middle class into the professional elite and sometimes higher. European schooling has gradually been extended to include a larger proportion of the population and to give the majority of the population more years of schooling. On the other hand, curricula have remained remarkably stable. Italian Renaissance humanists created a classical curriculum that from then on served to educate most of Europe's elite. Finally, almost all the political, religious, and private authorities who created schools intended to impart civic, cultural, linguistic, moral, religious, and social values as well as academic skills. Because the results have seldom satisfied the founders and because values change, every century has seen attempts to reform European schooling.

THE RENAISSANCE

Renaissance Europe inherited from the Middle Ages an uncoordinated and diverse school structure. Different kinds of schools competed with or complemented each other.

The organization of schooling, 1400–1500. One way to understand schools is to note their sponsors, that is, the institutions, entities, or persons who governed or paid the expenses for schools. A single schoolmaster wishing to create an independent school—the equivalent of an American private school in the twentieth century—typically opened a one-room school in his home or in rented quarters, and neighborhood parents paid him fees to teach their sons. His only qualifications were his teaching skill and his ability to persuade parents to send their children. The teacher might possess a university degree, which meant facility in Latin and acquaintance with higher learning in rhetoric, philosophy, law, or theology, or he might be little more learned than his pupils.

The tutor was another independent schoolmaster. He lived and taught in the home of a noble or wealthy merchant, or he visited the household daily. In both cases he taught only the children of the household or of two adjacent households. On occasion a tutor was the constant guide and companion, at home or in travel, to a single boy or youth of considerable wealth and social standing.

Other independent masters presided over their own boarding schools that housed, fed, and instructed children sent to them. A master of this kind became a substitute father to his charges. He taught boys in the classroom, chided their manners at table, and improved their morals throughout—at least parents hoped that this happened. Some of the most notable humanistic schools of the Italian Renaissance, operated by famous pedagogues such as Vittorino Rambaldoni da Feltre (1373/1378–1446/1447) and Guarino Guarini of Verona (1374–1460), were independent boarding schools.

The endowed school was an independent school that endured beyond the lifetime of a single teacher or founder. A wealthy individual left a sum of money for a school; endowment income paid the master's salary and rent for a schoolroom or building, where boys learned for free. In England before the Reformation, the master of an endowed school often had to be a priest so he could celebrate daily a mass for the repose of the donor's soul. Schoolboys learned reading, Latin, and sometimes chant. A very large endowment could create a boarding school, in which boys both studied and lived. An inadequate endowment might mean that boys had to pay supplementary fees. Sometimes endowed schools became municipal schools when the town council paid additional ex-

A Renaissance Schoolroom. Renaissance schoolmaster and his students. Illustration from *Parvulorum institutio,* 1512–1513. LIAISON AGENCY

authority or institution, such as a bishop, a cathedral chapter of canons, a monastery, or even the parish priest, were not numerous. In the seventeenth and eighteenth centuries church schools dominated the educational landscape.

Regardless of their sponsorship, actual schools were usually modest. Normally a single teacher instructed a group of boys of varying ages and abilities, anywhere from a half dozen to thirty, in a single room. If the teacher had forty pupils or more, he might have an assistant who drilled the younger boys in their lessons, such as Latin conjugations and declensions. The schoolroom might be in the teacher's home or in a separate rented room. It is unlikely that the school had an outdoor area for play or physical exercises. Drinking water and food had to be brought in. If the schoolroom had a stove, each pupil might be required to bring a stick of wood on cold days.

Only a minority of boys and a tiny minority of girls aged six to fifteen attended school. Probably about 28 percent of boys attended formal schools in Florence, Italy, in 1480, and 26 percent of boys attended formal schools in Venice in 1587. The girls' percentage was very low, probably less than 1 percent. About 20 to 25 percent of boys in England attended school in the sixteenth century and less than 5 percent of girls. About 40 percent of boys received enough schooling to become literate in the town of Cuenca (in Castile, Spain) in the sixteenth century, and perhaps 12 percent of Polish males attended school in the 1560s.

School attendance closely followed the hierarchies of wealth, occupation, and social status. Sons of nobles, wealthy merchants, and professionals, such as lawyers, physicians, notaries, high civil servants, university professors, and preuniversity teachers, were more likely to attend school than sons of craftsmen, artisans, small shopkeepers, wool workers, laborers, and servants. The primary reason for the different schooling rates was that schooling almost always cost money. The social and occupational expectations of parents were an additional factor.

Boys needed schooling, especially in Latin, in order to qualify for positions of leadership in society. But those positions and all the learned professions were barred to women. Hence few parents believed that daughters needed formal education. Some girls received informal teaching at home, but the number is impossible to estimate.

Urban dwellers were more likely to attend school than those who lived in the countryside or in farming villages because more teachers were available in towns and cities. Rural areas had few resources to dedicate to schooling and few available teachers. The distances

penses and took over direction. Some English endowed schools founded in the late Middle Ages or the Renaissance are still teaching boys and girls. Different kinds of independent schools existed all over Europe and probably made up a large majority of schools.

The local civil authority, such as the town council, might sponsor a school. The town government chose and paid the master, occasionally imposed curricular directives, and sent a visitor to see that teacher and pupils performed satisfactorily. Sometimes municipal schools were free; but they never enrolled all the school-age boys of the town and very seldom taught girls. The town government typically supported only one or two municipal teachers, who taught a small number, perhaps fifty or sixty, of the town's school-age boys. Often the town permitted the municipal teacher to collect fees from the students to augment his modest salary. Universal public education, with or without fees, did not arrive until the nineteenth century and only gradually won acceptance.

A third kind of school was the church school. Until the Protestant and Catholic Reformations of the sixteenth century, schools opened by an ecclesiastical

Seventeeth-Century Schoolroom. Teacher and students in Poland. Engraving by Matthias Morawa, 1657. NATIONAL MUSEUM, CRACOW, POLAND

that students might have to walk to get to school and the exposure of the schoolroom to the elements, a serious consideration in northern Europe, help explain the lower schooling rate of rural children. Although in theory schools taught all year, numerous saints' days and civic holidays, long vacations at Christmas and Easter, and carnival before Lent broke up the schedule. The need to work in the fields during harvest interrupted classes. And extremes of summer heat and winter cold closed schools or kept children home.

The classical Latin curriculum of the Renaissance. The most significant event in modern European schooling was the Renaissance adoption of a classical curriculum for the Latin schools in the fifteenth and sixteenth centuries. Medieval Latin schools taught a mixture of manufactured verse texts of pious sentiments, grammar manuals and glossaries, and limited material from ancient classical texts. Renaissance humanists discarded the medieval curriculum in favor of the works of Virgil, Cicero, Terence, Caesar, and other ancient authors. These authors taught grammar, rhetoric, poetry, history, and moral philosophy—together the humanistic studies that imparted virtue and eloquence to the free man, or so the Renaissance believed. Students learned to write Latin in the ornate and highly rhetorical style of the *Epistolae ad familiares*

(Familiar letters) of Cicero (106–43 B.C.), which was very different from the clear, functional, and sometimes graceless medieval Latin. They studied Virgil and Terence and read Caesar and Valerius Maximus for history. Humanist pedagogues sought guidance on Latin rhetoric and ancient pedagogy generally from the *Institutio oratoria* (Institutes of oratory) of the ancient Roman teacher of rhetoric Quintilian (c. 35–after 95). Italy adapted the classical Latin curriculum in the first half of the fifteenth century, and the rest of Europe followed in the early sixteenth century.

Because Latin was the language of law, medicine, science, and theology into the eighteenth century and beyond, attendance at a Latin school to learn classical Latin was the prerequisite for every professional career; all university lectures, texts, disputations, and examinations were conducted in Latin. To mention one scientific work among many, Isaac Newton (1642–1727) wrote his masterpiece, *Philosophiae naturalis principia mathematica* (Mathematical principles of natural philosophy; 1687) in Latin. Even after Latin ceased to be the universal language for learning, pedagogues and parents believed that the study of Latin and Greek grammar prepared the mind for any intellectual endeavor. Latin and Greek literature also conveyed the high purpose and lofty moral sen-

331

timents that society and parents wanted its leaders to emulate.

The adoption of a classical humanistic curriculum had profound social consequences. The division of European education into a classical Latin curriculum for the leaders of society and professionals, and a vernacular education for the rest (see below), made schooling the key to social hierarchy. Certainly social divisions existed before the adoption of the classical curriculum and would have continued without it. But at the time a Latin classical education was crucial for anyone who wished to obtain or hold a certain position in society. Even a bright child could not learn Latin without long and difficult study. Only parents possessing a certain amount of income could afford the fees to send a son and occasionally a daughter to Latin schools for many years, and to forgo the assistance and income that a working child brought to the family. From the Renaissance to the late twentieth century, the classical curriculum defined the academic secondary school, which divided the upper and middle classes from the working class. Using a classical education as the gateway to advancement also meant that boys, and later girls, of poor and humble origins might advance through merit if they could obtain a Latin education. Free Latin schools eventually became available to some children.

The remarkable but strange decision to adopt a curriculum based on the ancient works had far-reaching intellectual consequences as well. Ancient civilization, culturally Greek, spiritually pagan, and politically united under a militaristic Rome, differed greatly from contemporary European civilization, which was deeply Christian and politically divided into numerous states. Yet Europe's intellectuals and political leaders decided it was the study of the classics of ancient Rome and Greece that would render future leaders of society eloquent and morally upright. That decision held until the late twentieth century.

The classical curriculum also imparted a secular spirit to European schooling. Even though western European civilization was profoundly otherworldly in its ultimate goal, the Latin classical curriculum emphasized education for this life. Cicero, Virgil, and the other ancient pagan authors did not urge men and women to do what was morally right so as to enjoy union with the Christian God in the next world. Of course Renaissance educators were convinced that Christianity and the classics taught an identical morality of honesty, self-sacrifice for the common good, and perseverance. But the classics did not teach one to love either enemy or neighbor. Even though Catholic religious orders and Protestant divines added considerable religious content to the classical curriculum,

its secular spirit remained a significant part of European education far beyond the Renaissance.

Vernacular schools.

Vernacular schools also existed in every region of Europe. For example, in the major commercial city of Venice, half the boys in school attended vernacular schools in 1587 and 1588. The schools taught reading and writing in the vernacular, and often commercial mathematics to boys (and a small number of girls) destined for the world of work. This curriculum emerged from the practical experience and lay culture of the merchant community. Vernacular schools probably underwent little change during the Renaissance and beyond. Since church and state authorities did not hand down directives for vernacular schools, the teachers, who were almost always modest independent masters, taught what they pleased. Hence the children learned to read from the same adult books of popular culture that their parents enjoyed. Indeed Venetian boys sometimes brought to school from home popular vernacular books that parents wanted them to learn to read. The vernacular texts were a diverse lot, ranging from medieval saints' lives to Renaissance chivalric romances. Obviously they imparted conflicting moral values. Students would read about heroic saints who endured martyrdom for Christ, then read about knights who killed for revenge and ladies who committed adultery for love. Italian vernacular schools also taught advanced commercial mathematical skills and elementary bookkeeping. Vernacular schools in other parts of Renaissance Europe taught arithmetic, but not the rest of the commercial curriculum of Italian vernacular schools.

German vernacular schools were called *Winkelschulen* (backstreet schools) because they lacked official sponsors and might be found in humble locations. There male and female teachers of modest backgrounds taught boys and some girls basic literacy and elementary education as quickly as possible for small fees. Other European countries had similar vernacular schools.

Printing and the expansion of schooling.

Printing aided schooling by making available multiple copies of textbooks. The use of movable type began about 1450, and by the 1480s and 1490s publishers were producing significant numbers of reading primers and manuals of Latin syntax (the construction of sentences according to the rules governing the use of verbs) and morphology (the inflected forms of words). No longer would students have to rely on handwritten manuscripts available only to the teacher or to wealthy students. As the cost of printed books declined in the sixteenth century, all pupils could own a grammar manual and primer. Whether or not they did is impossible to determine.

Historians often assume that greater availability of inexpensive printed books accounts for the increase in schooling and literacy in the Renaissance. Rather, it was most likely this factor in combination with three others—greater availability of free or nearly free schooling, the desire of students and parents for more education, and society's willingness to reward those who took the trouble to learn—that increased the amount of schooling by 1600.

THE PROTESTANT REFORMATION

Martin Luther (1483–1546) argued for universal compulsory education, at least at the elementary level. When German princes accepted Protestantism, Lutheran clergymen drafted new arrangements for the church and state that almost always included a *Schulordnung* (school order). Protestant school orders firmly placed the state (prince or city council) in charge of the schools. By the 1560s and 1570s Protestant school orders created a relatively integrated set of schools, beginning with an elementary school to teach reading and writing. Abler students advanced to a higher school that taught Latin; the most gifted and socially more privileged went to an advanced secondary school that led to university. The goals were twofold: (1) to train future clergymen and administrators of the state and (2) to impart to a larger fraction of the male population enough reading and writing to function in an appropriate station in life. The students studied the same classical curriculum taught in Catholic lands along with a great deal of catechetical instruction in Lutheran Christianity. Protestant Germany and nearby border regions, such as Strasbourg, had a number of excellent secondary-level Latin schools.

It appears that the number and possibly the quality of schools increased during the age of the Protestant Reformation in Germany. But the Protestant Reformation did not mark the beginning of modern schooling. The goals were high, but the results were often modest, and the level of instruction was not always elevated. The schools still frequently charged fees, which poor parents could not afford. Sometimes parents could not even provide the stick of wood that a child was expected to bring for the school fire in winter. A school seldom enrolled all the boys in the village, and enrollments waxed and waned according to the work seasons. Even though the state was supposed to organize and direct schools, humble private schools, *Winkelschulen,* continued. Finally, because Protestantism abolished religious orders, it did not enjoy the new schools that religious orders of the Catholic Reformation provided. It seems unlikely that the Protestant Reformation produced more schooling than that available in Catholic Europe.

The thesis that Protestantism created a permanent expansion of schooling and literacy so that every individual could read the Bible cannot be proven on the basis of current research. The only example in which the Protestant Reformation achieved almost total reading literacy occurred in Sweden in the late seventeenth and early eighteenth centuries. There the state Reformed (Lutheran) Church undertook to teach the entire population, male and female, how to read. Thanks to great effort and governmental threats, such as refusing permission to marry to those who failed to learn to read, the effort succeeded. It was an impressive achievement but unique: nothing comparable occurred anywhere else in Protestant or Catholic Europe.

RELIGIOUS ORDER SCHOOLS IN CATHOLIC EUROPE

The Catholic Reformation religious orders of the sixteenth and seventeenth centuries altered the educational landscape of Catholic Europe. The Society of Jesus (founded in 1540) and other religious orders who followed their pedagogical example created new schools and sometimes took control of existing municipal schools. Because they did not charge fees, the schools of the Jesuits, Piarists, and other orders expanded educational opportunities and dominated education in Catholic countries in the seventeenth and eighteenth centuries.

The Jesuits. The Jesuits had not intended to become educators. In December 1547 the city government of Messina, firmly nudged by the Spanish viceroy who ruled Sicily for the Spanish Crown, petitioned Ignatius Loyola, the founder of the Jesuits, to send ten Jesuits to the Italian city, five to teach and the rest to undertake spiritual and charitable activities. The city government promised food, clothing, and a building. Recognizing this as an intriguing opportunity and understanding that one did not refuse a viceroy, Loyola managed to send seven Jesuits, including some of the ablest scholars of the young order. According to the agreement with the city, the Jesuit fathers would teach nine classes. In effect, they created a classical Latin elementary and secondary school, along with higher studies in philosophy. The city erected a building, the people of Messina supported the Jesuits through free-

Nuova Santa Croce

Per istruzione de' Fanciulli

will offerings, and the viceroy also helped. The school formally opened in October 1548. It was an immediate success, as two hundred boys enrolled by December. The school averaged an enrollment of about three hundred boys in the next two decades.

Free instruction largely explained the instant success of the Messina school. The Jesuits inaugurated the first systematic effort to provide free education for several hundred boys in a town, something entirely new for Italy and Europe. The opportunity must have seemed heaven-sent to the boys and their parents. In addition the Jesuit fathers were learned scholars and teachers. Many other Jesuit schools followed.

The Jesuit schools offered the same Latin curriculum that the Italian humanists of the fifteenth century had created and that Desiderius Erasmus (1466–1536) and other northern humanists promoted. But they made several additions: prayers, religious training, and insistence that the boys attend mass, confess, and communicate; better pedagogical organization, including imaginative teaching techniques; and higher subjects such as philosophy, mathematics, Hebrew, and theology.

The Jesuit schools soon refined their goals. Beginning in 1551 they phased out the introductory class that taught beginning reading and writing and the rudiments of Latin grammar; a boy had to learn these before entering a Jesuit school. The Jesuits decided to concentrate their energies on those likely to stay in school for many years. With this decision, partly provoked by a shortage of teachers, the Jesuits narrowed their educational mission chronologically and socially: they taught the Latin humanities to upper- and middle-class boys aged ten to sixteen. Since the Jesuits followed the policy of free education until the nineteenth century, they sought and received financial support from wealthy lay or ecclesiastical leaders of the community, and sometimes from the local town government.

A handful of Jesuit schools in large Italian cities, such as Rome and Milan, taught several hundred boys between the ages of ten and sixteen and a few older students. Jesuit schools in France, Germany, and Portugal often taught five hundred to fifteen hundred students. The large, famous Jesuit schools taught university-level philosophy, mathematics, and physics

334

MASSIME E PROVERBJ MORALI ¹³

In pri-mo luo go ri-cor-da-ti, che vi è un Di-o, che ha un es-se-re in-fi-ni-to, ed e-ter-no. Que-sto Di-o non ha cor-po, ma è pu-ris-si-mo Spi-ri-to, ed e in tre Per-so-ne di-stin-te, che si chia-ma-no Pa-dre, Fi-g liuo-lo, e Spi-ri-to San-to. Il Pa-dre e Di-o, il Fi-gliuo-lo è Dio, e lo Spi-ri-to San-to è Di-o. Que-ste tre Per-so-ne pe-rò so-no un Di-o so-lo. La se-con-da Per-so-na del-la San-tis-si-ma Tri-ni-tà, cio-è il Fi-gliuo-lo si è fat-to Uo-mo per ope-ra del-lo Spi-ri-to San-to nel se-no pu-ris-si-mo di Ma-ri-a Ver-gi-ne

Learning to Read. An Italian primer of the late eighteenth century. *(Left) Santa Croce* (Holy Cross) was the common name for primers in Italy from the Renaissance to the nineteenth century. *(Center)* The primer begins with a cross followed by the alphabet, consonants, vowels, syllables, and moral exhortations. Children learned by saying everything aloud and then reading. *(Right)* The opening page of moral maxims and proverbs, which were in fact Christian religious beliefs. The text begins, "In the first place, remember that there is one God, who has infinite and eternal essence." COLLECTION OF PAUL GRENDLER

to the older and brighter students. At the same time the vast majority of Jesuit schools enrolled only one hundred to two hundred students, who studied the Latin humanities curriculum and religious instruction under four or five teachers.

The Jesuit schools appealed to the community at large with their public programs. Students at Jesuit schools in Spain and Portugal began to give public performances of Latin tragedies with scenery, stagecraft, and music. They also presented what might be called achievement days, in which students orated, recited, and debated before parents and dignitaries of the city. The schools of other Catholic Reformation teaching orders, such as the Barnabites (Clerics Regular of St. Paul) and Somaschans (Clerics Regular of Somascha), did the same.

Schools for nobles.
Boarding schools limited to boys of verified noble lineage were a feature of the stratified society of the seventeenth and eighteenth centuries. Princes and other nobles founded boarding schools for noble boys, who mixed with their peers from different parts of Europe. Entering between the

ages of eleven and fourteen, they might stay until the age of twenty. The schools for nobles supplemented the standard Latin curriculum with lessons in singing, dancing, designing fortifications, French, and above all, horsemanship. These schools cost a great deal. Ranuccio Farnese (1569–1622; ruled 1592–1622), duke of Parma and Piacenza, founded a famous school for nobles in Parma in 1601 and gave the Jesuits direction of the school in 1604. It had a peak enrollment of 550 to 600 boys between 1670 and 1700, then began to decline. The Jesuits were the teachers in many noble schools and boarding schools with upper-class boys. Other religious orders followed their lead but to a lesser extent.

France.
In the early sixteenth century many French towns established Latin classical schools that were open to the boys of the town and were staffed by teachers who had imbibed the Renaissance humanistic curriculum in Paris. Then the Crown in the early seventeenth century encouraged the Jesuits and other orders to establish schools in the kingdom. Through financial subsidies or royal commands, King Henry

Notable Jesuits. Ignatius Loyola holding the Constitutions of the Society of Jesus, flanked by noted Jesuit theologians of the late sixteenth and seventeenth centuries: Leonard Lessius, Luis de Molina, Gabriel Vázquez, and Antonio Escobar y Mendoza. ©HULTON GETTY/LIAISON AGENCY

IV (ruled 1589–1610) persuaded the religious orders to take direction of the town schools. Sometimes the towns agreed because the schools were going poorly. The town could not provide enough funding, teachers were in short supply, enrollments were declining, academic standards were falling, and the students were disorderly. Under the protection of the Crown, the new religious orders of the Catholic Reformation became the schoolmasters of France.

Numerous towns across France replaced their secular schoolmasters with the Jesuits, the French Congregation of the Oratory, and the Doctrinaires (Secular Priests of the Christian Doctrine), all of whom established some remarkable schools. In 1603 Henry IV gave to the Jesuits a château in the town of La Flèche on the Loir River. The College Henri IV at La Flèche (usually referred to as La Flèche) began with that gift. The king provided additional financial support in the following years and encouraged members of his court to send their sons there. The school was an instant success, boasting an enrollment of 1,200 to 1,400 students, of whom 300 were boarders, in a few years. Among La Flèche's most famous pupils was René

Descartes (1596–1650). Entering in 1606, Descartes spent nine years at the school. He devoted the first six to studying Latin grammar, humanities, and rhetoric and the last three to studying philosophy, which included mathematics, physics, and Galileo's telescope discoveries. Although he eventually rejected the philosophy he learned there, Descartes in 1641 endorsed La Flèche for the excellence of its instruction, its lively students who came from all over France, and the spirit of student equality that the Jesuits fostered.

The Collège de Clermont (1560–1762), renamed the Collège Louis-le-Grand in 1682, was a Jesuit school in Paris that enrolled boys ages twelve to twenty. The number of students steadily rose from 1,500 (including 300 boarders) in 1619 to 2,500 to 3,000 students (including 500 to 600 boarders) in the late seventeenth century.

Students in the Jesuit schools and probably in most Latin schools in both Catholic and Protestant Europe were placed and promoted according to their achievement, not their ages. This meant that boys of many ages might be in a single class. For example, in 1677 the rhetoric class at the Collège de Clermont in

TABLE 1
JESUIT SCHOOLS WORLDWIDE, 1556–1749

Year	Total Number of Schools
1556	c. 35 (18 in Italy)
1575	121 (35 in Italy)
1599	245 (49 in Italy)
1607	293
1626	444 (80 in Italy)
1679	578
1710	612 (111 in Italy in 1700)
1749	669 (105 in France in 1762)

(Farrell, 1938, pp. 365, 431–435; Brizzi, 1976, pp. 20, 22; Brizzi, 1982, p. 919; and Palmer, 1985, p. 15)

Paris had 160 pupils (obviously taught by more than one teacher). One student was ten years old, three were eleven, eight were twelve, fifteen were thirteen, thirty-four were fourteen, thirty-seven were fifteen, twenty-five were sixteen, twenty-eight were seventeen, six were eighteen, two were nineteen, and one was twenty. While the rhetoric class normally took two years to complete, some pupils may have required more time.

Jesuit schools in Europe, Asia, and the Americas followed the program of studies minutely organized in the Society's *Ratio studiorum* (Plan of studies) of 1599. It prescribed texts, classroom procedures, rules, and discipline. The *Ratio* frowned on corporal punishment; if its use was unavoidable, a non-Jesuit should administer it. Other Catholic religious order schools offering Latin education copied Jesuit educational procedures to greater or lesser degrees.

Piarist schools. Not all schools of the religious orders taught a Latin curriculum to middle-class and upper-class boys. The Basque priest José Calasanz (1557–1646) had the revolutionary idea of offering comprehensive free schooling to poor boys, and he opened his first Pious School in the working-class area of Trastevere, Rome, in 1597. The first Pious School accepted only pupils presenting certificates of poverty issued by parish priests. It aimed to educate poor and working-class boys so they might earn a living in this

life and attain salvation in the next. The school offered free instruction in vernacular reading, writing, and arithmetic plus some Latin to bright boys, an early attempt to combine the vernacular and Latin curricula. It also furnished books, paper, pens, ink, and on occasion food, to needy pupils. In 1621 Calasanz established a religious order, the Poor Clerics Regular of the Mother of God of the Pious Schools, usually called the Piarists, to carry on his work. In time the Piarists dropped the certificate of poverty as a prerequisite for enrollment and accepted students from the middle and upper classes. Nevertheless, they continued to see the poor as their primary student constituency. Their schools enabled poor boys to move up the social ladder, those who learned Latin into professional positions. In 1784 the Piarists ran over two hundred schools, the majority in Italy and Spain and a smaller number in central Europe.

Education for girls. Boys and girls almost always attended separate schools in both Catholic and Protestant Europe. A large number of female religious convents educated Catholic girls as long-term boarders. Parents sent a girl to a convent for several years to be educated and to learn sewing and manners. She emerged educated, virtuous, and ready to marry. Some girls decided to remain as nuns. Indeed, professed nuns living in convents had a higher literacy rate and were consistently better educated than laywomen.

Church organizations also offered charity schools for poor girls. For example, in 1655 the papacy contributed funding to hire numerous female teachers to staff free neighborhood schools for girls in Rome. Each schoolmistress taught vernacular reading and writing to classes ranging from a few to more than seventy girls. These schools lasted until the Kingdom of Italy seized Rome in 1870. Catholic Europe also had an abundance of catechism schools, called Schools of Christian Doctrine, which taught the rudiments of Catholicism and a limited amount of reading on Sundays and numerous religious holidays to boys and girls in separate classes. Protestant Europe also had catechism classes or Sunday schools, about which less is known. Numerous clergymen who lacked benefices, livings, or parishes in both Protestant and Catholic Europe supported themselves as schoolmasters.

THE ENLIGHTENMENT

To this point central governments played no direct role in schooling, with the partial exception of state-church collaboration in some small German Protestant states. In the 1750s educational reformers argued that the state should become the directing force in education and that the church should be displaced.

Beginning of state schooling and attacks against church schools.

Enlightenment reformers, who always came from the upper ranks of society, believed that the absolutist state could and should improve humankind through reform from above. They accepted the psychology of John Locke (1632–1704), who held that the child was a tabula rasa (blank slate) on which anything could be written. Thus the right early education would impart useful skills to the child and instill the proper values, which included good manners and deference to authority. Children so formed would become useful and loyal citizens. Hence the central government, rather than local authorities, should control schools and choose the teachers. Church schools, which taught useless spiritual doctrine, in the opinion of the reformers, had to be eliminated.

The attack on church education occurred in Catholic countries just as the ruling classes were finding the most famous of the church schools, those of the Jesuits, less attractive. For example, enrollment at La Flèche dropped to four hundred, of whom two hundred were boarders, by 1760. The Society of Jesus was expelled from Portugal in 1759, France in 1764, and Spain in 1767; its schools (105 of them in France) were closed or assigned to other religious congregations. Bowing to pressure from governments, the papacy suppressed the Jesuits in 1773. But, needing to maintain educational institutions for their Catholic subjects, Frederick the Great of Prussia and Catherine the Great of Russia refused to publish the papal bull and maintained the Society's institutions in their domains. State authorities across Europe also confiscated numerous church buildings and properties during the last years of the eighteenth century and through much of the nineteenth century, further weakening the capacity of church groups to support schools. Governments seldom succeeded in eliminating church schools in either Catholic or Protestant lands, but they seriously weakened churches as rivals to the central state governments as the chief force in schooling.

Enlightenment reformers further believed that state schooling should be free for lower-class boys but limited to elementary education, ending at the ages of ten to twelve. Otherwise these boys would aspire to rise above their stations, thus depriving society of their labor and upsetting the right order of things. By contrast, the sons of the ruling classes seldom attended state elementary schools but continued to study with tutors or attended elite schools. They went on to secondary schools, including boarding schools, with the classical Latin and Greek curriculum. Despite its limited vision, the central governmental control of education fostered over the course of the next 250 years the slow expansion of free, compulsory elementary and secondary state education to a growing percentage of the population.

Prussia and France, 1750–1850.

Both Prussia and France were leaders in education. The Prussian government, the pioneer in state education, asserted state control over schools in several ways in the late eighteenth century. It reorganized the finances of local schools, established inspections, and organized some teacher training. Other German states followed the Prussian example in the first half of the nineteenth century.

France did the same. The different factions that ruled France during the French Revolution of 1789 to 1799 shared one belief about education, that is, the state should control the schools. Napoleon Bonaparte came to power in 1799 and in 1802 brought all education, from primary schools through the universities, under the control of the state by law. Although the immediate results were limited, he established the principle that every French government subsequently followed, that state control and uniformity of the schools is essential. In 1808 Napoleon established new secondary schools called lycées with a curriculum of Latin and Greek, French literature, logic, and mathematics. In a revolutionary precedent, entrance to the lycée became dependent on passing a rigorous examination that required considerable preparation beyond what a student could learn at an elementary school. Although the vast majority of pupils in lycées came from the upper-middle class and the aristocracy, a few students from other groups entered. Napoleon also established a state engineering school, École Polytechnique, and a state professional school, École Normale Supérieure.

Some German states established teacher training schools, the first of them in Berlin in 1756. The first French government écoles normales (normal schools) to train elementary teachers opened in the 1820s, and by 1863 half of the elementary teachers in France came from these schools. Teacher training schools also began in England in the 1840s. Although the normal schools mostly taught future teachers the same skills that they would teach their pupils, including orderliness and respect for the hierarchy of society, these schools helped men and women rise from peasant and working-class ranks to become teachers, especially at the elementary level. The graduates of French teacher training schools were often militantly antireligious and supporters of state education.

Teachers commanded some respect in a society in which not everyone could read and write and few people did so well. But a large social gulf separated teachers from the representative of the state or the local aristocrat who gave them orders. Moreover, the teacher was greatly enmeshed in the society of his or her local community and its values. Often teachers were required to perform other duties. For example, in Germany teachers were obliged to ring church bells, to assist at church services, and generally to help the local Protestant pastor or parish priest. They had to be pious according to the precepts of the local religion.

Another step in the process of creating state education was erecting buildings. Governments increasingly constructed either a building with multiple classrooms for several hundred students in large towns or a one-room schoolhouse in the country. The expression "go to school" began to have a physical meaning.

Individual classes, especially at the primary levels, still had many pupils, sometimes a hundred or more. State schools had more students per teacher than the Latin schools of the religious orders or the independent vernacular schools of previous centuries. The large classes meant that much learning consisted of simultaneous rote learning: students shouted letters and words in unison or did simple arithmetical calculations together.

CONSOLIDATION OF STATE EDUCATION, 1850–1918

As the national governments of England, France, Germany, Italy, the Netherlands, Russia, Spain, and Austria-Hungary grew stronger, they expanded centralized, compulsory, lay state education.

France. Because some 38,000 towns and villages in France lacked elementary schools, the 1833 Guizot law, named for the minister of education François Guizot (1787–1874), obliged every town to establish a public elementary school. But it did not order all students to attend them. Free primary education grew but was not universal. In the 1850s and 1860s Catholic religious organizations, again assuming an important position in French education, often operated local public schools under contract with towns. Between 1879 and 1886 the Ferry laws, named for the minister of education Jules Ferry (1832–1893), made public primary education free, tax-supported, and thoroughly secular. A law in 1882 required schooling for all boys and girls between the ages of six and thir-

TABLE 2
PERCENTAGE OF MALE CHILDREN AGED 6 TO 14 ENROLLED IN ELEMENTARY SCHOOLS

Country	1820	1850	1870	1883	1900
Prussia	59	81	93		97
Bavaria		83	84		96
France		60	88		94
England and Wales		66			90
Scotland			80		99
Sweden		59			90
Italy			34		57
Russia					29
Austria			57	83	97*

* Estimate

The Russian figure is adult male literacy in 1897, and the Austrian figures include boys and girls. (Maynes, 1985, p. 134; Florinsky, 1964, p. 315; Zeps, 1987, p. 11)

teen. As a result, literacy rates for the whole population, men and women, grew from 60 percent in 1870 to 95 percent in 1900.

Various Ferry laws practically eliminated Catholic schools in France and prohibited priests, brothers, and nuns from teaching, even in private schools, although Catholic schools returned in later decades as private schools. Other laws vastly expanded the ranks of teachers, especially female teachers, who replaced teaching nuns. The curriculum emphasized civil history and ignored France's religious past. For example, geographies passed over the great medieval cathedrals and paid little attention to Joan of Arc. In place of religious instruction, the public schools taught thrift, obedience to authority, and orderliness. The government in Paris dictated every aspect of French public education. Supposedly a minister of education looked at his watch at three o'clock on a Monday afternoon and said, "At this minute every pupil in every fifth-year class in France is studying Racine," referring to the dramatic poet Jean Racine (1639–1699). True or not, the story expressed the goal of the French educational system, the most centralized in Europe.

The standardization of schools and the establishment of links among primary, secondary, and higher schools probably had the most enduring effect on French society. Primary schools served the lower classes, while lycées were for the children of the upper and middle classes. Indeed lycées had their own preparatory schools, which began teaching Latin as early as age nine. In the 1860s and 1870s a new kind of secondary school developed, offering more practical instruction than the severely classical lycée. The new school provided what was called a "modern" education, consisting of general education in French, science, and history as well as commercial courses and manual training. Members of the lower-middle classes found them particularly attractive. In 1902 the French government placed the "modern" curriculum on an equal basis with that of the classics-oriented lycée.

At the age of eleven, the French pupil began a seven-year secondary school program divided into two parts. In the first four years the student followed either a classical or a modern curriculum. For the next three years a student chose more intense study of either Latin and modern languages or science or the other secondary school program of modern languages and science. In the second year of the second cycle (the sixth year overall), students took the first part of the *baccalauréat* (school-leaving certificate) examination. More than half of the students failed the first part of the examination and had to repeat the previous year. Those who passed spent another year preparing for the second part of the *baccalauréat* examination. Only those who successfully completed both parts of the *baccalauréat* were eligible for higher training at universities or other schools, such as the École Normale Supérieure. The fortunate graduates ruled France and became especially prominent in the civil service and the university professoriate—a fact of French life that remained constant through the end of the twentieth century.

France simultaneously created an inclusive, broad primary school system for the working and peasant classes and a rigorous, socially exclusive form of elite secondary education. A few talented children from the working and peasant classes, with financial assistance, made the transition from the standard primary schools to the secondary schools at the age of eleven. A somewhat larger number of lycée students came from the lower-middle class, the ranks of clerks and shopkeepers. But the majority of students in the elite schools came from the upper-middle and elite classes.

The rest of continental Europe.

Every other country in continental Europe developed a similar structure of state schools. All forced children to make a choice among three different secondary schools at the ages of ten, eleven, and occasionally twelve. A fortunate few, usually the offspring of upper and upper-

middle class and professional parents, went on to the secondary school with the classical curriculum, modern language training, and a limited amount of mathematics and science. Called *Gymnasium* in Germany, Austria, and Russia, *gimnázium* in Hungary, and *liceo* in Italy, the classical academic secondary school was the same everywhere.

From the Renaissance onward the classical secondary school was at the center of European elite education, even though classical Latin no longer had a practical use, except to some scholars, after the eighteenth century. Nevertheless, educational leaders, and probably the majority of society, believed that learning ancient languages and literature best enabled a boy and (later) a girl to realize his or her potential. The concept was called *Bildung* (cultivation) in German, *culture générale* in French, and liberal education in English. According to this view, the study of Latin and Greek grammar developed mental discipline, while ancient Latin and Greek literature offered examples of the highest human culture in the original language. The classical curriculum benefited the student regardless of future career because it developed the individual—but only a few. In 1883 the German historian Heinrich von Treitschke justified the classical secondary school and its social exclusiveness with the statement, "Millions must plow and forge and dig in order that a few thousands may write and paint and study."

Graduates of the classical secondary school went on to universities; took civil service positions; joined the professions of law, medicine, and theology; and became leaders of the nation. For example, until 1902 German students had to attend the *Gymnasium* to obtain the *Abitur*, the school-leaving examination certificate that permitted them to attend university. Only university graduates were allowed to sit state examinations for the civil service, the ministry, the medical and legal professions, and secondary school teaching. In 1902 Germany began to allow graduates of the other secondary schools to attend university under strict limitations, and other countries followed the German example.

The secondary technical school also developed in the nineteenth century. It combined a lesser amount of theoretical training and some ancient-language training with more scientific and technical education. Its graduates normally did not go on to the university, but they could attend advanced technical schools. Students from this stream often became managers and technicians in commerce and industry. In the late nineteenth and early twentieth centuries some countries developed nonselective secondary modern schools, offering vocational and practical training. They educated workers for occupations in which they would follow instructions. Finally, most countries added an additional three years or more of elementary school after the age of ten. Students who continued in elementary schools ended their schooling at the ages of thirteen, which was slowly raised to fourteen, fifteen, or sixteen. Some entered apprenticeships that might include limited additional schooling.

Only a few students attended a secondary school of any sort in the nineteenth and early twentieth centuries, and the majority of students entering secondary school at the ages of ten or eleven did not finish. In 1911 only 2.6 percent of students up to age seventeen attended secondary schools in France, and 3.2 percent of students up to age nineteen attended secondary schools in Prussia. Poorer countries, such as Italy, Spain, and particularly Russia, had fewer schools and a smaller percentage of the population in school, especially in secondary schools.

Neither the curricular streams nor the social exclusiveness of secondary education changed much from the late nineteenth century through the 1950s. For example, in one state of the Federal Republic of Germany in the 1950s, two-thirds of the students left elementary school by the ages of fourteen or fifteen. No more than 20 percent of German children tried one of the secondary schools. Of the age group ten to fourteen, 10 percent studied in an academic secondary school (Gymnasium), but only 3.3 percent graduated. Of Gymnasium graduates, 97 percent went on to higher education, normally university training. Only 5 to 6 percent of the students in all three secondary schools combined were the children of laborers, though laborers made up about half of the population. At the other extreme, 25 percent of the children in secondary schools had academically trained parents, usually Gymnasium or secondary technical school graduates, but the academically trained made up only 2.5 percent of the population.

Nineteenth-century governments across Europe decreed that all children must go to school to a certain age, which was gradually raised. An increasing number of boys and girls attended elementary schools, although the elementary curriculum was not extensive: reading, writing, arithmetic, and outside of France, religion. Governments provided more but never enough schools and teachers. Nevertheless, the expansion of schooling for the children of the working classes and peasantry across western Europe in the nineteenth century was impressive.

SCHOOLS AS BEARERS OF CULTURAL AND SOCIAL VALUES

European schooling in the nineteenth- and twentieth-centuries pursued cultural, national, and social goals

considered as important as academic skills and knowledge. The results were often tumultuous.

The nation and its minorities. Every national school system resolved the linguistic issue of multiple dialects by teaching one version of the national language, that of its most accomplished authors. For example, Italian schools taught Tuscan Italian, the language of the Florentine Dante Alighieri (1265–1321), instead of Milanese, Neapolitan, Roman, Venetian, or another regional dialect. In practice this meant that students, especially those in elementary school, learned the national language in school but spoke the regional language at home, in the street, and in the shop. Every national school system also taught a minority of children whose mother tongue was completely different from the national language. School systems sometimes permitted extensive bilingual education and other times imposed schooling in the national language on children of another mother tongue.

School officials and national leaders saw education, especially at the elementary level, as a means of creating national unity. For example, Italian schools, after Italian unification in 1870, taught a relentless patriotism emphasizing the exploits of Giuseppe Garibaldi (1807–1882), the attractive military hero of the battle for unification. Students wrote essays on such topics as "Why I love Italy." In 1886 Michele Coppino, the Italian minister of education, justifying this policy, issued a circular that stated, "We must not forget that the primary school aims at rearing a population as instructed as possible, but principally honest, hardworking, useful to the family and devoted to the Country and to the King." Other European governments made similar statements.

The desire to produce honest, hardworking, and loyal subjects led all governments outside France to allow religious instruction in state schools and often to permit the existence of religious schools, despite official anticlerical policies and rhetoric. For example, the Prussian state within united Germany wished to integrate both Catholic and Protestant children into the same schools, which would be nonconfessional. But strong opposition from both Catholic and Protestant church leaders caused the government to retreat. Successive governments found that maintaining good relations with the two religions through confessional primary schools was necessary to preserve the state's monopoly over education. By the early twentieth century almost all Protestant children in Prussia attended Protestant schools, while almost all Catholic children attended Catholic schools. Even in the Weimar government period, 1919–1933, 92 percent of Catholic school children attended Catholic schools, and 95 percent of Protestant children attended Protestant schools. Jewish children attended Jewish schools or Protestant schools where they had separate classes for religion.

When a minority both practiced a different religion and spoke a different language, toleration sometimes evaporated. The schooling of the Polish Catholic minority in the German state between 1870 and 1918 involved linguistic, national, and religious issues. Prussia, the largest state in united Germany, had a substantial number of Catholic Poles. It was reasonably tolerant of this minority and had permitted extensive bilingual education before unification of the German state in 1870. However, beginning in the 1880s the central German government, dominated by Prussia, increasingly imposed German language instruction on Polish children, with one concession. Bowing to the argument, advanced by both Polish Catholic and German Protestant clergies, that only religious instruction in the mother tongue could reach a child's heart and soul, it permitted Catholic religious instruction of Polish children in Polish.

Otherwise the German government increasingly attempted to germanize its Polish school population. It reduced Polish language instruction and teachers. It spent so little money on schools in Polish-speaking areas, whose population was expanding rapidly, that some elementary schools in Polish areas had three shifts a day, giving each child only about two hours of instruction, often in classes of well over one hundred students. When the government finally insisted that Catholic religious instruction should be delivered in German to Polish-speaking children, the children and their parents resisted. In 1901 a teacher caned pupils who refused to recite a psalm in German. In October and November 1906 up to 46,000 Polish-speaking school children refused to speak German during Catholic religious lessons. The government imposed fines on the parents and broke the strike by May and June 1907 without solving the dispute. This example and many other others demonstrate that governments often suppressed the religious rights and the languages of minorities in the schools or were forced into uneasy compromises. The creation of a Polish state in 1919 out of territories formerly ruled by Germany and Russia moved most of the Polish-speaking children out of Germany. Then it was Poland that had linguistic and religious minorities.

Fascist and Nazi schooling. Neither the Fascist government of Italy (1922–1943) nor the Nazi regime in Germany (1933–1945) made significant changes to the structure of schooling. Instead they added ideological themes to the curriculum. The schools stressed militarism, nationalism, and service to the country (*patria* or *Vaterland*) more strongly than before. They added material in the secondary schools that explained and promoted Fascism and National Socialism. Both governments taught an ideology that emphasized the leader (*duce* or *führer*) who embodied the will of the people and should be obeyed without question. Both promoted a conservative and traditional view of women's role, embodied in the Nazi slogan *"Kirche, Kinder, und Küche"* (church, children, and kitchen). But both regimes relied on youth organizations and a general indoctrination of the populace more than the classroom to propagate their views.

Italy expelled all Jewish teachers and students from elementary and secondary schools, some five thousand students and two hundred teachers, in October 1938. However, the government immediately established and financially supported Jewish elementary and secondary schools. With excellent teachers, some of the lowest teacher-pupil ratios in Italy, and dedicated students, they were among the best schools in Italy.

England. England followed the general European pattern, with the major exception of the English public school. England emerged from the seventeenth and eighteenth centuries with the educational mix, found all across Europe, of limited elementary schools, called "petty schools," teaching basic literacy in English, and grammar schools, which boys normally entered between the ages of nine and twelve, teaching Latin. In towns a host of endowed schools existed, usually founded through the modest bequest of a local patron and sometimes operated by a clergyman as part of the village church. England probably lagged behind the rest of western Europe in the percentage of children of school age who attended school in 1800.

The late-eighteenth-century industrial revolution created factories filled with working children, whose plight caught the attention of social reformers. The reformers set up Sunday schools, to which working children could go on Sunday or after working hours on other days, to teach elementary literacy skills and a catechism, usually that of the Church of England but sometimes that of other Protestant churches. The Sunday schools employed techniques of mass education, such as using older children to instruct the ablest younger children, who in turn instructed their peers, and recitation in unison.

Slowly the notion grew that the state should provide a limited amount of schooling to those without funds to pay fees or provide a school where one was lacking. But the question of the role of the Church of England, which wanted a strong voice,

ENGLISH PUBLIC SCHOOLS

Despite the name, English public schools were in fact expensive private schools. Seven boarding schools, Winchester (1382), Eton (1440), Shrewsbury (1552), Westminster (late sixteenth century), Harrow (1571), Rugby (1576), and Charterhouse (1611), were held in the highest esteem. Two day schools, St. Paul's, founded by the English humanist John Colet (1467–1519) in 1508, and Merchant Taylors (1561), completed the highest group. But England had many other boarding and day public schools of varying quality and prestige. All were independent, expensive, and filled with boys from the highest ranks of society. They taught a traditional Latin and Greek curriculum and maintained close ties with Oxford and Cambridge.

By the time the nineteenth century opened, the public schools had fallen into numerous abuses and difficulties. Thomas Arnold (1795–1842), headmaster of Rugby from 1828 to 1842, led a reform movement. He had three goals, listed in descending order: (1) he wished to imbue boys with Christian religious and moral principles, (2) he wanted them to conduct themselves as gentlemen, and (3) he wanted to train them intellectually. To achieve these ends, he emphasized Christian, specifically Church of England, religious training through the master's sermon and good example, and he gave the older boys a share in the governance of the school. They served as examples of leadership and good morality to younger boys. Arnold also emphasized sports as a means of fostering sportsmanship and loyalty, an emphasis that expanded greatly later in the century. He moderated but did not eliminate physical hazing and the faggot system, a form of bullying servitude imposed by the older boys on the younger ones.

Thomas Hughes (1822–1896), who began at Rugby at age thirteen, when Arnold was still headmaster, wrote *Tom Brown's School-days* (1857), which presents a wonderfully appealing picture of public school life. Thanks to the publicity generated by Hughes and others and an economic boom, which created a wealthy middle class that wanted its children to rise socially, the public schools enjoyed a golden age from 1860 to 1918 as more public schools, including some for girls, were founded. They spawned continental imitations, which never were as numerous or important as the English originals.

Boys went off to board at public schools as early as seven years of age, more often at ten to twelve, and remained there until they finished at eighteen. At their best the schools socialized boys into the habits of subservience and fellowship as younger students and of leadership and responsibility as older students. They also created lifetime bonds that had enormous practical benefits and social consequences. Old boys, graduates of a particular public school, helped one another throughout their lives. The public school ethos, including the view that gentlemanly behavior and loyalty were more important than intellectual achievement, permeated the higher ranks of English civil service, army, government, and society. Public school graduates comprised two-thirds to three-quarters of the judges, ambassadors, lieutenant generals and higher military officers, bishops, chief executives in the one hundred largest firms, and Conservative members of Parliament as late as the 1950s and 1960s. Public schools played a major role in perpetuating class distinctions and slowing the development of a merit-based society.

blocked massive state intervention and led to a series of partial measures. In the first, in 1833, the government made available funds to build more schools. An increasing number of reformers argued for greater state intervention in education on the grounds that the country needed a more educated citizenry to compete industrially with France and Germany, which already had state schooling. The Education Act of 1870 established that, where schooling was inadequate, a local school board of five to fifteen members elected by the local taxpayers would create and run schools, which would be financed by taxes, government grants, and pupil fees. It also permitted elementary schools operated by the Church of England. The overall result was much more elementary schooling. England had 1 million pupils in state elementary schools in 1870 and 6 million children in elementary schools, evenly split between board (that is, state) and church schools, in 1900. Thereafter the number of children in board schools increased.

Unlike school boards on the Continent, where complete authority over the schools resided with the central government, the English local school boards had extensive powers. Nevertheless in 1880 the central government obliged all children to attend school to the age of ten, the first compulsory school law in England. Elementary schools were still not free, but in the 1890s the central government began to grant schools small amounts of money to replace the fees previously paid by parents.

A series of reports followed that documented the inadequacies of secondary education, and the Education Act of 1902 abolished the school boards. In their place, the law made local county and borough governments responsible for both elementary and secondary education by constituting them as local educational authorities with all the legal powers of the former school boards and additional new powers. They were expected to coordinate primary and secondary education and to offer scholarships for poor children to attend secondary schools, which charged fees, and eventually to enter university. Local governments were obliged to provide scholarships (that is, free places) for a quarter of the students in the state secondary schools. They also provided partial financing to church schools operated by the Church of England, other Protestant churches, and the Catholic Church.

The English government slightly modified and extended educational benefits in the twentieth century. Scholarships were awarded on the basis of a competitive examination given to children at the age of eleven (the so-called eleven-plus), and the successful students studied at a grammar school for free. This became the English equivalent of the qualifying examinations for secondary school in continental Europe, the examination that determined a child's future educational career and life prospects. The grammar school remained classical in its curriculum; technical and vocational secondary education developed slowly.

The Butler Act of 1944 abolished fees for state secondary schools, provided more financial support for church schools, and proclaimed the principle that every child should receive both primary and secondary schooling. In recognition of the last, the government raised the school-leaving age to fifteen in 1947 and to sixteen in 1972. But only 20 percent of the children successfully passed the eleven-plus examination to enter the grammar (Latin) schools, which led to the university at that time. The others attended technical schools or modern secondary schools, which had a mixed curriculum. Many parents considered them inferior to the grammar schools. The failure to advance to the grammar school through the eleven-plus examination often left a legacy of bitterness among children and their parents. The Butler Act also made religion classes compulsory in state schools for the first time in English history, although almost all state and church schools already had some religious education.

In the late 1960s and early 1970s England moved toward comprehensive secondary schools intended to replace partially the grammar schools, still seen as the place for students of economic and social privilege as well as academic excellence. At the conclusion of secondary education, the General Certificate of Education, begun in 1951, was earned through examination and offered admission to the universities. The Certificate of Secondary Education, begun in 1965, was awarded to students of lesser achievement.

Scotland   Although ruled by the English Crown, Scotland followed a different educational path from England by more quickly developing a centralized state educational system.

In 1560 the Scottish Protestant leader John Knox (1513–1572) called for a system of parish schools; such a system developed over the next two hundred years. Legislation required landowners to appoint a schoolmaster for each parish, to pay him a small salary, and to build a schoolhouse. Parish schools enrolled both boys and girls, although girls' education emphasized reading and sewing rather than the broader range of academic skills imparted to boys. All children had to pay small fees, but the church or community paid the fees of poor children. Although parish schools were less numerous in remote and poorer regions of Scotland than in the affluent lowlands, it was a national system of elementary education, supplemented by a limited number of other schools. By the eighteenth century Scotland had one of the highest schooling rates, especially for girls, in Europe.

The parish schools provided the model for a national system of education. In the early nineteenth century secular leaders influenced by the Scottish Enlightenment, and clergymen of the Church of Scotland, agreed that the state should take the lead in education. Their efforts culminated in the Education (Scotland) Act of 1872, passed by the British Parliament, which transformed Presbyterian parish schools into state schools. The Act of 1872 established school boards to take direction of parish schools, to levy taxes, and to take other measures for the schools. It also decreed compulsory education for all Scottish children from the ages of five through twelve. The new state schools still provided Presbyterian religious instruction, but a conscience clause allowed children of other religions to absent themselves.

State-directed Scottish schools provided more elementary education than did the decentralized English system. In 1871 approximately 80 percent of Scottish boys and girls aged six through twelve attended school. But because schooling was not compulsory beyond age twelve, school attendance dropped to about one-third for boys and girls aged thirteen and fourteen. In 1901, 99 percent of Scottish boys and girls aged six through twelve attended school. The number dropped to 85 percent for boys and girls aged thirteen and to 35 percent for those aged fourteen. In the twentieth century Scottish education conformed more closely to the English system.

The Soviet Union, 1917–1989.

Russia lagged behind other nations in the percentage of children attending schools of any kind or level. In addition to the country's problems of vast distances and poverty, some tsarist governments feared extending education on the grounds that learning led to sedition, hence schooling was allocated according to class. Count Ivan Delianov, the minister for education in 1887, wanted the children of "coachmen, footmen, cooks . . . and other similar people . . . who should not be led to break away from the milieu to which they belong" barred from the classical *gymnasia*. Although this did not happen, in 1913 less than 40 percent of the population over the age of eight could read and write. Literacy was lower in the countryside and the vast Asiatic part of the Russian Empire.

After the 1917 Russian Revolution, the Communist government determined to change the schools and to provide free, compulsory state education for all. The educational ministry created a new unified school called the Free Labor School, which provided nine years of schooling for ages eight to seventeen, divided into five lower grades and four upper grades, for all. The schools were free and provided materials and lunches. The Free Labor School eliminated Latin, Greek, and religious education and attempted to integrate learning and life. The goal was for children to learn actively about farming and trades by caring for plants and animals and operating tools; about society by visiting institutions and organizations; and about the arts by drawing and singing. Subjects would lose their specificity. The schools also taught a considerable amount of Marxist-Leninist theory.

In reality, Russia had few schools, and those often lacked blackboards, pens, and paper. Despite the government's wish to open schools to all social classes, few children of workers and peasants remained the whole nine years. Sons and daughters of the middle and upper classes dominated the upper grades in the mid-1920s. In the 1930s, in a reversal of policy, the government forced some children of middle- and upper-class parents out of school. In that decade the

Stalinist purges, some of whose victims were teachers, and the extermination of the kulaks (free peasants) further disrupted the schools. Yet despite the lack of resources and the political and human disruptions, the Soviet Union did succeed in building more schools, educating more children, and sending more sons and daughters of the working class and peasantry into the secondary grades by the 1930s.

After 1931 Soviet education became less revolutionary and more traditional. The school system was oriented toward creating the workers, engineers, and technicians needed by the state for heavy industrialization. Examinations, stricter grading, and subject content were emphasized. Tuition fees for the upper grades of the secondary school were introduced in 1940, then abolished in 1956. Free boarding schools for boys and girls were established in 1956. On the other hand, the government in 1958 mandated that all applicants for higher education work for two years in industry or agriculture. They also needed the approval of organizations, such as trade unions and the Young Communist League. In the last decades before the collapse of the Soviet Union in the early 1990s, the social result of Soviet schooling was a contradictory mix. Soviet education attempted to create a classless society, but the sons and daughters of Communist Party officials, members of the government, and the professional classes enjoyed more educational benefits than the rest.

Eastern Europe.

Before 1945 the countries of eastern Europe—Poland, Czechoslovakia (later divided into the Czech Republic and Slovakia), Hungary, Romania, Bulgaria, Yugoslavia (later divided into several states), and Albania—had the same basic school structure, characterized by the same sharp social divisions, as western and central Europe. The major difference was that eastern Europe was poorer and, therefore, offered fewer schools and less opportunity, especially in the countryside. World War II had a devastating effect on education in eastern Europe. German special forces shot an estimated 27,000 Polish teachers. An estimated 10,000 teachers lost their lives in Yugoslavia, either in the struggle against the Germans or in the brutal fighting between ethnic and political factions. An unknown number of schools were destroyed. Immediately after World War II, Communist governments, supported by the Soviet Union and its conquering army, took control of all of Eastern Europe and part of Germany. The new Communist governments effected an educational revolution.

All education became state education, with the exception of a few remaining private schools in Poland. The eastern bloc countries often provided state

Kindergarten. English lesson in a kindergarten in Novosibirsk, Russia, December 1994. V. ZININ/ITAR-TASS/SOVFOTO

preschools, nursery schools, and kindergartens for children from one to six. These served as instruments of socialization as much as learning centers.

The fundamental unit was the basic school, which followed the Soviet model. The basic school had seven to ten (most often eight) years of compulsory schooling that was the same for all pupils from six or seven to fifteen or sixteen. In addition to reading and writing in the national language and mathematics, the basic school taught history and economics according to Marxist-Leninist principles; a foreign language, usually Russian instead of the French or German taught in pre-Communist years; and a considerable amount of biology, physics, chemistry, and polytechnical training. Latin and religious training were eliminated.

At the age of fifteen or sixteen the student either left school or entered one of three different kinds of secondary schools. If the student passed the appropriate examination, he or she entered the general secondary school, which concentrated on academic studies. Similar to the lycée or *Gymnasium,* it lasted three or four years and concluded with a certificate, like the French *baccalauréat* or the German *Abitur.* The certificate was a prerequisite for university entrance but not a guarantee of admission because places were limited. The second form of advanced secondary school was the vocational secondary school, also three to four years, which prepared students for a particular occupation, anything from engineering to kindergarten

teaching. Those who finished might also apply to enter universities. Third were trade schools, lasting one to three years, which offered both classroom and factory instruction, amounting to apprentice training, for particular trades.

Advancement also depended on ideological and political conformity. In the German Democratic Republic students had to participate in the *Jugendweihe* (youth consecration), a Communist ceremony that replaced the Christian religious rite of confirmation. School children had to be enthusiastic members of Communist youth organizations, such as the Young Pioneers and Free German Youth, whose leadership exercised veto power over a student's chances of entering a university.

The schools of the Communist bloc eliminated illiteracy and the social stratification characteristic of eastern European education before World War II. But they also developed their own social and political divisions. Sons and daughters of high Communist Party officials received educational preference, especially for coveted spots in universities. Higher education remained limited to a few. For example, the German Democratic Republic sent a smaller percentage of its university-age population to universities than did the Federal Republic of Germany. On 3 October 1990 the two Germanies legally reunited, and the five new states *(Länder)* of the former German Democratic Republic adopted the educational system of the German Federal Republic.

Western Europe. A series of educational changes swept across Europe in the 1960s, 1970s, 1980s, and 1990s. The school-leaving age was raised even before this, along with the expansion of state support for universities. The French government provided nursery school education to practically every child between the ages of three and five. Other French changes were designed to give all students some kind of secondary school graduation certificate and to increase greatly the number of university or university-level students. By the late twentieth century over a third of all French students went on to postsecondary institutions. France even gave local authorities some control over schools and involved parents in their operation. In Germany parents and the child, not the teacher or an examination, decided if the twelve-year-old child continued to the *Gymnasium* or another secondary school. Students more easily moved from one secondary school to another, and the classical secondary school lost some of its importance as the gateway to leadership positions in the state. Graduates of both the *Gymnasium* and the secondary technical school had the option to attend a university, but not the graduates of the secondary modern school. Similar changes were implemented in Italy and Spain, but slowly in the latter because of a shortage of state funding. Most state school systems offered optional religion classes, and central governments provided complete or limited funding to private and religious schools. Religion ceased to be an area of controversy.

Overall, the systems established by the late nineteenth century were modified but not undone. The social exclusivity of European education lessened, but did not disappear. The children of immigrant guest workers from outside the European Community presented a new area of concern because they usually landed in the secondary vocational school with little or no opportunity for further academic training.

CONCLUSION

The social history of European education after the Renaissance saw the extension of schooling to the entire population and the gradual lowering but not elimination of class barriers. The state assumed the commanding position in education that individuals, local authorities, and church organizations formerly held. Several features did not change a great deal over the centuries, notably the classical curriculum, religious training, and the belief that schools should also teach cultural and social values.

See also **Secularization** *(volume 2);* **Social Class; Students** *(volume 3);* **Youth and Adolescence** *(volume 4); and other articles in this section.*

BIBLIOGRAPHY

Social historians have devoted a considerable amount of scholarship to schooling, especially for France and Germany, from about 1750 onward. The period 1600–1750 for Europe outside of France and the impact of the Protestant Reformation in the German states have received less notice. Most historians have studied education within larger political, social, and religious contexts and have made excellent use of the abundant statistical information for the nineteenth and twentieth centuries. But statistics have been difficult to compile for earlier centuries. Historians have paid less attention to the intellectual content of schooling, that is, curriculum, textbooks, and how resources were used, except for the Fascist and Nazi periods. Some historians, especially in France, have seen schooling as social control or "policing the village," that is, as a means of compelling the lower classes to conform to social norms imposed from above. This approach risks missing the broader importance and complexity of education.

General Works

Cruz, Jo Ann Hoeppner Moran. "Education." In *Encyclopedia of the Renaissance.* Edited by Paul F. Grendler et al. 6 vol. New York, 1999. Volume 2, pages 242–254. A good pan-European survey.

Grendler, Paul F., ed. "Education in the Renaissance and Reformation." *Renaissance Quarterly* 43, no. 4 (winter 1990): 774–824. European coverage with an extensive bibliography.

Maynes, Mary Jo. *Schooling for the People. Comparative Local Studies of Schooling History in France and Germany, 1750–1850.* New York, 1985.

Maynes, Mary Jo. *Schooling in Western Europe: A Social History.* Albany, N.Y., 1985. A good survey for the period 1750–1850.

Ringer, Fritz K. *Education and Society in Modern Europe.* Bloomington, Ind., 1979. A good comparative study of secondary education and universities in France and Germany with some material on England c. 1850–1960.

England

Digby, Anne, and Peter Searby. *Children, School, and Society in Nineteenth-Century England.* London and New York, 1981. Contains 175 pages of interesting original documents.

Honey, John Raymond de Symons. *Tom Brown's Universe: The Development of the English Public School in the Nineteenth Century.* New York, 1977. A good account offering reasons for the appeal of English public schools.

Hughes, Thomas. *Tom Brown's School Days.* Harmondsworth, U.K., 1973. The novel describes in lively terms the education of a fictional boy at Thomas Arnold's Rugby; first published in 1857.

Lawson, John, and Harold Silver. *A Social History of Education in England.* London, 1973. A comprehensive account.

Martin, Christopher. *A Short History of English Schools, 1750–1965.* Hove, U.K., 1979. A good succinct account enlivened with many interesting quotations.

Tuer, Andrew White. *History of the Horn Book.* New York, 1968; reprint, 1979. A study of the primer with many illustrations; first published in 1897.

France

Anderson, R. D. *Education in France, 1848–1870.* Oxford, 1975.

Chartier, Roger, Dominique Julia, Marie-Madeleine Compère. *L'éducation en France du XVIe au XVIIIe siècle.* Paris, 1976. Statistical information.

Chisick, Harvey. *The Limits of Reform in the Enlightenment: Attitudes toward the Education of the Lower Classes in Eighteenth-Century France.* Princeton, N.J., 1981.

Corbett, Anne, and Bob Moon, eds. *Education in France: Continuity and Change in the Mitterrand Years, 1981–1995.* London and New York, 1996.

Delattre, Pierre, ed. *Les établissements des Jésuites en France depuis quatre siècles.* 5 vols. Enghien, France, and Wetteren, Belgium, 1949–1957. Articles on all the Jesuit schools in France.

Farrell, Allan P. *The Jesuit Code of Liberal Education: Development and Scope of the Ratio Studiorum.* Milwaukee, Wis., 1938.

Grew, Raymond, and Patrick J. Harrigan. *School, State, and Society: The Growth of Elementary Schooling in Nineteenth-Century France.* Ann Arbor, Mich., 1991. Useful statistics.

Huppert, George. *Public Schools in Renaissance France.* Urbana, Ill., 1984. Describes the municiple Latin secondary schools in sixteenth-century France.

Moody, Joseph N. *French Education since Napoleon.* Syracuse, N.Y., 1978. A general survey.

Palmer, R. R. *The Improvement of Humanity: Education and the French Revolution.* Princeton, N.J., 1985. Covers the French Revolution and the Napoleonic period.

Stearns, Peter N. *Schools and Students in Industrial Society: Japan and the West, 1870–1940.* Boston, 1998. A good brief account with some documents for France.

Germany

Albisetti, James C. *Secondary School Reform in Imperial Germany.* Princeton, N.J., 1983. Covers the period 1800–1914 well.

Blackburn, Gilmer W. *Education in the Third Reich: A Study of Race and History in Nazi Textbooks.* Albany, N.Y., 1985.

Friedrichs, Christopher R. "Whose House of Learning? Some Thoughts on German Schools in Post-reformation Germany." *History of Education Quarterly* 22 (1982): 371–377.

Lamberti, Marjorie. *State, Society, and the Elementary School in Imperial Germany.* New York, 1989. A good account of the religious, political, and linguistic issues.

Phillips, David, ed. *Education in Germany: Tradition and Reform in Historical Context.* London and New York, 1995. Good on developments since the 1960s and on the former German Democratic Republic.

Strauss, Gerald. *Enacting the Reformation in Germany: Essays on Institution and Reception.* Aldershot, U.K., and Brookfield, Vt., 1993. Includes several essays on schools in the German Reformation.

Strauss, Gerald. *Luther's House of Learning: Indoctrination of the Young in the German Reformation.* Baltimore, 1978. A critical assessment of the aims and results of schooling in the Lutheran Reformation.

Italy

Barbagli, Marzio. *Educating for Unemployment: Politics, Labor Markets, and the School System—Italy, 1859–1973.* Translated by Robert H. Ross. New York, 1982. An indictment of Italian education for training too many lawyers and civil servants and not enough engineers and others useful to the economy; first published in 1974.

Brizzi, Gian Paolo. *La formazione della classe dirigente nel sei-settecento: I seminaria nobilium nell'Italia centro-settentrionale.* Bologna, Italy, 1976. A study of Jesuit boarding schools for nobles in the seventeenth and eighteenth centuries.

Brizzi, Gian Paolo. "Strategie educative e istituzion: Scolastiche della Controriforma." In *La letteratura italiana.* Vol. 1: *Il letterato e le istituzioni.* Turin, Italy, 1982. Pages 899–920.

Grendler, Paul F. *Schooling in Renaissance Italy: Literacy and Learning, 1300–1600.* Baltimore, Md., 1989. A comprehensive study of all forms of preuniversity education in Italy.

Pelliccia, Guerrino. *La scuola primaria a Roma dal secolo XVI al XIX.* Rome, 1985. A comprehensive account of Roman elementary education from 1513 to 1829.

Toscani, Xenio. *Scuole e alfabetismo nello Stato di Milan da Carlo Borromeo alla Rivoluzione.* Brescia, Italy, 1993. A model study of schooling and literacy in Milan from 1560 to 1800.

Williams, George L. *Fascist Thought and Totalitarianism in Italy's Secondary Schools: Theory and Practice, 1922–1943.* New York, 1994. An excellent account with information on policy, textbooks, and preferred themes for compositions.

Woodward, William Harrison. *Vittorino da Feltre and Other Humanist Educators.* New York, 1963. A description of the most famous humanist schools and English translations of four fifteenth-century humanistic pedagogical treatises; first published in 1897.

Russia, the Soviet Union, and Eastern Europe

Alston, Patrick L. *Education and the State in Tsarist Russia.* Stanford, Calif., 1969. A general history of 1700–1914 that focuses on oscillation between centralization and local control of education.

Florinsky, Michael T. *Russia: A Short History.* New York, 1964.

Grant, Nigel. *Society, Schools, and Progress in Eastern Europe.* Oxford and New York, 1969. Covers Poland, East Germany, Czechoslovakia, Hungary, Romania, Yugoslavia, Bulgaria, and Albania in the twentieth century.

Hans, Nicholas A. *The Russian Tradition in Education.* London, 1963. Russian pedagogical thought in the eighteenth and nineteenth centuries.

Holmes, Larry E. *The Kremlin and the Schoolhouse: Reforming Education in Soviet Russia, 1917–1931.* Bloomington, Ind., 1991.

Muckle, James. *Portrait of a Soviet School under Glasnost.* New York, 1990. A first-person account of teaching in schools in Moscow and Leningrad in 1988 by an English teacher.

Sinel, Allen. *The Classroom and the Chancellery: State Educational Reform in Russia under Count Dmitry Tolstoi.* Cambridge, Mass., 1973. Describes conservative and progressive tendencies, 1866–1880.

Scotland

Anderson, R. D. *Education and the Scottish People, 1750–1918.* Oxford, 1995. An excellent account of the development of Scottish education.

Spain

Boyd-Barrett, Oliver, and Pamela O'Malley, eds. *Education Reform in Democratic Spain.* London and New York, 1995.

McNair, John M. *Education for a Changing Spain.* Manchester, U.K., and Dover, N.H., 1984. Focuses on the twentieth century.

Puelles Benítez, Manuel de. *Educación e ideología en la España contemporànea (1767–1975).* Barcelona, Spain, 1980. A good survey.

Other countries

Boucher, Leon. *Tradition and Change in Swedish Education.* Oxford and New York, 1982. After a brief historical survey, the book describes post-1945 developments.

Melton, James Van Horn. *Absolutism and the Eighteenth-Century Origins of Compulsory Schooling in Prussia and Austria.* Cambridge, U.K., and New York, 1988.

Rust, Val D. *The Democratic Tradition and the Evolution of Schooling in Norway.* New York, 1989. Norway developed a common school for all pupils before the rest of Europe.

Zeps, Michael J. *Education and the Crisis of the First Republic.* Boulder, Colo., 1987. A brief survey of Austrian education from 1770 to 1962, with a focus on 1919–1934.

The author is grateful to Professors Istvan Bejczy, Constantin Fasolt, and Erika Rummel, who recalled their schooling in the Netherlands, Germany, and Austria respectively, and to Catherine Schmitt for information on contemporary English schooling.

HIGHER EDUCATION

Charles R. Day

Universities have gone through several major phases in European history: a period of readjustment and then substantial decline in the early modern centuries, followed by revival and redefinition in the nineteenth century under the spurs of greater need for advanced training (particularly for expanding bureaucracies and professions) and the rise of specialized research. The twentieth century saw increasing enrollments, ultimately including significant numbers of women and some students of lower-class origin. The century was punctuated by the university-based protests of the 1960s, which led, though haltingly, to a diverse set of reforms.

THE MIDDLE AGES

European universities originated in the intellectual revival of the high Middle Ages. With the increasing order and security of the eleventh and twelfth centuries came the rise of towns and the development of cathedral schools. Originally intended for the instruction of the clergy, these schools broadened their curriculum during the twelfth century to meet the needs of a secular clientele training in law, Latin grammar, and the Roman classics. In Italy a school of medicine appears to have been established at Salerno as early as the tenth century, and a school of law at Bologna in the eleventh. In 1218 a school of law was founded at Salamanca in Spain. In France the University of Paris became a leader of northern intellectual life, especially in theology. A group of dissident students from Paris founded Oxford University in 1167, which produced another group of dissidents who established Cambridge a few years later. The first university in Germany was established at Heidelberg in 1386. By 1500 there were almost a hundred universities in Europe.

A university was originally a community of scholars and students interested in learning and organized as a corporation or guild possessing a charter guaranteeing its right to self-government and the ownership of property. Normally organized into four faculties—arts, theology, law, and medicine (with arts usually preparing for the other three)—universities were permanent institutions of learning possessing many of the characteristics of their modern counterparts: they had faculties of professors offering regular courses of instruction, holding periodical examinations, and awarding diplomas recognized throughout the Latin West. The bachelor of arts degree involved about four years of study, mainly in Latin grammar, rhetoric, and logic. The master of arts involved several more years of work in mathematics, natural science, and philosophy, and the doctorate required specialized training in theology, law, or medicine. Latin was the common language, so that students and professors could move freely from one university to another throughout Europe.

As centers of scholarly inquiry, the universities facilitated the rediscovery of the heritage of ancient Greece through the translation of Greek and Islamic texts into Latin. They were thus at the center of the high medieval synthesis of Greek and Arabic philosophy and the Christian philosophy known as scholasticism, which saw the beginnings of critical thought. Distinguished men of learning such as the French theologian Peter Abelard (1079–1142), the English scientist and Bishop of Lincoln Robert Grosseteste (1168–1253), and the Italian Dominican philosopher Saint Thomas Aquinas (1225–1274), were all associated with universities. The universities also played a vocational role, training administrators, lawyers, notaries, physicians, and ecclesiastics in response to growing demand.

FROM THE RENAISSANCE TO THE EIGHTEENTH CENTURY: REDEFINITION AND DECLINE

The new humanism, in contrast to scholasticism, was forged under the influence of Greek and Latin models, a development that aroused the opposition of many universities, notably the University of Paris. Although the new ideas did not alter the organization of the university, they did gradually penetrate the curriculum as human-centered studies based on Greek literature, rhetoric, poetry, history, and Platonic philosophy. It became fashionable for young men of good family to attend university in pursuit of polite learning, while others, of more modest origin, prepared for the clergy. Indeed, many religious reformers had studied the humanities in universities: Martin Luther and Philipp Melanchthon were professors at the University of Wittenberg, John Calvin had studied at the University of Paris, Huldrych Zwingli at Vienna and Basel, and various English reformers at Oxford and Cambridge. Many new universities were founded during the sixteenth century to train clergy, Protestant or Catholic, and to provide administrators for the growing territorial states; these included nine universities in Germany, Leiden in Holland, and seventeen universities in Castile founded from 1474 to 1620. Oxford and Cambridge, their statutes reformed, grew rapidly under the reigns of Elizabeth I and James I, from 1560 to 1625, and emerged as defenders of the monarchy and the Church of England. Many upper-class Englishmen attended Oxford or Cambridge, so much so that the Long Parliament of 1640 is said to have been the best educated in English history.

The Enlightenment of the late seventeenth and eighteenth centuries, as with the rise of humanism, took place outside of and often in opposition to the universities, many of which had become pillars of religious orthodoxy, both Protestant and Catholic. A minority of reformers argued that the function of the university was the advancement of knowledge through discovery and research, while traditionalists saw it as affirming and teaching truth. The latter generally prevailed, and intellectual and scientific work took place largely outside the universities, in royal societies and scientific academies under royal or aristocratic patronage. Advances in mathematics, optics, and statics were linked to the rise of new crafts and professions. Inventors and amateur scientists experimented in their own workshops and had little or no contact with the universities.

The upper classes gradually lost interest in higher education, and the lower were squeezed out. University students were reputed for bad behavior, drinking, rioting, and whoring. Consequently, enrollments fell in most European countries over the eighteenth century, declining, for example, in the twenty-eight German universities from nine thousand to six thousand students, mainly because of the excessive number of universities created in various German states, the poor quality of secondary education, and the shift of intellectual interest to learned academies and societies. In

A University Lecture. *University Lecture Room,* painting (1614) by Martin de Cervera. ©ARCHIVO ICONOGRAFICO, S.A./CORBIS

England, Oxford and Cambridge enrollments fell by one-half during the same period. In Spain they declined by the same percentage as universities withered as a result of strict government control, overemphasis on legal studies, and the increasing prominence of monks among students. The modernizing reforms of Charles III and Charles IV from the 1770s through the 1790s partially redressed the situation, but the long crisis of the Napoleonic years, which saw the closure of the universities, was only gradually compensated by reforms during the nineteenth century.

In England, Oxford and Cambridge trained clergymen and teachers, not lawyers, and the faculty was composed of clergymen rather than professors. Ninety percent of students were the sons of gentry, clergy, or military. In the later eighteenth century and the first half of the nineteenth, over one-half of Cambridge graduates and two-thirds of those from Oxford took holy orders. Teaching was done by college tutors, who taught all subjects, rather than by university professors, and so there was little academic specialization and scholarship languished. Religious dissenters were excluded from Oxford and Cambridge until the revocation of the Test Acts in 1854 and 1856.

The Dutch, the Scottish, and, in two cases anyway, the German universities were an exception to the downward trend. In Holland the Universities of Leiden and Utrecht pioneered in scientific research. In Scotland the universities of Glasgow and Edinburgh were nonresidential civic institutions, based partially on the model of the University of Leiden. Unlike Oxford and Cambridge, the Scottish universities employed professors for each discipline, modernized the curriculum to include the latest scientific advances, and accepted about a third of their students from the working classes. The broad range of subjects of study, the lecture system, the freedom of course selection and residence, the absence of religious tests, and the democratic character of the institutions influenced American universities. Finally, the reformed universities of Halle in Prussia (1694) and Göttingen in Hanover (1737) emphasized research and the advancement of knowledge in the social as well as natural sciences. Reforms were also introduced at Vienna in the Austrian Empire and at Uppsala in Sweden. The impulsion behind reform came from the emerging territorial monarchies, Austria, Prussia, Spain, and Sweden, which utilized the university for the training of state officials by endowing them with a monopoly over examinations leading to administrative posts.

In France the twenty-two universities fell into decline; the faculties of arts were gradually transformed into independent lower schools, or *collèges,* run by the Jesuits and other teaching orders, which were loosely connected to the universities. Only the law and medical faculties remained as independent professional schools, and their programs were often outdated. As a result the royal government began to open special higher schools during the eighteenth century in order to meet the demand for well-trained civil servants, military officers, and technical experts for the departments of mining, roads and bridges, and the military services, a trend that continued into the revolutionary period with the creation of the École Polytechnique in 1794 and the École Normale Supérieure in 1795. The Revolution suppressed the universities and closed most of the colleges. Revolutionary leaders talked of building a national system of schools but, diverted by war and unrest, they did little in practice to replace the old institutions.

Napoleon created a national system of secondary lycées and the state *baccalauréat* diploma for which they prepared. Anyone in possession of the *baccalauréat* could register in the university faculty of his choice; hence the "bac" was (and is) both the secondary school–leaving credential and the first higher education diploma. Napoleon reorganized the faculties of law and medicine but otherwise neglected the universities, concentrating instead on the development of specialized higher schools, the *grandes écoles,* as the sources of technical experts, military officers, and professors for his growing civil service, army, and lycées. He organized all secondary and higher educational institutions into a centralized public education corporation called the Université, which possessed a monopoly over education. The secondary and higher schools under its jurisdiction prepared for examinations for state diplomas, the *baccalauréat* and the *licence,* leading to the public services and emphasizing the transmission of knowledge, the memorization of self-evident principles, and stylistic elegance. Lycée professors, trained in the École Normale Supérieure, prepared for the *agrégation* examination instead of doing a thesis. The separation of teaching from research and the emphasis on the formation of competent but obedient civil servants tied education tightly to the needs of the state, impoverished the provinces intellectually, and all but destroyed the faculties of arts and sciences. France was still the leading country in the world in science at the time of Napoleon, but by the end of the century it would lag behind Germany and other countries.

THE NINETEENTH CENTURY

Over the nineteenth century professors in the French faculties of arts and sciences had few students, did little research, and contented themselves mainly with giving public lectures and administering and grading the *baccalauréat* exams. Scientific research was confined largely to the École Polytechnique, the Collège de France, and the Muséum d'Histoire Naturelle, all in Paris. Aware of the decline of research in France, Victor Duruy created the École Pratique des Hautes Études in Paris in 1868.

With the coming of the Third Republic, reformers such as Louis Liard and Ernest Lavisse sought to create six great university centers of teaching and research but instead had to be content with a weak law in 1896 establishing fifteen "universities" (one in each academy), which amounted to little more than administrative coordination of loosely organized groups of faculties. On the eve of 1914, there were about forty thousand students enrolled in French universities, mostly in law, medicine, and pharmacy, and only seven thousand in the faculties of arts and sciences.

Over the course of the nineteenth century, universities everywhere in Europe turned to the German idea of *Wissenschaft,* or the advancement of learning through research and discovery, as the preferred university model in an age of industrial growth. The origin of the reform of German universities dated to the defeat of the Prussian armies and the Frederickan state by Napoleon at Jena and Auerstädt in 1806. Intent on reform, the Prussian government hesitated between the model of the French specialized higher schools and that of the traditional German university. The decision in favor of the latter was based on the example of the reformed universities of Halle and Göttingen. This opened the way for the humanist ideas of Wilhelm von Humboldt and other reformers, for the idea of *Lernfreiheit,* of the internal motivation for study as opposed to external motivation (careers, passing exams, as in France), and of *Bildungsbürgertum,* a humanistic ideal of general culture and intellectual development. Henceforth the German elite, drawn from the aristocracy and bourgeoisie, was to be defined by university education. The introduction of the secondary *Gymnasium* in 1812 and of the *Abitur* diploma (1788, 1834) qualifying for university admission strengthened the philosophical (arts) faculties as institutions training professors and civil servants and brought them equality with the faculties of law, medicine, and theology. Henceforth the universities would be closely tied to the gymnasium preparing for the *Abitur* necessary for university admission. In 1809 the University of Berlin was established as a new, model university.

The Humboldtian university, combining research, teaching, and culture, differed at once from the Oxfordian residential university based on the tutorial system and the French *grande école* model. The German universities were relatively decentralized and flexible and allowed freedom to learn and to teach. They produced an extraordinary series of outstanding scholars. In chemistry, for example, professors like R. W. Bunsen at Heidelberg and Justus von Liebig at Giessen led teams of graduate students in conducting advanced research in their laboratories.

The weakness in the German system lay in the guildlike power of the professors, who dominated the corporate, self-governing structure of the German university and were thus able to prevent change. As each professor covered an entire field, he had a vested interest in keeping research centered in the basic disciplines, avoiding the creation of chairs in new subfields such as bacteriology, physiology, or sociology. As the century progressed, and the states increased their control over universities, professors of the imperial period became more and more conservative, supporting the empire against socialism at home and encirclement abroad.

As was the case among European universities generally, German universities were reluctant to admit fields based on applied knowledge, such as agriculture, engineering, clinical medicine, and architecture, which continued to be relegated to specialized schools or to apprenticeship. The *Technische Hochschulen,* for example, were engineering schools created on the French model of special higher professional schools beginning in the 1820s. Not until the kaiser's intervention in 1899 did they gain legal equality with the universities and the right to grant the doctorate. This accompanied reforms giving the nine-year programs and diplomas of modern high schools and technical institutions (*Realgymnasien* and *Oberrealschulen*) legal, if not social, equality with the gymnasiums. Finally, research institutes were established in 1887 and 1907 to provide for new scientific fields not covered by the universities. By the beginning of the twentieth century the German universities had lost their monopoly over advanced diplomas and research but had maintained the integrity of their programs and the distinction between pure and applied knowledge. Between 1870 and 1914, the number of university professors doubled but enrollments tripled. Universities became increasingly concerned with defending their superior social-cultural position against the rising lower classes and modern technical schools.

Faced with rapid strides in research and development in Germany during the nineteenth century, other countries reformed their universities. Oxford and Cambridge introduced honors examinations around the turn of the nineteenth century, abolished religious tests in 1854 and 1856, and introduced courses in the sciences, technology, and other modern subjects during the second half of the century, ending the monopoly of the classics. The tutorial system was reformed, celibacy abolished, and a body of professional teachers and researchers created, which helped restore the reputation of the two universities. Meritocratic reforms and examinations in the civil service at midcentury opened careers to university graduates that had hitherto not existed. Increasingly, middle-class families sent their sons to Oxford and Cambridge, and the percentage of students coming from the gentry and clergy declined.

The creation of civic universities, beginning with the University College of London in 1826, followed by Leeds, Sheffield, Manchester, and other schools beginning in the 1830s, made available courses in science, technology, economics, and other modern subjects, and provided access for social and religious groups that had long been excluded from Oxford and Cambridge and the "public" secondary schools that prepared for them. The introduction of secondary school–leaving examinations during the 1850s, the precursors of the O- and A-level exams, encouraged the reform of secondary education and the grammar schools.

Student Life in the Early Nineteenth Century. Student life at Oxford, aquatint (c. 1812) by Thomas Rowlandson (1756–1827). PRIVATE COLLECTION/ART RESOURCE, N.Y.

THE TWENTIETH CENTURY

From the nineteenth century to the middle of the twentieth, European universities successfully provided advanced education, fostered research, and contributed to the development of the nation-state. Higher education grew steadily, if not spectacularly, especially among the middle classes, as a result of the growth of white-collar positions in the professions, the civil service, and business and industry. In the first half of the twentieth century growth was limited by two wars and a depression and by the conservative organization of secondary and higher education, which provided access to only about 3 to 5 percent of the age group. European universities were closely tied to secondary schools—the gymnasiums, lycées, and so on—which prepared their students for difficult national examinations in the *Abitur,* the *baccalauréat,* and comparable diplomas in other countries, the possession of which enabled students to register in the university faculty of their choice. The solid general education received in secondary schools made possible specialization in university studies.

The universities, almost all of which were publicly financed, were considered part of a larger, national institution with uniform standards, goals, and requirements designed for a homogeneous upper-class clientele. They were governed from above by ministries of education, the councils of which formulated curricula, admissions standards, national examinations, and credentials. The ministry negotiated collective salary scales and working conditions with large national professional associations representing professors, nontenured teachers, and nonacademic staff. University presidents (usually called rectors or, in England, vice-chancellors) and deans were essentially state functionaries taking orders from ministry officials and inspectors and had little leverage against the guildlike power of the senior professors. The latter enjoyed the status of tenured civil servants holding their posts for life, lecturing, researching, and running their departments and research institutes as they saw fit. They defended the right of freedom of inquiry, the pursuit of pure rather than applied research, and the transmission of a general culture that included moral and civic values assumed to be necessary to the formation of elites.

The university faculties were not located on campuses but rather were scattered individually across the cities and prepared their students for examinations, usually after three years of study (the rough equivalent of the bachelor's degree), four years (master's), and eight years (doctorate). The universities provided little or no social life, for neither the administrators nor the professors took much interest in the programs of study or the success, failure, or general well-being of students.

In addition to universities, there were special technical-professional institutes such as the École Polytechnique in Paris, the Federal Institute of Technology in Zurich, the *escuelas técnicas superiores* in Spain, the *Technische Hochschulen* in Germany, the Imperial College of Science, Technology, and Medicine in London, and the Massachusetts Institute of Technology in the United States, plus various kinds of technical and pro-

357

Special Technical Professional Institute. Students at the École Polytechnique, Paris, c. 1880 ©HULTON GETTY/ LIAISON AGENCY

fessional colleges in Holland and Scandinavia and the land-grant colleges in the United States. In France, Switzerland, and Spain the special higher schools enjoyed more prestige than did the universities, but elsewhere they had equal or less status. The higher technical schools recruited from general secondary schools as well as from technical high schools and occasionally from vocational secondary schools.

The 1960s saw the advent of mass higher education, brought about by the extension in most countries of compulsory education to the age of sixteen and the introduction (with the exception of Germany and Holland) of comprehensive junior secondary schools. Although senior secondary education continued to be tracked into tripartite university-preparatory, technical, and vocational streams, most states eased the requirements for secondary credentials and modernized and professionalized programs. This attracted students of wider social backgrounds and career expectations. Women also began to attend universities in greater numbers, starting from about 20 percent in the 1950s and growing to over half of university students in many Western countries by the 1990s.

As justification for the expense of founding many new universities in the 1960s, proponents pointed to the demand for skills engendered by a rapidly developing technology, a changing workforce, and the need for broader social recruitment. Enrollments grew spectacularly throughout Europe, in France rising from 216,000 in 1960 to 586,000 in 1968, and in West Germany from 304,150 in 1960 to 525,300 in 1970. In England growth was substantial in the 1950s and 1960s (from 50,000 in 1945 to 258,000 in 1971) but slowed thereafter. In Sweden and Spain enrollments doubled in the 1960s and 1970s.

In response to student unrest of the late 1960s, which focused heavily on university issues from elitism to overcrowded classrooms, Italy watered down the requirements for the secondary *maturità* diploma, necessary for university admission; enrollments rose exponentially, from 270,000 in 1960 to around a million in the mid-1980s, before governments introduced stricter standards. The University of Rome had 160,000 students, the medical school alone 23,000. Though many students dropped out of school, the numbers of those obtaining the *laurea,* or bachelor's degree, addressed as "dottore," grew so rapidly that the university credential lost much of its appeal to employers.

Despite extensive building programs, the outdated universities proved unable to keep up with growth, causing severe inconveniences for many students. The dislike of paternalist social structures, the influence of marxist ideas, anxieties about the job market, particularly among those majoring in the liberal arts, and opposition to the war in Vietnam led to widespread student unrest and to the uprisings in Paris of 1968. As a result of student agitation, France, Germany, Italy, Holland, Spain, and the Scandinavian countries passed reforms increasing university autonomy, introducing American-style academic departments, and allowing the representation of junior professors and students in university councils. During the 1970s, however, senior professors and university officials reasserted their authority, and some democratic gains in university governance were reduced, notably in France and Germany.

A number of observers in the 1960s had predicted that the transition from elite to mass higher education would result in universal higher education, but the economic difficulties of the 1970s brought this hope to an abrupt end. Since then, public financing has seldom kept pace with enrollments and has sometimes declined. The 1980s and early 1990s saw economic problems, budget cuts, and in some cases slower growth in higher education enrollments. Universities were obliged by governments in several countries to eliminate departments and areas of study. This usually accompanied professionalization of existing programs to make them more relevant to the economy.

In England in 1980 the newly elected Thatcher government cut higher education budgets by 17 percent. During the following years universities were obliged to submit detailed reports on their activities and projects to the government, to introduce managerial techniques, to compete for funds, and to abolish tenure (after 1989). During the 1990s governments stepped back somewhat, and the universities recovered some of their autonomy.

Germany and France. In theory, the German universities, which come under the jurisdiction of the federal states (*Länder*), are decentralized and should be in a position to introduce changes. In fact there is considerable legal homogeneity and overlapping of functions in the German system (federal and state governments share responsibility for investments in buildings and major equipment), so that serious reform involves intervention at the system level, which is difficult to achieve. Internally, universities have the responsibility for courses of study and their content, research projects, and academic procedures, such as promotion and tenure (*Habilitation*), but beyond that they have little control over performance because professors have the legal status of civil servants with lifetime tenure and considerable freedom in teaching and research. In addition, the fifty-five German universities are obliged to admit students in possession of the *Abitur* and therefore have little control over admissions.

The seven-year German university program, comparatively long, leads to a diploma that is the rough equivalent of a master's degree in North America. About 70 percent of students in higher education study to obtain it; another 30 percent attend the four-year *Fachhochschulen,* which are mainly technical, business, and professional schools. The participation rate in higher education was over 25 percent of the age cohort by the mid-1990s, but the average dropout rate was 25 percent of that figure. About 18 percent of the age group succeeds in graduating from an institution of higher education.

At the end of the twentieth century German higher education was described as understaffed, underfunded, and overcrowded. In the mid-1990s, there were 318 institutions of higher learning, including the *Fachhochschulen,* having a total of 1.8 million students in a system set up for around 821,000. There were 50,000 students at the University of Cologne and 70,000 at the University of Munich. Since 1977 the number of incoming students has risen by 72.8 per-

cent, accompanied by only a 10 percent increase in building and laboratory space. These problems became worse in the 1990s as a result of the high cost of absorbing the East German system into that of the west. This diverted attention from the need for reform of the entire system of higher education in Germany.

In France higher education has been partially decentralized, professionalized, and modernized since the 1970s; however, the system has never been thoroughly reformed and still remains fragmented and segmented. Structural weaknesses were exacerbated by the rapid growth of the 1960s and again in the late 1980s as a result of the socialist government's decision in 1985 to raise the attainment rate of the *baccalauréat* and other secondary credentials from 30 to 80 percent by the year 2000. The growth rate of higher education between 1987 and 1995 averaged 8 percent annually, and attendance reached 1.5 million students in the universities and 2.1 million in higher education generally in 1997. In 1999 about half of the age cohort attended universities or other institutions of higher learning and a third obtained a diploma.

The main problem with the French system is that the universities are second-level institutions. While the universities must accept any *bachelier* who registers (with the partial exception of the medical faculties), the elite *grandes écoles* (École Polytechnique, École Nationale d'Administration, Haute École de Commerce, *écoles normales supérieures,* and others) recruit by very difficult examinations (*concours*) based on rigorous

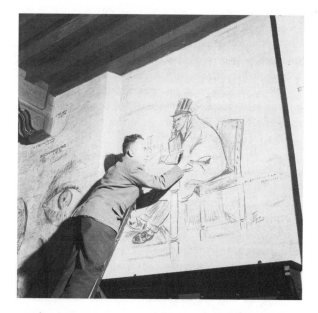

Exams. Student drawing graffiti in the University of Leiden sweating room, where students await the results of their examinations, c. 1955. ©HULTON GETTY/LIAISON AGENCY

two- or three-year programs located in special sections (*cours préparatoires*) of select urban lycées. With 5 percent of students, the *cours préparatoires* and *grandes écoles* obtain 30 percent of government funding for higher education. Their graduates monopolize the top positions of the civil service, business, and industry, and their powerful alumni and professional associations manage to block any serious reform of higher education.

Moreover, in the 1960s governments established two-year professional-technical schools, the *instituts universitaires de technologie* in the universities and the *sections de technicien supérieur* in the advanced sections of the lycées. In the early 1990s they also created a network of four-year technical-business schools called the *instituts universitaires professionnalisés* and unified teacher-training schools called the *instituts universitaires de la formation des maîtres* as special institutes within the universities. Together with the *grandes écoles,* these schools possess the right to set entrance examinations and draw about 40 percent of students in higher education. Though each type of school meets a need, such a variety of poorly coordinated institutions adds to the fragmented, segmented, and hierarchical nature of French higher education.

The universities are in theory one big uniform corporation spread across the country and have no control over admissions. As the ministry of education in Paris directs programs and personnel, the universities have few means of raising admission standards, improving their programs of study, or of demanding better performance from their professors. They have benefited, however, from government decisions, beginning in the 1970s, to introduce new professional diplomas and programs, and they have utilized the measure of autonomy accorded to them by the state to establish contacts with local and regional business and industry. The new professional diplomas have had considerable impact, particularly in computer and information sciences, where the universities have managed to outpace the *grandes écoles.* In response, the *grandes écoles* have invaded the domain of the universities by introducing extensive research facilities.

The Faure and Savary reforms of 1968 and 1983 increased the representation of faculty and students on university councils and made the universities more responsive to local concerns. In his bill, Alain Savary, education minister from 1981 to 1984, sought to transfer the *cours préparatoires* from the lycées to the first two-year cycle of the universities. The universities were to be allowed to impose entrance requirements after the first cycle for continuation into the second cycle (preparation for the *licence* and *maîtrise*), placing them at last in a position to compete with the *grandes*

écoles, which now had to select their students from the first university cycle. To complete the unification of higher education, all the *grandes écoles* were to be placed under the Ministry of National Education (almost half came under other ministries: Agriculture, Defense, Public Works, Industry, and Telecommunications).

Had it passed in its entirety, the Savary reform would have solved many of the problems of higher education in France. Unfortunately it came at a time of intense and divisive national debate over the future of private (Catholic) schools in France. Moreover, any possibility of the introduction of admission requirements in the universities arouses enormous hostility among students and many professors. Student riots erupted in the spring of 1983, which played into the hands of the powerful interest groups such as the Conférence des Grandes Écoles, the Société des Agrégés, and various pressure groups opposed to the absorption of the *cours préparatoires* by the universities and the unification of the *grandes écoles* under the Ministry of National Education.

The bill that finally passed in January 1984 broadened membership on academic councils and further decentralized and professionalized the universities, but the provisions unifying higher education were abandoned. Several ministers of education tried to introduce admissions requirements for the universities, but these efforts were met by massive student demonstrations, and they had to back down. During the 1990s every government projected reforms in higher education, but none achieved much.

Diversity and reform. The diverse nature of higher educational systems poses a significant challenge to efforts by the European Union to establish common admission requirements, programs, and diplomas. In a unified European system of higher education, it would be impossible, for example, to accommodate the French *grandes écoles,* the mass *baccalauréat* examinations in June, or the German seven-year undergraduate program. Moreover, some countries automatically admit students in possession of national secondary school credentials (France, Germany, Holland, and Italy), while other countries now recruit on the basis of grades and university admission requirements (Denmark, Sweden, the United Kingdom) or a preparatory year (Spain). It will be difficult, moreover, to democratize the many secondary systems that have for at least a century routinely tracked young people at an early age into university-preparatory, technical, and vocational sections, so that by the time most students reach sixteen or seventeen their future is already largely determined, frequently on the basis of their social origins.

University Lecture Hall. Students in class at Tartu University, Estonian SSR, early 1980s. SOVFOTO/EASTFOTO

As the twentieth century came to an end, it appeared that Europeans were contenting themselves mainly with developing exchange programs rather than with genuine unification of higher education; but the problem may not be insuperable, for several countries have attempted serious changes in higher education. In the mid-1990s the Italians launched much-needed reforms of secondary and higher education. The Dutch reduced university programs from seven to four years (in practice five) and promoted secondary vocational programs into higher education, creating the *hogescholen* in 1986, similar to the German *Fachhochschulen*. The Scandinavian countries pioneered in the 1950s and 1960s the granting of increased autonomy to universities and representation to nontenured faculty and students on university councils. In subsequent decades they decentralized their educational systems and successfully integrated various strands of higher education while retaining a diversity of institutions, general and professional.

The Spanish, whose rigid system was based on the French Napoleonic model, after 1970 managed to integrate the higher technical schools (*escuelas técnicas superiores*), the Spanish version of the French *grandes écoles,* into the universities, either directly as faculties or indirectly in the form of four technological universities. The Spanish thus managed to avoid many of the problems that the French encountered in coordinating special higher schools and universities. Their secondary schools prepare for the *Bachiller,* which opens the way to a preparatory year between secondary and higher education that determines university admission. The preparatory year avoids the dilemma of French, Dutch, German, and Italian universities of having to accept any student who has the *Abitur, baccalauréat,* or the equivalent. Finally, the Spanish began to decentralize higher education in order to accommodate regional demands (Catalonia, the Basque provinces). Such reforms exemplify the trend away from rigid centralized systems that could make European coordination easier in future years.

In response to rapid changes in the workforce, the universities began in the 1970s to add departments or programs of business education, computer studies, communications, criminology, environmental studies, microbiology, and other scientific specialties. But many established universities and higher schools have found it difficult to meet the steeply rising demand of students for access to these fields, especially to computer, information, and business programs, and this has stimulated the rise of competing private schools to fill the demand.

Since the 1960s governments have also attempted to diversify higher education by introducing short-course professional and technical schools outside the university: the polytechnics in England (1970s) and the former Soviet Union, the *instituts universitaires de technologie* (1966) and the *sections de technicien supérieur* (1962) in France, and the junior colleges in the United States and Canada, all two-year programs, plus the *escuelas universitarias* in Spain (three years), the *hogescholen* in the Netherlands (three to four years), and the *Fachhochschulen* in Germany (four years). Continuing education, distance learning, and other part-time programs have also been introduced in most countries, sometimes within and sometimes separately from the universities. Finally, public research institutes have been established (the Conseil National de la Recherche Scientifique in France, for example) that conduct research but do not teach. Thus during the twentieth century the university lost its monopoly over teaching and research almost everywhere in Europe.

CONCLUSION

Universities are among the oldest continuously existing institutions in Europe. Originally established to reaffirm and expound upon Christian certainties, they gradually evolved into institutions concerned with the discovery and advancement of knowledge through intellectual development and research, using scientific methods. They have also had a vocational function since the late Middle Ages, training professionals and higher civil servants for the state services. During the nineteenth century they played an important role in the development of national economies and the nation-state. During the twentieth century they increasingly educated specialists for business and industry and received augmented state support to advance knowledge and to achieve economic and technological goals.

Despite tremendous growth in enrollments and considerable efforts to achieve a greater measure of social justice in the recruitment of students, including scholarship payments, universities continue to be attended mainly by the children of the middle and upper classes, the vocational schools mainly by the children of workers. The University of Zurich was the first to admit women, in 1867, and since then women have become quite prominent in universities, often constituting the majority of students, though they are less numerous in industrial and technological fields. In the late 1990s an average of around a third to 40 percent of young people of university age (eighteen to twenty-four) in Europe reached higher education (though not all obtained diplomas), a percentage that is rising in most countries as European youth attempts to get as much education as possible as a guarantee against future changes in the workplace. The unemployment of young people aged twenty to twenty-four continues to be high, varying from around 15 percent in Germany to 25 percent in Italy and Spain, with England, France, and Scandinavia falling in between. Aside from certain sought-after fields, a university diploma no longer guarantees a good job.

The information revolution of the last several decades of the twentieth century is rapidly changing the nature of the university from the participatory model of the 1960s to a more managerial one. The explosion of knowledge outruns the capacity of universities to respond and creates competing sources of information. The modern mass university must deal with new and varying clienteles demanding ever more specialized occupational training. Business and industry provide much-needed subsidies and grants but at the same time seek increased influence. Governments expect more to be done at less cost. They have provided universities with more autonomy and self-government but retain their influence over programs, examinations, and personnel, while the professors and their well-entrenched associations are frequently opposed to change. This poses many problems for university administrators. Long used to taking orders from above, they are now asked to become innovative leaders reaching out to the community in quest of new sources of income, but they do not always have the experience or the means to do so.

In Great Britain and Scandinavia, particularly, some institutions have modernized and prospered, successfully establishing research parks, knowledge centers, alumni associations, and other forms of community outreach, partially liberating the institution from dependence on the state; but these tend to be smaller, newer institutions, created in the 1960s and frequently having a technical-professional bent, making outreach easier. The larger, comprehensive universities, in Germany and Italy, for example, have found it more difficult to adapt to change.

Because a knowledge-driven society requires substantial numbers of knowledge-trained people, the university, the existing institution capable of training such talent, is likely to survive. But it is difficult to predict the precise nature of the institution in the future. In an increasingly pluralistic and international setting, the university may not be able to define and transmit national culture and values. Social and professional advancement through higher education, never very marked, may suffer from increasing selectivity in sought-after fields; that selectivity tends to benefit young people from the educated upper classes. With continuing state intervention in university affairs, plus the growing activity of the private sector in research and development, freedom of research and teaching could be more difficult to assure. But there is little doubt that the research and development function, as well as the education of professionals for the public and private sectors, will continue in some form in the future.

Over the past eight hundred years universities have gone through many changes and endured many challenges, but none will test their ingenuity and capacity for survival as Europe's oldest institutions so much as the information age. The stakes are great, for the survival of European civilization and culture may well be linked to the survival of the university.

See also **Students; Student Movements** *(volume 3);* **Gender and Education** *(volume 4); and other articles in this section.*

BIBLIOGRAPHY

Altbach, Philip G., ed. *International Higher Education: An Encyclopedia.* New York, 1991.

Ashby, Eric. *Technology and the Academics: An Essay on Universities and the Scientific Revolution.* New York, 1966.

Becher, Tony, and Maurice Kogan. *Process and Structure in Higher Education.* London, 1992.

Ben-David, Joseph. *The Scientist's Role in Society: A Comparative Study.* Englewood Cliffs, N.J., 1971.

Bourdieu, Pierre. *The State Nobility: Elite Schools in the Field of Power.* Translated by Lauretta C. Clough. Cambridge, U.K., 1996. Translation of *La noblesse d'état: Grandes écoles et esprit de corps.* Paris, 1989.

Clark, Burton R. *Creating Entrepreneurial Universities: Organizational Pathways of Transformation.* Oxford, 1998.

Clark, Burton R. *Places of Inquiry: Research and Advanced Education in Modern Universities.* Berkeley, Calif., 1995.

Clark, Burton R., and Guy R. Neave, eds. *The Encyclopedia of Higher Education.* Oxford, 1992.

McClelland, Charles E. *State, Society, and University in Germany, 1700 to 1914.* Cambridge, U.K., 1980.

Morsy, Zaghloul, and Philip G. Altbach, eds. *Higher Education in an International Perspective.* New York, 1996.

Muller, Steven, ed. *Universities in the Twenty-First Century.* Oxford, 1996.

Organization for Economic Cooperation and Development. *Reviews of National Policies for Education.* Paris, 1990–.

Phillips, David, ed. *Education in Germany: Tradition and Reform in Historical Context.* London, 1995.

Phillipson, Nicholas, ed. *Universities, Society, and the Future: A Conference Held on the 400th Anniversary of the University of Edinburgh.* Edinburgh, 1983.

Ringer, Fritz. *The Decline of the German Mandarins: The German Academic Community, 1890–1933.* Cambridge, Mass., 1969.

Rothblatt, Sheldon, and Björn Wittrock, eds. *The European and American University since 1800: Historical and Sociological Essays.* Cambridge, U.K., 1993.

Rudy, Willis. *The Universities in Europe, 1100–1914*. Rutherford, N.J., and London, 1984.

Sanderson, Michael, ed. *The Universities in the Nineteenth Century.* London, 1975.

Shattock, Michael, ed. *The Creation of a University System.* Oxford, 1996.

Stone, Lawrence, ed. *The University in Society.* 2 vols. Princeton, N.J., 1974.

Weisz, George. *The Emergence of Modern Universities in France, 1863–1914.* Princeton, N.J., 1983.

TEACHERS

Scott J. Seregny

Sociologists of the professions have long recognized teaching as one of the least autonomous of professions, indeed a "semiprofession," distinct from medicine or law. Much of this has to do with teachers' ambiguous but decisive relationship to the rise of modern European states and state intervention in popular education, first in many of the German states in the eighteenth and early nineteenth centuries, later in France, and still later and less completely in Great Britain and Russia. The transformation of teaching from a part-time craft lacking formal qualifications to a full-time profession was directly connected to the establishment of state-sponsored mass education systems designed to discipline and integrate populations and maintain political and social order in response to the rapid population growth, economic transformation, and political upheaval (including the dramatic reshaping of state territories) that marked western and central Europe at the end of the eighteenth century and in the early nineteenth century. Teachers' responses to these developments were complex. Most teachers, when given the chance, identified state initiatives as "progressive" and supported state intervention as a means of emancipation from the local interests that had previously controlled schooling. Most supported and helped implement state projects for national integration. For example, French teachers under the Third Republic helped marginalize Breton and regional dialects in favor of the French language. In multinational states, however, teachers sometimes played significant roles in minority national movements seeking autonomy and language rights in schools. In revolutionary crises—1848 in Germany and 1905 in Russia—teachers often played visible leadership roles in popular movements for reform or revolution, although conservatives vastly exaggerated their participation.

Teachers' social and professional status was powerfully shaped by governments and the expectations of elites as to the role teachers and schools should play. To free themselves from community and parental control and to escape the uncertainty of local school financing, teachers often sought the security and status of inclusion in civil service ranks, even if such bureaucratization prevented them from attaining the professional autonomy won by physicians, lawyers, and other higher-status groups. Nevertheless, teachers had some success in shaping state policies to meet their corporate interests. Although teachers in most of Europe saw autonomy from local officials, clergy, and parents as a sine qua non for professional development and the state as a buffer against local pressure, they were not immune to the expectations expressed by local communities and the parents of their pupils. Since most teachers came from the same or similar social milieus, they readily identified with popular aspirations, particularly during revolutionary crises. In such instances, when teachers confronted both official resistance to reasonable professional goals and popular pressure to side with the population they served, they opposed the state.

Teachers' relationship to the communities they served was just as ambivalent. In training, ambition, and self-image, teachers accepted the mission to "civilize" peasants and workers. Teachers fought to detach schooling from communal control, and this struggle was central to their professionalization. In terms of social status and self-image, teachers distanced themselves from "the people." While the majority of teachers, especially men, came from humble origins, they aspired to a middle-class or at least a lower-middle-class status, for which their education, lifestyle, and dress supposedly outfitted them. Middle-class respectability, education, and notability, they assumed, would enhance teachers' authority in the community and facilitate their civilizing mission as role models of modernity, sobriety, and order. Most teachers embraced this professional image. So did states, and teachers' failure to live up to such respectability by frequenting taverns, playing cards, or engaging in improper sexual liaisons was often punished by school officials. Nevertheless, teachers also identified strongly with popular interests, such as pressures to democratize education by facilitating access for lower-class children to

Renaissance Teacher. Woodcut by Albrecht Dürer (1471–1528). GERMANISCHES NATIONALMUSEUM, NÜRNBERG

secondary and higher education. This in turn reflected teachers' resentment over the limitations placed in the way of their own educational advancement and mobility into the upper reaches of the education bureaucracy. The trajectory of teachers' professionalization was guided by their relations—sometimes marked by cooperation, at other times by conflict—with both the state and the people.

BEFORE PROFESSIONALIZATION— TEACHING AS A CRAFT

Before the nineteenth century most governments paid little attention to schooling. Nevertheless, after the Renaissance and the Reformation many children (especially boys) in western and parts of central Europe experienced some instruction. Local communities and religious congregations supported a bewildering variety of "schools." In terms of training, certification, remuneration, autonomy, and public expectations, few "professionals" taught in the schools of seventeenth- and eighteenth-century Europe. Teachers were "schoolmasters," a term suggesting that both community and teacher considered teaching a craft. Whether teachers were permanent residents in the community or sea-

sonal migrants, teaching was a part-time occupation, and parents sent their children for instruction when they grasped its utility and when economic circumstances allowed.

Teachers' skills varied widely. In seventeenth- and eighteenth-century Scotland teachers with university training offered instruction in Latin to village boys in church-run parish schools, and a few of these "lads of parts" went on to university. In England and Wales a diversity of charity and voluntary day schools sponsored by religiously affiliated societies, working-class-sponsored private schools, and other schools proliferated by the early nineteenth century. Teachers' qualifications also varied tremendously. By the 1830s, when the British state began offering grants to some of these schools with the requirement that they were subject to a new inspectorate, church organizations began providing teachers with formal training. By contrast, however, as late as 1851 some seven hundred private-school teachers could not sign the census form since they could not write even their own names. Everywhere, teachers were recruited from among marginal men, demobilized soldiers, or artisans who had failed at their chosen occupations.

In France and elsewhere the Catholic revival during the seventeenth century led to a proliferation of religious teaching orders, which offered basic instruction free of charge in communal schools. Removed from education during the revolution, the teaching orders rebounded after 1815. During the 1860s nuns constituted more than a third of all elementary teachers in France. Their formal qualifications often amounted to only a letter of obedience from their superiors, but they provided solid instruction in reading and writing to the increasing numbers of girls attending France's mostly sex-segregated primary schools. In 1870, three-fifths of the girls were taught by sisters who belonged to some five hundred congregations. In most cases teachers' qualifications were even less formal, and educational efforts were less organized. As in other crafts, teachers offered their services at fairs and markets. In the Vaucluse region of southeastern France, teachers from Alpine villages appeared at local markets, where they offered their skills to lowland villages. Migrant teachers sported feathers in their caps advertising their skills. One feather signified their willingness to teach reading and writing, two their ability to offer ciphering, and three their knowledge of Latin. Training, if it occurred, was limited to apprenticeship with a schoolmaster. In England and to some extent in France pupil-monitors worked with groups of younger children under the direction of a master teacher.

Teachers were often hired for a season between harvest and spring planting. Classes and teachers' lodging rotated among peasant homes, and teachers subsisted from the monthly fees they collected from parents, sometimes paid in bread or wine. In Bavaria, Baden, and other German states schools were more formal institutions with their own buildings and formalized financing. Until the mid-nineteenth century, salaries remained low, below those earned by unskilled laborers and petty clerks. In Russia this was still the case fifty years later. Contracts often stipulated that teachers would receive a plot of land that peasants would help work, and such arrangements persisted into the early twentieth century. Many arrangements placed teachers in a dependent and sometimes confrontational relationship with parents and community. Teachers often had to collect the school fees from poor parents, a situation guaranteed to make them unpopular, particularly during a period when peasants did not place a high premium on regular school attendance.

In much of Europe teaching remained a part-time occupation, and those who entered it usually combined it with other work, most commonly as "lay clerics" assisting the local priest or pastor. In France, the German states, and elsewhere teachers served as sacristans or sextons who rang the church bells, lit candles, dug graves, swept the church, and played the organ during services. These duties, enumerated in detail in the contracts local communities offered to teachers, reflected popular expectations. Parents expected teachers to lead their pupils to church, keep them silent during the liturgy, and help prepare them for first Communion. Clergy asserted their prerogative to visit the classroom at any time and report on their observations.

When schools began to proliferate in Russia, especially after the emancipation of the serfs in 1861, villages supported communal schools, where retired soldiers, unemployed sons of clergy (in Russia a legal "estate"), and other marginal types offered rudimentary instruction. In this way Russia followed patterns that had long characterized teaching in western Europe. Throughout Europe schools were largely supported and controlled by local communities before the nineteenth century. Teachers' qualifications were informal and uncertified. Where clerical supervision of schools existed, priests were more interested in the moral-religious influence teachers exerted in the classroom and beyond. States were remote from teachers' daily lives, even under Frederick the Great in Prussia, where the government issued decrees on compulsory schooling but lacked the means to implement them effectively. Everywhere teachers remained dependent

Schoolmaster. *The Village Schoolmaster,* painting by G. F. Cipper (c. 1670–1738). ©ND-VIOLLET

on local communities and clergy, neither of which supported an image of teaching as a professional vocation dedicated to a transcendent civilizing mission. Local interests and expectations prevailed in defining the teacher as a craftsperson. One teacher recalled his own days as a pupil in early-nineteenth-century Bavaria, remembering that on Shrove Tuesday it was the custom for the teacher to whip all of the children since local peasants believed that such beatings prevented worms in farm animals. Popular attitudes toward schooling, local financial control, and the neglect of schooling by European states meant that teaching remained an occupation of low and uncertain status.

STATE INTERVENTION AND TEACHER TRAINING

Official neglect began to give way at the close of the eighteenth century, and states asserted greater control over schools and teachers during the next century. Ministries of education established staffs of school inspectors who certified teachers' qualifications and supervised their classroom performance. States gradually assumed more of the costs of financing schools and offered teachers minimum salaries, a crucial development that lessened teachers' dependence on local communities and eventually supported a more secure, middle-class existence and professional status. To varying degrees and within limits, governments also supported teachers' efforts to form professional associations that fought for educational reforms and professional goals. The pace and extent of state intervention, however, was uneven. Germany led the way, followed by France, where the Guizot Law of 1833 mandated that local communes provide teachers with a minimum salary of two hundred francs and created an inspectorate that supervised schools and certified teachers' qualifications. Under the Second Empire (1852–1870), officials gained effective control over the hiring, transfer, and firing of teachers. Nevertheless, it was only in the 1880s, under the Ferry Laws, that state intervention was fully realized with the government assuming the cost of teachers' salaries, which significantly freed them from local control and raised their status.

In Russia most of these developments were incomplete before 1914. Not until the eve of World War I did the Russian government assume the cost of teachers' salaries. Elsewhere the minimum salaries that the governments of France, Britain, and Germany provided in the 1830s and later were critical to achieving teacher security (support for a teacher with a family), independence, and the respect that was believed inherent in a middle-class lifestyle. As a minor notable, the teacher's lifestyle had to be distinguished from that of the people. Nevertheless, teacher pay rose slowly and unevenly during the nineteenth century, and at mid-century many teachers still lived on the edge of poverty. When unskilled urban workers in France commanded incomes of 645 francs, three-quarters of the teachers earned between 450 and 500 francs. In Germany, France, Italy, and Britain teaching became materially secure only toward the end of the century. In Russia rural teachers with families still found it difficult on the eve of the war to provide their own children with a secondary education, a source of extreme bitterness and frustration.

Nearly everywhere the first effective state intervention in primary schooling occurred in the area of teacher training. The first normal schools were established in Prussia and other parts of Germany at the end of the eighteenth century. After the mid-nineteenth century, most teachers had received such training. Future teachers typically finished the public primary school at age fourteen, then took classes at a preparatory institution that augmented what they had learned at primary school, and finally at age eighteen entered a normal school, where they spent three years concentrating on pedagogy. Victor Cousin's favorable report on normal schools stimulated their expansion in France. The Guizot Law of 1833 mandated the establishment of a normal school in every department, and their numbers rose from fourteen in 1830 to seventy-four in 1837. Most of these trained men, but beginning in the 1880s a parallel network of women's normal schools was created. By 1869 France had seventy-six normal schools for men and eleven for women; by 1887 ninety and eighty-one respectively. Not all teachers graduated from normal schools. Some passed an examination to receive the teaching certificate that functioned as a kind of advanced degree for those with a primary education and that opened up employment as lower-level bureaucrats for the railroad. Not all normal school graduates remained in teaching, although rates of turnover decreased in the late nineteenth century as teachers' material security improved. Still, state training expanded so rapidly in France that by 1848 some 27 percent of teachers were normal school graduates and by 1863 half were.

In most European countries teachers were recruited from the peasantry, artisans, lower middle class, and working class. When women began to enter teaching in large numbers toward the end of the nineteenth century, they continued to come largely from the families of prosperous peasants, artisans, and minor officials in France, Britain, and other western European countries. In Russia, in light of the much slower development of girls' primary education, women teachers were drawn from the middle class, nobility, and clerical estate, but by the early twentieth century increasing numbers of peasant girls were entering the profession. Nearly everywhere an increasing percentage of teachers, male and female, were children of teachers. For such sons and later daughters of "the people," study in the relatively expensive secondary schools that opened a path to higher education for the children of the bourgeoisie was an unattainable goal. Normal school training, by contrast, offered a more realistic if modest prospect of educational and social advancement, one consistent with the nineteenth-century state's goal of creating schools that would civilize and acculturate the lower classes while maintaining existing social hierarchies. Most normal school students received scholarships covering tuition, room, and board in return for signing a contract that they would teach for a minimum number of years (ten years in France). When they emerged from the normal school, teachers could be counted among the small minority of the population who had received an education through the age of twenty. Nevertheless, in most cases they were not considered part of the educated middle class of nineteenth-century Europe, those who had passed through elite secondary institutions (often with classical curricula) and institutions of higher education.

When in the 1870s the Russian Ministry of Education and noble-dominated local governments, the *zemstvos,* established "teachers' seminaries" modeled after the Prussian normal school, preference and tuition stipends were given to peasant sons. The assumption was that these recruits would easily accept rural living conditions and would be less subversive than outsiders to the established social and political order. Normal schools were often established in remote areas, far from the temptations of the city, and students lived a rigidly monitored, almost monastic existence with little free time outside dormitory and classroom. Here Russians hewed closely to the model of teacher training developed in Germany and adopted in France earlier in the century.

In all countries normal school education was carefully limited. This was especially so during the decade following the revolutions of 1848, in which some teachers had played visible roles. Conservatives repeatedly warned against the dangers of overeducating future teachers and creating alienated, marginal men who might exercise a negative influence in classrooms and local communities. In Prussia, for example, the Stiehl Regulations (1854) limited normal school curricula and heavily emphasized religion. In France the conservative Falloux Law (1850) temporarily reinforced clerical supervision of teachers. Conservatives in Germany in the mid-nineteenth century and in Russia at the beginning of the twentieth century still proposed recruitment of former noncommissioned officers as teachers in place of trained professionals. However, from the 1860s teacher training began to deemphasize religion and to include subjects like pedagogy, science, history, and geography, in line with an expanded primary school curriculum designed to produce citizens and skilled workers. Such reforms left intact the educational caste-line that separated the closed systems of primary and elite secondary schooling, largely preventing teachers from continuing their education beyond the normal school. Teachers were educated, but within well-defined limits designed to keep them within the social orbit from which they came and to keep them in teaching. Their task remained to enlighten and socialize the children of the lower classes, who were expected to remain in their orbit as well.

Despite the limitations, normal schools offering standardized training, closer regulation of teachers' credentials, and the common experience of studying under the mentorship of supportive instructors nurtured an esprit de corps and professional identity among young men who entered teaching during the nineteenth century. A similar development occurred in France and other countries when normal schools were opened in the second half of the century to train women teachers. In both instances the schools instilled a new pride in academic achievement and a sense of mission to enlighten the people. In western and central Europe this professional identity was soon supported by teachers' associations, regular conferences, summer refresher courses, and a professional press. In Russia, due to the state's financial weakness and the vast number of teachers required to achieve universal schooling, the state never gained anything like the monopoly over teacher training that was established in the West. The number of normal schools training women teachers in Russia failed to keep up with the huge demand for teachers from this population, with the result that in the early twentieth century female recruits were still drawn from a wide variety of educational backgrounds, including secondary women's gymnasiums and the diocesan schools (mostly daughters of priests).

As teaching became more "professional," in the limited sense of becoming a full-time career with recognized qualifications, and as European states promoted teaching as vital to their missions of civilizing the lower classes and nation building, future teachers internalized a new ethos that clashed with the depressed realities of their social status and low pay. Consequently they were less willing to accept traditional arrangements of dependence on local community and clergy that had become codified (literally in some contracts of appointment) when their occupation had been defined as a craft. Steady salary increases in the second half of the nineteenth century freed many teachers of the need to accept subsidiary employment that increasingly was perceived as professionally demeaning, in particular the post of lay assistant to the clergy.

From France to Russia teachers' professional self-image was powerfully shaped by conflicts with the clergy, who tried to maintain the dominant position churches had previously held in schooling and who perceived teachers as potential rival figures of authority in the community. Teachers' professional identities included a strong commitment to laicity and a programmatic endorsement of secular education. Professionalization was defined in terms of emancipation from traditional subservience to the clergy, which teachers increasingly considered suffocating and demeaning. Their grievances involved some teachers in protests during the 1848 revolutions, and these resentments continued to smolder in the 1850s, when governments briefly conceded more influence to churches as an antidote to radicalism. In Germany salary increases helped free teachers from dependence. When German teachers created the most powerful professional associations in Europe in the late nineteenth century, they lobbied forcefully for an end to the clergy's continued role in school inspection, further secularization of the curriculum, and introduction of a ladder system that would permit easier access to secondary and higher education for lower-class children. Throughout Germany clerics continued to play a pervasive role in school inspection into the twentieth century. Teachers deeply resented this vestige of their former subservience, and German teachers' associations lobbied forcefully, but until the Weimar period unsuccessfully, for the removal of pastors and priests from the classrooms of the largely religiously segregated schools.

In France conflict between teachers and priests began in the 1830s, when the church attempted to regain its previous authority over schooling and teachers began to acquire a new sense of identity and competence through state-controlled training, certification, and inspection. Something similar began to occur in Russia at the very end of the century. There an overpopulated clerical estate ensured a ready supply of sacristans and deacons to assist priests, and the teacher-cleric relationship never attained the formal subordination that it did in the West. Nevertheless, Orthodox priests resented teachers' influence, and the competition between church schools and those established by *zemstvos* heightened tensions at the turn of the century. Well-publicized cases of cleric-inspired denunciations of teachers led to dismissals by police and inspectors. Moreover teachers complained that priests often failed to fulfill their obligation to teach the mandatory catechism classes with the result that teachers had to perform this function because pupils were examined in this subject.

Most historians agree that the price of teachers' emancipation was that in many countries teachers became lower-level bureaucrats by the close of the nineteenth century, never attaining the autonomy possessed by the so-called free or full professions. But with support by European states, teachers gradually achieved the status of lower-level or semiprofessionals, a status reinforced by standardized training, examination, improved pay, and full-time commitment. While state policy and teachers' own aspirations were central to this process, changes in popular attitudes toward schooling played an important role. As lower-class parents accepted regular attendance and longer terms of instruction for their children, they were more receptive to teaching as a full-time occupation deserving of respect.

TEACHERS AND THE COMMUNITY

In the long run two developments proved essential to improving teachers' social status in the communities where they served: popular acceptance of the utility of regular schooling for children and attenuation of the financial control—tyranny in teachers' eyes—that local communities had originally exercised. Teachers' authority in the community increased with their independence and with the respectability of middle-class standards of dress and behavior, which states, parents, and teachers themselves had all come to expect of the profession.

However, this does not mean that teachers isolated themselves from community affairs. In villages throughout Europe teachers pursued a clear strategy of transforming themselves into local notables by providing a range of extracurricular services that were vital to rural folk increasingly confronted with the broader world of bureaucracy, markets, and information. In rural France, where male teachers took advantage of salary improvements to abandon the demeaning post of lay cleric, they eagerly accepted the post of town clerk (or secretary to the mayor). Since it placed them at the strategic point where the village interacted with the official world outside, that position considerably raised teachers' prestige and influence. By 1884 over twenty-five thousand teachers held this post (almost 70 percent of teachers and nearly all male teachers in village schools). In France the Third Republic encouraged such activity, and teachers, men and women, helped organize cooperatives, clubs, and countless other village associations. Many sponsored adult classes in a conscious attempt to enhance their own prestige along with that of learning. As notables, they played an important role in sustaining the homefront during the final years of World War I, and the same was doubtless true in other countries. In the well-documented case of France, teaching had become by the turn of the century a materially secure, prestigious semiprofession, offering an avenue of social mobility, or at least status preservation, for the children of farmers, artisans, minor officials, and teachers, a reality reflected in declining rates of turnover and increasing length of service.

In Russia, by contrast, the government remained suspicious of teachers who attempted to carve out a wider role in peasant communities. Official memories of the participation of a minority of teachers in the revolution of 1905 were still fresh, conservative fears about the corrosive effects of schooling and teachers on the rural order were still salient fifty years after they had waned in western and central Europe, and teach-

Teachers in the Classroom. French school for apprentice telegraph operators, 1912.
©BRANGER-VIOLLET

ers had yet to achieve the gains in professional association won by their colleagues in the West.

THE EXPANSION AND FEMINIZATION OF TEACHING

Nearly everywhere in Europe the number of teachers increased dramatically during the second half of the nineteenth century and the early twentieth century. In England and Wales the number of primary schoolteachers increased three times between 1870 and 1880, from 13,729 to 41,426. By 1910 there were 161,804 teachers, ten times the number in 1870, the year Parliament passed the first Education Act that made the British state a substantial actor in the nation's schools. At that date teachers comprised less than one-tenth of 1 percent of the workforce, with eighty-nine teachers for every thousand workers, but by 1911 they accounted for nearly 9 percent. In Italy normal schools enrolled 6,000 students in 1870–1871, 14,200 in 1881–1882, and 20,000 by 1901. In the following decade the number of teachers-in-training more than doubled, with 50,000 attending normal schools by 1912. As was true in other countries, the expansion of schooling and the teaching profession in Italy reflected the liberal government's commitment to nation building, summed up in Massimo d'Azeglio's famous appeal, "Now that we have made Italy, we must make Italians." In Russia the prewar years saw a particularly dramatic expansion of the teaching profession from 105,355 teachers in ministry schools in 1910 to 146,032 in 1914, an increase of nearly 40 percent in in four years. Most of this expansion occurred in rural areas, where teachers constituted the most numerous representatives of an educated intelligentsia, much more visible than doctors and other medical professionals. In terms of education and potential authority, only the village priest rivaled the teacher.

Young men continued to enter the profession, but by the turn of the century new teachers were more likely to be women. Assumptions about gender roles helped legitimize the seemingly inexorable process of feminization. Some educators argued that women's nurturing role made them natural teachers, particularly in dealing with the tender emotions of children. But feminization was primarily a function of economics. In a period of rapid industrialization and state expansion, men with educations comparable to teachers and even some with normal school degrees were attracted to better-paying and physically less isolated clerical positions in administration and business. Educated women had fewer options and would accept lower salaries. Nearly everywhere before World War I, pay scales for women teachers were considerably lower than those for men. Nevertheless, teaching was more attractive to women than domestic, factory, or agricultural labor. In France only the postal service offered comparable civil service careers to women. Inevitably, with the rapid expansion of school systems and the increase in the number of teachers during the final decades of the nineteenth century, women came to dominate the profession in most countries. Teaching was perceived as a woman's occupation, which was a factor in its semiprofessional status.

The process of feminization was universal but uneven. In England, Wales, Italy, and Russia, as in North America, by the early twentieth century 60 to 70 percent of teachers were women. In France the proportions were closer to fifty-fifty, and the number of lay women teachers did not surpass that of men until 1909, with 58,396 women. In Germany, however, teaching earlier became a full-time profession, and the state moved aggressively after unification to improve salaries and pensions and to grant teachers the perquisites of civil service ranking and the privilege of serving as reserve officers in the army. There the profession remained overwhemingly male. Only 21 percent of elementary teachers in Germany were female on the eve of World War I, but the female proportion within the profession was increasing.

The effects of feminization are more difficult to gauge than the numbers. When women first entered the profession, some men resented them as competitors who would work for less and lower the profession's status. In France, where lay women began to move into the profession in the 1880s, male-dominated associations, the Amicales, at first prohibited women members. However, the fact that teachers, whether men or women, faced similar problems and similar enemies fostered solidarity and cooperation. In France conservative and clerical attacks on secular education and lay teachers during the Dreyfus affair induced men to accept women teachers as allies. In 1909 the national Amicale congress endorsed equal pay for women teachers, which was achieved in 1920. Men continued to dominate leadership posts in professional associations, but women established a more visible presence. In Russia, where teachers faced considerable problems of cultural isolation, clerical rivalry, and less support from the government, cooperation across the sexual divide eventually prevailed. The critical difference was that in Russia teachers found less support from the state, which shared some of the same concerns that the church and conservatives had concerning teachers' role.

Contrary to popular assumptions, most women entered teaching to pursue a career, not for a temporary interlude before marriage. In France by 1900 more than half of the women teachers had served for over fifteen years. Normal school graduates signed a ten-year contract to teach, and if they resigned early they had to repay the cost of training. More than half had married and continued to teach. Marriage was encouraged by French education officials, who wanted female teachers, like their male counterparts, to civilize peasants and workers and transform them into citizens. Married women teachers in particular would help socialize girls by inculcating middle-class domestic norms of hygiene and child care.

In the early decades of women entering the profession, they often faced difficulty winning popular acceptance, and many, particularly single women, lived lonely, isolated lives. Some contemporaries believed that feminization lowered the status of teaching, and this probably inhibited some men from entering the profession. Feminization also coincided with the increased subordination of teachers within educational bureaucracies, although the relationship was complex. Some scholars have argued that school administrators enforced marriage bans for women teachers as a way to prevent them from advancing to positions of authority and to keep salaries down. However, these bans were far from universal. Nevertheless, it is clear that from Great Britain to Russia men held positions of power and authority, such as principals and inspectors in the larger urban schools. Everywhere the powerful post of state school inspector, a figure of awesome authority over teachers' professional lives and often over their private lives, was held by men. Isolated but well-publicized cases of sexual harassment of teachers by inspectors underscored the fact that, while teaching was becoming increasingly feminized, power in the educational bureaucracies of European states remained firmly in male hands. In the Third Republic in France the inspectorate was opened to women, but their entry was slow. Evidence also shows that the first generation of women teachers faced more difficulty than men in gaining acceptance and authority in local, particularly rural, communities. This was true in France during the nineteenth and twentieth centuries, when a large percentage of men teachers also held the influential position of secretary to the mayor. Women did not hold this post, nor could they vote. In Russia men were more involved in community affairs, whether in the rural cooperatives that grew dramatically in the early 1900s or in rural politics during moments of upheaval like the revolution of 1905–1906.

TEACHERS, POLITICS, AND PROFESSIONAL ASSOCIATION

In many ways teaching was the most politically sensitive of the professions. Governments and elites recruited and trained teachers to integrate the masses into the evolving social and political order. At the

Teaching in the Red Army. A teacher conducts a literacy class for Red Army troops, Russia, c. 1917–1920. SOVFOTO/EASTFOTO

same time they remained wary of teachers' potential to disrupt that order. Given teachers' position as marginal and often poverty-stricken intellectuals whose work placed them in close contact with peasants and workers, official attitudes toward the emerging profession were often ambivalent, and they fluctuated over time.

In Germany, after the 1848 revolution, official discourse characterized the schoolteacher as a subversive pariah, but a mere twenty years later Otto von Bismarck and other architects of German unification extolled the Prussian teacher as the real victor at the Battles of Königgrätz and Sedan. Nevertheless, officials remained wary of teachers' loyalty in subsequent decades, even as they moved aggressively to meet teachers' professional goals to inculcate that loyalty. The same official suspicion existed in France, at least until the 1880s, when the Third Republic embraced lay teachers, men and women, as republican missionaries—the famous "black hussars"—who would civilize the peasantry and combat clerical and conservative political influence in the countryside. However, official suspicion then turned against the large numbers of women in religious teaching orders who still educated a large percentage of children, especially girls, in French primary schools. The Russian government remained extremely suspicious of teachers' potential to radicalize the masses until the very end of

the tsarist regime. An activist minority of teachers had been involved in revolutionary movements from the 1870s through the revolution of 1905. Because of financial constraints and the nature of the Russian autocracy, the government was never willing to adequately meet Russian teachers' demands for the material security, emancipation from local interests, or rights of professional association won by their colleagues in the West. In addition the Russian state failed to achieve the kind of monopoly over teacher training established elsewhere. Active opposition by teachers to the existing order was much less pronounced in western and central Europe by the end of the nineteenth century. However, teachers were not completely coopted by governments, and they were unable to shape state initiatives when these were viewed as inimical to their professional goals.

Imperial Germany provides a case in point. In 1889 Emperor William II issued a cabinet order that called upon teachers to combat the socialist movement in the classroom. Historians of German education once argued that teachers, coopted by civil service status, higher pay and pensions, and privileges like the coveted right to serve as reserve officers in the army, became subalterns, excessively subservient to the state, and helped indoctrinate pupils with a chauvinistic, antidemocratic ethos that contributed to Germany's political course during the twentieth century.

Research has shown, however, that while German teachers were patriotic like most teachers elsewhere by World War I, they resisted the call to struggle against the Social Democrats out of concern about alienating working-class parents. Instead, through their powerful national teachers' association of 125,000 members, they supported a program of education reform designed to democratize schooling (the ladder system), secularize the curriculum, and remove clerics from their traditional role in school inspection.

CONCLUSION

With the spread of schooling in nineteenth- and twentieth-century Europe, teaching became one of the most numerous professions. With support from states and growing popular acceptance of schooling, teachers' status changed dramatically in the course of the nineteenth century. While some teachers continued to perform supplemental work for economic or tactical reasons, like the secretary to the mayor in France, the prevailing trend was toward full-time teaching. Improved and standardized qualifications, relative material security, and emancipation from local control enhanced teachers' social and professional status. In a world where states and masses placed increased value on literacy and basic schooling, teaching offered the prospect of social mobility for the ambitious children of the lower class. However, this improvement often came at the the price of incorporation into the lower rungs of the state bureaucracy, and teachers consequently enjoyed considerably less autonomy than higher-status professions. In addition and paradoxically, the very success and spread of schooling ensured that teaching remained a semiprofession. With the rise of mass education, the services provided by teachers lost whatever mystique or esoteric quality they previously had. In contrast to doctors or lawyers, the knowledge and skills teachers possessed were generally within the competency of all who passed through the schools.

See also **The Liberal State** *(volume 2);* **Church and Society** *(in this volume); and other articles in this section.*

BIBLIOGRAPHY

Albisetti, James C. "The Feminization of Teaching in the Nineteenth Century: A Comparative Perspective." *History of Education* 22 (1993): 253–264.

Anderson, R. D. *Education and the Scottish People, 1750–1918.* Oxford, 1995.

Bergen, Barry H. "Only a Schoolmaster: Gender, Class, and the Effort to Professionalize Elementary Teaching in England, 1870–1910." *History of Education Quarterly* 22 (spring 1982): 1–22.

Day, C. R. "The Rustic Man: The Rural Schoolteacher in Nineteenth-Century France." *Comparative Studies in Society and History* 25, no. 1 (1983): 26–49.

Eklof, Ben. *Russian Peasant Schools: Officialdom, Village Culture, and Popular Pedagogy, 1864–1914.* Berkeley, Calif., 1986.

Harrigan, Patrick. "Women Teachers and the Schooling of Girls in France: Recent Historiographical Trends." *French Historical Studies* 21, no. 4 (fall 1998): 593–610.

Horn, Pamela. *Education in Rural England, 1800–1914.* London, 1978.

Horn, Pamela. "The Recruitment, Role, and Status of the Victorian County Teacher." *History of Education* 9, no. 2 (June 1980): 129–141.

Harp, Stephen L. *Learning to Be Loyal: Primary Schooling as Nation Building in Alsace and Lorraine, 1850–1940.* DeKalb, Ill., 1998.

Lamberti, Marjorie. "Elementary School Teachers and the Struggle against Social Democracy in Wilhelmine Germany." *History of Education Quarterly* 32, no. 1 (spring 1992): 73–98.

Lamberti, Marjorie. *State, Society, and the Elementary School in Imperial Germany.* New York, 1989.

LaVopa, Anthony J. *Prussian Schoolteachers: Profession and Office, 1763–1848.* Chapel Hill, N.C., 1980.

LaVopa, Anthony. "Status and Ideology: Rural Schoolteachers in Pre-March and Revolutionary Prussia." *Journal of Social History* 12 (spring 1979): 430–456.

Lawson, John, and Harold Silver. *A Social History of Education in England.* London, 1973.

Margadant, Jo Burr. *Madame le Professeur: Women Educators in the Third Republic.* Princeton, N.J., 1990.

Maynes, Mary Jo. *Schooling in Western Europe: A Social History.* Albany, N.Y., 1985.

Maynes, Mary Jo, ed. *Schooling for the People: Comparative Local Studies of Schooling History in France and Germany, 1750–1850.* New York, 1985.

Meyers, Peter V. "From Conflict to Cooperation: Men and Women Teachers in the Belle Epoque." *Historical Reflections* 7 (1980): 493–505.

Meyers, Peter V. "Primary Schoolteachers in Nineteenth-Century France: A Study of Professionalization through Conflict." *History of Education Quarterly* 25, nos. 1–2 (spring–summer 1985): 21–40.

Meyers, Peter V. "Professionalization and Societal Change: Rural Teachers in Nineteenth-Century France." *Journal of Social History* 9 (1976): 542–558.

Quartararo, Anne T. *Women Teachers and Popular Education in Nineteenth-Century France: Social Values and Corporate Identity at the Normal School Institution.* Newark, Del., 1995.

Ruane, Christine. *Gender, Class, and the Professionalization of Russian City Teachers, 1860–1914.* Pittsburgh, Pa., 1994.

Schleunes, Karl A. *Schooling and Society: The Politics of Education in Prussia and Bavaria, 1750–1900.* New York, 1989.

Seregny, Scott J. *Russian Teachers and Peasant Revolution: The Politics of Education in 1905.* Bloomington, Ind., 1989.

Singer, Barnett. *Village Notables in Nineteenth-Century France: Priests, Mayors, Schoolmasters.* Albany, N.Y., 1983.

Stephens, W. B. *Education in Britain, 1750–1914.* New York, 1998.

PRINTING AND PUBLISHING

Thomas Cragin

Johannes Gutenberg's movable-type printing press, invented around 1440, initiated a dramatic change in the communication of ideas throughout Europe. An author's text, though arguably no less subject to interpretation than earlier oral communication, became more enduring and less variable. As Walter Ong has argued, print promoted cognitive skills, especially comparative analysis and categorization that transformed the very nature of thinking. The printing press made book production cheaper and made books more plentiful. Long before most Europeans could afford a book, however, printers flooded Europe with cheap pamphlets, posters, and almanacs that spread the practice of reading with all its effects. Few innovations significantly altered printing mechanics between the fifteenth and nineteenth centuries, yet despite technological stasis, the printing trade played a crucial role in the dramatic social revolutions of the Renaissance, Reformation, Enlightenment, and French Revolution. Significant technological and business changes of the nineteenth century turned printing and publishing into modern industries, educating, entertaining, and informing a majority of Europeans. While technological and business advances continued to modernize the press and to diversify its forms and functions in the twentieth century, new media undermined its significance.

EARLY MODERN PRINTING AND BOOKSELLING

In the middle of the fifteenth century Johannes Gensfleisch, called Gutenberg, began a printing revolution with his invention of a movable-type printing press. His press combined the existing technology of woodblock printing, in which an engraved image is inked and pressed onto paper, with movable type, small metal blocks with a character or sign carved into one end and arranged together in a frame to form words. Gutenberg's printing press allowed printers to make hundreds of copies of books and thousands of copies of shorter prints at a time.

The success of Gutenberg's printing press depended on the earlier invention of paper and the dramatic growth in the demand for print. The significant growth of trade after the twelfth century offered substantial advantages to literate merchants, bankers, master artisans, and shopkeepers. The church also expanded the number of readers eager for the press's products by promoting clerical education. Finally, princes promoted the spread of reading by establishing in their territories new universities that educated the bureaucracy for their expanding administrations. A century before the invention of the printing press this growing demand for the written word inspired the invention of paper in Europe. Previously book manuscripts were written on animal-skin parchment. Bookmakers required countless sheepskins to produce a single manuscript, limiting production and commanding a high price. The papermakers of Fabriano, Italy, developed a series of innovations that facilitated papermaking, and imitators soon sprang up in cities in Italy, France, and Germany. Although paper remained the most expensive single element in manuscript and book production, it cost far less than parchment and was more plentiful, facilitating a dramatic increase in book production.

By 1480 twenty printshops operated in southern Germany, nearly thirty in northern Italy, fifteen in the Low Countries, and new ones sprang up in Breslau, Budapest, Copenhagen, London, Prague, and Seville. By the beginning of the sixteenth century printing establishments had spread to over 250 cities and towns across Europe. Most of these cities and towns were important sea and river ports concentrated in central and southern Germany, northern Italy, and southeast France. From these ports publishers exported prints to most European cities. Venice built its crucial importance to printing on its overseas trade and became Europe's printing capital in the fifteenth and sixteenth centuries. Despite the concentration of publishing in urban centers and the distribution of prints to other cities, printers made most of their products for local markets.

Gutenberg's Printing Press. Reconstruction of the printing press invented in the 1430s and 1440s by Johannes Gutenberg (between 1390 and 1400–1468) in the Gutenberg Museum in Mainz, Germany. In the foreground is a copy of the *Hypnerotomachia Poliphili,* first printed at Venice by Aldus Manutius in 1499. GUTENBERG-MUSEUM, MAINZ/ERICH LESSING/ART RESOURCE, NY

Printers quickly put Gutenberg's press to use in the production of pictorial images from woodblock engravings. At the same time printing changed the meaning and significance of pictorial images. Printed pictures ceased to be the focal point of a text's meaning and interpretation and instead became transparent illustrations of themes centered in the written text. Though they lost a great deal of their significance, illustrations remained important to sales. Engraving was time consuming and expensive, however. Fortunately an engraved plate lasted a long time, yielding tens of thousands of prints. A printer reused popular woodcuts by fitting new texts around them. Rivals in the trade often copied each other's popular woodcuts. Once the woodcut began to lose its popularity, however, the printer sold, rented, or traded it to a printer in another area. Merchants, clergy, and artisans decorated their walls with woodcuts. Copperplate engravings further revolutionized the trade in the fifteenth century because of their greater delicacy of detail. More expensive, copperplate engraved illustrations originally sold almost exclusively to the aristocracy. But by the end of the sixteenth century copperplate engravings had largely supplanted woodcuts except in the production of cheap prints for a mass audience. Printers that specialized in popular printing used worn-out woodcuts and fonts to print tens and even

hundreds of thousands of small pamphlets and large posters on cheap paper. Printers in England, France, Italy, and Germany produced this literature in cities and towns for peddlers to distribute to urban and rural readers.

For more than four centuries printing was the business of skilled master printers like Gutenberg and the artisans who lived and worked in their small shops. As the publishers of the learned, printers occupied a unique middle ground among their intellectually elite authors, their socially elite buyers, and their own origins as urban commoners. After the Reformation most printers received formal educations, often a year or two at a college that included study of Latin and Greek, the language of most books until the seventeenth century. Printers were, therefore, the most literate of skilled craftspeople, commanding particular respect. By the sixteenth century some printer-publishers had become so renowned that their names lent authority to the authors they published. Often politicized, they played significant roles in urban politics. But as artisans who worked with their hands, they were firmly planted among commoners, rarely able to rise above the status and position of a burgher. Gutenberg's ennoblement by the archbishop of Mainz was the exception that proved the rule.

Printers worked long hours, typically fourteen-hour days, printing two to three thousand sheets a day. Because paper was their biggest cost and labor their lowest, they refrained from printing too many copies of any book-length work. If more copies could be sold, these artisans remade the blocks for every page of the book and printed another limited edition. Because the cost of printing a book was so high, printers usually printed only works that had been contracted by a bookseller or book merchant who put up most of the money. In this sense booksellers operated as both sellers and publishers.

Until the nineteenth century the cost of setting up a print shop was relatively low. The printing presses and type were not inexpensive, but they represented a one-time cost since they did not wear out quickly and could be inexpensively repaired when they did. So while printing was at first dominated by a few large print shops, many small shops were in business by the sixteenth century.

In contrast to establishing a print shop, the high cost of books made the opening of a bookshop tremendously expensive. Booksellers worked closely with local printers, investing in the publication of a few books. To diversify their holdings without expending excessive capital on printing, booksellers traded books with one another throughout Europe. Because they often were published in Latin, books could be sold in any part of western and central Europe regardless of their point of origin. To keep track of each other's publications, booksellers corresponded regularly and soon began to coordinate their prices, distribution, and publication investments. Each bookseller-printer eventually published a catalog of his or her inventory. Bookseller-printers traveled a great deal to meet other booksellers, establish business exchanges, collect bills, and assess the market, especially by visiting book fairs. Through the networks that developed, booksellers attempted to reduce competition and redundancy. The rising demand for a greater variety of books for a growing legal bureaucracy, an increasingly academic church, and a professionalizing bourgeoisie encouraged booksellers to specialize their production for only one of these markets. Each sold his or her genre, be it legal, theological, medical, or business, through the networks of the European book trade.

Book production and sales began to make their marks on the urban landscape in the sixteenth century. Booksellers set up their shops and stalls near the working and living quarters of their target audiences. They sold scholarly and religious books from shops near colleges, universities, seminaries, and cathedrals. Booksellers sold legal texts from stalls and shops located near the law courts. In Paris they set up their stalls along the walls of the Palais de Justice, in London around the Hall of Westminster, at the Hague around the Palais des États, in Prague near the Royal Palace. Peddlers sold cheap prints throughout many parts of cities but especially at its most congested points, especially bridges and major intersections. Printing, whether secular, religious, or popular, came to dominate the city during the sixteenth century.

THE RENAISSANCE

The Renaissance's emphasis on learning greatly expanded publishing in the first century of print. Humanists advocated the extension of literacy to a greater portion of the society and demanded the translation of Latin works so they could be read in the vernacular languages. Inspired by these goals, religious and secular institutions amassed large libraries of handwritten manuscripts, especially classical works, many in the vernacular. When printing spread across Europe in the middle of the fifteenth century, a larger literate public snapped up cheaper print versions of these manuscripts.

Though classical and medieval texts dominated Renaissance publishing, printers published new works during the Renaissance, and many of those in turn spurred the expansion of publishing. Baldassare Castiglione's *Book of the Courtier* (written between 1513 and 1518) and works like it convinced the nobility that their success at court depended on a humanistic education based on extensive reading of history, poetry, and philosophy. To make works like these available throughout Europe, printers hired "rewrite men"

The Printer's Shop. Illustration from Diderot's *Encyclopédie*, 1762. COLLECTION VIOLLET

379

Selling the News. Newsmongers on the Quai des Augustins, Paris, 1681. Engraving by Margot BIBLIOTHÉQUE NATIONALE DE FRANCE, PARIS

to translate them from the language of the author's court into emerging national languages, spoken and read by a growing elite. Few well-known Renaissance works reached a truly large audience, however, because most printers published books, and few but the elite could afford them.

The majority of early prints were religious, though a historical understanding is skewed by the survival of clerical and aristocratic libraries and the disappearance of commoners' collections. The most notable products of early printing were vernacular Bibles. Gutenberg won fame for his. Printers also printed large numbers of pamphlets that taught litanies and commandments. Pictorial prints provided images of saints, the last judgment and the afterlife, and allegories of death. These prints not only constituted texts for use in the practice of religion but were considered sacred themselves. Hung on walls in homes and shops, they inspired awe but also stimulated

greater consideration of religion. Printers also catered to the special needs of priests by publishing guides to pilgrimages and instructions for confessors. Religious, such as the Brethren of the Common Life, an organization of Catholic humanists, set up their own printing presses to produce grammars so that the laity could read the Bible and other religious works in the vernacular.

Jewish communities quickly embraced printing as a means to expand the circulation of religious works. Jewish printers, many of whom were trained in Germany, reproduced a great number of religious works from their print shops in the Iberian Peninsula and Italy during the first century of European printing. In Venice, Jewish printers published the Babylonian Talmud and the Jerusalem Talmud. The common use of Hebrew by Jews throughout Europe made possible the greater circulation of these works to diverse communities.

THE REFORMATION

Religious prints outnumbered all others long before the Reformation. But both the Protestant and the Catholic Reformations expanded printing on an unprecedented scale, and their conflict altered the dynamics of the book trade. Though similar heresies preceded Martin Luther's movement, the Protestant Reformation was the first to spread by print and arguably owed its success to the press. No wonder Luther described printing as "God's highest and extremest act of grace, whereby the business of the Gospel is driven forward." Indeed the massive distribution of his cheap broadsides and pamphlets made Luther one of Germany's best-known authors even before he broke with the Catholic Church.

Protestant printers and booksellers worked together to spread Protestant religious propaganda, published in the vernacular for the widest possible readership. German printers also produced Protestant works in Latin for French audiences and in the Glagolitic alphabet for Slavic Croatians. Protestant Transylvanians, too, printed a great deal of religious literature in Slavic and Romanian languages. The Protestants' propaganda campaigns and their efforts to spread the practice of reading and religious study promoted the growth of literacy and greatly increased print's influence on East and West Europeans.

The Catholic Reformation also encouraged the printing and sale of religious works. Most important for its impact on the greatest number of readers was the massive Counter-Reformation propaganda, counterpart to the Protestants' religious broadsides and chapbooks. In particular Catholic printers produced hundreds of thousands of devotionals, often written by priests for their parishioners. The church also encouraged Catholic presses to print schoolbooks for use in Catholic seminaries in for the expanding education of priests and monks and pamphlets that outlined popular sermons, simplified doctrinal complexities and contradictions to answer the challenges posed by Reformationists, and classified sins and their penalties and pardons.

The Reformation created great rifts in the European book trade. Printers of differing faiths worked at cross-purposes in the production of rival propagandas and pirated each other's nonreligious books on a rapidly expanding scale. The European book market was also splintered by increasing linguistic divisions. The Reformation ended the preeminence of Latin as the main language in which books were published, spreading instead the use of the vernacular. French emerged as the most important of vernacular languages, replacing Latin as the language in which elites throughout much of Europe read and wrote. Vernacular book fairs flourished and produced bibliographies of books for sale by diverse printers in a single language. At the same time the print trade popularized national languages, reducing elites' use of diverse dialects. Increasingly printers and booksellers divided Europeans along national lines.

In an effort to exert greater control over publishing, Reformation era kings granted monopolies to printers and booksellers that limited the number of shops the Crown had to watch. The policy also made licensed printers and booksellers who enjoyed royal monopolies into allies of the Crown and the church. In England printer-booksellers united behind Henry VIII's effort to prevent the importation of foreign (heretical) prints and the immigration of foreign printers. The Crown formalized the association of English publishers in 1557, when it granted the great printers that made up the Stationers' Company nearly complete

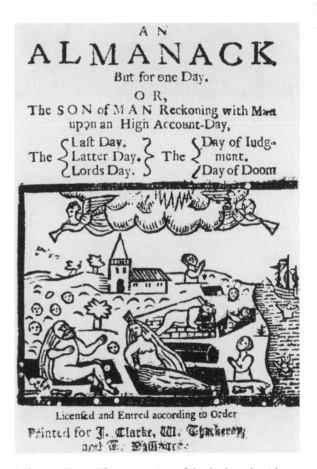

Religious Tract. The resurrection of the dead on the title page of "An Almanack But for One Day," from a collection of seventeenth-century religious tracts made by the English diarist Samuel Pepys (1633–1703). PEPYS LIBRARY, MAGDALENE COLLEGE, CAMBRIDGE

Reading and Religious Study. *Reading the Bible,* painting (detail) by Gérard Dou (1613–1675). MUSÉE DU LOUVRE, PARIS/©ND-VIOLLET

average of nine printing presses operated by twenty-four journeymen and apprentices.

Seventeenth- and eighteenth-century monarchs established new organizations within their governments to control of the press. Governments stepped up the prosecution of printers who pirated others' books, and most monarchs issued lists of banned books and punished those who printed or sold them. Inversely, kings rewarded printers and booksellers for publishing of works favorable to church and state. Most licensed printers and booksellers supported royal controls, since royal enforcement of their monopolies and copyrights increased their profits. By the beginning of the eighteenth century they had amassed considerable fortunes. When they could, however, even licensed printers and booksellers bent the rules to their advantage.

The impact of church and state on the control and development of printing was not limited to Catholic and Protestant lands. The Russian Orthodox Church also promoted the spread of printing, though on a far more limited scale than that seen in western and central Europe. Tsar Ivan the Terrible set up the first official printing house, or *pechatnyy dvor,* in 1563. Nearly all the works printed in Cyrillic were religious, and the press was controlled in large part by the Russian Orthodox Church.

Print also preserved religious and ethnic minority cultures against the power of kings and dominant religions within states, as in eastern Europe and the Mediterranean. Greeks, struggling to maintain their own press under Ottoman domination, turned to Venetian printers. Venetians printed nearly all Greek-language publications between the sixteenth and nineteenth centuries. Western European publishers also printed religious and secular works for Armenian readers throughout the world. These prints, like those for the Greeks, were critical to the survival of their faith and culture.

Reformation prints had tremendous social effects throughout Europe. They split the church and initiated an age of religious wars. For this reason, Elizabeth Eisenstein asserted that the printing press "contributed more to destroying Christian concord and inflaming religious warfare than any of the so-called arts of war ever did." Aside from its immediate religious and political impacts, however, the Reformation also spread print culture throughout Europe, gradually diminishing illiteracy. The English Stationers' Company records from 1587 suggest that, while the numbers of copies of ordinary works were no more voluminous in England than in Catholic countries, the company doubled its production of grammars and catechisms. Literacy grew rapidly and

control of printing and bookselling. By 1605 the king shifted the monopolies, previously granted to a few privileged printers, to all the members of the company, benefiting small booksellers and printers. By doing so he extended London publishers' influence and therefore his own throughout Britain and Europe. To prevent pirating, publishers registered a new book's title with the company, which granted and protected the publisher's copyright. Copyrights also were sold by one publisher to another. During the sixteenth century the kings of France granted similar monopolies to Parisian booksellers and printers, putting their competitors in the rest of France at a great disadvantage. Over the next two centuries these privileges caused the formation of large, specialized bookseller-printer companies and the disappearance of their weaker rivals. In 1644 Paris had seventy-six print shops, each with an average of only two printing presses, three journeymen, and one apprentice. By 1770, however, Paris had far fewer print shops, roughly forty, but each employed an

The Spread of Printing. Adapted from Elizabeth Eisenstein, *The Printing Revolution in Early Modern Europe* (Cambridge, U.K.: Cambridge University Press, 1986), p. 15.

with it the impact of print and the influence of writers.

THE AGE OF ENLIGHTENMENT

The dramatic growth of printing and publishing initiated by the Reformation accelerated during the eighteenth century. Printers produced and book dealers sold a growing number of expensive books to elite readers and cheaper books and ephemera to the middle and lower classes. Parisian booksellers offered more

than 100,000 books for sale along the rue Saint-Jacques and tens of thousands at the Palais de Justice. Estate records in western Europe, made at the death of independent peasants, artisans, shopkeepers, and merchants, suggest that most owned at least a few books, particularly religious works. For every book accountants noted, many pamphlets and other ephemeral works of too little value for notaries to mention probably existed.

In part the growing importance of the press is attributable to the economic growth of the eighteenth century. In fact the geographical shifts of the centers of the book trade closely mirrored the geography of economic power. In the seventeenth century the center of European book printing moved from Venice and Antwerp to Amsterdam, reflecting the shift of mercantile power from the Venetians to the Dutch. In the eighteenth century London printers outpaced their rivals in Amsterdam, mirroring the shift from Dutch to English mercantile supremacy.

More important than mercantile power, however, was the proliferation of clandestine printing that dramatically accelerated competition and lowered book prices. Since it was not illegal to pirate foreign books, publishers near borders flooded neighboring countries with pirated editions of new books. Book piracy was greatest across borders without linguistic barriers, as among the rival states in Italy and Germany. Many publishers, however, hired expatriate printers to produce pirated editions of their former country's books. Hiring French Protestant printers expelled from France by Louis XIV, printers in Geneva, London, Amsterdam, and Berlin pirated books for sale in France. Many of these clandestine networks began as a means to circulate Protestant books in Catholic lands but soon grew beyond their religious purposes. Genevan printers, originally Protestant propagandists, expanded into the publication of medical and legal texts, outpacing their Lyonnaise competitors. Ironically, Genevan printers eventually moved into the production of Catholic theological works, marketed throughout Catholic Europe and the Americas.

The book became more significant because it challenged the social, political, and cultural order. Governments' best efforts seemed powerless to prevent book piracy or to curtail the sales of banned books critical of church and state. By the mid-eighteenth century a government ban or clerical condemnation of an author's work actually promoted its sales. Inversely, the public often viewed permission to publish a work as proof of the author's duplicity with a corrupt government, diminishing sales. The spread of new publishing strategies also radicalized the press. By the mid-seventeenth century publishers began to free some authors from their dependency on wealthy patrons by giving advances on expected profits. Such independence freed writers to criticize their society and polity. The popularity of such daring works during the eighteenth century encouraged publishers to reward authors who penned them.

Printers and booksellers had to adapt their trade to cope with the competition posed by foreign, pirated editions. Knowing they would sell few copies once their books were pirated, many licensed publishers sold the first editions at the highest possible price,

narrowing the audience to the wealthy elite. Only one out of every ten such books sold in numbers sufficient to cover the losses incurred by the other nine. By encouraging licensed booksellers to raise prices and restrict sales, clandestine publishing and peddling diminished the circulation of the legitimate press and its significance. Banned books, meanwhile, proliferated. Later in the eighteenth century even licensed printers, unable or unwilling to narrow their target audiences, began publishing and selling pirated and banned books.

In the face of such widespread piracy, some monarchs took steps to better safeguard authors' and publishers' rights by extending copyright protection and expanding trade licensing. Britain's copyright law of 1709 gave greater protection to publishers that greatly stimulated the book trade. More printers appeared in London, and booksellers lined Grub Street, making it the center of the British book trade. A similar law passed by Louis XVI in 1777 initiated comparable changes in France on the eve of the French Revolution. During the eighteenth century old established booksellers and printers were overwhelmed by the vast numbers of newcomers to the trade.

Some kings encouraged the radical press to promote reform. Peter the Great, tsar of Russia in the early eighteenth century, encouraged the printing of scientific and philosophical works that challenged the rival authority of the Russian Orthodox Church. The nobility of Europe, too, encouraged the publication of hundreds of thousands of books, many radical works of the Enlightenment, that were housed in the private libraries of their estates and urban apartments. Ironically, elites' sponsorship of the radical press spread ideas that ultimately undermined their social and political power.

THE INDUSTRIAL AGE

Printers and publishers played a critical role in promoting social and political revolution at the end of the eighteenth century. Triggered by political publications like Thomas Paine's *Common Sense* (1776) in the American colonies and Emmanuel-Joseph Sieyès's *What is the Third Estate?* (1789) in France, liberal revolutions spread across Europe. The most dramatic and long-lasting result of the French Revolution was its destruction of privilege. By ending privileges the revolution swept away the guild system that had restricted the printing trade. The number of printers in Paris alone increased sevenfold in just a few months. Not only did the printing industry expand with the dismantling of government controls, it became far more politicized. In fact printers assumed roles as leaders and shapers of popular radicalism throughout the revolution.

After the French Revolution governments struggled to impose restrictions on the press. To forestall the politicization of the public, governments reimposed the licensing of printers and booksellers to restrict their numbers and reestablished the taxation of print to reduce its scale. Despite more intense efforts to enforce press censorship, the press became an increasingly significant tool of radical politics. The liberal revolutions of 1830 and 1848 rolled back these restrictions, which were finally eliminated in the late nineteenth century. In part the spread of the political press was the result of the growth of printing and publishing during the nineteenth century.

While printing technology changed little in its first three and a half centuries, technological innovations in the nineteenth century facilitated a dramatic proliferation of print. Improvements to the printing press in the late eighteenth and early nineteenth centuries accelerated the speed of printing while reducing its costs. More durable iron presses replaced their wooden counterparts in the late eighteenth century. Iron construction simplified the application of other innovations that sped production but increased the pressures exerted on the machine. The new application of rollers and cylinders that inked pages and pressed the image, for example, greatly improved and accelerated production. Innovations in papermaking were equally important in the dramatic changes to the printing industry. Inventors patented new machines in the early nineteenth century that produced paper in continuous sheets rolled onto a large drum that was then fed through a high-speed mechanical printing press. By the 1830s dozens of these machines produced vast quantities of paper. The development and spread of chemically processed wood-pulp paper in the second half of the century further increased paper production. Rising wages inspired the invention of labor-saving machines for typesetting that decreased the time and cost of putting a text into print. Not any one of these innovations but their combination triggered the dramatic revolution in printing and publishing. The rotary press combined the latest printing inventions with innovations in paper production. Powered by steam, the rotary presses of the *London Times* produced seven thousand sheets an hour in 1827. While thousands of small print shops survived in Europe at the end of the century, many still using human power, the majority of printing was done by large print shops operating enormous rotary presses.

The revolution in printing resulted from the dramatic increase in the number of those employed

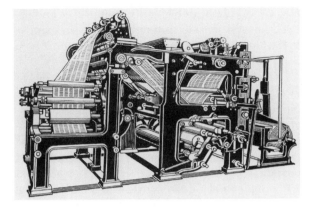

Rotary Press. The rotary press, steam or electricity driven, prints on a long roll of paper rather than on single sheets as did presses from Gutenberg to the eighteenth century.

in publishing at the same time that labor-saving innovations made each worker more productive. In Germany, the number of employees in the printing trade increased 150 percent between 1849 and 1875 and 600 percent by 1895. Over the course of the century the paper mills of Saxony increased their workforce 1,500 percent. New printing technologies made each worker far more productive. In Saxony innovations in papermaking made each worker fourteen times as productive. The vast increases in the numbers of more productive workers, therefore, created an explosion of print. Moreover technological innovations and economies of scale decreased the cost of raw materials from well over 50 percent of the total cost of making a book at the beginning of the century to about 15 percent at the century's end. As a result the cost of books fell dramatically throughout the century as their numbers increased.

Technological innovations also altered the appearance of prints. Developments in engraving and lithography facilitated the greater production of more accurate visual images. Photoengraving proved the most important among these innovations, allowing rapid reproduction of images for publication in newspapers.

The focus of printing changed as dramatically as its quantity and appearance. In the first four centuries of printing the bulk of printers' time was devoted to book production for an elite audience. Censorship records in early-nineteenth-century France suggest that publishers rarely printed more than a few thousand copies of most books and usually only a few hundred. Throughout Europe book publishers unable to sell to the wealthy usually went bankrupt in hard times. Even in England, where the innovations of printing were most advanced, books remained the preserve of elites with high prices. But the technological changes that made printing so much less expensive in the nineteenth century shifted printers' efforts from book publishing to printing for a larger market.

Commercial and political advertising, government publications, and newspapers became the main products of the press. Advertisements marketed products ranging from inexpensive patent medicines to bicycles and automobiles. Their proliferation reflected the growth of disposable incomes but also promoted the development of a consumer culture, in which sellers created popular desire for their products. Political prints, too, became increasingly important during the nineteenth century. Political parties distributed tracts and postered cities and towns with their candidates' names and slogans. Governments employed printers in the production of state propaganda to rival their opponents' prints. Mass politics feuled political printing and led governments to purchase primers and other textbooks in vast numbers for millions of European children, who were required to attend school. The spread of education had a reciprocal influence on the book market, as a larger literate public demanded more publications. In Russia, for example, the government mandated primary education in the 1880s. Consequently the number of copies of each published book doubled between 1887 and 1895 and tripled in the two decades that followed. Most important of all to the influence of print over daily life in Europe, newspapers became cheaper and more interesting to millions of readers during the century. Newspapers formed a bond that tied people of diverse social classes and regions to a nation, political party, and culture.

The mid-nineteenth century also witnessed a dramatic growth in book publishing, beginning in Britain, where a number of publishers issued cheap paperback reprints at less than half the normal book price. While these paperbacks sold to a larger middle-class audience, even at five shillings they remained out of reach of the lower middle classes. However, books began to reach lower-middle-class and upper-working-class readers throughout Europe with the gradual spread of lending libraries and subscription libraries. But these did little to stimulate the publishing industry. More significant to readers and publishers were the serialized novels, sold in installments. In the second half of the century publishers began to print cheaper paperbacks. First sold in railroad stations by pioneering booksellers such as W. H. Smith, they set a fashion among middle-class readers and soon became known throughout Europe as railroad novels. By 1856 Havard had published six thousand cheap paperback novels, each with press runs of around ten thousand. Once a single French publisher claimed to have sold 60 million copies, the book was no longer considered the preserve of elites or even the middle classes.

MODERN PUBLISHING

In the second half of the nineteenth century publishing became a large and complex industry. For centuries publishing was the business of booksellers and printers. Formerly the business of two partners, usually father and son, it became the business of great publishing houses in the late nineteenth century. English publishers led Europe in innovative business practices. The great publishers of the eighteenth century, such as Longman, Blackwood, and Macmillan, grew significantly and remained important into the twenty-first century. These emerging publishing companies were a business distinct from both printing and bookselling. The publisher recruited and guided authors, managed typesetters and printers, promoted specific books and periodicals, garnered government and industrial contracts, and engineered distribution to retailers.

Publishers became immensely powerful and influencial. Their managerial skills and salesmanship determined success. In France, Lévy excelled at picking bestsellers such as Edgar Allan Poe, and L.-C.-F. Hachette was renowned for his ability to win lucrative government contracts for textbooks. The death of one of these great publishers could destroy the business and often did. Publishers' influence, however, extended far beyond these business concerns. Many determined to publish works they felt had particular merit despite their potential unpopularity. Eugen Diederichs and Julius Lehmann in Germany, for example, attempted to publish fine works of literature that they believed would ennoble German culture. In Russia publishers tried to create a better-quality "people's literature" to replace the sensational pamphlets and serialized novels popular at the turn of the century. While more publishers throughout Europe remained concerned about the bottom line, many still refused to profit from the publication of works contrary to contemporary morals. The English publisher Mills and Boon, for example, published light romantic novels for women but refused to publish anything that pushed the boundaries of Victorian morality. Publishers wielded considerable editorial power over manuscripts. Herman Melville and Charles Dickens complained of editors' changes, and even where relationships between authors and editors were unstrained, manuscripts were greatly changed before publication.

The large British and French publishing companies were models for the rest of Europe in the late nineteenth century. Though German publishing remained decentralized and its major publishers did not grow to the size of their British and French rivals for many decades, German companies operated in a similar manner. By the end of the century modern publishing methods were well under way in western and central Europe. At the same time the competition posed by the pirating of foreign books declined as publishers honored international copyrights.

At the close of the nineteenth century more advanced technologies and industrial organization greatly increased the scale of publishing enterprises. The costs of printing technology escalated, especially because of the complexity of reproducing photographs for print and the use of diverse fonts. Photomechanical polychrome printing, photogravure, and offset printing allowed simpler and faster production of works combining text with image. As a result of the rising costs of printing technologies, the great multitude of presses was reduced and concentrated in the hands of a few large corporations. The status of the mechanical skills of an experienced printer fell dramatically. Even the skills of the owner of great publishing houses, though still important, moved away from aquisition, editing, production, distribution, and sale as owners delegated supervision of these tasks among large staffs. Publishing houses eventually further divided these tasks among branches, each responsible for a different kind of publication.

Publishing, like any other industry, became increasingly routinized. Publishers placed more importance on their editors' abilities to generate a successful list and less on editors' identification of artistic writers. Profits were more the editor's concern in the postwar period, as publishing joined the many businesses controlled by enormous multinational corporations. In West Germany, for example, a dramatic transformation in the 1960s took traditional publishers' emphasis away from great authors and their books and gave it to media conglomerates' mass marketing of diverse genres. Throughout Europe editors' relationships with authors became more distant and more formal in the twentieth century. Editors encouraged authors to conform to standardized plots and characters to insure the success of novels and short stories. Newspaper and magazine journalists, too, adopted standard formulas for their articles.

The growing scale of publishing decreased the unit cost of each print. As a result of declining sales and falling costs in the early twentieth century, publishers marketed books at radically reduced prices. In 1905 slumping sales encouraged the French publishing house Fayard to offer novels for less than one franc with press runs of more than 100,000 copies each.

Popular Books. A popular illustrated book, *The Glorious Knight Antipka: A Humorous Story from Village Life,* published in Moscow in 1914.

Their success greatly expanded novel reading in France. At about the same time British publishers introduced the pulp magazines that sold for a few cents. Pulps offered comics and adventure stories to children, fashion and beauty to women, and a variety of other specialized subjects to diverse reading interests. Magazine reading expanded greatly and further accelerated after World War I.

The severe economic collapse of the postwar period and the Great Depression and the simultaneous development of radio led postwar publishers to create cheap photographic magazines. They offered the visual stimulation that radio lacked to a public eager for sights and texts describing the luxuries of an affluent elite. Though the cheap novel and photomagazine revived publishers' profits in times of general economic decline, reading was losing its place as Europeans' principal means of entertainment. In the late twentieth century television and Internet communication greatly accelerated this trend.

While western European publishers faced falling demand and struggled to market new, cheaper prints at the dawn of the twentieth century, southern, northern, and eastern European printers and publishers experienced dramatic growth. Italian, Spanish, and northern European publishers rapidly expanded publishing at the turn of the century and after. Even in Russia popular book production increased nine times between 1887 and 1912.

Russian publishing was further transformed by the 1917 revolution. Between 1918 and 1919 the Soviet government nationalized and centralized the printing and publishing industries, forming the largest Russian publishers into a single State Publishing House. Publishing in the Soviet Union accelerated rapidly in the 1920s and 1930s but never kept pace with demand. The most significant changes in Soviet publishing came in the 1920s with expansion of publishing for non-Russian nationalities and in the 1930s with the Stalinization of publishing. By further centralizing and increasing the scale of publishing, Stalinization fostered the mass production of books and journals on an unprecedented scale.

East European publishers were unable to expand and modernize their presses until postwar Communist rule. Hungarian publishing, for example, remained small in scale until the postwar period. The nationalization of printing in 1946 and its expansion afterward finally produced a wider availability of newspapers and literary journals in the 1950s. Book production, too, increased notably, including the publication of international best-sellers. By 1984 book production exceeded 100 million copies.

The Stalinization of publishing in East Europe not only increased production but narrowed its titles and reduced its responsiveness to demand. East European publishers promoted works consistent with party ideology rather than those with the greatest appeal. Political censorship was considerable and moral censorship even more so. From the 1960s to the fall of the Communist state, Soviet and East European publishers failed to provide the variety and quantity of publications that their readers demanded.

Mikhail Gorbachev's policy of glasnost significantly reduced censorship, while his policy of perestroika promoted privatization. Together they began a process in the Soviet Union that quickly spread across East Europe. Accelerated by the fall of the Communist government, a more commercialized publishing industry emerged. However, the early transition to a competitive market proved ruinous for publishers who continued to print millions of unwanted books and journals. Falling standards of living further restricted the market, delaying the recovery of East European publishing.

Throughout Europe, as the century progressed, cheap books and serials became less significant to publishing profits, and three other sources of income became more important. Textbook production continued as a source of sizable earnings, especially as public education attendance was enforced more extensively, its duration lengthened, and its quality increased. Libraries generated profits for publishers, especially with the phenomenal growth of free public libraries. Publishers produced a growing number of academic books, printed in smaller numbers and sold at higher prices to private and public libraries. In turn education and libraries promoted the practice of reading that furthered publishers' sales of newspapers, magazines, and books. Finally, publishers looked to printed advertisements as their greatest source of income.

The future of publishing, still a major industry, is an open question in the twenty-first century. With great advancements in computer memory storage and the development of the Internet, many experts have predicted the disappearance of most prints in their twentieth-century forms. The impact this will have on the industry remains uncertain.

See also other articles in this section.

BIBLIOGRAPHY

Altick, Richard Daniel. *The English Common Reader: A Social History of the Mass Reading Public, 1800–1900.* Chicago, 1957.

Anderson, Patricia. *The Printed Image and the Transformation of Popular Culture 1790–1860.* Oxford, 1991.

Bellanger, Claude, et. al. *Histoire générale de la presse française.* Paris, 1969.

Booher, Edward E. "Publishing: The USSR and Yugoslavia." *Annals of the American Academy of Political and Social Science* 421 (1975): 118–129.

Brooks, Jeffrey. *When Russia Learned to Read: Literacy and Popular Literature, 1861–1917.* Princeton, N.J., 1985.

Carpenter, Kenneth E., ed. *Books and Society in History.* New York, 1983.

Censer, Jack R., and Jeremy D. Popkin, eds. *Press and Politics in Pre-Revolutionary France.* Berkeley, Calif., 1987.

Chappell, Warren. *A Short History of the Printed Word.* New York, 1970.

Chartier, Roger. *The Cultural Uses of Print in Early Modern France.* Translated by Lydia G. Cochrane. Princeton, N.J., 1987.

Chartier, Roger, ed. *The Culture of Print: Power and the Uses of Print in Early Modern Europe.* Translated by Lydia G. Cochrane. Princeton, N.J., 1989.

Darnton, Robert. *The Great Cat Massacre and Other Episodes in French Cultural History.* New York, 1984.

Darnton, Robert. *The Literary Underground of the Old Regime.* Cambridge, Mass., 1982.

Darnton, Robert, and Daniel Roche, eds. *Revolution in Print: The Press in France, 1775–1800.* Berkeley, Calif., 1989.

Dinerstein, E. A. "Soviet Publishing: Some Historical Landmarks in Soviet Russia." *Publishing History* 35 (1994): 65–80.

Dooley, Allan C. *Author and Printer in Victorian England.* Charlottesville, Va., 1992.

Edwards, Mark U., Jr. *Printing, Propaganda, and Martin Luther.* Berkeley, Calif., 1994.

Eisenstein, Elizabeth L. *The Printing Revolution in Early Modern Europe.* Cambridge, U.K., 1983.

Febvre, Lucien, and Henri-Jean Martin. *The Coming of the Book: The Impact of Printing 1450–1800.* Translated by David Gerard. London, 1976.

Lovell, Stephen. "Publishing and the Book Trade in the Post-Stalin Era: A Case Study of the Commodification of Culture." *Europe-Asia Studies* 50, no. 4 (1998): 679–698.

Martin, Henri-Jean. *The History and Power of Writing.* Translated by Lydia G. Cochrane. Chicago, 1984.

McAleer, Joseph. "Scenes from Love and Marriage: Mills and Boon and the Popular Publishing Industry in Britain, 1908–1950." *Twentieth Century British History* 1, no. 3 (1990): 264–288.

Neuburg, Victor E. *Popular Literature: A History and Guide from the Beginning of Printing to the Year 1897.* New York, 1977.

Ong, Walter J. *Orality and Literacy: The Technologizing of the Word.* New York, 1982.

Rectanus, Mark W. "Literary Publishing in the Federal Republic of Germany: Redefining the Enterprise." *German Studies Review* 10, no. 1 (1987): 95–123.

Spufford, Margaret. *Small Books and Pleasant Histories: Popular Fiction and its Readership in Seventeenth-Century England.* London, 1981.

Stark, Gary D. "Publishers and Cultural Patronage in Germany, 1890–1933." *German Studies Review* 1, no. 1 (1978): 56–71.

Sutherland, J.A. *Victorian Novelists and Publishers.* Chicago, 1976

LITERACY

R. A. Houston

At the end of the fifteenth century in Europe literacy of any kind was rare. Among the laity, the ability to read, write, and count was restricted to a small minority of wealthy, town-dwelling men. As late as 1800 no European country could claim that half its population could read and write. In most regions complete, if basic, literacy was still confined to town-dwelling men of middling status or above. Around 1900, however, many parts of Europe had achieved mass literacy. Perhaps 85–90 percent of adults were deemed to be literate in Britain, France, Germany, and much of Scandinavia. That success created an enormous cultural gulf in Europe, for in huge tracts of the east and south even the rudiments of reading and writing were denied to a majority of the population. Figure 1 and the map below show this development in different ways.

By the start of the twenty-first century literacy was regarded as a birthright, while illiteracy was seen as a personal shame and a national disgrace. This chapter looks at the timing, location, and social distribution of this change from restricted to mass literacy. It also explores more qualitative dimensions such as the reasons for and uses of literacy. Throughout, the acquisition and exercise of literacy in its different forms is understood in its social context, for the spread of literacy across space and time was determined by a complex interaction of factors such as wealth and social status, residence, cultural assumptions about gender roles, language, and religion.

Literacy is made up of several communication skills, which are best seen as bands in a spectrum rather than discrete categories. *Reading* of print or writing was possible at two levels. Some people could decipher texts, read them aloud, and memorize them in a mechanical or ritual way—although their personal understanding may have been questionable. We should not exaggerate the understanding and facility of those who possessed this intermediate or semiliteracy. Those with better education and a deeper immersion in printed and written culture could com-

prehend the text with greater precision, reading and thinking silently to themselves. They could understand new texts as well as familiar ones. However, "reading" was not restricted to written or printed words alone. People could gather information and ideas from *looking:* interpreting pictures and prints in broadsheets and pamphlets or watching and participating in plays and processions. Gesture remained a subtle and important form of nonverbal communication.

If they wanted to transmit their own thoughts other than through speech, people had to learn to *write,* or rather compose—an advanced skill that required considerable training and practice, and which effectively marked "full" literacy for most people. The other, more common, level of writing was in fact copying: writing without necessarily understanding. It was at this stage that people learned to sign their names on documents, and this ability is commonly used as an indicator that someone could read and understand printed and written texts in the vernacular, the language of everyday life. In other words, he or she was well along the road to "full" literacy. A small minority of men could also copy or compose in Latin, the international language of learning throughout the Middle Ages and the early modern period, or in another (later) pan-European language like French. Even those who had none of these skills were not culturally isolated for they could *listen*—hear a priest's sermons or a friend reading aloud, participate actively or passively in discussions with their peers. Associated with literacy is *numeracy,* which again covers a spectrum of skills from simple counting of objects to sophisticated accounting and complex mathematical calculations.

Since 1500, both reading and writing have increased in significance, sometimes simultaneously, sometimes independently; sometimes at the expense of oral and visual forms of communication, sometimes in tandem with them. The way to understand literacy in historic Europe is to assess the changing access which people had to the different bands in the spectrum and the ways they used them.

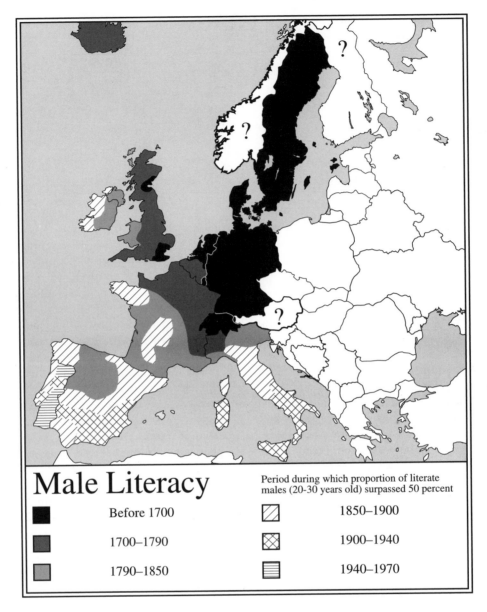

Male Literacy

Period during which proportion of literate males (20-30 years old) surpassed 50 percent

	Before 1700		1850–1900
	1700–1790		1900–1940
	1790–1850		1940–1970

Map 1.

PATTERNS

It was as late as 1995 that the first generally accepted comparison of international adult literacy attainments was published by the Paris-based Organization for Economic Cooperation and Development (OECD). The European countries included were Germany, Netherlands, Poland, Sweden, and Switzerland. Based on rigorous, direct, and standardized observations and tests, the study distinguished prose, document, and quantitative literacy, dividing each category into five levels of attainment. Social historians can touch on prose literacy (reports on, or summaries of, tests of reading ability) or elements of document literacy (signing), but quantitative historical studies of numeracy are absent. The social and geographical distribution of historic literacy is relatively easy to demonstrate using the "universal, standard, and direct" measure of ability to sign one's name in full on a document such as a court deposition, a contract, or a marriage certificate. Before the nineteenth century, reading is much harder to measure directly, but various indirect measures such as school provision or book production and ownership can be used. Until then, virtually all sources cover adults rather than children. Uniquely, the Lutheran churches of Scandinavia kept

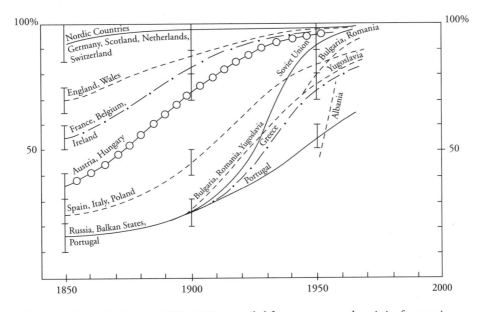

Figure 1. Literacy in Europe, 1850–1970, compiled from censuses and statistics for recruits, convicts, and signatures for bridal couples. Source: Johansson, *History of Literacy,* p. 72.

registers of reading and religious knowledge from the end of the seventeenth century. The Scandinavian example is a warning that comparison over time and place is rendered problematic by the many different sources and criteria of historic "literacy" used by churches, governments, social scientists, and historians. The figures given below may appear precise, but they are sometimes no more than broad indicators of different cultural achievements.

Fortunately, both direct and indirect indicators of literacy generally point in the same direction. Male achievements were superior to female, those of the rich to those of the poor; urban dwellers were almost invariably better able to write than peasants; Protestant areas of Europe tended to have higher literacy than Catholic. Expansion occurred first among the middling and upper classes, among men, and in towns. In northern England the illiteracy of the gentry fell from about 30 percent in 1530 to almost nil in 1600, but that of day laborers stayed well above 90 percent and did not fall substantially until the eighteenth and nineteenth centuries. Classified by economic activity, agricultural workers come lowest in the European hierarchy, industrial workers next, slightly inferior to commercial and service occupations, followed by professionals and landowners. Differences between the sexes were pronounced and enduring. A quarter of Amsterdam grooms marrying around 1730 could not sign the register compared with half of brides. In southern Europe sex was more important than status or residence in determining

achievements. Between 1540 and 1600 in the Spanish archdiocese of Toledo, 30 percent of town-dwelling men could not sign compared with 93 percent of women; the rural figures were 48 percent and 98 percent. In areas such as southern France, where the faiths coexisted after the Reformation, Protestant literacy was generally higher than Catholic until the eighteenth century. In other parts of Europe it remained so. Catholic illiteracy in Ireland fell from 46 percent in 1861 to 16 percent in 1901, but it remained higher than Protestant. Even among other apparently homogeneous social groups there were pronounced variations across Europe. Convicted criminals are an example. One English prisoner in three was wholly illiterate in the early 1840s. In contrast, "the intelligentsia of the criminal world" were the Germans, with fewer than one in fifty unable to read and write around 1860.

To these gradients can be added a bold geographical summary. If Europe was homogeneous in terms of its restricted literacy at the end of the Middle Ages, it had three massive cultural zones by the end of the nineteenth century: a literate, economically developed (and largely Protestant) north; a center with pronounced regional variations, notably France; and a less literate, underdeveloped (Catholic and Orthodox) south and east. The 1900 distribution was itself the result of four centuries of more robust advances in literacy in the northern parts of Europe than elsewhere. Within this broad-brush picture lay numerous local variations. A single English county at

TABLE 1
PERCENT UNABLE TO SIGN BY ESTATE (REGION)

Date	Fraugdegård (Funen)	Fussing (Jutland)	Lindenborg (Jutland)
1719–1725	92	88	78
1726–1750	88	62	57
1751–1775	90	24	31
1776–1800	87	7	11
1801–1825	65	26	32
1856–1850	33	29	26

the time of the mid-seventeenth-century Civil Wars might contain villages with proportions of literate men four times higher than others. Pronounced regional variations were reduced during the eighteenth and nineteenth century in some parts of Europe. However, this long-term trend disguises some astounding differences in the timing of change. Table 1 shows the percentage of Danish manorial peasants unable to sign their copyhold documents, 1719–1850. The dramatic improvement in signing ability on the northern, Jutland estates during the eighteenth century created a huge gulf in literacy between them and the Fraugdegård estate near Odense, which was not bridged until the middle of the nineteenth century. Similarly pronounced regional variations are found across northern Germany around 1800.

The pace of change was everywhere hesitant and irregular. At the time of Italian unification, analysis of the *censimento* or national census shows that 81 percent of females aged six years or older were illiterate, as were 68 percent of males. In absolute numbers that meant 17 out of 23 million inhabitants. Illiteracy was similarly prevalent in Spain at that date with figures of 81 percent and 63 percent respectively. Even in countries like Italy, where literacy did not advance rapidly before 1800, achievements since 1850 have been considerable. For every 100 illiterate females in 1861 there were just 5 in 1981. However, change has also generated some unexpected side effects. Whereas in 1861 illiteracy was evenly divided between males and females in Italy, by 1981 there were two illiterate women for every man.

The painfully slow pace of change and the late arrival of mass literacy finds its most extreme example in Portugal. Of those over seven years of age in 1890, 76 percent were illiterate, falling only slightly to 74 percent in 1900 and 70 percent in 1911. The figure was still 68 percent in 1930 and it was not until the 1940s that more than half of Portugal's population could read and write: two centuries after the most favored areas had passed that threshold. Portugal's 30 percent illiteracy in 1968 was the highest in Europe. Other peripheral zones were deeply illiterate well into the twentieth century. Greek men were 71 percent illiterate in 1870 compared with 36 percent in 1928; the respective figures for women are 94 percent and 64 percent. Levels of literacy were similarly low throughout the Balkans. In 1880, 90 percent of Dalmatia's people were illiterate and, as in southern Italy, towns were little better in this respect than the countryside.

The patterns outlined above are sometimes complex and varied, but the overall distribution and progress of writing ability is clear. Yet in many parts of Europe before the late nineteenth century reading was taught before writing. Given the discontinuous and brief training most children received (spending no more than two or three years in usually part-time schooling), it would be surprising if reading were not more widespread than the easily measurable ability to sign. For example, a case has been made that Lowland Scotland had near-universal reading by the mid-eighteenth century. The only convincing statistics are based on the Swedish *hustavla,* or registers of the Lutheran church's household literacy campaign. By c.1780 in Sweden and Iceland, male and female, young and old, rich and poor alike were almost all able to pass the Lutheran churches' tests. Signing ability was confined to less than 10 percent: largely town-dwelling males. As late as 1921, 30 percent of Finland's people could not read *and* write—an achievement inferior to Italy's. It is argued that the "Scandinavian pattern" may be more extensive, and that between c.1500 and c.1900 Europe comprised two zones: one where reading and writing were taught together; the other where reading alone was taught, this including many areas of Germany and a large part of southern and northwestern France as well as Scandinavia.

Tacitly or overtly, studies that show apparently extensive reading suggest that the breadth of cultural access in early-modern Europe was much broader than the signing statistics imply. The problem here lies with the nature of the reading that people did. It was normally religious and based principally on rote learning and recognition of well-known passages. Indeed, as late as 1750 one authority assigns critical reading ability in the German lands to just 10 percent of the population. Another reports that fewer than 5 percent of the men in the region of Arras and St. Omer in northern France were reckoned "well educated" in surveys conducted in 1802 and 1804. Subjective as such assessments are, they indicate the restricted impact that literate media could have had on ordinary people who were ostensibly "readers." Nevertheless, we must be alert to the possibility that reading was more widespread than writing, especially in certain parts of Europe and among certain social groups: poorer men and most women.

Females generally had less chance to learn writing than males. An investigation of 3,036 women aged above 20 years living in part of northern Italy in 1854 showed that just 410 could read and write though 1,103 could only read. It was not till the 1860s and 1870s that women began to approach complete literacy in this part of Italy. The existence of social forms that privileged visual, spoken, and sung communication (such as the French *veillée* or evening gathering), and which were dominated by ordinary women, suggests that their cultural lives continued to be cast in an oral/aural and visual framework.

There are prominent exceptions. Women of the eighteenth-century French and English upper-bourgeois and landed classes (and especially unmarried ones it seems) read periodicals and novels; used circulating libraries; joined reading societies; attended the theater and concerts; collected prints and bought paintings. Women seem to have been a crucial component of the anticipated audience for Enlightenment literature. Yet we should not exaggerate the social penetration of extensive female literacy. Book ownership of the kind recorded in *post mortem* inventories was growing during the eighteenth century (notably in France, Germany, and England), but it remained principally the preserve of middling and upper-class males.

If reading was almost certainly much more extensive than writing, elementary numeracy was probably ubiquitous. Even in the Middle Ages, one test of basic mental capacity was the ability to count to ten. However, formal accounting skills were much more restricted. Though written numeration had been known in the Latin west for several centuries, and paper was in general use, the abacus with counters was still often used in the seventeenth and even in the eighteenth centuries. The celebrated mathematician Leibniz used one. Roman and Arabic numerals coexisted (as did Gothic and Latin type or script), but there is also evidence across Europe of "peasant numerals"—symbols which represented numbers that may derive from roman numerals, but which are distinctive. As an advanced skill in the school curriculum and one more often learned as an adult for economic purposes, higher-grade numeracy probably progressed at the same rate as writing. There are no quantitative studies, but age reporting in documents shows growing precision and reliability in the eighteenth and nineteenth centuries, a fact which may indicate populations who were increasingly conversant with numbers.

EXPLANATIONS

Explaining these patterns and trends requires analysis of the central social, political, and economic relationships in historic Europe. The chances of being educated and of acquiring literacy depended on a wide variety of factors: wealth, sex, projected job opportunities and work experience, school provision and costs, community structures, employments for children, the power of landowners, access to literate media and the opportunities to use them, and even the language a person spoke in everyday life.

Schooling. Literacy and schooling naturally went hand in hand. For example, the German duchy of Württemberg had 89 schools in 1520 compared with over 400 by 1600, and across Germany in this period many rulers issued ordinances providing for or regulating elementary education. Catholics too expanded education. The first "school of Christian doctrine" was opened at Milan in 1536 to teach children the essentials of the Catholic faith. There were 28 such schools by 1564 and more than 120 in 1599. Postelementary education also expanded. Perhaps 1,000 new grammar schools were established in England, 1480–1660. Thus we find rapidly expanding literacy for some social groups in late-sixteenth- and early-seventeenth-century England, the German lands, and in the towns of northern Italy. Much of early-modern Europe truly experienced an "educational revolution."

The case of Italy shows the importance of schools in a later age. In the mid-nineteenth century 80 percent of children aged 6 to 12 years were at school in Savoy (later annexed by France) compared with just 9 percent in Sardinia. Small wonder that illiteracy among adult males was just 50 percent in the former provinces compared with 90 percent in the latter. In one southern province, Nuoro, only 337 of 61,479 women above the age of 20 years could read and write. Using broadly defined regions, proportions in school in the north of Italy grew from 67 percent in 1863 to 85 percent in 1901; figures for the central provinces are 28 percent and 50 percent respectively (incidentally, almost identical to Greece between these dates); for the south 22 percent and 44 percent.

Yet, until well into the twentieth century the vast majority of children anywhere in Europe could expect to receive only a few years of training in the rudiments of reading and writing. Children were contributors to the family budget from an early age in northwestern Europe until the nineteenth century, and until the twentieth century in the south and east. For them, leaving school might as easily mark the start of learning functional literacy rather than its culmination, for literacy has to be practiced as well as learned. As we chart the development of mass literacy we should also recall that schools became central to the acquisition of skills only by 1850 at the earliest. In Sweden, until 1858 the authorities assumed that children would have been taught to read at home; only after this did junior schools take over the tasks of basic education. The Nordic countries (notably Iceland and Norway) and some of the more thinly populated mountain and steppe regions of Europe relied on mobile teachers following a circuit until well into the twentieth century. As early as the eighteenth century, mountain regions of Austria like Tyrol or Vorarlberg seem to have had high literacy, but few schools. Fixed schools began to be common in the rural villages of Russia only in the decades following the emancipation of the peasantry in 1861. The total number of primary schools grew from 8 thousand in 1856 to 25 thousand in 1879 and then 100 thousand by 1911, the initiative coming from *zemstvos* (local authorities), the church, and the education ministry equally. The number of pupils rose from 450 thousand to 6.6 million between 1856 and 1911.

For all its importance, schooling was neither the only nor always the most significant cause of changes in literacy. Modern readers who live in states with powerful governments will be struck by how the progress of literacy in the nineteenth century was largely independent of major political events or, for that matter, educational legislation. From the sixteenth to the twentieth century, educational legislation was normally designed to consolidate, standardize, and enable rather than to innovate. Before the nineteenth century no European country had a school "system," but instead dozens of sometimes competing, sometimes complementary schools, which were organized and funded in different ways. Even major political upheavals like the French Revolution did little in the short term to change institutions or alter trends in literacy. By the time the republican statesman Jules Ferry realized the Revolutionary aspiration for free,

secular, and compulsory education in 1882, France was already a literate nation.

Religion and wealth. However slowly and hesitantly, literacy was increasing. Did the expansion favor Protestants more than Catholics? Protestantism is commonly described as "the religion of the book." Indeed, a glance at map 1 shows the enduring legacy of the sixteenth-century Reformation. The extensive literacy of the Dutch and Lowland Scots in the eighteenth century stands alongside their commitment to Calvinism. The Catholic conservatism of rural France, Poland, or Spain cannot be divorced from deep illiteracy. Was it simply a question of faith? In the north of Ireland during the seventeenth century Protestant farmers were better able to sign their names than Catholic ones, but they were also richer and lived in less remote areas. The point here is that Protestants and Catholics were not distributed equally among all sections of society. In seventeenth-century Poland virtually all the Calvinist minority were either nobles or town-dwellers. Crude divisions between faiths often break down under examination. Ability to sign was as common in staunchly Catholic northeastern France as it was in strongly Protestant England at the end of the seventeenth century. In France and Germany the differences between Protestant and Catholic were less in 1750 than in 1650.

Despite the hothouse atmosphere surrounding it, the early years of the Reformation saw only gradual improvements in literacy, which followed on from fifteenth-century developments and which were not unique to Protestantism. Seventeenth-century achievements were more substantial. The campaign to promote religious literacy in Sweden produced remarkable results in less than a century, widespread literacy being used to consolidate rather than cause religious change. In Denmark and Prussia, on the other hand, it was not the Lutheran Reformation of the sixteenth or seventeenth century that brought about widespread literacy, but the early-eighteenth-century campaign waged by the Pietists with the help of the new "absolutist" rulers.

No more than schools did the competing churches work in a cultural vacuum. Powerful economic, social, and political forces continued to influence literacy levels. The Protestant Vaucluse had lower literacy in the early nineteenth century than the Catholic province of Baden, the reason being that the German region had more communal property and could thus subsidize schooling. Indeed, on closer inspection, it is plain that across Europe factors other than religion entered into the equation. In the 1870s German Catholics were more accomplished than those of Ireland, who were in turn more literate than Italians. High Italian illiteracy cannot be divorced from its economic performance, for not until the 1930s were more than half the population employed outside agriculture. Religion was only one of many social, economic, and political forces that influenced the distribution of literacy.

The Italian and Irish examples just cited point to a connection between wealth and literacy at both an individual and a communal level. The most literate *départements* of nineteenth-century France were the prosperous open-field ones to the north and east of an imaginary line drawn between St. Malo and Geneva. Townspeople were more literate than rural dwellers because they were wealthier and followed occupations that required reading, writing, and counting. Illiteracy had been almost eradicated by 1700 among London's male merchants and artisans: a remarkable achievement.

Urbanization.

There is a connection between urbanization and literacy, but some cities were much more literate than others. Paris in 1850 was far superior to Naples, as London was to Madrid. Furthermore, some rapidly industrializing cities of northern England, northeastern France and northern Germany in the early nineteenth century saw literacy rates decline as overcrowding stretched the social fabric. The more general relationship between economy and literacy also involved positive and negative feedbacks. Literacy may serve to enhance a nation's economic performance, but it is also clear that growth (and political will) is needed to create and distribute the resources to fund the cost and opportunity cost of educating children, especially at the elementary level.

Urban children were likely to attend school longer than their rural cousins. When education was not compulsory, girls were taken away from school earlier than boys. The Russian school census of 1911 allows us to calculate the likelihood of a child attending school for a given period. Some 88 percent of boys would attend for a year compared with 52 percent of girls. But the chance that a boy would complete three years in school was just 39 percent and only 8 percent for a girl. In these circumstances, most functional literacy and other skills were picked up later in life. It was only in the late nineteenth century that regular and extended school attendance became a central part of growing up for British children and not until after 1945 in Eastern and southern Europe. A principal effect of this development was to fix childhood as a definable stage of life and as a social concept. Similarly, in the West, the expansion of secondary and tertiary provision after the World Wars respectively

has helped to create modern notions of "youth" and "youth culture" with, among other attributes, distinctive tastes in printed media.

Gender.

The Russian case is an extreme example of a common pattern. Males were educated to participate in the public sphere, females in the private or domestic one. This usually meant that girls gained religious knowledge, learned to read, and were given practical instruction in home-focused skills. In the Mediterranean lands, where gender roles were firmly delineated, it was long held to be positively undesirable to train girls in more than the rudiments of religion, reading, and housewifery. The legacy of such negative attitudes toward female education in those areas is clear in women's deep illiteracy well into the twentieth century. Such views are summed up in a French peasant's comment that girls in his canton (Quercy) had been taught to read, but not write, because the nuns did not want them penning love letters to their sweethearts. Reading was seen by educators as a passive skill. Writing enabled (among other things) unsupervised, long-distance communication and gave access to a different cultural world independent of teachers, pastors, family, and neighbors. Little wonder that secondary education for girls was not a serious subject of debate, let alone action, anywhere in Europe until the mid-nineteenth century—after 1868 in Spain, for example. Postelementary education for girls was only formalized in Britain from the 1850s. Previously, the daughters of the rich had been educated at home by governesses. Writing ability among women began to take off at the end of the nineteenth century in Scandinavia as they were drawn into teaching, clerical, postal, and service jobs. Even then, censorious attitudes toward educated women persisted among some sections of public opinion. Simply being literate was not always enough to transcend social conventions.

Because many women could only read, they did not have direct access to the full spectrum of literate culture. Worse, the growing dominance of written and printed forms in late-nineteenth-century Europe involved simultaneously devaluing the oral traditions of women and the elderly of both sexes, social groups who were commonly left behind in periods of rapidly advancing literacy. However, the presence of informal cultural intermediaries meant illiterates were never wholly isolated from the world of print and writing. Inability to decipher letters and words did not preclude access to the products of literacy. In the city factories and in the squares of small towns and villages of early-twentieth-century Spain and Portugal, newspapers might be read aloud by one person to anyone who cared to listen. Varieties of oral tradition survive

A Public Reader. Reading aloud from *La Feuille Villageoise* (The village news sheet), engraving (1777) by Clément-Pierre Marillier (1740–1808). BIBLIOTHÈQUE NATIONALE DE FRANCE, PARIS

in the mainstream until today, complementing rather than substituting for these traditions.

Linguistic variety. Intermediaries might bridge the gap between literate and oral culture, but the possibilities that literacy could open up usually depended on an individual possessing it for him or her self. In assessing why some areas or populations were less accomplished than others, it is hard to exaggerate how important linguistic variety could be. If education and writing or publishing were conducted in a language different from that of everyday life, literacy tended to suffer. Italy had had a relatively uniform written lan-

guage since the late Middle Ages, but a great diversity of spoken tongues: just 2.5 percent of Italy's population spoke "Italian" (Tuscan) with any fluency in 1861. Four-fifths of the inhabitants of Wales were habitual Welsh speakers as late as the 1880s, while at least a fifth of the population of France did not speak "French" (*langue d'oeil*) in 1863. It is no accident that the corners of France where Breton, Basque, and Occitan (*langue d'oc*) were the languages of everyday life were also the least literate in the eighteenth and nineteenth centuries.

Gaelic-speaking parts of the British Isles generally lagged far behind the advancing literacy of

English-speaking areas. The west of Ireland is an example. Roughly 55–60 percent of Ireland's people born in the 1770s spoke only Irish. Three quarters of those in the 12 counties of Munster, Connacht, and Donegal (with 45 percent of the population) were Irish speakers at the end of the eighteenth century compared with just 10 percent in the remaining 20 counties with 55 percent of Ireland's people. Irish speaking was low and literacy probably high in northeast Ireland even in the early eighteenth century because of the prevalence of English-speaking Presbyterians, many of them of Scots origin or descent. This example reminds us that language is not the whole explanation of literacy trends. Different religious priorities, a more balanced wealth distribution and greater aggregate prosperity in this region also contributed.

Irish was an oral and manuscript language, writing being confined to a very small learned class (almost a caste) in the sixteenth and seventeenth century. English possessed these attributes, but it was also a printed language and the medium of education. During the eighteenth century printed literature for Irish speakers was developed (albeit slowly) by Dublin publishers using a phonetic spelling based on English language orthography. This helped bring about growing English language literacy, but it also contributed to the decline of spoken and written Irish because print-literacy in Irish was secured through English, even for Irish speakers. There were almost no secular works printed in Irish during the eighteenth century and very few religious ones. Other parts of the so-called "Celtic fringe" experienced different fortunes. From the mid-seventeenth century, northwestern French Catholics used printed religious literature in Breton to further the Counter-Reformation, thus fueling the development of reading and writing in the language of everyday speech. Breton was not the language of education, but it was part of everyday religious life and this helped secure higher levels of literacy. Welsh became more deeply embedded as a literate language for this reason too, and because there was more literature available. There was a full Welsh Bible in 1588 and three thousand works printed prior to 1820 compared with fewer than two hundred in Irish. In the southern Low Countries at the end of the eighteenth century illiteracy was higher along linguistic frontiers and in mixed areas. However, the context here was also created by a legacy of ecclesiastical conflict and political fracture, which made education and literacy a weapon as much as a prize.

The state. Since 1500 Europe has seen the retreat of dialects and of separate languages like Gaelic, turning some from majority into minority tongues. Even in the late twentieth century, Europe had a sort of "fault line" between the speakers of Romance languages like French and Italian, and Teutonic ones like German (or its dialects like Alsatian). The influence over time of the state and of printed and later electronic media has been to standardize language as, say, French or German, leaving only the older generation speaking dialect variations. Attempts to revive regional dialects, suppressed or surrendered through political and economic change between the sixteenth and eighteenth centuries, began in the early nineteenth century. A Provençal revival led to the foundation in 1854 of the *Félibrige*—a society of regional poets who sought to codify and purify Occitan and to restore its usage by promoting it in literary works. Such movements remained uncommon compared with the late twentieth century. Gaelic was the first language of perhaps 50 percent of Scots around 1400, 30 percent in 1689, but just 20 percent in 1806. Gaelic-speaking

English Lesson in Scotland. Gaelic-speaking children in the Hebrides are taught English at school as a foreign language. As the islands become less isolated from the rest of Scotland, fluency in English becomes increasingly important.
©HULTON GETTY/ARCHIVE PHOTOS

in the Highlands of Scotland continued to decline throughout the nineteenth century as monoglots recognized the powerful advantages to be gained from literacy in English. At the end of the twentieth century, Gaelic in modern Scotland was spoken by just two percent of the population (most of them in the urbanized region of Strathclyde), having being artificially resuscitated in the guise of an independent "national" language—although it was never spoken by all Scots, even in the Middle Ages.

In the historical case of the *Félibrige,* language was used to assert particularism, in the modern case of Gaelic, nationalism. Historically, it was more often an alien imposition designed to create a "national" identity. For example, German was forcibly reintroduced as the language of government and teaching in the Hungarian lands from 1849–1867 following earlier efforts to Magyarize the country. From the 1880s a revived campaign used Magyar in elementary schools while secondary schools taught "national consciousness." The country's 92 teacher-training colleges used Magyar exclusively. However, this was not just against the German-speaking Austrian empire, but was also done at the expense of Rumanians, Ruthenes, and Slovaks. The effect was slow to be felt. Around 1880, 14 percent of Hungarians spoke Magyar and 23 percent in 1910 but, significantly, 90 percent of university students. Modern Swiss cantons allow the local majority the right to dictate the language used in courts and schools, but it is harder to learn in a language that is not used in everyday discourse. Both the modern Swiss example and the Hungarian one of the late nineteenth century were seen by some minorities as not only hindering literacy, but also as an unwelcome form of "linguistic cleansing."

However robust the generalizations about language and literacy, neither linguistic pluralism nor the spread of a dominant tongue necessarily meant low or only slowly improving literacy. German was the vernacular in the Alagna region north of Turin (near the modern Swiss frontier) until relegated to the home by the spread of Italian during the nineteenth century. The region also suffered other apparent disadvantages such as few settled schools and a dispersed, largely agricultural population. Yet, more than four-fifths of confraternity members, albeit from a privileged section of society, who subscribed a document in 1781 did so with their full names. The need of inhabitants of the Alpine foothills to migrate seasonally in order to find work and their location in an interstitial zone helped foster demand for multilingual literacy. In contested regions that frequently changed hands between the sixteenth and the nineteenth centuries—northern Italy is one example, Lithuania another—the languages of public affairs and education might change more than once in a generation. Overlying this were more enduring cultural relations with a single culture such as German. Ecclesiastical visitations of the seventeenth and eighteenth centuries revealed extensive possession of books in German and of manuscript (heretical) religious works. A long, heretically based tradition of vernacular literacy in manuscript and print may also help to explain the phenomenon, notably in the former Waldensian areas of northern Italy. Certainly, the Alagna district seems to have been unusually literate in the eighteenth century, the statistics backed up by contemporary comment. However, the advantages were selective, for high male literacy could coexist with low female, even in an area so apparently well-favored. In subscribed marriage registers, beginning in the 1840s, nearly all grooms could sign, but less than half of brides.

USES AND IMPLICATIONS

Being able to use a pen or decipher letters and words on a page opens up new possibilities. Literacy has economic and cultural uses, the latter including recreational and religious dimensions. The quantity of books grew from the Renaissance onward, and qualitative changes in their uses occurred, notably in the eighteenth century. Until the latter period, reading involved an intensive perusal of a small number of texts; thereafter readers sought out multiple titles and novel subjects. However, mass literacy does not necessarily mean the widespread functional use of literacy. For the majority of early-nineteenth-century Europeans, the literacy they possessed was a blunt tool, quite insufficient to reshape their lives. In western Europe as late as 1900 the ability to read and write fluently was confined to town-dwelling men of middle class status or above. Furthermore, while literacy potentially offered a singular commodity, the ways in which people related to its products were emphatically plural. Reading, as much as writing, was a creative process which involved selective appropriation.

Germany had businesses that typeset, printed, and sold books and pamphlets in most major towns by 1520, producing an unprecedented outpouring—perhaps 300 thousand copies of Luther's writings, 1517–1520. From the dawn of the Reformation new religious ideas were available to the reading public. By 1530 perhaps 4 thousand pamphlet titles had been produced in Germany and over the sixteenth century as many as 200 million copies may have been turned out Europe-wide. They could be bought from publishers or shops and stalls in towns, from itinerant peddlers in the countryside. For all faiths religious titles made up the bulk of books owned until the Enlightenment. Across southwest Germany, works of modern literature were largely to be found in the libraries of the upper classes. Even in the closing decades of the eighteenth century, no more than a fifth of books owned by people from Tübingen had an obviously secular tone and in the Württemberg village of Laichingen the figure was close to zero; more than a half of books owned were spiritually oriented. Book ownership was largely informed by the Lutheran revivalist movement called Pietism rather than by Enlightenment precepts. This does not mean that change was not occurring, for it may be that eighteenth-century people were more interested in devotions and meditations on practical morality rather than on old-style divinity.

More obvious changes, like secularization, that were associated with new developments in thought can nevertheless be detected in book collections. Pious books made up nearly half those owned at death in nine western French towns around 1700, compared with less than 30 percent in 1789. Another aspect of changing tastes was the new value placed on originality and novelty. The real growth area in reading material was not the staple texts, which people perused closely, but the more varied, ephemeral, and entertaining fare that was becoming available. Between 1700 and 1789 there were published 1,200 French-language periodicals of at least one year's duration. History and travel books became more popular. Also in France, pornography became a mature genre.

While the fully literate indulged themselves in its novelties, the semiliterate remained within their traditional mental world. In his autobiography, Goethe recounted childhood memories of enjoying a chapbook literature of magic, chivalry, and saints, which had changed little for centuries. Educational reformers were not slow to condemn the youthful preferences exemplified by Goethe. Whatever their faith in literacy (some argued that the poor should not be educated lest they got ideas above their station), its advocates from Luther onward can be found bemoaning the uses to which people put its products. It was cheap recreational pamphlets of perhaps thirty pages, known collectively as the *bibliothèque bleue* after the blue paper used as binding, which provided mass reading in France between the seventeenth and nineteenth centuries. Russian peasants who read newspapers in the 1890s were interested mainly in sensational events like wars or natural curiosities. The poet Matvei Ivanovich Ozhegov (1860–1933) wrote of peasant readers being interested only in "the news of the evils of the day or about the birth of a dog with twenty heads." Saints' lives remained the most popular mass-commercially-produced reading in early-twentieth-century Russia, long after more secular items had taken their place in the west. Yet, reading tastes were changing, as shown by the explosion in detective and adventure stories after the 1905 Revolution and of "women's novels" from the 1910s. The lesson here is that making people literate is one thing, controlling what they do with their abilities is quite another. Most people used their literacy primarily for recreation. In the 1970s a tenth of Russia's population never read a newspaper and a fifth hardly ever read books. For those who did, the focus on practical and escapist literature of a century ago remains, a pattern replicated in the west.

By the end of the Napoleonic wars the population of the urbanized provinces of Holland had come within easy reach of books and newspapers, even if most readers still preferred almanacs, chapbooks, and broadsheets. In contrast, rapid growth in the volume of novels and newspapers did not begin in Finland until the 1880s and 1890s. Norwegian postal subscriptions to such materials grew from 11 million items a year in 1880 to 56 million by 1900—this in a country where reading had supposedly been universal for over a century. Even then, the reading public for serious literature and current affairs was restricted to the prosperous urban middle and upper classes. Norway had 185 public libraries in 1837, but roughly 300 by 1860, almost all in small towns. In late-nineteenth-century France and Germany too, most subscribers to books and periodicals were townspeople and it is unlikely that most rural dwellers saw reading and writing as central parts of their economic, social, or cultural lives before the twentieth century. Literacy surely created the potential for increased cultural participation, but it could take a long time to be realized.

People were using their literacy more extensively as the nineteenth century progressed. All the journals printed in Paris in 1840 amounted to 3 million copies, but by 1882 44 million were being produced. Table 2, based on the *Statistique Générale du Service Postal*, gives the number of stamped letters and postcards sent per head of population in selected European countries in 1886 and 1900. This is not purely an indicator of the use of literacy because the density and reliability of the postal network also played its part. The German imperial postal service had already developed quite extensively by the mid-seventeenth century, but competition from the posts of individual states produced an increasingly dense and frequent (if no quicker) network thereafter. Two points are clear, however: first, in almost all of Europe, increased letter sending; second, the marked differences between the "core" coun-

TABLE 2
NUMBER OF STAMPED LETTERS AND POSTCARDS SENT PER HEAD OF POPULATION

	1886	*1900*
Belgium	17	26
France	15	22
Germany	20	44
Great Britain	45	67
Greece	2	2
Italy	6	12
Netherlands	18	26
Portugal	4	7
Russia	1	3
Switzerland	26	49

tries of western Europe and those on its eastern and southern fringes.

What was in the correspondence? Dictionaries were not widely used among the population at large until the nineteenth century. While copying was a central part of writing instruction, only the best-educated used standard spelling in their composition anywhere in Europe until the twentieth century. A careful study of writing among Danish soldiers was carried out by the Reverend J. L. Bang in 1882. He found that 32 percent could write well and 47 percent adequately, but only a fifth had good spelling and 44 percent were unsatisfactory. Of course, as long as what was written was understood, few letter writers worried about correct forms. Denmark was the first Scandinavian country to institute compulsory writing instruction in schools (1814), followed by Norway in 1827, Sweden in 1842, Finland in 1866, and Iceland in 1907. Most children were taught "passive" skills like reading. For example, a survey of over a thousand Danish rural schools in 1848, the year of revolutions across Europe, showed that 99 percent taught reading and 92 percent the rudiments of spelling (needed for writing). However, composition was taught in only a handful of schools and then only to the gifted few. This is reflected in the restricted use of writing among the population at large. For example, Danish rural diaries (*Bondedagbøger*) prior to 1850 record simple facts and were almost all written by affluent peasants.

Thereafter, these writings become more abstract and reflective (especially about religion). More cottagers and artisans, and for the first time women began to keep such personal records in the second half of the nineteenth century. Extensive use of literacy was spreading rapidly among more social groups in late-nineteenth-century northern Europe.

Religion. Issues of grammar and orthography illustrate that, even among the literate, the ways people related to writing could differ. We can also identify qualitative differences in the uses and importance of literacy that distinguished, for example, Protestants from Catholics. Reading the Scriptures was central to the reformed faith. Religious books were probably read more frequently among Protestants and the very status of reading was special. Studies of eastern France in the seventeenth century have shown that, despite having comparable basic literacy, Protestants tended to own more books on a wider variety of religious topics than their Catholic neighbors and to use them differently. Protestants accepted the overwhelming authority of what they knew or thought was in a religious book.

This does not mean that we should condemn Catholicism as obscurantist and antireading. Catholic leaders wanted literacy to spread, but in a controlled way, with the priest as intermediary in the process of understanding. They regarded some types of reading as a threat, rather than an invitation, to sound beliefs. An Italian priest, writing around 1530, could claim that "all literate people are heretics." Indeed, it is plain that being unable to read was construed by authorities in, for example, eighteenth-century Spain and Bohemia as a sign of Catholic orthodoxy, immunizing from contamination by this powerful force. Simply possessing a book was a sign of heresy. In short, there is no conclusive proof of the direction of the relationship between Protestantism and literacy, but the bond was stronger than that between Catholicism and literacy.

Limited literacy was not necessarily an obstacle to Catholic religious instruction. Illiteracy may have been an increasing disadvantage in everyday life, but the extent of any handicap was not uniform in all contexts or in all parts of Europe. Generally only the church imposed direct penalties on those without the rudiments of reading and religious knowledge. Illiterates might be refused religious rites such as communion or marriage in church—as in Sweden from 1686 and in Saxony from 1802. Literacy was not formally required for political participation and even in highly literate countries the franchise remained in any case highly restricted. One percent of adult males in Scotland could vote in parliamentary elections in the 1780s and 13 percent after the Reform Bill of 1832; just one Dutchman in ten could vote in 1853.

Advantages of literacy. In the course of the nineteenth century the practical, civil disadvantages of illiteracy became more apparent. After 1874 Russian conscripts who could prove they had been to school and had basic literacy were allowed to leave the military sooner than illiterates. Other countries used recruitment to foster literacy. The French army favored literate conscripts after 1872 and provided further training for soldiers. The rate of illiteracy among recruits to the Italian army fell much more rapidly than among the population at large: from 59 percent in 1870 to just 10 percent in 1913. For comparison, Swiss recruits had illiteracy as low as 6 percent in 1879 and 1 percent in 1900.

Access to the written or printed word could open up new horizons. Until the 1870s emigrants to North America came from Europe's most literate and economically developed countries. Within Europe, migrants to eighteenth- and nineteenth-century cities were generally more literate than those who remained in the countryside. Was it literacy that made them move or was this desire to learn part of a wider set of dynamic personality traits? French, Spanish, and Greek people who arrived in North America in the 1890s were much more literate than those who stayed in the old country. In contrast, Austrian, Belgian, German, and Italian emigrants mirrored the abilities of their former compatriots. Irish who emigrated to North America showed above-average literacy, but those who went across to Britain were indistinguishable in this respect from those in the counties they had left. Contemporary migrants toward Europe's eastern limits seem to have depended less on literacy (almost all were illiterate peasants) than on possessing an independent and pioneering spirit.

Those who stayed behind in Europe were not blind to the value of education and literacy. A marginal annotation made in a Bulgarian liturgical book in 1834 reads: "You should care for education not money, for education brings money." By the end of the nineteenth century in western Europe simply being able to read and write made little difference to a person's chances of being upwardly socially mobile. However, basic literacy may have helped to prevent those from the lower classes being adversely affected by a changing job market. The most pronounced benefits came increasingly from higher-quality literacy associated with prolonged schooling and the possession of certification to that effect.

Reading the Scripture. *Pastor Anslo and His Wife,* painting (1641) by Rembrandt Harmensz van Rijn (1606–1669). GEMALDEGALERIE, BERLIN/THE BRIDGEMAN ART LIBRARY

Education. During the nineteenth century education was also increasingly seen as a pathway to political participation, for example among the Norwegian workmen's associations who founded schools from the 1850s. Like workers all over Europe after the Revolutions of 1848, they recognized that education was one way of winning knowledge and freedom, of creating a sense of collective "class" identity while maximizing their potential as individuals. Optimism was tempered by experience. In the first flush of Italian revolutionary fervor during the 1790s and 1800s radicals advocated mass education in the principles of democracy. Later revolutionaries like Giuseppe Mazzini recognized that only the urban classes would be likely to pick up his propaganda. He was pessimistic about the opportunities to use literacy in the cause of political reform. He wrote: "As for speaking to the people . . . I would speak: but the paths are lacking, and we wander around in a circle . . . The people cannot read." Sicilian radicals of the mid-nineteenth century advocated extending the franchise to all men, but only those who could read and write.

The connection between politics and literacy is shown in twentieth-century Russia, but so too is the politicization of literacy. Lenin, the son of a school inspector, believed that "the illiterate person stands outside politics." Postrevolutionary Russia built on an existing liberal drive to promote learning and a growing mass desire for literacy and its products. Under Stalin, education made strong advances, but this was in the context of tight censorship and an obsession with the inculcation of political orthodoxy, including a vigorous attack on religion. Against a background of forced collectivization of the peasantry, rising literacy in 1930s Russia did not imply an invitation to understand and change the world in which the Soviets lived or to emancipate self and society, but a demand that they approve of an existing system.

There are other examples of literacy and education acting for stability rather than change. Take the example of the "fertility transition," which affected all parts of Europe between roughly 1870 and 1910. Until the second half of the nineteenth century, contraception was not widely practiced among the population at large. Couples could not, or did not, limit the number of children a woman would bear during her fertile years. The age at which a woman married for the first time was the primary determinant of fertility. The adoption of modern birth-control methods brought about a drastic reduction in fertility within marriage, couples had fewer children, and their standard of living improved as a result.

In some parts of Europe the relationship we might assume between education and modern attitudes is borne out. Regions of Italy and Spain with high basic literacy had low marital fertility by the early twentieth century, but in Germany the low illiteracy of adult males was only one precondition of an early and large reduction of marital fertility. In Brabant prior to 1920 it was in general only literate couples whose parents and grandparents had been literate who adopted new ways of limiting family size. In Portugal the expected relationship is reversed: marital fertility in 1930 and 1960 was lower in the less literate southern provinces than in the north. Indeed, we can turn the relationship between literacy and modernity on its head. Ron Lesthaeghe's *The Decline of Belgian Fertility* (Princeton, 1977, p. 194) concludes that: "the eradication of illiteracy through the development of primary-school education contributed more to the continuity of the existing moral norms than to their change . . . the degree of literacy in Belgium could be a better indicator of traditionalism than of modernization." Education and the literacy it brings is almost never value-free.

The Belgian example reminds us that education by itself may do little to alter the way people think. It can liberate an individual or society, but it can also be used to police attitudes and behavior. Its effect depends on whether the prevailing ideology supports continuity or change. The Belgian Catholic church effectively monopolized education in rural areas as late as 1900. Educational provision was excellent and illiteracy among adults under age 55 years was almost unknown by 1910. But the church was able to damp down changes in the moral climate that might have encouraged greater use of contraception.

At the same time, people may think or rationalize in a way that is "modern" thanks to their education, but behave traditionally because of the way they were socialized outside school. Literacy's growth may therefore sometimes have had limited effects. A further example is the continued dominance of middle-aged and older males in periods when their juniors were rapidly becoming literate. Reading ability was nearly universal among the under-fifties in mid-eighteenth-century Finland, but half the over-sixties could not read from the Bible. Illiteracy among Belgian men aged under 30 years was a fifth in 1880 compared with over a half for those aged over 80 years. But age brought wealth, status, and power in patriarchal families and communities, which illiteracy did little to diminish. It is the overall context of a society that makes literacy important or otherwise.

CONCLUSION

The areas and social groups that saw early and deep penetration of literacy were wealthier, more commer-

Literacy Class in the Soviet Union. Learning to read and write at the Krasny Bogatyr Works, Moscow, 1932. ITAR-TASS/SOVFOTO/EASTFOTO

cialized, and Protestant. Literacy became embedded in the society and culture of these regions and peoples, with the result that reading and writing were practiced more extensively and a "virtuous circle" was created. At different periods for different groups in different parts of Europe, the ability to read and write became a component of important areas of economic, social, political, and cultural life. In the seventeenth century, literacy was an integral part of Calvinist faith; in the eighteenth century it became central to the bourgeois and élite sociability that was a keynote of the Enlightenment; in the nineteenth century it was an agency both of political centralization and of particularism; in the twentieth century a firm connection with economic betterment became established as education and certification became synonymous.

Explaining the social and geographical distribution of literacy in historic Europe involves understanding failures as well as successes. Of the structural features of historic literacy, sex-specific differences have been all but ironed out in European countries covered by the OECD survey. The differences that remain reflect the other two historic givens, class and residence, which determine that in some countries, most obviously Poland, the population clusters into a much narrower (and lower) band of proficiency than others. Another international body, UNESCO, estimated that perhaps 15–20 percent of the population of late-twentieth-century France has some sort of literacy shortfall and perhaps 15–30 percent of Portu-

guese. "Residual" or "latent" illiteracy may exist even in nations with complete basic literacy. These figures are remarkably similar to the 10–15 percent illiteracy obtained in the more "advanced" European states of the late nineteenth century or in Russia in 1939. Perhaps at any given stage in social development after the introduction of mass education there is always a core of adults who are judged "illiterate." The reason is clear enough for some modern groups. For example, some Turkish *Gastarbeiter* in Germany run Koranic schools for their children as a way of preserving Islamic culture, but, since the same children are legally obliged to attend German state schools, a linguistic and cultural conflict arises, which inhibits learning. Elsewhere in Europe, older generations tend to be dialect speakers (or to use archaic Gothic or "black letter" script), and European educators perceive adult illiteracy to be their greatest remaining challenge. Any group left behind by mainstream cultural change, or which is socially or geographically marginalized may be so affected. Gypsies or "traveling folk" are another example.

Many of the positive implications of changing literacy are still with us. Scandinavia's early-modern reading campaign may be associated with the very high levels of book production there in the late twentieth century. Iceland had the largest number of published titles per capita of any Scandinavian country in the late 1980s and the highest average per capita book purchasing in Europe. Scotland's past literacy superiority may be exaggerated, but the very fact that people believe in it makes this vision of history a potent force for both continuity and change. In both tangible and intangible ways, the changing patterns of historic literacy have powerful legacies.

In the early twenty-first century, technological advances are said to be rendering obsolete the different literacies outlined above. Those with a calculator possess an electronic alternative to counting. Having access to a word processor may help us to dispense with all but a few uses of writing (including the need to authenticate by signature—and even that is being rendered unnecessary). However, television, radio, and electronic communication provide only imperfect substitutes for the ability to read. In some cases they actually require it. Indeed, economic and technological change may require the acquisition of new literacies to compliment rather than replace traditional skills. Two or three centuries ago being able to read and write marked a person out and gave him (rarely her) many opportunities denied to the illiterate. Simultaneously, the disadvantages of illiteracy were less pronounced. Since then, there has been an inflation of qualifications required of those wishing to use education to distinguish and advance themselves. The types of literacies and the levels of achievement needed to function in a modern society and economy have increased rather than decreased.

See also other articles in this section.

BIBLIOGRAPHY

Arnove, Robert F., and Harvey J. Graff, eds. *National Literacy Campaigns: Historical and Comparative Perspectives.* New York, 1987.

Bartoli Langeli, Attilio, and Xenio Toscani, eds. *Istruzione, alfabetismo, scrittura: Saggi di storia dell'alfabetizzazione in Italia (secolo XV–XIX).* Milan, 1991.

Chartier, Roger. *Lectures et lecteurs dans la France d'Ancien Régime.* Paris, 1987.

Furet, Francois, and Jaques Ozouf. *Reading and Writing: Literacy in France from Calvin to Jules Ferry.* Cambridge, U.K., 1982.

Graff, Harvey J. *The Legacies of Literacy: Continuities and Contradictions in Western Culture and Society.* Bloomington, Ind., 1987.

Houston, Robert A. *Literacy in Early Modern Europe: Culture and Education, 1500–1800.* London, 1988. A new edition is in preparation for publication in 2002.

"Lisants et lecteurs en Espagne, XVe–XIXe siècles." Special edition of *Bulletin Hispanique* 100, no. 2 (1998).

Literacy, Economy, and Society: Results of the First International Adult Literacy Survey. Paris and Ottawa, 1995. Report of the OECD.

Pelizzari, Maria R., ed. *Sulle vie della scrittura: Alfabetizzazione, cultura scritta e istituzioni in età moderna.* Naples, Italy, 1989.

Resnick, Daniel P., ed. *Literacy in Historical Perspective.* Washington, D.C., 1983.

Wagner, Daniel A., Richard L. Venezky, and Brian V. Street, eds. *Literacy: An International Handbook.* Boulder, Colo., 1999.

READING

Daniel P. Resnick and Jason Martinek

The ability to make sense of signs and images has been within the range of human capacity for close to five millennia, since the appearance of written scripts around 3000 to 4000 B.C. Yet for most of its history the combination of visual perception and brain processing that we call reading has been the practice and habit of elites. For Europeans, it is only since about 1500 that reading started to become the practice of substantial numbers of ordinary people.

Social historians have understood reading as an interaction between reader and text in specific social contexts. In arguing for this position, they deviate from narrower theories of context-free cognitive processing advanced by cognitivists. Historians have argued, for example, that the understanding of biblical texts of a voracious reader like the mid-sixteenth century miller Menocchio can be explained only by a careful examination of both his own life experience and the other books that he had read (Ginzburg, 1976). Less idiosyncratic readers in other times and settings have also brought to their texts lived experiences that have affected their way of referencing oral and written traditions.

But why read? Reading was a choice that increasing numbers of Europeans made to engage themselves in particular communities, real and imagined. Women and men, churchmen and nobles, clerks and secular administrators, merchants and artisans, and rural villagers and vagabonds did so for many different reasons. For some it was a necessary skill to make a livelihood, for others a way to challenge authority, but for many, largely among the young, it was a demand imposed upon them, intended to legitimate and uphold clerical and later secular authority. Nevertheless, reading had the potential to offer escape from the isolation of individual experience and to bind readers to a larger social body. To a real extent, the languages in which reading took place were binding readers to linguistic, national, religious, and economic communities (Anderson, 1991).

Despite advances in the accessibility of texts and the growth of opportunities for schooling over the last five hundred years, reading has persisted as a bounded "low literacy" experience for most of the European population, associated with the decoding of relatively simple and familiar texts. At the same time, a "high literacy" tradition—associated with unfamiliar texts, complex construction, inferential reasoning, and solitary reflection—has persisted for elites.

GROWING ACCESSIBILITY OF TEXT BEFORE 1500

Since the time of the first Sumerian tablets, reading had been understood as a vocal, difficult, and time-consuming exercise in which readers sounded out the text (Mangruel, 1997). Although some scholarly readers in the late Roman and medieval periods had been silent readers thanks to their familiarity with linguistic constructions and specific texts, most readers had had to turn written language into spoken words before they could understand it. No "take-off" for reading could take place without a more rapid and silent processing. The first steps in this direction were taken for Latin by the twelfth century and for the vernaculars of Europe in the three centuries that followed.

The vernacular languages became accessible to the reader through changes in the appearance of text. In the interest of more readers and easier reading, publishers of manuscripts copied by commissioned scribes changed the shapes and forms of letters, making them simpler and more distinct. The reader was helped along not only by the clean look of the letters, but by spaces between words, punctuation, and separations between paragraphs.

The alphabets of the European languages distinguished between vowels and consonants and made a place for both. The inclusion of vowel sounds made it possible for written languages and dialects to capture the vocabulary and usage of oral exchanges. At the same time, the accessibility of script was also advanced by changes in the appearance of text. Scripts were standardized and simplified, words were separated, spaces appeared between sentences and paragraphs. In this way written text became very accessible to novice readers. By the mid-fifteenth century, it was possible to read vernacular texts—French, Italian, Spanish, Dutch, and German, high and low, and in many dialects—as a silent reader (Saenger, 1989).

Silent reading, in turn, gave readers the possibility of moving through text discreetly, without alerting others to what they were encountering. In an age preoccupied with challenges to orthodoxy and rife with real and perceived heresies, this was very important. But silent reading did not bring about the demise of oral tradition or a wave of independent and critical challenge to received orthodoxies. Reading aloud to others continued to be a popular practice, whether in the home or the church, for instruction, entertainment, and information. In seventeenth- and eighteenth-century France and Germany, for example, men and women would listen to readers of stories as they worked evenings in homes and workrooms.

In the age of radio and then television, paid readers and broadcasters have continued the oral tradition so important to the spread of a rudimentary basic literacy. Religious programming, human interest stories, tales of heroic feats, and gossip about the well-to-do have remained the staples in the new media, relaying information that passes at the same time through newspapers and workplace conversations. The fears of early modern clerics and nineteenth-century social elites that the spread of reading would introduce novel and challenging ideas to a large public and thereby undermine authority has not been confirmed, although the spread of literacy has been associated with modernization, democracy, and economic growth.

READING IN THE SIXTEENTH AND SEVENTEENTH CENTURIES

Communication in sixteenth-century Europe remained largely oral. Estimates of those who could read are low and tell us little about the kinds of reading ability people had. Such estimates are based largely on the ability to sign one's name, an indicator of the ability to read that is useful in charting poorly mapped waters but not a reliable indicator. Perhaps only 3 to 4 percent of the population in German-speaking rural areas and 10 percent in towns could read (Engelsing, 1974). In England, we can estimate that possible readers were no more than 10 percent of the male population and a much smaller portion of women (Cressy, 1980). In Italian cities like Venice, which had enjoyed considerable commercial growth in preceding centu-

ries, reading rates were higher but did not embrace more than 25 percent of the male population.

Reformation and counter-reformation. Gutenberg's invention of the printing press in 1450, which in fact built on earlier European work and the Chinese precedent, began to increase the amount of reading material available in ways that would ultimately expand potential readership. Most initial printed material was religious, and it was the change in Europe's religious map, more than the new technology, that really launched a new stage in the social history of reading. The first movements to extend reading practice in northern Europe were led by religious reformers and their state backers in the first decades of the sixteenth century, when large portions of northern Europe rejected the hegemony of the Roman church in matters of creed, sacrament, and religious organization. Reformers made sermons, distributed flyers designed for public discussion, and argued for a revival of the early church practice of catechism, linking orality to the reading of text.

Catechism (to teach by word of mouth) had its origins in the effort to enlist recruits to Christianity in the early church and is referenced in the patristic writings. As oral instruction, it took on forms that were appropriate to the absence of written text: memorization, drill, and repetition of a set of beliefs. Later on, manuals for confessors developed the practice of defining what was to be learned by sets of questions and answers, which were also to be memorized.

Catechetical instruction in some form was maintained as a priestly obligation throughout the medieval period, and it served as the principal form of primary education. Manuscript texts were useful to priests and clerks engaged in teaching, and the extant copies of catechisms, songbooks, prayers, and lives of saints are evidence of this. Instruction clearly varied in quality and form from parish to parish, but in general it had limited aims.

Martin Luther's (1483–1546) own visits to parishes in Saxony in the 1520's had convinced him that religious instruction was moribund and that a new set of written guides to instruction was necessary for both pastors and laity. In the ferment of the sixteenth century, many reformers adopted the same strategy, among them John Calvin (1509–1564) and Johann Agricola (1494?–1566). In 1529, Luther published a "Little Catechism" along with an expanded one to assist in proselytizing for his movement.

The Little Catechism had a major role in guiding household reading habits in the areas of Lutheran influence. It began with the Ten Commandments, which was followed by the Apostles' Creed, the Lord's

Prayer (the Twenty-Third Psalm), and the sacraments. Reading of the text was designed to move the reader from fear of God to faith, prayer, and the promise of grace. Luther, who had demanded instruction and examination through catechism and developed texts that could guide both pastoral instruction and household reading, had many competitors in German areas that had broken with Rome (Strauss, 1978). More than a thousand catechisms have been catalogued in the holdings of the Weimar library (Reu), not counting the many that have disappeared.

Catechisms would be read on Sundays in churches and practiced in homes throughout the year, while schoolmasters used them as texts for their classes. Examinations of the young on their catechisms because a regular Lenten spring ritual for public authorities in the lands where Lutheranism was a state religion. The texts of these recitations were extended in some cases to embrace information about rulers, governments, and systems of justice. Public examinations on catechism thus served as civic exercises. The practice of examinations and home visitations was carried on into the eighteenth century in Lutheran Sweden, as confirmed by parish registers (Johansson, 1977).

Instruction in catechism had its own particular forms, associated with oral repetition, familiar text, and a set of memorized questions and answers. The blinders placed on reading by the outlook of catechetical instruction are well expressed in the observations of Tettelbach, a pastor and teacher in Saxony, in 1568:

> I have been noticing that schoolboys and other children merely memorize this precious book. This is a praiseworthy thing to do, to be sure. But they remember it without having thought or reflected on what it means, and they parrot the words with so little feeling that when one asks them a question about it, they can't explain even the simplest thing. (Strauss, p. 174)

Roman Catholic authorities, responding to the wave of challenges to orthodox belief and practice, developed and encouraged use of specially prepared digests of religious material and continued to limit the access of the laity to the Bible in the vernacular (Julia, in Cavallo and Chartier, 1999). Both Catholic and Protestant communities relied on guided reading of printed catechisms along with inspirational lives, prayers, and hymns. Direct access to the Bible itself, which Luther had at first promoted, was for some time opposed by both Catholic and Lutheran authorities and promoted only by those who were willing to leave interpretation of the texts open to the lay reader.

Vernacular translations of the Bible remained on the Index for two hundred years. Pius IV's (1499–

Reading the Bible. *Old Woman Reading the Bible,* painting by Gerard Dou (1613–1675). ©RIJKSMUSEUM, AMSTERDAM

1565) Index of Prohibited Books (1559) permitted reading of the Bible in translation by only two categories of readers. The first to receive this exemption were those who had the permission of their bishop and the support of their parish priest and confessor. The second group was the scholarly community— "learned and pious men" who were said to be "able to draw from that reading not harm but some increase of faith and piety."

Humanist elites. Humanists were a major part of the book buying market in these two centuries. They were noblemen, clerics, rulers, scholars, and civil administrators, people of some means who fostered the revival of respect for the contributions of Greece and Rome to later European values and institutions. As readers they identified with the Greek and Roman tradition in literature, history, and public administration. They were part of a movement to promote access to Greek and Roman texts in largely vernacular languages, a movement that began in the Italian city-states and spread throughout Europe. Although some, like Erasmus (1466?–1536) played a role in religious reform, many had markedly secular tastes.

Humanists called for major changes in the format of the book, the appearance of the page, and the variety of published texts, even before the introduction of the printing press (Grafton, 1997). They wanted and got small portable books, pleasing fonts, and a long list of titles. They promoted the habit and practice of reading in ways that affected the availability of varied reading material for all social classes. The genres of non-religious texts that they demanded, particularly romances and picaresque fiction, appeared in inexpensive editions for regional urban markets in the seventeenth century and then circulated more widely by the end of next century.

Humanist readers of the fifteenth and sixteenth centuries, before and after the introduction of the printing press, had an interactive and dynamic relationship with the publishers, middlemen, and printers who invested in the production and inventory of codex manuscripts and then printed books. As humanists reviving an interest in antiquity, their tastes ran predominantly to ancient Greek and Roman histories, literature, poetry, plays, biography, and autobiography of writers of antiquity, but they also read medieval Christian writers. They wanted to read the texts without the mediating apparatus of glosses on the page prescribing interpretation and the barriers to accessibility created by large, dark Gothic typefaces.

Reading had five characteristic features for the humanists. First, it was a social practice. They liked to discuss what they had read, hold symposia, and entertain one another with debates and readings. In succeeding centuries the practices they cultivated found their way into political discourse, entertainment, and the practices of book clubs and debating societies. Second, reading was used to shape and train memory. It was often simply the first step in a process that led to the memorization of a particular text. The recall and recitation skills of Joseph Justus Scaliger (1540–1609) and other sixteenth-century humanists were a source of celebrity among contemporaries.

Reading was also a step in the growth of personal knowledge, to be cemented by note-taking, copying, and paraphrasing. The personal libraries of humanists indicate their pride in creating their own comments and glosses on texts. "Whatever you read," wrote Guarino of Verona (1374?–1460) to a pupil, "have a notebook ready." Fourth, reading was an act of veneration. Just as the reading of lives of saints had shown consideration for Christian holiness, so did the reading of Greek and Roman literature and history indicate a reverence for the wisdom of pre-Christian antiquity. Readers of Niccolò Machiavelli (1469–1527) on Livy, like those who read Erasmus's *Adages*

(1500), were brought to deference by the act of reading.

Finally, reading was very often the occasion for tasteful and showy investment. Readers were eager to display to contemporaries and posterity the evidence of their personal reading tastes. The ornate covers and bindings of texts in humanist libraries of the sixteenth and seventeenth centuries, like the reader's comments on the pages, served as evidence of the association of reading and artful display. Jean Grolier de Servières (1479–1565), a leading French collector of the sixteenth century, inscribed in Latin on the cover of handsomely bound leather volumes that they were intended for the use of Grolier and his friends (British Museum, 1965).

The pedagogy of catechism heavily influenced the secular schools that were set up in the late eighteenth and nineteenth centuries. The German school system in Prussia, Bavaria, and other states established in the second half of the nineteenth century and greatly admired by the other European states was deeply rooted in the relationship between religious bodies and state power in the period of the Reformation.

READING AND SOCIAL MOVEMENTS: 1600–1900

Reading was not simply a solitary transaction between a reader and a text; the relationship between reading and social change was complex. On the one hand there were the interactions between readers, authors, and texts. Printed texts allowed authors who would have had a limited impact as individuals in preliterate societies to broadcast ideas widely. Texts could also provide political movements with a thread of ideological cohesion by providing individual readers with a shared set of beliefs and understanding of what was wrong with society and how to change it.

On the other hand there were interactions between readers, lived experience, and censorship. Reading could only lead to action if readers made a connection between the ideas contained in printed texts and their own experience. The viability of political tracts depended on readers' ability to believe what authors told them. Viability also depended on readers' access to printed material, which the state, because it had the most to lose from wide dissemination, tried to limit through strict censorship. When the state's ability to control what got printed and read was compromised, as occurred in England between 1640 and 1660, the world, as Christopher Hill has noted, could be turned upside down (Hill, 1972).

Prior to the English Revolution, the state's activities were shrouded under a veil of secrecy and privilege. Although newsbooks, the precursors to the modern newspaper, began appearing in the 1620s, readers learned little about domestic affairs from them because it was illegal to report on such matters. Instead, readers found information about events in other countries, in which merchants, the major consumers of the early newsbooks, had a great interest because their livelihoods depended on foreign trade. In the 1640s, however, the content of the newsbooks changed with the failure of the state, despite its own best efforts, to control what got into print.

Thus, what had previously been the private deliberations of the state became a matter of public discourse. This emergence of what historians have called the public sphere (Zaret, 2000) was due to the breakdown of censorship in the 1640s and 1650s, the wider availability of printed materials of an overtly political nature, increased literacy rates, and a heightened interest in political issues. In the public sphere, readers came together to discuss and debate arguments presented in journals, periodicals, and books. Collectively, these readers became the target for competing groups vying for power during the English Revolution.

The war between Parliamentarians and Royalists and among the factions in the Parliament was as much a war in print as a physical one. The war in print took two distinct forms. The first was a battle of righteousness and citation. Both sides tried to win over readers by using the Bible and religious imagery. "In the turmoil of the seventeenth century," wrote Hill, "the Bible became a sword to divide, or rather an armoury from which all parties selected weapons to meet their needs" (Hill, 1993, p. 6).

In a second arena, factions fought to win over readers through gossip, innuendo, and occasionally pornography. In the process, they borrowed deeply from oral traditions of gossip, bawdiness, and defamation. Printed gossip was passed on predominantly through newsbooks. In these newsbooks readers found detailed descriptions of the other side's transgressions and a view of events that reflected their prejudices, beliefs, and interests. The Parliamentarians' *Mercurius Britanicus* and the Royalists' *Mercurius Aulicus* carried on this war in the 1640s, at the same time that their troops took their arguments to the battlefield.

The use of the printed word to mobilize readers took place at the periphery as well as the political center. Levellers, Diggers, Ranters, and millenarian sects such as the Fifth Monarchy Men, who called for the abolition of the monarchy, the established church, and class distinctions, all used the printed word to attract supporters. Like the Parliamentarians and Royalists, they looked to the Bible for validation. In Acts 4:32, Gerrard Winstanley (1609?–1660?), a leading Digger, found support for his attack on private property: "All the believers were one in heart and mind. No one claimed that any of his possessions was his own, but they shared everything they had."

Reading clearly helped to fuel the French Revolution. Individuals have long noted the significance of reading to the revolutionary fervor of the late eighteenth century. The revolutionary texts in France were the great texts of the Enlightenment, authored by such men of letters as Voltaire (François-Marie Arouet, 1694–1778) and Jean-Jacques Rousseau (1712–1778), but influenced by Roman republican texts and classical example. Their texts criticized the absolutist state on what they saw as rational, not religious grounds. Readers found in these authors' texts an alternative way to construct society.

Voltaire's *Letters Concerning the English Nation* (1733, known in French as *Lettres philosophiques*), written during his exile to England, praised English customs, institutions, and intellectual life. The book's major implication was not lost on French readers; French customs, institutions, and intellectual life were, it suggested, far inferior to their English counterparts. French authorities suppressed the book and Voltaire was forced to flee Paris. Rousseau's work raised similar questions about the foundation upon which French society rested. In *The Social Contract* (1762), Rousseau argued that a legitimate government was one that rested on common consent, not oppression. Maximilien Robespierre (1758–1794) and other leaders of the French Revolution acknowledged a debt to Rousseau.

That such texts shaped readers' minds is clear by the lengths to which the state worked to suppress them. They were placed in the same category as pornography and censored as "bad books." Reading was dangerous precisely because it could lead readers to challenge the status quo.

Once the revolution started, the number of newspapers read and circulated increased dramatically. Readers found in these newspapers reports on the activities of the legislative body. Although politician publicists like Jacques-Pierre Brissot de Warville (1754–1793) envisioned newspapers as a means of establishing political legitimacy—"One can teach the same truth at the same moment to millions of men"—quite the opposite was actually the case. Newspapers presented a government being torn apart by internecine strife. Hence, just as reading could help inspire revolution, it could also work to undermine it (Popkin, 1990).

Reading the Paper. Bologna, Italy, 1975. ©OWEN FRANKEN/CORBIS

In the nineteenth century leaders of social movements continued to turn to readers for support and legitimacy, whether through newspapers, pamphlets, flyers, or books. Books such as August Bebel's (1840–1913) *Woman under Socialism* (1883) went through dozens of editions and reached many thousands of readers. Many leaders of the German Social Democratic party were also editors of newspapers. In Britain in the 1890s Robert Blatchford, who claimed to have been converted to socialism through reading, published one of the most popular socialist newspapers of the day, *The Clarion.* Reading never completely replaced the more traditional way of transmitting ideas—conversations in the market and workplace, political meetings, strikes, and demonstrations. But it raised the distinct possibility of reaching more dispersed populations over a more extended area than any speech ever could.

READING IN LIBRARIES

Until the nineteenth century, books were too expensive for all but wealthy individuals and institutions to purchase in great number. Most Europeans, if they owned books at all, had a collection limited to a catechism or book of hours, the life of a saint, a Bible, and perhaps an almanac. Martin's examination of 400 estate inventories in Paris in the seventeenth century indicates that merchants and artisans were rarely buyers of books, and when they did own books, they owned very few. Circulating libraries and reading cabinets appear in the eighteenth century to meet the demand for access to books without the requirement of purchase.

In the mid-eighteenth century the emergence of lending libraries and reading societies helped give readers access to a large number of texts. Middle-class readers often belonged to reading societies. In these societies, readers would have access to the latest books and journals, mostly of a political nature, which they would then discuss and debate. Unlike lending libraries, private reading societies were geared to the interests of their members. By the nineteenth century, however, reading societies were largely superseded by commercial lending libraries, which served a more heterogeneous population. (Wittmann, in Cavallo and Chartier, 1999).

In the nineteenth century municipal governments created municipal libraries, first in England and then on the continent. These libraries were aimed particularly at working-class readers and had a strong moral component. Reformers and employers hoped to elevate the moral sensibilities of the working classes, shape character, and ease social tensions. They saw the library as an uplifting alternative to the pub or alehouse, the traditional sites for male working-class leisure. Reformers discouraged workers from reading pulp fiction, urging them instead to read edifying literature. Despite these attempts, working-class reading continued to consist mostly of pulp fiction.

Even in non-capitalist countries, libraries served as a means to shape working-class minds. In the wake of the Russian Revolution, revolutionary leaders hoped to use libraries as a means to lift up workers, both morally and intellectually. One Party activist, for example, urged the citizens of Petrograd two years after the Revolution, "As the proletarian revolution wants you to be sober and clear minded you should not fail to obtain a book at your local library." (Lerner, 1998, p. 150). As this suggests, libraries were not value-free institutions.

Finland and Iceland, known for the high literacy of their adult populations, have had active circulating libraries and reading societies since about 1800. In Finland, where the public literacy of adults is among the highest in the world and where school-age children show the highest reading performance in international comparisons, circulating and public libraries seem to have contributed to this success. With strong financial backing from the Finnish government in the twentieth century and attention to community needs, Finnish library administrators have greatly expanded their holdings for children. They work closely with schools to stimulate children to read and teach children how to use the library. They have also offered on-site services for hospital patients and residents of nursing homes. To enrich the holdings of small rural libraries they started bookmobiles. Finnish libraries may be the most patronized in Europe, registering a full 25 percent of the population in a count made thirty years ago (Hatch, 1971).

READING FOR PLEASURE AND ESCAPE: THE NOVEL 1700–1900

In the sixteenth and seventeenth centuries there are many examples of readers who followed Luther's counsel and focused on a religious text with great intensity. They can be considered "intensive" readers, like the character Christian in John Bunyan's (1628–1688) *The Pilgrim's Progress* (1678). Christian's reading of apocalyptic portions of the Bible leads him to a catharsis of emotions and an affirmation of faith. Bunyan wanted his own readers to read his work with that same intensity, and he hoped that it would help them to find their own routes to salvation. Intensive reading involved a highly intimate relationship for readers, authors, and texts. It gave an individual reader the sense that the author's words were spoken directly to him. The trust bound up in this relationship could lead the reader to find in the author someone who could answer his deepest and most provoking questions or even completely redirect the trajectory of his life.

Some historians, such as Engelsing, have argued that reading changed in the eighteenth century. Not only did reading matter become more varied and secular, but the way of approaching a text changed for readers. Adapting to the more abundant literature, they turned to sampling, critical engagement with many different works, and perhaps a cursory examination of some of that material. Others, such as Darnton and Chartier, have disputed this argument, pointing to evidence of intensive engagement with novels

Reading Room. The working men's reading room at Carlisle, England. From *The Illustrated London News,* 20 December 1851. THE ILLUSTRATED LONDON NEWS PICTURE LIBRARY

in the eighteenth century and some examples of extensive reading by humanists in the two preceding centuries. One historian has even called the eighteenth century, because of its taste for the novel, a " 'revolution' in reverse—far more 'intensive' than before and not in the least 'extensive' " (Wittmann, in Cavallo and Chartier, 1999, p. 296).

Although the reading of religious texts remained an important staple of eighteenth century life, a shift had begun whereby readers increasingly turned from reading primarily for salvation to reading for information and pleasure. The growing popularity of novels, periodicals such as the *Spectator* (1711–1712), and newspapers over the course of the century demonstrates that readers' tastes were indeed changing.

That readers had begun approaching texts more superficially is evident in the emergence of the term "skim" in the English language to refer to a practice of readers. Only in the mid-eighteenth century did the term come to mean, "to glance over, without reading closely." According to the *Oxford English Dictionary*, the earliest record of the term used in this way dates to 1738 when Mary Granville Pendarves Delaney (1700–1788) described the practice in a letter to a friend: "I skimmed over [Your last letter] . . . to satisfy myself of your health." Three years later, Isaac Watts (1674–1748) used the term in a published work titled *The Improvements of the Mind*. "Plumeo," he wrote, "skimmed over the pages, like a swallow over the flowery meads."

Although extensive reading certainly gained ground in the eighteenth century, intensive reading persisted, particularly in the way readers approached novels like Samuel Richardson's (1689–1761) *Pamela, or Virtue Rewarded* (1740), Rousseau's *La nouvelle Heloise* (1761), and Johann Wolfgang von Goethe's (1749–1832) *The Sorrows of Young Werther* (1774). Historians have documented well the sentimental or empathetic responses these novels elicited from readers, particularly women, who were well represented among their readers.

Watt has noted the role of English women in ensuring the success of Richardson's *Pamela*. He attributed this appeal in part to the author's ability to write about women and their experiences with sensitivity and accuracy, far more so than any author before him. He also attributed it to the intimacy Richardson created between his readers and the text, which allowed for the "complete engrossment of their inner feelings, and the same welcome withdrawal into an imaginary world vibrant with more intimately satisfying personal relationships than ordinary life provided" (p. 196).

Darnton has shown how Rousseau's *La Nouvelle Heloise,* which went through at least seventy printings between 1761 and 1800, evoked a similarly strong emotional response among readers, male and female. In Germany, the emotional intensity with which readers read Goethe's *The Sorrows of Young Werther* is widely believed to have resulted in a wave of suicides. Thus, although what readers read had changed in the eighteenth century, how they read necessarily had not; they continued to have a passionate engagement with their texts. That novels aroused readers' emotions, however, made them a prime target for criticism. Critics also lambasted them for fostering unrealistic notions of romantic love and potentially compromising female chastity through their erotic suggestions. Novels were also imbued with the power to corrupt impressionable readers. Samuel Johnson (1709–1784) wrote that novels were "written chiefly to the young, the ignorant, and the idle, to whom they serve as lectures of conduct, and introductions into life. They are entertainment of minds unfurnished with ideas, and therefore easily susceptible of impressions." According to Samuel Taylor Coleridge (1772–1834) the long-term effects of novel reading on the mind were catastrophic. Novel reading, he believed, "occasions in time the entire destruction of the power of the mind" because it encouraged "no improvement of the intellect, but fills the mind with a mawkish and morbid sensibility which is directly hostile to the cultivation, invigoration, and enlargement of the nobler power of understanding."

Despite critics' best efforts, novel reading continued to be a popular leisure activity. Novels offered readers psychological mobility, opening up for them portals to other worlds. From the privacy of their own homes, individual readers could travel to the Swiss Alps, meet people from other classes, witness a barroom brawl, or attend a fancy ball. Novels also had the power to excite, scare, titillate, or depress. In short, they provided readers with a diversion from otherwise mundane ordinary lives.

By the second half of the nineteenth century extensive reading had become the dominant mode. For the sake of bourgeois propriety, readers were expected to read not only in silence, but with greater restraint and control. A text's success, therefore, was measured less by the feelings it evoked than its aesthetic qualities. The taming of readers' emotions occurred simultaneously with the taming of the novel itself, a process spearheaded by writers like Jane Austen (1775–1817) and Sir Walter Scott (1771–1832). No novel better illustrates the shift that took place than Austen's 1811 work, *Sense and Sensibility.* In this novel, sense reigns over sensibility. Even Marianne, a paragon of excessive emotionalism, settles down in the end.

The preeminent literary critic Matthew Arnold (1822–1888) codified the more restrained approach

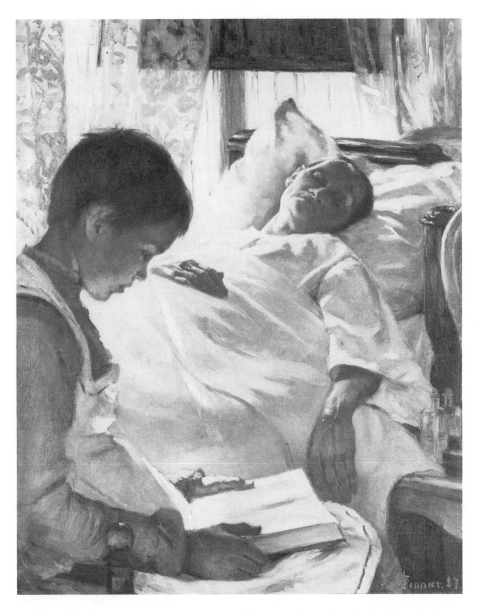

Reading Aloud. *Young Girl Reading to an Invalid,* painting (1887) by the Swedish artist Eva Bonnier (1857–1909). NATIONAL MUSEUM, STOCKHOLM/ART RESOURCE, NY

to reading in "The Function of Criticism at the Present Time" (1864): "Everything was long seen, by the young and ardent amongst us, in inseparable connection with politics and practical life. We have pretty well exhausted the benefits of seeing things in this connection, we have got all that can be got by so seeing them. Let us try a more disinterested mode of seeing them; let us betake ourselves more to the serener life of the mind and spirit." For Arnold, reason, not emotion, was to guide the reader.

The taste for novels was shared by urban workers who were who were emerging as readers of printed matter of all kinds in urban centers in Europe. Their tastes did differ from those of the bourgeoisie, ranging from the sensationalistic literature of the pulp press to moral and didactic literature generated by both socialist and evangelical movements. That said, clerks, office workers, shop assistants, workers, and laborers made up almost half of the borrowers in municipal libraries in Paris in the 1880s and 1890s, and more than half of the books that circulated were novels (Lyons, p. 336). The sheer proliferation of printed materials made it impossible to go back to the heyday of intensive reading.

READING FOR UTILITY AND INFORMATION

By the eighteenth century Europeans received so much information by way of the printed word that it had become an integral part of everyday life. It would have been hard to imagine a world without it. Since the seventeenth century and particularly in the nineteenth and twentieth centuries the amount of printed information Europeans had to process increased dramatically and made the ability to read even more necessary to function in European society. Europeans had to be able to make sense of the information found in such items as schedules and timetables, menus, advertisements, product labels, telephone books, recipes, how-to manuals, bills, and road signs.

The twin processes of state bureaucratization and the commercial revolution made reading an increasingly invaluable skill for Europeans to have at all levels of society. Even before the invention of the printing press, European states, which had previously relied predominantly on oral testimony, had become ever more dependent on written records. In the Middle Ages, the ability to read was not a prerequisite for holding office. That changed in the early modern period. The mid-sixteenth century witnessed the last illiterate high-ranking government officials in northern Europe—the first earl of Rutland in England and Constable Montmorency in France (Stone, 1968). Reading was required to process legislative initiatives, petitions, and other matters of state, particularly those relating to the military and taxation.

Similarly, the commercial revolution helped make reading a necessity of life. Merchants had long relied on written bills of exchange in their international trade. The printed word also impinged on the lives of farmers, shopkeepers, and artisans in the form of promissory notes, wills, and apprenticeship contracts. In addition, farmers and artisans increasingly relied on the printed word to provide them information about their occupations.

Since the early sixteenth century, Europeans had disseminated knowledge about agriculture in print. Humanists discovered Virgil's *Georgics* and further developed the genre. In Sir Anthony Fitzherbert's *Book of Husbandry* (1523) and other works that followed, readers found information on agricultural practices in different parts of England and recommendations on how to best raise crops and animals. In the eighteenth century, when agricultural improvement was of great concern to landowners, Arthur Young's (1741–1820) *Travels in France* (1792) was able to show a comparable concern with agricultural practices across the Channel.

In the sixteenth and seventeenth centuries manuals written by master craftsmen appeared for those already practicing the same craft. Manuals provided illustrations, patterns, and models. Although few sixteenth-century French artisans owned books, those who did were most likely, after religious texts, to own craft manuals or books of "pourtraicture" (Chartier, 1987, p. 150). These manuals were not intended for the general public because of the need for craftsmen to protect the secrets of their trades.

The dissemination of information about crafts could be a double-edged sword. At the same time that it could improve the quality of the end product, it could undermine the legitimacy of a craft's traditional practitioners. In the dairy industry in England before the eighteenth century, women played a leading role producing cheese for the family and perhaps a small surplus for sale. Dairywomen had learned the craft from other women, not from manuals or recipes. The process often lacked exactness, which meant that the product could differ greatly from batch to batch. In the eighteenth century, due to the commercialization of the dairy industry, men began to rationalize the process of cheesemaking by applying scientific knowledge to the craft. They published texts on the science of cheesemaking with recipes that encouraged product standardization. This led to the demise of dairywomen's control over the process (Valenze, 1995, p. 48–67).

In these two areas and in others, readers in the eighteenth century found that reading books offered an alternative to on-site apprenticeship for the development of skills and knowledge that were useful in the workplace. The genre grew again at the end of the nineteenth century with the decline of apprenticeship and became important to industrial education in schools and post-secondary institutes in the twentieth century. In the latter half of that century, this genre migrated in part to the television medium, where printed materials were a tie-in to demonstrations on screen. How-to manuals, however, persisted as an autonomous genre, responding to the demands of readers who wanted utility in their texts, and not simply pleasure and recreation.

THE FUTURE OF READING

By the late nineteenth century, nearly universal education in Europe had produced official literacy rates of 90 percent or more in countries like Belgium and Germany. Eastern Europe lagged, but both literacy rates and popular reading were growing there as well. Traveling book salesmen in rural areas throughout Europe complemented more organized bookstores and libraries found in urban areas.

The advent of mass reading raises several questions. Mass taste often differed from the reading matter recommended by social reformers. Trade union and socialist libraries, for example, urged working-class readers to consult serious works of philosophy and economics but found marked preferences for escapist novels. Children's books were divided between worthy, educational tracts, preferred by many parents, and more exciting fare sold directly to children, such as cowboy novels set in the American West, available in many languages. Mass-circulation newspapers offered large type and a simple vocabulary, as well as a sensationalist style that many social critics found repellent. Mass reading did not mean uniformity in the approach to reading.

BIBLIOGRAPHY

Anderson, Benedict. *Imagined Communities: Reflections on the Origin and Spread of Nationalism.* London and New York, 1991.

British Museum. *Bookbindings from the Library of Jean Grolier.* London, 1965.

Cavallo, Guglielmo, and Roger Chartier, eds. *A History of Reading in the West.* Translated by Lydia G. Cochrane. Oxford, 1999.

Certeau, Michel de, Dominque Julia, and Jacques Revel. *Une politique de la langue: La Révolution française et les patois: L'enquête de Grégoire.* Paris, 1975.

Chartier, Roger. *The Cultural Origins of the French Revolution.* Translated by Lydia G. Cochrane. Durham, N.C., 1991.

Chartier, Roger. *The Cultural Uses of Print in Early Modern France.* Translated by Lydia G. Cochrane. Princeton, N.J., Princeton University Press, 1987.

Cressy, David. *Literacy and the Social Order: Reading and Writing in Tudor and Stuart England.* Cambridge, U.K., and New York, 1980.

Darnton, Robert. *The Forbidden Best Sellers of Pre-Revolutionary France.* New York, 1995.

Darnton, Robert. *The Great Cat Massacre and Other Episodes in French Cultural History.* New York, 1984.

Darnton, Robert, and Daniel Roche, eds. *Revolution in Print: The Press in France 1775–1800.* Berkeley, Calif., and New York, 1989.

Eisenstein, Elizabeth L. *The Printing Press as an Agent of Change: Communication and Cultural Transformations in Early Modern Europe.* Cambridge, U.K., and New York, 1979.

Engelsing, Rolf. *Der Bürger als Leser: Lesergeschichte in Deutschland, 1500–1800.* Stuttgart, Germany, 1974.

Ginzburg, Carlo. *The Cheese and the Worms: The Cosmos of a Sixteenth-Century Miller.* Translated by John and Anne Tedeschi. Baltimore, 1976.

Grafton, Anthony. *Commerce with the Classics: Ancient Books and Renaissance Readers.* Ann Arbor, Mich., 1997.

Grafton, Anthony. "The Importance of Being Printed." *Journal of Interdisciplinary History* 11, no. 2 (1980): 265–286.

Hatch, Lucile. "Public Libraries in Finland." *Journal of Library History, Philosophy and Comparative Librarianship* 6, no. 4 (1971): 337–359.

Hill, Christopher. *The English Bible and the Seventeenth-Century Revolution.* London, 1993.

Hill, Christopher. *The World Turned Upside Down: Radical Ideas during the English Revolution.* New York, 1972.

Johansson, Egil. "Literacy Studies in Sweden: Some Examples." In *Literacy and Society in a Historical Perspective: A Conference Report.* Edited by E. Johansson. Umeå, Sweden, 1977. Pages 41–50.

Labarre, Albert. *Le livre dans la vie amiénoise du seizième siècle: L'enseignement des inventaires après décès, 1503–1576.* Paris, 1971.

Lerner, Fred. *The Story of Libraries: From the Invention of Writing to the Computer Age.* New York, 1998.

Manguel, Alberto. *A History of Reading.* New York, 1997.

Popkin, Jeremy D. *Revolutionary News: The Press in France 1789–1799.* Durham, N.C., 1990.

Resnick, Daniel P., ed. *Literacy in Historical Perspective.* Washington, D.C., 1983.

Resnick, Daniel P., and Lauren B. Resnick. "The Nature of Literacy: A Historical Exploration." In *Perspectives in Literacy.* Edited by Eugene R. Kintgen, Barry M. Kroll, and Mike Rose. Carbondale, Ill., 1988. Pages 190–202.

Resnick, Daniel P. and Lauren B. Resnick. "Varieties of Literacy." In *Social History and Issues in Human Consicousness: Some Interdisciplinary Connections.* Edited by Andrew E. Barnes and Peter N. Stearns. New York, 1989. Pages 171–196.

Saenger, Paul. "Physiologie de la lecture et séparation des mots." *Annales E.S.C.* (1989): 939–52.

Stone, Lawrence. "Literacy and Education in England, 1640–1900." *Past and Present* 42 (1968): 69–139.

Strauss, Gerald. *Luther's House of Learning: Indoctrination of the Young in the German Reformation.* Baltimore, 1978.

Valenze, Deborah M. *The First Industrial Woman.* New York, 1995.

Watt, Ian. *The Rise of the Novel: Studies in Defoe, Richardson, and Fielding.* Berkeley, Calif., 1964.

Zaret, David. *Origins of Democratic Culture: Printing, Petitions, and the Public Sphere in Early Modern England.* Princeton, N.J., 2000.

Victor Li provided research assistance in the preparation of this article.

JOURNALISM

Thomas Cragin

Europe did not see anything resembling modern journalism, the serial publication of news, until the seventeenth century. However, if the definition of journalism is expanded to include the regular printing of news and political, religious, and philosophical opinion, then journalism was born with the printing press in the middle of the fifteenth century. From the fifteenth to the nineteenth centuries most printed news catered to religious and sensational interests rooted in the popular oral culture that preceded print. After the invention of the printing press, journalists introduced radically new ideas and challenged the growing numbers of readers to rethink old assumptions. Religious dogma, the organization of the universe, and the legitimacy of constituted authority became issues for debate. Early journalists improved the communication of news and had a momentous impact on European society through their diffusion of the ideas of the Protestant and Catholic Reformation, the scientific revolution, the Enlightenment, and the French Revolution.

However, until the nineteenth century in western Europe and the twentieth century in eastern Europe illiteracy, poverty, and geographic isolation kept most Europeans from regular access to print journalism. All that changed in the nineteenth century and the early twentieth century, the newspaper's golden age. In that era mass-circulation dailies popularized the modern newspaper's blend of political, business, sports, and sensational news with special interest sections, reviews, and advertising. Accuracy, detail, speed, and investigation became ideals for the new professional journalist. In the twentieth century electronic media simplified journalistic style and greatly expanded its audience.

THE COMING OF PRINT

Before the invention of the printing press, most Europeans received news verbally from peddlers, travelers, soldiers, and beggars wandering through villages and towns. News of important international events could take years to reach peasant ears and would be greatly distorted when it arrived. False news could have serious effects, as when false reports of new taxes caused peasant revolts in the fourteenth century. Distortions of oral communication invested the written word with greater respect both for its authenticity and for its authority since it was the product of the learned elite.

In the mid-fifteenth century monarchs were among the first to use the printing press to communicate news. By the end of the fifteenth century kings often employed printers to publish their decrees for distribution to officials throughout their kingdoms. Especially in times of crisis, rulers used print to gain popular support. At the end of the War of the Roses, a struggle between rival factions for the English throne, the victorious king Henry VII printed and circulated the papal bull confirming his claim to the throne. Similarly King Charles VIII of France launched a major press campaign in the late fifteenth century to garner support for his invasion of Italy. Monarchs' use of print was quickly imitated by judicial, city, town, and church authorities. These publications usually were written by servants of the king, bishop, or mayor and were printed by royal or ecclesiastical printing houses or printers with royal privileges. Royal or ecclesiastic patrons exercised enormous direct influence over these writers and publishers. However, not all journalists wrote in the service of the church or the Crown.

Before the end of the Renaissance new kinds of journalism developed to serve the needs of commoners. The most important to the development of modern journalism were news books. Merchants' livelihoods depended on quick and accurate news of wars, plagues, famines, shipping disasters, and weather that would greatly increase or contract competition in the market. By the sixteenth century a number of individuals in Italy, Germany, and Holland capitalized on bankers' and merchants' need for quick and reliable news by selling handwritten newssheets reporting im-

Columbus Reports His Discoveries. First page of a letter Christopher Columbus describing his journey to what he supposed was Asia, printed in Spanish in Barcelona in 1493. RARE BOOKS AND MANUSCRIPT DIVISION, THE NEW YORK PUBLIC LIBRARY, ASTOR, LENOX, AND TILDEN FOUNDATIONS

portant business, military, and political events. These newssheets were destined for only a small readership, however, since the high costs of maintaining correspondents and couriers to collect and carry the latest news kept subscriptions beyond the means of most of the middle classes. But in the sixteenth century the printing press enabled news to reach a much larger audience.

THE REFORMATION AND
THE POPULAR PRESS

By the early sixteenth century a popular printed journalism flourished throughout Europe. A great variety of popular prints circulated in urban Europe at the end of the fifteenth century, and they were increasingly available to peasants in the countryside during the next century. Four hundred years before the advent of the mass newspaper press, these prints were produced by the tens and hundreds of thousands.

The popular journalists of the fifteenth, sixteenth, and seventeenth centuries ranged from great poets to lowly peddlers who produced and sold a broad range of literature to rich and poor alike. Their prints appeared in several sizes and formats, most combining text, song, and picture. Poster-sized broadsheets or broadsides, printed on one side for mounting on walls, were very popular in urban settings. More portable, small pamphlets were sold widely in cities and villages. The broadsides and pamphlets most commonly contained sensationalist news and information on religious debates and changes taking place in sixteenth-century Europe.

The Protestant Reformation initiated a war of words that greatly expanded the circulation of vernacular literature. Broadsides and pamphlets spread the ideas of the Protestant and Catholic Reformation in their most abbreviated forms. Martin Luther became one of Germany's best-selling authors through the circulation of hundreds of thousands of copies of his devotionals. While Luther's publications urged readers to decide theological questions for themselves, papal defenders circulated treatises demanding the complacence of "the ignorant and rebellious commoners." By 1521 official Catholic prints had done as much as Luther's to promote popular dissatisfaction with Catholic authorities, turning Luther's revolt into a mass movement. Though he was the most read Protestant journalist in Reformation Germany, Luther was by no means alone. Many of his followers published prints for mass audiences, sometimes in conflict with his views. In central and southern Germany, Protestant propagandists turned Luther's message into a call for social equality and political freedom, initiating the German Peasants' War of 1525. Afterward Luther, his princes, and their Catholic counterparts became increasingly aware of the dangers as well as the advantages of popular journalism.

Most of the Reformation broadsides and pamphlets were published in the vernacular language to reach the widest possible readership. In 1534 French Protestants touched off a dramatic conflict in Paris, known as the "affaire des placards," by posting anti-Catholic propaganda throughout the city. Millions of religious prints were circulated by both Protestants and Catholics in their struggle against one another. More than merely communicating the controversial issues relating to church doctrine, these prints reported miracles, detailed the stories of local saints, and described the actions of witches and demons. During the wars of religion spanning the sixteenth and seventeenth centuries, they heightened Europeans' fears of heresy, contributing to the violence of religious conflict and the persecution of so-called witches. Popular journalists in mid-seventeenth-century England, for example, reported miracles, monstrosities, and omens that fostered support for the reestablishment of monarchy.

Since church and state were united in Europe at this time, the religious conflict of the Reformation era was very much a conflict of states. Martin Luther won crucial support for his revolt against the Catholic Church through his printed appeals to the German princes. In England, Henry VIII distributed prints throughout Britain justifying his break with the Catholic Church. In France, Francis I issued prints defending the alliance he made between Catholic France and the Protestants in wars against the Spanish Catholics. In addition to using print to promote their interests, both Protestant and Catholic states fought the war of words by banning and burning their opponents' prints. This action, however, could have the opposite effect. As Elizabeth Eisenstein points out, inclusion in the Index of Forbidden Books often promoted the sale of a work that otherwise might have garnered little attention. Thus, to identify and prevent the circulation of banned works, nearly every government instituted elaborate controls over the press. Over time states made political and religious censorship more thorough and more repressive.

However, these controls were unnecessary for most popular journalism. Popular political news nearly always promoted the interests of the state and its established church. When reporting politics, journalists most often announced new laws and regulations, alliances, wars, battles, and peace treaties. They also made regular reports on the major political figures of the day, noting all royal births, deaths, processions, and weddings. Coercion by the state was seldom applied and usually unnecessary to gain good press for the government. In fact most popular political news was adamantly xenophobic and patriotic.

The vast majority of popular news, however, ignored government and politics in favor of sensational news stories. Lacking a loyal clientele, each print had to sell itself with attention-grabbing news. Violence sold best, especially reports of murders, trials, and ex-

1624

The crying Murther:

Contayning the cruell and most horrible Butche
of Mr. TRAT, Curate of olde *Cleaue*; who was first murthe
as he trauailed vpon the high way , then was brought home to his, ho
and there was quartered and imboweld: his quarters and bowels being
terwards perboyld and salted vp, in a most strange and fearefull manner. For this fac
the Iudgement of my Lord chiefe Baron TANFIELD, young *Peter Smethwicke*,
drew *Baker*, *Cyrill Austen*, and *Alice Walker*, were executed this last Summer
Assizes, the 24. of Iuly, at Stone Gallowes, neere Taunton
in Summerset-shire.

AT LONDON;
Printed by *Edw: Allde* for *Nathaniell Butter.*
1 6 2 4.

Crime Journalism. Violent crime and justice have been the subjects of the vast majority of news reports since the invention of the printing press. The cover of a news pamphlet, "The crying Murther," printed at London in 1624, carries a gruesome illustration designed to catch the attention of potential buyers. BY PERMISSION OF THE HOUGHTON LIBRARY, HARVARD UNIVERSITY

ecutions. News of natural disasters was also popular, especially when detailing mass fatalities. Reports of ghosts and monsters did not merely serve to inspire fiction, as they would in the nineteenth century, since early modern readers considered such reports to be factual. In addition to sensational reports, a large part of popular news related practical information. In town and country, newssheets announced the dates and locations of local fairs, festivals, and pilgrimages. Peasants prized the almanac above all other prints since they found so much use for its calendars, forecasts, horoscopes, and religious iconography. Such contents might be used to time planting and harvesting and to secure the protection of the saints for the year's crops.

Social historians look at the early modern popular press to expose the era's values and beliefs. Popular religious prints provide invaluable insight into the nature of religious belief and the early modern worldview. Miraculous divine interventions and satanic rites were not only reported as factual but were also pointed to as explanations for crime and injustice, acts of state, and natural calamities. Early modern journalism suggests that Europeans saw their world as the plaything of supernatural forces. Reports of violent crimes and punishments reveal the consistent affirmation of paternal authority, the vilification of independence in women and servants, and a widespread fascination with the grotesque. Read by elites as well as by the lower classes, these reports, especially those describing fantastical beasts and satanic monsters, suggest the distance between early modern and modern readers' acceptance of and belief in the marvelous.

Until the nineteenth century, broadsides and pamphlets were the most plentiful forms of printed news. But in the seventeenth century many of these prints lost their appeal for rich and poor alike. The upper classes began to disparage many popular genres as beneath their dignity. Scholars are uncertain as to how widespread this rejection of popular literature by elites was. A number of studies suggest that elites continued to buy certain popular pamphlets in the late eighteenth and early nineteenth centuries. Nevertheless, a new periodical journalism aimed at elite readers emerged in the seventeenth century.

THE BIRTH OF THE PERIODICAL PRESS IN THE AGE OF ENLIGHTENMENT

The first printed periodical appeared in Europe during the seventeenth century. In 1605 Abraham Berhoeven introduced *Nieuwe Tindinghe,* the first periodical newssheet. The Antwerp paper began as a weekly, but demand soon prompted three printings a week. By the middle of the seventeenth century weekly newssheets were printed in Holland, Germany, Austria, France, Italy, and Spain. While they had neither the format nor the content of the modern newspaper, these weeklies did provide subscribers with a regular source of news. The historian Henri-Jean Martin describes their proliferation as the birth of modern journalism. The speedier collection and publication of news in the early eighteenth century facilitated the introduction of dailies in Europe. The *Daily Courant,*

Europe's first daily, appeared in London in 1702, building its initial success on its updates on the progress of the War of Spanish Succession. England's first professional newspaper editor, Thomas Gainsford, adopted the popular pamphlets' narrative style to make newspaper reporting more engaging for the reader. The result was a hybrid journalism, more factual than before but still sensational.

While popular newssheets were notorious for distorting and falsifying information, newspapers achieved a better reputation among elites in the seventeenth century. Newspaper publishers earned a measure of respect by occasionally correcting errors from an earlier issue, creating the impression that journalists strove for accuracy. The Spanish *Gaceta de Zaragoza* (Gazette of Zaragoza) explained in a May 1688 report that it was "impossible always to satisfy quickly the public curiosity without sometimes making mistakes" but assured readers that its use of diverse sources that confirmed one another would guarantee accuracy. Yet the impressions these techniques gave were deceiving. Most reports were based on second- and third-hand information relayed from witnesses to foreign correspondents and then from couriers to the papers' publishers, distorted in each transmission. In the eighteenth century some newspapers addressed this problem by offering readers more direct information. The *Spectator,* a successful London daily, took its name from its reporters' and correspondents' first-hand accounts. Nevertheless, journalism was not yet investigative.

Early newspaper readers subscribed to the new weeklies and dailies to gain access to news critical for business, especially international news that they could not easily obtain otherwise. These texts provided readers with the latest details of European wars and equally important news on trade and conflict in America, Africa, and Asia. Though they reported on the great political and economic events of their day, the weeklies were by no means a medium for the spread of the most important ideas of their time. Few of them printed the scientific discoveries of the seventeenth century that revolutionized astronomy and physics. When discoveries were occasionally described, they were presented in the briefest and most simplistic terms. The early newspapers, like the news pamphlets, gave far more attention to sensations. The seventeenth-century newspaper subscriber could read more about strange births and monsters than about the scientific breakthroughs of Galileo and Johannes Kepler.

To read about the latest ideas relating to science, philosophy, and politics, readers could turn to periodical literary reviews that appeared in Europe in the late seventeenth century. Two of the most important, *Journal des savants* and *Philosophical Transactions,* appeared in Paris and London respectively in 1665. *Philosophical Transactions* published numerous articles on Isaac Newton's breakthroughs in physics, and both journals reviewed his *Philosophiae naturalis Principia mathematica* (1687). By the mid-eighteenth century dozens of new scientific, philosophical, literary, and professional journals spread the ideas of the scientific revolution and the Enlightenment. The dramatic change in Europeans' worldview during the eighteenth century is reflected in journalists' new explanations of events, attributing them to human and natural causes rather than to supernatural forces.

Journalists had established their influence over politics in the Reformation but wielded even greater power as a political force in the seventeenth and eighteenth centuries. Factions in the English government mobilized political writers to win popular support for their causes during the Glorious Revolution of 1688. Party leaders issued regular statements to their followers through printed pamphlets. By the early eighteenth century Grubb Street, the booksellers' street in London, was a center for the creation of political pamphlet propaganda purchased by rival factions in Parliament, and by the second half of the eighteenth century printers set up press shops in many of the smaller cities and towns of Britain. As a result the political pamphlet press made thousands of readers aware of the great debates of political philosophy and public policy.

While some early journalists, such as Jonathan Swift (1667–1745), enjoyed stable and profitable careers through service to the Crown, many were critical of their governments in a manner that appealed to a growing number of readers. As patronage shifted from the courts to the aristocratic salon, journalists became the tools of the nobility's attacks on absolutism. Moreover, coffeehouses and cafés provided these authors with a growing audience of middle-class readers, many of whom favored a more open society and polity. Pornographic *libelles* (lampoons) describing lurid details of the private lives of well-known personages, especially in royal courts, became the mid-eighteenth-century's best-sellers in many parts of Europe. Dressed up as philosophical treatises, they gave rise to a vast number of authors whom the historian Robert Darnton describes as "gutter Rousseaus." Throughout eighteenth-century Europe philosophes, radicals, and politically minded pornographers posed serious challenges to the authority and respect commanded by governments, earning those writers the reputation of constituting a separate and dangerous "republic of letters."

European monarchs attempted to counteract the threat by increasing controls over the press. Cardinal Richelieu, chief minister of French King Louis XIII, attempted to promote the development of royal absolutism in France by establishing in 1634 the Académie Française (French Academy), a formal body of writers with control of French printing. Governments throughout Europe attempted to buy off influential journalists with pensions and sinecures. Richelieu rewarded Théophraste Renaudot, editor of France's most important weekly newspaper, *La Gazette de France*, with a handsome salary, the exclusive privilege to print weekly news in Paris, and news updates from royal dispatches. In turn, *La Gazette de France* remained a firm ally of church and state, supporting, for example, the church's condemnation of Galileo for his heretical assertion that the earth revolved around the sun. Since newspapers and journals had to meet their subscribers' expectations for regular and timely installments, the threat of imprisonment kept most periodical journalists loyal to the Crown.

Though the periodical press grew throughout the eighteenth century and exerted great influence over its readers, it catered mainly to an elite audience of aristocrats and the upper-middle classes. Stamp taxes and censorship kept newspapers from reaching middle- and lower-class readers, who continued to depend on the cheaper broadsides and pamphlets instead. Journalism was deeply influenced by this situation. In describing the effects of censorship under the Old Regime, Martin asserts that the press was denied "the margin of liberty indispensable for it to flourish and treat the weightier topics" (Martin, 1994, p. 414). But in 1789 the Old Regime and its controls over the press came crashing down, granting the press a whole new political freedom and power.

THE RISE OF THE POLITICAL PRESS IN THE AGE OF REVOLUTIONS

Britain was among the first of the European states to grant the press limited political freedom. In 1771 Parliament granted the press the right to report parliamentary debates. In the two decades preceding the French Revolution, Britain was a refuge for Europe's most liberal critics of the church and absolutist monarchies. The English press became the most radical in Europe. The political power of the British press prompted the English statesman Edmund Burke to describe the journalists present in Parliament as "the fourth estate." America's war for independence, the radicalism of John Wilkes and his followers at home, and the French Revolution and its wars fueled the dramatic growth of newspaper and pamphlet circulation. The annual circulation of London papers alone

Revolutionary Journalism. Copy of *L'Ami du Peuple* for 13 August 1793 stained with the blood of its assassinated editor, Jean-Paul Marat. [For Jacques-Louis David's painting of the dead Marat, see the article "Artists" in volume 3.] BIBLIOTHÈQUE NATIONALE DE FRANCE/©COLLECTION VIOLLET

grew from nearly 10 million copies in 1760 to over 25 million in 1815. At the same time the provincial papers throughout urban Britain grew and exercised increasing influence on elections.

A great variety of political journalists, defenders and critics of the government alike, competed for the reading public's attention. By the early nineteenth century nearly every political party published its own newspaper. In Spain many newspapers were founded by *sociedades patrióticas,* political groups growing out of the informal discussion groups of Madrid cafés. Though no more numerous than conservative and nonpolitical writers, radical journalists inspired by Enlightenment ideas played a crucial role in bringing about a series of liberal revolutions in Europe, none more important than the French Revolution of 1789.

The French Revolution diminished censorship and generated a flood of new newspapers, pamphlets, broadsides, and almanacs. The power and radicalism of French revolutionary journalism surpassed mon-

archs' worst fears. Liberal nobles used the press in 1788 to undermine absolute monarchy in France, and the nobles' revolt was itself undermined by an even larger pamphlet campaign. Emmanuel-Joseph Sieyès wrote *What Is the Third Estate?* in 1789 and inspired the French to create a liberal constitutional and representative government. Politicians became journalists, and journalists such as Camille Desmoulins, Jean-Paul Marat, and Jacques Hébert became politicians who radicalized the revolution. Their role was significant because Parisian workers looked to them for insight and information. Because of the power they exercised and the fear they inspired in their political opponents, many journalists were murdered or executed at the height of the Revolution.

After 1793 French governments imposed strict censorship on political printing. Throughout Europe censorship was redoubled in the early nineteenth century to silence the political and social radicalism of journalists. Even Spain's brief moderate constitutional monarchy passed a law in 1822 that outlawed subversive prints that "injure the sacred and inviolable person of the King," warned against any attempt to stir rebellion, and even banned political allegory. But such strategies did not long stave off European liberals' demand for a free press. Increased censorship touched off revolution in France again in 1830, and journalists were crucial in the creation of a liberal monarchy. Journalists played an equally important role in the Chartist movement in England and in the 1848 revolutions on the Continent. While these were mainly urban revolutions in which journalists mobilized workers, democratic socialist pamphleteers created a peasant movement in France between 1849 and 1851 that demanded the liberalization of France's Second Republic. These peasants rose in revolt against Louis Napoleon's coup d'etat at the end of 1851, prompting his brutal repression of their democratic socialist movement and his reintroduction of severe press censorship. Though none of these revolutions succeeded in creating a lasting radical republic, the power of the press to mobilize the lower classes toward political ends encouraged journalists and politicians to expand the political press while governments made greater efforts to suppress it.

Among political periodicals, the socialist press has been of particular interest to social historians. Political repression and weak demand curtailed its success until nearly the beginning of the nineteenth century. Karl Marx's paper *Neue Rheinische Zeitung* (1848) could be considered exceptionally successful with only six thousand subscribers during the 1848 revolution, when the Prussian press was freed of political repression. By the end of the century, however, socialist editors such as Jean Jaurès, theorists such as Jules Guesde, and writers such as Anatole France reached a large and sympathetic audience through socialist newspapers. Studies of the socialist press suggest the gradual development of working-class consciousness and illustrate the transformation of socialist thinking over time.

The nature of journalism changed in the era of European revolutions. In the last decade of the eighteenth century three London papers, the nonpartisan *Times,* the Whig *Morning Chronicle,* and the Tory *Morning Post,* began a fierce competition to be the first to print the latest news during the French Revolution and the Napoleonic Wars. Couriers rushed the news, collected by domestic reporters and foreign correspondents, to waiting editors. The *Times* owners also invested in new techniques that decreased the time required to print a new edition. These papers assigned reporters to specific "beats," where they gained greater expertise and connections, enabling regular and more extensive reports. By the mid-nine-

teenth century readers showed a growing preference for fact over polemic, promoting a more factual journalistic style. Newspapers also encouraged reporters to move beyond mere description to investigate cause and effect. Taking advantage of the growing number of newspapers demanding the latest news, enterprising businesspeople, such as Charles Havas in Paris, Bernard Wolff in Berlin, and Paul Julius von Reuter in London, created agencies that collected news from foreign papers and correspondents and communicated it to their subscribers by courier, carrier pigeons, and eventually telegraph.

Although the speed of communicating news accelerated, the effect in Europe was limited to the few who could afford high subscription prices. Fearful of the political challenges of printed matter, governments prevented public sales and imposed stamp taxes sufficient to preclude middle- and lower-class subscriptions. In the early nineteenth century lower-middle-class readers accessed political papers by purchasing memberships in private libraries. Both middle- and working-class readers also found newspapers at subscribing bars and cafés. Few workers, however, read the political press through any means.

A few journalistic pioneers attempted to expand readership through three innovations. First, a number of French and British newspapers reduced the price of subscriptions by selling advertising space to the consumer industries of the industrial revolution. But even in 1846, after a decade of this practice, all the Parisian dailies combined could claim less than 200,000 subscribers throughout France. Though advertising did not create a mass audience for most European journals, it became a staple feature that manufacturers and sellers used to reach potential customers and that influenced marketing, business, and consumerism. Second, newspapers serialized popular novels. French newspapers printed great works by Victor Hugo, Honoré de Balzac, Alexandre Dumas, Alphonse-Marie-Louis de Prat de Lamartine, and Eugène Sue. Literature did indeed expand circulation among those who could afford subscriptions, but, more importantly, when newspapers eventually reached much larger audiences, the serialized novel greatly expanded fiction reading. Last, a number of magazine and newspaper editors applied new techniques of lithography to illustrate their serials. The English *Penny Magazine,* founded in 1830, and the German *Pfennig Magazin* (Penny magazine), begun in 1833, both featured woodcut illustrations. By mid-century more European publishers adopted the modern form of newspapers, offering the latest news, illustrations, and serial novels at prices reduced by extensive advertising.

Before the advent of mass circulation newspapers, journalism's greatest expansion resulted from the creation of countless professional journals, illustrated magazines, political newspapers, and provincial dailies that met the specialized interests of smaller readerships. While most of these publications remained prohibitively expensive for lower- and middle-class readers and none reached a large market, globally they brought variety to journalism. A truly mass newspaper press soon appeared.

THE MASS-CIRCULATION PRESS

After the mid-nineteenth century on the Continent, but earlier in Britain, a number of changes in the newspaper business converged with socioeconomic transformations to create a mass press in Europe. Growing disposable incomes and literacy in turn increased demand for the press. An important relationship existed between the expansion of literacy and the reciprocal growth of the press. Literacy rates from 60 to 80 percent in Britain, Germany, and France spurred the development of mass-circulation newspapers at mid-century, while low literacy postponed the expansion of the press until the late nineteenth century in southern and eastern Europe and the early twentieth century in Russia.

The development of mass presses also derived from changes in the newspaper business that increased supply and augmented demand. New printing technologies developed at mid-century made giant press-runs possible. More importantly mass-circulation newspapers increased consumer demand by downplaying politics and emphasizing sensationalism. After 1815 the *Times* of London outstripped its competitors in a climate of heavy censorship by remaining nonpartisan. John Walter, its founder, argued that a newspaper "should contain something suited to every palate . . . and by steering clear of extremes, hit the happy medium." The English "pauper press" began a newspaper revolution in the 1830s in part by de-emphasizing politics and refusing to pay the stamp tax. Halfhearted attempts to enforce the tax only generated publicity that boosted sales. In 1836 Parliament reduced the stamp tax to one penny and in 1855 abolished it, facilitating the dramatic rise in newspaper circulation. The "pauper press" also owed its success to its sensationalism. Henry Hetherington, publisher of *The Twopenny Dispatch,* emphasized crimes, fires, spectacles, and sports to make his paper one of the most popular in London by the mid-1830s.

In 1863 Polydore Milhaud's *Petit journal* (Small journal) touched off a similar newspaper explosion in France. The nonpolitical daily escaped the tax on political prints and sold at one-third the price of its competitors. Like its English counterparts, it published serialized novels and sensational news. By the 1880s *Petit journal* boasted over a million subscribers and soon had imitators. The illustrated mass-circulation dailies eventually replaced the news broadsides and pamphlets as the principal source of news for the lower classes.

Many social historians, anthropologists, folklorists, and sociologists have viewed the transition from the popular pamphlet and broadsheet press to the mass-circulation newspaper as a veritable cultural revolution. Eugen Weber describes it as the replacement of an oral culture in rural France with an urban-based written culture. While some historians have argued that these assertions overstate the differences between newspapers and their pamphlet and broadside predecessors, the mass-circulation newspaper did place newsmaking in the hands of more educated writers and editors and commercially oriented publishers. As popular news became the product of urban elites, their ideas gained broader acceptance. In dramatic reports of foreign massacres, vicious battles, heinous crimes, sensational trials, and executions, the newspapers addressed the topics traditional to broadside and pamphlet presses. Yet they did so in a manner that promoted new bourgeois ideas about nationalism and imperialism, social justice, moral order, masculinity, and femininity. The modern newspapers adopted traditional foci to gain a mass audience and spread elite ideas.

As newspapers reached a larger audience, journalists became more powerful. Reporters and editors gained notoriety through controversial press campaigns. William Howard Russell, a foreign correspondent for the *Times,* was famous for his scathing criticism of the mismanagement of the Crimean War. In the 1870s the passion and satire of two editors at *Petit journal* made their pseudonym, Timothy Trimm, a household word in Paris and provincial cities. French and German journalists fueled public support for the Franco-Prussian War in 1870, and western European journalists significantly promoted empire building in subsequent decades. Without doubt the most dramatic journalistic act of the century was Émile Zola's 1898 editorial "J'accuse!" decrying the army's scandalous injustice against Captain Alfred Dreyfus, who was falsely accused of passing military secrets to the Germans. Affirming what Edmund Burke had said a century before about the power of journalists, Zola and journalists like him brought down the French government. Moreover, Georges Clemenceau, who published Zola's article in *L'Aurore,* used the press to

Journalism in the City. Newsstand near the Gare St.-Lazare, Paris, 1899. ©BOYER-VIOLLET

build his own political career and eventually became France's president.

THE TWENTIETH CENTURY AND ELECTRONIC MEDIA

In the first decades of the twentieth century the sales of many mass-circulation dailies began to plateau in western Europe but continued to spread throughout southern and eastern Europe. Such dailies had already appeared in Italy at the end of the previous century, in Russia before World War I, and in Spain soon after

the war. In content newspapers continued to appeal to the largest possible audience by emphasizing sensational news and avoiding political partisanship. Even as the press increasingly escaped from government censorship in western and central Europe, political content undermined sales if the editors took a stance unpopular with a portion of their readers. This is not to say that newspapers ignored important political issues. On the contrary, they emphasized domestic and international politics heavily, but papers toned down their partisanship, even those papers serving as the mouthpieces of specific parties and political organizations. As they spread throughout Europe, mass-circulation dailies more than ever before shaped public responses to major issues, political and otherwise. As a result, businessmen and politicians hired professional "public relations" specialists to win them favorable press coverage.

In the twentieth century many dailies adopted new forms and content that improved sales and altered modern journalism. Editors added large headlines to front page articles to attract buyers and titled each story to facilitate selective reading. In content they won additional readers by covering sports, greatly extending that coverage after World War I. Indeed sports journalism became so important to working-class readers that Socialist and Communist Party papers featured it as well. Though satirical drawings had been a staple of many newspapers since the mid-nineteenth century, twentieth-century papers gave greater attention to comic drawings that eventually became comic strips. Also in the early twentieth century newspapers began to replace illustrations with photographic images, and those quick to adopt the new technology, such as *Paris-Soir,* won larger readerships. Moreover the photograph gave rise to an entirely new medium, the photomagazine. Photojournalism in the first half of the twentieth century shifted the attention of its largely middle-class readers away from the harsh realities of the post–World War I and Great Depression era to a glamorous material culture.

Journalism also changed as a business. Newspapers employed large staffs of editors, reporters, photographers, and correspondents, who pursued journalism educations. During the interwar years many journalists formed organizations to promote professional interests and standards. Expanding news agencies, such as Havas and Reuters, provided their subscribers with fully written news stories, background material, photographs, and illustrations. A complex variety of distribution agencies that circulated papers through retailers, wholesalers, and delivery services replaced postal subscriptions and street peddlers.

State control greatly altered journalism in many parts of Europe. The Russian tsar Nicholas II tried to increase state influence over the press by making the St. Petersburg Telegraph Agency, a government authority, a major source of information for Russian newspapers. After the Russian Revolution the Communist government successfully put all periodicals under state control.

At the same time it increased newspaper circulation to over three times that of the pre-Revolution level. Through the press the Soviet government promoted the spread of literacy, which jumped from 20 percent at the end of the nineteenth century to over

80 percent on the eve of World War II. The professionalism of early Soviet journalists gave way under Joseph Stalin to a political cadre that made the major media, such as the Soviet newspaper *Pravda,* into propaganda disseminators. Scholars debate whether Stalinist journalists exercised a degree of autonomy in the construction of state journalism or were merely puppets of the government. The willing duplicity of Nazi and Fascist journalists is debated less. The Nazis effectively used newspapers, magazines, radio, and films to promote state propaganda both in and outside of Germany. In the Stalinist Soviet Union and Nazi Germany thousands of journalists were willing government tools, hiding atrocities, promoting government policies, and distorting the public's perception of their state and society. So significant was their role in bringing about a world war that between 1944 and 1945 the victorious Allies abolished many of Europe's fascist and collaborationist newspapers and replaced them with new ones more suited to postwar politics. The war, however, did not end governments' control over the press. In Spain, Francisco Franco's government maintained strict controls over the press for thirty years. Even the more democratic states of postwar Western

Radio News. People listening to radio, Soviet Union, 1920s.
THE DAVID KING COLLECTION

Europe applied numerous controls, especially on new media. Swedish political parties, for example, controlled radio and television news until the late 1960s.

Not only a tool of government, journalism also continued to play a decisive role in the changing of governments. Polish journalists promoted the Solidarity movement's opposition to Communist rule in the 1980s. After 1985 Mikhail Gorbachev's policy of glasnost allowed journalists to criticize Communist governments in the USSR and Eastern Europe and undermined the governments' popular support.

The new electronic media of the twentieth century transformed journalism. In 1922 *Radiola,* France's first radio station, initiated a partial return to the tradition of spoken news. Subscribing to Havas news agency and reading reports from national daily newspapers, radio did not at first challenge the preeminence of the newspaper. Within a decade, however, radio stations throughout Europe employed their own reporters and correspondents and subscribed to news services catering exclusively to radio, making them the most up-to-the-minute news source. Realizing the importance of radio, both Stalin and Adolf Hitler used it effectively in the 1930s to extend their control over their states and their neighbors. Radio altered the style of news writing. As radio news reporting became simpler and more concise, newspapers also adopted the style, which quickly became the norm for modern journalism. To compete with radio, newspapers became larger and diversified their content to satisfy more tastes, producing the modern comic strip, weather forecast, and horoscope.

Journalists also communicated the news through film and television. The interwar years were the golden age of newsreel photography in Europe. Newsreels featured films of significant events and personalities and after 1927 included a narrator explaining the images. Shown in movie theaters, they made moviegoers witnesses to events, but weeks and months afterward. In this capacity newsreels played a crucial role in exposing Nazi atrocities in images that words could not. In the 1950s television further revolutionized journalism by adding video to the up-to-the-minute reporting offered by radio. Constrained at first by its own novelty and by the weight and bulk of cameras, television initially relied on newsreels for its images. However, television stations soon employed their own staffs of reporters and foreign correspondents. In 1949 France's first television news program aired coverage of a balloon race that ended with the destruction of the television cameramen's balloon and created an immediate sensation. In 1951 television news began to air twice a day in France, and by 1961 these telecasts reached nearly every part of the country. In contrast

Minitel. Woman using a Minitel, a computer terminal attached to the telephone that offers phone listings, schedules, and ticket ordering. Paris, 1989. OWEN FRANKEN/©CORBIS

to the United States, European television stations have been under the direct control of the government. In England, the British Broadcasting Corporation controlled television in the postwar period. Italian political parties directed all of Italy's national television networks until the late twentieth century. After the 1970s the proliferation of private cable and satellite stations distanced television from government control and promoted the development of stations specializing in television journalism.

Television accelerated the changes in journalism initiated by early twentieth-century media, continuing the trend toward shortened length and simplified content of reports. These techniques have influenced political campaigning, as politicians endeavor to present a pleasing image and to adopt an intimate tone for viewers. By adding the visual to radio's audio communication, television in a sense restored the audiovisual communication of news that preceded the spread of print. Yet television also continued the trend of the modern media to make news less interactive and less responsive to individual and small community needs and interests. By serving national publics, television, radio, and national newspapers have increased the distance between the event and the public.

The twentieth century closed with the spread of computer communications throughout Europe. Europeans began to rely on computer networks for communication and news in the late 1970s. Between 1978 and 1981 the French introduced TRANSPAC and TELETEL, public computer communication networks. Computer communications were not used widely because computers remained very expensive, however, Western European governments began to provide every home with access to national computer networks in the early 1980s. News, weather, transportation information, and a variety of other services became available through television sets or through small computer terminals, such as the French Minitel introduced in the 1980s. By 1988, 4 million French homes used Minitel, and computer communications increased fivefold. The Internet initiated the most dramatic transition by empowering the "Web surfer" to find news of particular interest. News agencies, television news networks, governments, corporations, and millions of other World Wide Web users offer a dizzying array of information. Print, audio, and video formats have become available at once, and the user can print a hard copy in seconds. The Internet has given Europeans a means to interact with news makers. While modern communications create easier access to more kinds of information, the overwhelming volume of available data gives greater significance than ever to the subjects chosen and judgments drawn by journalists. In the twenty-first century, journalists continue to shape public opinion and public policy. Despite the greater variety of information available to journalists, however, their foci and assessments remain very much informed by professional traditions.

See also **Professionals and Professionalization; Revolutions; New Social Movements** *(volume 3);* **Pornography** *(volume 4); and other articles in this section.*

BIBLIOGRAPHY

Altick, Richard D. *Writers, Readers, and Occasions: Selected Essays on Victorian Literature and Life.* Columbus, Ohio, 1989.

Bellanger, Claude, et al. *Histoire générale de la presse française.* Paris, 1969.

Boyce, George, James Curran, and Pauline Wingate, eds. *Newspaper History from the Seventeenth Century to the Present Day.* London, 1978.

Brake, Laurel. *Subjugated Knowledges: Journalism, Gender, and Literature in the Nineteenth Century.* New York, 1994.

Chartier, Roger. *The Cultural Uses of Print in Early Modern France.* Translated by Lydia G. Cochrane. Princeton, N.J. 1987.

Chartier, Roger, ed. *The Culture of Print: Power and the Uses of Print in Early Modern Europe.* Translated by Lydia G. Cochrane. Princeton, N.J., 1989.

Cheesman, Tom. *The Shocking Ballad Picture Show: German Popular Literature and Cultural History.* Providence, R.I., 1994.

Darnton, Robert. *The Forbidden Bestsellers of Pre-Revolutionary France.* New York, 1995.

Darnton, Robert. *The Literary Underground of the Old Regime.* Cambridge, Mass., 1982.

Darnton, Robert, and Daniel Roche, eds. *Revolution in Print: The Press in France, 1775–1800.* Berkeley, Calif., 1989.

De la Motte, Dean, and Jeannene M. Przyblyski, eds. *Making the News: Modernity and the Mass Press in Nineteenth-Century France.* Amherst, Mass., 1999.

Edwards, Mark U., Jr. *Printing, Propaganda, and Martin Luther.* Berkeley, Calif., 1994.

Eisenstein, Elizabeth L. *The Printing Revolution in Early Modern Europe.* Cambridge, U.K., 1983.

Esaiasson, Peter. "120 Years of Swedish Election Campaigns: A Story of the Rise and Decline of Political Parties and the Emergence of the Mass Media as Power Brokers." *Scandinavian Political Studies* 14, no. 3 (1991): 261–278.

Frank, Joseph. *The Beginnings of the English Newspaper, 1620–1660.* Cambridge, Mass., 1961.

Hardt, Hanno. "Pictures for the Masses: Photography and the Rise of Popular Magazines in Weimar Germany." *Journal of Communication Inquiry* 13, no. 1 (1989): 7–30.

Hollis, Patricia. *The Pauper Press: A Study in Working-Class Radicalism of the 1830s.* London, 1970.

Martin, Henri-Jean. *The History and Power of Writing.* Translated by Lydia G. Cochrane. Chicago, 1994.

McLuhan, Marshall. *Understanding Media: The Extensions of Man.* Cambridge, Mass., 1994.

McReynolds, Louise. "Autocratic Journalism: The Case of the St. Petersburg Telegraph Agency." *Slavic Review* 49, no. 1 (1990): 48–57.

McReynolds, Louise. *The News under Russia's Old Regime: The Development of a Mass-Circulation Press.* Princeton, N.J., 1991.

Neuberg, Victor E. *Popular Literature: A History and Guide from the Beginning of Printing to the Year 1897.* New York, 1977.

Nicholson, Eirwen E. C. "Consumers and Spectators: The Public of the Political Print in Eighteenth-Century England." *History* 81, no. 261 (1996): 5–21.

Palmer, Michael Beaussenat. *Des petits journaux aux grandes agences: Naissance du journalisme moderne, 1863–1914.* Paris, 1983.

Popkin, Jeremy D. *Revolutionary News: The Press in France, 1789–1799.* Durham, N.C., 1990.

Schulte, Henry F. *The Spanish Press, 1470–1966: Print, Power, and Politics.* Urbana, Ill., 1968.

Stephens, Mitchell. *A History of News.* New York, 1988.

Watt, Tessa. *Cheap Print and Popular Piety, 1550–1640.* Cambridge, U.K., 1991.

Weber, Eugen. *Peasants into Frenchmen: The Modernization of Rural France, 1870–1914.* Stanford, Calif., 1976.

Section 23

❧

EVERYDAY LIFE

Material Culture   435
Whitney A. Walton

Standards of Living   451
Norman J. G. Pounds

Housing   461
Craig Keating

Domestic Interiors   471
Rineke van Daalen

Clothing and Fashion   483
Beverly Lemire

Food and Diet   497
Kolleen M. Guy

Animals and Pets   507
Kathleen J. Kete

Toys and Games   521
Gary S. Cross

MATERIAL CULTURE

Whitney Walton

Social historians define material culture as the objects of daily life and the meanings that possessors, users, and observers invest in them. On one level the objects of daily life are stable over time. Food, shelter, furnishings, and clothes are common to all Europeans from the Renaissance to the present. On another level such objects vary enormously across different time periods, among different groups, and in different locations. They change drastically in terms of quantity, content, variety, and what their different forms signify to users and observers. For example, certain items of clothing have existed for centuries, like shirts, hats, skirts, and cloaks or coats. But new apparel articles, like long trousers for men, shirtwaist dresses for women, and underwear for everyone, and modifications of old ones, along with styles that change with increasing rapidity, make clothing highly variable. Moreover the connotations of clothing in terms of social standing, political positioning, and personal identity also vary greatly. Europeans have been drinking beer and wine and other fermented beverages since before the Renaissance. However, by the eighteenth century tea and coffee were becoming integral to the European diet, and the locations and manners of their consumption separated the sexes and gave rise to new utensils and social practices. Thus scholars find in material culture a rich source of information on the physical, daily existence of Europeans and how it changed. They also look to material culture for insights into the exercise of power, social relations, group values, and people's sense of themselves as individuals.

The influential historian Fernand Braudel drew attention to what he termed "material life" in his broadly conceived studies of Europe and the world from the fifteenth through the eighteenth centuries. In his works Braudel described in detail and in comparative perspective the objects of everyday existence, including food and drink, housing, furnishings, and clothing, in Europe, Asia, and Latin America during the Renaissance and early modern eras. Using a variety of texts and images he charted developments like the gradual introduction of the fork for eating food or the evolution of household furnishings from simple, carpentered storage boxes or trunks to elaborately decorated and variegated wooden chests of drawers, highboys, sideboards, stands, and desks. Such developments are significant because they reveal a refinement in manners and greater valuation of civility in the first case and more stable residences and an increased sense of security in the second. Braudel's interest was in delineating structures through this inspection of minute daily practices and objects. For Braudel material life, or the deeply internalized habits and implements of routine survival, was the dominant feature of preindustrial European society. He discerned the fundamental rhythms of human existence through close observation of things.

Numerous scholars are indebted to Braudel for his massive research and innovative analysis of everyday objects, and they have furthered the study of material culture by practicing new methodologies, introducing new analytical frameworks, focusing on particular geographic areas or social groups, and extending the time frame both backward and forward. One approach to material culture that several historians have employed fruitfully is to analyze the goods of rulers, aristocrats, and wealthy elites as reflecting certain cultural values and social and political power.

THE POSSESSIONS OF ELITES

The Italian Renaissance commonly is associated with great cultural achievements in the arts and in scholarship. These achievements were closely connected with extensive commercial networks and the accumulation of goods by wealthy Italian merchants, prelates, and princes. In addition to being works of art that represent innovations in perspective, color, and the treatment of the human figure, paintings of the Renaissance portray the settings and objects of everyday life and the values of their owners and patrons. They render in precise and beautiful detail the architecture of houses, the colors and designs of clothing fabrics and wall hangings, and the decorative carving on furniture and in household interiors. Painters represented few items of furniture—storage chests, tables, chairs, and beds—in domestic settings, but these were often skillfully carved and made of fine, polished wood. Plush fabrics, such as velvet, silk, brocade, and fine wool, appear frequently in dazzling colors—scarlet, green, ultramarine blue, russet, and lavender. Typical and opulent interior furnishings in fifteenth-century paintings include brass or silver-gilt candlesticks, tasseled cushions, embroidered cloths, and illuminated manuscripts bound in leather with jeweled clasps. The backgrounds of even religious paintings show rugs from Turkey, porcelain and silk from China, leather bookbindings from Spain, fur-trimmed, brocaded robes of the Ottoman style, and glass from Venice, reflecting the dynamism of the Levantine trade in the Renaissance and its contribution to the material culture of the rich.

The content of many paintings suggests that owners and patrons valued their material possessions and took pride in the prosperity and cultivation that accrued from successful commercial activity. Indeed paintings were commodities and furnishings whose value lay in the cost of the paint and the skill and reputation of the artist. Renaissance princes collected paintings and books as much to assert their status and influence as to promote fine art and humanist learning. The material culture of Renaissance elites reflects a daily practice of acquisitiveness and commercialism as well as erudition and art appreciation.

Patrons and collectors particularly prized antique artifacts because they provided an association between the present and a desirable past. The Renaissance poet Francesco Petrarch (1304–1374), for example, claimed that his possession of a book by Cicero (106–43 B.C.) made him feel like he possessed Cicero himself. In this case a material object embodied the knowledge of one of the ancients. Wealthy and cultivated persons of the Renaissance sought to tie their existence to ancient history through the acquisition of antique artifacts. When the supply of antique objects diminished or disappeared, collectors turned to artifacts of the Renaissance. Thus the private accumulation of historical goods became the foundation of public institutions to display the culture of the present and started a new, Western sensibility about the importance of preserving the past.

Material objects reflected power and wealth in other ways and in other contexts. Queen Elizabeth I (r. 1558–1603) of England spent lavishly in her court to impress the population with her authority and power and to coerce the nobility to spend extrava-

gantly as well. Paintings show the queen dressed in gorgeous silks and fine lace and covered with jewels. She filled her many palatial residences with elegant furnishings and entertained her guests with hunts, dances, performances, and huge banquets consisting of numerous courses and rare dishes. These practices required expensive objects for ritual proceedings that made visible the magnificence and hence the power of the monarchy, and these practices forced the nobility to do the same. Elizabeth wanted the nobles, the chief rivals to her authority, to spend their money and their time at court seeking her favors. This developed into a cycle whereby nobles who wished for royal beneficence spent large amounts to maintain their appearance and status at court. The more they spent, the more they depended on Elizabeth's largesse, and hence the more time and money they were required to spend at court. In this case, then, luxurious objects served as an instrument of power.

King Louis XIV, who ruled France from 1643 to 1715, exercised this technique notably, and his impressive material surroundings subsequently became the model for other rulers in Europe. Louis XIV built the magnificent palace of Versailles outside of Paris and furnished it with tapestries that recounted his glorious deeds on the battlefield. Paintings and sculptures portray the king as imposing, attractive, and effective, and to further enhance his self-image as absolute ruler he constructed the famous hall of mirrors to reflect and multiply his greatness. Surrounding the palace are extensive, carefully trimmed gardens and fountains with sculptures, refreshing and beautiful settings for parties, masquerades, and fireworks displays. Louis and his successors also constructed separate buildings on the royal grounds for more intimate gatherings and pleasures. Louis XIV claimed that he was the state, and his possessions were the visible manifestation of France's power.

In contrast to the absolute monarchies of France, Prussia, and Austria that attempted to construct national unity around royal splendor, the Dutch Republic of the seventeenth and eighteenth centuries suggests an alternative interpretation of material culture. Lacking an individual monarch to display publicly his or her power as representative of the state, the Dutch nonetheless placed and used material objects in a manner to assert an emerging national identity. Dutch people were intensely conscious of their Protestant faith and religious morality and sought to endow consumption and goods with moral meaning. They were no strangers to luxurious and exotic goods, since their efficient farming practices and growing trade networks provided them with abundant food, furnishings, and pleasures, even for successful artisans and modest

Dutch Interior of the Seventeenth Century. *The Life of Man,* painting by Jan Steen (c. 1626–1679). Photograph © Mauritshuis, The Hague

tradespeople. Dutch persons of the middling sort enjoyed satisfying meals of salads, stewed meat, vegetables, fish, and buttered bread with cheese or meat slices. They drank their favorite beverage, beer, out of pewter or silver tankards, some highly decorated. A room in a great merchant's house had walls hung with gold-stamped leather, fifteen paintings, and one ebonyframed mirror. The furniture consisted of an East Indian cabinet, a round nutwood table covered with a Turkish rug, a nutwood buffet, twelve chairs, a cupboard, and a harpsichord.

Yet the Dutch feared that excesses of materialism might lead them astray from a righteous and godly life. One solution was to encourage consumption in moderation. That is, goods in themselves, like alcohol and tobacco, were not inherently evil, but immoderate indulgence in them might hinder an individual from fulfilling a patriotic or civic responsibility. Another solution was discretion. The Dutch enjoyed food, furnishings, and clothing in the privacy of their homes, in contrast to the more public activities of the aristocracies of other European states. Yet another means of legitimizing private wealth was the Dutch valuation of cleanliness. Keeping their persons, homes, and cities clean was a sign of moral rectitude no matter how many possessions the Dutch had. Moreover cleanli-

ness connoted civic-mindedness for it distinguished the Dutch from less fastidious Europeans, and it was a prophylactic against disease that threatened to weaken the country.

ORDINARY PEOPLE

The paintings of princes, lace and jewels of royalty, and domestic comforts of merchants are fascinating in their sumptuousness and as manifestations of culture, power, and national identity. But in the early modern era the vast majority of Europeans did not have access to such goods. Indeed the poverty and simplicity of most people's existence contrasted sharply with the wealth and opulence of a minority. Yet the material culture of ordinary persons was no less significant than that of the privileged few during this period, and certainly the changes in daily life of the majority were slower but ultimately of far greater consequence.

Housing throughout Europe from 1400 to 1800 frequently consisted of wood. Peasant dwellings were simple, sometimes constructed of earthen materials along with wood. Their function was to provide shelter for humans and animals, and they often comprised only one room. Furnishings were also simple and might include a bench, a table, possibly some bed planks and sacks of straw, and basic cooking utensils, such as a pot, a pothook, and a pan. In some urban areas stone or brick replaced wood over time as the most common element in housing construction. Floors at the ground level, especially in poor dwellings, were of earth. Various types of tile floors appeared in the fourteenth and sixteenth centuries, and by the eighteenth century parquet floors were popular among the rich. Until the sixteenth century Europeans laid straw or flowers and herbs in ground-floor rooms; eventually this was replaced with woven mats and carpets. Walls were painted or covered with tapestry, though wallpaper became common in the seventeenth century. More expensive coverings, like leather or carved wood paneling, adorned the houses of wealthy families.

The staple food of Europeans was wheat, which they consumed, along with other cereals, in bread and gruel. In addition wealthy Europeans enjoyed plentiful and various meat dishes, like roasted and boiled fowl, beef, mutton, and pork. The poor settled for vegetables and some salt meat as accompaniments to bread and, more often, gruel. Eating practices in the fifteenth and sixteenth centuries were crude by modern standards. People ate off a wooden board or trencher instead of a plate. In many parts of Europe guests were expected to provide their own knives and cups or goblets. A common plate piled high with varieties of meat occupied the center of the table, and diners picked out what they desired with their fingers. Servants presented and removed dishes and filled cups with wine or water. Knives were essential eating utensils. Spoons became common in the sixteenth century, and individual forks spread slowly in the sixteenth and seventeenth centuries.

Peasant clothing changed little from 1400 to 1800. The most common fabrics were homespun linen or wool, and shoes were often a luxury. However the clothes of the rich changed rapidly during the same period, with distinctive regional variations. Women of the Italian Renaissance wore square-necked garments with wide sleeves and elaborate hairnets and headdresses. In the sixteenth century the black clothes of the Spanish court became popular throughout Europe, succeeded by clothing in brilliant colors from the French style in the seventeenth century. Although fashion trends affected all of Europe, regional variations were rife. Linen or lace neck ruffs could be huge and elaborate or small and modest. Face paint was popular in some places and frowned upon in others. The three-piece suit for men made its appearance in seventeenth-century England as the outward sign of masculine disdain for fashion and focus on serious matters like politics.

NEW PRODUCTS

In the seventeenth century and especially the eighteenth century material culture in Europe reflected the increased availability of goods from Asia, Africa, and the Americas. European trade with the Middle East, other southwestern portions of Asia, and northern Africa never entirely ceased after relations were established in ancient times. Europeans obtained silks, spices, and slaves from these areas throughout the late Middle Ages and early modern periods. Yet certain Renaissance princes, eager to bypass Muslim middlemen and acquire access to or a monopoly over larger quantities of highly valued goods, like spices and precious metals, subsidized sea voyages of exploration to other parts of the world. In terms of material culture, the long-term results of these voyages included the introduction of new products and larger quantities of known products and the subsequent transformation of daily European practices.

Tobacco from North America enjoyed immediate success among European men in the seventeenth century. Commentators believed that tobacco had a calming effect on the consumer while simultaneously stimulating intellectual activity. Pipe smoking was the most common form of tobacco consumption until the nineteenth century, though inhaling it into the nose in the form of snuff was also popular among certain eighteenth-century elites. Tobacco consumers acquired pipes and snuff boxes, new objects of pleasure. Additionally tobacco fostered public, largely masculine, taverns and coffeehouses, where men gathered to drink, smoke, and share news.

Coffee became an extremely popular beverage in Europe during the eighteenth century. Like tobacco coffee was initially consumed by men in public places, and coffeehouses became centers of information, business transactions, and, some governments feared, political subversion. Tea and chocolate were also drinks of choice among Europeans. Unlike coffee, they were often consumed in the home with new, largely feminine rituals, especially surrounding tea consumption. Ladies of the aristocracy and the middle classes bought pewter, silver, and porcelain tea services. A "public" ritual performed in the home, tea drinking became a social activity that ideally required comfortable and elegant tables and chairs and fashionable dress. These products and social practices have helped historians understand the meaning of material goods in the everyday lives of ordinary Europeans.

A Simple Interior. *The Comforts of Industry,* painting (1790) by George Morland (1763–1804). NATIONAL GALLERIES OF SCOTLAND, EDINBURGH

An extensive sampling and analysis of probate records in London and provincial England for the seventeenth and eighteenth centuries reveals both traditional and new patterns of domestic existence and sense of personal identity. Lorna Weatherill has maintained that the numerous cooking utensils in the homes of the comfortable classes were both traditional and reflective of the importance of food in this group's everyday life. While utensils were functional and unadorned, items for serving and eating food—dishes and cutlery—became more decorated and refined from the seventeenth to the eighteenth century. Wooden trenchers and bowls gradually were replaced by pewter dishes. Forks and knives were new in the list of personal and family possessions, as were tea services. These developments, according to Weatherill, indicated a new layout of table settings and a new habit of food consumption as a social activity. Additionally Weatherill noted an increase in mirrors in private homes, suggesting both a greater importance of the self and a desire to enhance the appearance of the home.

Similarly the diaries of Elizabeth Shackleton from 1751 to 1781 reveal a bourgeois Lancashire homemaker for whom the care and upkeep of household goods was a major source of identity and self-worth. According to the diaries Shackleton spent a considerable amount of her time ordering, mending, and maintaining household linens, clothes, dishes, and the like. She divided her domestic possessions into the categories of either "best" or "common," indicating her profound sense of distinction between private, family events, and social rituals. Although she was well aware of fashion trends and style changes in china and clothes on a national level, Shackleton was no giddy pursuer of novelty. She was a discriminating consumer who exercised a standard of tastefulness, beauty, and longevity in the items she bought. Regarding items of furniture in particular, Shackleton valued durability and recognized that quality pieces would outlast her own lifetime.

Poorer consumers also responded to the availability of new and more affordable goods, notably sugar. An expensive and highly prized item for several centuries, sugar became more widely available and cheaper in the eighteenth century with the establishment of sugar plantations in the Caribbean Islands. Owned by Europeans and worked by slave labor, these plantations produced sufficient quantities of sugar so that almost all Europeans could afford to buy some.

Over the course of the nineteenth century sugar became a mainstay of working-class diets in Britain. Combined with tea, it provided a quick, cheap, warm, and psychologically satisfying food for laboring men, women, and children with little time to spend cooking or consuming a more elaborate meal. The anthropologist Sidney Mintz suggested that sugar made possible the industrial revolution in Britain because workers in factories, sweatshops, and other operations regarded tea (almost always drunk with sugar), jam, and other sweets as convenience foods and compensation for long and difficult days or nights of continuous labor.

CONSUMER BEHAVIOR

An issue of great importance in the history of material culture and a subject of intense debate among historians has to do with changes in consumer behavior and the meaning of goods during the early modern period. Was there ever a consumer revolution, a dramatic and broad-based transformation in European attitudes toward things and in Europeans' daily practices involving material objects? If so, when did it occur, and how did it happen? Neil McKendrick and several other scholars have asserted that a consumer revolution did occur in the eighteenth century. They maintain that early industrialization was accompanied by increased domestic consumption in England. Working people acquired many possessions, like dishes, household adornments, ribbons, buckles, and trinkets, which were more affordable due to changes in production methods. Thus the laboring poor desired and enjoyed more material goods than ever before. McKendrick also discerned a revolutionary change in material culture among wealthier consumers. Enticed by innovative entrepreneurs, like the pottery maker Josiah Wedgwood, middle-class consumers wanted earthenware decorated with classical designs, which Wedgwood successfully marketed as fashionable among the elites.

By contrast, some scholars have maintained that the extravagant spending of Renaissance rulers and the somewhat more restrained acquisition of goods by wealthy commoners laid the foundation for the modern acceptance of consumerism as an integral part of daily life and personal identity. From this perspective, instead of a consumer revolution, a gradual "trickle-down effect" occurred over a few centuries. The purchasing of numerous household and personal items spread from the elite strata of society down to the less wealthy. Some research supports a bottom-up approach, indicating that working people, even the laboring poor, in early modern Europe made joint decisions at the household level about the allocation of their resources into production and consumption. Thus Jan de Vries posited "an industrious revolution" in the early modern period, referring to an increase in labor productivity stimulated by families' desires for more consumer goods. This interpretation challenges the idea of a consumer revolution because working people started to acquire more goods long before technology changed the manner of production and prices of goods. Moreover the desire for goods was internally generated at the family level and was not an imitation of elite behavior or the result of manipulative marketing.

Whether or not the increase in consumption was revolutionary or gradual and whatever the motives behind Europeans' desire for various furnishings and clothes, by the eighteenth century more goods were available and were consumed. Studies of notarial inventories of household possessions at the time of the owners' deaths in eighteenth-century Paris show a trend toward greater comfort, efficiency, and privacy in home life compared with earlier centuries. Room arrangements in apartments shifted away from a vertical organization, usually with the kitchen on the ground floor and other rooms serving multiple or separate functions in different levels above. A horizontal arrangement of rooms on one or two floors in the eighteenth century was more convenient for general movement and for hauling water and fuel to different parts of the home. Parisians at this time created more privacy in their homes with separate rooms for separate functions and the use of screens or partitions. Whereas in the early modern era a single room might serve for sociability, working, eating, and sleeping, by the eighteenth century urban dwellers were inclined to separate spatially these different activities. Lighting improved with more and better candles and lamps, clearer window glass, and less obstruction from closely packed, tall buildings. Mirrors were more common than ever before, suggesting both more sophisticated home furnishings and greater concern for personal appearance. Even the clothing of poor residents changed as the century progressed. Men had several changes of shirts and more variously colored clothes, while women added dresses, aprons, and even corsets to the standard petticoats.

The political significance of eighteenth-century consumption was apparent during the French Revolution of 1789–1799. An important contributing factor to the revolution was the inability of producers and distributors to satisfy popular demand for cheap knickknacks that imitated articles worn and used by the aristocracy, for example, stockings, umbrellas, and fans. The French Revolution eradicated the guild laws and other restrictions on production characteristic of the Old Regime.

Moreover the French Revolution imbued ordinary domestic products and clothes with political meaning. Dishes and wallpaper decorated with blue, white, and red and patriotic symbols became popular as consumers wished or felt compelled to communicate their revolutionary sympathies. Supporters of the revolution and the new republic abandoned the elaborate dress and powdered wigs of the Old Regime in favor of simpler styles of clothing and more natural hair arrangements. During this period male fashion shifted from silk knee breeches and stockings to long trousers worn with boots. Embroidered waistcoats and cutaway jackets gave way to more humble fabrics and long frock coats. Indeed English styles became the model in men's clothing, and the three-piece suit symbolized responsibility, masculinity, and the ascension of bourgeois men to political power. Dark, sober colors became popular among middle-class men in Europe in the nineteenth century. Unpowdered hair cut fairly short or arranged in falling curls hearkened back to classical antiquity. Such styles were named "à la Titus" and were worn, with some differences, by women and men alike. Women's dress also became simpler though more varied. Under the Directory (1795–1799) and during the Napoleonic era (1799–1814) fashionable women sported pale, diaphanous gowns with low necklines and high waists that revealed more natural figures than the corseted ones of the Old Regime. Eventually styles returned to a fitted look and tight-laced corsets, but the changes wrought in clothing by the French Revolution spread throughout Europe, fostered by the industrial revolution in manufacturing.

READY-MADE GOODS

For several centuries Europeans produced and dressed in woolens, linens, and occasionally silks. Sturdy wool or hemp fabrics were the foundation of the majority of Europeans' clothes, manufactured from the local indigenous sheep or grown in fields of flax. Wealthier persons also wore silk fabrics, lace, and embroidery produced in Europe from raw materials native to Europe. Cotton textiles, however, transformed Europeans' dress and way of life. Europeans came into contact with cotton fabrics through trade with Asia. In the eighteenth century Europeans were enamored with cotton calicoes from India with their brilliant colors and intricate designs. English producers of wool and silk objected to the importation of fabrics that

cut into sales of their own goods, and the government placed high tariffs and prohibitions on the calicoes. Recognizing the market for cotton textiles, ambitious craftspeople and entrepreneurs figured out a way to produce cotton textiles in England with a succession of spinning and then weaving machines. These methods of mechanical production and increased output were a significant part of the industrial revolution that started in England and spread to Europe. They also contributed to a dramatic change in the material culture of Europeans in the nineteenth century.

Plentiful and cheap cotton cloth constituted new and popular forms of clothing. Rarely worn in earlier times, underwear became a fundamental part of European dress as a result of the domestic manufacture of cotton textiles. Handkerchiefs, stockings, and other knitwear also were available to more consumers. The number of clothing items a person owned, even a relatively poor person, increased noticeably in the nineteenth century, though this trend was apparent earlier as well. Mass production methods required an agglomeration of workers, and migration from the countryside to urban areas proceeded apace. City dwellers were largely unable to produce goods for themselves, so increasing numbers of persons purchased larger proportions of household goods, clothing, and food. This demand for manufactured goods in turn fueled the quest for increased production. How did the mass-production methods of the industrial revolution affect the material existence of Europeans in the nineteenth century?

Wealthy Europeans could still obtain fine, handcrafted furnishings and tailor-made clothing throughout the nineteenth century. They might request a chest of drawers or a desk in a particular historical style, and craftspeople skilled in woodworking, veneering, design, and sculpting could produce an original and beautiful piece of furniture made out of valuable or attractive woods. Fashionable women and men also had many of their clothes custom-made, selecting a fabric and style. A dressmaker or tailor fit the garment to the customer's body and taste. Yet new items produced in new ways and ready-made goods offered a wider array of choices to consumers in the nineteenth century than in earlier times.

For example, a good bed was still constructed of wood, but box spring mattresses were an innovation in bedding brought about by more efficient methods of metal production. Beds made of metal were introduced and usually used by children, servants, the poor, or in hospitals. Knives, forks, spoons, and other tableware were fundamental items for many Europeans, but electroplating silver or gold on top of flatware made of baser metals enhanced their appearance. Rich and poor families liked to decorate their homes with art, and new alternatives were available to those who could not afford original paintings or sculptures. Print reproductions of varying quality adorned the walls of the comfortable as well as the working poor. For the middle class three-dimensional reproductive technology produced affordable versions of antique and contemporary statues and figurines.

A significant innovation of the industrial era was the manufacture of ready-made clothing. In earlier times many Europeans produced cloth and clothing for themselves and their families. An adult's worn-out jacket often provided suitable fabric for a child's trousers. Itinerant peddlers transported lengths of cloth throughout the countryside for purchase by rural inhabitants. Additionally a lively trade in old, used clothing was another source for the working poor, and employers passed on their old clothes to servants. New clothes were constructed for the most part for the wealthy, who selected fabric at a draper's shop, then proceeded to a tailor or dressmaker who fitted and stitched the garment for the individual customer. All of these methods of obtaining clothing continued into the nineteenth century, but a new method added a new array of cheap clothing choices, especially for male consumers of the working class.

In the years of economic slowdown cloth merchants could hire out-of-work clothing makers to cut simple patterns in men's trousers and jackets. The cut pieces were distributed to stitchers, usually female, who worked out of their homes. Merchants then offered for sale completed articles of clothing at low prices to working people. Gradually during the nineteenth century, with more and cheaper fabrics produced in textile factories and the patenting of the sewing machine in 1846, the ready-made process effectively produced more fitted, finer garments for sale in the department stores that appeared in France and England in the 1850s. In the nineteenth century urban dwellers in Europe had access to more goods than did their ancestors, though the middle classes were by far the greatest beneficiaries of this new abundance.

THE NINETEENTH CENTURY

Housing, the setting for these new goods, was also a significant aspect of material culture for nineteenth-century Europeans. Income from successful enterprises expanded housing options for the middle class from urban apartments above or behind shops to detached houses in the suburbs. In England the middle class invented suburbs in the early nineteenth century as a means to escape the dirt, noise, and crime of

densely populated urban centers. Building houses in the countryside surrounding cities, successful middle-class families enjoyed peaceful, healthy, and comfortable surroundings while men continued to operate family businesses or to work in other positions in the city. Removed from the site of trade and manufacturing, women and children became more home-centered, and domestic decoration and upkeep and child rearing became the primary functions of middle-class wives and mothers. To be sure many middle-class women had for a long time gained a sense of identity and self-worth through housekeeping, but in the nineteenth century this function assumed a new intensity. A flood of published housekeeping manuals testifies that more women were focusing on household cares and that they felt a need for professional assistance in the appropriate means of cooking, furnishing, maintaining, decorating, and entertaining in the home. Whether they lived in urban apartments or houses in towns, suburbs, or villages, middle-class women felt compelled to maintain comfortable surroundings for their families and suitable households for their status. The housekeeping manuals kept them abreast of changing styles in home furnishings and the manners and accoutrements appropriate for sociability.

While middle-class women fretted over the upholstery fabrics of their sofas and the carpet patterns on their floors, working people experienced a different material environment. Housing for the poor was usually makeshift, cramped, and overcrowded. A few rooms for a large family and simple, sparse furniture were luxuries indeed throughout much of the nineteenth century. In the cities workingmen especially sought warmth, light, companionship, and escape from dismal, cold, and uninviting living quarters in cafés or pubs. Women socialized on the front stoops and at the public laundering sites, where they washed their families' clothes and household linens. A vibrant public or street life compensated somewhat for the inadequacies of individual housing units. Urban renewal in major cities like London, Paris, and Vienna in the late nineteenth and early twentieth centuries made some improvements in working-class housing by razing areas of dark and hazardous buildings and erecting apartment buildings with uniform designs, more lighting, and modern conveniences like plumbing and later electricity.

New inventions of the nineteenth century also led to new items of material culture. Photography, invented and developed in France in the 1830s and 1840s, quickly affected European lives, especially those of the middle classes. Around midcentury stereoscopic viewers—decorative holders that put photographs side by side so a viewer could see an image that ap-

Home-Centered Women and Children. Receiving a visitor. *Aunt Emily's Visit,* engraving (1839) by E. F. Walker after T. Allom. MARY EVANS PICTURE LIBRARY, LONDON

proximated three dimensions or "real life"—were popular in comfortable Victorian homes. Visiting cards, made of photographic portraits reduced in size and mounted on a card, were exchanged and collected ubiquitously in both England and France. Family portraits became central items of home decoration. Picture postcards offered a means for people to communicate through the postal service that was less time consuming than writing an entire letter and that conveyed images to family and friends of, for example, a vacation site. Photography and travel increasingly were connected after the invention of small, cheap cameras at the turn of the century. Instead of relying on professional photographers, ordinary people could buy a portable camera, take pictures of scenery on holiday trips or informal snapshots of family members, and either develop the film themselves or send it to the manufacturer to be made into prints. People collected photographs in albums or put them in frames set atop a fireplace mantel or a piano. Pianos became common household furnishings in middle-class and eventually in working-class homes in the nineteenth century. Other new articles that made life easier, more pleasant, or more mobile during the late nineteenth and early twentieth centuries included matches, typewriters, electric lighting, telephones, gramophones, bicycles, and, for the very rich, automobiles.

Although urban populations grew steadily during the nineteenth century, the majority of Europeans still lived in the countryside, where traditional, re-

gional objects and rituals persisted. Rural people still slept in box beds, and women wore high, starched, white lace coifs in Brittany until World War II. Farmers and agricultural workers were not likely to use many candles or oil lamps, following the pattern of working in daylight and sleeping when darkness prevailed. The mass-manufactured goods that characterized urban life arrived slowly in the countryside. Yet even in Russia, a predominantly agricultural society at the beginning of the twentieth century, material culture became more urban and modern. Elegant, fixed-price shops competed with open markets in cities, and fashionable, Western clothing replaced traditional Russian shirts and shawls.

INTERNATIONAL RELATIONS AND DOMESTIC POLITICS

Although material culture is experienced by most people in the form of everyday activities and surroundings, it is inseparable from international relations and domestic politics. In the nineteenth and twentieth centuries European imperialism affected material culture in Europe itself in ways different from foreign trade and earlier forms of colonialism. Europeans continued to enjoy tea, coffee, chocolate, and tobacco from Asia, Africa, and the Americas. Art and artifacts from these continents contributed to Europeans' sense of themselves as distinct from other cultures and in most cases superior to them. In the nineteenth century European artists integrated a flat, two-dimensional Japanese aesthetic into paintings and decorative objects. Appreciation for Chinese art and Indian design also affected European porcelain, textiles, woodworking, and other goods. Cashmere shawls, originally imported from Asia but increasingly produced in England or France, were fashionable articles of clothing for middle-class women. English women who had lived in India returned to Europe with tastes and recipes for curry dishes. Although Europeans admired arts and crafts from other parts of the world, they represented these accomplishments as something less than the products of their own culture. By the late nineteenth century museums and exhibitions displayed textiles, furnishings, and decorative objects from Asia and Africa as exotic items produced by peoples whose inferiority to Europeans was obvious in Europeans' military conquests and domination over them. Indeed, some scholars have suggested that Europeans only "knew" the peoples of Asia and Africa through the artifacts they produced. Through museums, exhibitions, mass manufacturing, and department stores, many Europeans were exposed to non-European products or motifs and purchased them for use or decoration in their homes.

Material culture involved governments in other ways as well. By the nineteenth century the era of an absolute monarch associated with a particular furnishing or clothing style was over. Nonetheless, rulers and democratic governments patronized the arts and crafts and cultivated styles and designs that might promote a popular sense of national identity and state power. Following the Great Exhibition of 1851 in London, the first international gathering of products and machines, the British were gratified that the efficiency and output of their mechanized methods of manufacturing were unsurpassed. However, the men in charge of the exhibition were dismayed at the poor design and quality of British products in comparison with those from other parts of Europe and Asia. With the proceeds of the exhibition and selected items purchased from it, they established a museum of industrial design that later became the Victoria and Albert Museum. The purpose of the museum was to inspire British producers and consumers with examples of good taste in design and style. Although limited to an elite of intellectuals and artists, the arts and crafts movement in Britain was another systematic effort to manufacture objects of beauty and utility that defied the standardization and poor quality associated with mass-production methods.

French officials felt vindicated after the Great Exhibition that French goods were more beautiful than those produced in Britain, but they also were concerned about national manufacturing. All the more reason then for subsequent French governments to seek ways to maintain a competitive advantage. The government of the Third Republic (1870–1940) promoted both an ideal standard of good taste and an artistic style of art nouveau in the interests of economic prosperity and national unity. Cultivating the tastes of middle-class women was a major component of this effort. Through a reformed public education program for girls and in support of taste professionals who wrote books and articles, the Third Republic emphasized the importance of women's role as tasteful consumers for the home. A woman's civic function, according to the schools and the manuals, was to exercise good taste in furnishing her home. Similarly women were identified as major propagators of art nouveau, a graceful and fluid artistic style reminiscent of the rococo style from the eighteenth century. The Third Republic's intention in sponsoring the international exhibitions of 1889 and 1900 was, among other things, to encourage women as producers and consumers to revitalize handicraft production in France along with a distinctive French style of art nouveau.

Several scholars have deemed western Europe in the late nineteenth and early twentieth centuries a mass consumer society. More goods were available to more people than ever before, and even workingpeople had choices about the appearance and style of clothes and furnishings they purchased. Advertising in the popular press, on streetcars, and through pamphlets or catalogs urged people to buy particular products at particular stores. Women, especially of the middle class, were the primary architects of material culture in the home and were thus the main target of advertising and of advice on tasteful consumption. This function had alarming effects when wives purchased more than their husbands could afford, and in England legal authorities reduced men's liability for their wives' spending, setting back women's ability to obtain credit and hence individual autonomy. Even working-class women, in certain regions and depending on local manufacturing industries, assumed responsibility for feeding and clothing their families and furnishing the home. Historians have debated, however, to what extent this was an era of mass consumption, given the limited participation of the working poor in the world of department stores, leisure travel, national identity, and as the target of advertisers.

THE TWENTIETH CENTURY

The material culture of all Europeans changed dramatically during World War I. As national resources

A Nineteenth-Century Domestic Interior. *Hide and Seek,* painting of a London interior (c. 1877) by James Jacques Joseph Tissot (1836–1902). NATIONAL GALLERY OF ART, WASHINGTON, D.C., CHESTER DALE FUND

were increasingly channeled toward the war effort, even the wealthy experienced a variety of shortages. Following two or three years of murderous fighting, governments in England, France, and Germany restricted civilian consumption of fats, textiles, meat, bread, and other essentials, and imported goods of all kinds were limited or prohibited. Even before the first year of the war ended, bread and other foodstuffs were scarce in Germany, and authorities called on women in particular to exercise restraint in consumption. Although many Europeans made do with coarse-grained bread, margarine, and other food substitutes, frustration and discontent exploded in Berlin in October 1915, when women demonstrated against the high prices merchants charged for butter. As a result the government attempted to impose systematic rationing of goods in acknowledgment of consumers' legitimate concerns about the capacity of the regime to provide for its citizens during wartime. Germany's failure to effectively address the shortages was a significant part of its failure to prosecute the war itself. By contrast, Britons as a whole actually ate better in spite of wartime rationing and prohibitions.

Shortages of textiles and the new tasks women performed during the war in industry, agriculture, and the service sector led to long-term changes in feminine apparel. Even after the war ended more practical clothing remained, leaving behind the pre-war long skirts, elaborate bustles, and extravagant hats. Women's dress in the 1920s and 1930s was less fitted and confining and increasingly presented a vertical, androgynous silhouette. Daring, fashion-conscious women wore their hair bobbed, contributing further to the boyish look. Short hemlines, slim styling, and small cloches allowed women greater freedom of movement.

After the war the promotion of electric household appliances altered material culture in Europe. Electric irons, sewing machines, and vacuum cleaners were available for household consumption before the war, and clothes washers and water heaters appeared in the 1930s. Such appliances were touted as labor-saving devices, compensating middle-class women for the loss of servants at the war's end and promising modernity to households equipped with the latest appliances. However, research on both France and Britain reveals that diffusion of these machines was slow, taking decades to reach even half of British households. In addition to income and price, gender and leisure significantly affected who bought which appliances for what purpose. By and large families chose leisure products over those that would relieve women of some household labor. Working-class British households were more likely to have better interior electric

lighting and radios than electric cookers in the interwar years. The main reasons were economic. The cost of appliances, their installation, and their operation was more than most working-class families could afford. Consumers spent more on household furnishings, including bed and bath linens, curtains, cooking utensils, and dishes, and on clothing than on appliances, to say nothing of expenditures on food and leisure activities, including travel by train or motor vehicle, pubs, and movies. Producers of electricity and electrical appliances appealed to middle-class women to improve the cleanliness of their homes with these products. Although middle-class families were more likely than working-class families to own electric appliances, these devices actually confined women to the home more by raising standards of cleanliness. If appliances did not confine middle-class women, then working-class women who worked part-time for the middle class used the appliances in another person's home.

While electrical appliances and various forms of leisure and entertainment slowly permeated western Europe in the 1920s and 1930s, the inhabitants of the new Soviet Union experienced a drastic change in material life with the transition to a state-controlled economy in the 1930s. Severe shortages and deprivation were the common characteristics of the Stalinist experiment. Famine in the countryside in 1932 and 1933 along with collectivization forced millions of rural inhabitants to migrate to the cities, where they found little food and housing. Bread was scarce and adulterated, and people waited in line for hours at bakeshops, sometimes returning home with nothing. Bread and other hard-to-obtain necessities, including meat, milk, butter, vegetables, salt, soap, kerosene, and matches, were referred to as "deficit goods." As the government concentrated most of its resources in capital goods production, clothes were hard to come by, and shoes were sometimes unobtainable. Even persons with the skills to make and repair clothes and utensils could not ease the situation because thread, needles, and buttons were scarce and the state prohibited the private consumption of paint, nails, boards, or other raw materials. State ownership of housing meant the conversion of old buildings into communal apartments and the construction of barracks in new, industrial outposts. A typical communal apartment consisted of one room for an entire family with sheets or curtains dividing the space in which several people lived. Running water was not available, food was stored in sacks hung out the window, and building residents shared sinks, toilets, washtubs, and cooking facilities. Although more goods became available after rationing ended

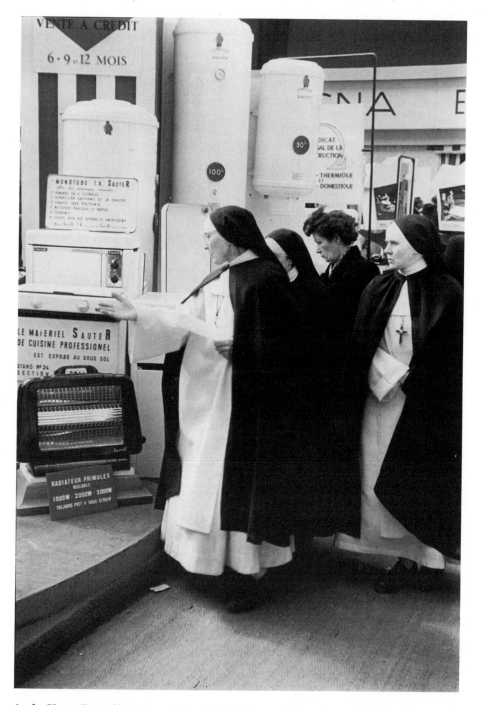

At the Home Furnishing Show. *Salon des Arts Ménagers, Paris,* photograph (1953) by Henri Cartier-Bresson. ©Henri Cartier-Bresson/Magnum Photos

in 1935, the practice of urban foraging never really ceased, and severe housing shortages persisted until the 1950s.

Shortages caused by war and the policies of totalitarian states fluctuated or contrasted with steady, sometimes astonishing, growth in the production and consumption of goods in Europe. In the two decades following World War II unprecedented economic growth and welfare states led to extraordinarily high levels of material satisfaction if not abundance. Refrigerators, washing machines, telephones, television sets, and cars became common possessions for all Europeans, even urban workers and rural farmers. People spent less of their incomes on food and housing and more on luxuries and leisure. Although the vast majority of Europeans gained access to the same objects of material culture, differences persisted in terms of style and quality and the meanings of objects for different social groups and individuals. The construction of diverse personal and group identities through the objects of everyday life requires more investigation. Scholars have begun to write the history of material culture in twentieth-century Europe and to examine the effects of wars, revolutions, changing capitalist and socialist economies, new media, and state policies on material culture.

See also other articles in this section.

BIBLIOGRAPHY

Appadurai, Arjun, ed. *The Social Life of Things: Commodities in Cultural Perspective.* Cambridge, U.K., 1986.

Auslander, Leora. *Taste and Power: Furnishing Modern France.* Berkeley, Calif., 1996.

Barringer, Tim, and Tom Flynn, eds. *Colonialism and the Object: Empire, Material Culture, and the Museum.* New York, 1998.

Bourdieu, Pierre. *Distinction: A Social Critique of the Judgement of Taste.* Translated by Richard Nice. Cambridge, Mass., 1984.

Braudel, Fernand. *Civilization and Capitalism, 15th–18th Century.* Vol. 1: *The Structures of Everyday Life.* Translated by Siân Reynolds. New York, 1982.

Brewer, John, and Roy Porter, eds. *Consumption and the World of Goods.* London and New York, 1993.

Briggs, Asa. *Victorian Things.* Chicago, 1989.

De Grazia, Victoria, ed. *The Sex of Things: Gender and Consumption in Historical Perspective.* Berkeley, Calif., 1996.

Findlen, Paula. "Possessing the Past: The Material World of the Italian Renaissance." *American Historical Review* 103 (February 1998): 83–114.

Fitzpatrick, Sheila. *Everyday Stalinism: Ordinary Life in Extraordinary Times: Soviet Russia in the 1930s.* New York, 1999.

Jardine, Lisa. *Worldly Goods: A New History of the Renaissance.* New York, 1996.

McCracken, Grant. *Culture and Consumption: New Approaches to the Symbolic Character of Consumer Goods and Activities.* Bloomington, Ind., 1988.

McKendrick, Neil, John Brewer, and J. H. Plumb. *The Birth of a Consumer Society: The Commercialization of Eighteenth-Century England.* Bloomington, Ind., 1982.

Miller, Daniel. *Material Culture and Mass Consumption.* New York, 1987.

Mukerji, Chandra. *From Graven Images: Patterns of Modern Materialism.* New York, 1983.

Pardailhé-Galabrun, Annik. *The Birth of Intimacy: Privacy and Domestic Life in Early Modern Paris.* Translated by Jocelyn Phelps. Philadelphia, 1991.

Roche, Daniel. *The People of Paris: An Essay in Popular Culture in the 18th Century.* Translated by Marie Evans. Berkeley, Calif., 1987.

Schama, Simon. *The Embarrassment of Riches: An Interpretation of Dutch Culture in the Golden Age.* New York, 1987.

Silverman, Debora L. *Art Nouveau in Fin-de-Siècle France: Politics, Psychology, and Style.* Berkeley, Calif., 1989.

Thomas, Nicholas. *Entangled Objects: Exchange, Material Culture, and Colonialism in the Pacific.* Cambridge, Mass., 1991.

Walton, Whitney. *France at the Crystal Palace: Bourgeois Taste and Artisan Manufacture in the Nineteenth Century.* Berkeley, Calif., 1992.

Weatherill, Lorna. *Consumer Behaviour and Material Culture in Britain, 1660–1760.* London, 1988.

Williams, Rosalind H. *Dream Worlds: Mass Consumption in Late Nineteenth-Century France.* Berkeley, Calif., 1982.

STANDARDS OF LIVING

Norman J. G. Pounds

A century ago a Polish peasant, who had been born a serf under Russian rule, wrote an account of his life. "About 1870," he wrote, "the peasants began to build proper brick chimneys, when the iron cooking stove came in, which [is] used everywhere in the kitchens." This simple innovation clearly made a great impression on him. It facilitated cooking, made his kitchen more comfortable, and marked a sharp improvement in his standard of living. Thus it has always been. Small increments, resulting from innovations made by unknown people, have been adopted and diffused. Individually they have been small; in the aggregate they have amounted to a series of revolutions.

The concept of standard of living is difficult to define and impossible to measure with any degree of precision. So many factors influence it, and those which seem favorable or unfavorable to one person might have the opposite effect on another. Standards of living are relative; they admit of no absolute measure, and comparisons between those of one society or community and those of another are always difficult and sometimes impossible. For any one person a satisfactory standard of living is that which he or she has come to expect. It is generally recognized that some people enjoy a higher and some a lower standard of living. There was a time when people were urged to be content with the lot which God had ordained for them. Now most people expect, or at least hope, that the human condition will, with or without their efforts, improve in the course of time.

The level of one's disposable income sets an upper limit to one's standard of living, and within the limits thus set there is an immense range of choices, so that, in effect, one "good" may be exchanged for another. The smaller the disposable income, the more restricted is this range of choice, and, at the very lowest levels, income covers only the barest necessities. An income below this level would, theoretically at least, fail to sustain life.

Standards of living are generally conceived or measured in terms of material things which one uses or enjoys. These range from things which are essential to maintain life to those which, however desirable they might appear, can nevertheless be dispensed with. Briefly stated, they can be said to fall into five categories: food and drink; housing; tools, appliances, and domestic equipment; entertainment and intellectual pursuits, including art; and, lastly, the satisfaction derived from parks and gardens and public buildings. Some of these "goods" are measurable. The possession of a television or a dishwasher or a bathroom is thus used to measure and compare standards of living, and for this reason questions are often asked about them in the decennial censuses. They measure current improvements. Lastly, the level of education, as well as physical and mental health and all the factors which influence bodily fitness, must be considered. In these spheres the progress made during the last century dwarfs all that had been accomplished during the whole preceding period of human history.

A key confusion about standards of living in early modern Europe involves the concept of a subsistence economy. Most peasants, who made up the bulk of the population, did produce most of what they consumed locally. But this did not mean, except for years of harvest failure, that all were confined to the barest survival. Some peasants had a wider margin, in terms of foods, festival clothing, and the like. Indeed, festivals themselves involved considerable village expenditure, and they were frequent occasions in many parts of Europe.

Further, standards of living clearly improved for many rural and urban west Europeans in the early modern centuries. Although a minority of propertyless people may have suffered deteriorating standards. This showed in better furnishings, new diet items like sugar and tea, and so on. By the eighteenth century, a full-fledged consumer society began to emerge, with eager attention to new clothing styles, manufactured china and other home items, clocks and watches, and so on. The definition of an appropriate standard of living was changing before the onset of industrialization throughout western Europe.

451

Waterborne Diseases. Father Thames presents his children—Diphtheria, Scrofula, and Cholera—to the City of London. Cartoon from *Punch,* 1858.

HEALTH AND LIFE EXPECTANCY

Health and life expectancy are major factors considered by historians in discussing standards of living. Both underwent a profound change during the later nineteenth and twentieth centuries. Life expectancy has increased, and certain causes of death have been virtually eliminated in the more developed countries. At the beginning of the modern period life expectancy at birth varied but averaged little more than thirty years. The death rate was especially high among children, and all ages suffered high rates of death from epidemic diseases, many of them induced by environmental conditions.

The plague, which had first appeared in Europe in the mid-fourteenth century, remained virulent for more than three centuries. Its last appearance in England was in 1665 and in France in 1720, but it remained endemic in the Balkans into the nineteenth century, and the Habsburg empire did not terminate its quarantine regulations against the Ottomans until the 1870s. The vector of the plague was the symbiotic relationship of the flea and the black rat. This nexus could be broken only by an improvement in living conditions which destroyed or at least reduced the rat

population. It is a measure of relative living standards within Europe that the plague disappeared from the west more than a century before it vanished in eastern Europe.

Other epidemic diseases which were environmentally determined were typhus and cholera, both of which ravaged society, especially in the crowded environments of congested cities. The vector of typhus was the body louse, which was able to multiply in the crowded, insanitary conditions of prisons and barracks—hence its alternative names, "jail" and "trench" fever. Both were eliminated only by more sanitary conditions and a liberal use of soap in personal hygiene and the laundering of clothes. Cholera was a latecomer on the European scene, though it had long been endemic in Asia. It was spread through polluted drinking water. It probably reached Europe first in the ships of Asian traders, but did not spread widely before the 1830s. Its spread was closely linked with the practice of taking water from underground sources which had been contaminated by sewage overflowing from cesspits. It was not wholly eliminated until a piped water supply, drawn from rural reservoirs, became available and a more effective system of sewers had been constructed.

Because the nature and source of disease were not understood before the later nineteenth century, there was little inducement to separate sewage disposal from the domestic water. Recurring epidemics of waterborne diseases were a fact of life. It was not until 1854 that John Snow, a London physician, plotted occurrences of cholera on a map and found that they clustered around a well in Soho, which supplied the neighborhood with water for drinking. The well was closed and the miniepidemic ceased. It was thus learned empirically that polluted water was likely to spread disease. But improvements came very slowly because the nature of pathogens was not determined until late in the century. The last severe outbreak of cholera from polluted water was in Hamburg, Germany, in 1890.

Other diseases both impaired the quality and reduced the duration of life, among them smallpox and a range of intestinal disorders. These have, at least in the more developed countries, been reduced to insignificance by developments in medical science and improvements in the environment. The medical advances of the last century and a half, which include the development of hospital design and management and the use of antiseptics and anesthetics, have together revolutionized both surgery and medical practice.

FOOD AND DRINK

Nothing illustrates better than diet the components of a standard of living. The level of calorie and protein intake essential for the performance of bodily functions varies between individuals and also depends to some extent on climate and the type of work to which a person is accustomed. Great physical exertion and a cold climate both demand a greater food intake. A good or high standard of living demands a diet considerably above the physiological minimum. In most developed countries a consumption of at least two thousand calories a day can be considered adequate, but a truly satisfactory diet also requires a certain volume of protein and specific vitamins. An adequate diet might consist of tasteless or unpalatable foods, but a good standard requires that more appetizing foods be substituted for those that merely satisfy one's biological needs. Eating becomes more than a physiological necessity; it is a pleasurable pursuit. A high-standard diet is marked by the consumption of a higher quality of food, inevitably at a greater cost. If the means are present to pay for them, the consumption of meat and other high-order proteins is likely to increase beyond one's physiological needs—sometimes with deleterious medical consequences.

In most societies there are occasions during the year when people indulge in excessive feasting. These convivial occasions can be regarded as part of the entertainment in which society at large participates. Some are celebratory, even religious, but among them are those which have an economic basis. In earlier European societies one year's harvest was expected to supply sufficient food to last until the next. As supplies one by one became exhausted, so a final, ceremonial eating marked the exhaustion of a particular comestible. Simnel cakes, a traditional Easter or springtime food in parts of Europe, marked the exhaustion of the supply of wheat of the highest quality. In similar fashion, the Christmas or midwinter feast followed the slaughter of the farm animals which could not be fed through the lean months of winter. The long-distance transport of foodstuffs, refrigeration, and other methods of preservation have, at least in the developed world, ended such seasonal periods of scarcity and made their accompanying feasts redundant. Some have, however, retained their importance in the social calendar, though they no longer possess any economic or dietary purpose.

Standards of living have sometimes been raised by the introduction of a new and particularly prolific crop. The potato, introduced into Europe from the New World, is an example. In some countries, notably Ireland, it quickly became a basic foodstuff and contributed to a sharp increase in population. Its failure

Food. *The Peasant's Meal,* painting (c. 1617) by Diego Velázquez (1599–1660). HERMITAGE, ST. PETERSBURG, RUSSIA/SCALA/ART RESOURCE, NY

in 1848 owing to a plant virus led to famine and severe mortality. Corn, or maize, has played a similar role, though more as animal feed than human. The development of refrigeration and the import of exotic and tropical foods from distant parts of the world has further extended the range of available foodstuffs, though usually at a high monetary cost, without any commensurate increase in the nutritional value of the diet.

HOUSING

Shelter from the elements has always been the second essential of human existence, and there is good archaeological evidence for some form of shelter from a very early date in human prehistory. The development of housing can be traced in considerable detail since structures have survived from the Middle Ages and earlier relatively intact. As a general rule, local materials were used, and, as far as Europe was concerned, the commonest and most widespread has always been timber. Good constructional timber was abundant everywhere except in a few arid regions, such as parts of Spain. Hardwoods, chiefly oak, were used for a framework, and the spaces were filled in with wickerwork and plastered with clay. Such homes have continued to be built until the present, and villages in much of central and eastern Europe remain mainly of wood. The rival to timber construction has been building in stone and brick and, in a few areas, of adobe, clay "lump," or "cob." The last has been important only in the absence of quality timber. Stone and brick construction represent a higher and more expensive mode of construction, even when the materials could be obtained locally. Broadly speaking, stone construction prevails in areas where a good quality of stone, usually limestone of Jurassic age, occurs. In England, for example, there is a "Stone Belt," within which masonry construction has prevailed. Brick making requires clay of a particular quality, and this is also highly localized. Brick building characterizes the historic cities of northern Europe, where good stone is scarce and clay relatively abundant.

From the Middle Ages most rural construction has been in timber, but urban building has been increasingly in stone or brick. The reason lies not so much in the greater wealth of cities as in their liability to disastrous fires. As early as the late twelfth century the city of London, for example, prescribed stone walls and slate or tile roofs as a precaution against its frequent conflagrations.

Standards of housing have risen during the past five centuries by countless small increments, achieved slowly and diffused gradually throughout the continent. Most innovations were made in the west, especially in France, the Low Countries, and Great Britain, and in the homes of the rich. The diffusion of these innovations took two forms, spatial and social. Most were adopted first by the well-to-do, who were able to afford the initial investment. Gradually they spread socially downward until, usually in simplified form, they were adopted in the homes of the poor. The downward diffusion of the masonry-built chimney, mentioned at the beginning of this article, was such an innovation. It called for capital rather than skill. A hearth could be built against an external wall, instead of being placed in the middle of the floor, and the smoke could pass upward through what was effectively a stone-built tunnel. Few innovations could have been more simple and few could have contributed more to the comfort of the home.

Glazed windows were a comparable innovation. They first made their appearance in the home during the Middle Ages, but remained very small and admitted little light. Then, in the sixteenth century, advancing technology permitted the manufacture of larger sheets of glass. This in turn encouraged architects to construct homes with large windows. The consequence was the well-lighted interior. The use of windows which could be opened and shut—casement or sash—spread socially downward and in the seventeenth and eighteenth centuries began to appear in the homes of the lower classes.

Another feature of daily life which underwent a gradual improvement throughout modern times was domestic illumination. One forgets how dark it was after the sun had set, how difficult to read or perform domestic tasks indoors, or to walk about outside. The importance of spinning as a domestic occupation was due in part to the fact that it was a simple manipulative task and could be performed in the glow of the fire smoldering on the hearth. Any more effective lightning had to be supplied by candles, usually of tallow and smelling abominably, waxed tapers, or oil-burning lamps. These gave way to gas lighting in the cities in the later nineteenth century, but it was costly since it required a network of iron pipes. It spread slowly to poorer homes and eventually to street lights. This was a development of great social importance, since it facilitated movement in greater security after dark.

A feature of homes from the sixteenth century onward has been greater attention to hygiene and privacy. The number of bedrooms increased, and they came to be better furnished with closets and beds. The indoor toilet first appeared in castles and fortified houses, where it might have been difficult or even

Laying Sewers. Building the common sewers in London, mid-nineteenth century. THE
FOTOMAS INDEX

dangerous to go far afield. In the grander homes they
began to appear in in early modern times, and there
were even attempts—with little success—to construct a flushing system. This called for a piped water
supply, which was nowhere available before the late
eighteenth or nineteenth century. Water was obtained
from wells and springs or from the nearest river, and
it was often polluted and always unreliable.

The lack of adequate provision for disposing of
sewage before the middle or even the later years of the
nineteenth century meant that the water supply was
often severely contaminated. Conditions were always
worse in cities than in the countryside because it was
more difficult to separate wells from the cesspits in
which human waste was collected. Where possible the
latter was discharged into a river, but this only removed
the source of infection to other communities farther
downstream. In some cities, such as London, cesspits
were even dug beneath the basements of houses. The
medieval coroners' rolls, which recorded the causes of
accidental death, even noted a case of drowning in such
a subterranean but nonetheless domestic cesspit. In no
sphere of human activity did the improvements of
modern times do more to raise standards of living than
in the provision of sewers, either of masonry or of
glazed pipes, to carry away domestic effluent.

A piped water supply complemented a sewage
system and brought about comparable improvements
in the living standards of all classes. It required, however, a reservoir to collect and hold water and, all too
often, a pumping mechanism to lift the water to a
level from which it could flow downhill to the homes
in which it was to be used. The city of Bath, England,
had such a system late in the eighteenth century, but
the lack of pumps limited the supply to the low-lying
homes, and these often found it more convenient—
and certainly cheaper—to continue to dip their water

from the river. The revolution in sanitation and water
supply did not take place in much of Europe until the
early twentieth century, and there remain areas, notably in eastern Europe, where even today it has barely
begun.

GOODS AND CHATTELS

The evidence for rising living standards is most apparent in items of domestic and daily use. Within
living memory they have increased in number and
sophistication, and what had once been available only
for the wealthy and privileged have now become necessities for the masses. This has resulted, on the one
hand, from expanding real incomes and, on the other,
from economies achieved in the mass production of
goods. New items are constantly being fed into the
body of consumer goods, while others pass out of
fashion, become obsolete, and cease to be made. The
types of goods with which people have furnished their
homes and which they have chosen to enjoy or display
have changed greatly over five centuries.

Fortunately, individual collections of durables
can be studied, not so much from surviving homes,
furnished and equipped, for there are few, but from
inventories of personal possessions made at the time
of death. The making of a will and the "proving" of
it after death fell within the jurisdiction of the medieval church. It was the duty of the ecclesiastical authorities to supervise the implementation of a will,
and this involved preparing a list, with their valuation,
of the chattels or movable possessions of the deceased.
These have survived in large numbers in England, but
less adequately in continental Europe. In each instance they listed the possessions of the deceased from
clothing and bedding to domestic fittings and furni-

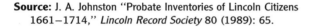

TABLE 1
ESTIMATED VALUE OF THE CHATTELS OF THE CITIZENS OF THE CITY OF LINCOLN, 1661–1714

Value	Number	Percentage
£1–5	91	18
£6–15	112	22
£16–35	138	27
£36–50	64	13
£51–75	47	9
£76–100	27	5
£101–150	20	4
£151–200	8	2
Over £200	3	1

Source: J. A. Johnston "Probate Inventories of Lincoln Citizens 1661–1714," *Lincoln Record Society* 80 (1989): 65.

ture. Such household goods as pots and pans and the wrought ironwork used to suspend pots and cuts of meat before the fire were all listed, together with the tools of whatever trade the deceased pursued. In using these probate inventories one must be aware of the fact that they may not be complete; occasionally a will bequeaths an item which is not mentioned in the accompanying inventory. Moreover, the poor were were not required to make a will. In England the cutoff point was the possession of chattels to the value of £5. Difficult though it may be to conceive of worldly goods of a lower total value, it is clear that a majority of the population possessed no more. An unusual Norfolk will of 1758 recorded a widow whose total assets were worth only £1 8s. 9d. ($2.20). Of this her bed made up £1 1s. In effect, she had no property beyond her clothes and a cooking pot. Table 1 illustrates how great was the spread between the rich and well-off and the mass of the impoverished population.

Among the categories of worldly goods, clothing is the least dispensable, although it performs obviously nonessential functions as well. Because it varies in style and quality and is subject to changes of fashion, clothing has become a status symbol, indicating a certain level of wealth or social importance. Hence some people have dressed above their station in life, leading authorities to prohibit excesses of dress for certain classes. Such sumptuary legislation has a long history. Control of both clothing and food was not unusual during the Middle Ages, but laws became increasingly difficult to enforce and were mostly abandoned during early modern times. Thereafter the question of dress tended to be influenced by fashion but controlled by the ability to pay for it. The regular laundering of clothes is a fairly modern development, as are many aspects of personal hygiene. It was restricted by the fact that soap was not generally available even in western Europe much before the nineteenth century and also by the fact that not everyone possessed a change of clothing. The prevalence of typhus was due in part to the prolonged wearing of soiled clothing infested with the body louse. Underclothes were rarely worn before a light fabric—at first linen and then, from the mid-eighteenth century, cotton—had become widely available. Such light fabrics lent themselves to more frequent washing, with consequent improvements in both health and comfort.

Historians have debated the standard of living under early industrial conditions, particularly in Britain. Optimists claim that wages went up, and point to signs of greater consumption of meat, purchase of cotton clothing, use of other new popular items like forks. Pessimists highlight high housing costs and frequent slum conditions, and some evidence of deteriorating health standards. The debate has been inconclusive overall, and is no longer active. There is general agreement that by the later nineteenth century, in western Europe, material standards of living were improving for most groups.

There was an underclass in most parts of Europe, and in some places it made up a majority of the population. It was undernourished, lived in cramped, unhygienic homes, and scarcely possessed the barest necessities for civilized living. Despite the progress in the material conditions of life between the Middle Ages and the twentieth century, this underclass scarcely benefited. At most, it can be said that it became numerically smaller until only small islands of extreme deprivation remained. The gap between the material conditions of the middle and upper classes and those of the humblest began to widen in the later seventeenth century, became wider still in the eighteenth, and in the nineteenth opened into the yawning gulf which did much to inspire the writings of Freidrich Engels and others.

MEASURING STANDARDS OF LIVING

While the fact of progress in material standards of living cannot be doubted, this advance is extraordinarily difficult to measure. It varies from place to place and from one class to another. Furthermore, it cannot be disputed that there have been times when standards declined, usually for a restricted period and often over a limited area. There is no effective measure of anything as subjective as a standard of living. The Bureau of the Census and comparable bodies in Europe make it a practice to inquire into living standards. Questions may range from the possession of a bathroom to domestic appliances. But these are only surrogates. It is assumed that a person who possesses them is likely also to have a certain range of other goods and, in material terms, to belong to a particular class. On this basis one might claim that people in one area enjoy a higher standard than those in another. But this is only a rough measure of material backwardness or well-being. It does not take into consideration the fact that people usually have a range of choice between the various "goods" available, and it cannot measure the levels of satisfaction they offer. In the last resort, the only objective measure other than life expectancy and stature is the disposable real income available to the family or individual, and even this is often very difficult to evaluate, especially where there is some degree of self-sufficiency.

A key question about standards of living involves how much one should go beyond material living conditions—food, shelter, consumer items—to different, sometimes less tangible aspects like health or even quality of work. In the industrial revolution debate, for example, it is more likely that workers suffered from a sense that their work life was becoming harsher and stranger than that their food standards were deteriorating.

If it is difficult to measure the degree of satisfaction afforded by material things, it is almost impossible to extend quantifiable comparisons to nonmaterial things. The length of the working day or week is a good example. We do not have to go back many centuries before we reach a time when the working day was as long as the human constitution could tolerate. During the early phases of the industrial revolution it could be ten to twelve hours for factory workers, and these would have been filled with hard, monotonous toil. After allowing eight hours for sleep, there was little or no time left for social or recreational activities. Such conditions, sometimes excused by the need to accumulate the fixed capital present in factories and machines, were described in horrifying and only slightly exaggerated detail by Engels in *The Condition of the Working Class in England* (1845) and by Charles Dickens in *Hard Times* (1854). In the course of time these conditions provoked a feeling of revulsion, and statutory limits were placed on the length of the working day. First its length was reduced in

stages of an hour or half hour, and then a half day off became the rule, at least in Western, industrialized societies. Without these reductions there could have been no organized sport, for there would have been no time during the daylight hours for a game of football (soccer). Organized football, as distinct from the unorganized brawls which took place between villages at certain seasons, dates from the second half of the nineteenth century, when for the first time working men had the leisure to play or to watch. The slow reduction in the length of the working day is the chief incentive in the development of those leisure activities which must be seen as major components of the standard of living. These developments represent an improvement in the standard of living which is both obvious and difficult to quantity.

Overall, the issue of standards of living looms less large in twentieth-century European history, although the pace at which consumer expectations rose was unprecedented and the pressure to keep up with innovations weighed upon many individuals and families. An important body of scholarship has assessed the impact of twentieth-century wars (especially World War I) on standards of living, particularly in Germany and Russia. Developments in eastern Europe after the

Slum Conditions. Glasgow, Scotland, 1868. MANSELL COLLECTION/TIME PIX

Rising Expectations. Nannies in Hyde Park, London. Photograph by Bruce Davidson. MAGNUM

Russian Revolution and then again during the decline of communism in the 1980s and 1990s also raise important questions. In Russia, living conditions, as evidenced by mortality rates, seemed to drop dramatically among some groups over the last two decades of the twentieth century.

But during the span of half a millennium human life has been transformed for the majority of the population. For most it has ceased to be, in Thomas Hobbes's words, "nasty, brutish, and short," and has become long, filled with interest, and freed from the prospect of imminent death from epidemic disease or medical ignorance. The gap between those best endowed with worldly goods and the rest has been narrowing. Life has also become fuller and more enjoyable in less material ways. Compulsory schooling has become the rule in all European countries, and illiteracy, even in the least-developed countries, has been reduced to a very small minority of the oldest of the population. This has opened up the pleasures of reading to a vast number, even if many do not take full advantage of their opportunity. Related to this rising level of education is increased interest in the arts, literature, music, and the theater. But underlying all these developments have been the reduction in the length of the working day, the increase in leisure, the rising gross national product, and the increase in real wages in even the least advanced of European societies. Without these underlying factors the truly revolutionary changes in Europe's living standards could not have been achieved.

But is there any kind of measure which can be used to appraise the chronology and extent of this improvement? It is possible to trace improvements in housing because enough early structures have survived, and in comfort because inventories tell us how they were furnished. But how well were people fed, and were improvements in this respect commensurate with improvements in material things? Records are highly selective. They tell of gargantuan feasts, but these were almost by definition only occasional, and for most people and certainly for all the poorer classes diet was usually coarse and at times unappetizing and nutritionally inadequate. If it were possible to throw all these components together, and thus to come up with a series of indices showing the overall improvement in standards of living, we should find, first, that the graph for the poorer classes would be much flatter than that for the better-off and, second, that growth was far from continuous; there were times when standards stagnated or even fell. Continental Europe was ravaged by intermittent warfare, in the course of which crops and farm animals were seized and homes and other buildings destroyed. The Thirty Years' War (1618–1648) was such a period, and it was continued in eastern Europe by the no less devastating *Potop* or "Deluge," when Russian, Swedish, and other armies lived for years at the expense of the land which they ravaged. Every decade or so the accumulated resources of parts of Europe were consumed or destroyed by marching armies. Bismarck claimed that there was evidence in the Germany of the late nineteenth century of the destruction wrought during the Thirty Years' War of two and a half centuries earlier. The longest period of peace ever known in western and central Europe was from 1815 to 1864, and this was also a period of significant growth in living standards.

Just as the chronology of progress was interrupted by periods of decline, so there were areas where the overall pace of progress was slower than elsewhere. Warfare, poor administration, and an oppressive class structure have sometimes caused this backwardness. The most backward area of Europe in these respects was without question the Balkans. It had suffered from an inefficient and shortsighted rule from the time of the Ottoman invasions in the fourteenth century, and to these factors were added the conservative attitudes and unwillingness to innovate or change which characterized Turkish rule. Not until the Ottomans were driven from most of the Balkans did attitudes begin to change. Rapid progress has been made in some parts, but areas remain where earlier attitudes to society and progress linger, where feuding and civil war are endemic, and living standards remain far below the European average.

Standards are also often below those of Europe as a whole in areas where physical conditions are harsh and the accumulation of capital assets slow and difficult. Such conditions occur in the far north of the continent, where climatic conditions are adverse and agriculture difficult and unrewarding. It costs more merely to live

Warfare. *Napoleon on the Field of Eylau,* painting (1807) by Charles Meynier (1768–1832). At Eylau the French faced the Russians and Prussians in an indecisive battle on 8 February 1807. CHÂTEAU DE VERSAILLES, FRANCE/PETER WILLI/THE BRIDGEMAN ART LIBRARY

in such environments, leaving less for discretionary uses. A dense rural population, with cultivated plots too small for economic exploitation, can also depress living standards. Before the land reforms of the twentieth century, there was an impoverished peasantry in much of eastern Europe, especially in Galicia, as well as in other overpopulated areas of Europe, such as southern Italy and Sicily. The situation has to a considerate extent been relieved by the breakup of large estates, thus making more land available for the peasantry, and also by migration to the cities and employment in manufacturing. In the perception of most of the rural population urban living offered advantages denied to them in the countryside. The city became the "Promised Land," as it is called in the title of a novel by Wladyslaw Reymont (1867–1925) about the industrial city of Łzodz, Poland. But it is doubtful whether all migrants from the countryside could afford to enjoy the amenities offered by the city. All too often the delights of the "Promised Land" have proved illusory.

See also **Cliometrics and Quantification** *(volume 1);* **Modernization** *(volume 2);* **The Population of Europe: The Demographic Transition and After** *(volume 2);* **Public Health** *(volume 3);* **Consumerism** *(in this volume);* **Literacy** *(in this volume); and other articles in this section.*

BIBLIOGRAPHY

Bakhtin, Mikhail. *Rabelais and His World.* Bloomington, Ind., 1984.

Bailey, Charles Thomas Peach. *Knives and Forks.* London, 1927.

Blum, Jerome. *The End of the Old Order in Rural Europe.* Princeton, N.J., 1978.

Braudel, Fernand. *Capitalism and Material Life, 1400–1800.* Translated by Miriam Kochan. London, 1973.

Braudel, Fernand. *Structures of Everyday Life.* Translated by Sîan Reynolds. New York, 1981.

Burke, Peter. *Popular Culture in Early Modern Europe.* London, 1978.

Burnett, John. *A Social History of Housing, 1850–1970.* Newton Abbot, U.K., 1978.

Cartwright, Frederick F. *Disease and History.* London, 1972.

Chapelot, Jean, and Robert Fossier. *The Village and House in the Middle Ages.* Translated by Henry Cleere. London, 1985.

Cipolla, Carlo M. *Clocks and Culture, 1300–1700.* London, 1967.

Davis, Dorothy. *A History of Shopping.* London, 1966.

Emmison, F. G. *Elizabethan Life.* 5 vols. Chelmsford, U.K., 1970–1980.

Ewing, Elizabeth. *Everyday Dress: 1650–1900.* London, 1984.

Forster, Elborg, and Robert Forster. *European Diet from Pre-Industrial to Modern Times.* New York, 1975.

Geremek, Bronislaw. *Truands et misérables dans l'Europe moderne (1350–1600).* Paris, 1980.

Hémardinquer, Jean-Jaques. *Pour une histoire de l'alimentation.* Paris, 1970.

Henisch, Bridget Ann. *Fast and Feast.* University Park, Pa., 1976.

Le Play, Frédéric. *Les ouvriers européens.* 2d ed. 6 vols. Tours, France, 1877–1879.

MacFarlane, Alan. *The Culture of Capitalism.* Oxford, 1987.

Malcolmson, Robert W. *Popular Recreations in English Society, 1700–1850.* Cambridge, U.K., 1973.

Mayhew, Henry. *Henry Mayhew's London.* Edited by Peter Quennell. London, 1969.

McNeill, William H. *Plagues and Peoples.* Garden City, N.J., 1976.

Mollat, Michel, ed. *Études sur l'histoire de la pauvreté.* 2 vols. Paris, 1974.

Moszynski, Kazimierz. *Kultura ludowa słowian.* Cracow, 1929.

Obrebski, Joseph. *The Changing Peasanty of Eastern Europe.* Edited by Barbara and Joel Halpern. Cambridge, Mass., 1976.

Pounds, Norman J. G. *The Culture of the English People: Iron Age to the Industrial Age.* Cambridge, U.K., 1994.

Pounds, Norman J. G. *Hearth and Home.* Bloomington, Ind., 1989.

Renbourn, E. T., and W. H. Rees. *Materials and Clothing in Health and Disease.* London, 1972.

Robins, F. W. *The Story of the Lamp (and the Candle).* Oxford, 1939.

Robins, F. W. *The Story of Water Supply.* London, 1946.

Roe, F. Gordon. *English Cottage Furniture.* London, 1949.

Spufford, Margaret. *Contrasting Communities: English Villagers in the Sixteenth and Seventeenth Centuries.* Cambridge, U.K., 1974.

Steer, Francis W., ed. *Farm and Cottage Inventories of Mid Essex, 1635 to 1749.* 2d ed. London, 1969.

Wace, A. J. B., and M. S. Thompson. *The Nomads of the Balkans.* London, 1914.

Warriner, Doreen. *Contrasts in Emerging Societies.* Bloomington, Ind., 1965.

Weber, Eugen. *Peasants into Frenchmen: The Modernization of Rural France, 1870–1914.* Stanford, Calif., 1976.

Wheaton, Barbara Ketcham. *Savouring the Past: The French Kitchen and Table from 1300 to 1789.* Philadelphia, Pa., 1983.

Yarwood, Doreen. *The English Home.* Rev. ed. London, 1979.

HOUSING

Craig Keating

Housing is of interest to social historians mainly to the extent that access to housing and to housing of a certain quality have long been important measures and determinants of social standing. Houses are capital and reflect a certain economic status. Tenancy, by contrast, often betrays a lack of economic wherewithal. More tellingly, tenancy tends to perpetuate socioeconomic divisions insofar as the percent of income spent on housing varies inversely with the amount of income. Yet housing is also interesting because many of the material aspects of the house (from its internal spatial arrangements to its proximity to the built human environment to its relation to the natural environment) play important roles in the cultural construction of class, gender, and individual identities, and in defining the boundary between public and private. Indeed, no discussion of the history of housing would be complete if it did not recognize that the ownership of a house or access to housing of different kinds and quality are not merely material facts of social existence but have symbolic and ideological values that have been important in the structuring of European society in the past.

EARLY MODERN EUROPE

Peasant houses in early modern Europe reflected the divisions in that omnibus social class, which included freeholders, farmers, tenants of a lord, sharecroppers, and day laborers. Houses reflected these divisions most importantly in their size. Houses of freeholders and farmers tended to be the most substantial. So-called long houses excavated in England and northern France and dating from around 1500 were from 40 to 90 feet long and 15 to 20 feet wide with steeply pitched timber beam thatched roofs and rock walls. While these houses may have had sleeping areas in the loft, the main floor was divided into two main areas: one for human habitation, the other for livestock. Often humans and livestock would share the same entrance. These houses were almost always enclosed be-

hind a fence or hedge and they tended to incorporate the yard area as an external extension of the house, an area where a variety of domestic chores were completed in the privacy that fence or hedge provided. For more marginal peasants (such as agricultural laborers or widows without family) houses were no more than huts, often comprising no more than one room.

The materials used in the construction of peasant households also varied. In part this was because of regional variations in materials available. Sod or wood and cob houses were commonly used in northern Europe, where large forests were common and readily accessible. In the south, stone of varying sorts was more common. But the materials used were also a matter of economics. Stone or brick were comparatively expensive, as were roofing tiles. Furthermore, the investment of a significant amount of labor and capital in the construction of a substantial house of wood or stone was a luxury not open to all.

As the foregoing indicates, peasant houses were functional, useful largely as aids to agricultural production. The cohabitation of humans and livestock as well as the very basic character of the human portions of peasant houses attests to this. So, too, does the evidence of an excavation at Wharram Percy in Yorkshire, where archaeologists have found that over three centuries nine different houses were built on the same site. Peasant houses were tools, and house and work were not distinguished as separate realms of everyday existence.

Nonetheless, the peasant house was not completely without cultural importance. However rudimentary, the physical form of the peasant house was intimately linked to certain social and cultural functions, especially to the notion of family. Indeed, as Emmanuel Le Roy Ladurie has pointed out in his study of Montaillou, peasants made no important distinction between physical house and family. The house embodied the family and was a symbol of stability and prosperity that distinguished substantial peasants from agricultural laborers, who were often

Flemish interior. Interior of a Flemish house, painting (c. 1555–1560) by Marten van Cleve (1527–1581). KUNSTHISTORISCHES MUSEUM, GEMÄDELDEGALERIE, VIENNA/ERICH LESSING/ART RESOURCE, NY

excluded from the compact of village society. It also formed the basis of possible future consolidation of wealth, standing, and privilege in the bringing together of goods, lands, and hearths through conjugal alliance. Also, the walls of both the house and its enclosure offered a measure of security, both real and imagined, against an uncertain world of war, beggars, and, often, wild animals.

By the 1600s, the houses of freeholding peasants and more substantial farmers were being built in two stories with stone foundations, wood construction, and, where available, slate or tile roofs (which posed less of a threat from fire). The cohabitation of animals and humans became less tolerated. Indeed, this commonplace of rural life (which persisted even into the twentieth century in some regions) came to be viewed as impossibly rustic and uncivilized by social observers as early as the 1600s. Increasingly, farm houses were separated from a variety of outbuildings, which served as barns and granaries. The houses of more substantial farms were built in two stories with clearly defined rooms for eating, sleeping, entertaining, and so forth. But if the traditional peasant cottage came to be viewed with disdain over the course of the fourteenth and fifteenth centuries, it ought to be remarked that rural peasants were all too well aware that there were other less savory alternatives: the one- or two-room

huts of agricultural laborers, just big enough for their family; or, to lose one's purchase on any house at all and become part of a mass (of indeterminate but clearly large numbers) of beggars who populated the countryside and who, if apprehended within the bounds of a city, would be imprisoned.

Equally notable both as a reflection of economic standing and cultural importance were the chateaux, manor houses, and seigneurial homes of rural Europe. In economic terms, the very size of these houses displayed the socioeconomic standing of their occupants. Owned by a single person, they housed, in some cases, hundreds of domestic servants. While the interior space of the peasant house in its sparseness and the melange of human and animal occupants manifested its functionality, the interior space of manor houses was clearly defined and divided. Different rooms were devoted not only to different daily functions (such as dining and sleeping), but some were clearly ceremonial in character. Nobles' houses, too, had exterior enclosures. Yet in the case of nobility these enclosures served as gardens or parks, created both for pleasure and as symbols of the refinement and culture of the owner.

As the very fact of the aristocratic garden implies, the houses of aristocrats and gentry were cultural entities rather than mere shelter. Accordingly, their function derived in part from their very aspect. They were meant to be seen. They were symbols of power and, to this extent, mechanisms of power. This specular function is manifested in countless contemporary prints in which castles are an almost omnipresent feature of the background. The symbolic presence of these houses also developed over the course of the early modern period, as the blank walls and stern towers of the fortified medieval castle gave way to the architectural flourish of the exteriors of the sixteenth and seventeenth centuries. The highpoint of this transformation was Louis XIV's construction of the palace of Versailles. Yet this palace, which set the standard for royal homes throughout Europe, differed only in size and scale from the kinds of houses that were constructed by the wealthiest aristocrats of this period. The important point for social historians in these developments is that houses were becoming cultural and ideological variables. Indeed, it seems that certain aristocratic ideas about houses developed in the early modern period (such as the relationship between house and nature, in the guise of the park) informed later, bourgeois notions of housing.

Urban housing in the early modern period reflects both similarities and differences with rural housing. Cities were distinct from the countryside in several respects. One of the most important differences was the very durability of cities and consequently of the houses within them. Construction was more often of stone with tile roofs and many of these kinds of houses (along with some of timber and mortar) survived into the twenty-first century. Early modern cities also had a distinct legal and political status that permitted a certain degree of land-use planning that sometimes limited the size and character of houses. But these powers were haphazardly enforced, leading to the housing densities and mazelike streets that virtually define the medieval and early modern city.

Cities were also unique because of their mixture of classes. Perhaps the largest single group in the city was artisans and shopkeepers. Most of these people would have occupied a single house that they also likely would have owned. As with peasant houses, there was no important distinction between the house as a place of residence and a place of work. The lower floors (including an enclosed courtyard) that opened onto city streets served as the location of workshops and offices as well as the kitchen, the larder, and the hearth. In other words, there was a thorough intermingling of what we would call the "domestic" sphere with the workplace. This blurring of the distinction between houses as homes and places of work was most advanced in the houses of master artisans, where the master and his family would sleep on the second story

and the journeymen and apprentices on the floors above, and all would share a common table.

A variety of other groups in society were housed in the city with an equal variation in the kinds of houses to be found. At the top of the social scale were aristocrats and wealthy merchants, whose houses were correspondingly grand. At the other end of the scale were day laborers, students, the aged, vagabonds, and others who had no position within a household. For these groups housing was defined by its scarcity, its consequent expense and its very poor condition. Merchants and artisans would rent out unused rooms in the uppermost floors of their buildings. These were dirty, pestilent, cold (by dint of their distance from the hearth) and hard to access. One family often occupied just one room. In periods of demographic crisis, cellars, *appentis* (lean-tos attached to the sides of buildings), and stables were pushed into service as housing. Rude huts were constructed in courtyards. The construction of speculative rental housing began in the eighteenth century in larger centers like Paris. But, here, too, the desire of landlords to extract profit from every possible inch of floor space merely added to the available stock of deplorable housing available to the poorest elements of society. Increasingly these included the bulk of the working population, as the

Eighteenth-Century Interior. *Le déjeuner,* painting by François Boucher (1703–1770). MUSÉE DU LOUVRE, PARIS/ ALINARI/ART RESOURCE, NY

463

guild structure that had in part supported the cohabitation of masters, apprentices, and other servants slowly faded. This also reflected the phenomenon, which emerged more clearly in the nineteenth century, of the literal social disintegration of cities as neighborhoods came to be divided along class lines.

THE NINETEENTH CENTURY

Throughout the early modern period, demographic changes played an important role in the social history of housing. Because houses were relatively expensive to build, the expansion and contraction of the European population directly affected the numbers of people who had to occupy them. In the eighteenth century, the expansion of the population of cities in particular (a function of the commercial revolutions of that century) was the chief demographic fact that affected housing. Population density per house increased significantly. Entire families living in just one or two rooms were common. In the nineteenth century, as the commercial revolution gave way to the industrial revolution, the steady growth of cities became an explosion. The scale of this growth in selected European cities is reflected in Table 1. Under these demographic conditions urban housing rapidly deteriorated in quality and became much scarcer. By the end of the century, housing was broadly recognized as a major social problem.

The declining condition of urban housing was documented and denounced as a social evil by social revolutionaries, social reformers, and social conservatives alike. The chief problem was the simple paucity of housing in urban centers. Migration from the countryside to cities was rapid and unplanned and easily outpaced the ability of already saturated housing markets to meet demand. For example, while the population of Paris grew by 500,000 between 1801 and 1851, only 4,000 new houses were built between 1817 and 1851. A variety of expedients to accommodate demand emerged. Among the forms of working-class housing that developed in industrial towns in England were cellars (the most degraded of urban housing, home to the city's most marginal elements), lodging-houses (intended for short-term stays by "tramp" labor, they were eventually pressed into service to house whole families on a permanent or semipermanent basis), tenements (preexisting houses subdivided into separate apartments), and the "back-to-back" or "one-up, one-down" (purpose-built speculative housing constructed in double rows where the front wall was the only nonparty wall). Shantytowns became common on the outskirts of industrial cities,

and huts and other makeshift constructions such as wagons housed the most marginalized of the urban poor, such as ragpickers.

A second major problem with worker housing in the industrial city was sanitation. Clean water and adequate sewage disposal were especially wanting in non-purpose-built housing such as tenements and cellars, although these were problems of far wider scope in cities lacking sufficient infrastructure in these areas. Once again taking Paris as an example, in 1851 only 82 miles of sewers serviced 250 miles of streets. Therefore, the streets themselves, as well as rivers, were open sewers. As a result, deaths outpaced births in many major cities in the first half of the nineteenth century. Also dangerous to the sanitary condition of working-class housing was its proximity to industrial enterprises, major sources of air- and waterborne pollutants.

By the middle of the nineteenth century, the conditions of cities and housing in particular had captured the attention of national governments. These conditions, it was believed, were the breeding ground of not only disease but also other vices such as crime and, more worrisome in the wake of the revolutions of 1848, social discontent. In 1850 the government of the French Second Republic passed the Melun Law, which gave municipal government the power to investigate and improve substandard housing. Subsequently the government of Paris established the Commission on Unhealthful Dwellings in 1851. Similar public health bodies with powers to investigate housing conditions of the poor were established in Britain and Belgium around the same time. These bodies were empowered to condemn houses as unfit for human habitation in the enforcement of public health standards.

While some have argued that these developments set the stage for a later, larger role for the state in matters relevant to housing and health, most European governments in the nineteenth century were reluctant to intervene in the question of housing. Indeed, many policies merely exacerbated what remained the central housing problem of the nineteenth and twentieth centuries: availability. Probably the most important outcome of the cultural construction of the problem of housing as one of social hygiene was the rebuilding of Paris begun in 1853 under Georges Haussmann, the prefect of Paris. Emperor Napoleon III gave Haussmann wide powers of expropriation, overriding the rights of individual property owners. The broad boulevards that Haussmann created using these powers were purposely planned to eliminate as much of the working-class slums of central Paris as possible. It is estimated that during his

TABLE 1
POPULATION GROWTH IN SIX EUROPEAN CITIES, 1800–1900

City	Year			Growth (Percentage)	
	1800	*1850*	*1900*	*1800–1850*	*1850–1900*
Amsterdam	220,000	224,000	510,850	2	128
Brussels	66,000	251,000	599,000	280	139
London	1,117,000	2,685,000	4,510,000	140	68
Paris	547,000	1,053,000	2,630,000	93	150
Rome	163,000	175,000	465,000	7	166

Source: Michael Wagenaar, "Conquest of the Center or Flight to the Suburbs? Divergent Metropolitan Strategies in Europe, 1850–1914." *Journal of Urban History* 9, no. 1 (November 1992): 62.

tenure as prefect, 27,000 residences were destroyed and their 350,000 occupants were forced to the outskirts of Paris. Industry, too, was cajoled into setting up on the fringes of Paris. Central Paris became a zone of apartment buildings of varying degrees of luxury inaccessible to all but the respectable middle classes. No plans were made to house the displaced poor and working classes, and the new working-class districts north and east of Paris merely replicated the grim realities of urban housing as they had been prior to Haussmann's reforms.

Haussmann's work in Paris inspired similar reforms of varying scope in Brussels, Rome, and Vienna. In all cases, cities became more socially distinct. Whereas the pre-nineteenth-century response to population pressure had been to build up, adding more floors to preexisting buildings (with the social class of occupants declining as one went up), later developments led to distinct and more socially homogeneous neighborhoods. In these cities the urban center became a bourgeois enclave, but in others such as London and Amsterdam, different political cultures that placed a greater emphasis on the rights of individual property owners impeded Haussmannian programs of social hygiene through slum clearance. In England, for instance, municipalities like London lacked the powers of expropriation given Haussmann. Indeed, each expropriation required a separate act of Parliament, making wholesale urban reforms almost impossible. Most housing improvements were left to the owners of individual properties, giving them a patch-

work character. The only exception to this role was Parliament's aid to railway companies in the purchase of five percent of the buildings in central London by the century's end. This displaced 100,000 occupants with no plans for their rehousing.

This is not to say, however, that ideas about urban reform were absent in England. On the contrary, the concept of the garden city advocated by the social reformer Ebenezer Howard launched a housing movement that spread to many places in Europe in the late nineteenth and twentieth centuries. Howard advocated the creation of estates of detached or semidetached houses separated from the city proper by the green spaces he deemed necessary for the physical and moral improvement of the lower classes. In so doing he was advocating for the less fortunate a mode of living that the English middle classes, having turned their back on housing in the city center, had already begun to practice.

The single-family, owner-occupied, suburban home, which the garden city epitomized, was at a cultural level arguably the most important housing development of the nineteenth century. For it incarnated a host of peculiarly modern ideas about housing, ideas that informed housing-reform initiatives well into the twentieth century. Perhaps the most important was the new separation of home and work, a separation daily ritualized in that peculiarly modern phenomenon of the commute. In part this was inspired by a desire to escape the urban conditions of industrial cities outlined above. But it cannot be understood without also taking into consideration ideas about gender and family that had become prevalent by mid-century. In many countries women's political and civil rights were officially limited. Laws restricted hours of work for women and children, justified by notions of the distinct physical and mental capabilities of women and men. The idea of a house physically separated from the hurly-burly of the industrial city was merely an extension at the cultural level of these developments. The very feminine nature of women (and, as some like Ferdinand Tönnies argued, of youth as well) demanded the separate space that the suburban house provided. Francis Place, secretary in the 1820s of the radical London Corresponding Society, spoke out against the morally degrading effects of the intermingling of men's work and women's work within the space of a single house, arguing for a separate study in which men might conduct their labor. The suburban house, proximate to nature through its garden, further recommended itself because of the perceived moral and physical benefits of that relationship. Also, home ownership, which the suburban house further embodied, was conceived by socially conservative paternalists as a great social stabilizer, endowing the owner with a greater sense of responsibility. And this house was above all a private space, the ground on which the family confronted society and public authority. Ideals of privacy further stipulated bedrooms clearly separating children and adults and, ultimately, individual bedrooms for children themselves.

However much this middle-class suburban house remained an ideal (it was hardly common in Europe as a whole and the middle classes of Paris, even as they espoused its virtues, betrayed in practice their preference for rental apartments), it was a powerful one. Beyond the garden-city movement, it formed the basis, in England at least, of working-class demands for housing. And it arguably informed the preference of government throughout much of the late nineteenth and twentieth centuries for housing policies that promoted private home ownership over government-owned and managed social housing.

The cultural construction of housing and the ideological commitment of governments to private enterprise solutions to the problem of housing supply help explain why, at the end of the nineteenth century, this problem still had not been adequately addressed. Nonetheless, all across Europe at this time, central governments undertook very modest interventions in the housing market. In 1890 the British government passed a Housing Act that empowered municipal governments to collect taxes for the construction of low-cost housing. The Belgian Housing Act of 1889, passed by a paternalist Catholic majority in parlia-

ment, offered low-cost loans to working-class families interested in buying or building a home. A home owning working class, it was believed, would be a respectable and politically stable working class. Elsewhere, tax incentives were used to encourage private-sector house construction. Ireland is exceptional in that some 48,000 rural laborers' cottages were constructed at the expense of the public purse between 1883 and 1926. Almost everywhere else the trend was to allow the private sector to take the lead in building houses and to encourage workers, either individually or through cooperative building societies, to find their own solutions to the general housing shortage.

Not surprisingly, attempts to address housing shortages by these means were far from successful. Given the wage rates of the urban working class and the relative expense of land and developments in the city, what private sector speculative house construction there was served an almost entirely middle-class market. Other private sector initiatives included company housing. Some company housing was on the military model, with dormitory accommodation and correspondingly martial discipline and regimentation of workers. Often it was simply exploitative, as in the case of coal miners' housing in the English Midlands which, despite its very low quality, was exorbitantly priced. Some employers, though, were of a philanthropic bent (a philanthropy bolstered by the economic necessity of retaining skilled workers in underhoused regions) and sought to create well planned colonies on the garden city model. The *Cité Ouvrière* created by the Mulhouse industrialist Jean Dollfus was a well laid out community of single-family homes that a worker, after fifteen years of payments, could own (though recent work suggests that this was only possible so long as wives and children also worked). It was a model copied by many large industrial concerns in Germany.

BETWEEN THE WARS

At the outbreak of war in 1914, neither the modest initiatives of the state, nor company housing, nor other, more honestly philanthropic plans, nor workers cooperatives had even come close to meeting housing needs in Europe. In Germany, where the proportion of the population living in towns of 100,000 or more had gone from 4.8 percent in 1871 to 21 percent in 1910, there was a need for 800,000 apartments for working families in 1914. By 1919 this figure was 1.4 million. Nor was Germany exceptional. But by the end of World War I, in the context of social revolution, real (as in Russia) or imagined (everywhere else), demands for housing could no longer be ignored. Britain's prime minister, David Lloyd George, fanned expectations by promising, with direct reference to the housing that returning soldiers might expect, "a country fit for heroes to live in." At the same time and for many of the same reasons, housing was further politicized by modernist architects like Le Corbusier, Ludwig Mies van der Rohe, Walter Gropius, and others associated with the Bauhaus movement, who believed that mass-produced, functional dwellings could not only house workers but could also aid in the transformation of society and culture at the dawn of what appeared to be a new age.

Both postwar political tensions and the utopian visions of modernist architects played a role in housing between the two world wars. So changed was the political and ideological balance of European society between the two wars that in the major industrialized nations there was bound to be some further move away from liberal solutions to the housing question. In Britain, no less than four Housing Acts were passed between 1919 and 1924 (eleven were passed between 1919 and 1945). These acts either provided national funds to local authorities to build what came to be called council houses, or paid out lump sums or ongoing payments to private interests building low-cost housing. Even in countries such as France, where politics shifted to the right after World War I, policymakers realized that the national state would have to assume a far larger role in the provision of housing. In France, Loucheur's Act of 1928 provided state funding for the construction of 200,000 low-cost dwellings and 60,000 medium-cost ones. Similar developments occurred in Germany, where the Weimar Constitution of 1919 gave the new Republic wider powers in the area of housing. In Scandinavia, where Social Democratic governments undertook reforms that set the stage for the modern welfare state, private house building and housing cooperatives far outstripped public housing.

The net result of all these initiatives was to radically increase the pool of affordable housing. In France, 300,000 new low-cost housing units were built between 1919 and 1931. In England the figure was a staggering 1.785 million. Yet even this level of construction failed to fill the need for low-cost housing. In some jurisdictions the failings of public housing initiatives were functions of ill-considered government intervention. For instance, in France wartime rent controls remained in force throughout much of the 1920s. This policy, which was supposed to make housing more affordable, deprived private builders of any incentive to construct low-cost housing at a time when the French government was relying

Public Housing in Austria. Apartment building constructed by the city of Vienna, 1929. ©BETTMANN/CORBIS

almost exclusively on the private sector to add to housing stock, thereby making housing scarcer and more expensive.

Perhaps the boldest experiment in public housing occurred in Vienna under the municipal administration of the Social Democratic Party elected after World War I. Here, too, rent controls severely depressed private house construction and augmented the need for new housing. To address these problems the Viennese government launched an ambitious plan of public housing funded by a steeply progressive income tax (which further depressed the private market). Eventually 64,000 new dwellings, mostly in large tenement blocks, were built under this program. But the initiative was distinct as well because of its broader social goals. Turning bourgeois notions about the social and cultural functions of housing on their heads, the architects of the "Red Vienna" experiment, as it came to be called, believed that the new communal housing would play a part in the constitution of a "new man" for a new, socialist age. Even though the socialist government rejected the designs of the architectural modernists, it embraced the modernists' utopianism as regards housing.

Utopian housing designs were given a fuller airing in the Bolshevik Revolution in Russia. Throughout the 1920s plans were proposed for the rebuilding of Russian cities and the provision of housing for the working classes. Here, too, the garden-city model had a certain currency. Indeed, the anarchist Pyotr Kropotkin, was a devotee of Howard's ideas, and the garden-city movement in Russia persisted into the 1920s and found its way into official plans (though without Kropotkin's involvement). Plans for communal housing were also advanced. Here, as in Vienna, the culturally and socially transformative potential of communal living was viewed by its proponents as integral to the transition to socialist society. By the 1930s, however, when the Soviet Union's industrial needs had emerged as the most pressing concern, experimentation in housing lost out to grim necessity. At Magnitogorsk, a new industrial town in central Russia, communal housing persisted as a preferred option for local communist authorities largely because of its efficacy in meeting the needs of the hundreds of thousands of workers who were coming to work there. While it was justified in local Party publications in terms of a collectivist social vision, when the preference of workers for independent living (manifested in the repeated erection of mud huts despite ordinances against them) became apparent, the construction of bungalows by workers was not only tolerated but eventually encouraged. In fact, as in Western Europe, the Communist authorities extended credit to workers for this purpose. Nonetheless, such houses remained a dream rather than a reality for most Russian workers.

POST–WORLD WAR II

The destructiveness of World War II increased the need for housing everywhere, although the response to this need varied from state to state. The war left 1.5 million dwellings in France uninhabitable. Added to preexisting housing needs, this meant that something like 2 million housing units were needed immediately and 14 million were thought to be needed over the following twenty years. By 1950, however, only 90,000 new dwellings had been erected. This feeble effort led to new measures, one of the most important of which in France was the creation of *zones à urbanisation prioritaire,* or ZUPs, which allowed governments to acquire land and to extend easy credit for the construction of large-scale housing projects. Some 140 ZUPs were established, mostly around Paris, and it was in these developments that the modernist architectural ideas of LeCorbusier, for instance, had their greatest effect. (Although only involved in four projects, he was an important influence on younger architects.) The average size of each development was 5,300 dwelling units, adding up to a total of three-quarters of a million.

Of course the ZUP projects, aided by public funds, were not the only source of new housing stock. Private sources contributed a great deal as well, such that between 1945 and 1990 French housing stock doubled with the addition of 14 million units, of which only 17 percent were social housing units. There was a significant increase in home ownership and an even bigger increase in rental social housing, both to the detriment of private rentals. Similar patterns prevailed in West Germany, where 16.5 million new dwellings were added to the national stock between 1945 and 1986, with a significant rise in home ownership. In Britain, only 9 million new dwellings were added between 1939 and 1989, but home ownership more than doubled, rising from 33 to 68 percent.

One of the important consequences of postwar housing developments was to offer an unprecedented degree of interior space. This is a function both of the raw increase in numbers of available dwellings (which by no means completely resolved the need for housing) and of the regulation of new housing stock when it was built. Governments around Europe established minimum size requirements for rooms, and in some cases also specified the kind and number of rooms that had to be built in dwellings. New regulations also required that amenities such as running water, toilets, baths, and central heating be installed. These regulations revolutionized housing in its material aspect. They also revolutionized the individual's relation to himself and others by providing a far greater degree of personal and private space than ever before. Earlier, the exile of children to corridors was often a necessary prequel to many couples' conjugal relations. The sharing of beds by two or more siblings (and sometimes even parents and children) had been the norm throughout European history. But by the mid-1970s, the average French home had 3.5 rooms, and there was a ratio of more than 200 square feet per person. This increase in individual private space is entirely consistent with the emergence of a consumer society that emphasizes as a chief marketing tool the fulfillment of personal needs through consumption. Space is not the only factor in housing's role in individualizing social experience. Running water, in-house laundry facilities, and the omnipresent radio and, later, television allowed tasks that were formerly done in a public space (such as a neighborhood pub, in the case of the communication of news) to be conducted in private. Detached housing estates integrated into broader transportation networks through the automobile served similar functions.

It is unclear, however, whether home ownership, which state policies continued to support throughout the postwar period, works in exactly the ways its original paternalist sponsors wanted. It has been assumed that the sale of over one million council housing units to their tenants under Margaret Thatcher's Right to Buy program (which was merely an expanded form of the selling of council flats that both Labour and Conservative administrations had pushed for decades) altered the political attitudes of their new owners and

Public Housing in Germany. Apartment buildings constructed by the city of Munich, 1955.
©BETTMANN/CORBIS

could account, at least in part, for the success of the Conservatives in the 1980s. Quantitative research suggests that new owners of council housing were no more or less likely to vote Conservative than any other voter. Qualitative evidence further suggests, against popular perceptions, that few of these new owners wanted to use the capital embodied in their homes as a means to escape their old neighborhood for a better one.

CONCLUSION

If housing emerged since 1800 as an important question for both the state and individuals, it is because of the linked demographic and economic changes that made it increasingly a scarce commodity. Yet as this essay has shown, it is not only in its simple material form that housing is important for social historians.

The efforts of the state, of individuals, and of other organizations to access and provide safe and affordable housing surveyed here were undertaken at a time when the house became an important cultural construct. Housing is indissociably linked to ideas about the family, gender, the environment, privacy, and respectability. Thus the efforts referred to above cannot be understood outside these cultural associations. Indeed, it may well be asked whether the general preference of both states and individuals to develop housing solutions based on private ownership is not a function of the fact that housing emerged as a social problem as it also came to be defined in cultural terms. It may well be asked whether the possibility of addressing the remaining major deficiencies in the available housing stock in Europe does not reside in moving beyond this particular cultural construct.

See also **The City: The Early Modern Period; The City: The Modern Period** *(volume 2);* **Peasants and Rural Laborers; Public Health** *(volume 3);* **The Household** *(volume 4); and other articles in this section.*

BIBLIOGRAPHY

Braudel, Fernand. *Civilization and Capitalism: 15th–18th Century.* Vol. 1: *The Structures of Everyday Life.* Translated by Siân Reynolds. New York, 1979.

Brumfield, William Craft, and Blair A. Ruble. *Russian Housing in the Modern Age: Design and Social History.* Cambridge, U.K., 1993.

Burnett, John. *A Social History of Housing, 1815–1985.* London, 1978, 1986.

Cole, Ian, and Robert Furbey. *The Eclipse of Council Housing.* London and New York, 1994.

De Vries, Jan. *European Urbanization, 1500–1800.* Cambridge, Mass., 1984.

Duby, Georges, and Philippe Ariès, eds. *A History of Private Life.* Vols. 2–5, Translated by Arthur Goldhammer. Cambridge, Mass., 1988–1991.

Forrest, Ray, and Alan Murie. "Transformation through Tenure? The Early Purchasers of Council Houses, 1968–1973." *Journal of Social Policy* 20 (January 1991): 1–25.

Gruber, Helmut. *Red Vienna: Experiment in Working-Class Culture, 1919–1934.* New York, 1991.

Guerrand, Roger H. *Les origines du logement social en France.* Paris, 1966.

Harloe, Michael. *The People's Home?: Social Rented Housing in Europe and America.* Oxford, 1995.

Hohenberg, Paul and Lynn Lees. *The Making of Urban Europe, 1000–1950.* Cambridge, U.K., 1985.

James, Simon, Bill Jordan, and Helen Kays. "Poor People, Council Housing, and the Right to Buy." *Journal of Social Policy* 20 (January 1991): 27–40.

Le Roy Ladurie, Emmanuel. *Montaillou: The Promised Land of Error.* Translated by Barbara Bray. New York, 1979.

Pensley, Danielle Sibener. "The Socialist City?: A Critical Analysis of *Neubaugebiet* Hellersdorf." *Journal of Urban History* 24 (July 1998); 563–602.

Pooley, Colin G., ed. *Housing Strategies in Europe, 1880–1930.* Leicester, U.K., 1992.

Power, Anne. *Hovels to High Rise: State Housing in Europe since 1850.* London and New York, 1993.

Shapiro, Ann-Louise. *Housing the Poor of Paris, 1850–1902.* Madison, Wis., 1985.

Sutcliffe, Anthony. *Towards the Planned City: Germany, Britain, the United States, and France, 1780–1914.* Oxford, 1981.

Wagenaar, Michael. "Conquest of the Center or Flight to the Suburbs? Divergent Metropolitan Strategies in Europe, 1850–1914." *Journal of Urban History* 19 (November 1992): 60–83.

DOMESTIC INTERIORS

Rineke van Daalen

Houses and their interiors provide a rich picture of the lifestyles of their inhabitants. They also represent and objectify the social relations of the people that designed them, built them, and used them. At the French court in the seventeenth and eighteenth centuries, typically the king and his wife each had separate sleeping apartments, an arrangement suggestive of their affective relationship. Nineteenth-century Londoners built their family residences away from business and pleasure, aspiring to privacy and safety from the cares and worries of the outside world within the impregnable castle of the home. Parisians on the contrary felt more attracted to life outside the home, in the streets, gardens, theaters, and restaurants. Viennese townspeople were more engaged in consumption than production. Both bourgeois and aristocrats relied on their luxurious houses as public representations of their status.

Houses, as the examples suggest, reflect the means of subsistence of their inhabitants, their affective relations and power relations, their family systems, marriage customs, laws of succession, and the composition of their households. Changes in these respects, such as the death of a parent or the formation of a new household, are reflected in changes in dwelling spaces. Houses also reveal the social relations between their inhabitants and the outside world. In small-scale, traditional socities there is no distinction between a public and a private domain and houses are more accessible than in differentiated societies. This contrast roughly corresponds to the dichotomy between countryside and city.

The social history of houses and domestic interiors may be told as a story of increasing differentiation: between home and work, between life in the household and in the extended family, between the community and the neighborhood, between different generations and sexes. During the Middle Ages, all-purpose rooms were characteristic of aristocratic, peasant, and artisan dwellings alike, but as people's daily pursuits became more varied and differences between people increased, the configurations of their houses

also changed. The function of domestic interiors as a display of status became more important as affluence increased, differences in power decreased, and status rivalry intensified.

Emulation and competition are driving forces in the development and spread of styles and fashions. Those to whom it mattered lost no time in acquiring the most up-to-date designs and fashions, and the rest followed slowly. Architects, designers, upholsterers, and later professional decorators were unfettered by national boundaries. Nevertheless, within Europe enduring regional building styles evolved as expressions of national and local qualities. General developments that affected Europe as a whole, such as industrialization, urbanization, and population growth, offer only a limited perspective on building styles. Local traditions, including those affecting homes and their design and decor, remained embedded in regional and national patterns of stratification and political organization. Taste in domestic interiors reveals not only people's actual social position, as notions of taste are usually acquired early and subconsciously, they also reveal people's deep-rooted dispositions. Thus the study of housing and domestic interiors opens the door on several areas of social-historical interest. This article, relying on several studies, sketches the history of housing in western European countries. More research on other parts of Europe is necessary, especially from a comparative perspective combining social history, sociology, and the history of art.

THE DIFFERENTIATION OF SOCIETY AND THE SUBDIVISION OF DOMESTIC SPACE

In his landmark work *The World We Have Lost* (1971), Peter Laslett drew attention to the scale of life in the preindustrial world. Nearly all people spent all their lives in small groups. Apart from going to church, people attended only gatherings that could assemble in ordinary houses, which were also the scenes of labor. The mean size of households was related to the status of their inhabitants: the laboring poor had few children, their life expectancy was low, and they sent their children at the age of ten as working servants to richer people. In England this group, the poor laborers, accounted for as many as two-thirds of the population. They lived in humble cottages whose construction cost less than three years' income. By contrast, members of the English gentry often had more than one mansion—some had as many as twelve seats—in various spots in the countryside; in their absence the houses were maintained by tenants. At the end of the preindustrial era, roughly three-quarters of the English still lived in villages and hamlets.

Although they do not supplant written materials, paintings and pictures offer glimpses of the simple lodgings of the majority, their interiors and uses. In *Visit to the Farmstead,* the Flemish painter Jan Brueghel the Elder (1568–1625) depicts a Flemish farmhouse consisting of only one room, with an open fire for cooking and heating in the center and a smoke hole above it. The room is dimly lit by small apertures. Of the peasants and children seen in the room, one woman is breast-feeding her newborn infant, two people are making butter in a churn, and another is entertaining three well-to-do visitors. The table has been laid for a meal, with a white tablecloth and several bowls of porridge, and someone is already eating. A cradle with a sleeping dog inside stands in a corner; a large box serves as storage space. Although the painting shows no bed, in reality one bed, which accommodated the whole family, always stood in the multipurpose living room of the houses of villagers in this period. The farmsteads functioned simultaneously as residence and economic unit of production. The dwelling provided shelter for the family and other inhabitants, the food provisions, harvested crops, tools, and even the cattle. Day laborers also lived in one-room dwellings. Within such a dwelling all human activities took place in the same space, and no boundaries delineated different pastimes or basic functions such as breast-feeding or sleeping. For centuries this spatial model was standard for the majority of the population, both in the countryside and the cities.

Gradually however, as social differentiation and stratification increased, the geography and the interior of the houses became more complicated. Among artisans and master artisans, growing commercial property translated into more elaborate interiors. According to an inventory drawn up in 1647 somewhere on the outskirts of Paris, the layout of the house of an artisan consisted of a downstairs kitchen giving onto the street, a living room behind the kitchen, and two rooms upstairs with a small attic. Up to the eighteenth century, and in some remote regions even into the nineteenth, beds stood in the heated living room, where people also stayed during the day. Even in the larger houses of farmers and burghers, people slept where they had fires—in the same place where they prepared and ate their meals.

The trend toward complexity and privacy.   Members of the gentry, the court nobility, and the merchant elite were among the forerunners in the trend toward more elaborate and complex houses. In their households the first provisions for privacy were created, and rooms became intended for specific purposes. The dwellings of the nobility of the ancien régime in France, called *hôtel* or *palais* depending on the owner's status, also housed a motley crowd of servants. The staff, from the coachman to the kitchen maid and the footman, lived behind the scenes, separated from the quarters devoted to the social life of the owners by one or more antechambers, in which servants waited for their masters and received orders. The German sociologist Norbert Elias observed that these rooms manifested the "co-existence of constant spatial proximity and constant social distance, of intimate contact in one stratum and the strictest aloofness in the other." (Elias, 1983, pp. 47–49). The same pattern is evident in the palace of the king. Noblemen and noblewomen took their humble place in the antechamber to await the king's orders.

The separate sleeping apartments for the king and his wife illustrate both their relationship in their marriage and their relations to their "houses" of descent. Husband and wife were primarily related as representatives of their lineage to the world outside. They had common social obligations to their families, but for the rest they were relatively free in their movement. They did not have what one might call a family life, and each had their own social circle and led their own social life. To allow them to perform their representative functions, the society rooms of their places were divided into two parts. Among the nobility the large salon was the heart of court society. In this *appartement de société* the master and lady of the house received a small circle of visitors and engaged in their more intimate social intercourse. Public and official visits took place in the *appartement de parade,* where the owners of the house arranged the affairs of court life as scions of a noble family, always endeavoring to live up to the demands of their social status.

Among these absolutist court circles, houses were built to meet the representative social obligations of their owners. Through their choice of materials, design, and decoration, architects tried to express the social status of the inhabitants. The cost was attuned

Visit to the Farmstead. Painting (c. 1597) by Jan Brueghel the Elder (1568–1625). KUNSTHISTORISCHES MUSEUM, VIENNA/ERICH LESSING/ART RESOURCE, NY

to the demands of their ranks. "A duke must build his house in such a way as to tell the world: I am a duke and not merely a count" (Elias, 1983, p. 63). In European absolutist societies, houses of the haute bourgeoisie and middle-class families were small-scale imitations of the houses of the nobility, with some significant differences. Sleeping arrangements of husbands and wives reflected their greater affective attachement. The bourgeois elite was not geared to social intercourse with many people but rather pursued contacts primarily related to business—hence the small size of their "society," or reception, rooms. Their homes had no *appartement de parade,* and their salon, or reception room, was less impressive than that of the nobility. Nevertheless, their houses were also built to display social status and prestige. In matters of interior design the French set the standard for civilized taste. It became fashionable for architects in the Netherlands and England to decorate interiors, window panels, doors, chimneypieces, ceilings, and vases in the French style. This style was transmitted by "advice books," illustrated with genre scenes and engravings of interiors that depicted the current good taste.

Family life and interiors. In the seventeen-century Dutch Republic, the wealthy ruling families in the city demonstrated their status by way of the comfort and luxury of the interiors of their houses. In addition to serving as living accommodations, these houses had separate areas for the use of business. Simon Schama (1987) has written of such homes as symbolic centers of decency, where morality was upheld. In the Dutch Republic family households were seen as the origin of authority and held a central place within the state. The special significance of the family is reflected in well-kept and carefully arranged dwellings. The Dutch attached great significance to tidy and well-kept interiors, and indeed exhibited a ritual cleaning mania. Wives and mothers had a pivotal function in fitting out and protecting hearth and home. They used their cleaning utensils to ward off the wickedness of the outside world and more generally to shield the house from evil. Careful tending and meticulous cleaning of the interior of houses demonstrated the solidity of family life and expressed at the same time feelings of patriotism and commitment to liberty and purity. A filthy and unattended house was seen as a breeding place for disease, creating opportunities for the spread of evil. Inventories of the houses of the elite attest to an array of carefully chosen furniture, cooking utensils, paintings, and household articles. All the accoutrements of domestic life were chosen to create a comfortable and well-maintained home and to express the social status and moral solidity of its owners.

As compared to earlier European housing arrangements, the houses of the Dutch elite showed a greater concern for privacy. This separation from the

Dutch Interior. *The Chess Players,* painting (c. 1670) by Cornelis de Man (1621–1706). SZÉPMŰVÉSZETI MÚZEUM, BUDAPEST/THE BRIDGEMAN ART LIBRARY

world outside is one aspect of broader processes of the modernization and growing intimacy of family life. In the Netherlands the modern family came into being relatively early. The seventeenth-century urban elite gave special attention to an intimate family event like childbirth by arranging *kraamkamers,* or lying-in rooms, to lodge mother and infant after delivery. The interior of these *kraamkamers* would be fitted up in accordance with fixed patterns and provided with special furniture for mothers and children. Objects like the *bakermat* (a rush basket for the dry nurse), the *kraamscherm* (a screen to protect mother and child from drafts and the inquisitive gaze of bystanders), the baby-linen basket, baby clothes, blankets, cradle, and pincushion were all meant to show the care and competence of mothers and to express the social status of

the family. Drawings of *kraamkamers* show the increasing value placed on privacy, with mothers and infants screened from outsiders. Whereas images from earlier in the seventeenth century depict visits from neighbors, relatives, and acquaintances to see mother and child, over the course of the century the childbed moved increasingly into the private sphere. As the number of visitors decreased, such scenes ceased to be community gatherings but rather became intimate, private moments within the nuclear family circle, concentrated in carefully arranged rooms.

This and other arrangements within the home correspond to changes analyzed by Norbert Elias in his landmark work of 1939, *The Civilizing Process* (2000). Elias showed that from the Middle Ages onward western Europeans became more sensitive and more reserved in their own behavior as well as in their behavior toward others. Bodily functions such as defecating, urinating, sleeping, and copulating began to arouse feelings of shame and embarrassment in the presence of other people. These feelings were reflected in the geography of houses and in the objects within the rooms. Houses became divided by more walls and gained more floors. Rooms acquired special functions for public and private behaviors and became accessible only from corridors and halls. Houses were adapted to these new needs, such as the replacement of one central, free-standing fireplace by several fireplaces built into the walls. The elite more and more put their beds behind the scenes and equipped them with curtains and hangings. People who were not familiar to each other less often slept in the same bed or the same room.

An important development in the trend toward privacy concerned defecating. In the countryside people continued to relieve themselves outdoors, but in the cities of the sixteenth century public conveniences were arranged and municipal ordinances forbade defecating outside these facilities. During the seventeenth century more and more well-to-do people acquired chamberpots, or *chaises percées,* for their own houses. These conveniences, formerly placed in the middle of dining rooms and salons, later were kept only in bedrooms; over time they were gradually ostracized to special nooks and crannies within the house, to cellars or under the doorsteps. Pots were also placed in bedside cabinets and cupboards or disguised as something else, for example as a pile of books. Conveniences for servants were still built in gardens and outdoor courtyards.

URBANIZATION, INDUSTRIALIZATION, AND THE INCREASED NEED FOR PRIVACY

During the nineteenth and in particular the twentieth century, houses underwent important changes, with urban dwellings leading the way. Two parallel processes, both characteristic of the breakdown of older social hierarchies, were significant: The social distance between family and servants lost its former clarity, prompting employers to increase physical distance between themselves and their staff. At the same time, relations between husband and wife, and between parents and children, became more egalitarian. These processes promoted further differentiation of the geography of houses and increased the individual need for privacy. Rooms and sections of the house were strictly divided on the basis of social, functional, and moral criteria. The interior decoration of the house now received more attention, and decorating the home became a profession.

Among the bourgeoisie, rooms acquired specific functions earliest and with greatest effect in England. Already in the sixteenth century a yeoman's house had a specialized geography, and in nineteenth-century country houses this specialization became elaborate. The preparation of the (quite simple) English meals was dispersed over specialized rooms: the larder, divided into store rooms; separate rooms for different kinds of cleaning; a scullery; and areas for cooking, baking, and washing up. By the middle of the century the medium-sized houses of the middle classes, small-scale imitations of Georgian houses, were also becoming elaborate. Masters and servants, men and women, visitors and family members had separate staircases and specialized spaces. Women gained their boudoirs, men their gentleman's room, and children their nurseries. The dining room was equipped with massive, simple furniture, expressing masculinity, while the drawing room showed feminine charm and elegance. In the planning of the house is evident the middle-class conviction that the private sphere belonged to women. Children were raised apart from their parents, tended by the nanny and governess. Rooms were preferably not connected by doors but rather separated by corridors and halls built at the expense of the size of the rooms themselves.

These houses allowed for a high degree of personal privacy, in particular for the adult owners, less so for children, adolescents, and servants. The layout of the house allowed English parents to avoid too much contact with their children. In contrast to customs on the Continent, English ladies never set foot in their kitchen domains. When the first English flats were built, architects tried to make the horizontal subdivision of the houses match the vertical subdivision in standard townhouses. But by the 1870s, in reaction to the elaborate Victorian houses, the suburban houses of the new middle class acquired a simpler layout. These houses had no basement, while the kitchen and reception rooms were arranged on the ground floor and the bedrooms were placed above.

The banning of beds to rooms that acquired the specific name of "bedroom" and their clear separation from the rest of the house became characteristic of the sleeping habits of much of the middle class. Hygienists of the nineteenth century recommended fresh air in the bedrooms and specified ideal sizes for the rooms. Curtains around the bed were preferably kept open. Gradually the idea became accepted that single beds for one person were preferable to cupboard beds and that spacious bedrooms were preferable to alcove bedrooms. A feathery eiderdown and pillow and too many blankets came to be seen as the breeding places of unpleasant odors and as an incitement to masturbation. Rooms for sleeping were to be kept free of odors of any kind—flowers, servants, animals, or foul laundry. Isolated houses were preferred, remote from the emanations of bustling crowds. In cities, windows were not to be opened for too long lest the polluted evaporations of the streets enter.

Although ideas about the desirability of privacy were similar in other western European countries, they varied in their realization. These differences were a consequence partly of the available economic resources and partly of traditions in family and societal life. French cities, for example, were more crowded than English, partly because of greater preference for urban over suburban life. The Parisian apartments that were built in the nineteenth century consisted of several ingeniously arranged, specialized one-purpose rooms, but their scale was very small and they did not offer as much privacy as English apartments. The French made the most of the available space and were less sensitive to the mingling of different atmospheres. Their bedrooms had a more open character and were seen as a comfortable extension of the drawing room; the kitchen and dining room were sometimes connected. English critics found such habits shocking. They saw the houses of the Parisians as uncomfortable, crowded, and even indecent. But compared to the dwellings of the ancien régime, these houses were not so bad, and compared to the houses in Vienna the new Parisian flats were paragons of compact and ingenious architecture.

The function of home as a display of status and wealth also varied among countries. English Victorians and Edwardians saw their houses primarily as a place for the family and eschewed ostentation, while the French home combined family uses with those of maintaining social relations, business, reception, and entertainment. The cultivation of this public side of life demanded more luxury, and thus the Parisian flats were lavishly furnished, with marble chimneypieces, velvet upholstery, embossed wallpaper, and abundant mirrors. In nineteenth-century Vienna, the continued social and political dominance of the aristocracy left the bourgeoisie in a subordinate position also in matters of culture and taste. The impressive lodgings of aristocrats came to epitomize good architectural taste and thus became models for bourgeois homes. Imitation of aristocratic styles often entailed a sacrifice of interior comfort in favor of external display and its suggestion of status. The petit bourgeoisie paid less attention to practical needs, such as places for sleeping, and sacrificed domestic comfort to create a salon

for receptions, where they exhibited their volumes of literature and poetry. They were rather slow to give their rooms differentiated and variable designations and late in introducing corridors.

Taking bodily functions backstage. Sanitary provisions are a special chapter in the social history of privacy in the home. Until the introduction of running water, people washed themselves with water from pitchers and washbowls placed on tables. In the houses of the rich, these tables would be elegantly tiled amenities, with towel rails, framed mirrors, and wooden or marble surfaces. Initially they were not placed in special bathrooms but were pieces of loose furniture that could easily be moved. In 1837 even Buckingham Palace lacked a bathroom. For a long time the ownership of baths and washbasins was a luxury. Water sellers served well-to-do customers without a bathtub of their own by carrying baths into their apartments. The first specialized bathrooms were spacious, in accordance with the recommendations of hygienists; they featured heavy furniture and walls covered with absorbent material. Alain Corbin (1986) has argued that the relatively late appearance of bathrooms was the most important event in the history of living accommodations in the nineteenth century and a decisive step in the specification of rooms for intimate purposes.

Great Britain was the first to implement the layout of houses according to the new sanitary norms, which were thought not only to be healthful but, in a more general way, civilized. Piped water supplies and the use of baths spread there earlier than on the Continent. As the custom of performing bodily functions in private became increasingly the norm and the ideas of the nineteenth century hygienists gained acceptance, people paid more attention to the interior of their bathrooms and toilets. Closet pots were made of vitreous china, often with elaborate floral decorations; seat, cover, and floor were made of oak and were neatly waxed. Water closets appeared as soon as running water was introduced in the nineteenth century, earlier for the rich than for the poor, and earlier in cities than in the countryside. But the majority of the population continued to lack such provisions. The pail-and-tub system, cesspools, and dunghills remained common. In France, where tolerance of bodily emanations was greater, the introduction of piped water took place later.

The new standards of privacy and sanitation depended on connecting houses to the public utilities of water pipes and sewers. And constructing these networks depended on two factors: The public needed to recognize that the living conditions of the poor increased the risk for both rich and poor of contracting contagious diseases. And they had to accept the notion that improvements in living conditions, sanitary amenities, and the removal of garbage and excrement from houses were issues that required municipal action in the construction of public works. Changing the behavior of individual poor people would not be sufficient. Houses in newly built districts, where residents were willing to pay for sanitary facilities, were the first into which fresh water was pumped via a branching network of pipes. The waste water and excrement was then drained away in a parallel but separate network of sewers. These public networks had far-reaching consequences for domestic facilities and conditioned the way people urinated, defecated, and washed themselves. Other innovations like gas, electricity, and the telephone had equally important implications for homes and domestic life in industrialized, urbanized societies.

Housing of the Poor. Woman in a courtyard of a slum in Newcastle, England. Photograh by Herbert Felton, c. 1875. ©Hulton Getty/Liaison Agency

The bourgeois home as a model for working-class dwellings.
Until well into the twentieth century, the majority of the working class lived in overcrowded houses of poor quality and without sanitary facilities. Over the course of the nineteenth century, the urban bourgeoisie began to see the houses of the poor as something to be ashamed of, a deficiency they were responsible for. Figures from the municipality of Amsterdam show that poor dwellings still commonly contained one or two multipurpose rooms: in 1899, 28.5 percent of the inhabitants lived in a one-room dwelling, 30.5 percent in dwellings with two rooms. The bourgeoisie was concerned that such dwellings would encourage men to frequent the pubs, while children would be prompted to roam the streets without adult supervision. The development of public housing, often organized by housing associations, was intended to provide affordable, functional, hygienic, and decent homes, and thus create the necessary conditions for a healthy and respectable family life. Rental regulations were drawn up, housing laws established norms for living accommodations, and model dwellings were built. Philanthropic female housing inspectors, who also collected the rent, instructed working-class mothers in proper living conditions.

Norms for good housing were attuned in particular to the family relations within the bourgeoisie, which in those days were taken as a model. Civilizing campaigns promoted a family life in which mothers and children were at the center, with a clear-cut division of tasks for husbands and wives and an inward-looking character. According to this model the necessary condition for a sound and decent family life was a house, preferably detached, with several one-purpose rooms: a living room, a kitchen for cooking only and not for socializing, bedrooms for parents, separate bedrooms for girls and boys, a separate toilet, and a special place for washing. Fresh air and sunlight were recommended as conditions for hygiene and good health, but only the well-to-do could afford such airy, light abodes. The design of houses was meant to allow the inhabitants to perform as many functions as possible—going to the toilet, cleansing the body, and doing the laundry—inside their homes. Collective spaces where members of different families met each other, like corridors and porches, were rejected as likely to promote gossip and indecent behavior. So as to ensure this introverted character, architects of the Dutch expressionist Amsterdam School (roughly 1920 to 1940) placed the windows in houses so high that the occupants were unable to look out.

As real wages rose, members of the working class could afford separate houses with several rooms, and they adopted some of these attitudes toward public space and domestic privacy. However, mapping the house according to existing family norms did not ensure that all people used their houses in the way the designers had intended. Many working-class families persisted in their old habits. They ate meals in their small kitchens, and some of them opposed hygienic campaigns directed at making feces both invisible and unsmellable in the house as well as outside it. Because of the popular belief that physical smells, including that of excrement, had a therapeutic and vitalizing effect, many families distrusted the bourgeois attitude toward bodily functions and saw it as a kind of conspiracy.

A Kitchen. An urban kitchen, color lithograph from a children's book by Eduard Walter, 1890. ARCHIV FÜR KUNST UND GESCHICHTE, BERLIN/AKG LONDON

In addition to the normalization of specialized rooms, the circulation of fresh air, and the construction of sanitary facilities, efficiency and functionality came to be prized attributes of the home. The idea that a rational household needed a rational division of the house was proposed in the first decades of the twentieth century by women advocates of labor-saving technology to lighten the housewife's workload, such as Christine Frederick in the United States, who was inspired by the American efficiency engineer Frederick W. Taylor; Paulette Bergère in France; and Erna Meyer in Germany. Feminist oriented, they saw housewives as managers running a business; their kitchens had to be efficient workrooms attuned to their professional activities. For modern housekeeping, housewives were to be guided by scientific principles and should have at their disposal the most practical kitchen furniture and household effects, preferably designed by professionals. Special exhibitions were organized to advertise such modern, rationally equipped kitchens.

The working class was also instructed in the choice of furniture and general taste in interior furnishings. Exhibitions showing model interiors demonstrated what was "good" and "bad" taste. Rooms were not to be filled with impractical furniture or ornamental trumpery. The "good" interior contained solid, functional objects that gave the inhabitants plenty of room for movement. Wallpaper and floor coverings were preferably simple and understated. Tasteful design was seen as symbolic of the "right" way to live, of being truly civilized. Industrially produced design furniture could provide tasteful, decent, and "correct" articles affordable to all.

This style of functional interior design was associated with the German Bauhaus school of architecture and design and the Dutch De Stijl movement, both influential in the 1920s. Bauhaus and De Stijl rejected what was seen as a bourgeois aesthetic, eschewing, for example, pillars, elaborate ornamentation, and pointed roofs. Modern architecture—represented by Walter Gropius, founder and director of the Bauhaus; Mies van der Rohe, who became Bauhaus director in 1928; Gerrit Rietveld, associated with De Stijl; and Le Corbusier, the highly influential Swiss-born architect and proponent of functionalism—may also be seen as a protest against the privacy of the bourgeois dwelling. These architects rejected conventional divisions between rooms and tried to diminish the distance between the inside and the outside of the house by the use of glass. The counterpart to the functional style in early-twentieth-century architecture and design was the Art Nouveau, or, in German, Jugendstil, movement, with variants all over Europe. This style, which flourished from 1890 to 1910, combined ideals of modernity with the tradition of handicraft and was characterized by a sinous, organic ornamentation.

VARIATION IN LIFESTYLES AND DOMESTIC INTERIORS

It was only after World War II that economic conditions permitted the widespread application of prewar ideas about housing and family life. In western European countries housing policies were still aimed at constructing small, standardized, functional family units, but over the years architects became less patronizing. Economic growth gave people the opportunity to arrange their own houses according to their own wishes, and "do-it-yourself" enthusiasts intent on renovating their houses and changing their layouts became common. In the twentieth century social inequality between men and women, between parents and children, and between different social classes gradually narrowed; as a result, in a process of informalization, manners became less rigid and a greater range of social behaviors and expressions became acceptable. Domestic interiors of ever greater variety reflected this trend. The geography of houses and the designation of rooms became more open and dependent on individual preferences. A strictly functional division of

houses was abandoned and multipurpose rooms adopted, although the bathroom and the toilet remained inviolate. The bedrooms of adolescents were used for study, listening to or playing music, and socializing. Kitchens were joined with living rooms to become "great rooms." In many houses televisions became fixtures in several if not all of the rooms.

Domestic design has become an important domain for cultural consumption and for expressing taste and, by extension, social identity. Everyday life has become aestheticized, not least in the way people arrange and decorate their homes. A range of magazines and stores addresses their desire to create the "house beautiful" and their ability to spend an increasing portion of their household budget to achieve that goal.

In the late twentieth century the Internet offered a new collective network linking people in their homes all over the world. Although the consequences remain uncertain, clearly the Internet allows people to carry out more functions within the confines of the home. At the same time, it brings the vast spaces out there into the private home, blurring far more than did radio and television the boundaries between inside and outside, and to a greater degree dissolving the line between work and home.

See also **The Urban Infrastructure** *(volume 2);* **Social Class; Public Health** *(volume 3);* **The Household; Cleanliness; Manners** *(volume 4);* **Consumerism** *(in this volume); and other articles in this section.*

BIBLIOGRAPHY

Bourdieu, Pierre. *Distinction: A Social Critique of the Judgement of Taste.* Translated by Richard Nice. Cambridge, Mass., 1984.

Collomp, Alain. "Familles, habitations, et cohabitations." In *Histoire de la vie privèe.* Vol. 3: *De la renaissance aux lumières.* Edited by Philippe Ariès and Georges Duby. Paris, 1985. Pages 500–541.

Collomp, Alain. *La maison du père: Famille et village en Haute-Provence aux XVIIe et XVIIIe siècles.* Paris, 1983.

Corbin, Alain. *The Foul and the Fragrant: Odor and the French Social Imagination.* Cambridge, Mass., 1986.

Cowan, Ruth Schwartz. *More Work for Mother: The Ironies of Household Technology from the Open Hearth to the Microwave.* New York, 1983.

Daunton, M. J. *House and Home in the Victorian City: Working Class Housing, 1850–1914.* London and Baltimore, 1983.

De Regt Ali. "Unacceptable Families: On the Origins of Social Maladjustment." *Netherlands Journal of Sociology* 18 (1982): 139–156.

Elias, Norbert. *The Civilizing Process.* Translated by Edmund Jephcott and revised by Eric Dunning, Johan Goudsblom, and Stephen Mennell. Oxford, 2000.

Elias, Norbert. *The Court Society.* Translated by Edmund Jephcott. New York, 1983.

Elias, Norbert. *The History of Manners.* Translated by Edmund Jephcott. New York, 1982.

Elias, Norbert. *State Formation and Civilization.* Translated by Edmund Jephcott. Oxford, 1982.

Featherstone, Mike. *Consumer Culture and Postmodernism.* London and Newbury Park, Calif., 1991.

Gleichmann, Peter R. "Die Verhäuslichung von Harn- und Kotentleerungen." *Medizin Mensch Gesellschaft* 4 (1979): 46–52.

Gleichmann, Peter R. "Die Verhäuslichung körperlicher Verrichtungen." In *Materialien zu Norbert Elias' Zivilisationstheorie.* Edited by Peter Gleichmann, Johan Goudsblom, and Hermann Korte. Frankfurt, 1979. Pages 254–278.

Gleichmann, Peter R. "Wandlungen im Verwalten von Wohnhausern." In *Wohnen im Wandel.* Edited by Lutz Niethammer. Wuppertal, Germany, 1979. Pages 65–88.

Goldstein, Carolyn. "From Service to Sales: Home Economics in Light and Power, 1920–1940." *Technology and Culture* 38 (1997): 121–152.

Laslett, Peter. *The World We Have Lost.* London, 1971.

Olsen, Donald J. *The City as a Work of Art: London, Paris, Vienna.* New Haven, Conn., 1986.

Schama, Simon. *The Embarrassment of Riches: An Interpretation of Dutch Culture in the Golden Age.* New York, 1987.

Shorter, Edward. *The Making of the Modern Family.* New York, 1975.

Sparke, Penny. *An Introduction to Design and Culture in the Twentieth Century.* London and Boston, 1986.

Stone, Lawrence. *The Family, Sex, and Marriage in England 1500–1800.* London, 1977.

Swaan, Abram de. *In Care of the State: Health Care, Education, and Welfare in Europe and the USA in the Modern Era.* New York, 1988.

Thornton, Peter. *Authentic Decor: The Domestic Interior, 1620–1920.* New York, 1984.

Thornton, Peter. *Seventeenth-Century Interior Decoration in England, France, and Holland.* New Haven, Conn., 1978.

Van Daalen, Rineke. "Family Change and Continuity in the Netherlands: Birth and Childbed in Text and Art." In *Successful Home Birth and Midwifery: The Dutch Model.* Edited by Eva Abraham-Van der Mark. Westport, Conn., 1993. Pages 77–94.

Van Daalen, Rineke. "Public Complaints and Government Intervention: Letters to the Municipal Authorities of Amsterdam, 1865–1920." *Netherlands Journal of Sociology* 24 (1988): 83–98.

Watkin, David. *A History of Western Architecture.* London, 1986.

Wohl, Anthony S. *Endangered Lives: Public Health in Victorian Britain.* London, 1983.

Wohl, Anthony S. *The Eternal Slum: Housing and Social Policy in Victorian London.* Montreal, 1977.

Wouters, Cas. "Formalization and Informalization: Changing Tension Balances in Civilizing Processes." *Theory, Culture, and Society* 3 (1986): 1–18.

Wright, Lawrence. *Clean and Decent: The Fascinating History of the Bathroom and the Water Closet and of Sundry Habits, Fashions, and Accessories of the Toilet, Principally in Great Britain, France, and America.* London, 1984.

CLOTHING AND FASHION

Beverly Lemire

STRUCTURE AND HIERARCHY IN DRESS

The European Renaissance flowered among a small but dynamic social elite who signaled their status through the cut and color of their clothes, as well as through the sumptuous fabrics from which their garments were made. Conscious of their rank, they gloried in their ambitions and their accomplishments. The symbolic use of dress to designate social or political status was ancient by the dawn of the Renaissance. However, in the fifteenth century the wealth at the disposal of the doges of Venice or the Medici of Florence eclipsed that of the preceding medieval period. Elite fashion and dress reflected that new affluence. Riches poured into Italy's trading cities. Local production of the highest quality silks and velvets supplied stunning displays of grandeur and privilege.

From the ancient world through the medieval period, dress signaled social status. Rank was accorded the monopoly of certain colors. As well, items of formalized attire were associated with specific social and political positions. Although apparel varied from region to region, the function of certain garments as social markers remained consistent. For example, in Venice men who held the rank of patrician or citizen upon attaining adulthood assumed a characteristic loose-fitting gown that they wore over their everyday clothes. This gown, called a toga, plus the long stole worn over the shoulders and a distinctive cap known as a *beretta* constituted the formal costume that set the gentleman and citizen apart from the artisan. These loose gowns remained signals of status. But from the fourteenth century on, clothing styles began to change rapidly, and following fashion became a mark of status. Dress followed new imperatives, becoming more revealing both for men and women. Patrician Italian youths sported waist-length jackets, revealing legs sheathed in close-fitting hose. Women of this rank wore gowns cut low across the breast, with a tighter fit around the body. The fashion cycle was set in motion, to the dismay of moralists. After 1400

it spread with growing speed from one corner of Europe to the other.

But even as fashion picked up momentum, some materials remained emblems of authority. Throughout Europe cloth of gold was the signal fabric of leadership. Woven in intricate brocaded patterns from gold and silk threads, it represented the apogee of material display. Indeed, in 1520 it formed the backdrop for one of the best known diplomatic rituals involving the Renaissance kings of France and England, Francis I and Henry VIII. The pageantry of costume and setting associated with the meeting was so magnificent that it became known thereafter as the Field of the Cloth of Gold. In a pavilion constructed of cloth of gold ranged people dressed in velvets, brocades, silks, and wools, with colors ranked from white, scarlet, and purples through blues, black, and browns. These colors, in combination with the textiles, communicated the standing of the wearer.

During the Renaissance, no region produced more lavish elaborations of dress than did Italy. Moreover, the modes of Renaissance Italy inspired nobles and royals of northern Europe, who looked to Italy for new kinds of social occasions suited to dramatic displays. One such event, the masquerade or masque, offered the frisson of sexual adventure in a formalized setting designed to exhibit the most elaborate costumes of court. In 1512 the first masque was held at the court of Henry VIII, to the great excitement of the lords and ladies, who were quick to see the opportunities presented by masked revels with anonymous suitors.

As trade and diplomacy carried trends from one court to another, the Renaissance brought a more intense preoccupation with fashion among the social elites and a gradual acceleration in the transformation of styles. High fashion flourished at the seats of political power. In this period fashion was the almost exclusive preserve of the mighty. Indeed, in court society ambitions and competing rivalries found expression through competitive expenditure on clothing. All over Europe luxurious apparel was the medium through which the great and would-be-great of both sexes, from aspiring royal mistresses to enterprising noblemen, jousted for preeminence. Their enormous collective expenditures were legitimized by their rank. Fashion and political power were inextricably linked.

Distinction in dress also preoccupied governments. The authorities asserted that an orderly society could not function without clear distinctions in ornamentation and dress within each social order. Sumptuary legislation ascribed specific colors, fabrics, and fashions to various social orders. In fifteenth-century England none but a lord was permitted to wear "any gown, jacket or coat, unless it be of such length that the same may cover his privy members and buttocks" (3 Edward IV, c.4, 1463). Lawmakers prized the rights that came with noble birth. Sumptuary laws were passed most vigorously from the fourteenth century onward, codifying the appropriate dress for each degree, with penalties assigned to transgressors. The fixed orders of society were to be visible. Thus, in seventeenth century France one's position on the king's council was confirmed through the cut and color of the ceremonial gown: the chancellor wore a long gown of crimson velvet; the councillors wore long violet gowns; the comptrollers wore short violet gowns; and the secretaries wore short black gowns. The intent was to differentiate social groups and give a stable, recognizable appearance to each segment of society. Ambiguity was to be avoided; presumption was to be squashed. In defense of this order the French government issued eighteen sumptuary decrees between 1485 and 1660; in England, seven acts and ten proclamations were issued between 1450 and 1600. This legislation was a response to insubordination, for a transformation in dress was under way, with or without official sanction.

Silk was one of the most hotly contested commodities. The nobility claimed a monopoly over the wearing of silk in most of Europe. However, silk did not remain the preserve of the aristocracy. Its attractions proved irresistible to ambitious bourgeois wherever silk novelties appeared. Stylish knitted silk stockings were brought as gifts from the Spanish to the English court early in the sixteenth century. By the 1560s informers were stationed at London's gates to hunt for commoners wearing these novel garments. Sumptuary legislation lapsed in England in 1604 and in France in the early eighteenth century. But with or without legislated prohibitions, European society was torn by competing desires. Growing numbers of men and women wanted new types of clothes made with new fabrics and designs. At the same time, representatives of the ancien régime struggled to limit fashions to the elite.

COMMERCIAL EXPANSION AND SOCIAL TRANSFORMATION

From the late Middle Ages, trade in the Mediterranean and Levant catapulted Italy to the forefront of Renaissance Europe, pouring undreamed-of wealth into state and private coffers. The riches that sustained noble families also brought new pressures to bear on the old order. Newly wealthy commoners and flourishing traders represented a threat to medieval regimes founded on hereditary feudal relations and inherited privileges. Growing cities attracted people from many backgrounds with less to gain from deference and loyalty to traditional authorities and more to gain through innovation, risk, and self-promotion. As the commercial momentum swept western and northern Europe, overseas trade with Asia, Africa, and the Americas created a growing cast of traders, merchants, and professionals who did not accept prescribed limits on their choice of clothing. Indeed, they rejected the very premise of sumptuary laws.

As expanding trade created a larger middling social order, so too did the development of European manufacturing. In addition, imported Asian textiles and new European-made fabrics increased the variety of materials available to a widening cross section of women and men.

Medieval Italy was the first European region to produce cotton and fustian textiles in quantity. Manufacturers realized that cottons were well suited to supply both domestic and export markets with low-priced goods. Spain soon followed suit. Throughout Europe popular tastes were changing. From the sixteenth century onward, the traditional heavy, durable woolen fabrics gradually lost their appeal. Middling and artisan customers wanted lighter textiles, known as the new draperies. Woolen-making regions in the Low Countries, France, and England were transformed under the pressure of these new consumer tastes. The new draperies offered mixed fabrics in wool, silk, linen, or cotton, as well as lightweight worsted wools. Modeled initially on light Italian wools, imitations proliferated. Italian cottons, fustians, and wools were copied by manufacturers in southern Germany, France, and the Low Countries; Flemish fabrics were adapted in England and imitated in Spain and Venice. For a growing number of Europeans, everyday clothing began to change. Whereas before a suit of clothing was expected to last a lifetime and even be handed down to heirs, now the selection of a coat, jacket, waistcoat, or cape became more a matter of personal choice than an investment for future generations. Less costly, more ephemeral commodities could reflect individual visions of appropriate dress.

FUSTIANS

Fustians (a blend of cotton and linen or just cotton) were made in ever greater quantities from the sixteenth century onward. They were produced in a great variety of styles, weights, and textures and included corduroys, moleskin, heavy twills, and velveteen. Some regions gave their name to fabrics that went on to be made in many other parts of Europe. Jean, for example, was known as coming initially from the city of Genoa; denim came from the French city of Nîmes, hence *de Nîmes*. Fustians were extremely popular fabrics, initially used by working people who needed sturdy clothing. The benefit of making garments from these fabrics was that they cost less than clothing made from heavy woolens and were easily washable. By the eighteenth century fustians were being substituted for a whole range of goods, including leather. For example, soft slippers could be made out of jean. And by this period, genteel and common consumers chose fustians for their daily apparel.

Lighter fabrics cost less and could be replaced more often. They were part of a revolution in dress, a revolution in self-presentation. The new fabrics enabled a greater preoccupation with personal display among the lower classes. Inevitably, the choices made by artisans and urban servants more closely mirrored prevailing upper-class modes. Their clothes did not replicate elite tastes. However, common clothing was being transformed and nowhere more dramatically than in northwestern Europe. From the 1500s plebeian dress began evolving from unchangingly drab coverings to a more varied range of apparel.

Dramatic alterations in dress continued during the seventeenth and eighteenth centuries. A proliferation of European textiles encouraged the wearing of body linens as an intermediary layer between the skin and outer garments. Shifts and shirts for men and women became commonplace; stockings were almost as ubiquitous. By 1700 linen shirts were a staple of the wardrobes of poor Parisian workingmen; workingwomen owned even greater numbers. Cleanliness, as well as display, was more readily attainable with the growing ownership of linen shirts and shifts. Shirts with lace at the cuffs and neck were well within the means of the bourgeoisie. Shirts, shifts, aprons, hand-kerchiefs, and stockings came in many qualities and at many prices. Accessories modified pedestrian garments. Textile wholesalers and retailers, peddlers and shopkeepers, offered an ever-widening range of choice to their patrons. In all social ranks garments and accessories made from these fabrics were more numerous than ever before, permitting a greater involvement with temporal modes.

Asian textiles also contributed to the refashioning of European dress. Brought in the 1500s to the Iberian peninsula, the floral-patterned fabrics caught the fancy of the Spanish royal family and moved gradually into wider markets. By the last quarter of the 1600s, trading companies from every major European country imported shiploads of calicoes and chintzes. For example, in 1684 over one million pieces of Indian cloth were landed at English docks. The brightly colored, washable East Indian textiles were unlike anything previously seen in Europe. Their richly colored botanical prints were a fraction of the cost of European silk brocades; printed chintzes inaugurated an era of even greater plebeian ornamentation. In the rural districts of the Netherlands, calicoes and chintzes were incorporated into everyday folk dress. Although the rate of diffusion varied among European nations, consumers could be found in every social rank, with England and the Netherlands providing the earliest and broadest markets. Even the laboring population of Paris owned quantities of the brightly patterned goods by the end of the eighteenth century.

East Indian textiles, with their vibrant floral designs, attracted legions of buyers—but also critics, who feared the contagion of social disorder for, as one English pamphleteer noted in 1719, "all the mean People, the Maid Servants, and indifferently poor Persons . . . are now cloathed in Callicoe, or printed Linen; moved to it as well for the Cheapness, as the Lightness of the Cloth, and the Gaity of the Colours . . . let any one but cast their Eyes among the meaner Sort playing in the Street, or of the better Sort at Boarding School" (*The Just Complaints of the poor Weavers truly represented*, 1719). The calico craze sparked the first public panic over plebeian luxury. In London wool weavers destroyed shops selling calicoes and attacked women on the street dressed in floral printed gowns. Most European governments banned printed cottons in an attempt to shore up the old order and the old distinctions in dress. But legal restrictions could not hold back consumer demand.

For one thing, men and women in eighteenth-century France, England, and Prussia found it thrilling to wear prohibited goods. The demand for contraband fabrics persisted through the eighteenth century. Increasingly those looking for light, bright

Washing Clothing. Etching by W. H. Pyne, 1802. BODLEIAN LIBRARY, OXFORD, U.K.

LAUNDRESSES

As the ownership of linens rose, so too did the number of women working as laundresses. In major cities thousands of women hired themselves out to wash, dry, and iron clothes and household linens. Usually these were poor women with few employment opportunities. For married women and widows with families this trade meant they could earn a living without having to live in as a domestic servant; they fit this work around their own family duties. As with most occupations, there were variations in the skills of laundresses, especially with regard to ironing. Complex lace ruffs, pristine cravats, and complex draperies on women's gowns required competent ironing with hot irons that came in a variety of shapes. The wealthy would employ their own laundresses, with a laundry room on the premises. But the majority of city dwellers depended on neighborhood laundresses. Improvements in urban housing in the nineteenth century meant that more middling and working women washed their family's laundry at home. Middle-class households typically hired extra help by the day to tackle soiled clothing and household linen. Washing and ironing was always heavy, tedious, and occasionally dangerous work, involving heavy cauldrons of boiling water, mountains of wet garments, and hot irons.

Throughout the nineteenth and early twentieth centuries, laundry work employed great numbers of female and immigrant labor, even as city laundries assumed a more capital-intensive pattern. Only with the widespread sale of washing machines after the Second World War did laundresses slowly disappear from the urban scene.

fabrics could find European-made equivalents. The ban placed on East India textiles throughout much of Europe stimulated the growth of indigenous linen and cotton industries, most particularly in Britain. By the second half of the century, Lancashire manufacturers could offer a wide range of substitutes for prohibited Asian textiles. As a result, customers, from court clerks to maidservants, wheelwrights to gentlewomen, owned a wider array of garments than ever before. Garments made from these new fabrics showed a sense of style, not that of the formality of the court, but a relative fashionability. Indeed, one regional study suggests that workingmen were willing and able to pay a premium for quality items of clothing that would reinforce their standing in the wider world. Even rural groups—particularly rural industrial workers—began to buy or make urban-style clothing rather than traditional garb. These patterns of expenditure concerned moralists, particularly when it came to young working females. Eighteenth-century commentators decried the priority given to the purchase of pretty gowns, hats, aprons, and shawls. And yet more young working women could be seen wearing stylish garb. In the nineteenth century, legislators and clergymen, dismayed at the independence and self-indulgence of workingwomen, suggested that an excessive material vanity could lead directly to prostitution. Restraint, self-denial, and moral control were recommended for all laboring people, but especially females. But the dynamics of production and the expansion of consumer culture made fashion a matter of general interest, with or without the acquiescence of court or clergy. Clothing changes reflected the decline of uniforms, such as guild attire for artisans. They came to serve new needs of self-expression.

From the seventeenth through the nineteenth centuries, popular fashions challenged the social hierarchy. Thus, young men and women from the middling and laboring classes denied the elites a monopoly of the social stage. The defenders of the waning status quo responded with a combination of derision and lectures on morality. Newspapers and magazines sneered at the "second-hand beaux," the red-armed belles and jumped-up apprentices who wore genteel costumes, confusing the social order in a masquerade. What would be the results, demanded the editorialists, if one could not distinguish a lady from her maid, or a master from his servant? Even more distressing was the sight of noble youths aping the appearance of coachmen, sporting fustian coats with handkerchiefs around their necks. From the eighteenth century onward, social boundaries were blurring; visible distinctions in dress were no longer absolute guides to social standing. The widening of the consumer base and the more elaborate displays arising from the lower social ranks heralded the transformation of European society.

Personal contacts with high society were not the only source of information on the latest styles of dress. Engraved prints of exquisitely gowned figures had been produced for a limited market intermittently throughout the sixteenth and seventeenth centuries.

Extremes of Fashion. "Eccentricities, Monstrosities, or Bell's and Beau's of 1799." English print, 1799. MUSEUM OF LONDON

Resplendence of the Sun King. Louis XIV, king of France, and Philip IV, king of Spain, meet at the Ile des Faisans, 7 June 1660. Sketch for a tapestry by Mathieu Antoine (1631–1673) after a painting by Charles Le Brun (1619–1690). CHÂTEAU DE VERSAILLES ET DE TRIANON, FRANCE/©PHOTO RMN–POPOVITCH

The more formalized reporting on fashion began in France with the appearance of the first fashion journal, *Le Mercure Galant,* in the 1670s. New trends were memorialized in illustrations, from which sharp-eyed readers could extract information on cut and finishings. News circulated with growing speed over the eighteenth century. In formally designated fashion journals, as well as through miscellaneous prints, literate customers found new sources of information, bringing them glimpses of the world of high fashion. *The Lady's Magazine* was the first English publication to produce regular fashion plates for its readers, from 1759 onward. Between 1786 and 1826, *Journal der Luxus und der Moden,* published in Weimar, brought German readers the latest fashion intelligence. Fashion journals multiplied throughout Europe, with ambitious publishers feeding the insatiable public interest in the latest vogue: *Cabinet des Modes* (1785–1792), *Gallery of Fashion* (1794–1804), *The Magazine of the Female Fashions of London and Paris* (1798–1806), *Journal für Fabrik, Manufaktur und Handlung und Mode* (1791–1808), *Repository of Arts, Literature, Commerce, Manufactures, Fashion and Politics* (1809–1828). Thereafter, publishers responded to the growing market for information with a range of magazines and catalogs rich in detail.

Beginning in the late seventeenth century, France claimed a unique place in Europe as the center of high fashion. The resplendence of the Sun King, Louis XIV, had elevated French creations to a peerless position. The preeminence of fashion was never in question in the Sun King's court. Indeed, Louis XIV's minister Jean-Baptiste Colbert asserted that he intended to make high fashion to France what the gold mines of Peru had been to Spain. French silks were synonymous with luxury; news of recent Parisian trends was eagerly awaited from Moscow to Dublin. During the intermittent wars of the early eighteenth century, French fashion dolls were permitted to pass between enemy nations. Blockades during the Napoleonic Wars interrupted, but did not reverse, French standing as the fashion Mecca, a status that was again unrivaled by the 1830s. Haute couture became synonymous with Parisian fashion house. Charles Frederick Worth (1828–1895), English born but French inspired, built the first gresat house of design and couture in the 1850s. La Maison Worth set the pattern for couturiers' houses, a pattern that would continue into the twentieth century. After 1850 one of the many profitable French exports was an immensely popular magazine, published in more than ten languages. All editions featured outstanding fashion plates produced in Paris. Called *Die Madenwelt* or *Le Follett,* it set the standard for fashion news throughout Europe. War once again interrupted communications during the siege of Paris in 1870. Silence from Paris induced panic in English editors, who were obliged to substitute Belgian and English fashion plates. Readers of *Le Follett* were congratulated for their patient stoicism when fashion news flowed again with the end of the conflict. French influence remained unrivaled for the rest of the nineteenth and much of the twentieth centuries.

The proliferation of fashion news was matched by changes in retailing over the same period. Up to 1800 most of the distribution of clothing fabrics and apparel relied on the traditional hierarchy of trades: mercers, linen drapers, and wool drapers. Each trade had a long ancestry, and practitioners were organized in guilds in most European cities. However, other patterns of retailing challenged their monopoly. Peddlers began appearing in increasing numbers from the sixteenth century onward, carrying necessities and humble luxuries to every quarter, encouraging trade, and generating wealth. General retail shops also multiplied, as did specialist shops that sold a range of clothing goods. As retailing became more complex, the traditional trade divisions began to break down. By the 1850s modern retail systems were in place, permitting consumers to buy a wider range of goods even outside the capital cities. Though elite fashions persisted, the meaning was altered. A well-developed trade in second-hand garments was also in place by the seventeenth century throughout Europe, changing the culture of fashion for elites and nonelites. Sumptuary laws were dead letters in the face of the vigorous market for silk gowns, wool jackets, and embroidered aprons, worn but still relatively stylish. Before the mass production of fashions, there was a mass trade in second-hand cloths that redefined fashion in the street. Popular fashions found a legitimate expression among the middle class and a growing portion of the working class of Europe.

THE POLITICS AND PRACTICE OF DRESS

The dress of ordinary Europeans was transformed by broad social and economic changes that took place over centuries. However, within this evolutionary process, dramatic episodes of political and religious upheaval inspired distinctive changes. Religious and secular revolts heightened the symbolic meaning of many material goods. From the beginnings of the Reformation, radical Protestants redefined their relations with other Christians and solidified group cohesion

Modern Retail Systems. Exterior of Harrod's Department Store, London, 1909. STAPLETON COLLECTION, UK/THE BRIDGEMAN ART LIBRARY

through symbolic forms of dress. For the Mennonites and Amish of northern and central Europe, the Quakers of Britain, and the Doukhobors of Russia, clothing reflected their relationship with God, their links with their coreligionists, and their distinctiveness from the wider society.

The perceived corruption of the Catholic and established Protestant churches produced a critique of luxury and personal adornment among many radical Protestant sects. Mennonites expressed their distaste for sixteenth-century Netherlands society through displays of public nakedness and used the destruction of clothing as a means of purification. Protestants in general were concerned to present a modest appearance, with no visible signs of opulence. Dress was often employed as a conscious mechanism to separate a religious community from the broader society, to exclude outsiders and enforce solidarity. In the 1690s the Mennonites of Switzerland, Alsace, and southern Germany divided on religious issues. Elements of dress became flashpoints for theological disputes. All subscribed to the ideal of simple, dark, utilitarian dress—worldly fashions were anathema to them. However, the leader of the new Amish sect broke with the rest of the Mennonite community and the Amish could not support the use of buttons. In their words, the Amish became the "hook and eye" people and the Mennonites were the "button people." In the succeeding centuries, including the twentieth, the size of men's hat brims, the cut of a jacket, and the kind of women's headgear were emblematic of one's position within the Amish and Old Order Mennonite communities, their dark archaic clothing setting them off from their neighbors.

Sober Elegance of the Dutch Elite. *The Surgeon Jacob Fransz Hercules with His Family,* painting (1669) by Egbert Heemskerck. The surgeon is perfoming bloodletting on his brother Thomas. AMSTERDAMS HISTORISCH MUSEUM

As norms of dress altered in tandem with shifting social, economic, and political movements, men's clothing exhibited perhaps the most striking adaptations. During the eighteenth century, middle-class men and even noblemen abandoned the rich decoration and lush colors that had characterized attire in the previous centuries. Gradually, they metamorphosed from the splendor of the butterfly to the utility of the moth. Clothes became darker and more restrained in cut. The standard components of male dress became trousers, waistcoat, and jacket, with the shirt visible beneath, the neck covered with a cravat or tie. This pattern of dress was an adaptation of workingmen's trousers and jacket, an example of the trickle-up effect in fashion.

This renunciation of excess is associated most strongly with the Netherlands and England. By 1600 dark, simple garb was a hallmark of the merchant class and nobility in the Netherlands. Sober garb suited the masculine culture of public probity; inspired by Protestant morality and commerce, this self-consciously sober look distinguished the Dutch from their more elaborate French and Spanish neighbors. The sober elegance of the Dutch elite traveled to England in the entourage of William of Orange and Queen Mary, following the Glorious Revolution of 1688. This style of dress was already entrenched among the nonconformist sects in England. By 1700 nationalist sentiment among the men of affairs, the Protestant stewards of English government and business, found expression in fashions distinct from those of autocratic France. Englishmen's coats became plainer, less ostentatious. Opulent apparel was deemed a corrupt, effeminate indulgence. Unadorned coats of dark wool cloth became the mark of a gentleman, of authentic public leadership. And in continental Europe England's liberalism and constitutional monarchy became synonymous with dark coats of unadorned fabric. Anglomania flourished in eighteenth-century France, inspired by a political critique of the ancien régime; these political sentiments were expressed in some circles by dressing in English modes. Enlightenment sentiments prescribed a modest attire.

The two late-eighteenth-century revolutions further eroded the old norms of elite fashions. As a representative of the new American republic, Benjamin Franklin wore undressed hair and plain attire to the French court, charming the assembled company. More dramatic still were the shock waves of the French Revolution. Throughout these complex events, clothing was often a political marker. Thus, the members of the Third Estate were authorized to wear only the plainest dark apparel. This unpretentious garb became part of the explosive critique of royal opulence and corruption. Dress frequently symbolized political positions through the tumult of early reforms, through revolution, the Reign of Terror, the reaction, and military dictatorship. Trousers, as worn by the laboring *sans-culottes* (those who did not wear *culottes*, the knee breeches worn by aristo-

HATS

Practical and fashionable, headgear was overlaid by a complex web of social meanings. For most of the period under study, soft caps and hats covered women's hair or decorated their heads. These coverings typically denoted life-cycle stages: the passage from childhood to adulthood, newly married to widowed. Among rural women distinctive caps or hats reflected regional folk styles. For many centuries religious dicta ensured that women's hair was covered in public. Only with the fashion for wigs in the eighteenth century did the public display of hair alter somewhat for those who followed this style. However, the utility and fashion potential of head coverings ensured their survival. The revolutions of the late eighteenth century marked the return to natural hair. But hats and head coverings remained an essential accessory for men and women, especially when in public. Throughout the nineteenth century the constraints imposed on women eased marginally. But women continued to wear hats for all formal public occasions well into the second half of the twentieth century, keeping their heads covered for ceremonies when men typically bared theirs.

For men as well as women, hats distinguished social rank and occupational standing. Hats also signaled defiance, camaraderie, or respect. Christian services required that men bare their heads as a sign of respect. In

the seventeenth century Quakers were the best known of religious egalitarians who refused to remove their hats, claiming a right to dispense with gestures of social deference. In their view equality before God made such gestures unnecessary. For this defiance before magistrates and nobles, Quakers suffered imprisonment and sometimes torture. In the nineteenth and early twentieth centuries, social status would be determined by the use of a hat, as opposed to a shawl, for workingwomen. Among men, the raising of one's hat was a masculine mark of courtesy offered to a social superior or an equal, male or female. But the niceties between relative equals were more problematic in cities where the social position of the person so honored was not guaranteed. Nonetheless, the doffing of a hat as a mark of respect was a courtesy expected by the elites from their social inferiors. Its daily or hourly repetition reinforced the social hierarchy. The erosion of these traditional displays happened slowly. Through much of the twentieth century, hats and hat honor resonated with social meaning, as did the particular types of hats worn by different social groups. However, with the gradual democratization of the West, hat use faded; outside an institutional context, it altered decisively in the second half of the twentieth century. Formal hats, and the customs associated with them, all but vanished from common usage.

Bloomers. The American reformer Amelia Bloomer (1818–1894) wearing her invention, loose trousers under a full skirt, that allowed freedom of movement while assuring female modesty. ©BETTMANN/CORBIS

crats and the well-to-do), certified adherence to Jacobinism, Maximilien Robespierre being a prominent exception to that rule. Plain caps worn by laboring men were reborn as liberty caps, powerful symbols of revolutionary authority for Jacobin men. Even amid the turmoil of revolution, however, they would not share this authority with female revolutionaries, who were forbidden to wear this cap. From shoes to buckles, hats to handkerchiefs, each refinement carried political overtones; during the Reign of Terror every citizen was required by law to wear a red, white, and blue cockade as a symbol of patriotism. When the political fury of the Jacobins was quashed, there were reactions in more than just the formal political sense. An explosion of highly stylized fashions worn by young men and women shocked visitors and older residents of Paris. *Les Incroyables* some were called, others *les Merveilleux;* the dress of these golden youth was characterized by outrageous extremes. Such excesses were short lived; thereafter, simplicity became the prevailing trend. Inside France and out, war accelerated the simplification of dress. For example, powdered wigs lost favor throughout Europe, more as a consequence of high wheat prices than as a reflection of generalized republicanism—finely milled flour being used as the powder for wigs. With the coming of peace, an aesthetic of restraint spread throughout the west.

Middle-class men adopted a more austere manner of dress well before the nineteenth century. After 1815 they continued their rhetorical claim to equality under the law and political responsibility by wearing identical black suits. Their bourgeois rectitude reinforced claims to political participation. In 1832 the debate in Britain was resolved with the extension of the franchise to middle-class men. Continental Europe enfranchised middle-class men less readily. However, throughout the nineteenth century, respectable apparel for men in business and government was the uniformly tailored, dark three-piece suit. Social rank could be determined through cut and quality and accessories. The suit remained a mark of authority and respectability for all classes. By the later nineteenth century, various types of suits were worn even by working-class men and radical trade union organizers, so general was the acceptance of this pattern of clothing. Mass production made suits easily available at an affordable price. And, though necessity demanded that poor men pawn their suits each Monday morning, they would be redeemed for Saturday night. Until the third quarter of the twentieth century, men from virtually every social rank displayed an extraordinary homogeneity in dress, all wedded to the respectable imperative of the suit.

If bourgeois masculinity was defined in attire by restraint, bourgeois femininity was defined by a prescribed indulgence. In the eighteenth century, women replaced the aristocracy as the group expected to define standards of beauty and fashion. In turn, fashion began to change frequently. The republican simplicity and physical liberation of the neoclassical styles of the Revolutionary and Napoleonic periods were short lived. The uncorseted female form did not survive for long. Social penalties were more severe for women who infringed the gender norms of dress than for men. In response, the advent of the "Woman Question" in the nineteenth century coincided with various movements for dress reform. In the mid-nineteenth century, the American reformer Amelia Bloomer proposed the wearing of long Turkish-type trousers under a skirt to free women for greater physical activity. Bloomers attracted legions of critics and were denounced in pulpits and editorials as dangerously unfeminine. However, the dress reform movement revived later in the century in most parts of Europe. Campaigns were inspired in equal parts by the feminist campaign for legal and social equality and a wish to promote healthier, more natural lifestyles. "Aesthetic" dress, developed by the British Pre-Raphaelite community, was marketed successfully from the 1860s onward. The dress for women consisted of loose-fitting gowns worn without corsets; men wore collarless shirts, soft felt hats, and flowing ties. By the turn of the century, Aesthetic dress had become an accepted alternative to styles that relied for their structure on confining corsets and petticoats.

The greatest transformation in women's clothing came with the new century. The First World War intensified the debates about women's place in society. Postwar changes in hair and clothing signaled the rebellion of a new generation of women, raised amid public campaigns for women's legal and political equality. Bobbed hair, short shiftlike dresses, and even trousers were their emblems in the 1920s. To French authorities these fashions were antimaternal and a threat to the state. Parents were urged to restrain their daughters; husbands were cautioned to control their wives, and many tried. However, these fashions were embraced by young women, for whom bobbed hair and shorter dresses represented the throwing off of shackles.

This critique of the gender status quo was matched later in the twentieth century by a rebellion of the young against the Paris-dictated "fashion" of their elders. In the mid-1950s young designers like Mary Quant produced affordable but dramatic clothes linking popular fashion with social rebellion. High fashion lost its defining authority. No longer restricted

A New Generation of Women. French evening dress by Jeanne Lanvin for the firm Mercie McHardy. Advertisement from *Le Bon Ton,* 1920. BIBLIOTHÈQUE DES ARTS DÉCORATIFS, PARIS, FRANCE/GIANNI DAGLI ORTI/CORBIS

to the factory and farmyard, jeans became mainstream dress over the next quarter century. New haircuts and clothes were linked to social and feminist critiques of the status quo, with particular emphasis on distinctive styles for youth. But here too, commercialization and mass production defused the initial political inspiration. Jeans stores and unisex boutiques opened in almost every community in Europe. Well-developed industrial and distribution industries responded to changes in taste, meeting the decisive shifts in fashion.

FROM MADE-TO-MEASURE TO MASS PRODUCTION

Just as clothing evolved for lord and laborer, so too did the process of production. From the fourteenth to the seventeenth centuries, people of almost all social classes relied on the tailors, hatters, and shoemakers resident in their communities to make clothes to order. Guilds controlled training and entry into the trades; the hierarchy within the trades offered opportunity for advancement for talented journeymen and a few journeywomen. At the same time, many thousands of artisans were employed making utilitarian articles under the direction of great and small masters. These trades made up a vital part of the corporate

Popular Fashion and Social Rebellion. Mary Quant with two models. ©REX FEATURES

Inevitably, the growing infusion of merchant capital undercut traditional guild structures.

No new technology was available to speed up manufacturing during the eighteenth century. Therefore, contractors reorganized labor, using women workers outside the guild systems. England's guilds were among the weakest in Europe, and in this context military ambition and fiscal innovation resulted in a new pattern of clothes production. Contractors competed for government contracts, employing hundreds and then thousands of needlewomen in an elaborate system of sweated labor. From 1700 onward this became one of the largest sectors of employment for urban women; but it was a largely hidden trade, a trade of attic and garret workshops. Journeymen tailors, in turn, found themselves becoming wage laborers when they had to compete with cheaper nonguild workers. Gender antagonism flared between tailors and seamstresses, with periodic public campaigns to bar women from all needle trades from 1700 through the 1800s. This process was replicated throughout Europe as capital and labor were reorganized in the clothing trades.

The development of ready-to-wear clothing transformed the types and cost of garments available. And there was a large and growing assortment of second-hand clothing traded from one corner of Europe to the other. People became accustomed to the convenience of ready-made clothes as a result of the used clothes market. The second-hand trade brought dated garments, worn but useful, to consumers in the middle and laboring classes. It flourished in most parts of Europe, recognized as an essential facet of the clothing trade. Garments outmoded in one country for one social group could be sold profitably in other markets. The used clothing trade persisted as a significant element in the garment industry until such time as mass production offered a sufficiently wide choice for all consumers. Thereafter it served niche markets only.

Ready-made clothing became commonplace during the eighteenth century, and by the nineteenth century specialist manufacturers expanded. With the advent of the sewing machine, after 1850 production networks integrated factory, workshop, and sweated home labor. The latter type of work was the particular resort of poor women and immigrants. The domestic use of sewing machines opened another method for the home production of garments from the late nineteenth century onward, with the aid of the latest patterns available through magazines and retailers. However, the enterprising women who set themselves up as dressmakers served a niche market only and offered no real challenge to manufacturers. Indeed, as mass production grew, high-quality, made-to-measure cloth-

foundation of Renaissance society. And the purchase of clothing by Europeans represented one of the most important areas of expenditure in that period. In England the total annual consumption of clothing accounted for about one quarter of all national expenditure at the end of the seventeenth century.

However, the seventeenth century also saw the beginning of decisive changes in the production and distribution of clothing. In France needlewomen received approval for the distinctly female occupation of mantuamaker or dressmaker, ending the monopoly of the tailors' guild. This division of labor was replicated in other parts of Europe. Furthermore, there were other pivotal pressures transforming the production of apparel. The seventeenth-century growth of national armies and navies required the creation of bureaucracies to support and provision these fighting forces. Large stocks of apparel were essential. Although we know more about England in this period, the economic momentum thus engendered was almost certainly a pan-European phenomenon. To ensure that soldiers and sailors were supplied with coats, breeches, shirts, stockings, and handkerchiefs, investors contracted out the process of production. Cost was a key factor; so too was the speed of production.

ing became less common, more the preserve of the affluent.

Menswear and women's accessories were the first mass-produced garments. By the late nineteenth century, virtually every article of clothing was made in the tens of thousands, through interrelated systems of factories and sweatshops. In the 1900s production became even larger and more diversified. The first historical examination of sweated labor, in the 1970s, was based on the assumption that government regulation had at last eliminated sweatshops. However, in the last two decades of the twentieth century, poorly paid piecework, in homes and workshops, was revived in response to the foundering of European textile and clothing companies faced with cheap Asian imports. As in previous eras, employers discovered no substitute for the flexible, low-paid work of women. From the seventeenth through the twentieth centuries, the gender division of labor remained a consistent component of the clothing trade as the market for ready-made grew.

Fashion was a more amorphous concept at the end than at the beginning of the twentieth century, yet some aspects of the clothing trade remained unchanged. Low-paid female labor was as much the organizational solution to economic challenges in the twentieth as it was in the seventeenth century. In addition, the constituents of clothing underwent changes as dramatic as those that began in the 1600s. High-tech apparel like anoraks and running shoes, plus the diffusion of artificial fibers, marked further alterations in common clothing that began first with the popularization of cottons. Simplification of dress continued with the erosion of age-specific garments and the emergence of unisex styles. As in earlier periods, economic structures, political priorities, and social signals were reflected in patterns of dress and the structure of clothing trades.

See also **Shops and Stores** *(volume 2);* **The Body and Its Representations** *(volume 4);* **Consumerism** *(in this volume); and other articles in this section.*

BIBLIOGRAPHY

Evolving Fashions

Boucher, François. *20,000 Years of Fashion: The History of Costume and Personal Adornment.* 2d ed. New York, 1987.

Breward, Christopher. *The Culture of Fashion: A New History of Fashionable Dress.* Manchester, U.K., 1995.

Buck, Anne. *Dress in Eighteenth-Century England.* London and New York, 1979.

Chenoune, Farid. *A History of Men's Fashion.* Translated by Deke Dusinberre. Paris, 1993.

Ginsburg, Madeleine. *An Introduction to Fashion Illustration.* London, 1980.

Newton, Stella Mary. *The Dress of the Venetians, 1495–1525.* Aldershot, U.K., 1988.

Perrot, Philippe. *Fashioning the Bourgeoisie: A History of Clothing in the Nineteenth Century.* Translated by Richard Bienvenu. Princeton, N.J., 1994.

Ribeiro, Aileen. *The Art of Dress: Fashion in England and France 1750 to 1820.* New Haven, Conn., and London, 1995.

Ribeiro, Aileen. *Fashion in the French Revolution.* New York, 1988.

Robinson, Fred Miller. *The Man in the Bowler Hat: His History and Iconography.* Chapel Hill, N.C., 1993.

Steele, Valerie. *Paris Fashion: A Cultural History.* New York, 1988.

Making, Buying, and Wearing Clothing

Breward, Christopher. *The Hidden Consumer: Masculinities, Fashion, and City Life, 1860–1914.* Manchester, U.K., 1999.

Bythell, Duncan. *The Sweated Trades: Outwork in Nineteenth-Century Britain*. London, 1978.

Coffin, Judith G. *The Politics of Women's Work: The Paris Garment Trades, 1750–1915*. Princeton, N.J., 1996.

Harte, N. B. "The Economics of Clothing in the Late Seventeenth Century." In *Fabrics and Fashions: Studies in the Social and Economic History of Dress*. Edited by N. B. Harte. Special Issue of *Textile History* 22, no. 2 (1991): 277–296.

Honeyman, Katrina, and Jordan Goodman. "Women's Work, Gender Conflict, and Labour Markets in Europe, 1500–1900." *Economic History Review* 44, no. 4 (1991): 608–628.

Lemire, Beverly. *Dress, Culture and Commerce: The English Clothing Trade Before the Factory, 1660–1800*. New York, 1997.

Lemire, Beverly. *Fashion's Favourite: The Cotton Trade and the Consumer in Britain, 1660–1800*. Oxford, 1992.

Levitt, Sarah. *Victorians Unbuttoned: Registered Designs for Clothing, Their Makers and Wearers, 1839–1900*. London, 1986.

Roche, Daniel. *The Culture of Clothing: Dress and Fashion in the "Ancien Régime."* Translated by Jean Birrell. Cambridge, U.K., and New York, 1994.

Sanderson, Elizabeth. *Women and Work in Eighteenth-Century Edinburgh*. New York, 1996.

Spufford, Margaret. *The Great Reclothing of Rural England: Petty Chapmen and Their Wares in the Seventeenth Century*. London, 1984.

Vincent, John Martin. *Costume and Conduct in the Laws of Basel, Bern, and Zurich, 1370–1800*. Baltimore, 1935.

FOOD AND DIET

Kolleen M. Guy

Historians recognize food and diet as significant aspects of social history, providing important insight into the material and cultural conditions of everyday life. Serious scholarly investigation of diet, ingredients, and rituals of consumption progressed rapidly over the last decades of the twentieth century. The founders of the influential *Annales* (1886–1944) school of historical analysis, Marc Bloch and Lucien Febvre (1878–1956), encouraged academicians to use archival documents, such as wills, household accounts, notarial records, and institutional inventories to study the diet and food habits of the past. Historians took up the challenge. By the 1960s and 1970s, research on European diet and food habits from the fourteenth to the eighteenth century focused on alimentation: food and drink production (planting and harvesting), distribution, and consumption. Quantitative studies dealt with a variety of specific historical questions from determining caloric intake to calculating per capita meat consumption. Despite a variety of criticisms about the incomplete or imprecise nature of the archival sources, notable *Annalistes,* such as Emmanuel Le Roy Ladurie and Fernand Braudel, went on to establish the study of food and diet as a legitimate means to better understand the structures of everyday life in European history.

Concurrently, other historians, influenced by the work of cultural anthropologists and ethnographers, began to explore the social importance of food and rituals of food consumption. Historians recognized food's symbolic importance and examined the production and consumption of food as expressions of social solidarity and stratification. By the late 1970s and early 1980s, those interested in the history of food and diet employed a variety of different approaches. Purely quantitative methods, favored by some early practitioners, gave way to looking at cultural contexts. Building on knowledge of the history of the family and women's work, historians made the family meal, including the preservation and preparation of food, a new focal point of study. Cookbooks, recipes, menus, etiquette books, and other gastronomic texts offered

new avenues of research. Culinary history, with its focus on food culture, exposed the layers of social production behind food choices and added to the rich documentation on alimentation.

New perspectives continue to proliferate. Given the centrality of food to most societies, historians turned their attention in the 1980s and early 1990s to researching the construction of social identity through dietary choices and culinary techniques in different countries and among different classes. Food and culinary techniques, as distinct expressions of ethnic or cultural identity, have a long and complex history that has only begun to be examined. Historians have also focused much new research on sites of consumption, such as restaurants, cafés, and public banquets. Research by social historians—past and present—on food, diet, and rituals of consumption continues to enrich our understanding of the history of everyday life.

Eating, with its quotidian repetition, may appear insignificant when placed next to the great deeds and events of history. Yet, historically, food has been a central preoccupation in most European societies where undernourishment and starvation were basic components of social life before the mid-nineteenth century. Proverbs from throughout Europe reflected the preoccupation with a full belly and exhorted listeners to stretch meager resources. From the urban beggar to the court nobility, it was understood that the fate of individuals and, according to French gastronome Anthelme Brillat-Savarin (1755–1826) in his *Physiologie du goût* (1825), the fate of nations intimately "depend[ed] on how they are fed."

How Europeans were fed historically hinged on a variety of factors that defy facile generalization. Shifts in food production and consumption in Europe were linked to the uneven pace of industrialization, urbanization, expansion of arable land, commercialization and transport, and agricultural specialization. Adding to the complexity, these factors were inextricably entangled with questions of political and social organization. Social historians, without minimizing

Outdoor Café. Tables at Quadri's Café on the Piazza San Marco, Venice, 1988. ©TODD GILPSTEIN/CORBIS

regional and national differences, however, have located a number of important trends in Europe's food and dietary history since 1400.

ISSUES IN FOOD HISTORY IN THE EARLY MODERN PERIOD

Food was a central preoccupation for most Europeans in the early modern period (1400–1800) as demographic growth, halted by the devastation of the Black Death, resumed across the Continent. Despite a brief slowing of population growth in the 1600s, the population of Europe increased from an estimated 61 million in the 1500s to 123 million by 1800. With demographic expansion came a surge in agricultural production. Historians generally agree that the amount of land under cultivation increased throughout Europe during this period, often at the expense of land reserved for grazing animals or hunting. In England the enclosure of common lands was under way and would pick up after 1530. Pastures were converted into arable land and in many places vineyards were destroyed to make way for more lucrative cereal crops. There was a decline in specialized production, particularly animal husbandry. As a consequence of changes in supply and demand, a large portion of the urban and rural population reduced meat consumption. Average annual meat consumption per capita in Germany, for example, plummeted from a high of 100 kilograms in 1500 to only 14 kilograms in the early 1800s. Similar patterns emerged across Europe.

Cereals became the primary source of nutrition for most Europeans; bread replaced meat in the popular diet. Despite the increase in cultivated land, agricultural production did not keep pace with population expansion. The price of grain in Europe climbed by 386 percent between 1500 and 1650 while purchasing power lagged behind. Statistical evidence reveals that cultivation of industrial crops, horticulture, and viticulture were highly dependent on the price and consumption levels of grain. The meager statistical data available suggests that many families changed their eating habits by further curbing meat consumption and increasing reliance on other plant products. Dried and salted fish might be added to the common diet as a surrogate for meat, particularly in urban areas, although generally it was not considered filling. Salaried workers, whose wages did not keep pace with prices, shifted a larger portion of their incomes to purchasing bread and other foodstuffs. In the countryside, even the peasants with a surplus to sell in the market reserved their best produce (including wheat and rye) for sale and subsisted on a diet of lesser grains (barley, millet, and so on), legumes, and chestnuts.

Between 1650 and 1750, the supply of daily bread for the bulk of Europe's population was affected by an agricultural depression. Although this depression was not as prolonged or severe as those that took place during the Middle Ages, the chief features were important to the bulk of Europe's inhabitants: decline in cereal prices, little land reclamation activity, expansion of animal husbandry and reduction of arable land, cultivation of fodder crops, and few agricultural innovations. The combination of the depression with the Thirty Years' War (1618–1648) and a series of epidemics brought fundamental changes to European agriculture and, subsequently, the European diet.

One change of particular importance was the upheaval in rural land ownership throughout western Europe as nobles, bourgeois, and royal officeholders gained possession of large expanses of farmland. Large-scale farms with regular access to markets prospered by experimenting with new crops and techniques. Land-poor peasants introduced potatoes to their gardens as their overall living standards declined. Similarly in eastern Europe, the nobility increased their control over agriculture and lucrative markets by subjugating the peasantry and increasing compulsory labor service. The process was complex and varied according to regions. With increases in the amount of labor and capital invested in farming, however, grain from the Baltic littoral created not only a flourishing internal trade but also flowed into Amsterdam to feed the hungry urban population of Europe.

As the proportion of grain in the popular diet increased, the crises provoked by grain shortages became more severe. There was a series of major grain shortages in France, Germany, England, Spain, Italy, and throughout northern Europe in 1555, 1597, 1630–1632, 1693–1694, and 1709. Shortages typically began with a harvest failure, which created a surge in prices. In some areas, there was a deterioration of bread quality as mixtures of grain (rye, wheat, and other grains) or substitutes (barley, oats, legumes, or, in severe cases, chestnuts) were used in bread making. The "hierarchy of bread"—white bread for the wealthy, brownish breads for those with some resources, dark bread for the least well-off—was a daily reminder of social distinctions. Lesser grains were better than no grains. Shortages resulted in malnutrition, vulnerability to disease, reduced fertility, and, at times, death. Rising grain prices (seen as unjust by the lower classes), adulteration of flour by millers, or the hoarding of wheat and bread often led to protests or bread "riots." Between the seventeenth century and the first decades of the nineteenth century, food conflicts—the possibility of popular disorders or rebellions due to bread shortages—resulted in greater state investment in stimulating grain production and trade, distributing bread or grain in times of shortage, and regulating markets. Famished crowds demanded that public authorities, particularly the mythical "baker king," feed the masses of hungry subjects. Responses such as the Elizabethan Poor Laws (1598 and 1601), for example, although known for their harsh treatment of the poor, did make English villages less vulnerable to famine. German principalities, similarly, administered prices, regulated market relations, and worked to relieve local shortages. As cereals came to

dominate the popular diet, the bread question became a major political issue.

The consumption of food and the social context for that activity was a clear expression of the opposition between the ruler and the ruled in early modern Europe. Abundance and variety characterized the table of the social elites; elaborate social rituals of consumption were an expression of their power. The contrast between the daily abundance on the dinner table of the wealthy and the daily dearth on the dinner table of the poor was striking. While the poor might have occasions of excess during important holidays or as markers of certain rites of passage, these were rare moments to be remembered. Elites and masses differed not only in the quantity regularly consumed, but the quality and variety of food consumed as well. Historians have concluded from the evidence in kitchen accounts and cookbooks of the wealthy that overall grain consumption decreased among the social elites in the early modern period in sharp contrast to growing popular consumption of cereal-based foods. Both the quantity and quality of prepared food available on a daily basis to the dominant classes represented and confirmed their social, economic, and political status.

Consumption of elaborate, expensive, refined foods, which were outside of the budget of the mass of Europeans, were deemed intrinsically appropriate for those with high social rank. Scientific and literary

Renaissance Banquet. *The Wedding at Cana,* painting by Paolo Veronese (1528–1588). Musée du Louvre, Paris/Erich Lessing/Art Resource, NY

Daily Abundance. *The Fat Kitchen,* painting by Jan Steen (1625–1679). Cheltenham Art Gallery & Museum, Gloucester, U.K./The Bridgeman Art Library

theories of nutritional privilege, whereby social class implied a certain type of "natural order" to food consumption, created a hierarchy of both food and people. Vegetables, particularly bulbs and roots, were believed to be among the lowest rank of the natural world and, therefore, most suitable for those of the lowest ranks of society. Fruits and fowl, by virtue of their distance from the element earth, were seen as the most appropriate food for the highest classes. Pheasant, partridge, and other "light" meats were seen as reflections of the refined character of those who consumed them. Spices, which were increasingly within reach of those outside of noble circles, were replaced with delicate flavorings such as chives, shallots, and capers, first used by French chefs. Where spices remained a luxury, such as in Germany, Poland, and Russia, their strong flavors continued to be part of the cuisine of the elite. Throughout Europe the wealthy table with its emphasis on quality food, elaborate presentation, and complex rituals acted as a daily reminder of the gulf between the ruling classes and the bulk of the population. Power was expressed through food.

PATTERNS OF DIETARY REGIMES

As power shifted in the waning days of the ancien régime so, too, did elite dietary preferences. By the eighteenth century, health considerations and issues of food hygiene became a part of the discourse of Enlightenment philosophers, encyclopedists, and technicians who turned their attention to the "science" of food, dining, and drink. The science of gastronomy created new taste professionals who enumerated some of the fundamental truths of the new food culture. Strong flavors of wild game and heavy meals with multiple courses of meat became symbols of old social and political regimes. The "enlightened" bourgeoisie and nobility adopted a more delicate, refined cuisine with mild cream sauces, more "white" meats, and increased varieties of vegetable foods. Restaurants featuring fine cooking opened in places like Paris in the late eighteenth century, and the idea of dining out not simply when traveling gained ground. The new attitude toward diet softened earlier rhetoric that had advocated the exclusive consumption of "quality" food by people of "quality." This changing ideological framework made proper nutrition and freedom of food choice an ideal; actual food consumption, however, continued to be a visible sign of rank and class membership.

Over the course of these centuries, changes in supply and demand and the introduction of new crops slowly altered the European diet. Rice, once an exotic import reserved for the wealthy, became a part of the

Daily Dearth. *The Lean Kitchen,* painting by Jan Steen (1625–1679). CHELTENHAM ART GALLERY & MUSEUM, GLOUCESTER, U.K./THE BRIDGEMAN ART LIBRARY

European diet from Spain to the Low Countries. Sugar, a dominant commodity of the European colonial trade, was consumed in vast quantities. A historian-anthropologist has argued that sugar became the first mass-consumption food, eagerly sought out and widely purchased, though not really necessary. As European long-distance trade became more sophisticated, new beverages, such as coffee and tea, were also introduced. While coffee, consumed in urban coffeehouses, became popular among European elites, tea became a basic beverage throughout European society. Hot, sweet tea was popular among the lower orders, particularly in England, where it was said to provide a quick burst of energy. Crops from the Americas, such as the tomato, potato, and maize (corn), were gradually assimilated as well. By the late eighteenth century, the nutrient-dense potato, which could feed more people per acre than grain, was an important staple of the popular diet. In the predominantly industrial countries north of the Alps, potatoes became a major crop in the gardens of peasant and wage-earning households. The lowly potato, believed to be fit only for peasants and animals when first introduced, gradually made its way into the recipes of the elite by 1800. Scholars attribute the variations in assimilation of new foods to climate and standard of living, as well as to differences in food cultures.

European dietary regimes underwent a perceptible shift starting in the eighteenth century (although there are significant differences in character and timing of change from region to region). One of the most remarkable things about the eighteenth century, compared to earlier periods, was that individual food consumption remained constant, while agricultural production was regulated to match. It is even likely that, for some classes, individual consumption went up, in spite of the great growth of population. Cities often demanded not only grain but also specialized produce, such as dairy products and fresh fruits and vegetables. The profit motive in agriculture worked against the practice of reserving certain foods for a select group of consumers. Between 1761–1790 and 1821–1850, high prices for agricultural products, which resulted from a combination of changes in consumption patterns, population growth, and demand for fodder crops (which reduced the amount of arable for cultivating grains for human consumption), led to an expansion of the area cultivated, increased animal husbandry, the introduction of new methods and inventions, and a renewed interest in agriculture. All of these factors stimulated development. But what was unique during this period was that the usual plowing under of grasslands for arable, which traditionally took place during periods of high cereal prices, was not undertaken. With the growth of demand for manure, the increase in the number of horses for transport, and changes in consumption patterns, animal husbandry did not decline in profitability in relation to cereal cultivation. Agricultural changes meant a greater variety of resources of food to sustain the population.

Desire for a variety of foods became increasingly more "democratic" in the modern period as old dietary hierarchies of exclusion were discarded. Greater food choices for a broader group of consumers did not necessarily result in more "democratic" diets. Despite enhanced agricultural productivity and progress in food supply by the eighteenth century, the mass of the European population had enough to eat only when harvests were good. Subsistence problems for both the urban and rural populations of Europe persisted well into the nineteenth century. Continued population growth, particularly in the later half of the eighteenth century, further exacerbated nutritional deficiencies. High cereal prices meant that food was the most important part of the budget of most working-class families; half of the family budget could be spent on bread alone. The poorer the family, the less varied the diet. This was also true of some members of the rural laboring classes who were hit by rising rents and food prices. For many, particularly among the lower classes, rising agricultural prices meant a diet that was monotonous (with the reliance on plant foods and cereals) and generally inadequate.

THE IMPACT OF INDUSTRIALIZATION

Historians note that there was an increase in demand for meat and dairy products early in the nineteenth century. This led to the spread of innovations pioneered in the Netherlands and in new crop rotations and livestock breeding and, according to some historians, a slow, perceptible improvement in the daily diet of the masses. Innovations were adopted slowly throughout Europe during the nineteenth century. The new husbandry, which generally meant a decrease in fallow, did not always, by itself, produce higher crop yields. But often the reduction of fallow was combined with new crop rotations that included fodder crops and growing herds of livestock—all of which provided more nitrogen to the soil through nitrogen-enriching crops and manuring. Greater demand and higher prices coupled with concomitant improvements in agricultural technology and technique stimulated European agricultural production between 1821 and 1850.

Whether this agricultural change resulted in an improvement in the diet of the growing number of working-class families in Europe has been part of an intense debate among social historians about the early effects of industrialization on the standard of living. Regardless of their conclusions, most historians agree that food remained a central part of the family budget, and a mother's role as a consumer was key to the family's well-being. Expenditures for food could take up between half and three-quarters of a working family's income even among the most skilled (and highly paid) workers. One estimate, based on calculations from a variety of different types of working families, showed that, between 1823 and 1835, the proportion of wages of the male head of the household that was spent on grains decreased. Nonetheless, grain and bread still absorbed around 55 percent of the man's wages. The last widespread European famine in 1846–1847, which had its most devastating effects in Ireland, attests to the extent to which the bulk of the populace continued to rely on grains and potatoes for nourishment.

For many working-class Europeans, any earnings above subsistence were dedicated first to modest improvements in diet. A bit of fat or, even better, butter on bread could be a cherished luxury. At times, the caloric needs of certain family members prompted difficult eating arrangements within working-class households. Mothers and children would often practice restraint in eating, in order to allow the male breadwinner to eat meat.

Around the middle of the nineteenth century there was a dramatic change in agricultural supply—due to intensive application of early nineteenth-century innovations—and demand—as an increasing industrial population wanted, and could afford, more meat and dairy products, and industry created new markets. Dearth, which had ruled everyday life for centuries, increasingly became an exceptional event. Nutritional standards improved as the century passed. Various studies of working families demonstrate that food continued to constitute the largest yearly expenditure. Aggregate figures for the French working class reveal that up to 60 percent of the family budget was dedicated to food; figures for England show no substantial difference. Bread remained a major item in the budget, but lower cereal prices made it possible for families to shift their spending to other food items, such as eggs, cheese, noodles, sugar, jam, and coffee. All but the poorest families consumed some meat. Even the bread consumed by the masses of Europeans changed. The long coveted white bread of wealthy consumers became the norm by the end of the century. Throughout Europe, consumption of wine, beer, and spirits, in both public and private drinking rituals, increased.

In the Restaurant. *The Gloppe Pastry Shop,* painting (1889) by Jean Béraud (1849–1936). ©MUSEE CARNAVALET/COLLECTION VIOLLET

A greater variety of food items in the family budget can be seen among the rural classes as well. At mid-century, peasants in some regions of France, for example, prepared daily meals that were a meager combination of black bread and *la soupe* (gruel, porridge, or, in some cases, just water with salt or fat added). Improved conditions by the end of the century might mean rye bread, potatoes, milk and cheese, soup with some fat, and, on Sundays, a bit of beef in the stew. A good meal, which everywhere included meat and wine, remained, however, an event to be remembered. Consumption of meat remained pitifully low outside of cities. The average city dweller consumed about 60 kilograms of meat per year while their rural counterpart was limited to about 22 kilograms per year. Continued reliance on grains could still bring disastrous results for rural residents as the harvest failures and horrifying famine of 1891–1892 in Russia attests.

Above all it was the increased consumption of meat that was revolutionary during these years with the floor on per capita consumption varying between 14 and 20 kilograms per year in places like France and Germany. Improvements in diet for both the rural and urban classes before World War I, however, were relative, judged from a low standard of evaluation. The consumption of milk and fresh fruits and vegetables among working families remained low. One study in 1904 found that 33 percent of English children were undernourished. While the bulk of Europeans consumed a greater variety of foods, malnutrition remained a common problem, particularly among women and children. Women often deprived themselves of nutrition when there was not enough food for the family. Shortages and high food prices, as in earlier times, could still lead to protest. In urban areas these disturbances were frequently incorporated into trade union activity and seen as a more general protest against the high cost of living.

Continued technological advances increased yields and led to a marked, although uneven, improvement in the European diet by the twentieth century. The combination of agricultural change, improvements in transportation, and the cultivation of new land put

Food Vendor. Kabob stand in Madrid, 1988. ©OWEN FRANKEN/CORBIS

an end to the cycles of famine that ravaged Europe in earlier periods. Shortages were not, however, a thing of the past. Hunger was widespread once again during World War I and World War II. During World War I, for example, near starvation conditions were reached in many countries by 1917, and food riots became a recurring event throughout the war years. These were man-made disasters: the result of wartime inflation, inefficient government policy, shortages of fertilizer, and hoarding of agricultural commodities.

Other developments affected European eating patterns in the twentieth century. The variety and number of restaurants increased. In Britain, fish-and-chips outlets provided new eating opportunities for the working class from the 1920s onward, a sign of new consumerism in the area of food. Beginning among the middle classes, particularly among women, there was an increased preoccupation with dieting or restraint in eating. In France this concern began to emerge in the last decades of the nineteenth century. Warnings about overeating and the need to discipline children's appetites proliferated. The decline of corsetry and the adoption of more revealing fashions made discipline of the body more and more desirable. Although rural regions and the working classes were somewhat exempt from these intense concerns, hostility to obesity ran high.

Dwindling numbers of traditional peasant farms in the West, the tragic results of Soviet collectivized farming, and the potential problems of genetically engineered crops have generated new discussions among

historians, economists, and policy makers over the relationship between economic modernization and nutritional choices in Europe. Without a doubt, the shift to an industrial economy in the nineteenth and twentieth centuries dramatically altered the history of food in Europe. Fast food, frozen dinners, and American soft drinks—all industrial food products—are now ubiquitous. Twenty-six percent of all restaurant meals in France were taken at fast-food outlets by 1990. Widespread, too, is a rich regional diversity in cooking techniques and gastronomic traditions that has developed in response to culinary homogenization. Uniformity at some levels of food production has not destroyed a rich tradition of diversity in food consumption. While speed of eating probably increased—the two-hour lunch began to decline in places like France and Spain, in favor of greater efficiency at work—Europeans resisted some American patterns. EuroDisney (opened in 1992 and later renamed Disneyland Paris) near Paris initially expected American-style willingness to snack at all hours, but the assumption proved wrong: European visitors wanted set meal hours, with wine and beer, and the Disney approach had to be adapted for their preferences. In a more serious vein, strong protests in the 1990s directed against American and other imports and against genetically altered foods demonstrated Europeans' fear of losing control over what they ate. Social historians have only begun to chronicle the unfolding story of culinary "traditions" and dietary transmutations of an ever-changing Europe.

See also other articles in this section.

BIBLIOGRAPHY

Aron, Jean Paul. *The Art of Eating in France: Manners and Menus in the Nineteenth Century.* New York, 1975.

Braudel, Fernand. *Civilization and Capitalism, 15th–18th Century.* Vol. 1: *The Structures of Everyday Life: The Limits of the Possible.* Translated by Siân Reynolds. London, 1981.

Butel, Paul. *Histoire du thé.* Paris, 1997.

Burnett, John. *Plenty and Want: A Social History of Diet in England from 1815 to the Present Day.* London, 1966.

Camporesi, Piero. *The Magic Harvest: Food, Folklore, and Society.* Translated by Joan Krakover Hall. Cambridge, U.K., 1993. Translation of *La terra e la luna: Alimentation, folklore, société.* Paris: Aubier, 1993.

Capatti, Alberto. *Le goût du nouveau: Origines de la modernité alimentaire.* Paris, 1989.

Clark, P. *The English Alehouse: A Social History, 1200–1830.* London, 1983.

Flandrin, Jean-Louise and Massimo Montanari, eds. *Food: A Culinary History from Antiquity to the Present.* Translated by Clarissa Botsford. New York, 1999.

Forster, Robert and Orest Ranum, eds. *Food and Drink in History: Seclections from the* Annales, Economies, Sociétiés, Civilisations. Vol. 5. Translated by Elborg Forster. Baltimore, 1979.

Hémardinquer, Jean-Jacques, ed. *Pour une histoire de l'alimentation.* Paris, 1970.

Le Roy Ladurie, Emmanuel. *Times of Feast, Times of Famine: A History of Climate since the Year 1000.* Translated by Barbara Bray. New York, 1971.

Livi Bacci, Massimo. *Population and Nutrition: An Essay on European Demographic History.* Translated by Tania Croft-Murray with the assistance of Carl Ipsen. Cambridge, U.K., and New York, 1991.

Mennell, Stephen. *All Manners of Food: Eating and Taste in England and France from the Middle Ages to the Present.* Oxford and New York, 1985.

Mintz, Sidney Wilfred. *Sweetness and Power: The Place of Sugar in Modern History.* New York, 1985.

Montanari, Massimo. *The Culture of Food.* Translated by Carl Ipsen. Cambridge, Mass., 1994.

Perrot, Marguerite. *La mode de vie des familles bourgeoises, 1873–1953.* Paris, 1961.

Rosener, Werner. *The Peasantry of Europe.* Translated by Thomas M. Barker. Cambridge, Mass., and Oxford, 1994.

Slicher van Bath, B. H. *The Agrarian History of Western Europe, A.D. 500–1850.* Translated by Olive Ordish. London, 1963.

Teuteberg, H. J. "Food Consumption in Germany since the Beginning of Industrialisation: A Quantitative Longitudinal Approach." In *Consumer Behaviour and Economic Growth in the Modern Economy.* Edited by Henri Baudet and Henk van der Meulen. London, 1982. Pages 233–277.

Unwin, P. T. H. *Wine and the Vine: An Historical Geography of Viticulture and the Wine Trade.* New York, 1991.

Weber, Eugen Joseph. *Peasants into Frenchmen: The Modernization of Rural France, 1870–1914.* Stanford, Calif., 1976.

Wheaton, Barbara Ketchum. *Savoring the Past: The French Kitchen and the Table from 1300 to 1789.* New York, 1996.

ANIMALS AND PETS

Kathleen J. Kete

In 1974 the *Journal of Social History* published a spoof on the history of pet keeping. "Household Pets and Urban Alienation" by "Charles Phineas" was a satire of the kinds of subjects Ph.D. programs were producing in the 1970s when social historians began to pay attention to the history of everyday life. In the same decade, however, a number of books and articles appeared which established the importance of attitudes toward animals in European, especially British and French, social history.

These studies make it clear that attitudes toward animals played an important part in the building of a sense of social identity in modernizing Europe. The history of Europeans' relationship to animals can be placed at times within a "left," and at times within a "right" political narrative of history. What is significant is the constancy of the the role of these attitudes in charting a shifting line between an "us" and a "them"—a line of exclusion that runs through the Puritan, bourgeois, feminist, nationalist, and even Nazi revolutions.

ANIMALS IN MODERNIZING EUROPE

Europeans had a greater acquaintance with animals in early modern times than had been the case in the Middle Ages. A rise in the numbers of domesticated animals went along with the agricultural revolution that began in Holland and England in the fifteenth and sixteenth centuries. Enclosure allowed for sheep farming and experimentation with new crops, some of which like alfalfa fixed nitrogen in the soil, some of which like turnips and clover provided fodder for animals. For the first time, it was no longer necessary to slaughter pigs and cows in the autumn. A motif of medieval art and culture was becoming obsolete.

Economic modernization initially shifted the ratio of animals to people in favor of animals. As Keith Thomas points out in *Man and the Natural World,* in the early 1500s there were three sheep for every one person in England. Animals and people lived in close proximity whether in the archaic longhouse, which contained humans and large domestic animals under one roof, or the increasingly common farmhouse. Although farmhouses primarily sheltered humans, they also warmed hens, lambs, calves, and goats. Jonas Frykman and Orvar Löfgren in *Culture Builders* present the observations of a sixteenth-century German merchant who visits a Swedish peasant farm. He bedded down on the farmhouse floor, and what seems to have bothered him most was being licked in the face during the night by hungry juvenile pigs. Young adults and family servants typically slept in barns in some rural areas into the twentieth century.

Urbanization in modernizing Europe also brought animals and people together. Authorities throughout early modern Europe legislated uselessly against the keeping of pigs within town walls. Alexander Cowan in *Urban Europe, 1500–1700* describes the failure of Philip II's administration to do so in Valladolid in the 1560s. In *Man and the Natural World,* Thomas explains how pigs caused fires and attacked children in English towns into the nineteenth century. Many sources note how cows were kept for milk and fowl were raised for eggs and meat. As cities grew so did the presence of the horse in the city. The waste products of all these animals joined with that of humans to foul the streets. So, too, did offal from the carcasses of animals slaughtered for meat.

Animals figured in the recreations of both urban and rural people. The so-called blood sports of modernizing Europe include cock throwing, cockfighting, dogfighting, bull baiting, and bull running which were conducted in villages, towns, fairgrounds—sites associated with festivities and drinking. They also include hunting, which was reserved by law for the elite and which will be discussed below. In Europe these sports triggered the first conflict between social groups over the treatment of animals, resulting in Europe's first animal protection law, the Protectorate Ordinance of 1654, promulgated during the radical Puritan stage of the English Civil War. The Ordinance of 1654 banned cockfighting and cock throwing. It also

Shearing Sheep. Shearing sheep and harvesting grain. The month of July from *Très riches heures du duc de Berry* by the Limbourg brothers, fifteenth century. MUSÉE CONDÉ, CHANTILLY, FRANCE/GIRAUDON/ART RESOURCE, N.Y.

set the terms for continued debate on the proper treatment of animals in England.

Cock throwing was a game that traditionally took place on Shrove Tuesday and at other festive occasions. The game began with tethering a cock to a stake with about a foot or two of slack in the tether. Contestants took turns throwing clubs at the cock until it was dead. Bull baiting was much like cock throwing. The bull was tethered with a rope long enough to provide mobility. Dogs were set upon the bull until it was weakened and bloodied from fighting. The bull then was slaughtered.

Bull baiting was said to tenderize the meat of these male animals, as did bull running, it was believed. Bull running took an entire day and was a townwide event. A bull was set loose, then was beaten by people, and chased by dogs through the streets of the town. At the end of the day, it was slaughtered for meat. Traditional recreations merged with the ritual slaughter of animals in the case of cock throwing, bull baiting, and bull running. In each case, these practices began to appear in the historical record as they were about to disappear from daily life.

An argument against these practices had been forwarded by the Puritans as early as the mid-sixteenth century, as Puritanism resonated with a more generally developing middle-class view. Blood sports and other popular recreations were associated with idleness and drunkenness. They profaned the Sabbath. They turned people away from their duties to God and society. Moreover, the Puritan reading of the expulsion of Adam and Eve from the Garden of Eden led to a recognition that humans owed it to animals not to enjoy or increase their suffering, a suffering which had become their lot after Adam's sin. In their sense of being lords of creation as revealed in Genesis 1 ("you will have dominion over the earth and the animals in it"), the European West began, with the Puritans, to develop notions of good stewardship over the earth and animals in it.

The Puritan argument was countered by the early Stuarts. James I issued the King's Declaration of Sports in 1618, which was reissued by Charles I in 1633. The *Book of Sports* was a defense of traditional recreations, and its insistence that these lay outside the purview of reform continued as the argument of some gentry and some rural poor into the nineteenth century and, with respect to hunting, throughout the twentieth century. The *Book of Sports* helped trigger a Puritan revolt against the state while Puritan interference in everyday life became a leitmotif of resistance to Puritan revolution.

The Ordinance of 1654 was overturned in the Restoration. Middle-class opinion in the next century, however, continued to form against blood sports. The valorization of happiness and benevolence expressed in latitudinarianism and more generally in Enlightenment thought was helping to shape middle-class attitudes toward animals in England. Robert Malcolmson in *Popular Recreations in English Society* shows how repulsion to these sports was expressed in the municipal press. By the end of the eighteenth century many towns were enforcing ordinances against cock throwing and bull baiting. Municipal ordinances were followed in 1835 with the Cruelty to Animals Act, which outlawed the "running, baiting, or fighting" of any animal.

One important shift in the pattern suggested by the mobilization of middle-class reformism against elite and popular conservatism in modernizing England occurred in Stamford in the 1830s. There middle-class opinion turned against the abolition of bull running when the London-based Royal Society for the Prevention of Cruelty to Animals (RSPCA) backed by the royal army forces mounted an attack on Stamford's bull running. The formation and the history of the RSPCA in the nineteenth century will be discussed below. Here it is seen that in England lines of conflict over the treatment of animals could be shaped not only by class but by a divide between the state and local traditions in ways that echo the conflict between London and the counties in the age of civil war and revolution.

On the Continent animal pain was also a part of traditional celebrations. Robert Darnton explains in *The Great Cat Massacre* how the "rough music" of a charivari could be produced by skinning a live cat. Cats also fared poorly in May Day and summer solstice festivities. Because they were associated with witchcraft, they were burned alive on maypoles or bonfires, their dying cries part of the fun. When it came to the problem of animals, however, the focus of reformers within the French elite and those surrounding the enlightened despots of Prussia, Russia, and Austria was to effect an agricultural revolution on the model of England's, that is, to improve the progress of animal husbandry and increase yields of grain. It was not until the nineteenth century that middle- and upper-class distance from lower-class cruelty to animals was institutionalized along British lines in animal protection societies. Meanwhile, early Enlightenment thought in France had produced two lines of argument about the relationship of humans to animals whose effects would linger in modern European culture. For followers of Montaigne, a lover of cats, animals were feeling creatures, akin in this way to humans. For followers of Descartes, animals could also be understood as living machines, sensate but unfeeling, whose secrets could be discovered through experimentation.

A Cockfight. *The Cockpit*, engraving (1759) by William Hogarth (1697–1764). ©HULTON-DEUTSCH COLLECTION/CORBIS

HUNTING IN MODERNIZING EUROPE

The patterns of social conflict associated with hunting in early modern Europe are distinct from those formed over the practice of popular blood sports. In England and on the continent hunting was reserved for the landed elites. The rural poor were allied in this issue with urban elites, not in opposition to hunting but in resentment of their exclusion from the sport. By the end of the eighteenth century, the romantic movement was developing an argument against hunting based on empathy with animal pain but, for the most part, notions of cruelty to animals were absent from the conflicts over hunting in early modern Europe.

Hunting and aristocracy. In the Middle Ages hunting was a type of practice warfare for the nobility. By the twelfth century forests were being reserved by important nobles and royalty for hunting. Although game could be a precious source of protein in the premodern economy, it is the political and cultural function of hunting that historians stress. In an age that depended on increasing the amount of arable land to expand the production of grain, the preservation of forests, or fragments of forests in deer parks,

was an exercise of power. The Robin Hood legends indicate the resentments that the royal forest law in England could trigger among those excluded from its benefits.

Hunting as an enduring attribute of monarchy is made clear in the biographies of the early modern monarchs of England and France. Even in old age Elizabeth I would go shooting. James I liked to bathe his arms in the steaming blood of a dying deer then anoint the faces of his entourage with its hot blood. Louis XIV's hunting parties appear frequently in the memoirs of the duc de Saint-Simon. It is in this context that Louis XVI's journal entry for 14 July 1789 makes sense. Simon Schama explains in *Citizens* that his entry, "rien" ("nothing") tells us not that the king was out of touch with one of the most important revolutionary events but that he was disappointed at not being able to hunt that day. His comment passes for premonition, for three weeks later, on the night of 4 August 1789, the hunting privileges of the noble elite were abolished along with all other aspects of feudalism.

Hunting had been a privilege of the ruling class since the establishment of manorialism. In France the exclusive right of the lord of the manor to hunt on peasant's land was one of the remnants of a system that economic modernity was making obsolete. Tocqueville points out in *The Old Régime and the French Revolution* that the right of the lord of the manor to hunt on peasants' fields was like the *banalité*—which included the obligations of peasants to use the lord's ovens and mills—less punishing in and of itself than as a reminder of an anachronistic system of power relations. Hunting's importance in defining social relations in rural France is indicated by the fact that it was both closely guarded by the nobility and contested by the peasantry. Isser Woloch in *Eighteenth-Century Europe* points to the prevalence throughout eighteenth-century Europe of poaching as a form of social protest. He also explains that complaints against the hunting privileges of the nobility were among the most frequent in the *cahiers de doléances,* the list of grievances solicited by the king on the eve of the French Revolution.

Poaching continued in France after the Revolution when it was redefined as a property crime. A permit system in the 1830s was designed by the state to combat the problem. But as Eugen Weber notes in *Peasants into Frenchmen,* hunting offenses remained more common than theft in rural areas through much of the century. At the same time, however, the romantic tide was turning some of the great landowners against hunting. Witness the romantic poet and revolutionary Alphonse de Lamartine's lament for a dying deer in his poem, *"Mon dernier coup de fusil"* ("My last shot").

In the German states and in Russia where serfdom hardened during the eighteenth century, hunting also marked power relations. The obligations of serfs included the beating of game, that is the obligation to process en masse through fields, woods, and underbrush driving game forward into clearings to be slaughtered by nobles. Readers of *War and Peace* will remember its wolf-hunting scene. David Blackbourn suggests in *The Long Nineteenth Century* that even in areas where the ties of serfdom were loosest, the hunting rights of the nobility were tightly held on to.

For the most part, early modern hunting on the Continent was a male pursuit although, as W. H. Bruford relates in *Germany in the Eighteenth Century,* German ladies were sometimes invited along to pig-stickings.

Hunting in early modern England.
In England conflicts over hunting were more complicated. Rural capitalism was destroying the medieval manor as urban capitalism was the guilds. By the eighteenth century London was the center of a commercial empire poised to dominate the globe. It is in this context of emerging capitalism that the game laws of early modern England and the opposition they generated can be understood. Though all English game laws were oppressive to the lower classes, it is the Game Law of 1671 that historians see as introducing class conflict into the arena of hunting.

The Game Law of 1671 followed the political logic of the seventeenth century in that it displaced the monarch as sole owner and protector of game by including in that definition the landed gentry. The gentry could hunt freely throughout the countryside (subject to a weak law of trespass) and they were charged with protecting game through the employment of gamekeepers and the enforcing of the game law through their offices of justices of the peace.

For P. B. Munsche, writing in *Gentlemen and Poachers: The English Game Laws, 1671–1831,* it is significant that urban elites—those merchant capitalist investors in the East and West India Companies who had previously joined with the gentry in resisting absolutism—were excluded by the game law from hunting. The game law qualified only large landowners, not those wealthy from mobile wealth. Munsche argues that the new law must be aimed at this group as the status of the lower classes with respect to hunting remained untouched by the law—that is, the penalties for poaching remained the same, a fine of about a day's wages for rural workers.

In Munsche's view the function of the game law was to enhance the social position of the gentry at the expense of the urban bourgeoisie, held to be responsible for the excesses of the revolution. Merchants were often Dissenters. More vaguely, but importantly, city life was associated with modernity, newness, rootlessness, and change. The importance of hunting in early modern England is that it allowed country gentlemen to build a positive social identity. Their exclusive association with hunting let them assert themselves as simple, natural, and English, a political move that shaped the divide between Tory and Whig in the Hanoverian century.

For Douglas Hay, whose "Poaching and the Game Laws on Cannock Chase" appears in *Albion's Fatal Tree: Crime and Society in Eighteenth-Century England,* the meaning of the game law lies in its enforcement, especially after the mid-eighteenth century when amendments made penalties for poaching harsher. Whipping, hard labor for night poaching in lieu of stiff fines, and by 1800 transportation for this offense were possible. The killing of deer in a park, that is, in an enclosed area, was punishable by death. Hay analyzed the application of the game laws on Cannock Chase, a great estate belonging to the Paget family. The laws were aggressively enforced through gamekeepers. They were also universally resisted by villagers. Unlike a crime of property which could alienate the perpetrator from the community, the hunting of game on land once viewed as commons was understood as morally right though legally wrong. Hay shows how villagers protected poachers from Paget's gamekeepers. Poaching, Hay shows, was—like wrecking, smuggling, arson, and rioting—a community crime, a form of protest, a way of building social identity among rural wage workers who were no longer feudal but not yet fully modern and class conscious.

In rural England one defined oneself in terms of one's relationship to hunting. Hay and Munsche would both agree. For Hay, unlike Munsche, the defining divide was between patricians—gentry and merchants—and plebeians, the working poor of rural and urban England. The game laws were part of a criminal code, a theater of power, based on the strategic deployment of penalties of capital punishment and transportation, which throughout England maintained the dominance of the propertied over the poor.

In any case, capitalism helped destroy the Game Law of 1671 and its amendments. Poaching was found to be fueled by the demand for game on the part of the urban elite; that is, game poached from the gentry found its way to the urban gullet. The status of game was such that it had become a necessary part of a gentleman's table and of a tavern menu by the early nineteenth century. The Game Reform Law of 1831, which opened hunting to anyone with a permit, was promulgated in part to increase the legal supply of game and make poaching less attractive and lucrative. In this it failed. In its other purpose, however, the law was more successful. Equalizing access to hunting by including professionals, doctors, lawyers, civil servants—nineteenth-century young professionals, such as one finds in the pages of Anthony Trollope novels—encouraged the adoption of Tory attitudes toward animals as the national attitude.

In a theme that strengthens as the nineteenth century wears on, Englishness comes to be set apart from other cultures by its special relationship toward nature. The democratization of hunting also results in the gentry finding new ways to express their status with respect to animals. The raising of prize pigs and cows is satirized in the endearing figures of Lord Empworth and his pig in the novels of P. G. Wodehouse and analyzed in the *The Animal Estate* by Harriet Ritvo.

ANIMAL PROTECTION IN MODERN EUROPE

In the nineteenth century attitudes toward animals took on unprecedented political importance. This is true for England especially, where the Society for the Prevention of Cruelty to Animals shaped both public opinion and public policy. Tocqueville indirectly signaled the importance of animal protection societies in *Democracy in America* when he spoke to the importance to liberal democracy of intermediate bodies between state and people. The RSPCA stands out as one of the most successful of European voluntary associations. Brian Harrison notes in *Peaceable Kingdom* that its legislative achievements both "reflected and enhanced their influence" (p. 84).

Animal protection societies were formed throughout Europe and the United States along the model of the British. The most important European society after the British was the French Société Protectrice des Animaux, founded in 1845. Societies were also formed in the German states and in Switzerland in the late 1830s and 1840s. The German cities of Dresden, Nürnberg, Berlin, Hamburg, Frankfurt, Munich, and Hanover established societies. In Switzerland, Berne, Basle, Zurich, Lausanne, Lucerne, and Geneva did so, too. According to Ulrich Tröhler and Andreas-Holger Maehle in "Anti-vivisection in Nineteenth-Century Germany and Switzerland," a German national organization, the Verband der Tierschutzvereine des Deutschen Reiches, in the early 1880s included more than 150 local animal protection societies. The Swedish national society was founded in 1875.

Marx specifically noted the role of animal protection societies within bourgeois Europe. In *The Communist Manifesto* he grouped them with other humanitarian organizations under the rubric of "Conservative, or Bourgeois Socialism." Marx saw the universalism of bourgeois culture at work in organizations whose object was the reform of lower-class behavior. "Members of societies for the prevention of cruelty to animals . . . like temperance fanatics, . . . organizers of charity, . . . improvers of the condition of the working class," Marx wrote, "wish for a bourgeoisie without a proletariat. The bourgeoisie naturally conceives the world in which it is supreme to be the best."

The transmission of bourgeois values was openly a goal of legislation prohibiting public violence to animals on the streets of urban Europe. To be kind to animals came to stand high in the index of civilization. It formed part of the project of civilization. The barbarian other—the urban working classes, continental peasants, southern Europeans, Catholic Ireland, Russians, Asians, and Turks—was defined in part by its brutality to beasts.

Animal protection in England and France. The Society for the Prevention of Cruelty to Animals was founded in 1824 in London. Its founders and early members included evangelical humanitarians but also Anglican ministers, Irish M.P.s, utilitarian radicals, and socially prominent Jews. One of the most important of these was William Wilberforce, otherwise famous for leading the campaign for the abolition of slavery in the British empire.

Throughout the century the society attracted royal and aristocratic patrons including Queen Victoria whose support explains its name change to the Royal Society for the Prevention of Cruelty to Animals in 1840. Members of Parliament could be called upon for advice and information. Its members included a large number of women from among the social elite. Harrison in *Peaceable Kingdom* credits its informal manipulation of the political system with its success in effecting legislation and changing attitudes toward animals. The RSPCA also developed a force of lower-class, paid constables who were highly disciplined and uniformed. Inspectors, whose job it was to discover and prosecute infractions of the animal protection law, wore badges from 1838, armlets from 1853, and hats and capes from 1856.

The first major achievement of the animal protection movement in England, however, preceded the formation of the SPCA. Martin's Act of 1822 was sponsored by Wilberforce, Thomas Fowell Buxton, and Richard Martin. Buxton, like Wilberforce, was an evangelical. Martin was an M.P. for Galway—"high-living" and "hard-drinking" according to James Turner's description in *Reckoning with the Beast*. The disparity in temperament and political orientation among the sponsors of the bill is an indication of how broadly shared among the British elite the new attitude toward animals had become. Martin's Act prohibited public cruelty toward horses and cows and most other farm and draft animals (though not bulls). Its significance lay in the fact that the law looked at animal cruelty from the point of view of animal pain, not the harm to or destruction of property.

Some observers noted that animals were protected by law in England before slavery was abolished and before children were protected from the worst exploitations of the factory system. The SPCA was accused of humanitarian inconsistency. It is true that only in 1833 were children under nine prohibited from working in factories and the work hours of older children regulated. Although the slave trade was abolished in 1807, slavery itself throughout the empire was abolished only in 1833. It is clear, however, that the protection of animals against public cruelty was part of an expansive process of reform. Martin's Act of 1822 and the more inclusive Animal Protection Act of 1835, which included dogs and cats—and like the

temperance movement, the ragged school movement, the first suffrage reform act of 1833—were responses to the advance of capitalism. In a more general way they were a part of that modernization of state and society that characterizes English culture in the first half of the nineteenth century.

It would be a mistake, however, to see the origins of the animal protection movement in industrialization per se. Not only did the movement to protect animals from cruelty begin in the seventeenth century but industrialization itself did not distance the English from animals. Ponies were used in mines, horses along canals and for the building of railroads. Horses provided transportation in cities for most of the century, and dogs pulled carts in London until 1839 and until 1854 elsewhere. The cavalry remained a basic unit of armies until World War I. Veterinary schools were founded to train people to treat horse and livestock diseases.

The animal protection movement in the nineteenth century is a chapter in the history of violence. It is only indirectly related to a romantic view of nature. It had an obvious though not exclusive class dimension. An outburst of anger, for instance, on the part of a London cabdriver that results in his beating to death an old weak horse on a London street is a recurring image of animal protection literature. From the point of view of the RSPCA and its sympathizers, it was a dangerously irrational act. Beating a dying horse will not make it work. Those who are vicious to animals will be murderous to others. From the point of view of workers and their advocates, however, the attempt to get a cab moving again is desperately rational, as Anna Sewell made clear in *Black Beauty* (1877). Fares were needed for survival

The RSPCA attacked the recreations as well as the livelihoods of the London poor. Dogfights as well as dogcarts were objects of attacks, but foxhunting by the professional and landed classes was left alone. Violence was sequestered, hidden away from the view of those susceptible to its pernicious influence. This explains the attempt in the first part of the nineteenth century to move London slaughterhouses to the periphery of the city, so the sights and sounds of dying animals would not disturb neighborhood life. Two principles informed the animal protection movement in the nineteenth century. The first was familiar to seventeenth- and eighteenth-century reformers: We have a duty to God to treat well each of his creatures who are dependent upon us. People should not cause animals unnecessary pain. The second was the need to quarantine violence, because like disease, it "communicates an immoral contagion of the worst and most virulent kind among those who witness it." Here

Defending Dogs. Dog lovers demonstrate in support of Sir Robert Gowers's Anti-Vivisection Bill, 1925, England. ©HULTON-DEUTSCH COLLECTION/CORBIS

Harrison in *Peaceable Kingdom* (page 120) is quoting the Bishop of St. David's at the 1846 annual meeting of the RSPCA.

In France a similar constellation of socialites, enthusiasts, middle-class reformers, and members of the political left as well as the right formed the Société Protectrice des Animaux. Its targets were similar to those of the British society—vicious cabbies and carters, slaughterhouses, and the treatment of animals by the rural poor. The target in peasant France was less the recreational use of animals than more pragmatic practices—the snaring of many little birds for food, the beating to death of unwanted dogs.

The first major achievement of the SPA was the Grammont Law of 1850, which prohibited public cruelty toward animals. In the aftermath of the Revolution of 1848, the National Assembly could be counted on to be receptive to arguments linking familiarity with violence to animals to criminal and radical political behavior among the *misérables* of Paris.

The second major success of the SPA was the integration of its principles within the national school system. Under the Second Empire, the Ministry of Education was persuaded to present a medal and prize money each year to the schoolteacher who best taught kindness to animals to students. This practice was continued under the Third Republic, an indication of how mainstream these attitudes toward animals were

among the political elite. Effectiveness was demonstrated by student essays on the subject of kindness to animals—"I used to destroy birds' nests but now know birds are mothers too"—that were forwarded to prefects and then to the minister of education in Paris. The National Archives retains copies of some of these essays, showing how love of animals became part of the catechism of the Third Republic and the Grammont law part of the Ferry reform of education.

In France as in England kindness to animals was equated with Atlantic civilization. Both the SPA and the RSPCA conducted crusades against Spanish bullfighting and inquiries into Arab disdain for dogs. As we will see in the discussion on antivivisection, however, this moral high ground was maintained by the British in their attack on French methods of physiology from the 1870s on.

PET KEEPING

New attitudes toward animals were focused by many people on pets. During the early modern period small dogs, cats, and monkeys had been kept as pets by members of the prosperous classes. This practice became obvious in the seventeenth century when Charles II was shown being openly demonstrative to his spaniels and Dutch genre painters depicted small animals as part of the material and symbolic apparatus of everyday life. Pets in this period, however, were considered luxury objects. Ladies' lap dogs (spaniels and pugs) had sometimes negative connotations of indolence and sexuality, and an association with aristocratic excess.

Most canine types were only roughly distinguished in terms of function. Johannus Caius's list of Tudor dogs, translated from Latin in 1576 as *Of English Dogges,* discussed seventeen varieties, which were divided into three categories according to their function: hunting and ladies' dogs, shepherds and guard dogs, and menial working dogs like spit turners. Hunting dogs included ordinary hounds and royal greyhounds in France. On the eve of the nineteenth century, very few breeds were distinguished as such. Ritvo in *The Animal Estate* notes the foxhound as an exception in England and points out that other breeds familiar to eighteenth-century people, such as the bulldog and collie, were transformed by nineteenth-century breeders. By the end of the century French experts could describe two hundred varieties of dogs. The British, more prudent here, recognized sixty

A Girl and Her Pets. *Doddy and Her Pets* (or *Little Girl Defending Her Cat*), painting (1886) by Charles Trevor Garland. BIBLIOTHÈQUE DES ARTS DECORATIFS, PARIS

A BIRD OF PREY.

Feathers and Fashion. A fashionable harpy's feathers spells death for the songbird. The caricaturist Linley Sambourne drew *A Bird of Prey* for the May 1892 issue of *Punch* to honor the newly founded Society for the Protection of Birds. COURTESY OF THE ROYAL SOCIETY FOR THE PROTECTION OF BIRDS

breeds, described and monitored by the newly formed British Kennel Club.

It was not until the eighteenth century in England, and the nineteenth century in France, that dogs began to take on their modern aspect of emotional necessities. Sources for the development of pet keeping include a tax on dogs in eighteenth-century London that chart an increase in the numbers of nonworking dogs—that is, dogs kept for pleasure and not for spit-turning, or for use in dogcarts, or as watchdogs. In France a tax on dogs in 1855 provoked middle-class protest indicative of the new attitude toward pets. Nonworking dogs, or pets, were to be taxed at a higher rate than working, useful dogs, like shepherds and guide dogs. In the law's eyes, pets were luxury objects. Like hunting dogs, they were for the rich. The tax was a sumptuary law meant to discourage pet ownership by the poor. Criticism of the tax in Second Empire Paris, however, centered, as Kathleen Kete shows in *The Beast in the Boudoir,* on the usefulness of pets. Pets were seen by the bourgeoisie as being integral to family life. They protected the home emotionally and physically. They were friends in need to the desolate.

Pet keeping in the form that became known in the twentieth century was established in France and Britain in the nineteenth century. There the dog became a cliché of family life. The rituals of pet keeping were also formed. Pet care books were written, dog and cat shows were established, and dog food companies formed. Spratt's Patent was the first commercial dog food. Boarding kennels, dog hospitals, and shops specializing in collars, leashes, and clothes were advertised to the middle classes. So, too, were stories about faithful family pets. Lord Byron's epitaph to his Newfoundland, "All the virtues of Man, without his vices" (1808) was reproduced on gravestones at the Parisian pet cemetery and at other final resting places. Pets by this point had clearly entered the history of the family, including changes in emotional emphases and, probably, the declining birthrate.

In this area, too, we find the nineteenth-century middle and upper classes monopolizing the virtue of kindness to animals. As Kete explains in *The Beast in the Boudoir*, dog care books imagined the pet as middle class. Clean, virtuous, and devoted, middle-class pets were contrasted with the dogs of workers, which, it was claimed, were abused, dirty, violent, and promiscuous. Animal refuges were in part established to rescue dogs from working-class violence.

Cats were less popular than dogs in the nineteenth century, though they attracted some enthusiastic admirers. In France their association with bohemian life set them in contrast to dogs, who were solidly bourgeois. In middle-class homes, birds were kept in cages, and plants in greenhouses and terrariums. The aquarium was invented and became wildly popular in the 1850s, 1860s, and 1870s.

By the twentieth century pet keeping was commonplace. At the turn of the twenty-first century, class biases no longer shape its practices as pets have become firmly a part of everyday life.

ANTIVIVISECTION

The issues of animal protection and the nineteenth century's love of pets come together in the antivivisection movement of the last third of the century. Vivisection—that is, experimenting on live animals to understand the mechanisms of the liver, the pancreas, the spleen, and other organs—was developed particularly by French and German physiologists. One of the most important in France was Claude Bernard, whose *Introduction to the Study of Experimental Medicine* was widely influential. Vivisectionists operated mainly on small animals, though sometimes horses were used in veterinary schools. Because of the availability and size of dogs, they were favored animals of vivisectionists.

The image of the faithful and loving family dog begging for his life in the laboratory of the vivisectionist was favored in antivivisectionist propaganda. The fear that the family pet, when lost, would end up on the vivisection table frightened children well into the twentieth century.

The antivivisection movement was important in western Europe from the 1870s to World War I. It was, first of all, an expression of conflict within the elite over the purpose of science and possibilities of its regulation. The question of whether scientists should be regulated was debated in Britain, France, and Germany. In Bismarckian Germany, antivivisectionists from the conservative and center opposition repeatedly petitioned the Reichstag in the 1880s and 1890s to abolish vivisection, but to no avail. The practice was left to the discretion of German scientists until the Nazi takeover. In Britain the Act to Amend the Law Relating to Cruelty to Animals in 1876 was the world's first restriction of vivisection by establishing a licensing requirement. Hostile public opinion forced the reopening of debate on vivisection, however. Both sides maintained a very active propaganda war until 1912, when the Royal Commission on Vivisection's final report upheld the practice of vivisection but subjected it to legal control. In France the question of whether to restrict vivisection was studied by the Academy of Medicine and by a committee of the SPA. As in Germany, and unlike in Britain, vivisection remained self-regulated in France in the nineteenth century.

In England and France within the established animal protection societies, there was a consensus that vivisection could be allowed if animals were caused no unnecessary pain and the use of anesthesia was urged. French scientists were dependent on vivisection to an extent that the British refused to be. Protests against visits of French physiologists to Britain became debates over the costs of modernity with British public opinion granting the English once again superiority in the realm of kindness to animals.

Vivisection stimulated an examination of the relationship between scientists and the state. More dramatically, it raised questions about women's roles and about the meaning of being female. Antivivisection is linked, therefore, to the development of feminism in the late nineteenth century. Some historians suggest that the antivivisection movement empowered women by providing them with leadership positions in volunteer organizations and a voice in the public sphere. Within the RSPCA and the SPA women played a largely decorative or behind-the-scenes role. But the leadership of antivivisection societies included very effective women. The Victoria Street Society for the Protection of Animals from Vivisection (established in 1876) was led by Frances Power Cobbe—already famous for her propaganda war in Florence against the German physiologist Moritz Schiff. Marie Huot and Maria Deraismes in France led the Ligue Populaire Contre les Abus de la Vivisection. Within the SPA the issue of vivisection moved ordinarily demure female members to speak out in opposition to it. Marie-Espérance von Schwartz, an ally of Ernst von Weber who founded the Internationale Gesellschaft zur Bekämpfung der Wissenschaftlichen Thierfolter (International Society for Combat against Scientific Torture of Animals) in 1879, was a member of its directing committee.

Mary Ann Elston, in "Women and Antivivisection in Victorian England, 1870–1900," points to the influence of women within the RSPCA, however. By establishing animal refuges, they saved dogs from hardhearted workers in mid-century and from evil scientists in the last part of the century. And, of course, men were leaders in the antivivisection movement, too. Its strongest supporters in England included men on both sides of the question of woman suffrage. In Germany its most famous supporter may have been Richard Wagner, who, as Tröhler and Maehle note, famously claimed not to want to live in a world "in which 'no dog would wish to live any longer.'"

Some women claimed an identification with animals mistreated by scientists, an identification that galvanized feminist consciousness. Women, like animals, were at the mercy of male rationalism. As Coral Lansbury asserts in *The Old Brown Dog*, Claude Bernard himself had "described nature as a woman who must be forced to unveil herself when she is attacked by the experimenter, who must be put to the question and subdued" (p. 163). In antivivisection imagery as well, the vivisector appears as a sexual predator, sadistically enjoying a perverse pleasure in causing prostrate animals pain. This is the image that appears in *Gemma or; Virtue and Vice* by Marie-Espérance von Schwartz, in *The Beth Book* by Sarah Grand, and in other works which Coral Lansbury, in *The Old Brown Dog*, compares with pornography.

The antivivisection movement emphasized the importance of feeling, rather than the use of scientific method, as a guide to understanding. It thus could serve as an interrogation of materialism, a rethinking of the aims and means of science. But the identification of women with animals abused by male science drew upon essentialist notions of female identity. It spoke to conventional binaries—woman and nature, men and culture, feminine emotion and masculine reason—and to an important degree served a conser-vative role. The antivivisection movement included suffragists in England, but also antisuffragists and conservatives in Bismarckian Germany.

For those involved in either promoting or opposing the antivivisection movement, society could seem divided into ruthless men of science and women, whose maternal roles of childbearing and nurturing gave them a special affinity with the world of nature and allowed them to critique the experimental method. In Germany, especially, this critique of materialism came to focus on Jews as well. In the minds of German and Swiss antivivisectionists, it was Jewish doctors who practiced vivisection and "Jewish" attitudes toward animals that allowed it. Arthur Schopenhauer had argued earlier in the century that, as Tröhler and Maehle put it, "it was time that the 'Jewish' view regarding animals came to an end" (p. 151). For anti-Semites like Wagner, this "Jewish" attitude was expressed in both vivisection and kosher butchering. (Its reverse, vegetarianism, was strongly promoted in Bayreuth.) The journal of the German antivivisection movement, *Their- und Menschenfreund*, as Tröhler and Maehle note, strongly supported the abolition of kosher butchering—which was achieved in Switzerland in 1893 and by the Nazis in 1933. The image of the kosher butcher practicing a private, bloody, orgiastic rite was much like the image of the vivisector, as a viewing of the Nazi propaganda film *The Eternal Jew* makes clear.

TWENTIETH-CENTURY TRENDS IN ANIMAL PROTECTION

Keith Thomas speaks in *Man and the Natural World* of the dethronement of humans, a process that begins in early modern Europe and continues through the nineteenth century. In the twentieth century the abandonment of the principle of the sanctity of human life and the hierarchy it presumes led to a radical right and a radical left rethinking of the relationship between humans and animals.

In "Understanding Nazi Animal Protection and the Holocaust," Arnold Arluke and Boria Sax discuss Nazi animal protection legislation in the context of the Nazi revolution of state and society. One of the first laws passed by the Nazis in April 1933 prohibited kosher butchering. Soon afterward, vivisection was first abolished, then restricted. Nazi animal protection extended far beyond these two overtly anti-Semitic acts, however. Laws covered the treatment of lobster and shellfish by cooks. To reduce their suffering, lobsters were to be thrown only one by one into rapidly boiling water. Another provision protected horses that were being shod. Endangered species such as bears, bison, and wild horses were protected.

Nazi animal protection legislation was not much more comprehensive than the British, Arluke and Sax point out, but clearly the Nazi understanding of the relationship between humans and animals was profoundly distinct from traditional European beliefs. Nazism "obliterated . . . moral distinctions" between animals and people, Arluke and Sax explain, a principle that allowed for a reordering of the chain of being. Some animal species rested above some human "races." So Aryans, German shepherds—"deliberately bred to represent and embody the spirit of National Socialism" (p. 14)—beasts of prey, and Teutonic acorn-eating pigs were far superior to subhuman "races." Jews were vermin that needed to be killed, as 6 million were in the death camps and in the German-invaded villages of eastern Europe.

The Nazi understanding of the natural world stands in contrast to that of the Soviets, who maintained Marx's nineteenth-century understanding of humans as being distinct from other animals by their control of the environment. The Soviet destruction of the environment of large parts of eastern Europe, made apparent after the fall of communism, warns against a naive celebration of this view as well.

The Animal Liberation movement of the 1970s renewed debate about the social meaning of the human relationship to animals. Peter Singer's *Animal Liberation* compared speciesism (a neologism) to racism and sexism. In each case, he argued, arbitrary characteristics were the signal for discrimination. In the case of the human species our ability to reason is our excuse to oppress other species. In the animal liberation movement of the 1970s and 1980s in Europe, antivivisection again became a cause. Protestors investigated animal research at university and private laboratories. Older causes, such as the transportation of animals to slaughter, were taken up in England by the Compassion in World Farming (CIWF) group.

The most important development of the late twentieth century may have been the global dimension of the environmental movement, which recognized the importance of consumer pressure on international trading practices and was captured in media images of demonstrators (in Oxford in 1997, for example) dressed as trees, skunks, butterflies, and squirrels.

But older themes as well as older issues prevailed in the late-twentieth-century animal protection movement. Hilda Kean notes in *Animal Rights* that in the CIWF campaign against Parisian Muslims' slaughter of sheep for the festival of Eid el Kebir, the British provenance of the sheep figured strongly. Kean notes, too, that recent campaigns against vivisection in England highlighted the fact that the animals used in British laboratories were imported from southern Europe, southeast Asia, and the Caribbean, speaking to an earlier British sense of themselves as uniquely civilized in the care of nature. In England, as well, the fight to abolish foxhunting seems likely to continue along not only class, but also rural-urban lines.

It seems clear from other late-twentieth-century events such as the outbreak of mad cow disease and the ensuing British-French enmity that Europeans will continue to find meaning in their relationship with animals along the lines of earlier structures of thought established since the Renaissance. Regional enmities as well as a sense of human guardianship of nature will likely prevail. Whether the logic of "dethronement" will also have social consequences in the twenty-first century is far more difficult to know.

See also other articles in this section.

BIBLIOGRAPHY

Agulhon, Maurice. "Le sang des bêtes: Le problème de la protection des animaux en France au XIXème siècle." *Romanticisme: Revue du dix-neuvième siècle* 31 (1981): 81–109.

Arluke, Arnold, and Boria Sax. "Understanding Animal Protection and the Holocaust." *Anthrozoös* 5, no. 1 (1992): 6–31.

Blackbourn, David. *The Long Nineteenth Century: A History of Germany, 1780–1918.* New York and Oxford, 1998.

Bruford, W. H. *Germany in the Eighteenth Century: The Social Background of Literary Revival.* Cambridge, U.K., 1971.

Cowan, Alexander. *Urban Europe, 1500–1700.* London and New York, 1998.

Darnton, Robert. *The Great Cat Massacre and Other Episodes in French Cultural History.* New York, 1985.

Elston, Mary Ann. "Women and Anti-vivisection in Victorian England, 1870–1900." In *Vivisection in Historical Perspective.* Edited by Nicolaas A. Rupke. London and New York, 1987. Pages 259–294.

French, Richard D. *Antivivisection and Medical Science in Victorian Society.* Princeton, N.J., 1975.

Frykman, Jonas, and Orvar Löfgren. *Culture Builders: A Historical Anthropology of Middle-Class Life.* Translated by Alan Crozier. New Brunswick, N.J., and London, 1987. Translation of *Kultiverade människan.*

Harrison, Brian. "Animals and the State in Nineteenth-Century England." In his *Peaceable Kingdom: Stability and Change in Modern Britain.* Oxford, 1982. Pages 82–122.

Hay, Douglas. "Poaching and the Game Laws on Cannock Chase." In *Albion's Fatal Tree: Crime and Society in Eighteenth-Century England.* Edited by Douglas Hay, Peter Linebaugh, John G. Rule, E. P. Thompson, and Cal Winslow. New York, 1975. Pages 189–253.

Kean, Hilda. *Animal Rights: Political and Social Change in Britain since 1800.* London, 1998.

Kete, Kathleen. *The Beast in the Boudoir: Petkeeping in Nineteenth-Century Paris.* Berkeley, Calif., 1994.

Lansbury, Coral. *The Old Brown Dog: Women, Workers, and Vivisection in Edwardian England.* Madison, Wis., 1985.

Malcolmson, Robert. *Popular Recreations in English Society, 1700–1850.* Cambridge, U.K., 1973.

Munsche, P. B. *Gentlemen and Poachers: The English Game Laws, 1671–1831.* Cambridge, U.K., and New York, 1981.

Phineas, Charles (pseud.). "Household Pets and Urban Alienation." *Journal of Social History* 7, no. 3 (1974): 338–343.

Regan, Tom. *The Case for Animal Rights.* Berkeley, Calif., 1983.

Ritvo, Harriet. *The Animal Estate: The English and Other Creatures in the Victorian Age.* Cambridge, Mass., 1987.

Ritvo, Harriet, *The Platypus and the Mermaid, and Other Figments of the Classifying Imagination.* Cambridge, Mass., 1997.

Schama, Simon. *Citizens: A Chronicle of the French Revolution.* New York, 1989.

Singer, Peter. *Animal Liberation.* 2d ed. New York, 1990.

Thomas, Keith. *Man and the Natural World: A History of the Modern Sensibility.* New York, 1983.

Tocqueville, Alexis de. *The Old Régime and the French Revolution.* Translated by Stuart Gilbert. Garden City, N.Y., 1955.

Tröhler, Ulrich, and Andreas-Holger Maehle. "Anti-vivisection in Nineteenth-Century Germany and Switzerland: Motives and Methods." In *Vivisection in Historical Perspective.* Edited by Nicolaas A. Rupke. London and New York, 1987. Pages 149–187.

Turner, James. *Reckoning with the Beast: Animals, Pain, and Humanity in the Victorian Mind.* Baltimore, 1980.

Weber, Eugen. *Peasants into Frenchmen: The Modernization of Rural France, 1870–1914.* Stanford, Calif., 1976.

Woloch, Isser. *Eighteenth-Century Europe: Tradition and Progress, 1715–1789.* New York and London, 1982.

TOYS AND GAMES

Gary S. Cross

Toys and games are the tools of play, and play is a large part of social life. Playthings have helped the small and powerless child overcome the frustrations and conflicts of adult life through imagination. Still, toys and games have never been exclusively for children. Playthings also convey messages from the older generation to the younger. Changes in toys and other playthings thus can reveal much about changes in the experience and meaning of childhood and how the broader cultural and material world has shaped youth. Because the historical record concerning toys is richer than that of games, the former will be stressed and the term "games" will refer to play objects rather than organized activities.

Before modern industrialization, childhood was brief and play not encouraged by parents. Especially for children of peasants and craftspeople, toys were rare. Adults gave them to children during festival times, and the young made toys for themselves in moments of freedom from control or work out of gourds, bits of wood, or animal parts.

Play was not especially associated with childhood and neither were toys and games. The word "toy" was associated with a child's plaything only at the end of the sixteenth century. Still, in Shakespeare's time, "toy" continued to mean anything frivolous or even simply a funny story. Adult and children's playthings were often not sharply distinguished until the eighteenth century. Sometimes it is hard to tell whether an object is a toy or an adult ritual object. Wide-ranging groups (including Hopi Indians and the medieval Japanese) passed on devotional images to their children for play after religious use. And in medieval Europe adult novelties were given later to children almost as an afterthought.

The French anthropologist Roger Caillois suggests that playthings vent four distinct needs: mimicry, vertigo (or giddiness), competition, and the excitement of chance. The toy has often allowed the individual to imitate the powerful and grown-up while also expressing the thrill of abandoning oneself (as in riding a roller coaster). Board games have rewarded personal skill in competition while requiring that players accept luck and thus the unpredictability of life. Cultures can be distinguished by their relative stress on competition or vertigo, for example, in their games and toys. Playthings have taught the young and reminded the old of the values and customs of their culture.

But in modern times, Europeans abandoned certain elements of play. They gradually gave up mimicking the gods with masks and dolls. For the most part, dolls have passed to children. Doll historians may exaggerate when they equate children's dolls with modern civilization, but clearly a mark of modernity is the turning of adult idols into children's play figures. Modern adults also gradually rejected vertigo—the ecstatic worship so common in ancient cultures that gave people the feeling of participating in a supernatural world. Instead, adult play slowly came to stress competition and chance in games of calculation and rules. Most modern adults have ceased toying with the dangerous and ecstatic and passed the objects they associated with this play to the young in harmless forms. This has been a long process involving basic changes in material and cultural life, affecting adult and child alike.

PLAYTHINGS IN EARLY MODERN EUROPE

Most early modern Europeans viewed play as a periodic catharsis, often associated with fairs or feast days but not specifically with childhood. Many modern playthings have origins in Mardi Gras or other quasi-religious festivals that were shared by adults and children alike. Some children's toys had origins as miniature souvenirs of late medieval religious pageantry. Churches displayed life-size manger scenes at Christ-

521

mas to delight and edify the congregation. Following a general cultural trend away from the community spectacle in the sixteenth century, these images were brought into the family circle when Italian and German craftspeople sold miniatures of these scenes for home display. From about 1470, engravings of secular scenes including battles and animals in natural settings were mounted on pasteboard for the amusement and edification of families. In the eighteenth century such miniature scenes were used as backdrops for home peep shows or toy theaters in Germany, Britain, and France. Toy theaters introduced the idea of the toy as a form of storytelling. Still, these miniatures were not children's toys as such, but festive and edifying household decorations.

However, miniature scenes eventually became children's play sets. Perhaps the earliest of these was the wooden Noah's Ark. This late-sixteenth-century German innovation offered religious training while allowing children to play with toy animals in a self-contained setting. Another example is the jumping jack, which had origins in the fourteenth century as a mechanical wooden figure that struck bells in church towers. By the sixteenth century, the jack of communal pleasure was miniaturized into a string-pulled jumping jack and was sold widely as a toy in central European fairs. Again, the jumping jack was a novelty as pleasing to adults at festive times as to children.

Some modern toys originated as diversions of adult aristocrats. Wealthy men had long been fascinated with mechanical movement. Automata, mechanical figures or animals powered by water and even steam, dated from the ancient world. By 1672 skilled craftspeople constructed automata powered by clockworks for Louis XIV of France. The eighteenth-century French artisans Jacques de Vaucanson and Pierre Jaquet-Droz made mechanical angels, pecking birds, and even models of children capable of writing. In the nineteenth century, with mass production, these novelties trickled down to children as toys. By 1836 walking dolls were perfected in Paris toy shops and survive today in remote control robots. Toy soldiers may have begun as pendants used by adults as charms rather than as children's playthings. The doll historian Karl Grober notes that miniature soldiers served as children's toys only from 1578 and that this was very rare. Kings and aristocrats collected handcrafted metal or wood soldiers to "play" war. Toys had little to do with the "innocence" of childhood. Amusements celebrating the macabre also have found expression as playthings. Toy guillotines were sold during the French Revolution, one of which was reportedly bought by the cultivated Johann Wolfgang von Goethe.

Similarly, fashion dolls originated as an effective way of displaying adult women's clothing. In 1309 the French royal court sent the English queen a miniature female mannequin dressed in the latest French style. In the seventeenth and eighteenth centuries clothing designers used these dolls to advertise Parisian fashion throughout Europe. They were a major reason for French success in dominating women's fashion. Mothers gave these dolls to their girls when no longer useful for displaying clothes. The history of dollhouses follows a similar course. First made in the form of a cabinet to include miniature furniture, dollhouses date from 1558 in Bavaria. But these replicas of exquisite domestic furnishings were models commissioned by wealthy women for their amusement and to display their taste and wealth. They were very expensive pieces of furniture, not toys for children. Aristocratic English women similarly collected dolls and doll furnishings in the eighteenth century. Only at the end of the eighteenth century did manufacturers build dollhouses specifically as toys designed to instruct girls in the arts of housekeeping. And even in Victorian England, dollhouses were commissioned objects d'art. Sometimes miniature upholstered chairs and doll dresses were made by adult members of the family to display craft skill. When the first hot air balloon ascended in 1783, French adults bought miniatures for souvenirs. Only later did the balloon become a child's toy. And hoops, tops, and ball games, which had traditionally been enjoyed by all ages, were only gradually abandoned by adults as childish.

Playthings were often miniatures of symbols of elite prestige and power. Thus most of the toys before the eighteenth century that have survived were made for the children of the aristocracy or wealthy merchants. In 1572 the king of Saxony gave his son a wooden play set depicting a hunting scene (complete with hounds, stags, wild boars, foxes, wolves, and hares) that allowed him to create minidramas of the leisure that he would enjoy when he grew up. By contrast, the princess received a doll's kitchen complete with 71 dishes, 40 meat plates, 36 spoons, and doll's furniture. Many toys were novelties that displayed wealth and taste.

Poor children, of course, enjoyed roughly made rag-and-straw stuffed dolls, and animal wastes provided materials for balls and knucklebones. Children made their own playthings. They improvised, creating fantasy worlds with whittled sticks and castaway bits of cloth. Traditional toys like hoops (from discarded wheels) pushed along the street with a stick survived until the end of the nineteenth century. And, of course, children played without toys or board or card games in a wide variety of chasing, racing, hiding, and role-playing activities in unsupervised groups.

MATERIAL CHANGES IN PLAYTHINGS, c. 1700–1850

The technological and economic revolutions that transformed general material conditions of European society also revolutionized the toy box. The modern European toy industry has its roots in Germany, where specialized craft production of playthings appeared in the sixteenth century. A key to their success was that they imitated both aristocratic and folk styles. In and around the small towns of Sonneberg, Erzebirge, and Berchtesgaden, as well as in Oberammergau in the Groeden Valley in South Tirol, families carved wooden animals and dolls in their cottages during the winter months, often to replicate local wildlife and people. From 1578 craftspeople from Nürnberg produced toy animals from tin. Later, about 1760, Andreas Hilpert of Nürnberg offered middle-class parents cheap tin adaptations of expensive silver or lead toy armies. Thereafter, Nürnberg set the standard for toy soldiers in Europe. This town also became famous for the Nürnberg Kitchen, a standardized play set for training girls in the essentials of domestic work in the nineteenth century. Gradually, German toy-making became a well-organized business. At first, peddlers sold handcrafted toys at fairs and door-to-door. Later, merchants centered in Nürnberg gained control over these traveling salesmen and forced village artisans to adopt uniform designs and to specialize.

In the nineteenth century especially, European toy makers also found new, cheaper materials. By 1850 papier-mâché, India rubber, and simple molding machines cheapened the cost of dolls. Porcelain doll heads were mass-produced from the 1840s and bisque (unglazed porcelain) from 1870. Simple mechanical contrivances also made dolls more lifelike. As early as 1823, dolls could say "mamma" when children squeezed simple bellows implanted in the doll's body. Technical improvements, including weight-activated eyes and ball-jointed limbs in dolls, became common by 1850. Paper dolls appeared in England and Germany in the 1790s, offering a cheap version of the three-dimensional fashion doll. In the 1840s and 1850s paper dolls featured the likenesses of celebrities (royalty but also ballerinas and famous singers like Jenny Lind). New materials were introduced to make dollhouses cheaper, including lithographed paper on wood and tin to simulate fancy wall coverings, doors, and other furnishings.

New manufacturing technologies also made playthings cheaper. By the eighteenth century simple wooden toys were fashioned from a ring of pinewood, turned on a lathe to form the outline of a figure or animal along the length of the ring, and then sliced

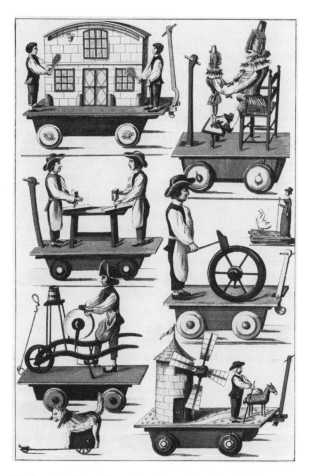

Mechanical Toys. Illustration from a French toy maker's catalog, mid-nineteenth century. Bowes Museum, County Durham, U.K./The Bridgeman Art Library

into multiple flat figures. About five thousand molds for casting lead figures were used around Nürnberg by 1840. By the 1890s chromolithography allowed mechanical printing to replace much hand painting on tin-plated toys. Cheap spring-work (windup) toys supplanted expensive clockworks, and hollow-cast toy soldiers put war toys in the hands of a broad middle class. Composition (a mixture mostly of wood fiber, bran, and glue) began to replace china and other clay materials for dolls' heads in 1895. These innovations not only introduced more playthings into a wider group of European children's lives, but they made it possible for manufacturers to produce more variety and to change their lines of toys and games, thus turning playthings into a fashion industry.

Deep into the nineteenth century, craft methods prevailed and families still made toys at home or in small shops. Children's goods were often mixed with adult trinkets in the packs of peddlers and in general stores. Toy manufacturing was often a sideline of "serious" industry (for example, common woodworkers made miniatures of carpenter and garden tools and toy horses and coaches with scraps, and cabinet makers produced dollhouses on special order). The Brio toy company of Sweden, for example, had its roots in basket making in the 1880s. Machines and factories were introduced only at the end of the nineteenth century.

Toy makers could be found throughout nineteenth-century Europe. By 1800, for example, small-scale English manufacturers from the Black Country were producing a variety of tin and wood drums, trumpets, whistles, soldiers, and farm and exotic animals. Paris became a center for high-quality handcrafted automata and porcelain dolls in the nineteenth century. But after 1860 larger, more sophisticated German toy manufacturers like Bing and later Maerklin and Lehmann offered distinct trademarked windup and military toys. German manufacturers bested British and French competitors with aggressive marketing that targeted regional cultural differences and appealed to a broad middle class. For example, Bing manufactured tin English battleships complete with English flags. By 1900 Germany was by far the world's greatest producer of toys, producing two-thirds of the dolls for Europe and exporting 75 percent of its output.

PLAYTHINGS AND CHANGING MEANINGS OF CHILDHOOD, c. 1700–1900

From the late seventeenth century, changes in the meaning and experience of childhood were reflected in new toy and game concepts. Historians of childhood stress the role of the Enlightenment on new attitudes about child rearing and playthings. John Locke's *Some Thoughts Concerning Education* (1693) asserted that play was not the "devil's workshop" but essential for the child's rational and occupational development. Children should have a variety of toys (but not all at once). In play children revealed those aptitudes that parents ought to encourage. Locke's ideas were passed on to nineteenth-century parents via popular child-rearing manuals. These books encouraged parents to protect their children from harmful influences and to find games and toys to guide the child's "progress" or training. The eighteenth-century French philosopher Jean-Jacques Rousseau stressed how parents should encourage spontaneity in their young children and provide an education that rewarded individual expression and personal development. Children were no longer seen as miniature adults; they were to go through developmental stages rather than be prematurely introduced to adult life.

These Enlightenment figures were hardly promoting permissive parenting. Advocates of children's toys and games throughout the nineteenth century stressed not undirected play and imagination but moral and intellectual training. The historian John Brewer argues that toys in the late eighteenth century were to teach children to value and care for property. A key figure in toys for learning was the German educator Friedrich Froebel, who founded the first kindergarten in 1837. Like other reformers of this period, he denounced rote memorization and argued that play should become a central part of early learning. According to these reformers, play was the young child's work and mode of learning. But it should not be left to chance. Froebel had a detailed program of play that prescribed step-by-step the child's activities. While later generations of kindergarten teachers would abandon Froebel's mystical views and rigid program, they stuck to the idea of managed play.

Accompanying this intellectual revolution in education was the transformation of the social context of childhood, especially for the middle classes. With the gradual removal of production from the home and from the training of children, toys and games became substitutes for preparing the young for adult roles. Moreover, play gradually replaced shared domestic work to create family loyalties and to train the child in the values of honesty and competition. In the home increasingly bereft of productive tasks and sometimes even baby siblings, toys became a way to imitate adult roles. They also served to help middle-class and socially aspiring parents isolate their young from an often unruly "child society" that might teach values inappropriate for upstanding families or social advancement. Toys then could protect the child in the sheltered environment of the bourgeois home while also providing antidotes for loneliness. Children were expected to learn the rational culture of self-control in the isolation of the nursery. Yet, with greater affluence in the course of the nineteenth century, the young were increasingly encouraged to enjoy spontaneity and the pleasures of their freedom from work and responsibility. Playthings were both vehicles to introduce the "real world" and fantasy objects that shut the child off from that world in a "secret garden." This contradiction became more evident as the century wore on and toys designed to please parents gave way to child-centered playthings.

NINETEENTH-CENTURY TOYS AND GAMES

Early-nineteenth-century toys were made mostly for the very young. Rattles, for example, were as much for the benefit of parents as children (and were sometimes called "child quieters"). The few toys available for older children were to distract them in that brief time before they could be put to work. Adults brought out miniatures only on special holidays. Into the nineteenth century, religious parents allowed their young to play with Noah's Arks only on Sundays or holidays. Didactic toys had roots in the seventeenth century. As early as 1656, we find the Scholers Praticall Cards, a teaching game for English children. Paralleling the publication of children's books in the mid-eighteenth century were a variety of information cards that taught geography, zoology, and even grammar. In the early nineteenth century French children learned about the prefectures of France and Austrians about exotic animals with card games. Moralistic themes predominated in English board games. For example, in the early Victorian Mansion of Happiness, children advanced a piece on a board by way of squares marked with character traits (Piety and Honesty, for example), moving toward the goal of Happiness. Landing, however, on Passion meant that you lost a turn.

The classic educational toy was, of course, the unadorned building block. It dates back to the time of John Locke in the late seventeenth century but was manufactured widely for the middle-class nursery in the mid-nineteenth century. A related, but predominately female, item was the sewing cards that appeared about 1880, often with improving mottos like "Waste Not, Want Not." Other improving toys were less moralistic, but they too were to be "worked on." Froebel's kindergarten play objects (called "gifts") were to awaken the mind and imagination of the child. The set was contained in six boxes and each successive box would be opened only as the child progressed in self-understanding. The first, for example, was filled with colored worsted balls. They were to teach the principle of "unity." Later the child would advance to more complex objects like cubes and cylinders and eventually a three-inch cube, divided to form twenty-seven solid oblongs, of which three were divided into halves to form four-sided prisms, and six into halves to form square half-cubes. Fourteen "occupations" activities prescribed proper use of the gifts, including paper folding, drawing, sewing, paper weaving, stringing peas, and clay modeling. A similar, if less abstract, ethos produced the notion that children should construct their own playthings. In 1859 and 1860 Ebenezer Landells published two primers on the construction of "useful things" like kites, bows and arrows, and cardboard fox-hunting scenes for boys and homemade cutouts of dancing dolls and paper bookmarks for girls. The former were to prepare boys for inventing and the latter to instruct girls on domestic crafts

A Boy's Plaything. *The Toy Castle,* painting by J. Byam Liston Shaw (1872–1919). CHRISTOPHER WOOD GALLERY, LONDON/THE BRIDGEMAN ART LIBRARY

and benevolence. So-called scientific toys emerged in the 1830s that taught children principles of optics, for example, with toy-sized magic lanterns.

Toys reflected conventional gendered work roles and the tools that went with them. A toy catalog from Nürnberg in about 1860 featured toy storefronts appealing to boys and tin dollhouses designed for girls. Military miniatures in tin plate, mostly produced by Bing and Maerklin, were common in the two generations before World War I, keeping boys up-to-date on the latest battleship in the European arms race and familiar with the armies of potential enemies.

Girls' playthings were mostly dolls, often semimanufactured, to be finished or assembled later. Thus dolls were sold in parts (heads, bodies, legs, and arms), and the customer was expected to make or purchase separately the clothes, doll furniture, and dollhouses. Handmade extras made toys affordable to many parents and allowed them and other relatives to contribute personally to the child's play. Doll accessories abounded. They included an amazing array of toy household tools, including washing boards, coal hods and shovels, and irons. Natural looking bisque-headed dolls, highly realistic with glass eyes, human hair, and ball joints, were made in Paris. Dolls manufactured by Jumeau were especially successful on the international market. Between 1860 and 1900 fashionably dressed "lady dolls" became a central part of the middle-class girl's life. Newly affluent mothers increasingly encouraged their daughters to play out the rituals of high society (from tea parties to funerals) with their dolls. The fashion doll also developed a girl's skill at identifying quality fabric and appropriate dress.

These talents were very important in a new age where middle-class women were expected to create a decorous home and become knowledgeable consumers. Dolls were used to instruct girls on the "proper" handling of objects and on the exercise of self-control.

Although these toys were utilitarian or (as in the case of porcelain dolls) for display, toys gradually became more playful and childlike, especially for younger children. Illustrative of this change is how didactic tales gave way to children's fantasy. Lewis Carroll's *Alice in Wonderland* (1865) abandons the dull world of adults for the comic literalness of Unbirthday Parties and Queens of Hearts while subtly parodying adult hypocrisies. Escapism from industrial society was projected onto children in Rudyard Kipling's *Jungle Book* (1894). And J. M. Barrie's *Peter Pan* (1904) treats the Darling siblings to Neverland, where nobody ever grows up, and spares Wendy of the fate of having to vacate the nursery until she is finally ready. As important, parents embraced these fantasies and the idea of purposeless play that they expressed. Late-nineteenth-century indulgence of children is shown in clothing, furniture, and medicines made especially for the young. The transformation of the communal festival of Christmas into a day featuring gifts for children is also part of this process. The Bon Marché in Liverpool, for example, introduced the first Christmas fairyland (toy department) in the 1870s, and by the 1890s Father Christmas was a regular visitor in December in British department stores. The late-Victorian poor may not have been able to afford toys at birthdays, but they saved and spent as lavishly as possible on their children at Christmas.

TWENTIETH-CENTURY TRENDS

Toys derived from popular characters in children's fiction became common after 1900. These playthings expressed parental indulgence for childish play while drawing on new and faddish elements from the wider popular culture. The British Golliwog, derived from a child's short story, became a fad doll from 1900. The Golliwog was a version of the black dandy and minstrel, dressed in blue swallow-tail coat and red bow tie—but with paws, not feet and hands, and with exaggerated eyes and lips. "Exotic" racial images were nearly as common in Europe as in the United States. Other popular dolls were the Katzenjammer Kids, who in comics endlessly played pranks on grown-ups, even if they got thrashed for it. These were images of a gentle rebellion from adult authority, a rebellion tolerated by parents, even embraced in the innocence of a plaything. Similarly, German windup toys often fea-

The Golliwogg. "The Golliwogg, Tired of Dancing," from a Victorian Christmas card. PRIVATE COLLECTION/THE BRIDGEMAN ART LIBRARY

tured whimsical adult characters in ridiculous situations in the 1900s.

Even more expressive of a new indulgence of childhood was the doll reform movement. Shortly after 1900, artists in Munich and Berlin designed dolls in the image of children. In opposition to the adult fashion doll with its detailed and realistic facial features and body, the doll reformers asked children what they wanted in a doll. This led to soft figures, sometimes with "unbreakable heads," that a child could hug and play with. Early examples of the doll reform were simple folk designs with abstract facial features and childlike in their construction. Most important, these dolls were to evoke the emotions of the child rather than to teach adult roles. The fact that most of these dolls looked like the child who played with them suggested that they were intended to be companions in childish play. The new doll's image also implied a growing toleration for the foibles of children. Some, for example, had impish looks on their faces with eyes askance. Common also was the wholesome and energetic look of the "Dutch boy" doll. Other doll reformers like Kaethe Kruse designed realistic baby dolls (often with the face and body of a newborn) with the hope of arousing maternal feeling in the child.

Another part of this trend toward more child-centered play was the plush or stuffed toy animal and figure. Unlike the wood or even cloth toy, these soft-centered toys with raised nap exteriors were ideal for young children seeking security and warmth. The German toy maker Margarete Steiff, who made stuffed elephants from 1880, claimed to have invented the soft and furry teddy bear (named for the American president Theodore Roosevelt) in 1902. Her company shifted production from cottage craftspeople to a modern factory in 1905, shortly after she gained access to an international network of buyers and had perfected her jointed plush doll design. The stuffed bear swept the "civilized" world in 1906–1907 (and was as popular in Europe as it was in the United States. Steiff sold one million in 1907 alone. So successful were Steiff's bears that other toy makers quickly copied them. In an effort to create an emblem of "authenticity," Steiff sewed a "button in the ear" of each plush bear that the company manufactured, thus creating a distinctive trademark. By 1911 Steiff was making cartoon characters and caricature dolls and advertising them through colorful postcards. These toys conveyed the message that children had the right to self-expression and fantasy. But they also attracted adults with the opportunity to join their offspring in a nostalgia for a "timeless" childhood free from the competition and change of the modern world.

The Victorian training toy had hardly disappeared. For older boys, it survived in the lead soldier that was given in complete and often expensive sets by parents as a rite of passage into robust boyhood. Electric trains offered a more positive image of growing up. They dated from 1884 in Germany, and Maerklin exported them by 1898. Electric trains combined accurate detail of the latest technology with a play setting that allowed boys to imagine themselves as powerful participants in an adult world of commerce and transportation. Construction toys, like Frank Hornby's Meccano of Britain, delivered boys to worlds of technological progress and business success. More than perforated metal strips that could be bolted together, Meccano showed boys how to construct the "world's mechanical wonders" as models. According to a popular biography, Hornby, as a boy, had dreamed of building a "perpetual motion machine," and his work on bridges inspired his Meccano toy. Hornby himself was to be a model for boys to emulate just as his toys were to prepare them to be engineers, scientists, and businessmen.

By contrast, early-twentieth-century girls' play included few miniatures of modern technology. Pet's Toy Grocery Stores, an English invention of 1909, was an update of the grocer's store play set common in the nineteenth century except that it included miniature trademark brands of packaged goods, teaching the girl "modern" shopping. But the doll remained central to girls' play. With it, girls learned to play expected roles by making their dolls into actors in domestic dramas of modern caregiving, conviviality, and consumption. The increasing tendency of dolls in the early twentieth century to look like children or babies may have reflected a trend toward smaller families. When girls lacked siblings to play with or babies to care for, they substituted dolls. As mothers bore fewer children, they took on more nurturing responsibilities. These mothers would rather have their young daughters play with baby dolls than risk their caring for their baby siblings. And baby dolls were intended to train girls into a maternal instinct that many social conservatives saw in decline early in the twentieth century.

AMERICANIZATION OF PLAYTHINGS IN EUROPE

Toys and games remained relatively static after 1920 in Europe. As in many areas of popular culture, American toy innovations penetrated European childhood. German toys lost their dominance in the United States during World War I, and after Hitler came to power in Germany in 1933, military priorities further weakened the German playthings industry. Radical change came from Walt Disney's aggressive marketing of character licenses to doll and toy makers in 1935. Mickey Mouse was as popular in Europe as in the United States, and Disney films like the feature-length *Snow White* introduced a new way of making story characters into playthings. The Americanization of toys meant a shift of play away from an adult world of training and toward an international culture of childhood created by linking children's movies and other media to toys.

Of course, older forms of toys survived after World War II. British Meccano and Hornby electric trains enjoyed a revival, and the Lesney "Matchbox" cars updated a tradition of play based on realistic miniatures of adult life. The Swedish Brio company perpetuated high-quality nonrepresentational wooden toys (simple trains, cars, animals, and blocks) and promoted them as an educational alternative to licensed character toys. Their "open-ended toys" were expensive, but they stimulated imagination and were advertised as a good investment in a child's development. Brio appealed to the relatively affluent parent who was eager for playthings that met a child's developmental needs. The German Playmobil company thrived by offering sturdy plastic updates of traditional wooden play sets. German toy makers abandoned war toys and specialized in electric trains and fine character dolls.

Nevertheless, despite the relative absence of TV advertising in Europe for children (as compared with the United States), European toy companies survived by imitating or becoming subsidiaries of aggressive American toy makers. In 1962 the venerable Lines Brothers of Britain made an obvious copy of Mattel's Barbie doll called Sindy. In 1966 Britain's Palitoy became the distributor for Hasbro's G. I. Joe (called Ac-

Lego. A visitor in a Lego boat rides past buildings made of Legos at Legoland near Billund, Denmark. BOB KRIST/ ©CORBIS

rapid change and an emphasis upon "blockbuster" hit toys. This plus the close integration of toy makers with an aggressive children's entertainment industry (comic books, movies, and TV cartoons) led to toy lines that served as props for playing a fantasy narrative. When American toy giants licensed the images of *Star Wars* characters for toys in 1977, European companies could not compete. In the 1970s and 1980s, for example, the independent British toy industry long used to a stable product line, nearly disappeared.

The most dramatic exception was Lego. In the 1970s and early 1980s, this Danish company built a toy empire against the trend toward action-figure fantasy. Instead, it perpetuated the construction-toy tradition with its interlocking blocks. Lego used museum and mall displays and its Legoland theme park to retain a reputation for quality and creativity. By the late 1980s, however, Lego compromised with the American fantasy-toy industry by introducing kits, or "systems," designed to construct a single model. While Lego did not provide a violent "back story," many of these systems came with exotic weaponry. Lego's construction-toy tradition adapted to many of the marketing techniques of the novelty makers.

Niche markets remained for educational and construction toys. For example, in the 1980s and 1990s Early Learning Centres in Britain sold Meccano, Brio, and other quality toys to parents of young children who opposed the commercialization of the young by international fashion toy makers. But the older child has become part of a global consumer culture through satellite TV, movies, comics, and, after 1991 especially, video games. By the 1980s the toy in Europe had become part of a global play culture. Toys are increasingly designed and marketed through American and Japanese companies and manufactured in south China adjacent to the international commercial center of Hong Kong. European parents, like affluent parents elsewhere, look to their children for emotional gratification and buy toys to please their offspring. Reduced family size and divorce probably have also accelerated this trend. The growth of satellite TV and privatization of the mass media have eroded the European's isolation from the power of the United States and the global children's fashion and fantasy industry.

tion Man in Europe). Even Brio distributed Mattel and Hasbro toys in the 1950s and 1960s. By 1985 the American warehouse retailer Toys "R" Us arrived in Britain and soon thereafter on the Continent, selling Barbie dolls and action figures similar to those offered in the United States.

The Americanization of toys was more than an economic fact. It also meant a new kind of plaything and experience of play that Europeans were unable to match. Especially from the 1960s, American toys were sold directly to children via TV ads on Saturday morning cartoon shows, bypassing the parent's values and memories of play. Intense competition made for

See also **America, Americanization, and Anti-Americanism** *(volume 1);* **Gender and Education** *and* **Child Rearing and Childhood** *(volume 4); and other articles in this section.*

BIBLIOGRAPHY

Ariès, Phillipe. *Centuries of Childhood.* Translated by Robert Baldick. New York, 1962.

Boehn, Max von. *Dolls and Puppets.* Translated by Josephine Nicoll. Philadelphia, 1932.

Brown, Kenneth D. *The British Toy Business: A History since 1700.* London, 1996.

Caillois, Roger. *Man, Play, and Games.* Translated by Meyer Barash. New York, 1962.

Carpenter, Humphrey. *Secret Gardens: A Study of the Golden Age of Children's Literature.* London, 1985.

Chapuis, Alfred. *Automata: A Historical and Technical Study.* Paris, 1958.

Coleman, Dorothy S., Elizabeth A. Coleman, and Evelyn J. Coleman. *The Collector's Encyclopedia of Dolls.* New York, 1968.

Cross, Gary. *Kids' Stuff: Toys and the Changing World of American Childhood.* Cambridge, Mass., 1997.

Fleming, Dan. *Powerplay: Toys as Popular Culture.* Manchester, U. K., 1996.

Froebel, Friedrich. *Education of Man.* Translated by N. N. Hailmann. New York, 1895. Translation of *Die Menschenerziehung* (1826).

Grober, Karl. *Children's Toys of Bygone Days.* Translated by Josephine Nicoll. London, 1928.

Humbert, Raymond. *Les jouets populaires.* Paris, 1983.

Kline, Stephen. *Out of the Garden: Toys, TV, and Children's Culture in the Age of Marketing.* New York, 1993.

Sutton-Smith, Brian. *A History of Children's Play: New Zealand, 1840–1950.* Philadelphia, 1981.

ISBN 0-684-80581-2

3M